A
MY CLUB HISTORY
Publication

MULLINAVAT

◄ A HISTORY OF MULLINAVAT GAA CLUB ►

1887-2024

VOL 1

BY JOHN POWER

PUBLISHED BY
MY CLUB HISTORY
LUCAN
CO. DUBLIN
IRELAND
Enquiries: Contact liam@myclubhistory.com

First Published 2024
Copyright © Mullinavat GAA Club

The moral and legal copyright of material produced in this publication, including text and photographs, is acknowledged and where possible due accreditation has been made. There is no claim to ownership of such material. The opinions and statements included in this publication are those of the author and not necessarily those of Mullinavat GAA Club.

Considerable care and research has been undertaken to ensure the accuracy of the content in this publication but, where error is noted, apology is sincerely offered and the good intent of the author should be accepted. Images are credited where possible. Many of these images are very old, in some cases faded or otherwise damaged, but the author felt it important that they be included.

No part of this publication may be reproduced, stored in or introduced into a retrieval system, or transmitted in any form or by any means (electronic, mechanical, photocopying, recording or otherwise) without the prior written permission of the copyright holders of this book.

Cover design and formatting: jessica@viitaladesign.com
Photographs: Mullinavat GAA Club
Cover Photos:
Front: Mullinavat Team, Courtesy Tom Brett (Kilkenny People); Kilkenny Team, Courtesy Nicky Brennan. Back: Courtesy Marie Morrissey.

Dedication
For the aspirations that drive us to scale new heights

Contents

INTRODUCTION

CHRONOLOGY

A BRIEF HISTORY

Part One: Gaelic Football (1887-2024) 35

Heroes Amongst Us Forever 209

Part Two: Hurling (1887-2024) 235

Mullinavat Hurling XV (1970-2024) 443

ROLL OF HONOUR

BIBLIOGRAPHY

Introduction

I AM PROUD and honoured to have been assigned the task of compiling this history of Mullinavat GAA Club.

In Autumn 2019, Mullinavat GAA entrusted me with the responsibility of writing a full history of the club. Having only a basic knowledge of what was involved, I gave myself eighteen months to complete the task. Four and a half years later, we finally have the two-volume finished product.

We love our GAA in Kilkenny, and in most South Kilkenny parishes, the GAA club is the backbone of the community. Mullinavat is no different!

Firstly, I would like to thank the club committee for their assistance and trust in myself, towards completing this project. As a 'blow in' to the parish from Waterford City, and originally from neighbouring Kilmacow, from day one I was always made welcome within the club.

John Power

My wife Brigid, sons JT and Brian, daughters Linda and Tara, along with my two grandchildren Sophie and Daithi, all have missed out on family time, at weekends especially, while I worked away on this project. Thanks for your support.

Many families and individuals have assisted me in gathering photographs and articles which we have used in this publication. The original club history, produced in 1984, was an excellent starting point, and I would like to thank each and every one of those people involved, from that project, all of forty years ago. Recorded minutes of AGMs from both the camogie and GAA clubs have also been of great benefit in compiling this history. Local newspapers such as Kilkenny People, Munster Express, Waterford News & Star and Kilkenny Voice have been used throughout this history, and all have provided great reference articles.

Thanks to my new friend Liam Hayes, and Hero Books, for their assistance in assembling this two-volume history. Liam, you promised me a history book that the club would be proud of, and you have assisted in professionally compiling and delivering same.

While I have attended numerous games at the well appointed Mullinavat GAA grounds over the years, many with my late father Sean, as a youngster, it is only in the past eighteen years, since moving here, that I realise the great people who made this club what it is today. I am extremely proud to now be a small part of this great GAA club.

This production has recorded both wins and losses, in so far as possible, of all the major games from the past 140 years, from underage to adult level, in all GAA codes.

An American journalist Christopher Hitchens is credited with a quote, 'Everyone has a book inside them, which is exactly where it should, I think, in most cases, remain'. Well, Mullinavat GAA now have two book volumes from yours truly!

Two volumes that almost certainly will have some errors and omissions, which will be totally my fault, and for which I apologise in advance. I enjoyed putting this Mullinavat GAA club history together, and I hope all readers will enjoy dipping in and out of it from time to time, in the days, months and years ahead.

The best way to predict our club's future is to create it, and I have no doubt we will by collectively building on what has already been achieved.

This club history is dedicated to all the individuals, past and present, who have in any way been involved in the history of Mullinavat GAA club.

John Power
Mullinavat GAA Club PRO
Author of *Mullinavat GAA Club History*

A Message from Mullinavat GAA Club Chairman
John Joe Aylward

A chairde gaeil go léir, is mór an onóir dom a bheith I mo chathaoirleach ar Cumann Luthchleas Gaeil Muileann an Bhata, go háraithe ag an am ríthábhachtach seo i stair ár gclub.

As Chairman of Mullinavat GAA Club, it gives me great pleasure on behalf of members and supporters of the club to welcome this history of Mullinavat GAA Club, covering years of sporting, social and cultural activity. There is much to reflect on within the book to prompt discussion and debate of great times past, games, players, events, milestones, achievements and disappointments. This book will become a reference point for Mullinavat people at home and abroad, and will prompt many a debate relating to the club and the community it has represented.

On behalf of our present members I wish to pay tribute to all our past clubmen and women whose enthusiasm, foresight and hard work brought the club from its foundation to its present standing. I would also like to take this opportunity to thank our current members, supporters and all those who continue to drive the club forward both on and off the field.

We have recently embarked on ambitious development plans for the club and these would not be attainable without the unwavering support we have within our community.

John Joe Aylward

As current custodians, it is our privilege to be able to continue on the fantastic work started by those who went before.

On behalf of the club I say a special thank you to author and PRO John Power for the enormous amount of time and research he has put into this publication. We fully appreciate the time and expertise you invested in researching and writing the book in a voluntary capacity. I am certain its contents will evoke discussion and interest, and many great memories will be recalled by Mullinavat people, both young and not so young, but above all else I hope it will inspire future generations to emulate the achievements of their predecessors.

The game is never over, the best is yet to come.

John Joe Aylward
Cathaoirleach
CLG Muileann an Bhata

A Message from GAA President

Jarlath Burns

A chairde,

Tá an-áthas orm an leabhar tábhachtach seo a sheoladh, ag ceiliúradh CLG Muilleann an Bhata.

It is my honour to add my voice to the chorus of celebration that marks the publication of this history of Mullinavat GAA and acknowledge the proud history that the club has had in its local community and in Kilkenny since 1887.

I want to commend John Power and all of those who have been involved in preparing this publication. The thing about a publication like this is that as welcome as it is now – its real value will only increase with the passing of time, and it will really serve as a guide and a reminder for future generations, who will be indebted to your work in recording all of this information, not just for today but for tomorrow.

What we don't try to remember we are certain to forget. Mullinavat, like every club, has a story worth telling and that needs to be told. The club is built on strong foundations – generations of fantastic players and club servants who have represented the club with distinction in hurling and football and in camogie, and who have brought further honour when called to serve in county colours.

Mullinavat's role in cementing the legendary status of Monsignor Tommy Maher and his contribution to the development of not just Kilkenny hurling but the great game itself is also worth acknowledging. What is equally important, is remembering that cups and medals and trophies only ever tell a small part of the overall story of a club's life and times. There is the deeper magic of the value that people can benefit from through their involvement in your club – the friendships and bonds and family ties that can be traced back down through decades and generations. The measure of that value is as precious as any cup.

Occasions such as this offer a chance to pause and reflect on the men and women who have built and steered this club since 1887 – on the field and off it and who continue to do so preparing teams and meeting the never-ending requirement for facilities and their maintenance.

It was 140 years ago that the dream and the vision of the GAA was set forth into uncertain and unchartered waters, but with a burning ambition. This book plays a role in recording how that vision has endured and prospered.

Thar ceann Chumann Lúthchleas Gael, Comhghairdeas agus míle buíochas.

Jarlath Burns
President, Cumann Lúthchleas Gael

A Message from Kilkenny County Board Chairman
PJ Kenny

Comhghairdeas go Mhuilleann an Bhata don an leabhar stairiúla seo a thiomsú. Tá súil agam go bhain sibh taitneamh as é a léamh.

It is a great honour and privilege for me as Kilkenny County Chairman to be asked to write a foreword for the latest publication of Mullinavat GAA History. I would like to acknowledge John Power for all the work in putting this publication together. I am sure it will provide countless hours of enjoyable reading – and looking at the old photographs – of the club history.

The importance of recording any GAA club history can never be underestimated; not only does it record all the victories and achievements, but it outlines where we came from, and the steps and sacrifices made by past generations for the love of the GAA club and the parish. It also shows the values and gives a sense of who we are today. It will hopefully inspire future generations in the coming years.

Mullinavat has a rich history and tradition from its earliest formation in 1887 to the present date. Many great hurling men have embellished the game at club, school and county level. Mullinavat, as a club, has provided many great players, coaches and administrators who have served Kilkenny with distinction. Much as I would like to mention names from the past and indeed the present, I feel it would be wrong to single anyone out as their names and deeds are well recorded in this publication.

Mullinavat has long been regarded as the geographical centre of South Kilkenny GAA.

The Mullinavat pitch has hosted many games in its history. The club always stepped up to the mark when hosting games, and the folklore surrounding games and legendary deeds of players will never be forgotten.

Mullinavat GAA club has been more than just one code; Bigwood was a force in Kilkenny football many moons ago. It recent times Mullinavat have had major success at Senior club football level in Kilkenny, annexing a number of titles and have been very unlucky not to win at provincial level. As a parish, Mullinavat has also excelled in the handball court, with numerous All-Ireland titles being accumulated.

Not to be outdone by the men, Mullinavat Camogie has also proved to be successful at local level at the Senior grade and also winning a Leinster Senior Camogie Championship

I will finish by thanking all who have served Mullinavat and Kilkenny GAA so well on and off the field of play. I wish the club all the best of success long into the future.

P.J. Kenny
Chairperson,
Choiste Cill Chainnigh

A Message from Former GAA President
Nicky Brennan

From its founding days in 1887, Mullinavat GAA Club has been an important part of the Kilkenny Gaelic Athletic Association community. Like many rural GAA clubs over the years, Mullinavat have had their challenges, but through the trojan effort of many loyal volunteers and players, the club continued to survive.

A double success in the Kilkenny Junior Hurling Championship in 1915 and 1916 hinted at a rewarding future for the new club, but that is not quite how it worked out. The reasons will, no doubt, be well documented in this publication, but Mullinavat are no different to many rural clubs that found the going very difficult over the years.

Successes were rare in the 1900s, but the hard work of club officials and players would eventually start to pay off in the 2000s. I suspect that many would see the highlight being the Kilkenny Intermediate Hurling championship success of 2014 and entry into the Kilkenny Senior Hurling Championship in 2015. The Rod Iron men, as the club is affectionately known, have more than held their own in Kilkenny's premier hurling grade. This publication will, no doubt, fondly remember the many players from Mullinavat who also enjoyed great success with various Kilkenny hurling teams.

If the dream of winning a Kilkenny Senior Hurling Championship remains as strong as ever, Mullinavat has been the dominant Gaelic football side in Kilkenny over the past decade, winning seven titles between 2007 and 2023.

I have fond memories of playing with Sarsfields (Conahy) against Bigwood (Mullinavat) when we won the Kilkenny Junior Football Championship in 1976 on a score of 0-8 to 0-1. This saw us complete a Junior Hurling/Football Championship double that year.

In recent years in the Leinster Intermediate Club Football Championship, Mullinavat has excelled. I was present when they lost by a narrow margin to Mattock Rangers (Louth) in the 2019 Leinster final.

One of Kilkenny's most memorable football days was winning the All-Ireland Junior Football final in Croke Park in 2022 against New York. I suspect that none of us ever expected a Kilkenny player to climb the steps of the Hogan Stand to be presented with an All-Ireland football trophy by the President of the GAA. The history-maker that afternoon was Mullinavat's Mick Malone. It was a very emotional day for all those who had kept the 'big ball' game alive in the county over many years. Incidentally, Mick Malone lined out with Kilkenny in the county's last National Football League game in Ennis against Clare ten years earlier in 2012.

Mullinavat has also made huge progress on the camogie fields over recent decades winning an array of county titles, with players from the club representing Kilkenny in many grades. The South Kilkenny club is also a handball stronghold in Kilkenny with players winning numerous county and All-Ireland titles at all grades and ages over the years.

Similar to many Kilkenny clubs, Mullinavat has continued to upgrade its facilities on the outskirts of the village and a newly installed walkway will ensure that parishioners of all ages have a top class leisure facility on their doorsteps.

I commend John Power on the painstaking research he has undertaken to produce this club history in two volumes. John has recorded all the highlights of GAA activity in the parish of Mullinavat and he especially recalls the many individuals who have brought glory to the parish, both on and off the field.

Congratulations to everyone involved with Mullinavat GAA Club on your century plus of Gaelic Games endeavour which has enhanced the lives of so many people in your parish.

Nicky Brennan

A Message from
Kilkenny Camogie Board Chairperson
Theresa Aylward

Is mór an onóir dom a réamhrá seo a scríobh ar son Coiste Chontae Cill Chainnigh. Comhghairdeas ó chroi le gach ball den club Muileann an Bhata. On behalf of Kilkenny Camogie County Board, I am delighted to have this opportunity to congratulate Mullinavat GAA on celebrating your history, 1887-2024. The club is well renowned for its success over the years in hurling, football and handball, and the Camogie club has also contributed hugely to your history and achievements.

Mullinavat Camogie won its first Junior A Championship back in 1948, and while it was 50 years before another Junior A title was recorded in 1998, an extremely successful period followed for the club. In 2000, the club won the Intermediate Championship title by defeating Tullogher and in the same year won the Under-21B title against James Stephens; this led onto Under-21A titles in 2001 and 2002, Minor A titles in 2003, 2004 and 2005 and a further Under-21A title in 2006. Given these successes it was only a matter of time before the club achieved Senior status, and this breakthrough was made in 2010 with just a one-point victory over one of your greatest rivals, St Lachtain's against whom Mullinavat also won the league title. The club proved dominant at the Senior grade in Kilkenny over the following years, with double success in both the League and Championship in 2012, 2013 and 2015.

The club also enjoyed Leinster success in winning the Leinster Senior Club championship in 2013 defeating St Ibar's of Wexford.

The highlight of 2016 was when Mullinavat had the honour of captaining the All-Ireland winning Kilkenny Senior Camogie team when Michelle Quilty climbed the steps of the Hogan Stand to accept the O'Duffy Cup on behalf of the county, a feat which had eluded Kilkenny for 22 years. Michelle was supported on that day by fellow teammates, Miriam Frisby and player of the match Julianne Malone.

Some notable achievements of Mullinavat adult players with Kilkenny County Camogie:

Elaine Aylward: Junior All-Ireland winner 2002, Div 1 National League, 2008 and 2014, All Star 2009
Amy Butler: National League Div. 1 2008
Michelle Quilty: Senior Team of the Year 2011; Div. 1 National League 2014, 2016, 2017, 2018; Senior All-Ireland Winner 2016; All Star 2014, 2016 and 2019
Julianne Malone: Senior All-Ireland Winner 2016 and 2022; All Star 2016 and 2022; National League Div. 1 2016, 2017, 2018
Leann Fennelly: Intermediate All-Ireland Winner 2008; National League Div. 1 2014, 2021; Senior All-Ireland Captain 2014
Claire Aylward: Intermediate All-Ireland Winner 2008
Angela Kenneally: Intermediate All-Ireland Winner 2016
Ciara Holden: Intermediate All-Ireland winner; Player of the Year and Soaring Star 2016

I would like to acknowledge and thank the Mullinavat club for your ongoing support of the Kilkenny Camogie County Board and note that the club continues to be well represented on our inter-county teams to date.

Congratulations and well done to all the past and present club executives, members and players for your hard work and dedication that has helped the club go from strength to strength. The ongoing development of the grounds and facilities are an indication of a fantastic community spirit, ensuring the future of the club for generations to come. Finally, I would like to compliment everyone who helped in any way in making this a memorable occasion for all connected with the club, and best wishes for the years ahead. Tá éacht déanta agaibh.

Theresa Aylward
Cathaoirleach Coiste Contae Cill Chainnigh
Camógaíocht

A Message from Kilkenny Handball Board

A chara,

Mullinavat Handball Club has been an integral part of Kilkenny Handball Board since its foundation in 1970. During that time the club has produced many fine players who have had tremendous success representing Kilkenny, along with producing two excellent Chairmen of the County Board.

However, long before the 'official' formation of the club, handball was played in the Mullinavat, and surrounding areas, for well over one hundred years. The hard-working committee, led by Secretary Billy Kelly, brought handball in Mullinavat to a new level when the court was erected in the late 60s.

Since winning its first All-Ireland title in 1977 – an Under-12 Doubles crown won by Joe Walsh – the Mullinavat club has enjoyed many successful days on the national scene. Along the way, family names such as O'Keeffe, Law, Anthony, Walsh, Foskin, Fitzpatrick, Aldridge and others have become familiar names in the handball world.

During that time one name that was synonymous with Mullinavat, and Kilkenny handball, was the late, great, Pat O'Keeffe, as he travelled the length and breadth of Ireland supporting local and county players. Along with providing support to the players, Pat dedicated his life to the promotion and development of young players in the handball court.

Also, to be remembered at this time was the contribution of the late Eamonn Law, a fantastic player who represented club and county with tremendous success, winning many All-Ireland titles in his career.

Along with producing great players, Mullinavat contributed to the successful running of Kilkenny Handball Board, with two delegates serving in the Chairman's position. For a number of years, Seamus Murphy held the position of Chairman, and in recent times, Joe Anthony took up the mantle to steer the Black and Amber to further success.

Kilkenny Handball Board are delighted to have been asked to contribute to the history of Mullinavat GAA and would like to wish the club the very best of luck in the venture.

Michael O'Shea (Chairman)
Martin Lalor
Kilkenny Handball Board

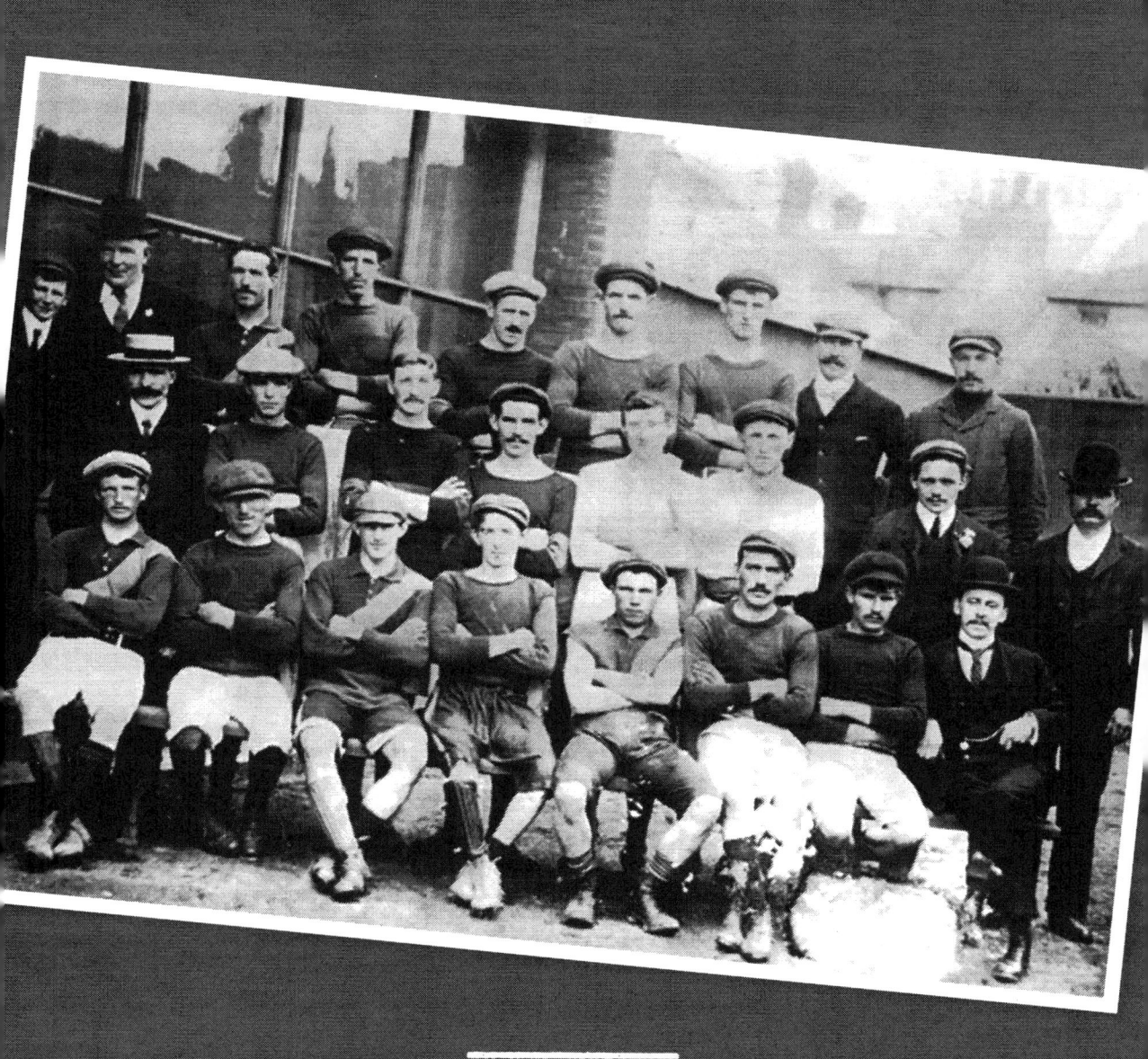

Kilkenny won 3 Leinster SFC titles (1888, 1900, 1911) and finished runners-up a further five times (1893, 1903, 1904, 1909, 1922). Here is the Kilkenny squad (Lamogue Rovers) which reached the 1903 Leinster SFC final: Mick Landy (capt), Stephen Davis, Tom Hyland, Pat O'Neill, Mick O'Neill, Bob Maher, Larry Comerford, John McGrath, Jim Donovan, Pat Power, John Fitzpatrick, Ned Conway, Nick Curran, Tom Phelan, Dan Stapleton, Mick Tobin, Davy Hoyne, Mick Tobin and Pat McGrath.

MULLINAVAT GAA
TIMELINE

- **MARCH 25TH, 1887:** Mullinavat played its first Senior County championship match in Gaelic Football at Piltown against the home team.

- **WINTER 1904:** Mullinavat appeared in their first Kilkenny SFC final, a loss versus Lamogue.

- **SPRING 1911:** Although Kilkenny had worn the black and amber as early as 1893, it was from this time that they were adopted as the official Kilkenny GAA colours.

- **FEBRUARY 2ND, 1913:** Mullinavat's first championship hurling match, this in the new South Junior Championship versus Kilmacow at Harristown.

- **JULY 20TH, 1913:** A first South Junior Hurling final for the club, versus Mong. The latter were awarded the title after an unfinished game, abandoned after 17 minutes.

- **AUGUST 4TH, 1916:** Mullinavat win a first County JHC final (1915) with a 2-4 to 0-1 victory versus Horse and Jockey.

- **APRIL 7TH, 1918:** Mullinavat win their second County JHC (1916) with a 2-4 to 1-2 victory versus Dicksboro at St James' Park, Kilkenny.

- **SPRING 1919:** Southern Board formed in 1919 with James Aylward of Mullinavat as its chairman.

- **APRIL 19TH, 1921:** A 23-year-old civilian James Hoban from Glendonnell was shot by Crown Forces on the Main Street in Mullinavat as part of "The troubles 1920-1922 inclusive."

- **APRIL 23RD, 1922:** At the Kilkenny GAA convention a reference was made by a delegate to a set of medals still due to Mullinavat club in connection with the 1917 championship victory.

- **JUNE 8TH, 1924:** Two Mullinavat men, John Murphy and Andrew McLaughlin, lost their lives in a road accident involving a lorry, when travelling with Mullinavat handball club to a match at Owning, Piltown.

- **NOVEMBER 22ND, 1924:** A fundraising dance held under the auspices of Mullinavat handball club in the new creamery store, Mullinavat was a huge success with 350 couples attending.

- **JANUARY 4TH, 1929:** Mullinavat make a fourth JHC final (1928) appearance in losing to Carrickshock, (the others were 1913/1915/1916).

- **SEPTEMBER 4TH, 1932:** Jack Duggan won the first of his three All-Ireland Senior hurling medals. With no parish rule, Mullinavat-born Duggan played his club hurling with both Knockmoylan and Mooncoin.

- **APRIL 4TH, 1934:** At Nowlan Park, Mullinavat carried off the honours in the County JFC (1933) with a decisive victory over Ballyfoyle in the final.

- **JANUARY 13TH, 1935:** Tullogher beat Mullinavat by six points when they met at Nowlan Park in the County Senior football final (1934).

- **MARCH 15TH, 1936:** A third County Senior football final (1935) loss for the club, this time by two points, versus Barrow Rovers (Glenmore and Slieverue United).

- **NOVEMBER 19TH, 1938:** Mullinavat suffered a four-point loss to Ballyline in the final of the County JHC, 3-5 to 2-4.

- **MARCH 19TH, 1939:** Mullinavat won its only Kilkenny County Minor Hurling Roinn A title (1938 final) with an eight-point victory over Dicksboro at Ballyhale.

- **DECEMBER 10TH, 1939:** Mullinavat, compensated for their defeat at the hands of Ballyline in the previous County JHC final last year and recovered the County title after a lapse of 22 years,

- **OCTOBER 13TH, 1940:** Mullinavat were now up to the Senior grade for the first time since the 1920s and reached their first ever Senior hurling final, losing by two points to Carrickshock.

- **AUGUST 8TH, 1943:** Mullinavat reached a second ever Senior hurling final, but lose to Carrickshock, who completed a four-in-a-row.

- **OCTOBER 28TH, 1952:** Fr Gallavan, who had arrived in the parish in July 1952, arranged a meeting at the Old School House, which resulted in the reformation of Mullinavat Hurling Club.

- **JUNE 1953:** The original Mullinavat GAA field was purchased for £590. This was the first official GAA pitch in the county, outside Nowlan Park

- **DECEMBER 20TH, 1953:** The Kilkenny GAA convention rescinded the three parishes rule and adopted a one parish rule for Senior, Junior and Minor hurling in Kilkenny from 1954.

- **SEPTEMBER 1ST, 1957:** Mullinavat clubman, John Sutton won an All-Ireland Senior Hurling Championship medal when Kilkenny beat Waterford in the final.

- **JULY 31ST, 1960:** The staging of the first ever Mullinavat Fete. The Aylward Cup was donated by James Aylward, a merchant in Arundel Square, Waterford, and 18 gaberdine overcoats was the winner's incentive. The very first game in the Fete's history was between Mount Sion and Castlecomer, which Mount Sion won by five points.

- **SUMMER 1961:** The county board introduced a break from the parish rule in 1961, which allowed Junior club players to participate in the Senior Hurling Championship as well as Junior. Four combination sides were allowed join the championship – the city, the North, the Near South and the Far South. Mullinavat were grouped in with the Far South selection, that included Carrickshock, Windgap, Piltown, Mooncoin and Carrigeen.

- **MAY 1963:** At a meeting of Mullinavat Handball club it was stated that preliminary work on the erection of the new handball court in the village had begun. It was expected to have the new alley ready for play during the summer.

- **MARCH 1967:** Mullinavat Hurling Club switched to current colours of black and all white, which in the main has remained the club colours to the present day.

- **JULY 1969:** A replay of the County Junior football final (1968) was ordered as Bigwood emerged victorious by 0-9 to 0-2 versus Barrowmount.

- **SEPTEMBER 3RD, 1972:** Mullinavat clubman, Mossy Murphy won an All-Ireland Senior Hurling Championship medal when Kilkenny beat Cork in the final.

- **OCTOBER 27, 1974:** Mullinavat win the Southern Divisional Junior Hurling final at Piltown for the first time since 1939 with a one-point victory versus Tullogher.

- **OCTOBER 1ST, 1978:** Mullinavat took Southern honours in the JHC at Piltown, beating Glenmore by a single point (2-6 to 0-11).

- **OCTOBER 21ST, 1984:** GAA Centenary Year and Mullinavat turned back the pages of history nearly 50 years when they scored this merited victory over Emeralds (Urlingford) in the JHC final at Callan. Previous wins were in 1939, 1916 and 1915.

- **DECEMBER 1984:** The original history of the GAA in Mullinavat in book form and over 100 pages in volume.

- **SEPTEMBER 24TH, 1989:** Mullinavat won their first ever County Intermediate Hurling Championship beating Young Irelands, Gowran before a 6,000 crowd at Nowlan Park.

- **APRIL 28TH, 1990:** Mullinavat played their first game in the Senior Championship since the 1940s, in the league stages, losing 1-18 to 0-10 to Shamrocks Ballyhale at Piltown.

- **OCTOBER 31ST, 1999:** Mullinavat beaten by John Lockes (Callan) by three points in the Kilkenny Intermediate hurling final.

- **MAY 14TH, 2000:** Mullinavat scooped their first County Intermediate football title following a convincing comeback versus O'Loughlin Gaels in Nowlan Park.

- **OCTOBER 21ST, 2001:** Mullinavat make up for the heartbreak of 1999 and step back into big time hurling with a three-point Intermediate final win v Clara.

- **APRIL 12TH, 2004:** Having been relegated from the Senior football ranks the previous year, Mullinavat bounced straight back, winning both the league and championship trophies.

- **APRIL 2004:** Four new dressing rooms and toilets completed at the club grounds

- **SUMMER 2005:** Work continued on the new spectator stand and training lights at Mullinavat GAA club.

- **SEPTEMBER 8TH, 2007:** A first Kilkenny SFC title for the club with a replay win versus Glenmore. This was the club's fourth final following 1904 (beaten by Lamogue), 1934 (beaten by Tullogher), and in 1935 (beaten by a Glenmore/Slieverue combination known as the Barrow Rovers).

- **SEPTEMBER 6TH, 2009:** Willie O'Dwyer is Mullinavat's most honour-laden player and on this date he won his fifth and final All-Ireland Senior hurling medal. He won previous medals in 2003, 2006, 2007 and 2008.

- **SEPTEMBER 25TH, 2010:** At the fourth attempt Mullinavat's Senior camogie team finally got over the line versus old foes St Lachtain's. They had lost finals to the same opponent in 2009, 2006 and 2005.

- **OCTOBER 17TH, 2010:** Playing in a fifth county Intermediate hurling final, we suffered a one-point loss versus city side Dicksboro.

- **NOVEMBER 11TH, 2013:** A historic day for our camogie club, winning a first Leinster Senior Camogie title versus St Ibar's/Shelmaliers of Wexford.

- **DECEMBER 8TH, 2013:** After 100 years Mullinavat won the County Under 21 Hurling Championship with a five-point victory over O'Loughlins Gaels.

- **NOVEMBER 11TH, 2014:** Mullinavat are back in the Senior ranks following a four-point Intermediate hurling final victory over St Patrick's (Ballyraggett).

- **NOVEMBER 23RD, 2014:** Mullinavat took their first Leinster Club hurling title (Intermediate) with a three-point victory over Kiltale of Meath at Pairc Tailteann, Navan.

- **DECEMBER 7TH, 2019:** Mullinavat were the first ever Kilkenny club to contest the Leinster Intermediate football final, and even though we lost by three points, versus Mattock Rangers, it was a proud day for the 400 or so Mullinavat supporters who travelled to Drogheda.

- **JULY 17TH, 2022:** All-Ireland Junior football final victory for Kilkenny at Croke Park. Has there ever been a prouder day for the parish? Eleven players out of 26, one selector also, represent the parish.

- **NOVEMBER 13TH, 2022:** Parish Priest Father Liam Barron has continued the tradition of clergy involvement in the Mullinavat GAA club. On this date the parish celebrated the Golden Jubilee of his ordination, and over 20 years service to parishioners in Mullinavat and Bigwood.

- **JUNE 30TH, 2023:** For the sixth time in seven seasons, and the seventh in the club's history, Mullinavat are once more the Kilkenny Senior football champions, beating Thomastown in the final.

- **DECEMBER 26TH, 2023:** The Mullinavat community walkway was officially opened in front of a large crowd at the GAA Grounds. Fr Liam Barron, who blessed the walkway, praised the great work of the local club in constructing such a tremendous facility for the people of the area.

The Mullinavat squad which claimed the Kilkenny SFC title in 2023

A Brief History

Mullinavat GAA Club was formed in 1887. In 1915 and 1916, Mullinavat won the Junior Hurling Championship, and the club entered a successful period again in the late 1930s and early 1940s winning Minor A in 1938, Junior in 1939 and contesting Senior hurling finals in 1940 and 1943.

The arrival of Monsignor Tommy Maher as Parish Priest in 1983 provided the catalyst for the club's future successes. Merging successful Minor and U-21 championship winning teams with some experienced players, Monsignor Maher guided the club to the 1984 Centenary County Junior Championship and the same group of players continued to win the Intermediate championship in 1989.

Winning the Minor B and U-21 B championships in 1998 and 1999 respectively provided the core group of players who won the Intermediate championships of 2001 and 2006. The club won its first ever U-21 A championship in 2013 having been beaten in the previous year's final, and this group along with a number of experienced players won the county and Leinster Intermediate Championships in 2014 and have maintained the club at Senior level since.

The club won the Senior Football Championship in 2007-2017-2018-2019-2020-2022-2023, and Intermediate Football Championship in 2000 and 2004, all milestone achievements, having amalgamated with Bigwood, who won Junior Football Championships in 1968 and 1979.

There is a long tradition of camogie in the parish also, and the club has been very successful in recent years, winning the Kilkenny Senior Championship four times, 2010-

2012-2013-2015. The club also won a Leinster Senior Club Championship in 2013, as well as numerous underage championships. Players from the club have won All-Ireland Senior medals and All Star awards, as well as having the honour of providing the captain of Kilkenny's All-Ireland Senior winning team in 2016.

HURLING FIELD

In the early part of the 1900s, hurling matches took place in several fields around Mullinavat village. Some of those venues were Purcell's field, and at a later stage John Dalton's field and also the Raftice field on the old N9 primary road to Dublin.

In June 1953, Mullinavat Hurling Club purchased the existing hurling field from the owner Ms Bernie Kelly. The plan was to erect an embankment so Senior and Junior games could be held there. To help defray the cost, a house-to-house collection was staged.

> 'Auction of Landsß – The land at Inchacanon, Mullinavat, containing 13 acres, statute measure, were put for sale by public auction at the salesroom, Gladstone St, Waterford on Tuesday last, by directions of the representatives of the late Mrs Mary McDonald, Lukeswell. After keen bidding between Mr Bernie Kelly, Mullinavat, and Mr John Walsh, Mullinavat, the former was declared the purchaser at £1,125. Portion of the land is let to the local hurling club. The auctioneer was Mr John J Phelan MIAA, Waterford, and Mr M M Halley, solicitor, Waterford had carriage of sale.'
> (Munster Express 5/6/1953)

> 'Gaelic Field Purchased – Mullinavat Gaelic Field has now been purchased from the owner, Mr Bernie Kelly, by the local hurling club, and a big scheme of alterations and improvements is contemplated. It is proposed to erect an embankment and make the venue suitable for county Senior and Junior championship games. To help to defray the heavy outlay, it has been decided to hold a house to house collection in the district in the near future, when it is hoped that a generous response will be forthcoming in order to bring the proposals to a successful fruition. The members of the hurling club deserve to be warmly commended on their initiative and enterprise, which should be a great boon to the "Rod-iron" village.
> (Munster Express 19/6/1953)

OUR STORY (1887-2024)

Since then, it is a story of continuous development:
- 1953 – Original field purchase @ £590. This was the first official GAA pitch in the county, outside Nowlan Park
- 2003 – Room and clubhouse development
- 2005 – Built
- 2021 – Second field purchased from Diocese for €30,000
- 2021 – Additional land purchase to facilitate walkway and Juvenile pitch
- 2022 – Additional land purchase to facilitate walkway and field extension
- 2023 – Community walkway and Juvenile pitch development.

OUR CREST

The Mullinavat GAA crest features three well known area landmarks; namely, Poulnassy Waterfall, Tory Hill and the Old Mill.

Poulnassy Waterfall is about one mile past the GAA grounds. The cross at the top of Tory Hill, which is also an area landmark, from where visitors enjoy a tremendous view of the local landscape. Finally, Mullinavat's Old Mill is where it is said that the stones used to build it were taken from the ruins of a nearby castle.

OUR COLOURS

Down the years Mullinavat GAA Club has had various sets of colours. In the early days the colours were 'chocolate and green'. In 1937, the colours were changed to 'blue and white'. In 1953 a new set of green and gold jerseys were presented to the club by Nicky McSweeney and Nicholas O'Neill (undertaker). In February 1967, via the Kilkenny People newspaper, Mullinavat send out an appeal to friends and traders for a new set of jerseys. £30 was raised and the Kilkenny People edition of 31/3/1967 reported: "Mullinavat hurling club have acquired a new set of jerseys of 'all white, with black bands' on the neck and sleeve." The colours were changed again in 1973, when a 'black and red' set of jerseys were purchased, at a cost of £49.

In 1976, the club decided to revert back to the 'black and white' colours. £56 was the outlay on this occasion, and whilst we have numerous variations of jersey style since then, we have always remained in black and white.

OUR PARISH HISTORY

The Mullinavat town name in Irish is Muileann an Bhata which translates as 'The Mill of the Stick'. Tradition has it that the name was derives from a mill which could only be approached by means of a rough stick over the Glendonnel River, where the bridge on the main road is now, beside the Garda Barracks.

AREA

The longest distance travelling north to south "as the crow flies" from Killahy in the upper end of the parish to Fahee, or Fahy as it is on the map in the lower end, is 11.9km The longest distance east to West, again as the crow flies, from Rathnasmolagh on one side to Listrolin at the other is 10.6km – giving a total area of 48.84 square miles (78.6km).

Mullinavat, prior to 1842, was part of Kilmacow parish. In 1801 the village had only 35 houses and 158 inhabitants. The building of the present parish church in 1805 improved matters and by 1841 there were 110 inhabited houses. In 1871, the population of Mullinavat was 531.

NAME

The name is said to have derived from the site of an ancient mill, which tradition has it could only be approached by the means of the large stick (probably a tree trunk) over the Glendonnell River. It is situated on the southern end of the village, near where the bridge on the main road is today. The Garda Barracks is also nearby.

Mullinavat originally comprised of the civil parishes of Kilbeacon, Killahy and Rossinan. The parish church of Kilbeacon was in use up to 1830. The Protestant community of the area used it at the time. Only the tower of the original building remained standing up to a few years ago. It was latterly demolished, as it was considered to be in a dangerous structural state. The surrounding stone wall and the graveyard remain today.

Killahy church was mentioned at the time of the suppression of religious houses around 1530. It was dedicated to the exaltation of the Holy Cross and very little of its remains are visible today. The church that stood in Rossinan was also mentioned during that time. It was dedicated to St Senan, patron of the adjoining parish of Kilmacow. The site of the church was to the south of the village, near the left bank of Blackwater River, on the main Waterford to Dublin Road. Both the road and railway line cut through its former location at present.

In 1946, the townlands of Clonassy, Listrolin and Rochestown were annexed from Mooncoin. The ancient church that served that district stood in Listrolin, in the laneway leading over the Assy River to Ballinacooley. The remains were uprooted and destroyed in the middle of the last century.

OUR STORY (1887-2024)

TORY HILL
(Ir. Sliabh Gcruinn, 'Round Mountain')

Tory Hill is one of the great landmarks of the parish of Mullinavat. It is said to have got its name from a famous outlaw called James Denn. Denn used its superb vantage as an ideal spot for a hideout. The word Tory derives from the Irish Toraidhe, meaning outlaw, or more precisely, one who is pursued. It stands 10.4 metres (34 feet) short of a mountain. Spectacular views can be had from its summit on a clear day.

Tory Hill reaches a height of 290 metres in elevation.

There is a pattern held each year on Tory Hill on the second Sunday of July. This is locally called 'Tory Hill Sunday' and 'Frocchans Sunday'. It never was a religious celebration, but merely consisted of the people of the neighbourhood gathering to pick the wild berries called 'Frocchans'. In the Holy Year of 1950, a large cross was erected on the summit of the hill, and since then the rosary had been said by the people who gather beneath the cross.

Visit Kilkenny website states: "If you're looking for a 360 view over the surrounding counties Waterford, Wexford, Tipperary and Kilkenny, then there's no better beauty than the top of Tory Hill. Suitable for families, friends and hikers alike, this loop has a gravel track most of the way for when the mountainous terrain becomes too much. Tory Hill can be completed in a 2-hour hike and is one of our favourite Off the Grid Kilkenny spots for sure!'

INCHICARRON CASTLE

This was the dwelling of one Walsh clan and was occupied by a John Mac Walter Walsh. This gentleman was a poet of considerable merit and has a dance tune called 'Tatter Jack Walsh' named after him. His property was confiscated, and he died in 1660. Tatter Jack's remains were buried in Killbeacon cemetery. The site of the original castle was located in the field beside the parish GAA grounds.

CLONASSY CASTLE

The remains of the foundation of this other Walsh clan castle is to be found in the townland of the same name. It is located in a field overlooking the village, appropriately called "The Castle Field". Its last occupant was Robert Walsh, Member of Parliament for Kilkenny. He was slain in 1691.

POULANASSY WATERFALL

This is situated 3km from Mullinavat on the road through Clonassy towards Piltown and Carrick-on-Suir. Poulanassy waterfall flows into the river Blackwater. Visit Kilkenny website says: 'The picturesque Poulanassy Waterfall, located just outside Kilkenny, is a natural beauty. Surrounded by forestry terrain and overhanging trees, it's a guaranteed great day out for family or friends. Or even if you need some time alone with nature, this is the ideal tranquil spot! The waterfall's pool is the ideal spot for a peaceful swim and in the summer, you have full access to picnic areas and portable BBQs.'

PART · ONE

GAELIC FOOTBALL

1887–2024

CHAPTER 1

1887-1939

'P. Aylward (Hon Secretary Mullinavat) wrote on behalf of the club objecting to Dungarvan being awarded the match played at Thomastown on 31st May, in the Junior Football Championship, on the grounds that Dungarvan played an unregistered man named Richard Dalton; and (2) that Dungarvan played in the same colours as Mullinavat, contrary to the rules, the latter club, being the longer registered, having priority of claim to colours.'

1931
South JFC R1
Dungarvan 1-3; Mullinavat 0-0

1887-1939

While we all know both Kilkenny and Mullinavat as counties and clubs that prioritise hurling, in the past two decades Mullinavat have proudly become one of the football strongholds of the county, joining the likes of Glenmore, Thomastown, Railyard and Muckalee. While the lure of county and club hurling championships deprives Kilkenny of its best footballers, our club has performed heroics in the Gaelic football code in recent years. In this section of our history, we look at both the club's recent successes, along with the adjacent story of the difficult task it is for those running the big ball code in a hurling county such as Kilkenny, to keep the game going.

FIRST KILKENNY SFC 1887

MARCH 25, 1887

Kilkenny SFC: Piltown 1-02; Mullinavat 0-03

The first definition of a parish rule was created for the 1887 championship. Clubs could only use players living or working in the parish of each club. Nineteen teams entered the first county football championship. The draw was: Mullinavat v. Piltown, Mooncoin v. Ballyhale, Kilmacow v. Slieverue, Johnstown v. Sart, Lisdowney v. Crosspatrick, Kilkenny v. Killamory, Kilmanagh v. Kells, Working Mens Club v. Conahy, Tullaroan v. Castlecomer and Callan bye.

The Mullinavat v. Piltown game was played on March 25th, 1887 as part of a triple header with the Mooncoin v. Ballyhale and Mooncoin v. Ballyhale games.

So, on 25th March, 1887 Mullinavat played its first Gaelic football county championship match at Piltown against the home team. The team and supporters travelled in wagonettes, common carts and every available mode of transport, whilst a good many also accomplished the journey by shank's mare (it was no trouble to walk 20 to 30 miles to a match in those days). Despite very unfavourable weather, Piltown was invaded by a big hosting of Gaels that day, and considerable enthusiasm prevailed between the neighbouring rivals.

The game involving Mullinavat was the third game at Piltown that afternoon.

The Mullinavat selection included the Aylward brothers (Clonassy), Tom Thompson (Clonassy), Mick Power (Clonassy), Jim Costelloe and Patsy Power (Bawnageloge), Patsy Hurley (Rossinan), the Forristal brothers (Buckstown), Jackson Dalton (Buckstown), Pat Kinsella (Rathkieran) and Tom Burke (Ballinacooley).

The victorious Piltown team were under the captaincy of Bill O'Donnell, Ballyhenebry. Others of the team on that occasion were the Dunnes of Ballyhenebry, Mick Conway and Sam Tobin, Tybroughney; Ned Quinn, Tybroughny; Mick Farrell, Castletown; the brothers O'Shea from Owning, and L Fitzgerald of Raheen, a native of Catsrock.

SECOND KILKENNY SFC 1888

Thirty-four teams participated. Mullinavat lost to Slieverue but objected that Slieverue had three Kilmacow men on their team.

THIRD KILKENNY SFC 1889

The draw for the 1889 Kilkenny Hurling and Football Championships took place on Friday, 8th March, but Mullinavat were not involved in either. Glenmore v. Prospect (Kilkenny), Inistioge v. O'Connells (Ballyhennebery) Thomastown v. Kilkenny Commercials, Thomas Larkins (Kilkenny) v. Tullaroan, Tullogher v. Ballyouskill, Killamery v. Callan, John Mandevilles (Temploerum) v. Kells, Ballyhale a bye. However, the club did participate in a couple of Gaelic football challenge games.

MARCH 17, 1889
ST PATRICK'S DAY 1889 FOOTBALL TOURNAMENT AT MOONCOIN
Mullinavat 0-02, Ballyhenneberry 0-00 (abandoned early in first half)

This was the third game in a footballing programme that day also involving Waterford Commercials versus Carrick Young Irelanders, and Slieverue versus John Mandevilles (Temploerum).

Mullinavat started well with the wind, before a major row developed, which caused the game to be abandoned. Referee Mr Pat Fogarty, who had also took charge of the previous games, found that he could not continue, with players and spectators involved in the melee.

The Munster Express reported: 'Daniel O'Connell's (Ballyhennebery) lost the toss and kicked against the wind, Mullinavat having the advantage and scoring a point. They followed up with another, which should have been a goal, and then added two points to their score. The O'Connell's goalkeeper then amused himself by striking one of the Mullinavat men, when

Foskin, the captain of the "Rod Iron" men, at once very properly decided on withdrawing his men, the match being awarded to him. The conduct of some of the men playing for Ballyhennebery was simply disgraceful, and calculated to bring discredit to the association.

Mullinavat: John Foskin, John Raftice, John Walsh, Martin Corcoran, Pat Kinsella, Pat Shea, Michael Power, T Foskin, M Hynes, Pat McEvoy, Michael Aylward, Thomas Aylward, D Grant, E Grant, John Whitty, James Costelloe, P Power, P Hurley, W Darmody, T Forristal and P Aylward.

Mullinavat also played Slieverue at Bishop's Hall. And two months later, on May 11th, Mullinavat played a challenge SF game versus Mooncoin at Rathcurby, losing 0-3 to 0-0.

1890-1895

Very little by way of GAA activities in much of South Kilkenny, including Mullinavat, due to political disturbances at the time.

1896

Mullinavat beat a Ferrybank selection in Kilmacow, in a fundraiser for the Kilmacow Fife and Drum band. Later that year Mullinavat played Slieverue at Christendom in a football contest.

In October 1896, Kilmacow and Butlerstown drew 0-3 each in a charity fundraiser for two families evicted from their farms in Kilmacow parish.

In November 1896, a Waterford Commercials selection beat Mullinavat 2-2 to 0-0 in a physical contest in Doody's Field, Lower Kilmacow. Local man, Patrick Doody of Tinlough refereed the tense contest.

1904

Kilkenny SFC Final: Lamogue beat Mullinavat

Lamogue, a team from the Windgap area, beat Mullinavat to complete a three in a row.

From the newspaper accounts it appears that GAA clubs in the early decades of the twentieth century engaged in fundraising by hosting tournaments among other activities. To entice teams to a tournament medals or jerseys were advertised and provided for the winning team members. On the 31st of July 1904 a 'highly successful tournament' took place at Glenmore (The Waterford News and Star, 5 Aug. 1904). It was held in a field given by Dr. Philips, of Rochestown House (Mount Ida). Two matches were to be held that day. The first was a championship match between Slieverue and Nore Rangers, and the other a friendly between Mullinavat and Campile. It was reported that the young and inexperienced men of Slieverue proved that they were equal to their opponent though they did not win. The Campile team failed to appear for the friendly, so the Glenmore team took to the field to play Mullinavat and the game ended in a draw. The article concluded that the Glenmore Football Club Committee are to be congratulated on the silver medals awarded, the excellent field arrangements and it was noted that the 'new extension railway line affords unique facilities to meet in Glenmore' with a field convenient to the Aylwardstown station.

1905

Kilkenny SFC Final: Lamogue beat Harristown

This win completed a Lamogue four in a row for the team from the Windgap area.

1913

First South JFC Final: Tullogher drew with Harristown
First South JFC Final Replay: Tullogher 2-04; Harristown 0-01

'On Sunday, 31st August, an important fixture will be brought off at the above centre under the auspices of the Ballyhale Hurling Club. In football, Harristown is billed to meet Tullogher in the final of the first division of the County Championship South, and a friendly hurling challenge is being arranged between Callan and Mullinavat. The prowess of the Harristown and Tullogher footballers is so well known that the names alone are sufficient to ensure a record attendance and an exciting contest for Co. Championship honours. The gate receipts are to go to the funds of the Harristown Club, and we need scarcely remind Southern Gaels that it is their bounded duty to grant their patronage and practical support to a club which has done, ana is doing, so much to uphold the prestige of our national pastimes.'

1914

South JFC Final: Harristown beat Kells

Even though beaten in the Southern final it was Harristown who competed in the County final, losing to Burnchurch.
Kilkenny JFC Final: Burnchurch 1-00; Harristown 0-02

1915
South JFC Final: Kells 2-00; Glenmore 1-02

1916
South JFC Final: Cappagh beat Glenmore

1917-18
No Championship played

1919
South JFC Final: Glenmore 2-01; Harristown 1-00 (unfinished due to darkness)
South JFC Final Replay: Glenmore 2-03; Hugginstown 1-01
Glenmore went on to beat CYMS (Kilkenny) 2-4 to 0-1 in Junior County final.

1920
South JFC Final: Cotterstown 0-3; Hugginstown 0-1
Cotterstown went on to win county Junior final beating Castlecomer.

1921
No championship.

1922
South JFC Final: Barrow Rovers (Tullogher) 1-04; Glenmore 0-01
Barrow Rovers went on to beat Muckalee United 2-3 to 0-1 in Junior County final.

1923
South JFC Round 1: Tullogher beat Mullinavat
South JFC Final Cotterstown 2-01; Glenmore 1-02
Cotterstown won County final on a walkover from Cuffesgrange.

1924

South JFC Final: Knocktopher 3-01; Glenmore 1-01

Knocktopher won County Junior final, 3-4 to 1-2 versus Conahy. Mullinavat were not in the draw, where 6 South JFC clubs were affiliated along with 17 in hurling.

1925

Mullinavat were not competing in Gaelic football in these years; the six who did compete in the South Junior football were Glenmore, Grove, Coolroe, Kilmacow, The Rower and Dunnamaggin.
South JFC Final: Glenmore 2-01; The Rower 0-03

1926

Mullinavat did not compete with eight teams competing in the South Junior football championship. The eight were Killarney, Coolroe, Slieverue, Tullogher, Glenmore, Hillsboro, Emmets, Kilmoganny and The Rower.
South JFC Final: Coolroe 1-03; Glenmore 0-00

1927

Twelve teams entered the South Junior Football Championship with four new teams being Knocktopher, Civic Guards, Raheen and Knockroe.
South JFC Final: Cotterstown 0-06; Glenmore 0-04
County Final Replay: Cotterstown 2-04; Conahy 1-02

1928

South JFC Final: Tullogher 0-03, Glory Rovers (Dunnamaggin) 0-01

Tullogher won County Junior football final versus Cloneen 1-3 to 1-1.

1929

JUNIOR

Thirteen teams entered the South Junior Football Championship with Mullinavat back competing. The first round draw being: Hugginstown v. Thomastown, Blacks and Whites

v. Tullogher, Glenmore v. Mullinavat, Cotterstown v. Brandon Rovers No 1, Ferrybank v. Inistioge, Skeogh V Brandon Rovers No.2, Templeorum a bye.

South JFC R1: Glenmore 2-03, Mullinavat 1-00
   (Match refixed as Glenmore used an illegal player)
South JFC R1 Replay: Glenmore 1-03, Mullinavat 0-00
South JFC Final: Tullogher 1-02; Brandon Rovers (The Rower) 0-05
South JFC Final Replay: Brandon Rovers 0-08; Tullogher 0-07
   (Tullogher were later awarded the title on an objection)

Kilkenny county had three successful periods in Gaelic football, 1887/88, 1900/1913 and 1920's. After this hurling was the prominent sport in the county, a situation that continues to today. In the later years of the 1930s decade many Mullinavat men played with Carrickshock, Kilmacow, Slieverue and Glenmore amongst others, particularly in years when Mullinavat failed to field teams.

1930
JUNIOR

Twelve teams were registered for the South Junior football draw.
South JFC R1 Mullinavat v. Raheen scr.
South JFC R2: Mullinavat 2-07; Knocktopher 2-00

'The above teams met at Knockmoylan on Ascension Thursday 29/5/1930, in the initial round of the Southern Junior Football Championship when the representatives of the "rod iron" village were deserving winners on the score of 2-7 to 2-0, after a good game. The weather conditions were ideal and there was a fairly large attendance of spectators. The scores were level at half time, but Mullinavat were superior in the closing moiety and ran out comfortable winners by a margin of seven points.'

'Mullinavat pressed from the start and D Maddox sent in a point within the first few minutes of the game. Floodhall were away per Carroll and Fitzgerald, but "Gill" Murphy made a splendid save in the Mullinavat goal. From a free to Mullinavat, Forristal drove wide. Mullinavat continued on the offensive, but sent many wides. Forristal added a neat point from a free close in. From a further free Power cleared effectively for Knocktopher and attacked to send over, J Aylward put Mullinavat further ahead with a point from a free. Knocktopher attacked in determined fashion and forced a "50." The kick was well placed by Connors and the forwards finished for a good goal to level the scoring. From a free P Aylward saved for Mullinavat, but the forwards pressed again for Murphy to bring off a brilliant save in goal at the expense of a "50", which was well cleared by the backs, of whom Sullivan at full was an outstanding performer, and his many stylish clearances were enthusiastically cheered. Tobin placed to advantage from a free to Mullinavat but Maddox spoiled by fouling.'

'Carroll broke away for Knocktopher on the resumption, but the backs cleared to advantage. Mullinavat attacked and from a neat passing movement Aylward finished for a grand point. Mullinavat again pressed, and Maddox drove wide from far out. P Aylward was conspicuous on the back for Mullinavat and nullified many hot attacks by Knocktopher. Forristal was fouled, and from the free Aylward finished for a neat point. Murphy saved well in goal, but the forwards were again in possession to send through for a goal, which gave Knocktopher the lead for the first time by a point, Exciting bouts of play followed, and with the margin so close the spectators were kept at a high pitch of expectancy. Hoiden was fouled, but the free brought no reward. Mullinavat made many gallant attempts to equalise, but Egan came to the rescue for Knocktopher on the back line and saved many dangerous situations. Mullinavat were away again, and from a grand pass from Maddox, J. Aylward shot over the crossbar for the equaliser amidst great cheering. Egan saved from a free taken by Maddox. A further free to Mullinavat (taken by Tobin) struck the cross-bar and Hyland cleared from the danger zone, but J Aylward cleverly eluded two opponents to score a brilliant point.'

Mullinavat: W Sullivan (captain), M Murphy (goal), John, James, Patrick and William Aylward, Philip, Thomas and David Maddox; W Walsh, J Murphy, P Holden, J Tobin, E Conway and L Hanrahan,

COOLROE V. MULLINAVAT

'The above match in the second round of the Junior Football Championship, which was fixed for Inistioge on Sunday 20/7/1930 did not take place as Mullinavat wore notified on Saturday evening that Coolroe were not travelling. It was rumoured that Mullinavat were claiming the match on the grounds that they did not receive sufficient notice of the postponement of the fixture, but we learn since that such is not the case.'

South JFC Final: Carrickshock 1-03; Brandon Rovers 0-04

1931

JUNIOR

Sixteen teams took part in the 1931 South Junior Football Championship.
South JFC R1: Dungarvan 1-03: Mullinavat 0-00

(Match awarded to Mullinavat as Dungarvan had used unregistered player)

'P Aylward (Hon Secretary Mullinavat FC) wrote on behalf of the Club objecting to Dungarvan being awarded the match played at Thomastown on 31st May, in the Junior Football Championship, on the grounds that Dungarvan played an unregistered man named Richard Daiton, and (2) that Dungarvan played in the same colours as Mullinavat, contrary to the rules, the latter club, being the longer registered, having priority of claim to colours. J Aviward, in support of the objection, provided the copy of the Dungarvan players as registered with the County Secretary and such list did not contain the name of Edward Daiton. The Dungarvan representative stated that it was a slight error on their part in filling up the form. The Chairman said that Dungarvan fielded a player who was not registered according to rule and he had no option but to award the match to Mullinavat.'

South JFC Semi-final:

'Before a good attendance of spectator at Knocktopher on Sunday 15/11/31, Killarney defeated Mullinavat by the narrow margin of two points, on the score of 2-3 to 2-1'

South JFC Final: Brandon Rovers (The Rower) 2-00; Killarney 1-00

1932

JUNIOR

South JFC R1: Mullinavat w/o Cotterstown

South JFC R2: Mullinavat 4-05; Knocktopher 1-00

'Mullinavat scored a decisive victory over Knocktopher in the Southern Junior Football Championship, after a keen and vigorous game, on the score of 4-5 to 1-0. The play all through was characterised by dash and determination rather than brilliance, and though Knocktopher missed a few likely openings, their opponents excelled at passing and combination, and dominated the play in the concluding stages. Towards the end one or two ugly scenes developed when altercations arose between opposing players resulting in invasion of the playing pitch by rival supporters but, happily, order was restored and the game ended quietly.'

Mullinavat: Tom Conway (captain), Edward Walsh (goal), John, James, William and Pat Aylward, David, Thomas and Philip Maddock, T Walsh, Jack Farrell, Jim Phelan, Pat Holden, M Woods, J Tobin.

South JFC Semi Final: Hillside Rovers (Glenmore) 4-02; Mullinavat 2-00

South JFC Final: Start 4-02; Hillside Rovers (Glenmore) 3-05

South JFC Final Replay: Start 1-04; Hillside Rovers (Glenmore) 1-03

1933
JUNIOR

Nine teams participated in the South JFC first round: Kilmoganny v. John Lockes, Inistioge v. Kilmacow, Blacks and Whites v. Slieverue, Lamogue v. Mount Juliet. Mullinavat a bye.

South JFC R2: Mullinavat 3-00; Kilmoganny 1-03
South JFC Semi Final: Mullinavat 2-05; Lamogue 1-05
South JFC Final: Mullinavat 3-05; Slieverue 0-02

'Before a rather small attendance, due no doubt to the unfavourable weather conditions, Mullinavat scored a decisive victory over Slieverue in the Southern Junior football final played, at Ballyhale on Sunday 24/9/1933, on the score of 3-05 to 0-02. David Maddock, of University College, Dublin, who put in serviceable work all through for Mullinavat, scored a goal and two points in the opening half, and John Aylward added a point. On the turnover Slieverue made a few spirited assaults on the Mullinavat citadel, but the latters defence was too good for the opposing forwards, who at times finished weakly. Jim Phelan, who was a force in South Kilkenny hurling and football circles some years ago, and who also played in the United States, was a tower of strength in the Mullinavat defence, and effected many brilliant clearances. Jack Farrell, the well known Carrickshock hurler, was very accurate with frees from which he obtained a goal and two points after the resumption. Tom Conway put the issue beyond doubt with a fast goal some minutes later, and Mullinavat continued on the offensive to emerge comfortable winners by a margin of 12 points.'

'Hard knocks were given and taken and the game throughout was played in a good sporting spirit, with the exception of a slight incident at the Slieverue goal early in the game through interference by spectators, which was quickly got under control.'

Mullinavat: Tom Conway (captain), J Tobin (goal), David Maddock, Thomas Maddock, Philip Maddock, John Aylward, Pat Aylward, William Aylward, J Barron, Jim Phelan, P Holden, Jack Farrell, T Walsh, J Dwyer and Edward Walsh.

County JFC Final: Mullinavat 6-03; Ballyfoyle 0-03
FIRST COUNTY JUNIOR FOOTBALL WIN FOR SOUTH IN 5 YEARS

'At Nowlan Park, Kilkenny, on Sunday 15/04/1934, Mullinavat carried off the honours in the County Junior Football Championship (1933) by a decisive victory over Ballyfoyle in a final on the score of 6-3 to 0-3. This was the first County Junior Football win for a South side since Tullogher in 1928. The small attendance numbering about 200 was due, no doubt to the adverse weather conditions, a strong southerly wind making matters very unpleasant both for players and spectators alike.'

'Stylish football, under such a handicap, was out of the question, and the game resolved itself into a duel between the defences and the opposing forwards in either half, the prevailing high wind playing an important factor in the procuration of scores. However, taken all round, and apart from the assistance derived from the elements, Mullinavat were the more polished footballers, and their methods of attack and defence came with a machine like precision which left no doubt as to their superiority in each department.'

'Playing with the wind, Mullinavat obtained all their scores in the opening moiety, and Ballyfoyle, who only secured a point in this half, found the task of reducing such a big lead beyond their ability, and apart from two minor scores for the Northern representatives, the score sheet in the concluding half was practically blank.'

'The winners gave a sound exhibition, and each man played his part in contributing to the victory, from the "culbaire" right up to the last line of forwards. Most of their scores were obtained by David Maddock, University College, Dublin (who hails from Ballyquinn), and Jack Farrell, the well known Carrickshock hurler.'

'Mullinavat won the toss and played with the gale in their favour, but the Northmen pressed with vigour from the commencement and experienced ill luck when the ball struck the crossbar and upright in succession. Tobin cleared and Mullinavat broke away for the opening score when, following a neat centre by Conway, the forwards finished for a major after a tussle in the goalmouth after six minutes play. The Southern men returned from the delivery, and John Aylward raised a second green mark flag. Bowling was wide of the mark on a free to Ballyfoyle, and shortly after Mullinavat forced a "50", from which Farrell, with a low, swift shot crashed into the net for a great goal, which was a splendid solo feat. Mullinavat now led by three to nil and continued to dominate the play.'

'The Ballyfoyle backs, of whom Brennan, Lawless and Bowling were prominent, were sorely tried and broke down intermittently under sustained pressure. David Maddock from a passing movement, initiated on the wing, increased the lead by a further goal. A free cased for Ballyfoyle and from the kick close in Brisbane notched a point. Mullinavat continued to harass the opposing defence, and David Maddock and Jack Farrell added a goal each and T Walsh a point before the interval, when the scores were: Mullinavat, 6-3; Ballyfoyle 0-01.'

'On the restart Barron was cautioned for fouling. Ballyfoyle, now aided by the breeze, pressed strongly, but the Mullinavat backs, assisted by their colleagues in the forward line, who had moved down for defensive work, broke up repeated onslaughts. Jim Phelan, the old veteran of many memorable games, Dwyer, Holden and Walsh were doing heroic work for the "Rod Iron" men, and despite spirited attacks by the Northmen, nullified every effort at scoring. A "50" to Ballyfoyle brought no reward, and the battle waged furiously in Mullinavat territory until Brennan, from an opening far out, sent over the bar for a point. Farrell was injured but resumed. Ballyfoyle kept up the pressure, and Bowling added a third point, which was the last score of the match, shortly after Conway and Holden (M.) were injured but resumed.'

Mullinavat: Tom Conway (captain), J Tobin (goal), L Maddock, T Maddock, P Maddock, J Aylward, William Aylward, Pat Aylward, J Phelan, P Holden, J Farrell, EC Walsh, J Barron, P Dwyer, and T Walsh.

1934

SENIOR

SFC R1: Mullinavat 1-04; Glenmore 0-00

'Before a big attendance at Ballybeg on Sunday, Mullinavat defeated Glenmore in the Senior Football Championship by 1-4 to nil. Mr M Connolly refereed. The winners (who are last year's Junior champions) showed excellent combination and good teamwork. Scorers for Mullinavat were Tom Maddock (goal), Jack Farrell (3 points) and Tom Conway (point).

Mullinavat: Tom Conway (captain), W Aylward, P Aylward, Jack Duggan, P Holden, Tom Walsh, Ed Walsh, J Barron, Jim Phelan, D Maddock, T Maddock and P Dwyer.

SFC Semi Final: Mullinavat v. Blacks and Whites (abandoned after 20 minutes)

County Board Meeting (December 1934) on the abandoned game.

'The referee's report on the recent game at Thomastown between Mullinavat and Blacks and Whites in the SF semi-final, which had to be called off after 20 minutes play, was read, but was not available for the Press.'

Mr Maddock (Mullinavat) – "It is a most disgraceful report, and I hope the delegates won't further disgrace themselves by adopting any petty attitude here today. I take serious objections to some of the statements in that report. As far as Mullinavat are concerned, we have taken part in the championship for the past two years and never became involved in any trouble, so that the statements contained in that report, could not be accepted. When a man is on trial for his life it is his past record that counts chiefly, and we are ashamed of none of our players. They have shed lustre on the county, and we are proud of them. They have won high honours on many fields of play."

Mr Walsh (Blacks and Whites) – "The referee states he was obliged to order Jack Duggan and A Healy to the sideline, but to their credit it must be said that neither was responsible for the row, which was caused by outsiders."

Mr Farrell – "The Blacks and Whites were responsible for the row, because the whole time their followers shouted threats towards the Mullinavat players. Mullinavat had only about ten supporters the same day."

Father Brennan – "Apparently there is an element of roughness creeping into football of late which was not to be glossed over. We had the same position in the county twenty years ago, and we don't want to have it renewed again. If it continues, we may as well draw the line first as last and see also that spectators as well as players be severely cautioned. It is a serious report and must be accepted in its entirety. I propose its adoption."

Mr Walsh – "It wasn't very serious, and the primary cause was an old spleen between the Juniors of Mullinavat and Blacks and Whites."

Mr Maddock – "A County Board serves a dual purpose in making hurling and football more popular, and at present there was a welcome revival in Kilkenny following a slack period, so that it would be a pity to check the efforts now being made towards a revival in the county. I suggest that the match be replayed at a neutral venue."

Mr M Egan seconded, and it was eventually decided that the match be replayed at Nowlan Park, admission to the sideline to be strictly limited to two officials from each team.

Suspensions: Jack Duggan (Mullinavat) and A Healy (Blacks and Whites), who were reported for striking, were suspended for one month from the date of the game.

SFC Semi Final Replay: Mullinavat 2-02; Blacks and Whites 0-01

'At Nowlan Park, Mullinavat qualified to meet Tullogher in the 1934 county final on 13th January. The South Kilkenny team played in winning vein throughout and were superior on the general run of the play. Maddock, Holden and Duggan scored for the winners, and Kelly obtained the solitary point scored by Blacks and Whites.'

SFC Final: Tullogher 1-04; Mullinavat 0-01

'Tullogher beat Mullinavat (last season's Junior champions) when they met at Nowlan Park. Kilkenny, on Sunday 13/01/1935 in the county Senior football final, 1934.'

'A very interesting feature of the game was that two sets of brothers were in direct opposition. Jim Dwyer was on the Tullogher team, whilst his brother Paddy lined out with Mullinavat. Furthermore, Tom Conway captained Mullinavat, whilst his brother Ned was in the black and amber of Tullogher.'

'Heavy rain which fell on the previous day, which left the ground in a greasy condition, which made the handling of the football very difficult, but it made no difference to Tullogher, who swept into the attack from the start. With the game only a minute old, Tom Bird send over the bar for the first score of the game. Jack Duggan saved well for Mullinavat shortly afterwards. In another fierce attack by Tullogher, Wat Ryan made a great run and rattled the net for a splendid goal.'

'Dick Barron sent over a point, and the flying Wat Ryan received from Martin J Malone, and shot a great point, to leave Tullogher leading at halftime by 1-3 to 0-00. John Farrell gave Mullinavat some hope with an early second half point, which turned out to be Mullinavat's only score of the game, but the Tullogher men came back in style and Tom Bird put a clear six points between the sides, 1-4 to 0-1. Mullinavat's best were Jack Duggan John Farrell, Jim Phelan and Leahy.'

JUNIOR

South JFC R1: Blacks and Whites beat Mullinavat. (Mullinavat got game replayed following a successful objection concerning illegal players)

South JFC R1 Replay: Mullinavat 0-05; Blacks and Whites 0-04

'The game was keenly contested, an altercation between players, at one period leading to blows, but matters ended, quietly.'

Mullinavat: J Holden (captain), J Gaule (goal), William Dalton, Phil Maddock, William Maddock, M Barron, Bob Aylward, J Phelan, William Walsh, D Duggan, William O'Sullivan, James Hendrick, T Tobin, J Aylward, and Jas Hayes. Scorers: Holden (1 point), Duggan (2 points), and Hayes (2 points). The latter scored the winning point.

South JFC Semi final: Nore Rangers (Inistioge) 2-00; Mullinavat 0-02

Mullinavat: J Holden (captain), Jack Gaule (goal), W Maddock, P Maddock, W Walsh, J Walsh, J Phelan, M Barron, T Tobin, J Aylward, Robert Aylward, J Hendrick, W Sullivan, J Hayes and J McDonald. Sub: E Leahy.

South JFC Final Slieverue 3-04; Nore Rangers 1-02

1935

Mullinavat again competed in both Senior and Junior in 1935.

SENIOR

SFC R1: Mullinavat w/o Confederation (city) scr.

'The team to do duty for Mullinavat in the 1935 Senior football championship was chosen from Tom Conway (captain), J Tobin (goal), John, William, Patrick and Bob Aylward, Tom, James and John Walsh, E Walsh, Tom and Phil Maddock, Jack and Denis Duggan, P Holden, James Phelan. M Barron, J Farrell and J Roughan. The squad includes Jack Duggan and J Walsh of the Kilkenny All Ireland hurling team.

SFC Semi final: Mullinavat 2-04; Cloneen 2-00

'The game was played under bitterly cold weather conditions, which imposed a trying handicap on the players. The winners led at the interval by 2-3 to nil and emerged worthy victors in an exciting finish. Tom Conway, the Duggan brothers, Paddy Holden and Jack Farrell were outstanding for Mullinavat.'

Mullinavat: T Conway (captain), J Tobin (goal), W Aylward, J Duggan, D Duggan, J Walsh, T Walsh, P Holden, J Roughan, J Farrell, C Doogue, M Barron, J Aylward and R Aylward. Mr W Doogue Kilkenny, refereed. The winners meet Barrow Rovers in the final.

County SFC Final: Barrow Rovers (Glenmore and Slieverue United) 0-05; Mullinavat 0-03 (January 13, 1936)

'Before a good attendance at Barrett's Park Now Ross, on Sunday, Barrow Rovers (Glenmore and Slieverue United) defeated Mullinavat in the final of the County SF Championship for 1935 by 0-05 points to 0-03, after a stern hard fought game played under ideal weather conditions.'

Mullinavat squad: Tom Conway (captain), J Tobin (goal), Patrick, William and Robert Aylward, James, John, Edward and Tom Walsh, Jack and Denis Duggan, J Farrell, J Roughan, T Coleman, C Doogue, M Barron, J Phelan and T Maddock.

JUNIOR

Nine teams competed in the South Junior Football Championship. The first round draw was: Barrow Rovers v. Blacks and Whites, Nore Rangers v. Knocktopher, P H Pearse v. Mullinavat, John Locke's (Callan) v. Avonree Starlights (Callan); Lamogue a bye.

JFC R1: Mullinavat v. P.H. Pearse Ferrybank (abandoned after 11 minutes due to continuous heavy rain)
JFC R1 Refixture: Mullinavat 1-03; P.H. Pearse Ferrybank 0-03

'An unusual situation arose at the commencement of the game when it was discovered that neither side had brought a ball and a long delay ensued until one was procured from Ferrybank by car. Kilkenny All-Ireland hurlers figured on opposing sides, Jimmy Walsh being with Mullinavat and Locky Byrne assisting P. H. Pearse, both of whom figured prominently throughout. The teams were level at half time. Mullinavat, a goal, scored by T Tobin, and PH Pearse three points (Power, O'Grady and Carroll).'

'The latter team lost a few likely chances in this moiety, sending a few narrow overs, and on the turnover Mullinavat forged ahead by 2 further points from J Aylward and J Walsh, adding another minor just on the call of time to win by a margin of three points.'

Mullinavat: J Holden (captain), J Gaule (goal), Edward, Robert, John and James Aylward, John, James and Thomas Walsh, Thomas and Phil Tobin, James Hayes, John Long, Phil Maddock and M Barron.

South JFC Final: Tullogher 2-01; Mullinavat 0-01

'Tullogher beat Mullinavat in this battle of neighbouring parishes in the 1935 South

JFC Final, played at Ballyhale on 15/12/1935. The Tullogher goal had a narrow escape early in the first half, the ball being practically on the line, but Malone cleared safely. Malone, who played full-back for Tullogher, was outstanding throughout. The game was vigorously contested, no quarter being given or taken. Tullogher turned over at halftime with a lead of 2-1 to nil, M. Morrissey being the scorer. The Mullinavat backs defended well in the second half, the Aylwards and Walshs being effective, but the forwards could make no impression on a stout Tullogher defence. J Walsh (of hurling fame) had a point for Mullinavat in the second half, the only score recorded in this moiety, and with the light failing fast the game lost interest towards the end. The full-time scores was: Tullogher 2-1; Mullinavat 0-1.'

'During the course of the Southern football final at Ballyhale on Sunday, James Holden, of the Mullinavat team, sustained an injury to his shoulder in an accidental collision with a colleague, for which lie had to be subsequently treated by Dr. Coughlan of Newrath.'

Mullinavat: R Aylward (captain), J Garde (goal), William Aylward, John Aylward, James Aylward, J Walsh, T Walsh, James Walsh, William Walsh, T Tobin, D Doherty, J Barion, J Holden, Edward Aylward and J Hayes.

Tullogher: M Cody (captain and goal), James Malone, John Malone, T Malone, J Purcell, Peter Purcell, W Lawlor, J Hendrick, Stephen Murphy, M Doolan, M Morrissey, Edward Moore, Pat Gaule, J Walsh and E Moore.

1936

SENIOR

Having competed in both the Senior and Junior Football grades in both 1934 and 1935, there was suddenly a scarcity of players in 1936. Mullinavat were unable to compete at Senior as many players had regraded to Junior to play with Moonrue.

The Kilkenny Co. GAA Board Meeting of late June 1936 received the following plea from Mullinavat club secretary, Mr J Conway, secretary, Mullinavat FC wrote: "On behalf of the above Club I desire to inform you that we cannot field any Senior team this year, as a number of our best men are regraded Junior to play with Moonrue, and more of them have left the parish. There are only four or five Senior men here now, and if you could possibly regrade them we would try to have a Junior team." There was no further order made."

JUNIOR

South JFC R1: Mullinavat w/o Kilmoganny
South JFC R2: Mullinavat scr.
South JFC Final: Nore Rangers 0-1; Moonrue (Harristown area) 0-1
South JFC Final Replay: Nore Rangers w/o Moonrue scr.

1937

JUNIOR

JFC R1: Mullinavat v. Knocktopher scr.

Knocktopher and Mullinavat were to meet at Ballyhale on Sunday 25/7/1937 in the initial round of the Southern J.F. Championship, with Sergeant Kehir as referee, but Knocktopher conceded. Mullinavat had a successful year afterwards in hurling, and may have withdrawn from the footballing competition.

South JFC Final: Clover Brand 4-06; Glenmore 1-01

The Kilkenny Football Board held its first meeting in 1937. Chairman Mick Heffernan (Glenmore). Secretary Liam Mac O'Daly (Clomanto).

1938

JUNIOR

Mullinavat did not compete.

The Bigwood club was formed in 1938, and would, in the main, take over the football activities in the parish from Mullinavat. The first Bigwood club officers were Dick Vereker (chairman) and Tom Byrne of Ballincrea (secretary).

'Bigwood and Newtown Rovers met in a challenge football game at Ballinerla on Sunday 13/11/1938 when an exciting contest was expected. Bigwood, as a newly formed combination were preparing to become affiliated to the Kilkenny Southern Board for the 1939 championship. A set of new jerseys was purchased following a players collection, by Ned Kelly, from James Aylward, for £2 10s. They were worn for the first time on that Sunday. Newtown Rovers were a talented team, and already had recorded a number of victories over local sides, so this was a good preparation game for the Wood boys, and would provide a useful pointer. The match was timed for 2.30pm, and was played in a field kindly given by Mr John Healy.' The result is unknown.

Bigwood: Ned Freyne (captain), T Freyne, J Freyne, Edward Kelly, J McDonald, P McDonald, M McDonald, R Vereker, J Vereker, J Bergin, P Durney, T Durney, M Bolger, P Fitzgerald, T Fitzgerald, W Grace and R Atkins.

1939

JUNIOR

Mullinavat did not compete.
JFC R1: Bigwood beat Glenmore by one point
South JFC R2: Slieverue 0-08; Bigwood 0-02

'The winners, who led at half-time by 0-01 points to nil, had the services of many well-known Carrickshock and Kilkenny hurlers, including Jimmy Walsh, Jimmy Kelly, Jack Phelan, Jimmy Cassin, Paddy Donovan, et cetera, whilst Bigwood had the services of Tom and Willie Walsh of Mullinavat. Pete Sutton, who won the Kilkenny county Minor hurling championship recently with Mullinavat, and Dave Kenneally (Kilmacow). Walsh, Kelly, Phelan and Donovan had the scores for Slieverue whilst, Freyne, Vereker and Walsh were involved in the points for the losers.'

Bigwood: Edward Freyne (captain), M McDonald (goal), P McDonald, Willie Walsh, Tom Walsh, Richard Vereker, James Vereker, Dick Vereker, T Fitzgerald, T Durney, Tom Maddock, P Sutton, Edward Kelly, Dave Kenneally and P Durney.

South JFC Final: Slieverue 0-09; Black and Whites 2-00

Junior Football League Round One: Bigwood 2-03; Glenmore 0-03

'Bigwood gave a fine display of fast dashing football and had a definite pull over their opponents in every position. Facing the hill and breeze in the first half they led by one point at the interval. Playing with the wind advantage in the second half, they definitely took the upperhand, and increased their lead by six points. Glenmore fought back gallantly but never showed any sign of breaking through the "Wood" defence.'

Bigwood: Edward Freaney (captain), Jim Vereker, William Vereker, Dick Vereker. James McDonald. Michael McDonald, Pat Durney, Tom Durney, Peter Sutton, Edward Kelly, Freyne, Byrne Tom Fitzgerald, Matty Reddy, Tom Byrne and Edward Kelly.

CHAPTER 2

1940s

Bigwood Junior football 1940 (v Glenmore)

Front row: Tom Byrne, Pat Durney. *Second Row* - Willie Vereker, Tom Fitzgerald, Ned Freyne, Peter Sutton, Michael McDonald, Tom Freyne, Willie Durney. *Back Row:* Pat McDonald, Dick Vereker, Tim Vereker, Michael Vereker, Ned Kelly, Tom Durney. Also included are J Freyne J Keogh, John Roche, Jim McDonald, James Purcell, Jimmy Power, Pat Gaule, Tom Durney, Andy Freyne, Statia Foskin, Mary Fitzgerald, Bridie McDonald, Michael Freyne, Michael Purcell and Nan Fitzgerald.

1940s

1940
JUNIOR

Bigwood, appearing in the championship for the first time the previous year, went out in the initial round to Slieverue (who later went on to take county honours), but came back even stronger this second season.

South JFC Round One: Bigwood 1-04; Glenmore 1-1
South JFC Semi Final: Bigwood 1-03; Tullogher 0-02

'Tullogher led 2 points to 0-00 at half-time, but failed to score in the second half. Bigwood failed to score in the first half but finished strongly and put up 1-03 in the second period, with no reply from Tullogher, to give them a four point victory margin at the finish.'

Bigwood: E Freyne (captain), Michael Vereker, Dick Vereker, R Vereker, William Vereker, P McDonald, M McDonald, Paul Fitzgerald, Tom Fitzgerald, Tom Freyne, Peter Sutton, S Bergin, Willie Durney, Tom Walsh and Ned Kelly.

SOUTHERN JUNIOR FOOTBALL FINAL VENUE DISPUTE

In connection with the southern final between Bigwood and The Rower, postponed on 29th September, the following correspondence in reference to the matter was read at the subsequent Southern Board meeting at the Concert Hall, Thomastown, on Thursday 29/12/1940.

"A Chara, I have been obliged to call off the Junior Football game, The Rower v. Bigwood, fixed for Robinstown on Sunday next, 29th September, as I am informed that the field at Glenmore is staked, and, therefore, not available. I wrote to both teams suggesting Ballyfacey as a suitable venue. Bigwood agreed but the Rower would not agree, but stated they are satisfied to play at Ballyreddy, Thomastown or New Ross. I have communicated The Rower's offer to Bigwood. Liam Mac Oda."

The following reply was read from the Secretary of the Rower Club: "A Chara, our letter of the 18th inst. re football game, The Rower and Bigwood, received on Saturday. I am sorry to say The Rower team are refusing to travel to Ballyfacey. The match was fixed for Glenmore (Robinstown) at a meeting of the Football Board. It was agreed to toss for Ballyreddy or Glenmore on conditions that the game would not be played at Ballyfacey should Glenmore win the toss. We would not agree to this at all, as Bigwood are at home in Glenmore, only it was pointed out that it would help the Board's finances considerably by playing at the above mentioned venues. It is with reluctance we are compelled to take this step, as the winter is approaching, and we don't want to delay tho championship, but The Rower cannot be expected to play Bigwood at home. Ballyreddy is a neutral venue, and we are prepared to play there, otherwise Thomastown or New Ross. Glenmore were aware of the field being staked long ago, and it should have been brought to your notice before now, as it means the game, will have to be postponed. Let me know by return if game could be played at any of alternative venues suggested. Is mise, Marty Butler."

Mr T. Fitzgerald (Glenmore) – the field at Robinstown could be put into order again for the match.

Mr Lyng (The Rower) – suggested Ballyreddy as an alternative venue which would still be neutral.

Mr T Byrne (Bigwood) – Glenmore is neutral also.

Mr Lyng (The Rower) – Not for us, we would be playing Bigwood at home.

Mr T Byrne (Bigwood) – How do you make that out?

Mr Lyng (The Rower) – Isn't Glenmore in Bigwood parish?

Mr T Byrne (Bigwood) – You're mistaken this time. Bigwood is in Mullinavat parish, and either Robinstown or Ballyfacey would be neutral for the teams concerned.

Chairman – It is a pity the game was not played on the date fixed as it was one of the finest of the year and I'm afraid we'll never get such a good day again.

Mr Byrne – What ruling did the Co. Chairman give in connection with the recent Senior hurling semi-final. Doesn't the same thing apply in our case? There was a rule quoted on the matter.

Chairman – Yes, but this is a different case. The Rower didn't actually refuse to travel. The match was fixed for Robinstown and could not be played owing to the field being staked. That difficulty will now be overcome, and as the venue has already been fixed at a meeting of the Board, it must stand. As the ground will now be in order, I think both teams should have no objection in having the match played there, and allowing the fixture originally made to stand.

OUR STORY (1887-2024)

South JFC Final: The Rower 1-03; Bigwood 0-02

'In ideal autumn weather, and before a record attendance of spectators, The Rower defeated Bigwood in the South Kilkenny Junior Football Championship Final at Robinstown, Glenmore, on Sunday 27/10/1940, by a margin of four points, on the above score. It was a keenly fought game, in which some hard knocks were given and taken, but overall, it was sportingly contested throughout, and held the interest of the crowd to the last whistle.'

'Bigwood were strongly fancied for divisional honours this season by their many supporters, but they failed to touch their usual form on Sunday, and seemed to want for training. They never rose to the same standard shown against Tullogher in the semi-final at Ballyfacey, and though playing well in the opening half, they faded out in the second moiety, when The Rawer upped gears to have the upper hand. The winners fielded the same team which defeated Kilmacow in the semi-final, and have now qualified for the decider alter many years of earnest endeavour.'

'Sunday's big attendance indicates the keen interest which is being evinced in the efforts at a revival of the game in the South, and judging by the enthusiasm displayed, there is every manifestation of a welcome return to the football code, which in former years held high estimation in the hearts of southern followers. Playing in their first divisional final, Bigwood battled gamely to the last, and went down with flying colours. Though beaten, they were by no means downhearted and were the first to extend the hand of congratulation to their opponents, a gesture which was warmly appreciated and returned by their worthy rivals. Beautiful weather conditions further enhanced the fixture, and both sides had a big following, which included many famous players of the past, and a large sprinkling of the youth, all interested in the outcome of this long and eagerly-awaited clash.'

'Lively exchanges followed the throw-in, and Marty Butler was early in the picture for The Rower, sending well down, but the forwards spoiled by fouling. The free eased for Bigwood, who broke away on the wing to send over. Two frees to The Rower in succession were beaten off, and following good work by Freyne and Vereker, Bigwood moved in and a neat bout of combination play between the forwards was capped by a point from Tom Walsh, which opened the scoring after seven minutes play. Keen play followed, in which hard knocks were given and taken without demur, and both sides were visited in turn. Twenty minutes of the opening half had elapsed before John Grace, receiving from M. Butler, set the teams level with a great point from the corner. The Rower lost a further chance of a score from a close up free, but were away again in the next minute for John Grace to give his side the lead for the first time with a goal. Tom Walsh sent wide at tho other end for Bigwood in a good try for a score. The half-time scores were: The Rower, 1-1; Bigwood, 0-2.'

'The Rower pressed from a free on the resumption but Mick Vereker saved in goal. A further free to The Rower, taken by Eddie Kehoe, was finished for a point to leave the scores 1-2 to 0-2. Bigwood opened up from the kick-out, Vereker and Durney being prominent in a movement which carried play right into their opponents territory, forcing a "50" taken by Ned Kelly, which put the forwards on the offensive, bur they spoiled by fouling. Jim Grace was wide off the free to The Rower. Edward Kehoe was injured, but resumed. From a free the same player placed right in front of the posts, but Paul Fitzgerald cleared splendidly. Pat Durney (Bigwood) retired injured, and was replaced by Tom Durney. Ned Kelly placed well from a "50" to Bigwood, and when Fitzgerald and Freyne centred in turn a hard tussle waged around the posts, but was finished for an over. Bigwood again pressed, but were unable to make any impression on a sturdy defence, which nullified repeated onsets. Kehoe and Butler, who were tireless workers for The Rower throughout, were again in the van of a neat increment which was wided in the corner. A free to The Rower, and one to Bigwood in succession brought no reward. A further free to The Rower (Edward Kehoe) was cleared by Jim Vereker but the forwards returned to finish for a point, which made the issue safe. The Rower now seemed to have the upperhand and had two overs in as many minutes.'

Bigwood: Edward Freyne (captain), Mick Vereker (goal), Jim Vereker, Dick Vereker, William Vereker, Richard Vereker, Willie Durney, Pat Durney, Pat MacDonald, Michael MacDonald, Tom Freyne, Tom Walsh, Paul Fitzgerald, Edward Kelly and Pete Sutton. Sub: Tom Durney.

The winners have now qualified for the County final, in which they meet either Ballyouskill or Muckalee. The gate receipts, which go to Kilkenny County Football Board, amounted to £11 pounds, 11 shillings, 0 pence which was a record for a divisional football final.

1941

JUNIOR

South JFC R1 One: Kilmacow 2-03; Bigwood 0-01

Bigwood objected saying Michael Kelly (Dunkitt) was non-resident in the parish 6/7/1941: General Meeting of Kilkenny Football Board.

Chairman Mr Luke Roche (Tullogher). Bigwood delegates were Tom Byrne, Edward Freyne, W Durney, Pat McDonald, James Power Kilmacow delegates William Walsh, W Kelly, Liam de Cleir. Secretary (Mr T Butler, the Rower) read the following objection from Bigwood Football Club:

'On behalf of Bigwood Football Club. I object to Kilmacow being awarded the Junior Football Championship tie, Bigwood v. Kilmacow, played at Dunkitt on Sunday, June 1st,

1941. I object on the grounds that Michael Kelly, whose name appeared on the official Kilmacow list of players, played with Kilmacow, contrary to rule 12. page 71, Official Guide of the GAA.

'The rule states – "Any club including in its team in county championship any player who has already played with another club in the same county championship, and any team including in its team any player who has already played with another county in county, inter county or All Ireland matches, shall be disqualified and shall forfeit the match.'

'No player shall play for more than one club in the same competition (subject to rule 12, county committee) under pain of suspension, and any club playing a non member in its team in county championship shall forfeit the match. No player to play for a club outside the county in which he resides in county, inter county and All Ireland matches, except as set forth in rules 15 clubs and 14 championship.'

'Rule 15 clubs also page 39 states – "A player who has commenced a championship in any county shall be eligible to finish that championship for his club or county for that year, even though he leaves the county, and plays in another county, provided he does not play for the second county in the same year's championship. A player employed outside his county and coming back to the latter every week-end, may declare his residence. Any player having participated in championship, who again takes part in the same year's championship in a lower grade, even with his own club, shall be automatically suspended. Rule 14 (championships) has no bearing on this objection. My submission is that Michael Kelly, who had been residing in Dublin prior to the game (and is still there), played with Kilmacow, contrary to the rules I have quoted, thereby rendering the Kilmacow team illegal. I enclose P.O. for £1, as required. Do cara – Tomas O Broin, Runaidhe.'

Mr T Butler, The Rower, Secretary – The objection is in order. Are Bigwood going ahead with it?

Mr T Byrne – Yes.

Kilmacow Delegate – Before you go any further, Mr Chairman, I would like to have a ruling on one particular point, which might save a lot of time and discussion. The objection is based on the fact that one of our players is employed outside the county. We hold that a player who is only employed in a temporary capacity outside his county does not come within the scope of the non resident rule at all. The player in question, Michael Kelly, is an employee of the Department of Posts and Telegraphs, with Waterford as its normal headquarters. When in Waterford, he resides at his home at Dunkitt, Kilmacow, each night, and this fact will not be contradicted by Bigwood. In the course of his duties, he has to travel to various places occasionally outside the county, required sometimes for a few days, and sometimes for a few weeks, as the case may be. It has been ruled that such players, of whom there are many, could not be classified as non-resident players. In case there is any doubt about Michael Kelly being on such temporary work outside the county from time to tune, here is what the Department District Engineer, who is in charge of this particular section, says:

"A chara,

"In reply to your letter of the 1st inst., I desire to inform you that Mr Michael Kelly's duties in this Department are of a mobile nature, entailing employment in any part of the 26 Counties under the Government of Eire, as occasion should require. His normal headquarters are Waterford city. Mise, le meas, – B. C. McNeill, District Engineer."

'There are many similar cases which would be in the same category, including as well as Department employees, railway men, insurance inspectors, hackney car owners, who were playing members of the Gaelic Athletic Association, both past and present, in Leinster, Munster and Connacht. Even in their own county, they had the case of Sean O'Brien, the well-known Eire Og and Kilkenny All-Ireland hurler, who, as they all knew, was a plasterer by occupation, and was in temporary work outside the county. There is no precedent with any Board or Council to show that a player engaged in work of a temporary nature outside the county comes within the scope of the non-resident rule at all. It this point is not sustained, and it is not for me to say, it is a matter for the Chairman to decide, and we have to accept his decision, but if it is held that Michael Kelly, the player in question, does not come within the same category, then the various Boards and Councils concerned with similar cases in the past must be wrong, which all boils down to the fact that the men who framed the rules must be wrong in their interpretation of them.'

Mr T Byrne – We had a similar case, where a member of our club was residing in Dublin, and he could not play.

Mr Luke Roche, Tullogher, Chairman – Did you get a ruling to that effect?.

Mr Byrne – Well, we did not get it officially, I approached the Kilmacow Secretary before the start of the game and told him that Michael Kelly would be illegal, and that if he played and Kilmacow won, we would object, but he only walked away and said nothing.

Kilmacow Delegate – The fact that Bigwood maintained we had an illegal player did not decide the matter. There is a higher authority than that, Michal Kelly was not illegal, because he was only outside the county temporarily. It would be different in the case of a man employed in a permanent capacity in Dublin, such as the case of Jackie Power, the Limerick hurler, where it was ruled by the Central Council that he should return to his home each weekend if he desired to play with Ahane. That does not apply in the case of a player who is only on temporary work or on loan outside his county.

Secretary – It is the same case as Jim Coney, and he was ruled perfectly legal to play. There are several of that kind where a man can play who is only outside the county temporarily..

Mr W Kelly – Bigwood could have played Tom Freyne also, and he would not be illegal, as he is only doing a course in Dublin.

Chairman – It is stated here in the letter that Michael Kelly's normal headquarters are Waterford and we can't go beyond that fact. Sometimes he is outside the county for short periods, but that is only temporary, and I hold that Michael Kelly's place of residence is Kilkenny County, and that he is perfectly entitled to play with Kilmacow in this year's championship. We have seen from the referee's report that Bigwood were beaten by eight points, and I must say that their objection is very technical.

Mr Byrne – We are satisfied to replay the match, when there is a technical point involved.

Kilmacow Delegate – The question of a replay doesn't arise; we stand or fall by Michael Kelly, and we hold he was legal to play.

Chairman – I have given my ruling, and if Bigwood are not satisfied they can appeal to a higher authority.

Mr Byrne – We cannot take it beyond the County Committee.

Secretary – Are you appealing to the County Committee?

Mr Byrne – Must we give notice to Kilmacow, if we are?

Secretary – No, it is against the Football Board the appeal is, but Kilmacow will, of course, be notified in the usual way.

Mr Byrne – We have to put the matter before the club.

South JFC Final: Carrickshock 2-03; Kilmacow 1-00

1942

JUNIOR

South JFC R1: Bigwood 2-02; Tullogher 1-00
South JFC Final: Kilmacow 3-02; Bigwood 0-02

1943

JUNIOR

South JFC R1: Glenmore: 1-01; Bigwood 1-00

'It was a hard fought game in which rivalry was exceptionally keen throughout. Rain fell during the first moiety and spoiled play to some extent, ground conditions resulting in a greasy ball imposing a severe handicap on the players. During the course of the game Jim Bergin of Bigwood sustained a hard knock in a collision with other players, and had to retire injured. Bigwood strove hard to score the equaliser in the closing stages, but the opposing defence held out under sustained pressure, Glenmore maintaining their lead to the close of a strenuous game. Both sides had a number of changes from last year's teams. Mr Michael Morrissey, Tullogher refereed. The winners now meet either Ballyhale or Carrickshock in the Southern Divisional semi final.'

South JFC Final: Coolagh 0-06; The Rower 1-03
South JFC Final Replay: Coolagh 1-03; The Rower 1-03
South JFC Final Second Replay: Coolagh 1-02; The Rower 0-01

1944

Mr Paddy Walsh of Bigwood took up the role as third chairman of the football board for 1944 and was also there for 1945.

Twelve Junior football teams entered for the 1944 South Junior championships, showing an improvement in numbers over the previous years. In view of the big number of teams in the Junior grade, and the difficulty of transport during this period, it was unanimously agreed to divide the teams into three groups, with four in each section. Bigwood got drawn in Group Two along with Coolmore, Glenmore and Tullogher.

Also in 1944 Tom ("Builder") Walsh of Bigwood was selected on the Kilkenny Senior Football team that played Wexford in the Leinster Senior Football Championship.

JUNIOR

South JFC R1: Bigwood 1-02; Coolmore (Hugginstown) 1-01

'It was the first time for a county championship game was played on a week evening, and the initial venture proved a good success. The winners led at the change over by 1-1 to 0-1. Following an altercation in the last few minutes of the game, a Bigwood player was sent to the line. The match, however, was conducted in a good sporting spirit in general.'

Bigwood: Michael McDonald (captain), Pat Durney (goal), T Durney, Dick Vereker, P Sutton, T Sutton, J Holden, Michael Holden, S Bergin, Tom Walsh, P Foskin, Paul Fitzgerald, Michael Purcell, W Atkins and T McDonald.

South JFC R2: Glenmore 4-00; Bigwood 0-04

'Before a big attendance at Mullinavat, Glenmore defeated Bigwood. The O'Connor brothers, Walsh, O'Rourke and Furlong starred for the victors, whilst Holden. Foskin, Sutton and Fitzgerald did good work for Bigwood.'

Bigwood: Jim Bergin (captain), Pat Dumey (goal), Tom Durney, Tom Walsh. Tom ("Builder") Walsh, John Holden, Michael Holden, Stephen Bergin, T McDonald, Dick

Vereker, Tom Sutton, P Sutton, Paul Fitzgerald, Michael Purcell and T Fitzgerald

South JFC Final: Glenmore 3-04; Kilmoganny 0-03

1945

Bigwood elected the following officers for 1945: Chairman, Mr James Vereker; Secretary, Mr James Phelan; Treasurer, Mr Richard Vereker.

JUNIOR
South JFC Round One: Glenmore beat Bigwood
South JFC Final: Kilmoganny w/o Glenmore scr.

MINOR
South Minor Final Roinn A: Bigwood 4-01; Lamogue 2-01
County Minor Final Roinn A: Bigwood 1-01; Railyard 0-03
(A first county Minor football championship win for Bigwood).

1946

JUNIOR
Bigwood did not feature in the thirteen team 1946 Junior Football draw.

1947

'The annual general meeting of Bigwood Hurling and Football Club was held on Friday night 18/4/1947 when a satisfactory year's progress was reviewed and the members of the committee were also complimented on the sound financial position. Congratulations were extended to the Minor football team on winning the County Championship. The following officers were elected for the current year: Chairman. Michael McDonald; Vice-chairman. Philip Purcell; Secretary. Michael Purcell; Treasurer. Peter Foskin; Committee: Richard Vereker, William Vereker, Patrick Walsh, James Phelan, Kieran Dollard, James McDonald, and Thomas Sutton. It was decided to affiliate a Junior football team in the County Championship, and all members were asked to turn out for practice as soon as the tillage drive was over. For the 1947 season, Bigwood now had the assistance of a number of former Kilmacow players, as well as members of the disbanded Harristown Club.'

JUNIOR

South JFC Round One: Glenmore beat Bigwood

Glenmore v. Bigwood was fixed for Mullinavat on June 29, but was subsequently postponed. It was rescheduled for 31/08/47 but again did not occur. It got a third time for 28/9/1947, but as the Munster Express reported the following week, 'for the third successive occasion, football followers who assembled at Mullinavat on Sunday last were disappointed when the two South Junior football championship ties between Kilmoganny and Slieverue, and Glenmore and Bigwood failed to materialise. Only two teams, Kilmoganny and Glenmore, put in an appearance, and a friendly game was played between them, resulting in a victory for the former by 0-4 points to 0-2. Unless something is done by the County Football Board with regard to the carrying out of fixtures the game will lose much of its popularity in the south in the future, as spectators have too often disappointed, and clubs have been put to much unnecessary expense of fruitless travelling which can be ill afforded at the moment.'

The game was eventually staged at Mullinavat on 19/10/1947, when Glenmore had a victory over Bigwood in the County Junior Football Championship, after a vigorous game, in which tempers became frayed towards the end. Mr Pat Aylward refereed. It had taken four months for the first round fixture to be completed. The matter of the state of football in the county generally was raised at the annual convention of the County Football Board was held at Thomastown on Sunday 7/12/47.

Incidentally, there was just 13 delegates present for the entire county! In his report Mr Seamus Lyng, Secretary, stated that the number of clubs affiliated were six Senior, 23 Junior and 11 Minor. Owing to clubs failing to fulfil their engagements all three championships remain unfinished.

South JFC Final: Tullogher 2-03; Black and Whites 0-01

1948

JUNIOR

South JFC R1: Slieverue 1-03; Bigwood 1-01

'On Sunday 18/7/1948 at Glenmore, the first round South JFC meeting of Slieverue and Bigwood took place at 2.30 pm (old time) before a big attendance. Slieverue defeated Bigwood by 1-3 to 1-1, after a close and keenly contested game. The winners led at half-time by 1-1 to 1-0. The teams in opposition always had a friendly rivalry in existence and this encounter was no exception. For the losers Bigwood, the Sutton brothers,"Butcher" Fitzgerald and Willie Durney stared.'

South JFC Final: Tullogher 2-01; Glenmore 1-03

1949

JUNIOR

South JFC Round 1: Bigwood 1-06; Knocktopher 0-00

'Before a big attendance at Mullinavat on Sunday 5/6/1949, Billy Atkins (1-1), Dick Aylward, Bunty Walsh, Mick Walsh and Ned Kelly scored for the winners, who led at half-time by 0-5 to 0-0.'

Bigwood: P Reddy (captain), J Phelan (goal), Pete Sutton, Tom Sutton, John Sutton, Paddy Sutton, M Walsh. W Walsh, Ned Kelly, Sean Connolly, W Atkins, W Durney, T Fitzgerald, Jim Phelan and Richard Aylward.

South JFC Round 2: Bigwood beat Blacks and Whites
South JFC Semi Final: Glenmore beat Bigwood

'Glenmore defeated Bigwood in the Southern Junior Football Semi-final by a big margin, after a robust game. Glenmore had the services of a number of the Kilkenny inter-county Junior football team, including Garda Sean O'Connell, Ferrybank. Both sides had come through the earlier rounds impressively, Bigwood defeating Knocktopher and Blacks and Whites, and Glenmore overcoming strong opposition from Tullogher and Grennan Rovers.'

'The Sutton brothers, Walsh and Kelly were the pick of the losers. Early in the first half, a player from either side was sent to the line for engaging in a bout of fisticuffs, and despite some keen tussles, the rest of the match passed off without incident.'

South JFC Final: Kilmoganny 2-02; Glenmore 1-04

Bigwood participated in the South Junior Hurling championship also in 1949, taking Knocktopher to a replay.

Jim Conway served as club treasurer from 1962-2019, and above are pages from his 'ledger' relating to payments and receipts from 1956 and 1957. Also below are minutes from the club's AGMs in 1981 and 2004.

CHAPTER 3

1950s

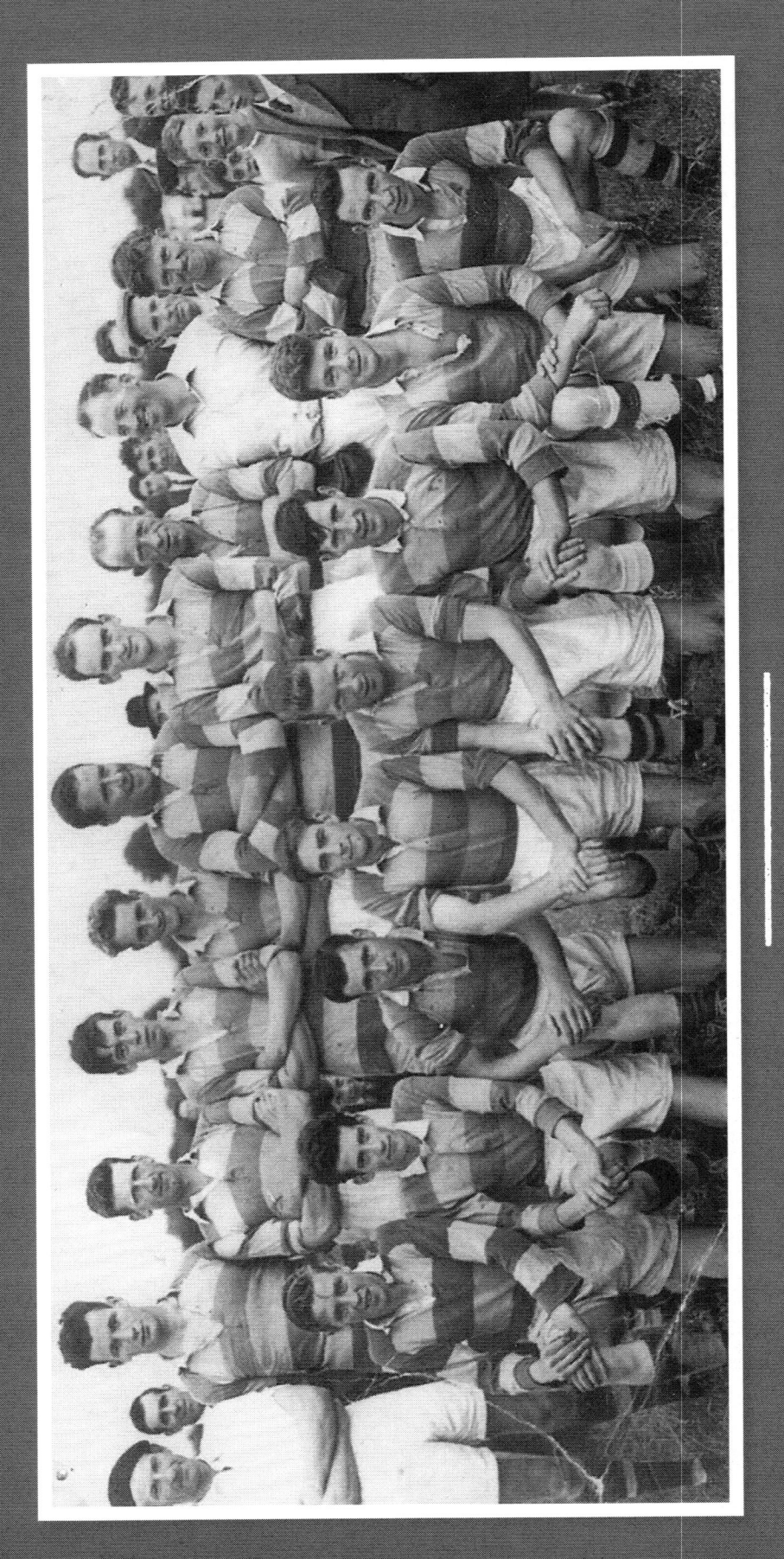

The Bigwood team which competed in the Junior Football Championship in 1958
Back Row (from left): Pakie Reddy, Garda Liam Quane, Tom Sutton, Tom Henley, Ned Delahunty, Matty Woods, Jim Power, Tom Fitzgerald, Paddy Reddy, Stephen Quinn. Front Row (from left): Philly O'Neill, Johnny Irish, Tommy Quinn, Tommy Reddy, Seamus Foskin, Paddy Phelan, Seamus Sutton, Donie Geary.

1950s

1950
JUNIOR
South JFC R1: St Canice's (Tullogher) 1-07; Mullinavat 0-04
South JFC Final: Eoghan Ruadhs (Callan) 2-01; Tullogher 2-01
South JFC Final Replay: Eoghan Ruadhs (Callan) 2-00; Tullogher 1-02

1951
JUNIOR
Neither Bigwood or Mullinavat featured in the twelve team South Junior Football championship for 1951. At the end of year GAA Convention held at City Hall, Kilkenny on 16/12/1951, a motion by the Cotterstown that the football championships be played during the Summer months was adopted.
South JFC Final: St Canice's (Rosbercon) beat Graiguenamagh

1952
JUNIOR
Eleven teams were in the draw for the 1952 South Junior Championship for the Southern area, again with no involvement by either Mullinavat or Bigwood.
South JFC Final: St Senan's (Kilmacow) 2-01; Kilmoganny 2-01
South JFC Final Replay: St Senan's 3-03; Kilmoganny 0-04 (AET)

1953
JUNIOR
Eight teams were in the draw for the 1952 South Junior Championship for the Southern area, again with no involvement by either Mullinavat or Bigwood.
South JFC Final: St Senan's (Kilmacow) 2-03; Coolagh 0-04

1954
JUNIOR
Ten teams were in the South Junior Football draw for 1954 South Junior Championships with again no involvement from either Bigwood or Mullinavat.
South JFC Final: Coolagh 1-02; Kilmoganny 0-00
South JFC Final Replay: Kilmoganny 2-01; Coolagh 0-04 (ordered following an objection)

1955
JUNIOR
South JFC R1: Mullinavat 3-08; Kilmoganny 0-03

Mullinavat defeated Kilmoganny in rather easy fashion on the first round of the South Junior Football championship on a score of 3-8 to 0-3.

Mullinavat: Paddy Holden (goal), John Holden, J Holden, John Sutton, Tom Sutton, Billy Kavanagh, Seamus Foskin, Martin Raftis, W Walsh, Larry Carew, Pat Durgan, Matty Woods, Larry Shea, John Dwyer and Paddy Tynan.

South JFC R2: Coolagh beat Mullinavat
South JFC Final: St Canices (Rosbercon) 4-03; St Senan's (Kilmacow) 0-01

1956
JUNIOR
South JFC R1: Slieverue beat Mullinavat
South JFC Final: St Senan's beat Slieverue

1958
JUNIOR

The South Junior football championships first round draw for 1958 resulted in the following fixture: Coolagh v. Glenmore, St Canice's (Rosbercon) v. St Senan's (Kilmacow), Knockmoylan v. Ballyhale, Slieverue v. The Rower.

1958 South JFC Final: Slieverue 0-11; St Nicholas 1-02

1959
JUNIOR

South JFC R1: Bigwood v. Knockmoylan

Though eleven meetings were held and some matches were refixed three times, the championships were not completed in any Gaelic football grade, and there were still three Senior, five Junior and five Minor games championship to be played in Kilkenny, stated Mr James Lyng, secretary when he appealed for an 'honest effort' to have the championships completed, at Co. Kilkenny Football Board's Convention.

'Fetes have an upsetting effect on championship games'. a delegate said during, the discussion of a motion at the annual convention of the Football Board at Thomastown on Tuesday 11/12/59.

'Though eleven meetings were held and some matches were refixed three times, the championships were not completed in any Gaelic football grade, and there were still three Senior, five Junior and five Minor games to be played in Kilkenny, stated Mr James Lyng, secretary, when he appealed for an "honest effort" to have the championships completed.'

1959
Kilkenny Football Board Convention

CHAPTER 4

1960s

The 1969 Bigwood Senior football squad

Back Row: Philly O'Neill (secretary), Jim Dollard, Michael Fitzgerald, Jim Freyne, Sean O'Neill, Sean Fitzgerald, Tommy Reddy, Tom O'Neill, Garda Vincent O'Regan, Eddie Doyle, Michael Dollard. **Middle Row -** Paddy Phelan (chairman), Martin O'Shea, Denny Duggan, Davy Aylward, Tony Atkins, Jim Phelan, James Aylward, Larry Forristal, Pat O'Brien, Willie Doyle. **Front Row:** Pat Atkins, Tommy Duggan, Jimmy Reddy (treasurer).

1960s

1960
JUNIOR

Bigwood Football Club annual general meeting. The following officers were elected for the current year: Chairman, Paddy Phelan, Coolnaleen; Secretary, Philly O'Neill, Fahee; Treasurer, Paddy Reddy, Bawnagelogue. It was decided to affiliate a Junior team in this year's county football championship.

South JFC R1: Bigwood v. Glenmore

Bigwood were involved in a three game first round trilogy with Glenmore in the championship. On Thursday 9/06/1960 they played a 2-04 each draw at Mullinavat, scores were at a premium in a 0-03 each replay at Ballyhale on 24/07/1960, before finally they lost to the Glenmore men 1-02 to 0-07 on August 5th in a third contest.

Bigwood (second game): Stephen Quinn (captain), Tom Quinn (goal), Tom Sutton, Seamus Sutton, Garda Quane, Jim Power, Matty Woods, Seamus Foskin, Pat Phelan, William Delahunty, Pat Atkins, Philly O'Neill, Tommy Reddy, John Irish, Tom Fitzgerald and T Henley. Pakey Reddy was also a panellist.

South JFC Final: St Nicholas (Cotterstown/ Kilmoganny) 1-06; Thomastown 1-04

1961
JUNIOR

South JFC R1: Bigwood 1-04; Piltown 0-02
South JFC R2: Bigwood beat Tullogher
South JFC Final: Bigwood 2-08; Slieverue 2-01
(Bigwood won the South final played on 22/04/1962)

County JFC Final: Barrowmount 1-08; Bigwood 1-03 (played on 8/07/1962)

'The game was played in conjunction with the Kilkenny S.H. Championship tie between Freshford and Bennettsbridge with the football, game commencing at 3.45pm following the hurling. The game was well contested throughout with very little between the teams but the greater opportunism and combination of the Barrowmount men paved the way to victory. The winners hail from Goresbridge area, and had the services of Andy Comerford, the well-known Kilkenny hurler who was outstanding at centrefield. Bigwood played well in the opening period and turned over a point ahead at half time, 1-3 to 0-5. However they failed to register a score in the second moiety, when a few good chances were lost.'

Bigwood: Seamus Sutton, Michael Harney, J Reddy, Stephen Quinn, J Phelan, S Foskin, Tommy Quinn, Stephen O'Neill, Tommy Reddy, John Irish, J Power, Wattie Walsh, Sean Atkins, J Sutton and H Smith.

On August 15 we had a clash between "Mullinavat Veterans" and "Bigwood Old Timers". Tom Sutton was the referee and Bigwood won by a point.

Bigwood beat Kilmacow in conjunction with Kilmacow Fete.

MINOR
South Minor Football Final: Lamogue 1-05; Bigwood 0-01

1962
JUNIOR
South JFC R1: Bigwood beat Thomastown Rangers
South JFC Semi Final: St Senan's (Kilmacow) beat Bigwood
South JFC Final: St Senan's 1-08; The Rower 1-00

MINOR
'An unusual situation occurred in the county Minor football championship game between Bigwood and Lamogue at Ballyhale on 25/8/1962 when the ball got punctured within a few minutes of the end play and the match had to be called off as no other ball was available. At the time of the abrupt stoppage Lamogue were leading by one point and it looked to be anybody's game when the referee called it a day.'

South MF Final: Bigwood 3-06; Lamogue 2-4 played 24/03/1963
County MF Final: Railyard 2-06; Bigwood 0-04, played 25/08/1963

'Bigwood making their first appearance in a county Minor football final for many years almost upset the champions, Railyard in the 1962 final at Nowlan Park. It was only in the last ten minutes that Railyard showed their traditional form. Up to then, there was little between the sides entering the last quarter. Bigwood, in fact, led by 0-4 to 0-3.'

'Played in torrential rain, which militated strongly against good football, the game throughout was a very mediocre affair, and offered little in the way of entertainment. Bigwood led 0-3 to 0-1 at half time, and remained on top for the opening five minutes of the second half, but entering the final ten minutes, Jimmy Byrne shot to the net and seconds later James Byrne pointed from a free. Brennan who had come to centrefield had a beautiful goal two minutes afterwards, and during the time that remained Nash and Dwyer had further Railyard points.'

Bigwood: P O'Connor (goal), Ned Mernagh, S Walsh, S Freyne, Durney, T Duggan, L Walsh, T O'Neill, S O'Neill, T Atkins (0-1), P Sutton (0-1), J Irish (0-1), M Fitzgerald (0-1), D Vereker and F Shaughnessy. Sub: M Fitzgerald for Freyne.

1963

JUNIOR

South JFC R1: Sleverue and Bigwood played a draw
South JFC R1 Replay: Slieverue 2-04; Bigwood 1-05

MINOR

South Minor Football Final: Lamogue 4-04; Bigwood 0-02

1964

JUNIOR

South JFC Final: Mooncoin 4-05; Bigwood 0-02
(Played March 7, 1965)

'In their first year in the Junior football championship, Mooncoin accounted for Bigwood in the 1964 southern Junior football final played in perfect conditions at Thomastown on Sunday. After a shaky opening quarter, they got completely on top and, leading by 2-3 to 0-2 at the interval, they had matters all their own the second half, scoring 2-2 without a reply from Bigwood. Apart from a 10 minute period midway through the first half the football was of a very poor standard, and the game was marred by a disgraceful fracas in the second half.'

'Star of the Mooncoin side was left half forward, Clause Dunne, who, apart from scoring a goal and a point, had the Bigwood defence in a split frame of mind on many occasions.'

'John Fitzgerald was outstanding in the| Bigwood defence, and he got most assistance from Jim Phelan, Seamus Foskin, and Tom Quinn. Tom Reddy tried hard at midfield, and Tom O'Neill also had his moments. Denis Duggan, Larry Phelan, and Sean Condon were best in an attack that never got going.'

Bigwood: S Sutton, N Delahunty, S Foskin, S Quinn, T Duggan, T Quinn, J Phelan, T Neill, T Reddy, L Phelan, S Condon, D Duggan, P Neill, J Fitzgerald and S Atkins. Subs: T Atkins and M Conway.

THE SOUTHERN DISTRICT BOARD ANNUAL CONVENTION

Chairman, Mr Michael O'Neill said they were in the happy position in Kilkenny of having one club in every parish. Some clubs however felt that if they fielded a team or two in the Championships and took part in a few tournaments, they had done their duty. This was not enough. 'A club in a parish was something to be admired, and it should be an honour to be a member of a club. It should be the ambition of every club to own its own playing field, a pavilion which could be used as a dressing room, and a club house for members. There was money available for the purchase of playing fields, and every club should take advantage of it and get to work on the buying of playing fields.' He knew there were a lot of clubs in the county making great strides in that direction.

1965

JUNIOR

JFC R1: Bigwood 1-03; St Senan's Kilmacow 1-03
JFC R1 Replay: Bigwood 1-03; St Senan's Kilmacow 1-03

'By a remarkable coincidence St Senan's Kilmacow and Bigwood played a draw for the second time in two weeks, when at Mullinavat on Sunday 3/10/1965 they again failed to decide who goes into the second round, to meet Slieverue, on the score of 1-3 each, which was the exact same score as in their previous game.'

'Bigwood had first advantage of a fairly strong breeze but made very poor use of it, and at half time their lead of 0-2 to 0-0 did not seem adequate. Kilmacow took up the running on the resumption to shoot a goal and 3 points for a 4 points lead midway through the second half.'

'Bigwood's Tom Neill who fielded many high balls held sway at midfield and was probably the best footballer afield. Right half back Jim Phelan was another who was always in the picture and Reddy a hard worker throughout, Liam Condon, Philly Neill, and Fitzpatrick were also outstanding.'

Bigwood scorers: P Neill (1-0); L Condon 0-2); and T Neill (0-1).

Bigwood: T Power, E Delahunty, P Sutton, N Fitzpatrick, J Phelan, T Reddy, D Freyne, R Carroll, T Neill, T Atkins, L Condon, P Neill, T Duggan, J Fitzgerald and J Sutton. Subs: S Neill and J Dollard.

JFC R1 Second Replay: St Senan's Kilmacow 3-02; Bigwood 0-08

'Two goals, the first of which came midway through the second half, by Kilmacow's Paddy Hoban, who had switched from corner back to the forward division, saw Kilmacow on the road to victory and thus ended this marathon between the sides, which had two postponements, one unfinished game due to a burst football, and two drawn games on the score of 1-3 each. This sixth meeting concluded the issue.'

'After Hoban's opening goal, Kilmacow were well on top, and well deserved their victory, which gave them the right to meet Slieverue at the same venue, in the second round next Sunday. At half time Bigwood led by 0-3 to 0-0, and right through this half it looked as if they would win, as they were playing the more attractive football, and had the Kilmacow defence at full stretch, forcing them to foul in an effort to stem some good attacking movements. However the first Kilmacow goal, which could be attributed to a defensive blunder, saw their defensive become uncertain and Kilmacow gaining in confidence completely changed the pattern of play.'

'Corner back John Fitzgerald was a hard worker throughout for Bigwood, and other defenders to catch the eye were Tom Quinn, and Pat Sutton. Tom Neill played his usual stylish game at midfield until an injury slowed him down. Denis Duggan had a fine game in the Bigwood attack, getting most assistance from Tony Atkins, and Philly Neill.'

Bigwood scorers: D Duggan (0-4), T Atkins (0-2), T Neill and J Aylward (0-1 each).

Bigwood: J Dollard, J Fitzgerald, T Quinn, T Power, J Phelan, P Sutton, T Duggan, T Power, J Phelan, P Sutton, T Duggan, T O'Neill, T Reddy, D Duggan, P O'Neill, L Condon, J Aylward, J Sutton and T Atkins. Sub: N Delahunty for T Power.

South JFC Final: Slieverue 0-06; Coolagh 0-04

1966

At the annual meeting the following officers were elected: Chairman – Michael Harney, Fahee; Chairman – Thomas O'Neill, Fahee; Secretary – Philly O'Neill, Fahee; Assistant Secretary – Seamus Sutton, Rosslnan; Treasurer – James Reddy, Rahard; Junior captain – Tommy Doyle, Coolnaleen. It was decided to affiliate Junior and Minor teams in the 1966 county championships.

First Mullinavat and Bigwood GAA Club Dinner Dance held at Springhill Hotel Kilkenny

JUNIOR

JFC R1: St Senan's beat Bigwood after four games
JFC R2: Slieverue drew with Bigwood
South JFC Second Round Replay: Bigwood 2-07; Slieverue 1-01

'Some disgraceful scenes were witnessed at Mullinavat on Sunday 16/10/66 when Bigwood met Slieverue in the replay of their second round of the Junior football championship. With 25 minutes of the second half still to be played Bigwood were leading by 2-7 to 1-1 when the game came to an unsavoury end. Rivalry between these neighbouring teams has been over keen in the past with a number of over robust games, and when an early bout of fisticuffs between three or four players from each side occurred on Sunday there was always the possibility of the game getting out of hand. The match itself was an over rugged affair with too much spoiling by both sets of backs and up to the time the game was abandoned what ever good football had been seen, had been served up by the Bigwood side.'

'There was far too much kicking and use of fists allowed to go on and after about five minutes of the second half with Slieverue mounting a series of attacks in the Bigwood goal, a Slieverue player was fouled as he tried to break through. When he wasn't awarded a free, he retaliated by attempting to strike the offending opponent. Within seconds a number of players from both sides had joined in the fracas, and this was the signal for invasion of the pitch by spectators who joined in the fighting. In a few minutes, the field was the scene of several fights with players and spectators being knocked to the ground. One player was kicked on the ground and had to be assisted to the dressing room when some semblance of order was restored. The referee had no option but to abandon the game as more serious incidents might have occurred with spectators and players in an ugly frame of mind. It was fortunate that no one received serious injuries, though five or six players and spectators from both sides had black eyes, thick ears and bruises to show for their endeavours. The player who had to be assisted from the field seemed to be alright when the teams were leaving the dressing rooms.'

'Slieverue broke away from the throw in and have the tonic of an early goal when Michael Meagher shot a good goal from the right-wing. Next item of note twas the bout of fisticuffs which broke out about 40 yards from the Bigwood goal. Bigwood at this stage were getting a grip on the game and with Tom Neill playing soundly at midfield they began to dominate the exchanges, and the forwards were getting a good supply, and made very good use of the openings that came their away. First Philly Neill broke through for a well taken goal to level the scores, and Tony Atkins, a real will of the wisp forward, was causing much bother to the Slieverue defenders. When he was fouled, Dennis Duggan, who was to prove a very reliable place kicker, send over the bar from a free. Duggan added a further point from a 14 yard free, and at this stage, apart from odd breakaways, the Slieverue forwards were getting little opportunity of increasing their score. Tony Atkins, who was making good use of his speed, added a brace of points. Duggan had another point from play and added a point from a free gave Bigwood a comfortable lead of 1-6 to one goal. Bigwood continued to show up much better than the Slieverue team and Tony Atkins slipped a defender and slashed the ball well out of the goalkeepers reach for a good goal. The last score of this half, a point for Bigwood, also fell to Tony Atkins, when he dispossessed a Slieverue defender after a short kick out, and send over the bar, to leave Bigwood ahead by 9 points as half-time, 2-7 to 1-0.'

'On the resumption, Slieverue were backed by the strong breeze and after holding out against early Bigwood pressures they managed to mount an attack which resulted in a free on the 40 yard mark, which was sent over the bar by Richie Walsh. Slieverue now seemed to have settled down better and there was an improvement in their play But the game had to be called off when the fracas broke out. Best for Bigwood were Tony Atkins, their star forward Denis Duggan, Philly Neill, Tom Neill, Tom Reddy, Jim Phelan and Martin O'Shea.'

Bigwood: E Bolger, S Fitzgerald, T Quinn, J Dollard, Jim Phelan, Tom Reddy, T Duggan, T O'Neill, Martin O'Shea, Denis Duggan, Philly Neill, W Freyne, P Phelan, S O'Neill and Tony Atkins.

JFC R2 second replay: Slieverue 2-03; Bigwood 0-07
(Kilkenny People report)

'At the third attempt, Slieverue overcame the challenge of Bigwood in the Junior football championship when, in perfect conditions at Piltown on Sunday 30/10/66, they defeated their neighbours by two points (2-3 to 0-7) after a thrilling hours football. Slieverue stepped up considerably on their form of the previous games and in the second half they really asserted themselves to gain a goal lead midway through this period, and had to fully extend themselves to hang on to their lead in the last ten minuses. Bigwood fought back strongly to reduce the lead to two points and had several strong movements beaten off in the closing stages. In the 58th minute, they were awarded a "50" when the Slieverue defence, under heavy pressure sent over his own end line, but the Slieverue defence managed to clear the ball, and they were mounting another attack when this very sporting game was called to a halt by referee James Murphy, Tullogher, who handled the same very well.'

'The game produced a good standard of football with Bigwood shaping very well in the opening half, and with the sides level on three occasions during the hour, and the lead alternating the fairly large attendance got good value for money. Bigwood must be considered the unlucky team in southern football as four years ago they were defeated by Mooncoin in the southern final, Mooncoin going on to win the championship. Three years ago they went under to Slieverue, and last year after two drawn games, they went under to St Senan's, Kilmacow. This year after their first game with Slieverue ended in a draw, they were leading by 2-7 to 1-1 early in the second half hour when a bout of fisticuffs broke out amongst the players and the crowd invaded the pitch and the game had to be abandoned. On Sunday, as on the previous occasions, they were again in the lead at half time but this time it was only by a point and they missed a great opportunity of being further ahead as they had been awarded a penalty which was taken by Denis Duggan and saved by Tim Murphy in the Slieverue goal. Duggan's shot was a strong one which was going over Murphy's head when he managed to break down the ball and get it away in spite of the in rushing forwards. On the other hand Slieverue missed several chances from placed balls and over the hour they only scored one point from a free. Bigwood from an equal number of opportunities had five points from play.'

Bigwood: N Bolger, J Fitzgerald, T Quinn, J Dollard, J Phelan, T Reddy, T Duggan, M Shea, T O'Neill, T Atkins, D Duggan, S O'Neill, P Phelan, J Aylward and P O'Neill. Subs: W Doyle and M Fitzgerald.

South JFC Final: Slieverue 1-09; St Senan's 0-03

At the football board convention, held at Nowlan Park in December, Secretary Mr Michael Morrissey, said he had mixed feelings about the past year. It was with regret he had to report that the championships were not finished within the year. In the North the Junior championships were finished in good time to have the final played, but in the South the semi final and final have still to played The main reason for the delay in the South was that two games were drawn, one game was unfinished, and all had to be replayed. An objection held up the Southern Final.

1967

At the annual meeting of Bigwood Football Club in February 1967 the following officers were elected: Chairman – Michael Harney, Fahee; Vice Chairman – John Irish, Melville; Secretary – Philly O'Neill, Fahee; Treasurer – James Reddy, Rahard, Junior captain – Tommy Duggan Vice Captain – Dennis Duggan, Minor Captain – Willie Doyle, Coolnaleen.

It was decided to affiliate Junior and Minor teams in the 1967 county championships.

JUNIOR
JFC R1: Kilmoganny 2-02; Bigwood 0-07

Kilmoganny were a newly formed club, mainly made up of Dunnamaggin hurlers. Included in their team were Ollie Harrington and Jim "link" Walsh, both former Kilkenny inter county hurlers. 31 Junior and 21 Minor teams entered the 1967 Kilkenny football championships. Whilst "foot and mouth disease" caused delays, at the time of the football convention in January 1968 the football club finals had again not yet been played yet.

South JFC Final: Rower Inistioge beat Lamogue

1968
JUNIOR

South JFC R1: Bigwood 2-05; Kilmaganny 1-00
South JFC R2: Bigwood 3-06; St Senan's Kilmacow 1-04
South JFC R3: Bigwood v. Thomastown or Thomastown Rangers Oct 13
South JFC Semi Final: Bigwood 0-07; Mooncoin 0-04
South JFC Final: Bigwood 2-06; Glenmore 2-04

'Bigwood beat local rivals Glenmore by two points in a tough Southern Junior Football Final, played in atrocious weather conditions at Piltown. This was a well contested contest with the issue in doubt right to the finish. All 5 goals came in the opening half, with the sides level at the interval, 2-2 each. Bigwood took the lead early in the second half, but Glenmore fought back in the final quarter. In fact, it took a late save from Bigwood goalie Eddie Doyle to save the day.'

Bigwood panel: Eddie Doyle, Jack Fitzgerald, Michael Fitzgerald, Tom O'Neill, Sean O'Neill, Jim Phelan, Jim Dollard, Larry Forristal, Tommy Reddy, Martin O'Shea, Davy Aylward, Denny Duggan, Pat O'Brien, Tony Atkins, Willie Doyle and James Aylward.

County JFC Final: 1968 Bigwood 0-06; Barrowmount (Goresbridge) 0-06 (abandoned with 90 seconds remaining, replay ordered)

'The 1968 Junior football final between Barrowmount and Bigwood at Nowlan Park on Sunday evening 27/4/1969 was called off by the referee Louis Feeley, one and a half minutes from the end, when Barrowmount were leading by 0-6 to 0-4. A Bigwood goal was disallowed, and their supporters invaded the pitch. They refused to leave. Up to that stage it was a clean and very sporting game. Worst feature of the whole matter was that an umpire was attacked and assaulted. The matter will be dealt with by the Football Board.'

'E Doyle in goal, J Fitzgerald and T Reddy were good in the Bigwood defence, while

T Atkins and P O'Brien starred in the attack. Andy Comerford opened the scoring with a Barrowmount point from a free and D Duggan replied, also from a free. Fitzharris pointed a Barrowmount free, but two Bigwood points by Atkins left the halftime score Bigwood 0-3 to 0-5 for Barrowmount. P Keyes levelled soon after the restart, and J Gough put Barrowmouot in front with two good points. P O'Brien had Bigwood's only score in this half, and P Keyes ended the scoring with a point.'

Bigwood: E Doyle, J Dollard, J Fitzgerald, W Doyle, J Phelan, T Reddy, D Aylward, T O'Neill, D Duggan, S O'Neill, P O'Brien, T Atkins, L Forristal, P O'Neill, and M Fitzgerald.

Bigwood were later awarded the title due to "illegal constitution" on the Barrowmount (Goresbridge) team. The Goresbridge outfit logged an appeal and counter objection concerning the constitution of the Bigwood team. An investigation committee was set up, comprising Michael O'Neill (Kilmacow), chairman of the county board; F O'Brien MC (Kilmoganny), chairman of the football board, and Seamus Delaney, (Kilkenny), secretary of the football board. Eventually a Final Replay was ordered for the end of July 1969, and Bigwood emerged victorious: Bigwood 0-9; Barrowmount 0-2.

1969

Having won the 1968 Junior County Final, Bigwood were now playing in the 1969 Senior Football Championship. The first round draw was: The Village v. Clann na Gael (ref M. Meally), The Rower Inistioge v. Railyard (ref S. Delaney), Tullogher v. Thomastown (ref F. Walsh), Muckalee v. Mooncoin (ref S. Delaney), Junior champions (Bigwood) a bye.

SENIOR

Kilkenny SFC Round Two: Tullogher 3-09; Bigwood 0-07

'Tullogher won well at Piltown Gaelic Field on Sunday 5/10/1969, they beat Bigwood 3-9 to 0-7 in the second round of the Kilkenny Senior Football championship. But Tullogher were hard pressed for long periods by last year's Junior champions. Bigwood, started better and led 0-3 to 0-0 after 10 minutes. Tullogher came storming back and scored 1-3 without reply. But Bigwood kept pressing and at half time ware only a point behind, 1-3 to 0-5.'

'Things looked rosy for them when they had a point to level the game immediately after the restart to level the scores. Then Tullogher put on the pressure. They took the lead with a point, then rammed in two goads which put them on the road to victory. The game, which was always entertaining, was played in a fine sporting spirit. Tullogher always looked the better team, principally because they adopted more direct methods whereas Bigwood over did the short passing. But the winners at times seemed to ease off and this is something that needs to be rectified if they hope to advance further. For Bigwood, E. Doyle (goal), D. Alyward, Fitzgerald and Sean O'Neill played well.'

Bigwood: E Doyle, J Dollard, J Fitzgerald, W Doyle, T Duggan, L Forristal, D Aylward, M O'Shea, T O'Neill, D Duggan, J Freyne, S O'Neill, M Fitzgerald, P O'Brien and J Aylward.

SFC Final: Railyard 0-11; Mooncoin 0-06

JUNIOR

Bigwood were also in the draw for the South Junior football championship for 1969.

South JFC Round Two: Bigwood 2-04; Coolagh 1-03
South JFC Final: Kilmoganny 3-06; Mooncoin 1-00

'An unusual situation occurred in the game between Bigwood and Lamogue at Ballyhale when the ball got punctured within a few minutes of the end of play and the match had to be called off as no other ball was available. At the time of the abrupt stoppage, Lamogue were leading by one point and it looked to be anybody's game when the referee called it a day.'

1962
Bigwood Vs Lamogue
Kilkenny MFC

CHAPTER 5

1970s

The Bigwood Junior football team which won the county championship in 1979: Back Row (from left) - Philly O'Neill (secretary), Michael Duggan, Nick Fitzgerald, John Delaney, Michael Delahunty, Paudie Holden, Jim Walsh, Timmy Gough, John Fitzgerald, Jim Dollard, Davey Aylward, Pascal Power. Front Row (from left) - Eamon Kelly, Michael Dollard, Andy Aylward, Sean O'Neill, Tommy Duggan (captain), James Aylward, Michael Fitzgerald, Leo Carroll. John Foskin, Pat Duggan.

1970s

1970

At the annual general meeting of Bigwood Football Club, held in the local Old School, the following officers were elected for the current year: Chairman, Jim Dollard, Ballincrea; Vice-Chairman, Michael Harney, Fahee; Secretary, Philly O'Neill, Fahee; Assistant Secretary, Willie Doyle, Coolnaleen; Treasurer, Jimmy Reddy, Rahard; Senior and Junior Selection Committee: Pat Atkins, James Reddy and the Chairman; Senior Captain, Larry Forristal; Junior Captain, Michael Power, Vice-Captain, Paschal Power. Minor and Under-16 Selection Committee: Pat Atkins, Willie Doyle and Tommy Duggan.(Mullinavat); Minor Captain Michael Fitzgerald, Fahee; Vice-Captain, Matty McDonald, Ballyhomuck.

It was decided to affiliate Senior, Junior, Minor and Under-16 teams in the County Football Championships. The latest date for payment of membership fees was fixed for 31st March. Arrangements were made for the presentation of the 1968 County Junior Championship medals to the members of the victorious team at the annual dinner dance of the club, to be held in the Tower Hotel, Waterford, on Saturday night, 14th March.

FIFTH MULLINAVAT AND BIGWOOD GAA CLUB DINNER DANCE AT TOWER HOTEL, WATERFORD ON 14TH MARCH, 1970

'Presentation of Trophies – The Lyng Cup (which is a memorial trophy of the late Seamus Lyng, Inistioge, who was a former secretary of Kilkenny County Football Board), and medals won by Bigwood in the 1968 county Junior football championship, were presented to the members of the victorious team.'

'Mr Jim Dollard, Ballincrea, Chairman of the club, presided, and the attendance of over 200 included Very Rev Dr. Hughes, P.P. V.F. Mullinavat; Rev D O'Hanlon, C.C. Mullinavat; Mr Michael O'Neill, Kilmacow, Chairman of Kilkenny County Board GAA and, Mrs O'Neill; Mr Francie O'Brien, M.C.C., Kilmoganny, Chairman of the Kilkenny Football Board in 1968 (who presented the medals to the players), and Mrs O'Brien; Mr Michael Carroll, Rossinan, chairman of Mullinavat Hurling Club, and Mr Seamus Delaney, Kilkenny, Secretary of the County Football Board.'

'Mr Jim Dollard welcomed all present, including the priests of the parish, and congratulated the players on winning the title, and for their excellent behaviour and sportsmanship. He thanked Paul Fitzgerald for so kindly giving them the use of his field. 'They owed a debt of gratitude to him, and only for his co-operation the club would be badly stuck.' He thanked their loyal supporters for showing their appreciation in winning the championship, and for patronising the annual function that night.'

'Very Rev Dr. Hughes P.P. V.F. Mullinavat congratulated the clubs on organising such a happy function, and hoped that everyone would enjoy the night. His first experience of football was in the South, as in his youth in North Kilkenny there was hardly any football at all, as it was all hurling. He extended sincere congratulations to Bigwood in winning a football title, and hoped they would go on to win a championship in hurling.'

'Mr Michael O'Neill (Kilmacow – Chairman of Kilkenny County Board GAA) thanked the committee for their invitation to Mrs O'Neill and himself, and said it was great to see such a big crowd present at the celebrations of the two clubs, Bigwood and Mullinavat. Great credit was due to Bigwood on winning a Junior championship, and they should do well in the Senior grade. Mullinavat had not won a hurling title for many years, and though they usually do well in Fete and tournament games, they seem to make an early exit in the championship.' However, 1970 may be their year."I played with Mullinavat hurling teams in former years," he continued, and not alone did we never win a title, we never even won a match (laughter). One year we were beaten by Slieverue in Glenmore by one solitary point, and Slieverue went on to win the county final, but lost on an objection. I was also on the Bigwood team which played Knocktopher in Ballyhale on one occasion, and we were in the lead with some minutes to go when somebody swiped the ball and the match was not finished. To make matters worse, we lost on the replay!"'

'Mr O'Brien, who was Chairman of the Kilkenny County Board in 1968, presented the Lyng Cup and medals to the victorious team. Those who received medals were – John Fitzgerald (captain), Eddie Doyle (goal) Jim Dollard, Willie Doyle, Davy Aylward, Tommy Reddy, Tom O'Neill, Philip O'Neill, Sean O'Neill, Larry Forristal, Pat O'Brien, Denis Duggan, Tommy Duggan, Tony Atkins, Pat Atkins. Michael Fitzgerald, Martin O'Shea, Vincent O'Regan, James Aylward, James Freyne, Jim Phelan, and Michael Dollard.'

SENIOR

SFC Round one: Bigwood played versus James Stephens at Thomastown
SFC Final: 1970 Railyard 0-08; Muckalee 0-04

JUNIOR

South JFC First Round: Coolagh 4-09; Bigwood 1-03

Powered by Kerry-men Jimmy Lane and Ted Griffin and Muck McHugh from Galway, the Coolagh boys went ahead right from the start, and never looked like being caught. They led by 2-5 to 0-1 at the interval.

South JFC Final: Glenmore 0-06; Slieverue 1-03
South JFC Final Replay: Glenmore 1-07; Slieverue 1-03

1971

'BIGWOOD AGM January 1971 (Bigwood Club decided to oppose ban). Officers elected were: Chairman Jim Dollard, Ballincrea; Vice Chairman Jim Phelan, Coolnaleen; Secretary W Doyle, Coolnaleen; Assistant Secretary: P O'Neill Fahee; Treasurer Noel Power Loughcullen; Delegates to County Board and Southern Board, chairman and secretary. Selection committee, Senior and Junior Paddy Phelan, Coolnaleen, L Forristal. Ballincrea, Pat Atkins, Ballincrea, Tom and Philly O'Neill, Fahee; Senior captain, James Aylward, Ballinacurragh; vice captain, Tom O'Neill; Minor and Under-16; selectors, J Aylward, P Atkins and L Forristal; Junior captain, J Freyne, Fahee; vice captain, T Duggan, Mullinavat; Minor captain, Jim Walsh, Ballincrea; vice captain: Dick Doyle, Coolnaleen. Under-16 captain, M Kelly, Rathlikeen, vice captain, Peader Kelly, Rathlikeen.'

'By 25 votes to 11, it was decided to support the abolition of all Ban rules.'

SENIOR

Kilkenny SFC Round One: Bigwood 1-07; Thomastown 2-03

'At Mullinavat on Thursday (Corpus Christi – 10/6/71) Bigwood defeated Thomastown in the opening round of the county Senior football championship. It was a close and exciting game, with the issue in doubt to the last whistle, and though Thomastown fought hard to get the equaliser in the closing stages, the Bigwood defence held out well under sustained pressure. The winners led at half-time by 1-5 to 1-0, but Thomastown showed up well in the second moiety, and had the assistance of Kilkenny inter county goalie, Paddy Dempsey, who was a sound custodian.'

Bigwood: Ned Doyle, Luke Nolan (0-1), Sean Fitzgerald, Willie Doyle, Jim Freyne, Jim

Dollard, James Aylward, Michael Power (0-1), Dave Aylward (0-1), Michael Dollard (1-1), Larry Forristal, Sean O'Neill (0-2), Noel Power (0-1), Jim Walsh, Mick Fitzgerald. Sub: Philly O'Neill for J Freyne.

Kilkenny SFC Round Two: Bigwood 0-02; Northern Selection 5-01

'Pat Henderson made his return to the GAA scene following his recent accident in which he received rather severe burns. He helped the Northern football selection beat Bigwood in the Senior football championship, and on this form the winners could be a force in the championship.'

'There was a distinct difference between the two sides, and this had quite a lot to do with the game. The Northern Selection chosen from Junior clubs from Galmoy to Goresbridge, had a big advantage in weight and size, and this gave the very young Bigwood boys very little scope for their football. There is no denying the merit of this win for the North. They had the advantage almost everywhere, but what football we saw from Bigwood was worth seeing and it was a pity they could not get more into the game. This is a very young side and their stylish crisp football deserved a better reward. Willie Doyle was outstanding in an overworked Bigwood defence, while Dave and Seamus Aylward worked hard in the half back line with Jim Dollard doing reasonably well against Pat Delaney. Michael Power, a stylish player, and Eddie Doyle had their moments at midfield, while in an attack that saw little of the ball until the closing stages. Tony Atkins, Michael Dollard, Larry Forristal and Sean O'Neill tried hard.'

Bigwood: D Vereker, P Nolan, J Fitzgerald, W Doyle, D Aylward, J Dollard, S Aylward, E Doyle, M Power (0-1, free), M Dollard, L Forristal, S O'Neill, M Fitzgerald, P Power and T Atkins (0-1).

SFC Final: Railyard 3-10; Thomastown 0-03

JUNIOR

South JFC R1: Slieverue beat Bigwood
South JFC Final: Slieverue beat Graiguenamanagh

MINOR

1971 South Minor Football Final: Kilmoganny beat Bigwood

1972

SFC R1: Clann na Gael (Kilkenny City) beat Bigwood

'Clann na Gael (Kilkenny City) defeated Bigwood in the initial round of the current year's county Senior football championship at Piltown on 21/5/1972 by a wide margin. Both Clann na Gael midfielders, and particularly Vincent O'Shea, dominated in the first half, and they build up a sizeable lead which Bigwood could never peg back.'

(Mooncoin and Bigwood met in the losers group of the county Senior football championship at Piltown on Sunday 18/6/1972.)

SFC Final: Railyard 2-10; Clann na Gael 0-09

JUNIOR

South JFC R1: Bigwood met Glenmore
South JFC Final: Graiguenamanagh 0-04; Lamogue 0-03

KILKENNY FOOTBALL CONVENTION 1972

"It was regrettable that in 1972 Kilkenny footballers made a very poor showing in the Leinster football championship," Mr Mick Meally, chairman, told delegates at the annual convention of the Kilkenny; Football Board on Tuesday 23/01/1973.

'A contributory factor to this was the fact that they had no matches and could not see their players in action, as the hurling selectors did. In addition to this, there was a lack of training and lack of interest by some players. The Kilkenny Minors had given fair displays, although the Minors had no time to practice, and the Under-21s had just two evenings practice.'

1973

MULLINAVAT AND BIGWOOD GAA CLUB'S SEVENTH ANNUAL DINNER DANCE

For the first time in 13 years, the MacCarthy Cup was back in Waterford on Sunday 21/1/73 when the clubs held their seventh annual Dinner Dance at the Tower Hotel, with over 200 members in attendance. Noel Skehan of Bennetsbridge, who captained the winning Kilkenny hurling team the previous September against Cork was the guest of honour on the night.

BIGWOOD FOOTBALL CLUB AGM

'Mr Jim Dollard Ballincrea, outgoing chairman, presided at the annual general meeting of Bigwood Football Club on Tuesday 30th December, 1973. At the AGM the question arose as to whether the club should revert back to Junior status. The club, having won the Junior title in 1968, had been playing in the Senior grade, but now relegation was proposed, as it was proving difficult to field a Senior side against other stronger teams in the county. The motion was carried by 22 votes to 5, so it was decided to apply for regrading from Senior to Junior for the year ahead. The following officers were elected: Chairman, Seamus McDonald, Ballyhomuck; Vice Chairman Larry Forestal, Ballincrea; Secretary Pendergast Kelly Rathlikeen; Treasurer Noel Power, Loughcullen; Delegate to County Football Board Willie Doyle, Coolnaleen; Selection committee: Paddy Whelan, do; Johnny Phelan, do; Ned Kelly. Rathlikeen; Philly O'Neill, Fahee, and the chairman; Junior captain. James Walsh, Ballincrea; vice-captain, Denis Vereker, do: Minor captain, deferred to a later date. It was agreed to affiliate Junior and Minor teams in the county championships for 1973, and club membership fees were increased.'

JUNIOR

With Bigwood back in Junior there was 12 teams in the 1973 South Junior Football Championship draw. The first round was: Bigwood v. Glenmore, Graignamanagh v. St Senan's, Tullogher v. Mooncoin, Piltown v. Coolagh; Lamogue v. Kilmoganny, Slieverue v. Shamrocks.
South JFC Final: Slieverue 1-04; Mooncoin 0-05

1974

Bigwood GAA Club held its annual meeting in February 1974. Officers elected were: President, Rev D O'Hanlon, C. C, Mullinavat; Chairman, Jim Dollard, Ballincrea; Vice Chairman Philly O'Neill, Fahee; Secretary Willie Doyle, Coolnaleen; Treasurer Philly O'Neill; Selection committee, chairman, vice chairman, Sean Fitzgerald, Knockbrack, Michael Harney, Fahee, and Liam Walsh, Farnogue; Junior captain, Michael Dollard, Ballincrea; vice captain, Willie Doyle, Coolnaleen. It was decided to affiliate Junior and Minor teams in the 1974 county championships.

JUNIOR
South JFC R1: Graignamanagh v. Bigwood
South JFC Final: Slieverue 1-05; Lamogue 0-07

GAELIC FOOTBALL IN THE COUNTY

Kilkenny football looked like getting a much needed lift with plans the County Football Board had in mind for 1974. Following Kilkenny's dismal showing in the National Football League, the county selectors decided to take definite steps to improve football at inter-county level. The board set up of a county schooling panel. The formation of the panel, depending on the success of a special sponsored competition. This competition was run on a league basis, and involve five specially picked teams. The fact that Kilkenny were back competing against Senior teams in the Leinster championship proper had prompted this move. Kilkenny had not participated in the Leinster SFC from 1964 to 1973 inclusive. These teams consisted of players who were considered good enough for the inter county team. They played in a special AIB sponsored competition and later a panel was chosen as the one to represent the county in 1974. These players were later having special training and coaching sessions together. All clubs were asked to release players for these sessions. Clubs already having been asked to send in nominations of possible prospects from the panel. Up to 1974 the championship was for Junior teams but this had been abolished this year.

It was the first time in almost 10 years that Kilkenny were due back competing against Senior opposition. In the first round of this new competition, Kilkenny faced Carlow and had they overcome this obstacle then they would have had a home game with Louth. The purpose of the selected panel was partly to ensure that Kilkenny would always have a good panel available for selection. This was to do away with the problem of dual stars such as Mick Brennan and Kieran Purcell upsetting the team if and when they have to withdraw due to hurling commitments. After a special meeting on Thursday 23/2/1974 arrangements were made to contact each club, and get their nominations, so the plan can go into operation immediately. The success of the campaign depended on the co-operation the Co Board would get from individual clubs.

17 CLUBS AT FOOTBALL FUTURE MEETING

A heated County Board meeting, during which players were slammed for lack of interest, was intended to herald the beginning of a new era for Gaelic football in Kilkenny. Delegates from 17 clubs attended the meeting at Delaneys in Patrick Street, Kilkenny. Unfortunately, Bigwood did not send representatives.

The ills of Kilkenny football were discussed and plans were outlined to try and put Kilkenny on the football map. To give the game a much needed boost the Board had decided to start the already mentioned new football league competition and plans had been made to get more interest in the county sides. Team selectors told delegates that they believed it was the complete lack of interest by players in the past which had put Kilkenny in the football doldrums.

It was agreed to pick two panels of players from the North and South of the county. These were to take part in a trial and the best picked would form the squad to represent Kilkenny in all competitions. The new league was also intended to help the selectors.

The following were the teams selected to get the new Kilkenny football revolution under way in Nowlan Park on Sunday 10/3/74. So that everybody would get a fair trial the selectors placed many established players on the list of substitutes. Most of these have already played for the county in the league. Tom Walsh the former Laois footballer, had declared for Kilkenny. A full turnout by players and substitutes was expected.

Northern: Bill Walsh, Mick Moore, Kieran Mahon, John Maher, John Murtagh, Pat Henderson, John Byrne, Niall Morrissey, Mick Meally, Billy Harte, Tom Loughlin, Mick Daly, Fan Larkin, Mick Brennan, Pat Delaney. Subs: T Cunniffe, T Walsh, S Brennan, N Geoghegan, P Hurley, M Fitzgerald, C O'Brien, B Morrissey and S O'Brien.

Southern: Pat Dempsey (Thomastown), Matt Hogan (Kilmoganny), Pat Walsh (Shamrocks), John Dempsey (St Senan's), Dick McNamara (St Senan's), Tony Hoyne (Thomastown), R Alyward (Glenmore), Tom Waters (Rower), V Hoyne (Thomastown), Jim Dempsey (Rower), Kieran Purcell (Lamogue), Liam Cody (Graig), John Phelan (Glenmore), Mick Tierney (Rower), Ted Dollard (Glenmore). Subs: S Connolly, James Phelan, Pat Coady, Ger Kenny, M Hoyne, B O'Sullivan, G Fennelly, J Walsh, G Culleton, H Ryan, T Kinsella and P Kavanagh.

POST TRIAL

'Kilkenny football selectors got a good insight into what to expect when they sorted their new football selection scheme at Nowlan Park on Sunday 10/3/1974. In a special game to get the ball rolling, and iron out some difficulties, a Northern selection proved twice as good as their Southern opponents. From every point of view this game proved a valuable exercise. Well over 50 players arrived and got games in this first of the football boards planned team finding games. The Co Board's enthusiasm certainly seems to have rubbed off on players. Very few of those selected were absent, and many sent apologies for non attendance.'

'After an entertaining first half in which the Northerners were on top the score stood at 0-7 to 0-1 in favour of the winners. The pattern was the same on the restart. The southerners came more into the game but were always battling against the tides. Good for the winners were M Moore. T Walsh, J Murtagh, N Geoghegan and M Brennan, while T Waters, Dick McNamara, T Dollard and T Hoyne tried hard for the losers.'

1975

JUNIOR

South JFC R1: Bigwood beat The Rower
South JFC R2: Bigwood 6-14; Piltown 0-00
South JFC: Bigwood 0-12; Tullogher 1-08
South JFC Final: Shamrocks 0-10; Bigwood 1-02

'Bigwood won the toss and had the advantage of a strong breeze in the opening half, but failed to make use of it, and were a point in arrears at the break, 0-3 to 0-2. Shamrocks, who had the assistance of a number of the Carrickshock hurling team which went under to O'Loughlins in the county final recently, went further ahead in the second moiety and were worthy winners.'

Bigwood: E Doyle, W Doyle, N Fitzgerald, S Fitzgerald, D Aylward, J Aylward, J Dollard, M Dollard, J Phelan, T O'Neill, S O'Neill, P Grant, T Considine, J Walsh and M Fitzgerald.

COUNTY

INTERVIEW WITH MR MICHAEL MEALLY, CHAIRMAN OF THE CO. FOOTBALL BOARD

"The response from some players and clubs to the call to county football duty is the worst in a quarter of a century." That is the view Mr Michael Meally, chairman of the Co. Football Board, expressed in a frank interview with the Kilkenny People.

"In my 25 years' reign as chairman this is the poorest response I have ever seen. In the early 1950's, we got into four Leinster finals and the same can be done again. It is not that the players are not getting the opportunities. Trophies have been put up for competition, one set by a former chairman, Mr Mick Gibbons, and all arrangements have been made, but some players and clubs just don't want to know".

"Kilkenny are now out of all Leinster championships Minor, Under-21 and the final team, the Senior side, made an undistinguished exit at Athy on Sunday June 1st (Westmeath 2-14; Kilkenny 2-2). That was the last straw. Before that game several of the selectors were said to have been touched by the apparent apathy. When a meeting for them was called there was only a 50% response. Only three turned up and no excuse was forwarded by the missing men.

That gave way to talk of withdrawing from all intercounty competitions altogether. Bravely, the Co. Board decided to go ahead with the fixture on the coming Sunday, knowing they would be under strength. Muckalee, who had reached the final of the Allied Irish Banks sponsored football league, had told the Board that their players would not be available. For that warning the Board were at least grateful. Other clubs who seemed to have no intention of sending players didn't bother to send word."

1976

JUNIOR

South JFC R1: Bigwood w/o Glenmore scr.
South JFC R2: Bigwood beat Lamogue
South JFC Semi Final: Bigwood beat St Kieran's (Kilmacow & Mooncoin Utd)
South JFC Final: Bigwood 1-07; Rower Inistioge 0-05

'At Knocktopher on August 1st, Bigwood defeated The Rower-Inistioge in the southern Junior football final by a margin of five points, on the score of 1-7 to 0-5. The winners were in front at the interval by 0-4 to 0-2 and went ahead in the last quarter to win comfortably. Bigwood last won the county Junior championship in 1968 beating Bennettsbridge in the final.'

Bigwood: Mick Dollard (captain), Ned Doyle (goal), Willie Doyle, John Fitzgerald, Michael Fitzgerald, Micky Fitzgerald, Tom O'Neill, Sean O'Neill, Davy Aylward, Seamus Walsh, Tommy Duggan, Noel Freyne, Jim Dollard, Tony Atkins, Tom Considine. Sub: Ger Freyne for Tony Atkins.

County JFC Final: Conahy Sarsfields 0-08; Bigwood 0-01

'Conahy Sarsfields won their seventh football title when they defeated Bigwood by 0-8 to 0-1 in the Junior football final at Nowlan Park on Sunday. Bigwood is a club with a fine football tradition and they last collected the honours in 1968. But on Sunday week last, Conahy, with a good blend of youth and experience, came out on top whereas the losers had better individual players.'

'Bigwood never gave up the chase and to the final whistle gave all they had. Great credit must go to each team for the sporting manner in which the match was played. The game was free flowing and frees were very few and far between. Sean Buggy made some fine saves in the Conahy goal, and Ned Mulhall was very impressive at full-back, and got able assistance from Seamus Nolan and John Muldowney. Young Michael O'Regan who replaced Pat O'Shea who was ill, gave a fine display.'

Bigwood: Ned Doyle, Jim Dollard, John Fitzgerald, T Doyle, J Duggan, J Walsh, Davy Aylward, F Considine, N Fitzgerald, M Dollard, G Freyne, Micky Fitzgerald, J O' Neill and F O'Neill. Sub: P Power.

Conahy Shamrock: J Buggy, J Muldowney, S Mulhall, S Nolan. M O'Regan, L Butler, P Brennan, M Buggy, P Mulhall (0-1), K Mulhall (0-4), N Brennan (0-1), K Brennan, S Muldowney (0-1), P Morrissey and E Conway (0-1). Sub: P Lacey.

COUNTY
KILKENNY'S NO SHOW 21/11/1976 NFL DIVISION 2B SOUTH V. WATERFORD AT PORTLAW

'The Kilkenny footballers will have their third outing in the National Football League when they take on Waterford at Portlaw on Sunday. Already the Noresiders have fallen to Carlow and Wexford. However, this weekend they will have an even stronger selection available as there is no hurling clash. But as James Stephens are involved in the Senior club championship their players are tied up.'

Kilkenny panel selected: J Cullen, N Morrissey, B Henriques, J Bracken, D McNamara, G Walsh, J Moran, M Regan, G Fennelly, D O'Hara, R Dunne, T Maher, K Fennelly, M Dowd, M Ruth, K O'Shea, T Moran, J Morrissey, J Grace, M Culleton, J Heffernan and M Fennelly.

(Kilkenny People article 26/11/76)

'The majority of clubs in Kilkenny just do care about the fortunes of the County football team. But when it comes to hurling the same clubs will be falling head over heels to get into the limelight. This in the opinion of football chairman Nicholas McGrath is the root of the problem.'

'All the problems came to a head on Sunday 21/11/1976 when only 10 players turned up for Kilkenny v. Waterford in the National Football League at Portlaw. Twenty five had been nominated but this was cut by the exclusion of James Stephens, Carrickshock and Conahy Shamrocks players, all of whom were on club duty.'

'But those who failed to put in an appearance showed a disgraceful, and disrespectful attitude towards the Football Board. Nicholas said some clubs just do not give a damn. But when a player is picked from some of these clubs to play for the county hurling team, then he will be accompanied by the club secretary, chairman and a few more what can be called helpers.'

'This is all part of the attitude towards football', in Kilkenny, he added. What a lot of people do not realise is that the county Is obliged to field a team in the National Football League. Financially the Co. Board loses nothing. He described Sunday's turnout as "disgraceful" but thanked the ten players who showed up, and those who sent excuses as to why they could not attend. But he warned the non-attenders as to their future conduct. 'There is a rule whereby a player can be banned from playing for a year if he does not play when selected for county duty. We do not want to enforce this rule, but it is there in the book. Were the rule used, then the players would be out of bounds for hurling Inter county duty as well," he pointed out.'

'The ten who made the journey on Sunday were: John Joe Cullen, Nicky Morrissey, Barry Henriques, John Bracken, Jim Moran, Jack Morrissey, Dick O'Hara, Ger Fennelly, Tony Maher, Dick McNamara. One selector who was to collect three players never arrived either, but he is an ever present at all other football games.'

KILKENNY FOOTBALL CONVENTION 1976

'Kilkenny Football Board Chairman Nicky McGrath (Kilkenny): "Footballers in Kilkenny have no pride in playing for their county and sometimes give the impression that to be seen in the county jersey is embarrassing. And despite a hidden fear that may be harboured by some members of the Co. Board, football on the Noreside can be built up at no cost to the Co. Board." Those and a few more points were touched on by Football Board chairman, Nicholas McGrath in his annual address to the Football Convention at the City Technical school on Wednesday of last week. Mr McGrath alleged that some county players did not want to be seen representing their county in football.

"In Kilkenny, there is no dignity attached to playing football for your county. Some players sneak out on the pitch to play and look as if they are ashamed to be seen playing for their county", he remarked. "This attitude will remain until there are big changes," he added.

Opening, Mr McGrath conceded that the Football Board had problems, but they were not insurmountable ones. Later he hinted that County Secretary, Paddy Grace was afraid to promote football because it might cost the Co. Board money. Nicholas stated: "Paddy Grace has done great work and has helped pay off the debt on Nowlan Park, but I fear he was afraid to promote football because it might cost the Co. Board money. We have to prove that we are not draining the Co. Board. If football is not going well then the Co. Board must hit out and ask why things are not being done and why games are not being played," he stressed.

"The Co. Board must see that football is run right and is functioning properly, and if it is not, then it should be got rid of," he remarked. The former Kilkenny Senior hurling team trainer said that GAA games must be made attractive to young people. And as well as the playing side, the social side of the Association should also be developed. "Since the removal of the ban young people have the opportunity to play all games. The GAA must have facilities to offer these young people and attract them into the Association," he said.

There were 17 motions from 8 clubs before the 1976 Football Board Convention. Nine were, for one reason or another, deferred but those adopted were:

1. That a manager and two selectors be appointed to the Kilkenny Senior team (Piltown).
2. That all football championships be held on a knockout basis (Blacks and Whites).
3. That all clubs be given an opportunity to participate in a league (Blacks and Whites).
4. That a coaching course be held in the county and a coaching panel be appointed (Gaels).
5. That the Football Board appoint selectors and team managers for the Under 21 team (Sarsfields, Conahy).
6. That a Senior B all-Ireland football championship be organised for weaker

counties (Dicksboro).
7. That the Minor league be started straight away (Muckalee).
8. And that a special committee be appointed to look after county Minor teams (Dicksboro).

1977
JUNIOR

The 1977 South Junior Football Championship draw was as follows: The Rower (bye); Carngeen (bye); Shamrocks (bye); Coolagh (bye); Kilmacow (bye); Bigwood; Slieverue; Mooncoin; Piltown; St David's and Lamogue.

Kilmacow, Bigwood and Slieverue were scheduled to play off to balance up the number of teams. Then the competition was run off in pairs down through the list.

South JFC R1: Slieverue 0-10; Bigwood 2-03
South JFC R2: St Senan's 3-04; Slieverue 1-04
South JFC Final: St David's (Glenmore-Tullogher) 0-09; Rower Inistioge 0-06

"Organisation and cooperation vital in football plan."
(Kilkenny People report)

'Football championships in Kilkenny must be organised properly and the only way this can be done is by cooperation between everyone involved. In 1978, all the championships will be completed within the year. In one of the most sensible and frank reports to the Football Board convention, chairman Nicky McGrath spelled the message out loud and clear for all clubs. This year there will be changes, all for the better, he hoped. To an outsider seeing one year's championship being completed in the middle of the following year's championship would appear ludicrous. To us it didn't, he remarked. He admitted that the Football Board had contributed to this chronic situation. Lack of communication and cooperation were the prime reasons for the fall down. Starting, he quoted a general piece from the Charter or the GAA read: "The Association shall foster, promote and control the National games of hurling, Gaelic football and handball and such other games as may be sanctioned and approved by Congress."

"How can we be playing our part properly?" he asked. "My reason for reading that extract is to point out that in order for the aims of the GAA to be carried out, there must be cooperation between all those who play and all those who are administrators.

"When I took over as chairman two years ago, the various boards in Co. Kilkenny were noted more for their lack of communication with one another, than for their communication. My first year as chairman was to assess the problems and work out structures which would overcome these, he said. To this end I issued a calendar of events in February 1977, plus a complete fixtures list for all Championships, which were distributed to all clubs and boards. For that I feel I can take a certain amount of credit. But much more credit is due to the clubs in attempting to adhere to this set schedule, he added. He continued, "If you cast your minds back to when Tony Hanahoe was in Kilkenny, you will remember he said that before you can even think of going anywhere in football, you must have properly organised and properly run championships. With your cooperation I have managed this year to run-off, with two exceptions, two years championship."

1978

Bigwood Football Club A.G.M: At the annual general meeting, the following officers were elected for the current year. President – Very Rev Dean Hughes, Mullinavat P.P., V.D; Vice president – Rev N Collier. C.C., Mullinavat C.C.; Chairman – Willie Doyle Ballincrea; Secretary – Philip O'Neill Fahee; Treasurer – Edward Doyle, Ballincrea; Committee – J Reddy, P Kelly, M Freyne, J Phelan and J Fitzgerald.

It was decided to affiliate Junior and Minor teams in the county championships for 1978 and a 7-a-side tournament for a set of plaques will commence at the new pitch in Fahee on 1st March. A "30" card drive in aid of the club funds was to be held in The Shanty, Smartscastle every second Friday night.

JUNIOR

The three parish rule still operated in Kilkenny football in 1978, and the South Junior Football was partly played on a league basis. In the South Junior first round draw it resulted in the following fixtures: Carrickshock v. Coolagh, St Senan's (Kilmacow) v. Piltown, Bigwood v. Slieverue, St David's (Glenmore and Tullogher United) v. Rower Inistioge; Shamrocks (Ballyhale) v. St Patrick's (Smartscastle). Lamogue, Carrigeen and Mooncoin were awarded byes in the first round.

Bigwood lost to Slieverue on 21/4/78 at Mullinavat. In the final group stage it was Bigwood v. Shamrocks, Piltown v. St David's, Thomastown v. Mooncoin. Kilmacow (bye).

1978 South JFC Final: St David's 2-09; Carrickshock 2-03

BIGWOOD & MULLINAVAT 9TH ANNUAL FUNCTION

'The 9th annual dinner and social under the joint auspices of Mullinavat Hurling Club, Mullinavat Handball Club and Bigwood Football Club was held in the Tower Hotel in January 1978, and was attended by a total of 247 members, guests and supporters.'

'Ned Conway "Beaupre" Garrandarragh, was master of ceremonies, and the speakers included Rev D Collier, C.C., Mullinavat; Rev J Gallavan, P.P., Newmarket; Messrs Michael O'Neill, Kilmacow, Chairman of Kilkenny County Board, GAA.; Tommy O'Brien, N.T., Kilkenny, Chairman, Leinster Handball Council; Seamus Murphy, Mullinavat, Chairman, Kilkenny County Handball Board; all of whom paid tribute to Mullinavat Junior hurlers on reaching the county final, and winning the local Fete Tournament, county juvenile titles, and All Ireland honours in various grades, as well as Bigwood football team on reaching the southern Junior final.'

'Andy Aylward, Chairman, Mullinavat Hurling Club; Tom Anthony, Chairman of the Handball Club; and Jim Dollard, representing Bigwood Football Club, suitably replied, and also thanked their respective supporters during the past year. The southern Junior hurling championship medals were presented to the members of the victorious team by Mick O'Neill, County Board Chairman, and the Fete trophies by Noel Kent, on behalf of Kent Brothers, Kilmacow, sponsors of the Tournament. Music for dancing was provided by The Rhythm Kings from Waterford.'

1979

JUNIOR

South JFC R1: Kilmacow 1-04; Bigwood 1-06
South JFC R2: Bigwood 3-03; Carrickshock 2-05
South JFC R3: Bigwood v. Rower Inistioge or St David's
South JFC Final: 1978 Bigwood 3-04; St Patrick's Kilmacow 2-04

County Junior Football Final: Bigwood 3-02; Dicksboro 1-05

Three times Mullinavat teams have won the Kilkenny County Junior Football Championship - 1933 as Mullinavat, and both 1968 and 1979 as Bigwood.

The 1979 victory over city club Dicksboro featured an 18-year-old opponent, who later had a distinguished rugby career ahead, namely Willie Duggan.

Willie, despite a stated hatred for training, went on to play 41 times for the Irish rugby team, making his debut in 1975 v England. The Kilkenny man was also a star performer on the 1977 British & Irish Lions tour of New Zealand, playing in all four test matches. Willie, who sadly passed away in 2017, is remembered as much for his love of 'life', as for his undoubted rugby qualities. He had 'shovel- like' hands and certainly was not one to mess with. So the next time you come across survivors of the Bigwood 'Men of 1979' (appearing in this book), remember they too must have had a powerful presence on the playing pitch, when winning their 1979 Junior County title.

Bigwood squad: Michael Duggan, Nick FitzGerald, John Delaney, Michael Delahunty, Paudie Holden, Jim Walsh, Timothy Gough, John FitzGerald, Jim Dollard, David Aylward, Pascal Power, Eamon Kelly, Michael Dollard, Andy Aylward, Sean O'Neill, Tommy Duggan (captain), James Aylward, Michael Fitzgerald, Leo Carroll, John Foskin, Pat Duggan and Phil O'Neill (secretary).

MINOR

South Minor Football Final: Mooncoin 1-04; Bigwood 0-03

Bigwood Panel: Tommy Duggan (captain), Timmy Gough (goal), Pat Duggan, John Delaney, Paudie Holden, Nicky Fitzgerald, Michael Fitzgerald, Michael Dollard, Andy Aylward Farnogue, Davy Aylward, Ballydaw; Jim Walsh, Ballincrea; Eamon Kelly, Rathlikeen; Sean O'Neill, Fahee (Bigwood). Subs. Michael Duggan, Sean Foskin, Leo Carroll (all Mullinavat); Jim Dollard, Ballincrea; Willie Doyle, Coolnaleen; Sean Kelly Rathlikeen; Larry Forristal, Ballincrea, Michael and William Delahenty, Fahee (all Bigwood).

COUNTY
FOOTBALL BOARD MEETING

Post Leinster U21 Football Championship: Wicklow 1-13; Kilkenny 1-03

(Kilkenny People report)

'For the recent Under-21 football championship game between Kilkenny and Wicklow only 12 of a panel of 26 turned up. A chap who wasn't able to walk out to the 21 yard line to place the ball played in goal, and a 12 year-old was considered as a substitute. There were the facts put before the Football Board. It was pointed out there was a rule whereby those who did not turn up could be suspended for six months. The matter was referred to the Co. Board for a ruling. Board chairman, Nicky McGrath said it was the worst case he ever came across. "With half a team we could have won looking back," he said. One team selector told of the player who was barely able to walk, and another, Peter Flannery said that for an away challenge match against Wexford, Kilkenny had 20 players."They were all notified at the game that the championship clash was coming off. Until we reached Aughrim we didn't know if we could field a team. If we could reach 15 it was the maximum," he stated.

> # CHAPTER 6
>
> ---
>
> # 1980s

Mullinavat GAA History 1884-1984, 'The Green Book' which was published for the Centenary Year and the four men who compiled it (Sean Maher, Ned Haberlin, Jim Conway and Mossy Murphy).

MULLINAVAT
G.A.A. HISTORY

1884   1984

1980s

1980

Jim Dollard, Ballincrea, outgoing chairman welcomed old and new to a very well attended AGM of Bigwood Football Club. The Chairman also thanked those who helped in any way to bring the 1979 County J.F. Championship to Bigwood, and also those who helped to raise funds for the Club throughout the year and looked forward to the same support in the 1980 Championships. The following officers were elected: President, Very Rev D. Collier, P.P.; Vice President, Canon D. Hughes, Dean of Ossory; Chairman, Jim Dollard (outgoing); Vice chairman, Willie Doyle (outgoing); Secretary, Phil O'Neill, (outgoing); Treasurer, Eddie Doyle; Selectors: Jim Dollard, R. O'Neill, Jim Reddy, James Aylward and Larry Forristal; Delegates to County Board: W Doyle, P O'Neill, J Dollard and Andy Aylward; Senior Captain: Eamonn Kelly; Vice-captain: John Fitzgerald.

SENIOR

Only 4 teams competed in South: Shamrocks, Graignamanagh, Thomastown and Bigwood.
SFC R1: Thomastown 1-08; Bigwood 3-01
SFC Final: Shamrocks 4-07; Muckalee 1-01

JUNIOR

South JFC R1: Bigwood 0-14; Mooncoin 0-04
South JFC Final: Slieverue 4-09; Glenmore 2-06

UNDER-21

South U-21 R1: Mooncoin 2-03; Bigwood 1-03
South U21 B Final: Thomastown 1-06; Mooncoin 0-08

MINOR

South MFC R1: Bigwood 3-03; Graignamanagh 2-05
South MFC R2: South Bigwood 2-06; Mooncoin 2-04
South MFC Semi Final: Bigwood 2-11; Shamrocks 0-02
South MFC Semi Final: Thomastown 3-04; Bigwood 2-03

BIGWOOD FOOTBALL CABARET

'Guest artist at a well attended cabaret run by Bigwood football club, held in The Shanty, Kilmacow on Thursday 10/01/1980 was Fr. Michael Cleary, Dublin, who contributed a first class programme of songs and comedy, which was thoroughly enjoyed. A number of raffles were also held. The attendance included members of the Bigwood team, winners of the county Junior football championship last year, led by their captain, Tommy Duggan, Mullinavat.'

1980 FOOTBALL BOARD CONVENTION

'In an at times hard-hitting and certainly comprehensive report, Football Board chairman Nicky McGrath threw down the gauntlet to the top body." In 1979, I suggested that the Football Board should be financially self sufficient, I still believe this. I would ask that the Finance Committee of the Co. Board for 1981 would produce a balance sheet which would clearly show the cost of football to the county is nil, or perhaps it makes a slight profit." 'Stepping down from his post after five years, the city vocational school teacher leaves the game in as healthy a position as it ever was. This year all the championships have been completed, and the slate has been wiped clean for a new beginning. "I have at times been highly critical of procedures and events that took place in the name of football, and I make no apologies for doing so. I did it in the interest of football. I believe these criticisms have brought about major changes for the better in certain areas at least," he argued.'

1981

SENIOR

Five teams in SFC South Championship: Thomastown, Shamrocks, Slieverue, Graiguenamanagh, Mullinavat.
South SFC Semi Final: Bigwood 4-03; Graiguenamagh 0-03
South Section SF Final: 1981 Thomastown 1-09; Bigwood 1-04
County SFC Final: Thomastown 2-06; Muckalee 0-06

JUNIOR
South JFC Semi Final: Carrickshock 1-10; Bigwood 1-09
South JFC Final: Glenmore 3-10; Coolagh 2-03

UNDER-21
South U-21 FC Final: Thomastown 1-09; Bigwood 0-03

MINOR
South MFC Roinn A: Graiguenamagh 0-03; Bigwood 0-01 (unfinished – both teams disqualified)

COUNTY
Bigwood players were involved in the Kilkenny Senior, Under 21 and Minor football squads in 1981. The threat made in April to players of not turning up finished with a strange county board meeting in May. A rarely used GAA rule 44 was brought into the discussion: Rule 44 states: "County Committees shall have power to suspend for six months a player who refuses to travel or play for his county"

'The Kilkenny Under-21 footballers play Longford in the Leinster championship at Nowlan Park on Sunday week as a curtain raiser to the Offaly v. Laois National Hurling League semi-final. The Football Board are holding a trial at Nowlan Park on Thursday (7pm) between the Senior county team and the Under-21 team. A big panel has been notified. All clubs are requested to see that their players attend. The Board has issued a statement to the effect that any players who refuse to turn out for football will not be included in the county hurling panel. The declaration refers in particular to Under-21 players.'

Kilkenny Under 21 F panel: B O'Hara, S Brennan (Thomastown); E Dowling, S Fitzpatrick, J Tyler, T Haberlin (Slieverue); P Heffernan, E Walsh (Tullogher); W Lannon (Thomastown); L Walsh (Kilmacow); **P McDonald, S Duggan (Bigwood)**; D Fennelly, Grace (Shamrocks); J Ryan (Dunnamaggin); J Murphy, E Aylward, M Heffernan, S Boyle (Glenmore); J O'Dwyer (Coolagh); O'Leary, N Boyd, P Brennan, R Kelly, S Fitzpatrick (The Village); M Byrne (Gowran); M Cleere, J Mulcahy, M McGrath (The Gaels); M Ryan, P McGuire (Galmoy); E Mansfield (Railyard); P Doheny (Tullaroan); M Walsh (Dicksboro); J Holland (Ballyragget); G Brennan (Conahy).

Kilkenny Senior F panel: D O'Hara, J Costelloe (Thomastown); J and G Walsh (Slieverue); L Bird, M Walsh (Tullogher); J Murtagh, M Fitzgerald, N Power (Railyard); J, Roche (Kilmacow); C Heffernan, D and F Ennett, P Murphy (Glenmore); M Hogan (Dunnamaggin); M Morrissey, B Grace, P Cahill (Graignamanagh); J and M Fitzgerald (Bigwood); M Carroll, G Woodcock, C Barry, R Dunne (Danesfort); D and P Connolly

(Clara); P Neary, J Hennessy, JJ Cullen, J Murphy (The Village); P Kennedy (Coolagh); M O'Hanlon, P Grace (Mooncoin); J O'Donnell (Castlecomer); E Maher, P Phelan, G Ryan (Freshford); R Keneally, M Kelly, S, K and B Fennelly (Shamrocks); K O'Shea, J Ruth (Ballyragget); W Purcell (Johnstown); N Brennan, K Brennan, K Mulhall (Conahy); **T Goff (Bigwood)**.

(John McDonal, Dan Power and Donal Harney were on Kilkenny Minor Football panel)

Leinster U21F First Round: Longford 1-10; Kilkenny 3-03
Leinster SFC First Round: Kilkenny 2-04; Wexford 2-11

(Based on Kilkenny People report)

'Nine players who refused to kick football with Kilkenny at Senior and Under-21 level, escaped suspension at the Co. Board meeting at Nowlan Park last week when a recommendation to do so from the Football Board was defeated. On an 18 to 15 vote, with many delegates abstaining, the requests, in the form of letters signed by football secretary, Seamus Delaney, were marked "read and left at that". In one letter, the secretary named Joe Hennessy, Paddy Neary (The Village), Syl Hennessy (Paulstown), John Costello (Thomastown), Kieran Brennan (Sarsfields) and Michael Cleere (The Gaels) for not turning out for the Seniors and Michael Morrissey (Graignamanagh) and Paddy Heffernan (Tullogher-Rosbercon) for not playing at Under-21 level. It was stated in the latter that a similar recommendation will be submitted to Bord na nOg with regard to Minors who failed to turn out, all this being decided at a Football Board meeting on May 11, 1981. Then in a second letter, Michael Walsh (Dicksboro) was singled out as another to be suspended with a recommendation that "the strongest possible action be taken with regard to this player". It was stated he turned up for an Under-21 match against Longford limping and with six stitches in his head. It has transpired that he played a soccer match on the morning of the game," the secretary wrote. Again outlining the feeling of the Football Board members, the secretary stated: "There was serious condemnation of representatives to allow the Minor football fixture against Wexford to be fixed on the same date as the all-Ireland colleges final, thus depriving our county of the services of at least five of our best players. Football Board chairman, Barry Henriques explained that every step was taken to notify players for the matches in question. Five weeks prior to the Wexford match (Senior) he wrote what he called a begging letter to players letting them know in advance when the match was on and when training was going to be held. He said the last line of the letter asked the players to notify the chairman or secretary if they were not interested. If no notice was received, it was taken as a sign of interest. Two telephone numbers were given. A few players rang to say they were not interested. The chairman said a fortnight before the Senior game he wrote to the panel again, this time about training, three sessions were arranged but they were all a farce, as only an average of four players turned out each night."

"I think we were very fair to all," Mr Henriques said. "Later, as far as I know, cards were sent out to all the same panel." Toddy Lacey (Conahy Shamrocks or Sarsfields in football) asked the football chairman what notice Kieran Brennan (Sarsfields) had received. The chairman said the letter was sent five weeks before the game; another two weeks before and a card sent to his house. Toddy Lacey pointed out that there were three Kieran Brennans living in the one area, and the one in question had not received notice. Jim Rice (O'Loughlin Gaels) said Michael Cleere (The Gaels) claimed he got no notice either. Football secretary, Seamus Delaney said he met Cleere's father on the Friday before the match and he (Mr Cleere) said Michael would have to miss his brother playing in the All Ireland colleges final because he was going to kick football."How many of these players listed actually trained with the team?" asked the Co. Board chairman, Michael O'Neill. Football Board Chairman: "None". John Healy Tullogher/Rosbercon) said Paddy Heffernan (Tullogher/Rosbercon) had informed the football secretary that he wouldn't be available to play if it was a fine day because he had farm work to do. "That was a flimsy excuse," declared the football chairman. Eamon Doyle (O'Loughlins Gaels) said they were responsible for getting match programmes out for big games at Nowlan Park. He said the football secretary was unable to supply them with a team or panel days before the day, so he found it impossible to fathom how the players were contacted with such precision and then this situation still arose. He said no match programme appeared. "The question of notification is being made a lot of here", declared Kieran Meally (Erin's Own). "If I had my way a lot of delegates would be suspended. For years this notification thing has been used as an excuse". He felt the people involved with the county football team were putting more work in than those with the county hurling team. He said "If people stop paying lip service to football and do a bit of work for it instead, it would be better. A little positive help from everyone who pretends to be interested would be better". '

1982

SENIOR

SFC R1: Bigwood 0-06; Graiguenamagh 1-03
SFC R2 Thomastown 2-04; Bigwood 0-05
SFC R3 Bigwood 3-05; Glenmore 0-09
SFC R5: Shamrocks 3-11; Bigwood 0-06
SFC Final: Shamrocks 0-06; Thomastown 0-06
SFC Final Replay: Shamrocks 0-07; Thomastown 0-02

JUNIOR

South JFC R1: Bigwood 4-07; Graiguenamagh 0-07
South JFC R2: Mooncoin 9-07; Bigwood 0-01
South JFC Final: St Patrick's (Kilmacow) 2-11; Mooncoin 1-06

UNDER 16

County Under 16B Football Final 1982 – Bigwood 5-09; Gowran 0-02

A first win at this grade for Bigwood.

1983

MULLINAVAT FUNCTION

'The annual meeting of the three clubs involved in GAA activities in Mullinavat and Bigwood took place in the Bridge Hotel, Waterford, on Sunday 23rd January 1983, for their annual reunion. 150 attended and the MC for the night was Mr Ned Conway. Secretary of the local hurling club. In attendance was Fr Daniel Collier. P.P., Mullinavat, Fr T Carriuan. C.C, Mullinavat and Fr J Galvin. P.P. Newmarket and a former curate to the Mullinavat district. They were joined by the President of the GAA Mr Paddy Buggy and Mrs Buggy; Mr Michael O'Neill. Chairman of Kilkenny Co. Board and Mrs O'Neill. Presentations were made to the winning Mullinavat Junior hurling squad in the Kent sponsored Gold Watch Tournament, run by the Mullinavat Fete Committee in the summer of 1982.'

'Mr Thomas Duggan, Garrandarragh, spoke on behalf of both the Handball Club and Bigwood Football Club and again, looked forward to a good year and thanked everybody for their help in the past.'

SENIOR

SFC R1: Paulstown 1-14; Bigwood 3-01
SFC Final: Thomastown 1-05; Railyard 1-02

JUNIOR

South JFC R1: Coolagh w/o Bigwood scr.
South JFC Final: Coolagh 1-06; St Patrick's (Kilmacow) 1-04

UNDER-21

SFC Semi final: Glenmore 6-03; Bigwood 2-02

COUNTY

POST Leinster JFC Round 1: Offaly 2-16; Kilkenny 0-5

'It was like throwing lambs to the slaughter when a hastily put together Kilkenny took on a far superior Offaly team in the Leinster Junior football championship at Tullamore on Wednesday. For years Kilkenny had been firm backers of the idea to bring back the inter county Junior football championship. But after this match, and the events leading up to it, they need never have bothered. The Noresiders didn't train for the game. The selectors, at least, showed a bit of interest and picked a panel. At first people said they were interested, then it turned out they weren't. So the night before this tussle six players who were not listed on the original panel were asked to come along and help out. They did. But it didn't help the cause at all that on the same night the county Junior hurlers played a challenge against Tipperary. Surely one or two players involved there could have helped out in Tullamore?'

COUNTY BOARD MEETING

'Kilkenny should pull out of the National Football League because the top brass in the county are just not interested in the game. "There is only one team that matters in this county, the elite 15", fumed an irate Barry Henriques, chairman of the Football Board, when he suggested involvement in the Football League should be terminated. "To pull out of the NFL would be the right thing for this county to do", he urged during a stormy debate on football at the Co. Board meeting at Nowlan Park. The Football Board chairman's remarks were uttered when he voiced his annoyance at the way the Kilkenny Junior football team was treated before, and on the night, of the Leinster championship game against Offaly in Tullamore. "It was a football farce," the John Lockes (Callan) official opened. "The events that led up to it were a disgrace. We hear nothing from this Board only sanctimonious crap about football from people who pretend they are interested. They say they will do all they can for football, but they don't care." The football chairman said there was a "ban in existence" on the night the game was played. "Some players were banned from playing with the Junior football team," he accused, "I know that for a fact." He said that in the lead-up to the match everything possible was done by the Football Board and selectors to make sure the best possible team was fielded. Four times the players were notified and most gave a commitment to play. "We also got a commitment from the Co. Board that everything would be done to help this team out," he reminded delegates. "What happened? One night we ended up flying around the city looking for an acre of land to train on."

"Some players were told if they did not travel to the Junior hurling challenge they would lose their places on the team altogether," he pointed out. He exonerated Co. Board secretary, Paddy Grace, from all blame, because he knew the secretary had tried to get players to kick football.

1983 FOOTBALL BOARD CONVENTION
(BASED ON KILKENNY PEOPLE SUMMARY)

"No matter what, hurling will come first in Kilkenny. It is just the way things are and no one can do much about it." That was the suggestion from Co. Board chairman, Michael O'Neill, when he addressed the Football Board convention in January 1984. "It was implied here that the Co. Board doesn't support football as it should. But does anyone?" the Kilmacow official asked.

"The majority of clubs are first hurling clubs and after that they are football. That is not unusual in counties like Kilkenny. You will get the reverse situation in other counties."

He said that there was no reason why football should be neglected. Kilkenny has a football tradition, and some of the early championships the county were won at football. He felt the county Senior final of 1983 did great credit to football.'

1984

'Mullinavat Hurling Club and Bigwood Football Club joined forces for a dinner dance at the Bridge Hotel, Waterford on 20/1/1984. It was presided over by Mr Ned Conway, secretary of the hurling club, and he welcomed the 124 guests. Fr T Maher P.P., Fr L Dunne C.C. and Fr J Galavan P.P. Newmarket all attended. Fr Tommy Maher said that this was his first time attending this event, and as it was the GAA centenary year it's also worth looking back at the club's history. He wished the club well in the coming year and will be available to help.

Hurling chairman Michael Carroll expressed the hope that the club would win a championship title at the end of the year. Tommy Duggan, as chairman of the Bigwood football club said football had gone through a very lean period, but perhaps 1984 could be their year. He also spoke on behalf of the handball club, in which he stated it had been one of the most successful years to date.'

SENIOR

SFC: Glenmore 0-07; Bigwood 0-04
SFC: Bigwood 1-05; Gaels 0-03
SFC: Paulstown 5-05; Bigwood 1-04
SFC: Railcard 3-05; Bigwood 1-04
(Did not reach KO stages)
SFC Final: Thomastown 1-09; Railyard 0-04

JUNIOR

South JFC: Coolagh v. Bigwood
South JFC Final: 1984 Mooncoin 2-09; Coolagh 2-00

UNDER-21

U-21 FC R2: Bigwood v. Lamogue

MINOR

South MFC Final: Bigwood 2-03; Thomastown 1-06
South MFC Final replay: Bigwood 3-07; Thomastown 2-04
County MFC Final: Dicksboro 2-07; Bigwood 1-01

CENTENARY SFC

R1: Bigwood 2-08; Slieverue 2-02
R2: Bigwood: 0-06; St Patrick's, Kilmacow 1-04
R3: Replay: Bigwood 1-06; St Patrick's 1-06

COUNTY

Leinster JFC Round 1: Wexford 1-07; Kilkenny 0-05

'Kilkenny made a brave effort but were scuttled by a late Wexford goal in this entertaining Leinster Junior football championship game at sundrenched Thomastown on Sunday. The deciding score came six minutes from time when Seamus Kennedy got his fist to a cross and diverted the ball into the Kilkenny net. That put the winners 1-6 to 0-4 in front it a time when the losers were improving and looked to have a real chance of scoring an historic win.'

'The football in the opening half was generally mediocre, but in the second period the standard improved a bit. The winners opened the scoring in the third minute when Michael Walsh kicked a point. That was answered by one from Eamon Maher before Sean O'Shea landed a brace to leave the winners 0-3 to 0-1 in front at the halfway mark.'

'The home tide showed improved form on the change around. They enjoyed a good start when Paddy O'Dowd pointed. But Sean O'Shea did likewise for the visitors. There O'Dowd had another to reduce the leeway to the minimum (0-4 to 0-3) after only 36 minutes. Wexford were a bit unsteady for a while, but they fought back to get points from frees by O'Shea. Again Kilkenny came back and Paddy O'Dowd pointed to gain reward for a lot of team effort The losers went chasing just then, but then came the Kennedy goal that put too much of an obstacle in front of them. The visitors were never going to be beaten afterwards. They had fine players in Michael Walsh, Sean O'Shea, Noel Barry and Michael Finn while the losers best were John Lawlor, Michael Galway, Dermot Fennelly and Paddy O'Dowd.'

Kilkenny: J Brennan, M O'Dowd, M Galway, J Lannon, M Walsh, J Lawlor, P Lawlor, D Hoyne, M Fitzgerald, D Fennelly, A Hoyne, E Maher, P O'Dowd, M J Ryan and G Walsh. Subs: P Hughes and T Brennan.

FOOTBALL CONVENTION
(BASED ON KILKENNY PEOPLE SUMMARY)

Seamus Delaney – Kilkenny Football Board Chairman: "The Leinster Junior football championship is there for the taking, if Kilkenny would only organise themselves properly for a serious assault on it. That goal is obtainable, and we proved that during 1984", are the encouraging words from Seamus Delaney, in his annual address which he delivered to convention at Nowlan Park.

"The Juniors were beaten by five points by Wexford in the first round", he points out. "A goal 10 minutes from the finish was the decisive score. Wexford later went on to win the Leinster championship and qualified for the All Ireland only to be beaten by Cork." He appeals to everyone involved in football to forget their grievances, real or imaginary, and pull together and make a serious assault on the Leinster Junior championship.'

1985
SENIOR

SFL: Mooncoin v. Bigwood
SFL: Graignamanagh beat Bigwood
SFL: Glenmore 1-11; Bigwood 1-04
SFC R1: Bigwood 2-03; Sarsfields 0-08
SFC R2: Railyard 2-10; Bigwood 0-02
SFC Final: Thomastown 5-03; Railyard 1-05

UNDER 21

Under 21 F Roinn B: Mooncoin 2-07; Bigwood 0-02
South Under 21B F Final: Graigue Ballycallan 2-10; Mooncoin 2-02

MINOR

Minor F Roinn A: Railyard 2-10; Bigwood 0-02
Minor F Roinn A: Thomastown 3-11; Bigwood 3-04

FOOTBALL CONVENTION

POST 15/5/85 Leinster JFC Round 1 – Meath 1-04; Kilkenny 1-03

'Defeat was the lot yet again, but all things considered, this was one of the most encouraging performances by a Kilkenny football team in the modern day history of the game. In the end, a lone second half point by Meath gained them passage through the second round of the Leinster Junior championship. And there was even a reply to that score from Kilkenny, but an interval deficit of a single point was still there at the finish. So a lot of good, honest and determined effort once again gained no reward. The truth here wasn't the familiar old tale of a respectable performance, and that being it. The losers had chances to win, they kicked 8 first half wides against Meath's two. Then they were treated very harshly by the referee seven minutes from time, when Pierce Phelan was fouled as he attempted to kick a score from five yards, but the official waved play on. As in the overall context, Kilkenny deserved better luck then.'

Kilkenny: J Brennan (Thomastown); T Brennan (Railyard), M Galway (Thomastown), J Lannon (Bennettsbridge), M Delaney (Railyard), B O'Hara (Thomastown), G Power (St Patrick's), D Hoyne 1-0 (Thomastown), E Maher (Freshford), P Phelan (Freshford), J Coyne 0-2, frees (James Stephens), D McBride 0-1 (James Stephens), G Walsh (Thomastown), A Hoyne (Thomastown) and M 'Cloney' Brennan (Railyard). Sub: M Morrissey (Graignamanagh).

Four days before he stepped down as chairman of Kilkenny Co. Board, Michael O'Neill was elected chairman of the football board. At the football board convention at Nowlan Park, the Kilmacow official beat the man who held the post last year but who resigned before the end of his term, Barry Henriques (John Lockes). In a straight contest between the two, Michael O'Neill won by 39 to 26 votes. "The reason I allowed my name go forward for the election was I want to try and do something for football", said Mr O'Neill, who last year took on the job of selector with the county football team. "The games doesn't enjoy a high profile in Kilkenny, but if we all work hard together, things just have to improve." The new chairman paid tribute to Barry Henriques, who, during his time, worked very hard to promote the game in this hurling mad county. Mr Henriques wished the chairman well. He said Mr O'Neill was leaving the easiest job in Kilkenny and taking on the hardest one, so he needed all the luck and support he could get. In a contest for the post of vice-chairman, Jim McGrath (Danesfort) beat Jack O'Neill (Paulstown) by 42 votes to 22. Secretary, Seamus Delaney was returned unopposed. Delegates to Co. Board – S Delaney, Tom Ryan (Glenmore), Tommy Duggan (Bigwood), Teddy Holden (Graignamanagh).'

1986

'The annual general meeting of the Bigwood Football Club was held at the School in Bigwood. A good attendance of members were present and they were welcomed by their Chairman Mr Sean Kelly. The following officers were elected for the coming year: Chairman, Sean Kelly; vice chairman, Michael Delahunty, Fahee; secretary, Phil O'Neill do.; treasurer, James Aylward Newtown, Gaulsmills; Selectors: Liam Walsh Bigwood; James Aylward and John Fitzgerald, Fahee; County board representatives: Tommy Duggan, Mullinavat.'

'The Chairman congratulated Tommy on his appointment as referee for the All-Ireland Inter Firms Final played in Cork, between Our Lady's Hospital, Cork and Crown Control, Galway, and also on his election to the Kilkenny Hurling Board from the County Board Convention recently. A discussion took place on the Senior team in the club and it was decided that that team would seek entry to the Junior grade at the football board when grading and re-grading of teams would take place.'

JOINT SPORTSMEN CELEBRATE

'A joint dinner-dance for the members of Mullinavat/Bigwood GAA Clubs and the Handball Club of the parish was held recently in the Tower Hotel, Waterford. Ed. Conway, "Beaupre," Garrandarragh, Mullinavat secretary of the hurling division, welcomed all. Guests were Mons. T Maher, Rev J Galvin, Newmarket; Rev Liam Dunne, Mr Michael O'Neill. Chairman of the Kilkenny Co Board and his wife; Mr Joe Mackey, Chairman of the Southern Board, and his wife. On behalf of the hurling club, Mr Andy Aylward, Farnogue, thanked all for their continued support and looked forward to be a good year in 1986. Mr Sean Kelly, Bigwood spoke as Chairman of the Bigwood Football Club and again thanked all for their help last year in the running of the club. Mr Tommie Duggan, Garrandarragh, Mullinavat, spoke on behalf of the Handball Club.'

JUNIOR

South JFC R1: Bigwood 0-09; Kilmoganny 1-03
South JFC Semi Final: Carrickshock 1-03; Bigwood 0-03
South JFC Final: Tullogher Rosbercon 1-07; Carrickshock 1-07
South JFC Final Replay: Tullogher Rosbercon 0-09; Carrickshock 0-01

OUR STORY (1887-2024)

1987

MULLINAVAT FUNCTION

'A very pleasant function was held under the auspices of Mullinavat Football Club and the local GAA Club on Friday 23/01/1987 in the Ardree Hotel, Waterford. Presiding was Edward Conway, "Beaupre," Mullinavat, secretary of the hurling club. He welcomed all to the function run by the hurling club, Bigwood Football Club and the local Handball Club. Guests were Mons. Thomas Maher, Rev Liam Dunne, C.C; Joe and Mrs Marie Mackey, Dunamaggin, Chairman of the Southern Board GAA. He also welcomed Liam Fennelly of Knockbrown, an All-Star Award winner for the second year running. The night also marked a presentation to Mons. Maher, on his retirement last year from active involvement in GAA both in the parish and county.'

'Michael Carroll, Chairman of the Hurling Club, presented Fr. Maher with a Waterford Crystal decanter. He thanked him for bringing to Mullinavat, while coach and trainer of the team, a Junior hurling championship and a "B" special Junior hurling championship. He wished him well in his "retirement" from the game and in his continued position as Parish Priest of the district.'

'Monsignor Maher in returning thanks referred to starting involvement in the game as a coach and trainer in Dublin in 1948, and if he had known then it would be 1987 before he would finally call it a day, he doubted if he would have taken up the call. He loved his association with the Gaelic Athletic Association, but he commented: "You cannot put young legs on old shoulders." He thanked the members of the club for the nice gesture and would be around to hopefully see an Intermediate championship landed in the Rod-Iron Village.'

'Michael Carroll thanked the two main sponsors – South Eastern Bungalows and Waterford Foundry Ltd. They have continued to support their tournament and the finance had been considerable. He congratulated John Dunphy and Pat Hoban, a Kilkenny Minor star on winning a Winter League medal playing for the Kilkenny team. He welcomed the high numbers of camogie personnel that were present at the function. He paid special word of thanks to Sean Kelly, Chairman of the Football Club, for all his work. Joe Mackey thanked the Committee for their kind invitation. As Chairman of the Southern Board he paid special attention to the work done by the host club and although now under the control of the County Board as an Intermediate club, he stated that the Gaelic pitch in Mullinavat was always made available to the Board. He praised both Richard Carroll and Thomas Duggan for their work as referees for the Board. He congratulated the special Junior team in their victory and to the gallant performance made by the Under-21 hurlers in the South final v. Glenmore. Tom Anthony, Chairman of the Handball Club, was also present, as was the secretary of the Camogie Club, Miss

Margo Slattery, together with their Chairperson, Miss Martina Holden, Knockbrown, and Miss Catherine O'Keeffe, Ballyluskey.'

BIGWOOD GAA CLUB AMALGAMATE WITH MULLINAVAT GAA

At a special meeting held in February 1987 it was decided to disband the Bigwood GAA club. It was not now financially feasible to have two clubs in the parish. The cost of public liability insurance was the main reason. At this meeting four football selectors were picked to act with the chairman going forward. So to conclude the amalgamation of the Bigwood football club into the Mullinavat GAA club the following football selectors were appointed:

Sean Kelly, Bigwood; John Fitzgerald, Fahee; Tommie Frisby, Red Acres; Eamonn Kelly, Bigwood and Michael Carroll, Mullinavat GAA chairman. The captain of the football section chosen was Michael Delahunty, Fahee. The Under-21 captain was William Haberlin and Minor captain Bill Walsh, Bigwood.

The Bigwood club had lasted 49 years (formed in 1938) and had taken over the football activities in the parish of Mullinavat until 1987. The first Bigwood club officers had been. Dick Vereker (chairman) and Tom Byrne of Ballincrea (secretary).

SENIOR

R1: Mullinavat 1-04; Young Irelands, Gowran 1-03

Mullinavat: P Laherty, M Harney, J Fitzgerald (0-1), S Kelly, J Dunphy, D Harney, E Kelly, W Haberlin, T Frisby, B Power, W Delahunty (1-1) A Walsh, M Law (0-2), P Frisby, and H Waters.

JUNIOR

South JFC R1: Mullinavat v. Slieverue
South JFC R2: Mullinavat 1-07; Carrigeen 0-05
South JFC R2: Semi Final: St Patrick's (Kilmacow) 1-07; Mullinavat 1-04

Mullinavat: P Laharty, W Fitzgerald, J Fitzgerald (0-2), M Laharty, W Haberlin, P Hoban, E Kelly, P McEvoy, T Frisby, H Waters, P Frisby, A Walsh 1-2), N Harney, B Walsh and B Power. Subs: M Law, M Knox.

South JFC Final: St Patrick's (Kilmacow) 2-07; John Lockes (Callan) 0-06

UNDER-21

South Under-21 B FC R1: Mullinavat v. Shamrocks

COUNTY

Billy Walsh stars for Kilkenny footballers.

Kilkenny celebrated their first football title win in 76 years. The title won was the Leinster Minor league. In a replayed final, Kilkenny beat Wexford by 2-8 to 0-10. Earlier the team had played a draw, Kilkenny 0-7 to Wexford 1-4. The last time Kilkenny won anything in football was way back in 1911 when they took the Leinster Senior crown.

Leinster Minor Football League Final: Kilkenny 0-07; Wexford 1-04
Leinster Minor Football League Final Replay: Kilkenny 2-08; Wexford 0-10

'Kilkenny Minor Footballers wrote their names into the history books when they won the county's first football trophy in 76 years. One had to go back to the 1911 Leinster Senior Football Final for the last Kilkenny football final victory. This latest win was in the South Leinster Minor football league final against Wexford at Wexford Park on Monday 11/5/1987. The sides had played a draw a few weeks earlier at Nowlan Park.'

Leinster JFC Round 1: Dublin 1-09; Kilkenny 1-07

'The county Junior footballers put in a brave performance in the championship at Parnell Park. Away to Dublin they lost by just two points, 1-7 to 1-9. Subsequently Dublin qualified for the all-Ireland Final.

GAELIC CONVENTION (JANUARY 1988)

'Pat Mulrooney – Kilkenny Football Board Chairman: "We won our first title in 76 years when the Minor team won the South East League by beating Wexford. Great credit is due not alone to the players who gave their all, but also to the selectors and trainers". The Clara official also had a look at the past year's activities, and he was encouraged by what he had to report. "Things were improving at local level, and Nickey Brennan had commenced what should be a rewarding programme at Senior county level. Of course, Senior champions, Mooncoin played a big part and put an excellent effort into the game. The year has been a demanding and difficult one, but it was also exciting", the chairman disclosed.'

1988
JUNIOR

South JFC: Mullinavat 4-04; Mooncoin 1-03
South JFC: Mullinavat 2-10; Carrickshock 1-02
South JFC Final: Mullinavat 0-08; Piltown 0-05
County JFC Final: Graigue Ballycallan 2-06; Mullinavat 0-04

Mullinavat: P Laherty, S Kelly, P McEvoy, T Frisby, P Frisby, P Hoban, D Harney, J Fitzgerald (0-3), J Walsh, B Walsh, L Aldridge, E Kelly, M Fitzgerald (0-1), P Holden and B Power. Subs: N Harney, W Haberlin.

UNDER-21

South U-21 Roinn B semi final: Mullinavat 1-06; Piltown 0-07
South U-21 Roinn B Final: Mooncoin 1-06; Mullinavat 0-05

OPEN DRAW FOOTBALL CHAMPIONSHIP

Mullinavat v. Thomastown at Mullinavat

COUNTY

It was an excellent year by Kilkenny football standards. Club wise James Stephens won the Senior football championship in October 1988 by beating the Railyard by 0-7 to 0-5 in a Senior final replay. On the County front there was a notable happening in the NFL. Kilkenny beat Waterford by 2-10 to 2-8. It was the county's first win in the NFL since 1981, which was also versus Waterford.

KILKENNY 2-10; WATERFORD 2-8

'The outcome of this seventh and final round of the 1987/88 NFL series involving near neighbours kilkenny and Waterford at Fraher Field, Dungarvan on Sunday afternoon may have been purely academic, and no doubt this was reflected in the smallest crowd ever to patronise such a fixture visitors, it was a most refreshing experience as they recorded wins at Senior football level, at the expense of a home side that was lethargic in the extreme. Fair play to Kilkenny who recovered well after conceding a goal inside 60 seconds, and gaining a crucial grip on the exchanges at a vital period in this lively affair, held out in the finish to record a slender but richly reserved victory.'

Kilkenny: L Purcell, N Maher, N Geoghegan, T Brennan, P Drea, C Hayes, E Kelly, D Connolly, L Cassin, J Conion, M Morrissey, R Minogue 0-2, M Kennedy 1-1, E Maher 1-0 and B Smyth 0-7. Sub: J Casey for J Conlon.

LEINSTER JFC

'The Kilkenny footballers experienced mixed fortunes in 1988. First, they beat Carlow in the Leinster Junior championship. This was their first win in 17 years (since 1971) in an adult championship. Mark Kennedy shot the deciding goal in the 56th minute that gave Kilkenny a memorable 1-9 to 1-8 victory. The same week an impressive Laois team destroyed the dream of glory, when they won a Byrne Cup semi-final clash at Nowlan Park by 1-11 to 0-6. That was followed by a defeat at the hands of Dublin in the Leinster Junior

OUR STORY (1887-2024)

Championship semi final, 1-14 to 0-4). The footballers enjoyed the good run while it lasted.'

Leinster JFC Quarter Final: Kilkenny 1-09; Carlow 1-08

'Kilkenny's football bubble was almost burst at Dr Cullen Park by a battling Carlow team in this first round Leinster Junior Football championship tie. However superior fitness enabled them outscore more naturally gifted opponents, but they left it very late before clinching a place in the semi-finals. Not until the 55th minute did Kilkenny inch ahead for the first time, but Mark Kennedy's goal, at that stage proved this game's decisive score. The Mooncoin man ghosted in behind the home defence, which was caught napping by a wind assisted clearance.

Carlow keeper, Sean Kearns quickly advanced, but Kennedy beat him to the draw and first timed a goal that saved Kilkenny's blushes and ensured a big crowd at Nowlan Park tomorrow night for their O Byrne Cup semi final against Laois. Carlow led by 1-6 to 0-3 at the interval after being aided by the strong breeze, but Kilkenny trailed by only three points by the 38th minute. Points from M. J. Grace and Johnny Nevin left Carlow four points clear with 12 minutes remaining and they looked like holding out until Kennedy pounced for that all important goal.'

Kilkenny: L Purcell, J Mahon, T Brennan, M Delaney, E Mansfield, C Hayes, E Breen, D Connolly (0-1), L Cassin (0-1), E Kelly (0-1), M Morrissey (0-1), R Minogue, M Kennedy (1-0), A Maher and B Smith (0-3). Subs: M O'Dowd (0-1) for Minogue, E Maher (0-1) for Morrissey, J Maher for Kelly.

Leinster JFC Semi Final 1988: Dublin 1-14; Kilkenny 0-04

'The great Kilkenny dream of appearing in the county's first Leinster football final in 17 years was well and truly kicked into touch by dynamic Dublin in the provincial Junior championship semi-final at Nowlan Park. Bad and all as things were for Kilkenny then, they nosedived at the throw in for the new half when midfielder Liam Cassin fell awkwardly and was forced to leave the field with a suspected broken arm. Kilkenny just weren't in it after that against what Sean Kelly might term a 'super team'. While one felt pity for the demoralised losers in their plight, some were often left lurching at shadows, it was something to watch the swift, constructive moves pieced together by the Dubs, who looked to be coached to perfection. The way the game should be played, and who knows, Kilkenny might get there some day. At least they improved this year. That was a start.'

Kilkenny team and scorers: L Purcell, J Mahon, N Geoghegan, M Delaney, R Mansfield, T Brennan, K Breen, D Connolly (0-1), L Cassin, L Bird (0-1 free), M Morrissey R Minogue, M Kennedy, (0-1), T Maher, and M Dowd (0-1). Subs: E Maher for T Maher, E Kelly for L Cassin (injured), J Maher for M Dowd.

1989

Open Draw R1: Mullinavat 3-10; Lisdowney 0-06
Open Draw R2: Tullaroan v. Mullinavat

JUNIOR

South JFC R1:| Mullinavat 1-08; Mooncoin 0-04
South JFC semi final: Mullinavat 4-09; Windgap 0-09
South JFC Final; Mullinavat 0-07; Piltown 0-06
County JFC Final: Bennettsbridge 2-09; Mullinavat 2-06

UNDER-21

South Under 21 Roinn B: Graignamanagh v. Mullinavat

COUNTY

Leinster JFC Semi Final: Kildare 1-12; Kilkenny 0-11

'Kildare withstood a late Kilkenny recovery bid in the second half at Newbridge to qualify for the final with four points to spare. Kilkenny led on two occasions during the first half, but they were overwhelmed in the third quarter when the home side added an uninterrupted 1-5 to their tally.'

Scorers: Kilkenny: W Blanchfield (04): B Smith (0-3); E Connery (0-2); L Cassin and M Morrissey (0-1 each).

FOOTBALL CONVENTION

'It may have raised a few eye-brows, even made the hair stand on the back of a few necks, but one Kilkenny GAA official has suggested local fixtures should be fitted in around the World Cup soccer matches this coming year. Hard-working secretary of the Football Board, Pat Mulrooney, made the suggestion that is sure to have upset some and pleased others, in whatever proportions no one knows, when he delivered his annual address to the Football Board Convention. "Looking to the playing side in the coming year we must guard against taking on the television during the Summer screening of the World Cup soccer finals," he declared. "I hope the Fixtures Committee will avoid confrontation during this period, because it is difficult enough for clubs to exist on the meagre gates of the past few years without trying to get people to attend games when there is an alternate attraction on the television.'

'And Pat wasn't finished at that: "The Ban is gone, so we must get on together. Clubs will be severely stretched because of players on holidays in Italy during this period. We will have to accommodate them if we are to survive This may mean a doubling of fixtures prior to, and immediately after the World Cup finals," he declared.

The Mullinavat squad which lost to Graigue-Ballycallan in the Kilkenny JFC final in 1988.

# CHAPTER 7

1990s

Kilkenny star John Power and the Liam MacCarthy Cup visit Mullinavat in 2000:
Top: *John Joe Aylward, John Power Tommy Frisby, Father Liam Barron.* **Middle:** *John Power, Deirdre Aylward, Anna Woods.* **Below:** *Peggy Hoban, Maureen McEvoy, Martin O'Brien, Brigid Haberlin, Kathleen O'Brien.*

1990s

1990

South JFC R1: Mullinavat beat Kilmacow
South JFC Semi Final Mullinavat 4-08; Thomastown 2-03
South JFC Final Mullinavat 4-06; Piltown 1-04
County JFC Final: Dicksboro 0-09; Mullinavat 2-02

'Dicksboro created a bit of history at Danesfort on Saturday when they beat Mullinavat in the Junior football county final to register their first win in the competition. But before taking home the silverware they had to endure a nail-biting closing 10 minutes. Pat McEvoy punched a goal for the Southerners to give them a one point lead entering the closing stages.

The 'Boro stared defeat squarely in the face, but they met the challenge head on. Late points from Sean Moore and reserve, Michael Walsh helped them to a bit of history and their second county title of the year.'

'The closing minutes were frantic. Mullinavat poured forward in search of the equaliser and Dicksboro hung on desperately. With time ticking away a Dicksboro attack broke down 40 yards from the Mullinavat goal. From this mistake the losers stormed down the field and following a nice interchange of passes, worked themselves into a scorable position. However, the effort was off-target. A relieved 'Boro captain, Tom Maher went on to accept the Lyng Cup on behalf of his team. The first half was keenly contested. It was Mullinavat who got off to the better start, scoring two unanswered points through Michael Duggan. Shortly afterwards, Dicksboro opened their account. Stephen Kennedy pointed a free following a foul on Mark Dowling. There were only three other scores during the remainder of the half. All fell to Dicksboro and all were scored by the outstanding footballer on the field, centreforward Martin Handrick. This left the city side 0-4 to 0-2 ahead at half-time.'

'This margin should have been greater. The 'Boro forwards missed several chances and Stephen Kennedy had a penalty saved by Mullinavat goalkeeper, Pat Laherty. Michael Kennedy was also very unlucky when a powerful ground shot struck the post.'

'Dicksboro got into their stride quickly in the second half and increased their advantage. Martin Handrick and Stephen Kennedy shot unanswered points. They appeared to be pulling away at this stage. Then came the boost Mullinavat badly needed. Liam Walsh expertly converted a penalty to leave just a point between the sides with 15 minutes to play.'

'Anthony Teehan kept a sound goal for the winners. He got excellent cover from all the backs with Niall Morrissey, Frank Colcough and David Beirne most effective. Tommy Bawle and Stephen Kennedy, when brought out from half forward, dominated midfield. Up front best were Martin Handrick, Sean Moore and second half substitute Mickey Walsh. Mullinavat were best served by goalkeeper Pat Laherty, Pat Hoban, Liam Aldridge, Michael Duggan, Eamonn Kelly and Joe Walsh.'

Mullinavat team and scorers: P Laherty, S Kelly, J Fitzgerald, T Frisby, P Frisby, D Harney, P Hoban, M Dunphy (0-2), J Walsh, E Kelly, L Aldridge, B Walsh (1-0), M Duggan, P McEvoy (1-0) and H Waters. Subs: T Duggan and K Power.

Dicksboro team and scorers: A Teehan, T Butler, N Morrissey, T Maher, D Beirne, F Colcough, T Maher, T Bawle, P Stapleton, F O'Meara, M Handrick (0-5), S Kennedy (0-2), M Kennedy, S Moore (0-1), M Dowling. Subs: R Dalton, M Walsh (0-1) and L Scott.

Referee: C Whelan (Dunnamaggin).

FOOTBALL CONVENTION 1990
(HELD JANUARY 1991)

(POST 5/5/1990 Leinster JFC First Round Dublin 1-12; Kilkenny 1-2 at Parnell Park)

Football Board secretary, Pat Mulrooney (Clara): "A little bit of planning and common sense could eliminate a lot of problems with regard to football in Kilkenny." That was the conclusion of Football Board secretary, Pat Mulrooney (Clara) when he delivered a well thought out address to Convention. The secretary admitted the worst moment of the year was when Kilkenny failed to fulfil a National League tie away to Clare, because they hadn't enough players. But the Clara official felt that dark moment could be the beginning of a bright new era for the game by the Nore, if the right spirit was forthcoming. "That was an awful blow to the Football Board and selectors, who had just taken up their new posts", Mr Mulrooney said in relation to the Clare affair. After that non-event there was a meeting between players and officials, and the result was a much improved showing against Limerick the following week. With the commitment of players and management we can look forward to a promising effort in the Leinster Junior championship", he thought. If nothing else comes out of that Clare fiasco, it showed us that if football is to continue in

Kilkenny, then clubs will have to wake up and put their full backing into the effort instead of paying just lip service, as is the situation at present".

Mr Mulrooney said the Co. Board would have to recognise that football will have to receive the same treatment as hurling, even in its secondary position. Team mentors involved with hurling sides will have to be told that football championship games take precedence over hurling challenges. "No club should have to play a football championship game without their full panel of players. This shouldn't be the case to facilitate a hurling challenge".

1991
SENIOR
SFL: Mullinavat 1-08; Black and Whites 0-01
SFL: Mullinavat 2-04; Tullogher Rosbercon 1-05
SFL: Mullinavat 1-10; Mooncoin 3-01

JUNIOR
South JFC R1: Mullinavat beat Mooncoin
South JFC Semi final: Shamrocks 2-08; Mullinavat 2-04
South JFC Final: Shamrocks 1-08; Coolagh 2-05
South JFC Final Replay: Shamrocks 2-06; Coolagh 0-10

1992
SENIOR
SFL: Mullinavat v. Thomastown
SFL Semi Final: Mullinavat v. James Stephens

JUNIOR
South JFC: Mullinavat 3-14; Carrickshock 3-04
South JFC: Mullinavat 4-12; Slieverue 1-06
South JFC Fina:l Piltown 2-03; Mullinavat 1-05

Mullinavat: P Laharty, Joe Kelly, J Fitzgerald, L Power, N Harney, T Frisby, E Kelly, M Dunphy, B Walsh (0-1), B Aldridge (1-1), R Carroll (0-1), P Mansfield (0-1), W Atkins (0-1) and P Kelly, D Dungan.

COUNTY
Leinster JFC Round One: Kilkenny 1-08; Westmeath 0-11

Leinster JFC Round One Replay: Westmeath 4-08; Kilkenny 1-11

Westmeath were slow to get into their stride, but then did a lot of damage in a five minute spell which ultimately beat Kilkenny in this Leinster Junior football championship replay at St John's Park, Kilkenny.

Kilkenny: J Brennan (Erin's Own, 1-2), Brendan Smith (Railyard, 0-4), Liam Kenny (Piltown, 0-2), J Dooley (Muckalee, 0-1), S Kennedy (Dicksboro, 0-1) and B Maguire (Railyard, 0-1).

FOOTBALL CONVENTION
(Held December 1992)

'Kilkenny County Board chairman Nicky Brennan, and football board chairman Kieran Meally both dealt with the structures of football in a Kilkenny. Both men felt that there were footballers in areas where clubs are not organised to play the code, who should be catered for elsewhere. Kieran Meally asked that clubs support players who want to kick football with the county, and stop putting obstacles in their way. Nickey Brennan hinted there might be a change in the parish rule for football, so that everyone who wanted to play the game could do so. There was also an address from Football Secretary Pat Mulroney who said Kilkenny had set their Sights on winning the Leinster Junior football championship next year, and if they don't do it there will be at least one very disappointed man.'

1993
JUNIOR

South JFC: Mullinavat 4-11; Rower Inistioge 2-05
South JFC: Mullinavat v. Coolagh
South JFC: Mullinavat beat Slieverue
South JFC: Mullinavat beat Carrickshock
South JFC: Thomastown 1-11; Mullinavat 1-11
South JFC Final Piltown 1-10; Thomastown 3-04
South JFC Final Replay: Piltown 3-11; Thomastown 4-04

FOOTBALL CONVENTION

'Clubs not interested in promoting football at county, as well as local level, should forget about the game altogether, because they are only messing things up. That was the two-barrelled blast from Football Board secretary Pat Mulrooney in his annual address to Convention. Mr Mulrooney opened his delivery by promising to "set out some of the ills which keep football at the bottom of the national ladder." He exonerated the team trainer, management and players from all blame, and put the cause of the ills squarely with clubs. "There was no training from the end of the National League up to the Championship," Mr Mulrooney blasted. "The reason being that clubs would not release players for training, even for one night."

1994

JUNIOR

South JFC: Thomastown 2-07; Mullinavat 1-07
South JFC: Mullinavat 2-08; Carrickshock 1-04
South JFC: Mullinavat v. Coolagh
South JFC Semi Final: Kilmoganny 4-19; Mullinavat 1-06
South JFC Final: Kilmoganny 4-14; Thomastown 0-07

COUNTY

Leinster JFC Round One: Laois 2-13; Kilkenny 0-07

Tony Dunne, a man who in the past helped Kilkenny City's soccer side, proved the Cats' greatest enemy as Laois reached the Leinster JFC semi-finals at Portlaoise on 2/5/94.

Kilkenny: Damien Walsh (Railyard, 0-5), Bernard Maguire (Railyard, 0-1) and Pat Brennan, St Patrick's, 0-1 each).

The Players Committee set up to examine "The Way Forward" for football in Kilkenny made many important points during its 5-page report, issued in November 1994.

The 16 most important ones were:
1. Football has been in a state of crisis for years.
2. Kilkenny has the resources to make progress, but attitudes and structures are not helping.
3. Players do not currently have the proper level of skill or fitness to make decent progress in the intercounty game.
4. Prayers only get from three to five club games a year, and about eight inter-county matches. Everyone must get more matches,
5. Current structures for football are similar to those in other counties, but they are not adequate for Kilkenny's needs
6. Playing the local championships between March, April and May, as was currently the case, was fine. But that period between September and February when most hurling games are out of the way, should be used to improve skills.
7. Floodlit football leagues should be organised when the new all weather pitch

becomes available at Scanlon Park, Loughboy.
8. More football tournaments should be organised, and clubs should be obliged to run one bi-annually. These could be for 7, 9 or 15-a side teams.
9. The current situation of allowed unattached Junior players join Senior clubs should be continued for at least one more season. Alternatively, Junior North and South sides could be formed and be allowed into the Senior championship.
10. Matters concerning football cannot be decided at Co. Board by a mere majority vote because the Board contains members who have no interest in the game.
11. Snacks of some sort must be provided after training. Meals only after matches or training on Sunday.
12. Accommodation provided for overnight trips was "excellent", but some of the buses hired were "dreadful".
13. Proper gear, and at least 12 footballs, must be provided for training.
14. Opportunities which exist during the current National League must be exploited to attracted the better players. The footballers have an away trip to London in the new year.
15. Positive developments will take time, and progress may only be achieved after a considerable length of time.
16. Clubs must have a fundamental change of heart, and actually encourage and facilitate the playing of football at club and inter-county levels.

1995

JUNIOR

South JFC: Mullinavat bye
South JFC: Mullinavat beat Rower Inistioge
South JFC Final: 1995 Carrickshock 1-08; Mullinavat 0-02

Mullinavat team and scorers: Brian Conway, J Geary, J Fitzgerald, Lenny Power, Joe Kelly, N Harney, E Kelly, Joe Walsh, R Carroll (0-1), O Aylward (0-1), P Keneally, M Dunphy, H Waters, P Kelly, and D Dungan. Subs: M Duggan, R Power

COUNTY

Leinster JFC Round One: Dublin 1-14; Kilkenny 0-10

'The Junior footballers of Dublin produced some lovely passages of flowing play when they defeated Kilkenny in the Leinster JFC at Ballyragget yesterday evening. In the end, three late points from the sharpshooting Padraig Doherty earned the Dubs a slightly bigger win than they might have expected against hard-chasing opponents. There was little

between the two sides during the opening half apart from the only goal of the game in the 12th minute when Alan Toft tucked away a rebounded penalty from Alan McNally. That score helped shoot the Dubs into a 1-5 to 0-7 interval lead.'
Kilkenny: D Walsh 0-6, J Grace, P Brennan, S Kennedy, P Drea 0-1 each

KILKENNY CONVENTION

'Football is losing out very badly during the height of this season in the current hurling-football mix of games in Kilkenny. In fact, in many cases football teams are turning out in competitions without any preparatory work. Even worse many clubs are simply opting out.

This was the none too encouraging news chairman of the Games Administration Committee. Ned Quinn (Mooncoin) said the time has come for Kilkenny GAA to seriously attempt to provide an appropriate slot in the fixtures calendar for football. The fact all inter-county teams play in June congests the fixtures schedule for many players. This makes the proper preparation of county teams, other than Senior, very difficult. Some players are expected to turn out in important games for club and county within days.

1996
JUNIOR
South JFC Semi Final: Mullinavat 5-05; Kilmacow 1-01
South JFC Final: Carrickshock w/o Mullinavat scr. (Was fixed for 12/7/96 but not played)

UNDER-16
County Under 16B Football Final: Mullinavat 2-01; Shamrocks 1-02
 A first win at this grade.

COUNTY
Leinster JFC Round One: Kilkenny 0-11; Kildare 1-08
Leinster JFC First Round Replay: Kilkenny 0-04; Kildare 0-03
Leinster JFC Semi Final: Meath 1-13; Kilkenny 2-07

Totally committed Kilkenny gave fancied Meath the shock of their lives before bowing out with all guns blazing in the Leinster Junior football championship semi-final at Navan. The winners were delighted to hear the final whistle because they were really stretched to cope during the closing 10 minutes of so when the gutsy Cats threw everything into attack in a bid to force at least a draw And Kilkenny went close, and on more than one occasion, to getting the goal that would have earned them a replay. Ken O'Shea put a late low effort into the side netting, and Pat Brennan and James Young were also unlucky when they pierced the Meath defence But the winners had their luckiest escape in the dying seconds when Bernard Maguire was twice deprived by goalie, John O'Sullivan, who was acclaimed a hero.

Pat Drea was outstanding for the losers, as was Liam Cassin when he joined him at midfield in the second half. Liam Kenny did really well when shifted to centre back. Damien Walsh was very good on the frees, and kicked six points Jimmy Walsh and Seamus Crean, Kenny O'Shea and Eddie Roche also played very well.

Kilkenny team and scorers: D O'Neill, J Teehan, E Roche, F Hickey, J Walsh, D Beirne, S Crean, P Drea (1-0), W Blanchfiel, B Maguire (0-1), J Grace (captain), L Kenny, J Young, D Walsh (0- 6) and K O'Shea (1-0). Sub: L Cassin.

1997
JUNIOR

South JFC: Mullinavat 0-05; Shamrocks 1-02
South JFC: Mullinavat v. Graignamanagh
South JFC: Mullinavat v. John Lockes
South JFC: Mullinavat 4-07; Rower Inistioge 2-08
South JFC: Mullinavat v. Thomastown
South JFC Final: Carrickshock 0-09; Mullinavat 0-09
South JFC Final Replay: Carrickshock 0-12; Mullinavat 0-09

UNDER-21

U-21 FC Roinn B: Mullinavat 2-10; Carrickshock 0-06 (played January 1998)
South U-21 FC Final: Mullinavat 1-10; Mooncoin 0-09 AET (0-8 each at 60 minutes)
South U-21 FC Final Replay: Mooncoin 1-10; Mullinavat 0-09

1998
JUNIOR

South JFC: Mullinavat v. Rower Inistioge
South JFC: Mullinavat v. Graignamanagh
South JFC: Mullinavat v. Kilmacow
South JFC Semi final: Mullinavat 5-14; John Lockes 0-05
South JFC Fina:l Mullinavat 2-09; Kilmacow 0-09
Kilkenny JFC Final: Young Irelands 0-09; Mullinavat 0-06

UNDER-21
South Under 21 FC Semi final: Mullinavat 0-9; Piltown 1-10
South Under 21 FC Final Mullinavat 3-5; Mooncoin 0-8

'These teams met in a repeat of last year's Southern Under-21 football (Roinn B) final, but this time it was Mullinavat who emerged victorious. Although the dividing margin was six points, the issue was in doubt until Liam Murphy goaled for Mullinavat in the 59th minute to seal a victory which was fully deserved. Mullinavat should have been well clear at that stage, but they were guilty of wasting chances. The winners enjoyed a dream start. A Stephen Roche shot went all the way to the net in the second minute. It was a lead they were never to relinquish. Conor Conway increased the lead when he pointed two minutes later. Mooncoin's first score came from a Paul Fewer point after six minutes. Seamus Holden scored a goal for Mullinavat to put them six points clear. Mooncoin got their act together and put pressure on the 'Vat defence. Vincent Power scored two points inside a minute, and two more from Billy Ryan reduced the deficit to a pair of points by the 23rd minute. Both sides missed chances which left the half time score: Mullinavat 2-1, Mooncoin 0-5.'

'Tommy Walsh pointed early in the second half to reduce the arrears to the minimum. Conor Conway replied for Mullinavat. Conway then set up Keith Madigan for a point to edge Mullinavat three points clear. Vincent Power pointed a minute later. Billy Ryan pointed to leave the minimum between the sides after 44 minutes. It was to be Mooncoin's final score. Midway through the half Ollie Dalton in the Mullinavat goal saved brilliantly at point blank range. Mullinavat seemed to find their feet again, and with Keith Madigan now operating at centre forward they began to put their opponents under pressure.'

'However, chances went astray at both ends. Two further points from Conor Conway and Keith Madigan put Mullinavat three clear with five minutes left. There was still time left for a Mooncoin rally. But the Vat defence, ably led by Walter Burke and Paul Aylward, held out. Liam Murphy ensured a Mullinavat victory when he goaled just before full time.'

'Best for Vat were Walter Burke and Paul Aylward in defence, Keith Madigan, who was outstanding throughout the field. Martin Knox worked hard in midfield. Up front Conor Conway, Liam Murphy and Andrew McGovern were prominent.'

Mullinavat team and scorers: O Aylward, PJ Aylward, W Burke, J P Dungan, J Duggan, P Aylward, M Walsh, K Madigan (0-2), M Knox, A McGovern, L Murphy (1-0), C Conway (0-3), D Duggan, S Holden (1-0) and S Roche (1-0). Subs: A Duggan, K Slattery, A Wall, J Rohan, M Roche, and M Duggan.

County Under 21 Final: Mullinavat 0-07; Railyard 0-05
(Unfinished, Mullinavat awarded title)

MINOR

MFC Roinn A: James Stephens 1-8; Mullinavat 1-8
MFC Roinn A Replay: Mullinavat 2-5; James Stephens 0-9
MFC Roinn A Semi Final: O'Loughlins 3-7; Mullinavat 2-6

1999

Mullinavat footballers were up to Intermediate in 1999 and competitions in Kilkenny re-organised, with more games for everyone. The Co. Board gave the go ahead for the re-structuring, and the Senior and Intermediate competitions were run much like the hurling league/championship. The Senior and Intermediate divisions were divided into two groups of four teams. The top team in each qualified for the league final, with the Moremiles Cup on offer in the Senior grade. These two teams, Senior and Intermediate, will also go through to the championship semi-finals. The second teams in each group qualified for the championship quarter-finals. The bottom two teams in each division played off for the remaining quarter-final places. And the losers of the latter matches would contest the relegation play-off. First round matches in both grades were fixed for March 20. The second round was fixed for April 3.

SENIOR

SFL: Mullinavat 2-05; O'Loughlins 0-05
SFL: Mullinavat 3-06; Mooncoin 0-05
SFL: Mullinavat v. Clara
SFL Final: Mullinavat 3-05; Black and Whites 1-10

INTERMEDIATE

IFL Final: Mullinavat 3-05; Black and Whites 1-10

Mullinavat Team and scorers: O Dalton, W Burke, Mossy Murphy, JP Dungan, P Mansfield, Joe Walsh, Michael Murphy, M Knox, P Aylward (0-1), M Dunphy, O Aylward, L Murphy, A McGovern (1-4), S Holden (2-0) and C Conway. Subs: D Duggan, K Slattery.

UNDER-21

Under 21 South FC Roinn B: Mullinavat beat Carrigeen

'Mullinavat became the first winners of the newly inaugurated Intermediate football league when they overcame the spirited challenge of Blacks and Whites in an exciting final in Thomastown. The standard of football was quite good, with Blacks and Whites in particular scoring some excellent points Mullinavat scored three goals during the first half and they were crucial. They missed a number of good opportunities afterwards.'

'Playing into the wind, Mullinavat opened the scoring when Andrew McGovern pointed in the second minute. James Doyle levelled with a free after five minutes. David O'Neill pointed to put the losers ahead. Then lead was short lived however. Seamus Holden netted for Mullinavat. Within three minutes Blacks and Whites had levelled with two points from David O'Neill and another from Michael Doyle. In the 16th minute, Seamus Holden again netted for the 'Vat to put them three points clear. Their opponents hit back smartly, and had four points without reply.'

'Then came the best move of the match. Andrew McGovern netted for Mullinavat following a slick passing movement involving Paul Aylward and Conor Conway. Half time score: Mullinavat 3-1, Blacks and Whites 0-8. The winners looked to be in a strong position after playing against the wind. Blacks and Whites took the game to them afterwards. Peter Cleere pointed in the 36th minute to leave a mere point in it. There was no score during the next 10 minutes, although both sides had a number of chances. In the 46th minute Andrew McGovern pointed, and two more from him saw Mullinavat lead by four with five minutes of normal time left.'

'James Doyle pointed for 'Whites, and Paul Aylward kicked a reply. There were a number of stoppages for injuries during the half, and as the match went into stoppage time, Ned Kelly goaled for the losers to cut the deficit to the minimum. However, Mullinavat held out against great pressure and took the title by the minimum margin. Best for Mullinavat were Walter Burke and John Paul Dungan in defence, Martin Knox in midfield. Andrew McGovern and Seamus Holden were good in the forwards, while Paul Aylward had a fine second half.

Mullinavat: O Dalton, W Burke, Mossy Murphy, JP Dungan, P Mansfield, Joe Walsh, Michael Murphy, M Knox, P Aylward (0-1), M Dunphy, O Aylward, L Murphy, A McGovern (1-4), S Holden (2-0) and C Conway. Subs: D Duggan, K Slattery.

COUNTY

Leinster JFC Quarter Final: Laois 0-14; Kilkenny 1-06

The Laois Junior footballers qualified for a Leinster semi-final meeting against either Wexford or Dublin thanks to a comprehensive victory over Kilkenny in Portlaoise. Paul Carroll scored a brilliant goal for Kilkenny after just four minutes, but they added only one more point to their total in the opening half. Laois finished the game with 14 men after Mark Rooney shown the red card while he was being stretchered off the field.

Kilkenny: Eddie Mulroney, John Gaule, Niall Morrissey, Ger Campion; John Lonergan,

MULLINAVAT GAA CLUB

Paddy Mullally, Richie Mullally; P Brennan, Jim Murphy (0-1): Michael Dunne, Liam Kenny, Colm Connolly (0-1); Paul Carroll (1-0), John Phelan (0-1) and D Walsh (0-2). Subs: P Mullins (0-1) for J Lonergan, P Fewer for M Dunne, M Jordan for J Murphy.

CHAPTER 8

2000s

The Mullinavat squad which claimed the Kilkenny Intermediate league and championship titles in a glorious 2004.

2000s

2000

INTERMEDIATE

IFL R1: Black and Whites 2-07; Mullinavat 1-04
IFL R2: Mullinavat 1-09; O'Loughlin Gaels 1-02
IFL R3: Mullinavat 1-08; Mooncoin 0-03

IFC R2: Mullinavat 0-15; Bennettsbridge 0-05
IFC Semi Final: Mullinavat 2-05; Conahy Shamrocks 0-08
IFC Final: Mullinavat 1-04; O'Loughlin Gaels 0-6

'Mullinavat scooped the first Intermediate title of the new Millennium following a convincing comeback in Nowlan Park. Andrew McGovern's goal for the Southerners turned the tide against city side O'Loughlin Gaels, who had reversed a two point half time deficit with a miniature scoring spree to take the lead.'

'The first football final of the year looked set to be an engrossing tussle between the teams until the weather intervened. The week long sunshine finally broke and Nowlan Park was shrouded in a steady misty drizzle on Sunday, which made the pitch very greasy. When the first score of the game finally came before the 20 minute mark, through a Conor Conway free, you could sense the relief from the Mullinavat supporters that the eagle of the football calendar wasn't about to turn in to a lame duck. Mullinavat forged ahead and increased their lead on the half-hour. Conway raised the white flag with another pointed free, and some good work by Seamus Holden teed up Liam Murphy for his first score of the game. After some early misses, Colin Furlong notched up O'Loughlins first score before the break to leave just two points between the sides. O'Loughlins awoke in the second half and took the game by the scruff of the neck inside the first minute. They snatched the ball straight from the throw-in and set up Furlong for his second point. They could and should have levelled the game on 37 minutes. Somehow Furlong missed a relatively easy free, letting Mullinavat's indiscipline go unpunished.'

'However, they drew level on 38 minutes through wing back Brian Skehan, following a poor kick-out. O'Loughlins took the lead for the first time six minutes later through Skehan and looked set to go on to victory. However, Mullinavat blitzed their hopes of victory on 46 minutes. Substitute Ollie Aylward pumped a free dangerously towards the O'Loughlins goal. Teammate Seamus Holden was first to react. After grabbing the ball, he quickly passed it to the advancing Andrew McGovern, who blasted past the helpless keeper Paul Cleere. O'Loughlins tried hard to come back after that devastating blow. Two mare points from the boot of Furlong brought them level again, but Mullinavat stepped up a gear. With only two minutes left the Southerners scored what proved to be the winner. As the ball broke well inside the O'Loughlins half. Tony Doyle was adjudged to have fouled corner-forward Michael Duggan. As time ticked by, Conway remained calm and coolly kicked the free high and over the bar. While the scoring may not have been high, the level of heart and effort put in by both sets of players was off the Richter scale. Best for Mullinavat were Liam Murphy and the sharpshooter Conor Conway, while Skehan and Furlong gave their all for the Gaels.'

Mullinavat team and scorers: D Duggan, W Burke, M Murphy, J P Dungan, P Mansfield, J Walsh, M Murphy, M Knox, P Aylward, S Holden, K Madigan, L Murphy (0-1), A McGovern (1-0), C Conway (0-3, all frees) and M Duggan. Subs: O Aylward for M Knox, 35 mins; M Dunphy for J Walsh, 38 mins; R Carroll for K Madigan 57 mins.

UNDER-21

Kilkenny U21 Roinn A Football Final: Mullinavat 1-08; O'Loughlin Gaels 2-04

'All action Mullinavat won their first Roinn A Under-21 football county title when they edged out O'Loughlin's in dramatic fashion in Thomastown. Three points behind with five minutes remaining, it looked all over for Mullinavat. Then Lady Luck appeared to smile on them. They were awarded a penalty when Keith Madigan was fouled. However, Andrew McGovern's shot went inches wide. The cup looked destined for O'Loughlin's. However McGovern made amends two minutes later when he superbly finished to the net a brilliant passing movement involving Tomas Frisby and Michael Duggan The scores were level. The drama was far from finished. In the closing minute, Conor Conway swung over the winning point with his left foot from a difficult angle to give the Southerners an exciting victory.'

'Mullinavat dominated the opening period and were three points up after 10 minutes thanks to Conor Conway (2) and Tomas Frisby. Two more points from Conor Conway increased their lead before O'Loughlin's had their solitary score of the half, a pointed free from Niall Bergin after 25 minutes Mullinavat replied with a fine point from sharpshooter, Conor Conway. That left them 0-6 to 0-1 ahead at the break. The winners should have been even better off, such was their dominance Their forwards wasted a lot of possession. The 'Vat started the second half brightly. Conor Conway increased their lead with a point from a free.'

'O'Loughlin's were not prepared to give in. With Brian Hogan starting to assert himself at midfield, they began to get back into the game. Hogan led the revival, and pointed after five minutes. Shortly afterwards Jimmy Foster had their supporters cheering when he netted to leave just two points between the sides. Brian Hogan pointed a free in the 41st minute to narrow the gap to the minimum. O'Loughlin's were on top throughout the field. Their pressure was rewarded in the 50th minute when they were awarded a penalty. Brian Hogan coolly stepped up and blasted the ball to the net to put O'Loughlin's ahead for the first time. When Johnny Roe increased the lead to three points, it looked as if O'Loughlin's had the momentum to carry them to victory.'

'Mullinavat responded magnificently During a frantic closing five minutes, despite missing the penalty, they got the vital scores to give them a dramatic but deserving victory. The winners had strong defenders in Seamus Farrell, John Paul Dungan, Pat Butler and Walter Burke. Martin Knox and Andrew McGovern worked hard at midfield. Conor Conway and Tomas Frisby showed great skill up front.

Mullinavat team and scorers: M Walsh, S Farrell, J P Dungan, D Butler, P Butler, W Burke, M Murphy, M Knox, Andrew McGovern (1-0), T Duggan, K Madigan, M Duggan, Thomas Frisby (0-1), Conor Conway (0-7, 4 frees) and D Conway. Subs: E Maher, B Kenneally, S Frisby and R Raftice.

2001
SENIOR

SFL: Mullinavat 2-12; Graigue Ballycallan 1-02
SFL: Kilmoganny 2-04; Mullinavat 0-08
SFL: James Stephens 4-11; Mullinavat 0-06
SFL: Mullinavat 2-11; Young Irelands 2-05

SFC R1: Mullinavat 2-06; Dicksboro 1-08
SFC R2: Muckalee 2-04; Mullinavat 0-04

2002
SENIOR

SFL: Muckalee 0-08; Mullinavat 0-01
SFL: Mullinavat 2-05; James Stephens 1-07
SFL: Dicksboro 3-03; Mullinavat 2-04

SFC R1: Mullinavat 4-10; Young Irelands 1-06
SFC R2: Dicksboro 5-09; Mullinavat 0-07

2003
SENIOR

SFL R1: Mullinavat 1-07; O'Loughlin Gaels 1-04
SFL R2: Muckalee 0-14; Mullinavat 1-05
SFL R3: Erin's Own 0-12; Mullinavat 0-04
SFL R4: Kilmoganny 1-07; Mullinavat 1-06
SFC Relegation: Glenmore 1-07; Mullinavat 1-06

2004
INTERMEDIATE

IFL R1: Mullinavat 1-07; Conahy Shamrocks 0-09
IFL R2: Mullinavat beat Black and Whites
IFL R3: Mullinavat W/O Young Irelands
IFL R4: Mullinavat 3-02; Shamrocks 0-08
IFL Final: Mullinavat 3-06; Carrickshock 3-06
IFL Final Replay Mullinavat 2-07; Carrickshock 1-05

IFC Semi final: Mullinavat beat Black and Whites
IFC Final: Mullinavat 4-07; Conahy Shamrocks 0-06

Mullinavat dominated the Intermediate football campaign in 2004. Having been relegated from the Senior ranks the previous year we bounced straight back winning both the league and championship trophies. The club went on to battle bravely versus opponents from Wicklow and Wexford in our second Leinster campaign. This was Mullinavat's second title, the first being in 2000. We were unbeaten in the league campaign where we defeated Carrickshock in a replayed final.

As league winners Mullinavat were straight into the championship semi final where we beat Blacks and Whites. The Intermediate Final was played in Bennettsbridge on Easter Saturday. Early goals from Jamie Fennelly and Conor Conway (2) gave Mullinavat a lead they were never to relinquish. At the interval Mullinavat led 3-2 to 0-4. After the interval Mullinavat quickly recorded a fourth goal. Willie O'Dwyer fielded a high ball, set off goalwards, laid the ball off to Michael Duggan, who struck beautifully to the Conahy net. The Northerners kept battling but it was a bridge too far as Mullinavat went on to win by eleven points, 4-7 to 3-6.

The still new competition for the Leinster Club Football Championship was continuing, and we were again grouped in with the Carlow and Wexford champions. As mentioned previously these Mullinavat teams laid the foundations for the five Senior football wins we have achieved since.

UNDER-16

County Under 16 B Football Final: Mullinavat 2-6; St Patrick's (Ballyragget) 1-4
(A second win at this grade for Mullinavat)

2005

SENIOR

SFL R1: Mullinavat 1-09; Railyard 2-05
SFL R2: Piltown 2-05; Mullinavat 1-07
SFL R3: Mullinavat 3-07; Dicksboro 0-04
SFL Final: Mullinavat 0-09; Muckalee 0-07

SFC R1: Glenmore 2-19; Mullinavat 0-09

UNDER-21

Kilkenny Under 21B Football Final: Mullinavat 3-08; Mooncoin 2-04

'A superb display of ball handling, vision and scoring process from Mullinavat full forward Jamie Fennelly was the main difference between the teams in this Under-21B football final played in ideal conditions at Piltown. Mullinavat scored three goals in the opening quarter, with Fennelly involved in all three, scoring the first and assisting in the other two. In truth, Mullinavat were far superior to the southern neighbours. Dominant in the central positions where Richie Raftice, JT Murphy, midfielders Willie O'Dwyer and Pat Farrell, and Nicolas Anthony were outstanding, they possessed a full forward line of real scoring policy which accounted for 2-4 of the winners total.'

'Mooncoin had plenty of possession but couldn't match their conquerors in front of goal as they shot 11 wides and missed numerous other chances. Both teams showed a good sporting attitude to the game from the outset with Mooncoin starting the brighter but they were off target on two occasions before Mullinavat's first attack. At half-time Mullinavat were ten points ahead, 3-4 to a goal.'

Mullinavat team and scorers: Tom Fitzpatrick; John Dalton, Richie Raftice, Derek Aylward; Joe Wall, JT Murphy, Michael Farrell; Willie O'Dwyer (0-1), Pat Farrell; Richie Cunningham, Nicholas Anthony (1-2, 1 free), Stephen Ryan (0-1,"45); Patrick Raftice (0-1), Jamie Fennelly (1-2) and Paul Fitzgerald (1-1). Sub: Patrick Jones (0-1).

2006
SENIOR

SFL R1: Mullinavat 1-05; Muckalee 1-05
SFL R2: Mullinavat 2-08; Dicksboro 1-06
SFL R3: Mullinavat 1-08; O'Loughlin Gaels 1-06
SFL R4: Mullinavat 3-08; Glenmore 2-03
SFL Final: Railyard 2-06; Mullinavat 0-09

SFC R1: Mullinavat 0-09; Glenmore 0-09
SFC R1 Replay: Mullinavat 0-08; Glenmore 0-07
SFC Semi Final: Mullinavat 0-12; Kilmoganny 0-06
SFC Final Erin's Own 1-05; Mullinavat 1-03

'The ability to make better use of the ball and scoring two opportunistic goals gave Railyard victory in this keenly contested Senior football league final in Bennetsbridge. Mullinavat had some fine individual players but never worked to the same level as a team against a more experienced opponents. Dominating the opening quarter Mullinavat led 0-2 to 0-1. It should have been more, but over elaboration and some poor decisions cost them dearly. Railyard got a fortunate goal in the 15th minute that transformed their challenge and they proceeded to completely outplayed of opponents during the following 10 minutes to lead 1-4 to 0-2 by the 25th minute. But stubborn Mullinavat battled their way back into the match and landed 4 points to trail by the minimum at half-time 1-4 to 0-6.'

'The decisive score came in the fifth minute of the new half when a free was floated in under the Mullinavat crossbar; the ball was well held by the Mullinavat keeper Declan Duggan, who passed the ball out to a defender, Railyard full forwards Damian Walsh intercepted the attempted clearance, and shot to the roof of the net. Mullinavat could never make up the deficit from then to the finish.'

Mullinavat: Declan Duggan; Walter Burke, Maurice Murphy, Seamus Farrell; Michael Farrell, Dinny Butler, Michael Murphy; Paul Aylward (0-1), Willie O'Dwyer; Michael Duggan (0-1), Ger Anthony (0-1), Liam Murphy; Tony Duggan, Jamie Fennelly (0-1) and Conor Conway (0-5, 3 frees). Subs: Paddy Raftice and Damien Reid.

2007

SFL R1: Mullinavat 1-06; Kilmoganny 1-06
SFL R2: Mullinavat 1-10; Dicksboro 1-07
SFL R3: Mullinavat 1-05; Railyard 0-08
SFL R4: Mullinavat 2-06; Muckalee 1-09

SFC R1: Mullinavat 2-11: St Lachtain's 2-06
SFC Semi Final: Mullinavat 2-06; O'Loughlin Gaels 1-06

'The old adage about how goals win games certainly rang true for Mullinavat's Senior footballers. Beaten finalists last year, the men from the south hit the net twice in a powerful first half performance in Ballyhale. Their first 30 minutes were good enough to see off the challenge of O'Loughlin Gaels. Better still, it was good enough to get them to the county final. While both sides had their fair share of chances to raise several green flags, the 'Vat elected to take theirs, and at vital stages.'

'They didn't have to wait long for the first opportunity, grabbing it little over 60 seconds after the throw-in. The game was barely into its second minute when Jamie Fennelly collected and long free and found room to cut through the Gaels defence. Aided by some good handling from Andrew McGovern and Tomas Frisby, Fennelly made his way towards the Gaels square. He broke through the centre, then clipped a shot that looped over 'keeper Kevin Cleere and into the top right corner of the net. One goal almost became two, as Mullinavat went close to doubling their lead in the fourth minute. Again, hesitancy at the back from O'Loughlin's allowed their opponents to advance without any real challenge to block their path.'

'Racing on to a crossfield pass from Willie O'Dwyer, Paul Aylward did well to steer his low shot beyond the outstretched Cleere, but corner-back Stephen Tyrrell slid in to toe-poke the ball on to the base of the post before a colleague scrambled it clear. Mullinavat were firing on all cylinders, but the loss of Aylward with a knee injury (the player was stretchered off after just eight minutes), checked their stride somewhat. They did get going again, but it took some time, McGovern finding their next score with a pointed free in the 19th minute.'

'Driving through the Gaels defence Dinny Butler was given time and space to surge, through for a shot at goal. Butler's low, shot was kept out by a strong one-handed save by goalkeeper Cleere, but the rebound fell kindly for Mossy Murphy, who tapped it home from close range. Sub Michael Duggan ended the first half scoring for the Vat right on the half hour, but only after his dipping shot was pushed over the bar by the diving Cleere.'

'With the breeze at their backs it was no surprise to see O'Loughlin's get the upper hand in the second half possession stakes but, try as they might, they couldn't bridge the two goal gap. Scores proved hard to come by, but when they did both sides moved quickly to cancel each other out. The Gaels shot points through Jason Lawlor and Alan Geoghegan, but like scores by Andrew McGovern (0-2) and Jamie Fennelly had O'Loughlin's still behind by seven with eight minutes to play (2-5 to 0-4). They may have looked down, but the Gaels were not out of it by any means. With their midfield well on top, Alan Geoghegan point kept the Gaels newfound momentum going. Their hopes were boosted even further when Jason Lawlor coolly fired a penalty to the net after Cummins had been taken down in the square.'

'The city side were buzzing now, even more so when Peter Dowling fizzed a shot over the bar in the last minute of normal time. With the gap now down to two points, it was the 'Vat who looked the more flustered. They had it all to do to keep the Gaels at bay, with the half-back line of Michael Farrell, Walter Burke and Tony Duggan working overtime to snuff out any threatening moves.'

'They did threaten one good breakaway and won a penalty when Andrew McGovern was fouled when en route to goal in injury time. Rather than risk going for goal, Fennelly showed a composed head and took his point.'

Mullinavat: C Conway, P Raftice, G Anthony, S Farrell, M Farrell, W Burke, T Duggan, Michael Murphy, W O'Dwyer, T Frisby, D Butler, P Aylward, Jamie Fennelly (1-2, 0-1 pen), Fennelly, Mossy Murphy (1-0), Andrew McGovern (0-3, 0-2 frees). Sub: Michael Duggan (0-1) for Aylward.

O'Loughlin Gaels: K Cleere, D Dwyer, B Murphy, S Tyrrell, A O'Brien, Peter Dowling (0-1), N Bergin, Martin Comerford (0-1), Alan Geoghegan (0-1), Kevin Morrissey (0-1, free), S Cummins, J Comerford, S Shortt, Jason Lawlor (1-2, 1-0 peno, 0-2, frees), C Bergin. Subs: A Comerford for Murphy, 23 mins; R Leydon for Dwyer, 28 mins; O O'Connor for Shortt, 31 mins; D Loughnane for Morrissey, 47 mins.

Referee: D Connolly (Mooncoin).

SFC Final: Mullinavat 0-09; Glenmore 1-06

'Mullinavat were going for their first Senior county title, and they almost put the match beyond Glenmore's reach within four minutes of the restart as Michael Duggan raced through on goal, but shot was brilliantly saved by veteran Glenmore goalkeeper PJ O'Connor.'

'That moment seem to inspired Glenmore somewhat as they played with greater confidence throughout the field, despite not always taking advantage of the good position they enjoyed. However they manage to engineer a crucial goal in the 39th minute when a well worked movement saw Paul Phelan set up substitute Eoin Murphy who palmed the ball to an empty net, 1-4 to 0-7, to level the game. A minute later Paul Phelan kicked over a straight forward free and Glenmore never relinquished the lead.'

'There was only three scores during the final 20 minutes as Andrew McGovern kicked over two free, while Mark Phelan kicked over a fine point for the Glenmore men, after good work by John Phelan.'

'Andrew McGovern got Mullinavat off the mark with a pointed free from 40 metres, before we had to wait until the 12th minute when he expertly struck over another placed effort from the 40. Paul Phelan opened Glenmore's account with a pointed free three minutes later before McGovern converted a 20 metre free in the 16th minute, following a magnificent 70 yard solo run by Jamie Fennelly. The opening score from play came in the 19th minute, when Michael Duggan high long-range delivery was fisted down by Mossy Murphy and McGovern raced through to fist over and extend their lead to 0-4 to 0-1.'

'Good work by the Glenmore midfield duo saw Richie Mullally kick over an inspirational point from 40m, before Paul Phelan with another free reduced the margin to a single point.

However Mullinavat finished the first half and the score of the game came approaching first-half injury time when Nicholas Anthony won possession and cut loose onto his left before shooting over a fantastic score, while another delivery by Michael Duggan was knocked down by Mossy Murphy before Jamie Fennelly blasted all over from close range. Mullinavat led 0-6 to 0-3 at half-time.'

'Mullinavat extended their lead to four points within three minutes of the restart, as another long delivery by Duggan found McGovern in space. The latter raced through before steadying himself to kick over an excellent point after showing terrific composure. PJ O'Connor kept Glenmore in touch a minute later, when pulling off a fantastic stop from Duggan, and between the 37th and 40 minute, Glenmore scored 1-2 that proved decisive to the outcome of the game.'

'Emme Vereker set up Paul Phelan for a very good score, before the hard-working Vereker was taken off and replaced by super sub-Eoin Murphy who level matters up when fisting home from close range, following good work by Paul Phelan. Phelan tagged on a free to push Glenmore ahead for the first time, 1-5 to 0-7. McGovern's free in the 45th minute levelled matters up to set up an exciting final quarter, before Glenmore regained the initiative as Mark Phelan operation at wing forward kicked over a well executed effort.'

'Another free for McGovern in the 53rd minute proved to be the final score as Glenmore dominated the closing minutes, but couldn't take advantage, with Paul Phelan off target with three frees while Richie Mullally's attempted effort went narrowly wide. Overall throughout the sixty minutes, Mullinavat were the better side as they were more economical in front of goal, and Glenmore only started to get going after the equalising goal.'

Mullinavat: Conor Conway; Paddy Raftice, Ger Anthony, Seamus Farrell; Michael Farrell, Dinny Butler, Walter Burke, Michael Murphy; Tony Duggan, Willie O'Dwyer; Nicholas Anthony (0-1), Tomas Frisby, Andrew McGovern (0-7, 5 frees). Jamie Fennelly (0-1), Mossy Murphy and Michael Duggan. Sub: Liam Murphy

SFC Final Replay: Mullinavat 3-07; Glenmore 0-11

'It was an evening to remember for the footballers of Mullinavat at Mooncoin on Saturday evening last. In the replay of the Kilkenny Senior final, they had five points to spare over a gallant Glenmore team and so become the first team from the parish to claim the county Senior title, albeit at the fourth attempt. They had appeared in the final of 1904 (beaten by Lamogue), 1934 beaten by Tullogher, and in 1935 they fell to a Glenmore/Slieverue combination known as the Barrow Rovers. So, this was a great victory for the Rod Iron which was richly deserved.'

'Football will always rank a poor second to the game of hurling in Kilkenny, but Mullinavat and Glenmore showed here – was a little more determination to the game in the county, the standard can improve. The final was much better than the drawn game and both teams went at it hammer and tongs. Both sides fought to bring home the Edward Langton Memorial Cup. Mullinavat varied their tactics combining the passing with some long probing balls into the Glenmore square. This paid dividends because any fouls were severely punished by the excellent Andrew McGovern. Then when similar indiscretions occurred at the other end the deadly Paul Phelan showed how a free should be taken. But as the game war on Mullinavat gradually asserted their influence and in the end were worthy winners.'

'Jamie Fennelly opened the scoring with a fine paint for Mullinavat in the fourth, but a Paul Phelan free tied up the scores two minutes later. Midfielder Kenneth Cotterell finished off a great solo run sending the leather high between he posts. Again the sides were tied as Andrew McGovern pointed a free. Paul Phelan put Glenmore one up, but the wiley Jamie Fennelly cut in from the wing and shot a great paint. Paddy Murphy set up full forward Michael Phelan and when Paul Phelan send over another Glenmore led again by a two point margin. Then there came the first of Mullinavat's three goals. Right halfback Willie O'Dwyer ranged up field, tore through the Glenmore defence, had a shot saved initially but when it came back to him he crashed it into the net for a superb score. Andrew McGovern increased the Mullinavat lead with another pointed free, but two like scores from razor sharp Paul Phelan tied the score once more.'

'Then came that crucial goal as we approached the half time whistle. A lovely piece of combination by the Mullinavat forwards ended with Tony Duggan sending a cracker of a shot past Glenmore goalie PJ Aylward to leave the half-time score 2-4 to 0-7 in favour of a Mullinavat. Within two minutes of the second half Paul Phelan from yet another free cut back the deficit to two points. Another eight minutes had elapsed before the next score – but it was well worth waiting for. From practically out on the corner flag Andrea McGovern swung over a peach of a point. Glenmore got a like score again from Paul Phelan. McGovern pointed a Mullinavat free, but hard-working Mark Phelan countered with one of his own. It was Andrew McGovern who raised a white flag for the Mullinavat men from a free but Paul Phelan put over his eight point of the game and again there was only two points between the teams. Then came the clinching score which put the issue beyond all doubt. Jamie Fennelly bore down menacingly on the Glenmore goal and was hauled down in ceremoniously inside the small square.'

'Fennelly's penalty would have done credit to any penalty taker in the English Premiership. That was that, and the final whistle sounded shortly afterwards to leave Mullinavat Senior football champions by a five pot margin, 3-7 to 0-11.'

'In the fine team display by Mullinavat, Conor Conway dealt with anything that came his way on goal and was ultra-safe under the high ball. Paddy Raftice, Joe Anthony and Seamus Farrell constituted a rock solid full back line. Water Bure, until injured, with Michael Murphy and rampaging Willie O'Dwyer, who played a stormer were excellent further out. Dinny Butler and Michael Farrell had a great hustle with their opposite numbers at centrefield. Nicky Anthony, Liam Murphy and Thomas Frisby worked hard in getting the ball to do inside colleagues. Jamie Fennelly, Andrew McGovern and Tony Duggan were the trio who put up the winning tally for the 'rod iron' boys. Michael Duggan too made an impression when coming on for the injured Burke.'

'Man of the Match – Andrew McGovern'

Mullinavat team and scorers: Conor Conway; Paddy Raftice, Ger Anthony, Seamus Farrell; Michael Farrell, Walter Burke, Willie O'Dwyer (1-0); Dinny Butler, Michael Farrell; Nicholas Anthony, Liam Anthony, Tomas Frisby, Jamie Fennelly (1-2), Andrew McGovern (0-5) and Tony Duggan (1-0). Sub: Michael Duggan for Burke (injured).

2008
SENIOR

SFL R1: Mullinavat 2-09; Dicksboro 0-06
SFL R2: James Stephens 0-11; Mullinavat 0-09
SFL R3: Mullinavat 1-06; Carrickshock 1-06

SFL R4: Mullinavat 2-05; O'Loughlin Gaels 0-08
SFL Final Railyard 0-11; Mullinavat 1-06

'This contest saw Railyard hang on for a two-point victory over defending Senior champions Mullinavat in a game of two halves. Railyard completely dominated the first half and built up an 0-9 to 0-2 lead at the interval. After the break it was the Southern men who dominated. However they were let down by poor shooting in front of goal.'

'An Andrew McGovern point from play in the third minute gave Mullinavat a lead they held just once, but Railyard responded and six unanswered points in an eleven minute spell between the 7th and 18th minute put the Northern men, 0-6 to 0-1 in front. The full forward line accounted for all but one of their first half total with Sean Brennan and full forward Paul Donnelly adding a brace of points during the opening period, while there were on target from a Calendar Roche and Sean Dowd. McGovern replied with a pointed free before the Northern men added unanswered points from three Celeb Roche frees as an unforgettable first half saw Railyard lead 0-9 to 0-2 at the interval.'

'Mullinavat made a number of significant substitutions at the interval introducing James Culleton and JP Dungan, while Michael Murphy moved from defence to attack. Jamie Fennelly blasted home a goal immediately after the restart and that urged Mullinavat on to greater efforts, before a Kevin Philips point restored Railyard's grip. Mullinavat dominated the second half but had great difficulty finding the target, only scoring two points from play over the closing 25 minutes.'

'Points from McGovern (free) and Jamie Fennelly left just three between the sides. A golden opportunity went a begging in the 49th minute when a terrific movement involving sub James Culleton and Tommy Holden combined to set up Brian Kenneally, but his shot was well saved by John Mansfield. The Southern men were cutting lose through the Railyard defence and Holden finished off an excellent five-man movement for a well taken score. Five minutes of injury time were added on as Eoin Boran required attention and he was taken to hospital by ambulance. A McGovern free cut the lead to the minimum but a Celeb Roche free in the fifth minute of injury time concluding the scoring after a lively corner forward Sean Brennan was fouled to round off the contest.'

Mullinavat: Declan Duggan; Brian Kenneally, Walter Burke, Paddy Raftice; Michael Murphy, Dinny Butler, Michael Farrell; Willie O'Dwyer (1-0), Paul Aylward; Ian Duggan, Tommy Holden, Brian Power; Stephen Ryan, Jamie Fennelly and Andrew McGovern. Sub: James Culleton and JP Dungan.

SFC R1: Mullinavat 1-08; Glenmore 0-08
SFC R1: Erin's Own 1-08; Mullinavat 1-05

2009

SFL R1: Mullinavat 3-10; Mooncoin 3-03
SFL R2: James Stephens w/o Mullinavat scr.
SFL R3: Mullinavat Dicksboro
SFL R4: Railyard 2-11; Mullinavat 3-06

SFC R1: Mullinavat 2-07; Carrickshock 0-5
SFC Semi Final: Muckalee 1-09; Mullinavat 0-09

COUNTY
Leinster JFC: Wicklow 0-13; Kilkenny 1-6

Kilkenny: JJ O'Sullivan (St Patrick's), David Walton (James Stephens), Richard O'Hara (Thomastown), Martin Dowling (Muckalee), Eoin Kavanagh (Rower Inistioge), Kieran Joyce (Rower Inistioge), Michael Gannon (St Patrick's), John Brennan (Erin's Isle), Sean Mahony (Thomastown), Aidan Mackey (Windgap), Eddie Brennan (Erin's Own), David Lyng (Rower Inistioge), Robert Shore (Muckalee), Graham Lawlor (Railyard), JJ Dunphy (Kilmoganny). Subs: Michael Malone and Stephen Ryan (Mullinavat).

The Mullinvat squad which won the Kilkenny SFC title in 2007.

CHAPTER 9

2010-2024

The Mullinavat squad which reached the Leinster Intermediate football final in 2019.

2010-2024

2010

SENIOR

SFL R1: Mullinavat beat James Stephens
SFL R2: Mullinavat 1-12; Dicksboro 1-04
SFL R3: Mullinavat 1-10; Railyard 1-06
SFL R4: Mullinavat beat Erin's Own
SFL Final: Mullinavat 1-06; Muckalee 0-06

Mullinavat won a second Kilkenny Senior Football League title in 2010, adding to the 2005 win. In a first game for the club since June 2nd, the Senior footballers of Mullinavat defeated Muckalee in the delayed Senior league final, on Saturday 4th September in Thomastown.

This game was played on the eve of that "Drive for Five" All Ireland hurling final game v. Tipperary. The result was a three point win for the Rod Iron men and with it the title of Senior league champions for 2010.

Having played good football in a first half they we totally dominated, we led by 1-6 to 0-1. However we failed to score in the second half but still defended stoutly and held out to gain a three point victory, on a score line of 1-6 to 0-6.

SFC Quarter Final Mooncoin 0-11; Mullinavat 0-10

COUNTY

Leinster JFC Quarter Final: Meath v. Kilkenny

Kilkenny: JJ O'Sullivan (St Patrick's), Aidan Mackey (Windgap), Richard O'Hara (Thomastown), Thomas Kehoe (James Stephens), JJ Grace (Grange Nolvin), Seoirse Kenny (St Patrick's), Paddy Raftice (Mullinavat), Michael Malone (Mullinavat), Sean

Mahony (Thomastown), Eoin Kavanagh (Rower Inistioge), Ger Staunton (St Patrick's), Sean Mooney (St Patrick's), James Culleton (Mullinavat), Padraig Grace (Rower Inistioge) and Michael Saunders (Danesfort). Subs: Michael Duggan (Mullinavat).

2011
SENIOR

SFL: Mullinavat v. Thomastown
SFL: Mullinavat v. Railyard
SFL: Mullinavat v. Dicksboro
SFL: Muckalee 1-10; Mullinavat 1-05

SFC R1: Muckalee 2-09; Mullinavat 2-07

Leinster JFC Quarter Final: Kilkenny 3-5; Wexford 0-13
    Kilkenny: JJ O'Sullivan (St Patrick's), Declan Grennan (Tullogher Rosbercon), Thomas Kehoe (James Stephens), Paddy Raftice (Mullinavat), Seoirse Kenny (St Patrick's), James Mackey (Windgap), Darren Fitzpatrick (Kilmoganny), Michael Malone (Mullinavat), Michael Mahony (Thomastown), Emmet Vereker (Glenmore), Michael Duggan (Mullinavat), JJ Grace (Grange Nolvin), David Prendergast (Thomastown), JJ Dunphy (Kilmoganny) and Robert Shore (Muckalee). Subs: Joe Fennelly and James Culleton (Mullinavat).
Leinster JFC Semi Final: Cavan 0-13; Kilkenny 0-4

2012
SENIOR

SFL R1: Mullinavat 2-04; Erin's Own 2-04
SFL R2: Mooncoin 4-04; Mullinavat 2-05
SFL R3: Mullinavat 1-11; Thomastown 0-02
SFL R4: Mullinavat beat Railyard
SFL R5: Mullinavat beat Dicksboro

SFC R2: Mullinavat 3-10; James Stephens 1-03
SFC Semi Final: Mullinavat 1-07; Thomastown 0-07
SFC County Final: Muckalee 1-10; Mullinavat 0-07
    It was two days before Christmas when Mullinavat lined out in their seventh Kilkenny

Senior Football Final at Palmerstown. Defeat was again our lot, as was the case in 1904, 1905, 1934, 1935 and 2006. The big crowd that travelled to Palmerstown for the 2012 Kilkenny Senior football championship final, got an exhibition of all that is good about football when it is played with skill, heart and determination, from two well-prepared sides.

Mullinavat were first to show their hand with two early points, before Muckalee got off the mark in the 10th minute with a point from John Mulhall after a John Maher pass. Colin McGrath added another from play when finishing a move started by Michael Morrissey in the half backline. The only goal of the game was set up by a Paul Maher pass to John Mulhall, who made good ground, and set up Bryan Byrne, who finished well. Captain Shane Coonan fisted a point after a good through ball from Bryan Byrne. Tom Morrissey put Colin McGrath through for another point from play, and two fine frees from Colm and John Maher left the half-time score: Muckalee 1-7; Mullinavat 0-3.

The game was far from over at this stage, as Mullinavat took a grip of the match. Sterling defending was required by the full back line of Canice Maher, Oliver Walsh and Aidan Murphy, who got great cover from Michael Morrissey, Patrick Nolan and Martin Dowling in a solid half back line that were not afraid to attack. When this sextet was breached, two mighty saves from John Coonan when the game was in the melting pot were crucial. Robert Shore scored Muckalee's first second half point in the 20th minute, after a pass from Joe Maher, a score that proved to be very important as Muckalee finish strongly. There was further points from Robert Shore, who took a pass from Canice Maher after a strong run out of the defence, and a pointed sideline kick from John Maher. Others like Joe Maher, James Maher and Fionn Lawlor did well when called upon.

Mullinavat were beaten but can be very proud of the part they played in a well contested contest. History was made with Muckalee completing the first ever three in a row, to add to the league won early in the year, County Board chairman, Tom Brennan congratulations both teams for their skill and sportsmanship and Muckalee for winning the treble.

COUNTY

Leinster JFC Quarter Final: Kildare 0-18; Kilkenny 1-02

Kilkenny: JJ O'Sullivan (St Patrick's), Declan Grennan (Tullogher Rosbercon), Paul Donnelly (Railyard), JJ Grace (Grange Nolvin), John Mulhall (St Martins), Ollie Walsh (Muckalee), Sean Mooney (St Patrick's), Darren Fitzpatrick (Kilmoganny), Brian Byrne (Muckalee), Richard O'Hara (Thomastown), Robert Shore (Muckalee), Graham Lawlor (Railyard) and James Culleton (Mullinavat). Subs: Joe Fennelly and Paddy Raftice (Mullinavat). Selectors: Tommy Duggan (Mullinavat).

2013
SENIOR
SFL R1: Dicksboro 0-11; Mullinavat 0-08
SFL R2: Railyard beat Mullinavat
SFL R3: Mullinavat v. Kilmoganny

SFC R1: Mullinavat 4-06; O'Loughlin Gaels 0-09
SFC Quarter Final: Muckalee 0-12; Mullinavat 0-06

COUNTY
Kilkenny were now competing in the British JFC Championship
British JFC R1: Kilkenny 2-14; Hertfordshire 0-06 at Luton
 Kilkenny: JJ O'Sullivan (St Patrick's), JJ Grace (Grange, Kildare), Bob Aylward (Ballyhale Shamrocks), Noel Darcy (Muckalee), Paddy Nolan (Muckalee), Mark Aylward (Ballyhale Shamrocks), Declan Grennan (Tullogher-Rosbercon), Joe Maher (Muckalee), David Lyng (Rower-Inistioge), James Phelan (Fenians), Ger Purcell (Windgap), Pat Kinsella (Mooncoin), Stephen Duggan (Mullinavat), Graham Lawlor (Railyard) and Brian Egan (Dicksboro). Subs: John Mulhall (Muckalee), Fionn Lawlor (Muckalee) and Kevin Byrne (O'Loughlin/Gaels)
British JFC R2: Kilkenny v. Lancashire in Birmingham
British JFC R3: Scotland 2-08; Kilkenny 2-06 in Edinburgh
 2013 Selectors: Michael Duggan (Mullinavat). Squad: Tommy Duggan and Michael Duggan (Mullinavat).

2014
SENIOR
SFL R1: Mullinavat 1-06; O'Loughlin Gaels 0-07
SFL R2: Mullinavat 2-05; James Stephens 2-04
SFL R3: Conahy Shamrocks 3-07; Mullinavat 1-04

SFC R1 Clara 2-11; Mullinavat 2-08

British JFC R1: Warwickshire 0-10; Kilkenny 1-02 at Nowlan Park
 Kilkenny: JJ O'Sullivan (St Patrick's), Peter McBride (Young Irelands), Bob Aylward (Ballyhale Shamrocks), JJ Grace (Grangenolvan, Kildare), Paddy Nolan (Muckalee), Noel

Darcy (Muckalee), Declan Grennan (Tullogher-Rosbercon), James Whelan (Fenians), Ger Purcell (Windgap), Brian Egan (Dicksboro), Paul Maher (Muckalee), Michael Farrell (Railyard), Robbie Walsh (Kilmacow), Colin McGrath (Muckalee) and Robert Shore (Muckalee).

British JFC R2: Kilkenny 3-08; London 1-12 at Ruislip
British JFC R3: Kilkenny 4-11; Kilkenny 1-12 at Manchester
British JFC Semi Final: Scotland 0-18; Kilkenny 0-07

Panellists: Joe Fennelly, Tom Aylward, James Culleton, Stephen Duggan, Conor Conway (Mullinavat).

2015

SENIOR

SFL R1: Mullinavat 3-07; Glenmore 0-08
SFL R2: Mullinavat 0-07; Railyard 0-06
SFL R3: Mullinavat 1-08; Conahy Shamrocks 1-05
SFL Semi Final: Mooncoin 0-14; Mullinavat 2-04

SFC Quarter final: Glenmore beat Mullinavat

COUNTY

British JFC R1: Kilkenny 4-14; Gloucestershire 2-05
British JFC R2: Kilkenny 1-13; Lancashire 1-11
British JFC Semi Final: Kilkenny 1-16; Gloucestershire 0-01
British JFC Final: Kilkenny 2-07; Scotland 0-08 in Edinburgh
First win for Kilkenny

All Ireland JFC Semi Final: Mayo 1-12; Kilkenny 1-08

An impressive opening twenty minutes from Mayo that saw them fire 1-5 without reply laid the foundations for a win over Kilkenny to send them through to the All-Ireland JFC final. They left Tullamore on Saturday as convincing winners as Kilkenny failed to deal with their firepower up front. The Kilkenny men did rise a gallop before the break with four points but that was in response to Damien McGing's low strike to the net that helped Mayo to a 1-5 to 0-0 lead. Mayo added another through Gavin Conway to move them to 1-6 to 0-1 before Kilkenny's late burst saw Mayo lead 1-6 to 0-4 at the break. Kilkenny started the second half brightly and got another score back but Ronan Malee and Gavin Conway were a constant threat up front for Mayo and the Cats had no answer for the duo in the second half, as they kicked 0-5 with a brace from Malee putting them 1-9 to 0-6 ahead.

Kilkenny: JJ O'Sullivan St Patrick's), Stephen Duncan (Danesfort), Bob Aylward (Shamrocks), Noel Darcy (Muckalee), Joe Fennelly(Mullinavat), Paddy McConigley (Railyard, 0-1), Philip Roche (Railyard), Michael Malone (Mullinavat, 0-2), James Culleton (Mullinavat), David Herity (Kilmoganny), Caleb Roche (Railyard, 0-2 both frees), Cormac McDonald (Railyard, 0-1) Michael Bolger (Graiguenamanagh, 0-1"45"), Paul Donnelly (Railyard, 0-1), Brian Egan (Dicksboro). Subs: David Lyng (Rower Inistioge) for McDonald, (half time), JJ Grace (Grangenolvan, Kildare) for Lyng (Black Card 38 minutes), Cormac McDonald for Fennelly (41 minutes), Jason Shelley (Tullogher Rosbercon) for Bolger (50 minutes), D O'Connor for Donnelly (59). Panel also included Stephen Duggan, Stephen Ryan and Michael Duggan (Mullinavat).

2016

SENIOR

SFL R1: Mullinavat 2-08; O'Loughlin Gaels 0-09
SFL R2: Railyard 2-15; Mullinavat 1-11
SFL R3: Mooncoin beat Mullinavat

SFC R1; St Patrick's 1-07; Mullinavat 1-04

COUNTY

British JFC R1: London 4-6; Kilkenny 2-9 at Nowlan Park with Dubs v. Laois
British JFC R2: Kilkenny 8-18; Hertfordshire 1-7 in Glasgow
British JFC R2 Quarter Final: Scotland 1-9; Kilkenny 1-7

Kilkenny 2016 squad included Ger Malone, James Culleton, John Walsh (Mullinavat).

2017

SENIOR

SFL R1: Mullinavat 3-12; St Patrick's 1-06
SFL R2: Mullinavat 3-13; James Stephens 3-06
SFL R3: Mullinavat 2-12; Glenmore 0-07
SFL Semi Final: Railyard 1-11; Mullinavat 1-10

SFC Quarter Final: Mullinavat 1-11; Clara 1-11
SFC Quarter Final Replay: Mullinavat 2-09; Clara 1-07
SFC Semi Final: Mullinavat 3-07; Kilmaganny 0-08

SFC County Final: Mullinavat 3-12; Railyard 2-05

'Mullinavat infrequent visitors to the winners enclosure at this level, did things the hard way when winning their second Kilkenny Senior Football title. The South Kilkenny outfit had to win the game twice against utterly defiant defending champions Railyard at Nowlan Park on Saturday. The Vat took control of the ball from the throw in but even if they carried an eleven point lead into the break (2-6 to 0-1), they should have been an awful lot better off. They kicked nine wides during the half, surely the game should have been over?'

'Railyard who just weren't at the races from the off, found the right gear and were motoring after the break. Within 10 minutes they were back in the game, big time, having cut the deficit to 2-7 to 2-4. The Rod Iron men needed to show their mettle, and they did during the following ten minutes, to more or less make or break Railyard and their four in a row bid, and a 22nd title overall. Post match, Mullinavat manager Michael Aylward said: "That was terrific, these lads have a great track record at under age level, They have great ability, this was about bringing that ability to the fore." In the league semi final, Railyard had beaten Mullinavat by one point.'

'Mr Aylward said: "We knew we had a real chance and we went for it. Now if we get the chance we will put in a good effort in the Leinster Club Championship." In that competition, Mullinavat will be operating at Intermediate level. The winners dominated the play early on, but a single point from a free by Mullinavat's attacker Ian Duggan following a foul on Adam Mansfield, was all they had to show for a lot of good football during the opening quarter.

Their second point, virtually at the end of that quarter was from Michael Malone. He made a great catch from one of their own kick outs, before bursting up the pitch to the County end goal and hitting the target from 35 minutes. The winners had shot five wides during the first period, plus Railyard goalie John Mansfield brought off a class save from Duggan after a lovely sweeping move involving Tom Aylward and Jamie Fennelly.'

'The winners' play was really impressive as Railyard were pinned in their own half for long spells. Tom Aylward, Joe Fennelly, Ian Duggan, Michael Malone and the nippy John Walsh when sprung from the bench, knitted some lovely moves together and Mikey Jones was powerful at full back. Then within the space of 90 seconds Railyard were hit for two goals, both scored by Jamie Fennelly. The first was at the end of a move involving John Walsh and Michael Malone. The second when he dived to fist home at the edge of the square following a cross from the left by Walsh. The losers were struggling big time. They didn't open their account until the second minute of "lost time" when free taker Caleb Roche converted a free after a defender was hounded into over carrying the ball. Half time Mullinavat 2-6; Railyard 1-1.'

'From the start of the new half Railyard were a different team as players began to show for the ball all over the field. The same Roche kicked a free in the 31st minute. He repeated the act within another minute. The hugely impressive Philip Roche punched a hole in the winners defence with another determined burst, and when he off loaded to Colin Phillips racing up on his shoulder, we hardly saw the ball before it fell dead in the back of the net, a great score (2-6 to 1-3). The Vat were back-pedaling big time. They conceded a Minor to Ronan Walsh, with an assist from Ciaran Whelan, in the 35th minute before Malone placed Brian Phelan for a like score. On 40 minute the Railyard jumped right back into the match, which was reward for the great work done by Philip Roche, Colin Phillips, Noel and Caleb Roche and Paul Kelly. A scramble in front of the Mullinavat goal ended up with Phillips being fouled. Caleb Roche drilled home a low hard penalty. (2-7 to 2-4).'

'The game was running away from Mullinavat but they arrested the slide in a rare break upfield a foul on Joe Fennelly earned Ian Duggan a point from a free. John Walsh then kicked a great point from 45 metres off his left foot. Suddenly the game had swung. Mullinavat had a goal chance in the 48th minute, but Liam Fennelly shot wide when clean through. However, the goal was on the way. On 50 minutes Jamie Fennelly and Brian Phelan ripped the Railyard defence apart leaving John Walsh with the easy task of rounding the keeper and planting the ball in the net. The score was 3-9 to 2-4. There and then Kilkenny County SFC Final was decided.'

Mullinavat: Killian Dunphy; Ryan Bland, Mikey Jones, Darren Kenneally; Simon Aylward, Ger Malone (0-1), Mark Mansfield (0-1); Tom Aylward (captain), Joe Fennelly (0-1); Michael Malone (0-2), Ian Duggan (0-2, frees), Conor Duggan; Adam Mansfield, Jamie Fennelly (2-2) and Brian Phelan (0-1). Subs: John Walsh (1-2) for A Mansfield; James Culleton for M Jones (inj); Liam Fennelly for C Duggan.

COUNTY

British JFC R1: Kilkenny 4-17; Scotland 0-08
British JFC R2: Kilkenny beat Warwickshire
Semi Final: Kilkenny 1-14 ; Lancashire 0-15
Final: Kilkenny 3-16; Warwickshire 1-06 (in Birmingham)

(All British Inter County JFC Second win in three years for Kilkenny)

All Ireland JFC Semi Final: Meath 2-21; Kilkenny 2-08

'Meath took a while to get on top but when they did they proved much too strong for "British" champions Kilkenny at a sunny Nowlan Park. Having led by just three points at the break (0-8 to 0-5), the Royals tacked on seven points in seven minutes as they powered to victory. A 40th minute goal from Michael Malone stopped the rot, but Mayo green flags from Stephen Coogan and Daire Rowe underlined the Westerner's supremacy. Tullogher Rosbercon's Cian O'Donoghue got the second Kilkenny goal.

Kilkenny Football Squad v. Meath: JJ O'Sullivan (St Patrick's), James Mackey (0-1,

Windgap), Richard O'Hara (Thomastown), Joe Fennelly (Mullinavat), Pat Hartley (Tullogher Rosbercon), Paddy McConigley (Railyard), Ger Malone (Mullinavat), Michael Malone (1-1, Mullinavat), Tom Aylward (Mullinavat), Philip Roche (0-1, Railyard), James Culleton (Mullinavat), Tom Phelan (Conahy Shamrocks), Bill Sheehan (0-2, frees, Dicksboro), Ian Duggan (0-1, Mullinavat), David Kelly (Rower Inistioge), John Mansfield (Railyard), Tom Kenny (Dicksboro), James Nolan (Clara), Ronan Coffey (Kilmoganny), Eddie Moylan (0-2, 2 frees, Dicksboro), Cian O'Donoghue (1-0, Tullogher Rosbercon), Michael Jones (Mullinavat), Conor Joyce (Rower Inistioge), Darragh Brennan (Carrickshock), James Power (John Lockes), John Walsh (Rower Inistioge) and Conor McDonald (Railyard).

2018
SENIOR

SFL R1: Mullinavat w/o Glenmore scr.
SFL R2: Mullinavat James Stephens
SFL R3: Kilmoganny 4-08; Mullinavat 2-08

SFC R1: Mullinavat 5-14; Clara 3-07. 22/05
SFC Quarter Final: Mullinavat 3-14; Kilmaganny 1-05
SFC Semi Final: Mullinavat 3-13; O'Loughlin Gaels 1-03
SFC County Final: Mullinavat 5-11; Muckalee 2-09

'It was celebration time for Mullinavat when they won their third Kilkenny Senior championships in late July 2018 at Bennetsbridge. The winners were backboned by six members of the Kilkenny British Junior championship winning side, and they looked good all over the field. They led at half time by 2-5 to 1-4 after missing a penalty and a second chance of a goal as well. Tomas Breen opened the scoring for Muckale with an early point. Mullinavat bounced back smartly shooting 1-2. When Sean Maher goaled for the losers it helped them keep in touch with smart moving opponents who still held a lead of 1-4 to 1-2.

A goal from a penalty by John Walsh and a pointed free left Mullinavat well clear. Michael Malone then burst through the Muckalee defence and when he was foot tripped he was awarded a penalty. Walsh's penalty effort came back into play off an upright, but they were still in a strong position at the interval. They hit back for 1-4 but when Jamie Fennelly scored two late Mullinavat goals it simply served to underline their dominance.'

Mullinavat: Killian Dunphy; Shane Kelly, Simon Aylward, Mikey Jones; Ryan Bland, Mark Mansfield (0-1), Joe Fennelly (0-1); James Culleton, Michael Malone (0-2); Conor Duggan, John Walsh (1-1, goal penalty, point free), Liam Fennelly (0-1); Adam Mansfield, Jamie Fennelly (3-4, 2 points frees) and Brian Phelan. Sub: P Gahan (1-1).

COUNTY

British JFC R1: Kilkenny beat Warwickshire
Semi Final: Kilkenny 2-13; Scotland 1-08 (in Leeds)
Final: Kilkenny 6-12; Warwickshire 0-09
All Ireland JFC Semi Final: Galway 2-22; Kilkenny 2-08

'Galway struck for three points within two minutes of the start of this game, before Mullinavat's John Walsh finished a lovely move by punching the ball into the net to draw level. The gulf in class became evident as the game progressed and by the interval led 2-12 to 1-3. Galway first half goal scorers were Johnny Ryan and Matthew Reddington

Galway continued to dominate after the break, although the Cats battled bravely. It was another Mullinavat player, Mikey Jones, who got the Cats second goal in the 51st minute. The fact that there is a big divide in standards between the British Champions and Galway was evident throughout, and can also be seen from these three All Ireland semi final losses v. Mayo (2015), Meath (2017) and now Galway. However it has to be said that Kilkenny once again gave a good account of themselves here.'

Kilkenny Squad: JJ O'Sullivan (St Patrick's), Aaron Duggan (Dicksboro), Richard O'Hara (Thomastown), Paul Kelly (Railyard), Martin Gaffney (Dicksboro), Paddy McConigley (Railyard), Shane Kelly (Mullinavat), Sean Dowd (Railyard), Michael Malone (Mullinavat capt.), Michael Kenny (Lisdowney), James Culleton (Mullinavat), Shane Stapleton (Dicksboro), Edward Moylan (Dicksboro), Ian Duggan (Mullinavat), John Walsh (Mullinavat), Jamie Fennelly (Mullinavat), Luke Hickey (James Stephens), Michael Jones (Mullinavat), Conor Joyce (Rower Inistioge), James Power (John Lockes), Conor O'Carroll (Lisdowney), Brian Cahill (Railyard) and Ben Hickey (James Stephens).

2019

SENIOR

SFL R1: Mullinavat 6-12; Clara 2-07
SFL R2: Mullinavat 5-10; O'Loughlin Gaels 1-12
SFL R3: Mullinavat 1-13; Tullogher Rosbercon 2-06
SFL Semi Final: Mullinavat 3-09; Conahy Shamrocks 1-06
SFC Quarter Final: Mullinavat 2-06; O'Loughlin Gaels 1-09
SFC Quarter Final Replay: Mullinavat 1-10; O'Loughlin's 0-07
SFC Semi Final: Mullinavat Mullinavat 2-16; Muckalee 1-11
SFC County Final: Mullinavat 1-07; Railyard 1-07

'It was a contest in which there was obviously no winner, not even the game of football, and there was both regret and relief in possible equal measure, on both sides afterwards.

OUR STORY (1887-2024)

That was the story after a card littered, sometimes rugged, oft times unsavoury, but rarely engaging Kilkenny Senior Football Final at John Lockes Park in Callan. Mullinavat, who finished with fourteen men, definitely had regrets. After coming back to equalise with a point from Adam Mansfield in the 59th minute they drove on. However three chances from frees, two of which offered decent chances of scores, failed to produce what would have been the winning point.'

'Mullinavat manager Michael Aylward agreed that the bid for three in a row was let slip: "We had chances from frees to win it in the end. We let a real chance slip. Credit to the Railyard, they are good. They are a dogged team who chase games to the very end. It was a peculiar sort of game. The couple of cards took a lot from the game for everyone. The referee ruled according to the book and that was it. There is more in both sides. We can both play better, and now we will get another chance at it." Railyard finished with thirteen men, a situation they found themselves in before the break, so they were pleased enough to escape without a defeat.'

'The weather turned bad shortly before the start with rain driven by a largely cross field wind. Mullinavat opened the scoring with a point from a free in the second minute from Brian Phelan following a foul on Mansfield. The next score was the Railyard goal, Ian Booth tucked the ball away in the tenth minute from close range after Caleb Roche had knocked down a long high ball driven towards the country end goal. Railyard didn't add to their account until the 26th minute, a point from a free by Roche, by which stage they were 1-4 to 1-1 behind and a man down. Noel Roche engineered a point for Roche on 28 minutes but before the call for the rest, Railyard had a second man dismissed. At half time the score was Mullinavat 1-4; Railyard 1-2.'

'The flurry of cards continued after the break. There was another red, this time for Mullinavat. Two black cards were also flashed, plus Railyard had a team official send from the playing area. And they lost midfielder Eoin Regan, who was playing well, with concussion we were told, and he didn't appear for the second period. Against expectations the Railyard took hold of the game. Philip Roche had been their playmaker throughout, but Caleb Roche upped his game big time to help inspire things. Caleb Roche kicked the equaliser from a free in the 41st minute (1-4 each) as the Vat surrendered all control of the game. Railyard drove on and Roche got them in front, Brian Phelan equalised. Phelan then fisted the lead point for Mullinavat as the full concentration was on football, and the quality of fare rose substantially.'

'That man Roche dragged Railyard back level before a foul on Philip Roche saw him shoot them in front on the 57th minute (1-7 to 1-6). Mullinavat nearly had a goal through Brian Phelan subsequently, but goalie John Mansfield brought off a great save at the expense of a 45. The effort fell short but Adam Mansfield gathered possession and levelled it. After that Mullinavat had three chances from frees to win it. Brian Phelan kicked the first wide after Jamie Fennelly had been fouled. Goalie Killian Dunphy came up the field and had a go from the next free, but the range was beyond him. As Railyard tried to kill the game and hold possession they surrendered the ball and committed a foul nearing 65 minutes. From 35 metres on the right, Phelan kicked the ball wide of the far post.

Mullinavat team and scorers: Killian Dunphy; Mikey Jones (captain), Joe Fennelly, Darren Kenneally, Padraig Gahan, Shane Kelly, Ger Malone, Tom Aylward, Michael Malone, Conor Duggan, Ian Duggan, Brian Phelan (0-3, 1 free, 1 "45"), Jamie Fennelly (1-0), Adam Mansfield (0-4). Sub. Oisin Knox.

SFC County Final Replay: Mullinavat 1-13; Railyard 0-10

'At the second time of asking, Mullinavat consolidated their position as the Kilkenny Senior football champions when they presented a sturdy defence of the title in this replay against Railyard at Nowlan Park. After a bit of early shadow boxing, Mullinavat's lively wing forward, Adam Mansfield posted a point after two minutes, to get his balance sheet up and running. The imposing Railyard centrefield, Paul O'Neill balanced the book with a delightful point from 38 metres out from the Arus O'Cearbhaill stand. Eight minutes of inter-passing from both teams elapsed before another mark was registered. Mullinavat's nerveless free-taker Ian Duggan slipped over a beauty, and then the Railyard enjoyed a let off. A Mullinavat attack, crafted from midfield by the impressive Tom Aylward, saw the ball passed through the hands of Duggan and corner-forward Brian Phelan, before being delivered to Jamie Fennelly. His shot was brilliantly stopped by John Mansfield in the Railyard goal. As the ball came back off Mansfield's hands, Oisin Knox thundered in to half volley a shot, which was again saved by Mansfield at the cost of a "45". Three points by Ger Malone (2) and Adam Mansfield had the winners out by 0-5 to 0-1 by the 12th minute.'

'They were dominating the middle third of the park with Aylward and Michael Malone dictating matters. Two points by the lively Kieran Whelan and Pat McConigley reduced the deficit to two, but three Ian Duggan points – two of which were free shots – and a terrific Michael Malone 40 metre effort, saw Mullinavat approach half time leading by 0-9 to 0-3. A smart left footed effort by the clever and talented Kieran Whelan left the score reading: Mullinavat 0-9; Railyard 0-4.'

'Within 90 seconds Ger Malone slipped over a grand point for Mullinavat, to which Railyard's most impressive operator, McConigley replied with a like score. Alas for Railyard they were knocked back in the 38th minute. Brian Phelan combined with his opposite corner forward colleague, Oisin Knox to deliver. Winning the ball some 20 metres from the Railyard goal, Phelan beat two defenders with a dribble the would make many professional soccer players green with envy. Espying Knox languishing all alone at the edge of the

Railyard small square, Phelan hit a daisy-cuter across the square. The smart Knox knew exactly what to do. Duggan added a point from a free in the 40th minute. Already the Rod Iron lads could look forward to the celebrations.'

Mullinavat team and scorers: Killian Dunphy; Mikey Jones (captain), Joe Fennelly, Darren Kenneally, Mark Mansfield, Shane Kelly, Ger Malone (0-4), Tom Aylward, Michael Malone, Conor Duggan, Ian Duggan (0-6, 4 frees), Adam Mansfield (0-2), Brian Phelan, Jamie Fennelly, Oisin Knox (1-1). Subs: Simon Aylward for Shane Kelly, Ryan Bland for M Malone (black card), Mark McNamara, Padraig Gahan, John Walsh, Michael Walsh, Daniel Walsh, Robert Malone, Gavin Maher, Robin Davis, Jack Byrne Doyle, Conor Frisby, Sean Fitzpatrick, Jack Walsh, Ian Mansfield, Damien Aylward, Stephen Law, Eoin Maher, James Culleton and Liam Fennelly.

COUNTY

British JFC R1: Kilkenny 3-16; Warwickshire 0-06
British JFC R2: Kilkenny 0-13; London 1-06 (at Nowlan Park)
British JFC Semi final: Scotland 1-15; Kilkenny 0-01 (at Clydebank)

2020

SENIOR

SFC Quarter Final: Mullinavat 1-12; Railyard 0-02
SFC Semi Final: Mullinavat 3-06; Clara 1-10
SFC County Final: Mullinavat 5-07; Mooncoin 1-04

'Mullinavat are Kilkenny Senior football champions once again after they were comprehensive winners over championship newcomers Mooncoin in UPMC Nowlan Park. It was a fourth title win on the trot for the South Kilkenny club and the result was rarely in doubt after the 2019 Leinster Intermediate finalists found the net on five occasions with corner forward Brian Phelan getting in for a hat-trick. It only took three minutes for Mullinavat to get the opening goal of the game and Mooncoin didn't help themselves with full back Sean Wall losing the ball in a dangerous area and with goalkeeper Eoin Purcell stranded, Liam Fennelly was able to kick the ball into an empty net. Mooncoin responded with Sean Gannon shooting narrowly wide when taking advantage of indecision but normal service soon resumed when Brian Phelan palmed in a goal to give Mullinavat a six point lead. Further scores from Conor Duggan, Ian Duggan and John Walsh soon followed as the defending champions led 2-4 to 0-0 at the first water break'.

'Mooncoin then got something of a lifeline when wingback Sean Gannon got forward to rifle a shot past Killian Dunphy in the Mullinavat goal. The 2019, Intermediate champions were unable to build and that stroke of luck however and they were relatively fortunate to only trail by seven points at the break. The second period began in similar circumstances to the first with Mullinavat on the attack, and within 60 seconds of the resumption they had a third goal with Phelan finishing on the back of a flowing move, involving Joe Fennelly, Mark Mansfield, and Ian Duggan. Mooncoin has a couple of opportunities to make a game of it, but they were proving pretty wasteful in front of goal as Mullinavat stopped a few chances near their goal line. Cormac Daly and Paul Hennebry did knock over successive points for the Eugene Dunphy managed side, but once Padraig Gahan netted Mullinavat's fourth goal in the 37th minute, the game was almost over as a contest. Mullinavat then finished off the game in style, with a Conor Duggan point arriving before Phelan netted his third goal of the final that saw his side run out 5-7 to 1-4 winners.'

Mullinavat: Killian Dunphy, Joe Fennelly, Shane Kelly, Simon Aylward, Mark Mansfield, Ger Malone, John Walsh (0-1), Tom Aylward, Michael Malone, Conor Duggan (0-2), Ian Duggan (0-3, 0-2 frees), Adam Mansfield, Padraig Gahan (1-1), Liam Fennelly (1-0) and Brian Phelan (3-0). Subs: Robin Davis for Duggan 49 minutes, Michael Walsh for Liam Fennelly 53 minutes, Ian Mansfield for Joe Fennelly 55 minutes, Damien Aylward for Adam Mansfield 57 minutes, Richard Devine for Walsh 58 minutes.

2021
SENIOR

SFC R1: Mullinavat 5-19; Danesfort 1-06
SFC Quarter Final: Mullinavat 5-13; Tullogher Rosbercon 4-06
SFC Semi Final Mullinavat 2-14; Clara 0-04
SFC Final Thomastown 2-06; Mullinavat 1-05

'A moment of individual Mullinavat brilliance sealed the county Senior football spoils for Thomastown. Rory Monks was the toast of the 'Town after his late, late goal helped the boys in blue claim the county crown. A final which had twisted this way and that, seemed certain for a dramatic penalty shootout ending after both sides were deadlocked entering the final 60 seconds of normal time. Then Monks made his move. Coming out the field to gather a low ball he picked up possession and, with one quick shimmy, slipped the attention of defenders Ger Malone and Simon Aylward. With a clear path to goal, Monks surged forward towards the City End posts, leaving the Vat defence in his wake. He didn't stop until he had closed down the posts, then showed incredible coolness to clip a sweet strike into the top right corner of the net. As far as match-winning moves go, it was something else.'

'Proving they would not be intimidated by the champions, Thomastown made a sharp start to proceedings, forcing Mullinavat net-minder Killian Dunphy into a smart save to deny Stephen Donnelly a goal, within 30 seconds of the throw in. Mullinavat had to survive another scare soon afterwards; Dunphy was mightily relieved to see Brian Staunton's bouncing fifth minute delivery come back off the top of crossbar and then hit the post before coming out. While the Vat drew first blood, with Padraic Gahan's opening point it wasn't long before they were behind. Full forward Stephen Donnelly showed quick reactions to watch as Diarmuid Galway's pass broke his way before he slammed an instinctive shot into the Mullinavat net.'

'The wind was in Thomastown's sails, something they highlighted when Davy Prendergast dashed through the centre to add a quick point to Donnelly's goal. Ten minutes in and Thomastown were cruising (1-1 to 0-0). They went close to adding another goal just 60 seconds later when Daithi Barron's shot beat Dunphy, but Simon Aylward made a brilliant goal line clearance to rescue his side. Mullinavat cleared their heads after that scare, pulling back two points via the impressive James Culleton and Oisin Knox (free), while Prendergast clipped over a fine point with his left foot. An equally good score by Michael Malone meant the Vat were within one point of the leaders at the first water break (1-2 to 0-4). Thomas O'Hanrahan made it a two point game soon afterwards, taking his point after a hefty shoulder challenge, but Mullinavat showed the pedigree of champions when they tested the town with their next attack. Culleton started the move with an excellent solo forward before releasing the ball to Knox, but net-minder Patrick Khan pulled off a superb save to deny the forward. While Thomastown recovered their composure, Rory Monks and Prendergast (free) adding points, another Oisin Knox free meant Mullinavat were just three behind at the interval (1-5 to 0-5).'

'The champions ramped up the pressure in the second half. Rather than get frustrated Mullinavat kept going forward and looked to have a real chance to get back into the game when they were awarded a 40th minute penalty. Oisin Knox drilled a low shot towards the bottom right corner, but Khan guessed correctly and dived to his left to beat the shot out. When the following rebound, and subsequent 45 were spurned, it looked like curtains for Mullinavat. However, they shook of the disappointment of those misses and hit back to raise the green flag six minutes later. Started by a mark and quick pass from Culleton the Vat pressed forward working the ball around through Michael Malone and Brian Phelan. The final pass to Padraig Gahan, who drilled an inch perfect shot across the square, just beyond Khan's outstretched left foot, and inside the far post (1-5 to 1-5). Inspired by that goal Mullinavat went looking for more scores to turn the game their way. They pressed and pressed, working the ball from right to left, but the shooting gaps they needed weren't given by Thomastown, who defended with incredible resolve. Then, just when it looks. Like normal time would finish all square – Thomastown missed two frees in the final quarter – the Grennan men made their move.'

'With Mullinavat on the front foot, searching for that final score to win it, they were caught cold when a low ball was drilled forward and seized by Monks. One speedy break later the Mullinavat net shook. The win was within Thomastown's grasp now and they were determined to hold on. A sweet and swift strike from Thomas Hanrahan, who picked up an excellent pass and fired the ball over the bar via the outside of his right boot, sealed the title, their first at this grade since 1985. For Mullinavat their influential captain James Culleton, Centre back Ger Malone and the roving Liam Fennelly wee the most impressive.'

Mullinavat: Killian Dunphy; Ryan Bland, Shane Kelly, Simon Aylward, Joe Fennelly, Ger Malone, Padraig Dempsey; James Culleton (0-1), Michael Malone (0-1), Conor Duggan, Liam Fennelly, Adam Mansfield; Padraic Gahan (1-1), Oisin Knox (0-2) and Brian Phelan. Subs - Darren Kenneally for Bland, 58 mins; Conor Walsh for Gahan, 60 mins.

2022
SENIOR

SFL R1 Tullogher Rosbercon 2-06; Mullinavat 0-07
SFL R2 Mullinavat 3-12; Conahy Shamrocks 1-01
SFL R3 Mullinavat 2-07; Railyard 0-05
SFL R4 Mullinavat 2-12; Mooncoin 1-03
SFL Final Mullinavat 1-07; Dicksboro 1-01

SFC Quarter Final: Mullinavat 2-15; Danesfort 1-10
SFL Semi Final: Mullinavat 1-07; Dicksboro 1-01
SFC Final: Mullinavat 1-12; Thomastown 0-08

'This was a sixth title for Mullinavat, adding to successes in 2007, 2017, 2018, 2019 and 2020. Thomastown deservedly took their fifth title in beating Mullinavat last year, but on this occasion, most of the time, there was really only going to be one winner. The holders did actually make the better start, and when Mullinavat centre back Ger Malone got an early black card, Rory Monks opened the scoring from the resulting free. The same player got a point from play two minutes later.'

'Mullinavat captain Michael Malone opened their scoring with a point, and shortly afterwards Brian Phelan had a clear goal chance saved by Paddy Khan in the Thomastown goal. Richard O'Hara burst through the Mullinavat defence to score a point from 40 metres out, to leave the Town 0-3 to 0-1 ahead on ten minutes. The next three scores were for Mullinavat, a 60 metre free by goalie Killian Dunphy, Padraic Gahan and Michael Malone. A fine score from Peter Connellan levelled matters on 0-4 each, but Mullinavat then took control.'

'By the interval three further points had been added by Mikey Jones, Michal Malone and a second Killian Dunphy free. In this period also Thomastown lost Rory Monks through what looked to be an unfortunate leg injury. Half time Mullinavat 0-7; Thomastown 0-4.'

'Brian Phelan got Mullinavat the opening score of the new half, to move four points ahead. On 35 minutes, Dunphy made a fine save from Thomastown's Daithi Barron, and with that, may have went their chance of a comeback. Danny Monks took over the free taking and pointed to reduce the margin to three. Tom Aylward (Mullinavat) and Monks exchanged further points, 0-9 to 0-6 on 40 minutes. Adam Mansfield added a Mullinavat point, and then the game clinching goal by Brian Phelan after a fine passing move. 1-10 to 0-6 as we headed in the last quarter.'

'In the last ten minutes there was just two further scores, Brian Staunton (45) for Thomastown, and the final score of the game was by Adam Mansfield for the winners. Mullinavat star man on the day was Michael Malone, but as with the recent successes at the club, it's more about the collective than the individual.'

Mullinavat team: Killian Dunphy (0-2); Joe Fennelly, Simon Aylward, Mikey Jones (0-1); Shane Kelly, Ger Malone, John Walsh; Jim Culleton, Tom Aylward (0-1); Conor Duggan (0-1), Michael Malone (0-3), Adam Mansfield (0-2); Brian Phelan (1-1), Liam Fennelly and Padraic Gahan (0-1). Subs - Sean Fitzpatrick for Pádraic Gahan, Peter McDonald for Ger Malone.

COUNTY

2022 All-Ireland JFC Final: Kilkenny 3-12; New York 1-09

'Things you don't see every day, the Kilkenny footballers enjoying a lap of honour around Croke Park to the delight of tens of thousands. A restructuring of the All-Ireland Junior Football Championship presented a window of opportunity this year which Christy Walsh's Cats have jumped straight through. With mainly overseas teams participating, Kilkenny and New York emerged victorious from a double header of Junior semi-finals on Friday evening, franking their passes to Croke Park for a novel decider ahead of the Dublin/Kerry Senior game. Both sides also managed to give the impression of being teams more used to the grand stage than they actually are, and the nine-point win flattered Kilkenny. Like Friday's semi-final win, they glossed the scoreline with two late goals, Mick Kenny and John Walsh both netting in stoppage time on this occasion. Still, it wasn't an undeserved win, nor anything like it, with Kilkenny leading from pillar to post and showing no little quality throughout the hour. Kenny finished with 1-4, matching his tally from Friday, while Jamie Holohan also netted, and there was a familiar figure seen at full-back – four-time hurling All Star Paul Murphy.'

Kilkenny: Killian Dunphy (Mullinavat); Paul Murphy (Danesfort), Tom Kenny (Dicksboro), Ger Malone (Mullinavat); Kevin Blanchfield (0-1, Graignamanagh), Ciaran Wallace (Erin's Own), Shane Kelly (0-1, Mullinavat); James Culleton (0-2, Mullinavat), Tom Aylward (Mullinavat); Conor Hennessy (0-1, Tullogher Rosbercon), Michael Malone (Mullinavat), Mick Kenny (1-4, 4 frees, Lisdowney); Rory Monks (Thomastown), Jamie Holohan (1-2, Erin's Own), Adam Mansfield (Mullinavat). Subs - Ethan Phelan (0-1, Glenmore) for Monks and John Walsh (1-0, Mullinavat) for Mansfield (h/t); Shane Murphy (Glenmore) for Hennessy (45); Shane Stapleton (Dicksboro) for Malone (52); Joe Fennelly (Mullinavat) for Kelly (61).

Other panellists: Jimmy Dermody (Fenians), Ger Malone (Mullinavat), David O'Carroll, Kevin Blanchfield, Jack Kavanagh, Kieran Whelan, Philip Roche, Kieran Cooney, Edward Moylan, JJ O'Sullivan (St Patrick's), David Griffin, Tom Roche, Mikey Jones (Mullinavat) and Liam Dunphy.

2023

SENIOR

SFL R1: Mullinavat 1-08; Railyard 2-05
SFL R2: Mullinavat 3-11; Muckalee 2-08
SFL R3: Mullinavat 4-12; Clara 0-07
SFL Semi Final: Mullinavat 1-14; Mooncoin 1-09
SFL Final: Mullinavat 2-07; Tullogher/Rosbercon 0-10

'While this final, played in perfect Spring conditions, was always well contested, the football was often average throughout the afternoon, but was still always interesting, as there was never much between the sides throughout. Tullogher Rosbercon took advantage of early Mullinavat sloppiness in the attack with three unanswered points from Cian O Donoghue, two from frees, sandwiching a point from play by the same player, after a blocked goal chance. Mullinavat got off the mark on 14 minutes with a goal from a James Culleton penalty, this after Ger Malone was fouled close in. Points from Ian Duggan (18 minutes) and Liam Fennelly (21 minutes) put the "Rod Iron" boys 1-2 to 0-3 ahead. Similar Minor scores from Niall Mooney (23 minutes) and a Conor O'Donoghue free, meant it was all square at the interval, 0-5 to 1-2.'

'Two early second half points from an Ian Duggan free, and a Mikey Jones score following a Liam Fennelly pass, got Mullinavat two clear. Mullinavat now looked like they were going to move through the gears; Darren Kenneally had a close-in goal chance saved, before Tom Aylward did raise a green flag, this after good work by Ger Malone and Liam Fennelly (2-4 to 0-5). To their credit Tullogher Rosbercon battled back quickly, and knocked over three points in a row with scores from Cian O'Donoghue (free), Donnacha O'Connor with the best point of the game from distance, and Cian O'Donoghue again, this from play (0-8 to 2-4).

Ian Duggan (M) and O'Donoghue (TR) exchanged frees between the 16th and 18th minute.

Two further frees from Ian Duggan restored a Mullinavat four point lead (2-7 to 0-9) but it was Tullogher who finished strongest with Danny Glennon pointing from play and a half chance of an equalising goal was blocked before the finish.'

'Best for Mullinavat were Simon and Tom Aylward, Ger Malone and Ian Duggan from frees.

Cian O'Donoghue was Tullogher's main man in attack, whilst Pat Hartley, James Lyng, Tarek O'Connor and Danny Glennon were others who tried hard.'

Mullinavat: Mark McNamara; Mikey Jones (0-1), Joe Fennelly, Ian Mansfield; Simon Aylward (captain), Shane Kelly, Darren Kenneally; Tom Aylward 1-0), Ger Malone; Conor Duggan, James Culleton (1-0, pen), Ian Duggan (0-5, free); Fiachra Knox, Liam Fennelly (0-1) and Sean Fitzpatrick. Subs - Michael Walsh for Conor Duggan, Conor Power for Sean Fitzpatrick.

SFC Quarter Final: Mullinavat 3-07; Dicksboro 0-07
SFC Semi Final: Mullinavat 5-06; Tullogher Rosbercon 0-06
SFC Final: Mullinavat 3-07; Thomastown 1-09

'For the sixth time in seven seasons, and the seventh in the club's history, Mullinavat are once more the JJ Kavanagh & Sons Kilkenny Senior football champions. For the third season in a row, Mullinavat and Thomastown were the final pairing, tied at 1-1 in the trilogy series going into this game, Thomastown having stopped Mullinavat from doing an unprecedented five-in-a-row in the 2021 championship. Mullinavat raced into an early lead, hitting the back of the net with five minutes on the clock but Thomastown kept pressing, clawing their way back up the scoreboard towards the end of the first half and into the second, hitting a goal of their own to tie proceedings at 1-05 apiece.'

'With 15 minutes to go, momentum was swinging Thomastown's way as they pulled two points clear but the never-say-die attitude that carried Mullinavat through to a Leinster Intermediate semi-final last season prevailed with two late goals making sure the Senior title stays with the holders. An opening half Zach Bay Hammond goal had given Thomastown early hope of trumping the holders and while they led by a point at the half-time break, they largely relied on the free taking accuracy of Rory Monks.'

'Mullinavat on the other hand saw all their scores come from play bar one and their forward unit created many goal opportunities with efforts from Michael Malone, Oisin Knox and Liam Fennelly netting game defining efforts. Mullinavat are a side that has gained a lot of football experience in the past few seasons and their multiple trips into provincial competition is certainly serving them well as they overpowered Thomastown in the end.'

'Thomastown made a bright beginning to a final that was played in front of a small enough crowd when Rory Monks converted a third minute free. The Vat responded in fine style when a quickfire 1-2 gave them a four point lead by the seventh minute. Points from Tom Aylward and Ian Duggan got the scoring momentum going for the champions before Ger Malone batted off a couple of challenges on the way to finding Liam Fennelly who combined with Michael Malone as the centre forward blasted a shot past Luke McNena in the Thomastown goal. Adam Power replied with a point from distance for the challengers and the sides then went tit for tat over the following minutes.'

'Jonjo Farrell and Rory Connellan continued the scoring for Thomastown while Michael Malone and Ian Duggan kept the winners ticking over. Mullinavat then saw a number of goal opportunities go abegging where Adam Mansfield had a close in effort blocked as well as a disallowed goal when a fisted attempt went all the way to the net past Luke McNena. Those squandered chances looked like they'd come back to bite when a second Rory Monks free reduced the deficit to two points before the aforementioned corner forward set up Zach Bay Hammond for a cracking goal in first half stoppage time. That proved to be the final score of the half as Thomastown led 1-5 to 1-4.'

'The second half turned into a real tactical affair where there was only two points in the opening 10 minutes and they both came for Mullinavat. Those efforts from Ian Duggan and impact sub Oisin Knox edged Mullinavat in front but Thomastown were refusing to go away quietly. A 40th minute Monks free levelled up matters for the third time and when the Thomastown top scorer then extended his tally the other side of an Adam Power point from play, there looked to be an upset on the cards.'

'Mullinavat were having none of it though and they dominated the final quarter as they pounced for a 2-1 tally that stalled the Thomastown momentum. When a combination of Michael Malone and Liam Fennelly forced in Mullinavat's second goal, the overall tone of proceedings changed. Things then got very scrappy and a mini scuffle broke out behind the O'Loughlin end goals that resulted in Mullinavat's Shane Kelly getting a straight red card.

Monks followed up with his fifth free to leave just the minimum between the teams but just when extra-time seemed a possibility, Mullinavat went down the other end and struck the game winning goal when a flowing team move ended with Oisin Knox finding the net.'

Mullinavat: Mark McNamara; Mikey Jones, Joe Fennelly, Ian Mansfield; Shane Kelly, Ger Malone, Simon Aylward; James Culleton, Tom Aylward (0-1); Conor Duggan, Michael Malone (1-1), Ian Duggan (0-4, one free); Adam Mansfield, Liam Fennelly (1-0), Padraic Gahan. Sub: Oisin Knox (1-1) for C Duggan (halftime).

OUR STORY (1887-2024)

COUNTY

All Ireland JFC Semi Final: Kilkenny 1-13; London 0-15

'Kilkenny are back in the All Ireland Junior Football Final for the second year in a row with a hard earned victory over London tonight at Abbotstown. As with last year, Mullinavat again had great representation, with six starters and three substitutes. The starters were Shane Kelly and Ger Malone in defence, Tom Aylward in midfield, with Mick Malone, Jim Culleton and Ian Duggan in the forward division. Joe Fennelly, Mikey Jones and Adam Mansfield were among the thirteen named Kilkenny substitutes. Kilkenny led by four points at half time, 0-12 to 0-8. All six Kilkenny forwards had scored in the opening half, with James Carroll of Bennetsbridge, outstanding with 0-5 from play. Kilkenny were actually very accurate in the opening period, with 12 scores from thirteen shots at the post.'

'London started the second half stronger and were well back in the game until, on 38 minutes, Darren Lynch of London got a black card, and during this period James Carroll of Bennetsbridge got a vital Kilkenny goal. This put Kilkenny 1-13 to 0-12 ahead on 49 minutes. While we did not score again, Kilkenny held on for a one point victory.'

Kilkenny team and scorers: Ciaran Farnan; Shane Kelly, Tom Kenny, James Darmody; Kevin Blanchfield, Nathan Sherry, Ger Malone; Conor Hennessy, Tom Aylward; Mick Malone (0-1), Jim Culleton (0-2), Mick Kenny (0-1, free); James Carroll (1-5), Ian Duggan (0-1) and Jamie Holohan (0-3). Subs: Ciaran Quilty for Dermody, Adam Mansfield for Houlihan, Rory Monks for Duggan, Sean Gannon for Hennessy,

All-Ireland JFC Final: New York 0-13; Kilkenny 1-09

'Brian Coughlan capped a terrific New York fightback with a dramatic stoppage time winning point as the Exiles claimed a maiden All-Ireland JFC title success. They did it the hard way because they trailed by two points with just four minutes of normal time remaining having watched Kilkenny dominate the majority of the second-half. But three late points from Shay McElligot left it on level terms before Coughlan, part of an entirely New York born and bred team, popped up with the winning point at the Hill 16 End three minutes into stoppage time.'

'Kilkenny won last year's final by 3-12 to 1-9 though former county hurling stars Paul Murphy and Ciaran Wallace, their full-back and centre-back in 2022, were notable absentees this year. CJ Molloy, who had a brief spell on the Donegal panel under Jim McGuinness, didn't feature last year but lined out in Friday's semi-final win over Warwickshire and again today. Living in Donegal and part of the Ardara club, the nephew of 1992 All-Ireland Donegal hero Anthony Molloy struck New York's opening score from a free. That tied the scores up at 0-1 apiece and they were level again at 0-2 apiece before Kilkenny briefly took the lead through Mick Malone.'

'But five New York points in a row, including two each from free-taker McElligot and the impressive Conor Mathers, left the Exiles sitting pretty at 0-7 to 0-3 clear at half-time.

McElligot stretched their lead to five with a pointed free after the restart though New York didn't score again for almost 20 minutes. In the meantime, a dynamic Cats outfit ran hard at the New York defence and hauled themselves into a winning position with an unanswered 1-3 between the 36th and 48th minutes. Kenny's last act before being substituted was to strike their 44th minute goal, rounding the goalkeeper and shooting home off his left foot after bursting onto a clever ball across goals from the right. Emmet Loughran's 51st minute point for New York got it back to level terms briefly but Kilkenny scores from Ciaran Quilty and Carroll nudged them into a two-point lead which put them on the verge of back to back titles.

They couldn't hold on though, and 12 wides overall cost them as New York proved the hungrier and more efficient in the crucial closing minutes.'

Kilkenny: Ciaran Farnan; Shane Kelly, Nathan Sherry, James Darmody; Kevin Blanchfield, Tom Kenny, Ger Malone; Tom Aylward, Jim Culleton; Conor Hennessy (0-1), Jamie Holohan, Mick Kenny (1-2, 0-2 frees); James Carroll (0-3, 0-1 free), Ian Duggan and Mick Malone (0-1). Subs - Joe Fennelly h/t, Ciaran Quilty (0-1) for Aylward h/t, Rory Monks (0-1) for Duggan 36, Adam Mansfield for Kenny 44, Mark Hender for Culleton 57.

Gaelic Football
IN PHOTOS

County Intermediate football champions 2000

Back Row (from left): Liam Murphy, Martin Knox, Pat Hoban, Paul Mansfield, Ollie Aylward, Michael Murphy, Conor Conway, Michael Duggan. Front Row (from left): Declan Duggan, Walter Burke, JP Dungan, Andrew McGovern, Keith Madigan, Paul Aylward and Maurice Murphy.

Peil na nÓg June 2002

Senior Football League champions 2005
Back Row (*from left*): *Joe Kelly (selector), Willie O'Dwyer, Brian Kenneally, Maurice Murphy, Michael Murphy, Conor Conway, Tony Duggan, Ger Anthony, Dinny Butler, Daniel Monk.* **Front (*from left*):** *John Paul Dungan, Seamus Farrell, Walter Burke, Andrew McGovern, Paul Aylward, Michael Duggan, Jamie Fennelly, Declan Duggan, Nicholas Anthony, Liam Murphy and Paul Whelan (coach).*

SFL winners 2010

Jamie Fennelly, captain of the Mullinavat Senior football champions 2018.

*Mikey Jones, captain of the
Mullinavat Senior football county champions 2019.*

Senior football county champions 2019

Back Row (from left): Mark Mansfield, Robin Davis, Eoin Maher, Sean Fitzpatrick, Brian Phelan, Adam Mansfield, Danny Walsh, Killian Dunphy, Ryan Bland, Ian Dugan. **Middle Row (from left):** Jamie Fennelly, Stephen Law, Michael Walsh, Shane Kelly, Ger Malone, Tom Aylward, Michael Malone, Joe Fennelly, John Walsh. **Front Row (from left):** Oisín Knox, Mark McNamara, Darren Kenneally, Simon Aylward, Mikey Jones (captain), Gavin Maher, Jack Byrne Doyle, Conor Duggan, Jack Walsh and Michael Aylward (manager).

Senior football county champions 2020

Back Row (from left): Fiachra Knox, David Maher, Conor Walsh Mark McNamara, Liam Fennelly, Joe Fennelly, Tom Aylward, Mark Mansfield, Damien Aylward, Conor Frisby, Killian Dunphy, Michael Malone, Luke Byrne Doyle, Ian Mansfield, Robin Davis, Brian Phelan, Adam Mansfield. **Front Row (from left):** Jack Walsh, Padraic Gahan, Darren Kenneally, Ian Duggan Richard Devine, Ger Malone, Simon Aylward, Mikey Jones, Shane Kelly (captain), John Walsh, Conor Duggan, Gavin Maher, Sean Fitzpatrick and Michael Walsh.

Shane Kelly celebrates another triumph in 2021.

Below: *A total of 12 Mullinavat men (11 players and selector Ian Duggan) were part of the Kilkenny panel that won that All-Ireland Junior Championship final in July 2022. A great afternoon to see Kilkenny footballers lift silverware in Croke Park.*

Michael Malone lifts the All-Ireland Junior Football Championship trophy.

Senior football county champions 2022

Back: Michael Aylward, Darren Kenneally, Brian Phelan, Conor Duggan, David Maher, Peter McDonald, Donnacha Walsh, Mark McNamara, James Culleton, Padraic Gahan, Tom Aylward, Joe Fennelly, Ian Mansfield, Michael Malone, Mikey Jones, Shane Kelly, Jamie Fennelly. **Front:** Killian Dunphy, Ryan Bland, Ian Duggan, Ger Malone, John Walsh, Liam Fennelly, Gavin Maher, Shane Aylward, Sean Fitzpatrick, Adam Mansfield, Simon Aylward

While off the field, our stewards continue to make sure the club always works hard.

Mullinavat hit the national headlines with our brilliant exploits in 2022.

'Vegas boys' are planning to hit jackpot and put Kilkenny club football on the map

Hurling is at the heart of the Cats, but Mullinavat are showing the way in terms of the big ball

MICHAEL VERNEY

THERE'S a famous yarn that centres around a high-profile Kilkenny hurler asking legendary boss Brian Cody if he could play a club football game, in which the player was met with "if you want to further your football career, then by all means go".

Needless to say that player was subsequently at Kilkenny training on the night in question and it paints a picture of where the big ball comes in the scheme of things on Noreside.

Mullinavat are helping to buck that trend somewhat, though, with another sensational run in the Leinster club JFC but coach/selector Jamie Fennelly, son of Kilkenny legend Liam, knows where they stand.

Fanatical

"Football is probably the distant fourth or fifth, cousin in the county, to be honest about it – and it's not going to be an easy job to change that. It's a fanatical hurling county, and we're no different in Mullinavat," he says.

"I don't think that's up to us to try and force a change, whatever the appetite of the county board is and the clubs, I'm not sure. We love playing it and it's probably up to the county board to look more into that, and we'll concentrate on ourselves."

Mullinavat, known locally as Mullinavegas due to the strip through the town which resembles the famous Nevada city, have been flying the flag in style with victories over Offalyside Bracknagh and Wicklow's Shandough.

There has been much debate about the gap between county and provincial champions in some quarters, but the Vegan boys have had little love given that their fifth Kilkenny SFC success in six seasons came back in May.

"It's kind of run-of as soon as possible to get out of the way for the hurling,"

Fennelly says matter-of-factly. "It's no different to us, because we were looking to concentrate on the hurling ourselves anyway.

"From the middle of May until we were knocked out of the hurling, it wouldn't have ever registered with us. Full focus would have been on the hurling and we would have even liked less time to prepare for Bracknagh, because it would have meant that the senior hurlers went a bit further.

"Football would never have even crossed our minds. As soon as they were knocked out of the hurling, we gave them a week and then left it up to the players.

"We said we'd facilitate whatever they wanted to do – and they were really up for it and eager for it."

Fennelly, now 37 and a former minor/U-21 hurler with the Cats, played lock Rangers in the 2019 Leinster JFC final before switching to coaching under manager Michael Aylward.

Little did he think that he would still be venturing down to the club grounds in November, but this is a Mullinavat side with plenty of pedigree, as they had a dozen players involved with Kilkenny's All-Ireland JFC success in Croke Park earlier this year.

They include captain and talisman Michael Malone – who also skippered the Cats' footballers to a rare success at GAA HQ – and former Kilkenny under-age hurling sensation John Walsh, while many learned their football trade during secondary school in Good Counsel College, New Ross.

Several of the squad – as well as Fennelly himself – would have fostered a love of the big ball across the Wexford border, and they well collide with many former class mates when they take on Model side St Miogrel's of Foulard in Callan on Saturday.

Mullinavat are backboned by their senior hurling team but Tyrone native Shane Kelly is an outlier, having moved to the area – "he even picked up the hurl the last couple of years to play with the

Mickey Jones of Mullinavat during the launch of the AIB Leinster GAA Club finals in 2019. Below: The Twelve Apostles – the Mullinavat players involved in Kilkenny's 2022 All-Ireland JFC win in Croke Park – (back row l-r) Tom Aylward, Ger Malone, Joe Fennelly, James Culleton, Michael Malone, Conor Duggan, John Walsh; (front row) Ian Duggan, Mikey Jones, Shane Kelly, Adam Mansfield, Kilian Dunphy

junior F side" – and they have no intention of ending their Leinster journey just yet.

Both sides will know plenty about each other as they chase a provincial final place – and Fennelly, whose brother Liam is left-forward while another sibling Ken is corner-back, is keen to make the most of the glorious opportunity before them.

"Lads are dedicated to it but it isn't the be all and end-all, it's not the hurling. We'd much prefer to be in (Ballyhale) Shamrocks' situation preparing for a Leinster semi-final in the hurling even though we're delighted to be here and we're taking this seriously.

"Every game we go into we're going to be the underdogs so we won't start dreaming of Croke Park yet, but we'll give it a good rattle and see where that takes us," he says.

Sherlock joins Westmeath set-up

INCOMING Westmeath manager Dessie Dolan has confirmed his backroom team for the new season which sees Dublin's Jason Sherlock come on board as a "performance coach".

The highly-rated Sherlock was an integral part of Jim Gavin's Dublin management set-up as they secured a record-breaking five All-Ireland titles in a row, and his acquisition represents something of a coup for Westmeath.

Earlier this year, Sherlock was strongly linked with the vacancy in Monaghan before the Farney men eventually settled on Vinny Corey.

Meanwhile, Derry club Slaughtneil are reportedly close to naming former Tyrone manager and current Louth supremo Mickey Harte as their new manager.

Leinster Football Campaigns

2000/01

JUNIOR

Leinster JFC Group: Marshalstown (Wexford) 3-15; Mullinavat 0-03
Leinster JFC Group: Mullinavat 0-07; St Andrews (Carlow) 0-05

Mullinavat had won the Kilkenny Intermediate Football Championship in their first ever final. A new competition for Leinster football had been created, and we were grouped in with the Carlow and Wexford champions. This Mullinavat team laid the foundations for the seven senior football wins we have achieved since.

'Football in Kilkenny received a badly needed boost when determined Mullinavat scored a deserved win over St Andrew's (Carlow) at McGrath Park on Sunday 19/11/2000. Two weeks earlier Mullinavat had been beaten by the Wexford champions, but they bounced back to score a fine win here. Tommy Duggan and Conor Conway kicked the two opening scores for the winners. St Andrew's hit back for a point from Ciaran Kelly, and after Morgan Drea and Ken Hickey rose the white flag, they went on to lead by 0-3 to 0-2 at the break. During that half Mullinavat kicked a penalty wide, and they also wasted a number of other opportunities. Early in the second period St Andrew's increased their lead. John Nolan was downed in the square and they were awarded a penalty. Trevor Nolan was content to tap the ball over the bar. Surprisingly, that was the loser's only score for 20 minutes. Four points from accurate Mullinavat free taker Conor Conway put his side in front for the second time. Sub Fergus Bolger earned parity for St Andrew's, and a draw looked the likely outcome. In a daring late effort, Mullinavat had points from Conor Conway (free) and Tommy Duggan to score an unlikely victory. Stars for the winners were goalie Ollie Dalton, the Butlers, Pat and Ken, Liam Murphy, Conor Conway, Tommy Duggan and Seanie Holden.'

Mullinavat: O Dalton, Pat Butler, Ken Butler, JP Dungan, Ollie Aylward, Walter Burke, Liam Murphy, Martin Knox, Andrew McGovern, Conor Conwav (0-5, frees), Keith Madigan, Michael Duggan, Tony Duggan (0-2), S Holden and Declan Duggan.

2004/05
JUNIOR
Leinster JFC Group: Mullinavat 1-09; Valleymount (Wicklow) 1-06

Mullinavat had won the Kilkenny Intermediate championship for the second time in 2004. The previous year had been a very poor year for the club, with relegation from the Senior grade in both hurling and football. Football wise we bounced back immediately, with a second Intermediate win. The still new competition for Leinster Club Junior Football was continuing. This time we were grouped in with the Carlow, Wexford and Wicklow champions.

'Kilkenny football received a timely boost when Mullinavat recorded a notable victory over Wicklow's Valleymount in the first round of the Leinster Junior Football Championship in Mullinavat on 12/11/2004. The home side had to work very hard for the win. The visitors looked to have the better of their opponents when two points ahead as the match drew to a close. However, the home team didn't give up the chase, and a great goal by Michael Murphy, when he soloed into the oppositions defence and blasted the ball to the net to give to give his side a one point lead. The home team fully deserved the win, as they matched then opponents in all areas of the pitch. At half time the winners led by 0-5 to 0-3. They should have been further in front, because they squandered two good goal chances. Best score of the half was a brilliant point from the sideline by Michael Duggan. Thanks to Michael Murphy's late goal, and a point from Jamie Fennelly, the Rod Iron side ran out deserving winners.'

Mullinavat: Declan Duggan, Walter Burke, Maurice Murphy, Seamus Farrell, Ger Anthony, Dinny Butler, Michael Murphy (1-0), Tony Duggan, Paul Aylward, Willie O'Dwyer, Michael Duggan (0-1), Liam Murphy, Jamie Fennelly (0-1), Conor Conway (0-4) and Andrew McGovern (0-3).

Leinster JFC Group: Mullinavat 0-05; Shamrocks (Wexford) 0-05

Kilkenny champions Mullinavat travelled to Enniscorthy on Saturday and came away with a hard earned draw in the final game of the round robin series in the Leinster Junior football championship. By doing so they finished top of the group, which also included Valleymount of Wicklow. The Noresides had to dig deep for everything they got. The weather conditions were poor and conditions were difficult. Mullinavat found themselves a point down as the final whistle approached. However, a point from Andrew McGovern two minutes from the end earned the Noresiders a draw and a place at the top of the group. The winners qualified for the Leinster semi final. They now travel to Ballinagar in Offaly on Saturday when they take on Kilclonfert.'

Mullinavat: Declan Duggan, Walter Burke, Maurice Murphy, Seamus Farrell, Ger Anthony, Dinny Butler, Michael Murphy, Tony Duggan, Paul Aylward, Willie O'Dwyer, Michael Duggan, Liam Murphy, Jamie Fennelly, Conor Conway (0-3), Andrew McGovern (0-2).

Leinster JFC Semi Final: Kilclonfert (Offaly) 0-13; Mullinavat 1-04

'In what proved to be a surprisingly one-sided encounter, at least as far as the scoring was concerned, Mullinavat lacked the scoring power to match their hosts, despite enjoying an almost equal share of possession throughout the hour. Nor did the visitors have the resources to make changes in an effort to instil greater "bite" to their attack, for although they had eleven substitutes listed on the panel published on the match programme, they actually had only two players available, one of whom was drafted in as a late starting replacement for wing forward Willie O'Dwyer.'

'The fact that the visitors were restricted to just two points from play bore testimony to the strength and resourcefulness of the Offaly side's defence in which Joe Moore, Shane Dunne and Terry Brennan were real stalwarts and goalkeeper Fergal Smyth distinguished himself with a number of fine saves that included a second half penalty. Mullinavat's best players were to be found in defensive roles, their key players being Dinny Butler, Ger Anthony, Maurice Murphy and goalkeeper Declan Duggan who did well to keep a clean sheet on what proved to be a busy afternoon for him. Paul Aylward worked really hard at midfield, but there was a dreadful lack of finishing ability up front, with Michael Duggan and Jamie Fennelly the only visiting forwards to impress.'

'An early exchange of points between Fergal Beacon from a free awarded for a foul on Alan Daly and Jamie Fennelly following a very good passing movement left the sides on level terms for the only time during the hour. The Wasps might have had a goal early on, but Alan Daly's good effort was clawed out from under the bar by goalkeeper Declan Duggan. Instead, Kilclonfert had to settle for a string of seven points before a pointed free in injury time by Conor Conway for Mullinavat closed the first half scoring, sending Laz Molloy's side in leading by 0-8 to 0-2. There was little change in the pattern of scoring on the change of ends. The Kilkenny side continued to do well enough outfield, but once within scoring range their attacks fizzled out as their forwards came up against an unyielding home defence.'

Mullinavat: Declan Duggan; Walter Burke, Maurice Murphy, Seamus Farrell; Ger

Anthony, Dinny Butler (0-1), Michael Murphy; Tony Duggan, Paul Aylward; Nicholas Anthony, Michael Duggan (captain), Liam Murphy; Jamie Fennelly (0-1), Conor Conway (0-2, frees) and Andrew McGovern.

2007/08
INTERMEDIATE
Leinster IFC Preliminary Round: Mullinavat 0-10; Clonmore (Carlow) 1-06

'This first ever appearance of Mullinavat in the Leinster Intermediate championship set the scene for future years, with a creditable single point victory over Clonmore.'

Mullinavat Squad: Conor Conway, Paddy Raftice, Ger Anthony, Seamus Farrell, Michael Farrell, Dinny Butler, Walter Burke, Michael Murphy, Tony Duggan, Willie O'Dwyer, Nicholas Anthony, Tomas Frisby, Andrew McGovern, Jamie Fennelly, Mossy Murphy, Michael Duggan, Paul Aylward, Liam Murphy Liam Anthony, John Paul Dungan, Kenny Slattery, Stephen Ryan, Declan Duggan, Damien Reid and Pat Farrell.

Leinster IFC Quarter Final: Edenderry (Offaly) 3-14; Mullinavat 2-03

'Credit Mullinavat with giving this second round Leinster intermediate club championship game in Mullinavat on Sunday 11/11/2007, the best shot that was in them. They came up somewhat short, but they never accepted the inevitability of the situation and came away with their credibility intact. Bear in mind that Edenderry were relegated to the intermediate grade last season, primarily on a technicality, and they returned with a vengeance in 2007. They have always been a proud senior football club in Offaly with a plethora of senior titles to their name. Ostensibly Mullinavat were facing a pseudo senior outfit from one of the leading football counties in the province. Whilst the winners were more familiar with the basic rudiments of the game, Mullinavat lacked nothing for effort or a willingness to do the best they knew. Their play lacked fluidity, some kicking skills and there was a lot of wrong option taking. Mind you, the more vaunted Offaly side did not have a footballer on board better than Pat Raftice, Tomas Frisby or Jamie Fennelly. In addition, Walter Burke showed a fierce determination. Even if his play was a little unorthodox, nevertheless, he never flinched from confronting the Edenderry attack as it bore down on his patch, and neither did he resist the challenge of carrying ball into the heart of the opposing defence whenever the opportunity presented itself. Another star for Mullinavat was goalkeeper, Conor Conway. Time and again he threw himself in front of the many goal-bound shots by rampant Edenderry. One save in particular in the 22nd minute defied physics, never mind the human abilities any normal goalkeeper is endowed with. An Edenderry attack had their full-forward clean in on Conway's goal. James Merrick, no mean operator for Edenderry, tried to sell a dummy to Conway. As he shaped to kick the ball to Conway's right side, he flicked off the outside of his boot to Conway's left. The Mullinavat man, as if redirecting himself in mid-air, twisted his body in a kind of reverse jack knife and palmed the ball out for a "45." The crowd applauded, included Merrick.'

'After 20 minutes the losers were giving a fine account of themselves, although adrift by 0-1 to 0-5. Raftice was practically unbeatable on the full back line, and while Mossy Murphy had to resort to much punching of the ball at that stage, any port in a storm seemed to be the tactic. Jamie Fennelly and Tomas Frisby were combining well and causing not too little trouble. Fennelly got a grand second point before the break. However, the winners had amassed 10 points: Edenderry 0-10, Mullinavat 0-2. Mullinavat never stopped trying. Like a punch-drunk boxer, they were hanging on the ropes, but they wouldn't go down. Frisby got a fine second Mullinavat goal in the 59th minute.'

Mullinavat: Conor Conway, Paddy Raftice, Michael Murphy, John Paul Dungan, Tony Duggan, Walter Burke, Michael Murphy, Michael Farrell, Dinny Butler, Andrew McGovern (0-1, free), Willie O'Dwyer, Tomas Frisby (2-0), Jamie Fennelly (0-1), Kenny Slattery (0-1) and Stephen Ryan. Subs: Declan Duggan, T Reid.

2017/18

INTERMEDIATE

Leinster IFC Preliminary Round: Durrow (Offaly) 2-17; Mullinavat 3-05

Mullinavat returned to the Leinster Championship for the first time since 2007 but suffered a nine-point loss in an away game against Durrow of Offaly.

Mullinavat Panel: Killian Dunphy; Ryan Bland, Mikey Jones, Darren Kenneally; Simon Aylward, Ger Malone, Mark Mansfield; Tom Aylward (captain), Joe Fennelly, Michael Malone, Ian Duggan, Conor Duggan; Adam Mansfield, Jamie Fennelly, Brian Phelan, Brian Kenneally, Padraic Gahan, John Walsh, James Culleton, Liam Fennelly, Jack Byrne Doyle, Conor Frisby, Shane Frisby, Seamus Farrell, Damien Aylward, James Brennan, Sean Brennan, Nathan Malone, Aaron Tynan, Joe Gahan, Willie O'Dwyer, Robbie Malone, Jack Walsh, Gavin Maher.

Durrow team and scorers: J Smith; D Magner, O Cusack (0-1), J O'Brien; J Maher, G Spollen, M Hughes; B Geraghty (1-1), M Mooney (0-2); B Fogarty (0-2), P Murphy (0-1), P Kinnarney (0-6); J Fogarty (1-0), A Geoghegan (0-3) and D Wyer (0-1). Subs used: J McKeogh, S Duignan, D Wyer, S Hughes, and S McDermott.

2018/19

INTERMEDIATE

Leinster IFC Preliminary Round: Horeswood (Wexford) 3-14; Mullinavat 1-05

'Recent star Wexford attacker PJ Banville led Horrswood to an assured victory over Kilkenny Senior champions, Mullinavat in round one of the Leinster Club Intermediate Championship at a sunny but blustery O'Kennedy Park, New Ross on Saturday. Mullinavat were hoping to repeat their success in this competition from 2007 against Clonmore (Carlow) and to chalk up a first Kilkenny win since Railyard's surprise elimination of Augrim (Wicklow) in 2014. But fresh from having secured an immediate return to Senior championship action in Wexford, Horeswood showed their season's work so far as a slick first half performance had them home-and-hosed by half time (3-8 to 0-1). In fairness it was July 29 when Mullinavat completed back-to-back Kilkenny SFC title wins, before their hurling challenge brought them to the Senior quarter finals on September 30. Horeswood in contrast had won the Wexford title the week before. They sank their claws into Mullinavat when going close with two goal chances, before PJ Banville disposed the Mullinavat keeper and swept the breaking ball to the net for the icebreaker in the fourth minute. Ian Duggan replied with a pointed free on 10 minutes, before Horeswood out-classed them to storm clear by 3-8 to 0-1 at half-time. The Kilkenny standard bearers resumed in the second half with a couple of pointed frees from Ian Duggan. The losers didn't go down without a fight. Jamie Fennelly pointed before Adam Mansfield pulled it back to 3-11 to 1-4 on 44 minutes when being put through for a one-to-one with the 'keeper after a superb delivery from midfielder Jim Culleton. Ian Duggan followed with a point to have it down to 3-11 to 1-5 after 46 minutes. Horeswood roused themselves to finish with a flourish.'

Mullinavat: Killian Dunphy; Mikey Jones, Simon Aylward, Darragh Kenneally; Liam Fennelly, Ger Malone, Joe Fennelly; Jim Culleton, Michael Malone; Ian Duggan (0-4, 3 frees), John Walsh, Conor Duggan; Adam Mansfield (1-0), Jamie Fennelly (captain 0-1) and Brian Phelan. Subs: Pauraic Gahan for Conor Duggan (54 minutes), Ryan Bland for Mikey Jones (57 minutes).

2019/20

INTERMEDIATE

Leinster IFC Preliminary Round: Mullinavat w/o Wexford champions
Leinster IFC Quarter Final: Mullinavat 3-11; Ballyboughal (Dublin) 2-11

'It was a day to remember for mighty Mullinavat on 9/11/2009. They upset all the odds when they beat Ballyboughal of Dublin in the Leinster Intermediate Football Championship in Thomastown. Inspired by the majestic Michael Malone, who was exceptional at midfield, and scored 0-5 from play, Mullinavat took control from the outset. Backed by a strong first half wind they build up a 3-7 to 0-3 lead by halftime. Malone opened the scoring with a well taken point, before Ian Duggan doubled their account from a free. In the 11th minute Malone added another point, after he took advantage of slack defending as the opposition goalie had soldiered 50 metres up the field. Mullinavat were in dreamland in the 13th minute when Oisin Knox went on a brilliant solo run before passing to the on-running Brian Phelan. The latter punched the ball to the net, 1-3 to 0-0. Phelan almost added a second goal moments later, but he slipped when about to pull the trigger. However, Adam Mansfield was on hand to fist another point. Ballyboughal were under serious pressure. The Vat confirmed their superiority with goals in the 16th and 17th minute. First a glorious long range diagonal ball from Ian Duggan found Jamie Fennelly who slotted home. Brian Phelan added his second when he walked the ball into the net. The gap was a staggering thirteen points, 3-4 to 0-0. Adam Mansfield, Ian Duggan and Michael Malone added points as the Vat maintained their thirteen points at the interval, 3-7 to 0-3.'

'The losers were a different animal after the break and got off to a blistering start. With the strong wind behind them, the Mullinavat defence was tested to the limit. Mullinavat responded admirably. The defence never panicked and refused to yield. The full back line of the tigerish Mikey Jones, the masterful Joe Fennelly, and the close marking Shane Kelly was dominant and authoritative. John Walsh at wing back, and Tom Aylward in midfield, drove forward to add to the magnificence of Michael Malone. The Noresiders managed to steady the ship and they outscored the Dubs by 0-3 to 0-1 between the 35th and 41st minute. Michael Malone, Conor Duggan and Tomas Aylward all pointed as they stayed 3-10 to 1-6 in front. Mullinavat remained in control, and after Gerry Seaver pointed twice from frees, Michael Malone replied with his fifth point from play in the 53rd minute. Mullinavat still had a nine-point lead (3-11 to 1-8). The Dubs piled on the pressure in the dying minutes. Points in quick succession from Gerry Seaver and Cormac Flynn, and Seaver again from a free narrowed the gap to six points. An injury time goal by Ballyboughal left just three points between the teams. Mullinavat were hanging on. The visitors surged forward in one last attack, but Adam Mansfield's attempt went wide.'

Mullinavat: Killian Dunphy; Mikey Jones (captain), Joe Fennelly, Shane Kelly; Mark Mansfield, Ger Malone, John Walsh; Michael Malone (0-5), Tom Aylward (0-1); Conor Duggan (0-1), Ian Duggan (0-2, one free), Adam Mansfield (0-2); Brian Phelan (2-0), Jamie Fennelly (1-0) and Oisin Knox.

Leinster IFC Semi Final: Mullinavat 2-10; Rosenalis (Laois) 1-07

'The Mullinavat men have taken the Leinster Intermediate championship by storm. Following on from their memorial victory over the Dublin champions, Ballyboughal in Thomastown two weeks ago, Mullinavat followed up with another power packed performance on Saturday 23/11/2019 against Rosenalis of Laois. John Walsh epitomised the Mullinavat spirit, and he turned in a wonderful individual performance. Despite picking up a yellow card in which Rosenalis were reduced to 14 men after their full forward Ronan Murray was sent off, following an off the ball clash, Walsh stormed into the game. His goal from the penalty spot in the 25th minute set the trend for victory. Walsh was consistently picking up breaking ball around the half back line, and he surged forward at every opportunity to provide inspiration and opportunities to all around him.'

'Defensively Mullinavat were solid. They never flinched under pressure. Mark Mansfield charged forward at every opportunity, and he capped a super second half with a glorious point. The midfield duo of Tom Aylward and Michael Malone contributed handsomely once again. They both scored 0-2, while Ian Duggan led the way in attack. He was terrific in the way he pulled the strings and orchestrated things, constantly causing the Rosenalis defence all sorts of bother. Mullinavat simply charged into the match. They led by 1-4 to 0-3 at the interval. John Walsh's goal from the penalty put them in a very strong position, while Michael Malone shot two points from play. Tom Aylward, who kicked a point at the start and an Ian Duggan free completed the first half scoring for the winners.'

'Mark and Adam Mansfield added points early in the second half to stretch the lead out to six points. While Eoin Dunne replied with a point from play for Rosenalis, the clinching score came around the 40th minute. Initially the Rosenalis defence did well to halt a Mullinavat attack, but they were slow in releasing a ball. Jamie Fennelly swiftly pounced to rifle an unstoppable shot to the net that gave goalie Tommy Shelly no chance, 2-6 to 0-4. Cilluan Callally and Ian Duggan exchanged points after that, and despite being down to 14 men, Rosenalis kept plugging away. Rosenalis refused to yield, and a James Jackson goal from a penalty gave Mullinavat some anxious moments, especially so as they had to play the last 14 minutes with 14 men, after Michael Malone was dismissed on a black card. As the Mullinavat midfielder had been booked earlier on, he received his marching orders for the second offence. It was a tight and nerve testing battle at the finish. Ian Duggan pointed around the 55th minute which concluded the scoring.'

Mullinavat: Killian Dunphy; Joe Fennelly, Shane Kelly, Mikey Jones; Mark Mansfield (0-1), Ger Malone, John Walsh (1-0, penalty); Michael Malone (0-2), Tom Aylward (0-2); Conor Duggan, Ian Duggan (0-4, 2 frees), Adam Mansfield (0-1); Brian Phelan, Jamie Fennelly (1-0) and Oisin Knox. Subs: Darren Kenneally, Liam Fennelly, Simon Aylward, Damien Aylward, Padraic Dempsey.

Leinster IFC Final: Mattock Rangers (Louth) 1-14; Mullinavat 0-11

Mullinavat were the first ever Kilkenny club to contest the Leinster Intermediate final, and even though we lost, it was a proud day for the 400 or so Mullinavat supporters who travelled to Drogheda, on a December Saturday in 2019.

The Irish Examiner report said: 'Mattock Rangers digged deep into their reserves to see off a gutsy Mullinavat. The Louth champions had to come from behind to do so, in what was an eleven-point turnaround triumph at the Gaelic Ground on Drogheda. Brian Corcoran's goal five minutes into the second half was the first time the Collin men led the game. Up until that point the Kilkenny champions were in the ascendancy. Full forward Jamie Fennelly landed two points in a row to deservedly put the underdogs 0-7 to 0-2 in front after 20 minutes. Mattock had closed the gap to one by half time, and Corcoran pounced for the match defining goal shortly after the restart. Mattock managed the lead from that point onwards to see the Louth men home to a famous victory'.

John Knox in the Kilkenny People wrote: 'The pity was that the whole of Kilkenny wasn't there to bear witness. People would have been proud, surprised and delighted too. Mullinavat's extended run in the Leinster Club Intermediate championship brought them wins over Ballyboughal (Dublin), and Rosenalis (Laois). Alas Mattock Rangers (Louth) proved a challenge too big in the provincial final in windswept Drogheda on Saturday. The Rod Iron men, making history as the first ever Kilkenny team to contest the final, departed the scene with heads held high. For me Mullinavat's level of performance was a revelation. They played with confidence and without fear. They were comfortable on, and in their use of the ball. They knew what they were about, swarming around colleagues in possession to offer options, and looping run after looping run. Long high and hopeful passes were off the agenda. It's keep-ball stuff, playing the percentage game, to cut errors to a minimum. And it worked to a large degree. History was left at a first appearance in the final by a Kilkenny team, but the occasion wasn't marked with silverware'.

Mullinavat: Killian Dunphy; Shane Kelly, Joe Fennelly, Mikey Jones; John Walsh (0-1) Ger Malone (0-1), Mark Mansfield; Tom Aylward Michael Malone (0-1); Conor Duggan, Ian Duggan (0-4, 3 frees), Adam Mansfield (0-1); Oisin Knox (0-1), Jamie Fennelly (0-2) and Brian Phelan. Subs: Padraic Dempsey for Mansfield (49 minutes), Liam Fennelly for Phelan (49 minutes), Simon Aylward for Jones (51 minutes), Darren Kenneally for Conor Duggan (58 minutes).

2020/21

Not held due to COVID.

2022/23

INTERMEDIATE

Leinster IFC R1: Mullinavat 2-06; Bracknagh (Offaly) 1-07

'Five months after winning the Kilkenny Senior football title, Mullinavat upset the odds again as they defeated Bracknagh of Offaly in the opening round of the Leinster Intermediate Football Championship at John Lockes Park, Callan on 22/10/2022. Bracknagh dominated the opening half, but their 1-4 to 0-2 half-time advantage was scant reward for their play, and they were made pay for a number of misses when Mullinavat turned the tide in the second half. Mullinavat captain Michael Malone kickstarted the Kilkenny side's revival when scoring a fantastic individual goal at the start of the second half and they then completed the comeback when subs Padraic Gahan and Oisin Knox scored a goal and a point respectively.'

'Bracknagh were well fancied coming into the game, and all looked to be going to plan when Stefan Geoghegan knocked over the first two points from play. Mullinavat responded with their first point via Michael Malone in the 8th minute, but just two minutes later they were on the back foot when Bracknagh got the opening goal of the game. Mullinavat replied with a John Walsh free but despite hitting eight first half wides, the visitors kicked the last two points of the half as Robin Galbrith and Michael Cunningham both found the target."

'Geoghegan and Ian Duggan exchanged points at the beginning of the second half before the tie was turned on its head when Mick Malone goaled for Mullinavat in the 36th minute. Malone's effort left only two between the teams and it soon became one after a Tom Aylward score. Peter and Michael Cunningham both pointed in the 45th and 47th minutes for Bracknagh but remarkably they wouldn's score again in the final 10 minutes. As a result, Mullinavat rallied and after Ian Duggan converted his second free, they struck for goal when Padraic Gahan kicked a shot to the net after being set up by Liam Fennelly and Oisin Knox. Knox then kicked the insurance score in stoppage time as Mullinavat claimed a big victory.'

Mullinavat: Killian Dunphy; Joe Fennelly, Simon Aylward, Mikey Jones; Shane Kelly, Ger Malone, John Walsh (0-1, one free); James Culleton, Tom Aylward (0-1); Adam Mansfield, Michael Malone (1-1), Conor Duggan; Ian Duggan (0-2, two frees), Liam Fennelly and Brian Phelan. Sub - Oisin Knox (0-1) for Phelan half time, Padraig Dempsey for Conor Duggan 43 minutes, Padraic Gahan (1-0) for Mikey Jones 45 minutes, Peter McDonald for James Culleton 61 minutes.

Leinster IFC Quarter Final: Mullinavat 3-09; Shandonagh (Westmeath) 0-15

'Mullinavat showed their opening round victory over Bracknagh was no fluke as they overcame Westmeath side Shandonagh at John Locke Park in Callan on Saturday afternoon. Like against Bracknagh, the Kilkenny side's goal threat played a huge part in the victory with Michael Malone putting in a fine individual display for the winners. In that round one victory, the Vegas boys were slow out of the blocks and that was the case here again with their first score from play only arriving in the 22nd minute from the boot of Ian Duggan. With Brian Kavanagh scoring 11 points in total for Shandonagh, they had opened up a three-point lead, but Michael Malone's goal changed all the momentum as Mullinavat levelled matters by half-time.'

'Michael and Ger Malone then added further goals in the second period and despite Shandonagh finishing strong, Mullinavat held on to claim a three-point win. Brian Kavanagh and Michael Malone shared early points before Shandonagh took control when moving into a 0-4 to 0-1 lead by the 11th minute. Malone kept Mullinavat in touch with a pair of frees but Shandonagh were playing all the football at this stage. With Kavanagh knocking over a series of superb efforts from play, the visitors led by three points. After Ian Duggan reduced the deficit on the back of a well worked move, Mullinavat began to get their game going. While Kavanagh replied with his fifth point of the half, the home side soon got the opening goal of the game. With Liam Fennelly and Adam Mansfield finding a hole in the Shandonagh defence, the ball found its way to Mick Malone. He found the bottom corner with a precisely taken left footed attempt. The goal put Mullinavat into the lead for the first time although Tom Molloy did equalise before the end of the half.'

'Hitting 1-1 without reply at the beginning of the second half pushed Mullinavat into a commanding lead when a brilliantly palmed goal from Ger Malone was followed up by a point from Liam Fennelly. Kavanagh kept Shandonagh ticking over with a free in the 39th minute, but after the Westmeath side squandered a number of opportunities Mullinavat took full control with 1-2 on the trot as Michael Malone's second goal gave the winners a 3-8 to 0-9 lead. A black card to Mullinavat midfielder Tom Aylward allowed Shandonagh to mount a late revival as they aimed to overturn the sizeable deficit. A pair of points from both Kavanagh and Molloy left three points between the sides but the clock was on Mullinavat's side as they held on to secure another big win.'

Mullinavat: Killian Dunphy; Joe Fennelly, Simon Aylward, Mikey Jones; Shane Kelly, Ger Malone (1-0), John Walsh; James Culleton, Tom Aylward (0-1); Adam Mansfield, Michael Malone (2-5, three frees), Oisin Knox; Ian Duggan (0-2), Liam Fennelly (0-1) and Padraig Dempsey. Subs - Conor Duggan for Mikey Jones 49 minutes, Padraic Gahan for Oisin Knox 54 minutes, Brian Phelan for Fennelly 56 minutes, Peter McDonald for Ian Duggan 59 minutes.

Leinster IFC Semi Final: Fethard St Mogue's (Wexford) 0-07; Mullinavat 0-05

'It was a tight and tactical affair, but Wexford side St Mogue's did enough to edge Mullinavat out of the Leinster intermediate club football championship at John Locke Park in Callan. A big travelling support descended on the Kilkenny venue, and they left the happier as St Mogue's claimed a two-point victory. Both teams lined out with a full-time sweeper and, as a result, defences were very much on top. While Mullinavat will be disappointed at the end result, the visitors had the better of proceedings. Unlike their previous two Leinster championship victories against Bracknagh and Shandonagh, the Kilkenny side started quite well, and they were on the scoreboard within three minutes when Ian Duggan converted a free. The lead didn't last long though, with successive St Mogue's efforts from Morgan Ellis and John Tubritt putting the visitors into a one-point lead. St Mogue's then pushed their advantage out to two points when Cian Byrne knocked over a free, before Ian Duggan doubled his and Mullinavat's tally a couple of minutes later. Mullinavat's main asset in attack was again their captain Michael Malone. The championship top scorer had two big goal chances in as many minutes for the Vegas boys but, after shooting wide originally, the centre forward then squandered another opportunity when St Mogue's goalkeeper William Doyle made a great save from close in. St Mogue's were more economical from play and by the half-time break they led 0-4 to 0-2 when Cian Byrne curled a beautiful effort between the posts.'

'The visitors continued to dictate the tempo at the start of the second half but, after a couple of careless wides, Mullinavat hit back with their opening score from play when a quick free from Ian Duggan found James Culleton who found the target in style. The Fethard based Wexford side soon restored their two-point buffer when John Tubritt scored from play, and they looked in control by the halfway mark of the second half. While Mullinavat struggled to get scores from play, and credit must go to the St Mogue's rearguard for that, the home side were still getting scores on the board and there was only a point between the teams when Ian Duggan converted his third free of the game. Mullinavat corner back Mikey Jones then got forward to score as he equalised the game at 0-5 apiece. Mullinavat seemed to have all the momentum as the game crept into the final 10 minutes. Michael Aylward's team looked to have a big penalty claim when Padraic Gahan appeared to be pulled back in the square, but Offaly referee Fergal Smyth waved away the Mullinavat complaints. That opportunity for a goal really came back to haunt the Vat as they wouldn't score again in the remaining time allotted. After a Cian Byrne pointed free helped the Wexford side retake the lead, the result was then settled with an insurance score from John Tubritt.'

Mullinavat: Killian Dunphy; Joe Fennelly, Simon Aylward, Mikey Jones (0-1); Shane Kelly, Ger Malone, John Walsh; James Culleton (0-1), Tom Aylward; Ian Duggan (0-3, frees), Michael Malone, Conor Duggan; Adam Mansfield, Liam Fennelly and Oisin Knox. Sub: Padraic Gahan for Conor Duggan 38 minutes.

2023/24
INTERMEDIATE
Leinster IFC R1: Ballylinan (Laois) 1-14; Mullinavat 0-07

'Mullinavat exited the 2023 AIB Leinster Intermediate Football Championship following a 10-point defeat by Laois side Ballylinan at a sunny afternoon in Stradbally, on Saturday. The overall Mullinavat showing was better than the final result suggests, where they were just 0-6 to 0-3 behind at the interval, and only behind by a single point, five minutes into the new half. Ballylinan had won their county title on the last day of September, the Kilkenny side three months previously, on the last day of June. Football wise Mullinavat were "ring rusty" and it showed, against an opponent who are exclusively a football club, and a serious one at that. They had been relegated from the Senior championship last year, after 50 years in the premier grade of Laois football.'

'Ballylinan were first off the mark with a point from Cathal Dunne. Three minutes later Mullinavat replied with a Padraig Dempsey score. The next four-pointed scores were all from the Laois representatives (0-5 to 0-1). Michael Malone pulled a point back for Mullinavat, replied to by a Gary Walsh point from play, this shortly after a fine save by Mark McNamara in the Mullinavat goal, following a close range shot from the same player. Adam Mansfield reduced the margin to just three points with a point before the break. Half Time – Ballylinan 0-6; Mullinavat 0-3.'

'Ryan Brady of Ballylinan had been black carded in the two minutes added time of the first half, so Mullinavat resumed with a numerical advantage. They took advantage with scores from John Walsh with a fine catch and point, and a Michael Malone free. The lead was now just a single point. A feature of the game was breaks upfield from the Ballylinan number three Seamus Lacey, and on one such sally he pointed (0-7 to 0-5). When Mullinavat's Simon Aylward picked up a black card the tide seemed to turn against Mullinavat. Gary Walsh increased the lead with two points, the first a free. It was now 0-9 to 0-5. On 44 minutes Mullinavat had a real goal chance when John Walsh and Oisin Knox combined well, but the Laois keeper Tom Wright intercepted to foil the attack. One minute later Ballylinan grabbed a goal that really altered the pattern of play. Another one of those Lacey breakaways, and a lay off to full forward Ciaran Fennessy, who finished emphatically (1-9 to 0-5). The same player pointed a minute later.'

'Michael Malone got a much-needed Vegas score from a free, but a sequence of four points from the excellent Gary Walsh, three from play, concluded their scoring (1-14 to

0-6). To their credit Mullinavat kept going, and a fine move involving James Culleton and substitute Sean Fitzpatrick, was pointed by the fist of Oisin Knox.

Mullinavat: Mark McNamara; Mikey Jones, Joe Fennelly, Ian Mansfield; Shane Kelly, Ger Malone, Simon Aylward (captain); James Culleton, Tom Aylward; John Walsh (0-1), Michael Malone (0-3, one free), Padraig Dempsey (0-1); Adam Mansfield (0-1), Oisin Knox (0-1) and Padraic Gahan. Subs: Conor Duggan for Shane Kelly (blood), Conor Duggan for Simon Aylward, Sean Fitzpatrick for Pauric Gahan, Fiachra Knox for Adam Mansfield, Jonathon Cawley for Mikey Jones.

Heroes Amongst Us Forever

MULLINAVAT GAA CLUB
PRESIDENTS EVENING (15/2/2020)

The club held a special evening, to recognise the excellent service to our club by our four club Presidents on February 15th, 2020. The evening was extremely well attended, and all four club presidents, Richie Carroll, Jim Conway, Ned Haberlin and Liam Kenneally were overwhelmed that the club would recognise them in such a way. A Waterford Crystal clock each, was presented to the Presidents to mark their many years of service to the club.

Sadly, we lost one of these four gentlemen in January 2024… Jim Conway (RIP).

Back Row: Tommy Frisby, Andy Aylward, Michael Law, Ned Conway. Front Row: Ned Haberlin, Liam Kenneally, Jim Conway, Richie Carroll.

JIM CONWAY RIP

Everyone remotely involved in Mullinavat GAA club, and indeed Mullinavat parish and further afield, were saddened in January 2024, to hear of the death of Mr Jim Conway. Jim was a former player, almost lifelong treasurer (1962-2019), and unofficially Mr Mullinavat GAA Club.

'President Jim'. We gave him that title officially in 2020, but he was a man who never sought recognition for a lifelong commitment to the GAA and particularly to his local club. Whether fund raising, lining pitches, acting as umpire, treasurer and numerous other tasks he took on over the years, and way too many to list here, it's safe to say there's practically nothing Jim wouldn't do for Mullinavat GAA club. From cutting the grass, to sorting out All-Ireland Final tickets for club members, no job was ever too big or small for Jim. Even in recent times, whilst not at meetings or matches, he always had the inside track on everything that was going on inside Mullinavat GAA Club.

Jim received a Sports Volunteer Award back in 2004 from then President Mary McAleese, and in the time since then he probably did enough to earn such an award again, perhaps many times over! We reprint below an article from the Kilkenny People (16/07/2004), when Jim was bestowed with that volunteer's award at Áras An Uachtaráin. 'Normally he can be found on duty as an umpire at games in the local field. But last week one of the most discreet workers in sport in Kilkenny enjoyed tea with the President. Mullinavat GAA club official, Jim Conway, discarded the white coat of an umpire and instead donned his finery for a meeting with President Mary McAleese. Mr Conway of Killandrew, Mullinavat, was one of the chosen few honoured during a day for Sports Volunteers in Áras an Uachtaráin.

'He has served as treasurer of Mullinavat GAA club for 43 years. He organised the famous Gold Watch Tournament in the town, which attracted teams for all parts of the country for over 28 years. And he has been caretaker of the club grounds virtually since he was able to push a pitch marker. Mr Conway has been an umpire for over 30 years, and only recently he was on duty by a post during a Kilkenny camogie final at Nowlan Park. Anything that needed doing in Mullinavat, Jim Conway was prepared to put his shoulder to the wheel. "He has gracefully given his life to the GAA," Mr Hickey added. "He is a gentleman, a person any club would be proud to have involved".

' "If you ever want to find him, he will be the umpire on the duty at the right-hand post of the goal at the town end in Mullinavat on match days," advised County Board chairman, Ned Quinn. "The GAA is blessed to have people like Jim Conway in its ranks," he added. "

RICHIE CARROLL

Player, selector, referee, dance ticket seller and in recent years chief Piltown draw ticket seller, President Richie has always had his shoulder to the wheel for the Mullinavat club.

Whilst probably most noted and remembered as a top-class referee, prior to this he had a 20-year playing career with the Mullinavat club. He has two Southern Junior Hurling Championship medals to his name (from 1974 and 1978), along with numerous tournament victories.

Richie has refereed the 1996 Kilkenny County Junior Hurling final, numerous South Junior Hurling finals, and many big games within the county, at both Senior and Intermediate. Richie lives at Rosscinan, Mullinavat and was married to his late wife, Breda. He has served the club as Vice Chairman, underage selector and several other roles.

In his working life, Richie was employed at Shaws Department Store in Waterford, and he has taken his sales experience gained there into fund raising for the GAA club. In former days, he was one of the chief dance ticket sellers for Mullinavat Fete, and nowadays he is equally the chief ticket seller of Piltown draw tickets for our club.

All clubs in the county would be envious of having an active member such as Richie, and we are delighted to have him, still very much involved in fund raising, and a worthy President of our club.

NED HABERLIN

Lorry driver, bus driver, shopkeeper, whilst always also a servant of the club he loves, that's President Ned Haberlin. Ned came to the parish from Glenmore and married local lady, Breda McEvoy.

The club has always been a major part of Ned's life, where he has served at committee level at both adult and particularly juvenile level. He commands the respect of people not just within the club, but within the parish also. He was an active member of the Mullinavat Fete committee and would be best remembered as one of its trusted and reliable dance ticket sellers. Within the GAA club itself, Ned often operated dual roles, with both the adult and juvenile sections of the club. He has been PRO and Bord na Nog secretary for many years. In the latter role, he has always stressed the importance of good behaviour, and always encouraged parents to take part in supporting their youngsters on the playing field.

Ned stepped aside from full committee involvement in 2005 but can still be seen at almost all club games. We were delighted to add Ned as a club President a few years back and thank him for his service to his club and parish over many, many years.

LIAM KENNEALLY

Liaison officer, driver, coach, umpire and friend to all children at the St Beacon's primary school, President Liam has always been an active club member.

At our 2019 AGM, a letter was sent in directly from the school, concerning Liam, stating how much he had given to the community, via his school liaison officer role, over a 40 plus year period. For every one of those 40 plus years, Liam threatened to retire, only to be back in action the next month, next week and sometimes even the next day!

Liam loves the Mullinavat club, and equally loved his role as school liaison officer. In his working life, Liam was employed at Grannagh Paper Mills amongst other things, and is married to Kitty. They resides at Ballynooney.

Liam has made a lasting impression with all the kids in the school; they loved to see Liam arrive, and proof of this is that whenever a wedding happens involving a former St Beacon's pupil occurs, Liam is generally on the guest list! Even though officially now retired from his role, we in the club have no doubt that Liam won't be far away when the Mullinavat school line out in future hurling and football competitions.

OPENING OF MULLINAVAT COMMUNITY WALKWAY (26/12/2023)

The cutting of the ribbon to officially open the walkway was done by three of the club's four Presidents, Richie Carroll, Ned Haberlin and Liam Kenneally on St Stephen's Day, 2023. The club's fourth President Jim Conway was unable to attend. With the ribbon cut, the locals set about walking or running their GOAL mile on a crisp December morning. The GAA Club would like to encourage all to now use this facility in the years ahead.

A FEW CLUB STALWARTS NO LONGER WITH US

Below we remember a few individuals no longer with us, but fondly remembered within Mullinavat GAA Club. Hundreds of others could have featured under this heading had space allowed. RIP to all.

Deep are the memories, precious they stay
No passing of time can take them away

GARDA PAT O'NEILL

Pat O'Neill was an outstanding young hurler for the Mullinavat club. He captained Kilkenny in the 1939 All-Ireland Minor final loss to Cork, on the day when World War Two broke out, Pat's father, also called Pat, had been stationed in Mullinavat as a Garda for around 50 years. Pat featured on two of the most famous days in Mullinavat GAA club's history. He starred as full-back on the 1938 Minor winning team v. Dicksboro (4-5 to 2-3) and in 1939 he came on as a substitute for the Mullinavat Junior team on the day the club won a first Junior County Hurling final since 1917 in a 5-0 to 3-1 victory over Freshford. Pat came on as a substitute that famous day, when Willie Durney was injured. As a Garda Pat served most of his career in County Wexford, and when he died in 1984 his funeral was attended by representatives from both Mullinavat GAA club and Kilkenny GAA County Board. Pat O'Neill is only one of four Mullinavat players who made the 20-man squad for the 1939 Minor All Ireland Final, a 5-02 to 2-2 loss to Cork. Fr Michael Holden (missed county final due to clerical studies), Philip Hoban and Mick Walsh were the others. Not on the final squad but credited with seeing Kilkenny Minor action in 1939 were Danny McLaughlin, and J Purcell.

JOHN WALSH, THE MILL

The death occurred in Waterford Infirmary on Friday 3/3/1967 of Mr John Walsh, The Mill. Mullinavat, following a brief illness. Son of the late Mr and Mrs John Walsh, Mullinavat, he was a member of a family long associated with the business, farming, sporting and social life of the parish. A former well-known Junior hurler and footballer, he won a Junior Hurling Championship with his native parish in 1939. He later figured in many hectic Senior games, including a number of county finals. In the football grade, he won a number of county Senior hurling titles with the neighbouring parish of Glenmore, and was also a member of Kilkenny Senior hurling selection committee in 1954 and 1955. A keen follower of outdoor sport, particularly racing and hunting, he was from a family long associated as horse racing owners and trainers. He was secretary of Mullinavat Harriers for many years up to the time of his death

WILLIAM DURNEY, BIGWOOD

The death occurred in August 1992 of Mr William Durney. He was a native of Bigwood, Mullinavat and was the second of two sons born to the union of the late John and Margaret Durney. From farming stock, the late William was approaching his 80th year. For some time, he was employed in England, returning some years ago to reside in Waterford. He was a noted hurler in his day and played his games with Mooncoin and Mullinavat selections in Kilkenny Championship hurling. Many indeed would have felt during his playing career that he was county calibre; he usually lined out at centrefield and in the great Mullinavat team that reached Senior hurling final stage in 1940 partnered Paddy Holden in that position. He was buried in his native Bigwood after Requiem Mass was celebrated by Monsignor Tommy Maher, PP, Mullinavat.

He was uncle to John Durney, Bigwood; Margo Power, Inistioge: and Brenda O'Farrell, Tinneranny, New Ross. He was brother of Tom Durney, Bigwood, who passed seven years earlier, in 1985. William Durney was mentioned in all reports during the Senior hurling final of 1940 which saw Carrickshock beat Mullinavat, and also in the Junior hurling championship win in 1939. Durney gave star performances m both games. Even when injured in the 1939 encounter, with Freshford players getting the best, they reintroduced the injured Durney, and it was not long until the gallant Bigwood man had this in control.

The 1939 victory is recorded elsewhere in this publication.

JOHN SUTTON, RAHARD (1928-1989)

John Sutton, Ballyrobin, Slieverue, who died in May 1989, was one of the Gaelic Games best exponents in both codes. He was born in Rahard, Mullinavat, to the late Peter and Mrs Margaret (nee Foskin) Sutton. From farming stock, his family were long associated with the greater South Kilkenny area in a variety of ways. In the Mullinavat Centenary History, John was described as one of the outstanding hurlers to have graced the Gaelic Athletic Association pitches in both grades. He played for his beloved Kilkenny and in the famous black and amber he won an All-Ireland SHC medal in 1957. He featured prominently against Waterford in 1957, a day which he cherished in his mind for many a year. He went on to play for Leinster, to travel to America and be feted by the Gaels in New York and to have played for an Ireland Selection in 1955. His popularity was widespread. When his death reached South Kilkenny people, it was said by one admirer: 'You are saying goodbye to a great hurler'.

He played for Mullinavat, Glenmore and Carrickshock in hurling, and a St Senan's Selection in the football code. He played competitive hurling up to his 37th year when he lined out for Glenmore in a Senior Kilkenny Hurling Championship final. In 1966, he was nominated as a county hurling selector. He was a hero to many.

For his native Mullinavat he played all his Juvenile and Junior hurling with the club. Then he moved to the neighbouring club of Carrickshock and thereafter to

Glenmore. John had very few enemies and many friends. He was a great character, though not in great health for some time prior to his death. He was a familiar figure at many matches and watched with a careful eye on his son's performance in the jerseys of the Slieverue teams. John also loved the regular flutter on the horses, and it was in the process of going about his favourite pastime that he fell ill and died a short time afterwards. The obsequies on both days of his funeral were massive. He was a hero to many, hurlers from all quarters attended. Local parish priest, Monsignor Thomas Maher, who had trained Senior hurling teams for Kilkenny, flanked (with former colleagues from the late 50s) his coffin as it was taken to its resting place in St James' Cemetery, Glenmore.

He was married to the former Nell Doyle from Glenmore village and bore nine children: Sons: Peter, Australia; Michael, England; and John, Paul and Brendan, Ballyrobin, Slieverue. Daughters: Margaret Duggan, England; Geraldine Kirwan, Glenmore; Ann Cleary, Ferrybank; and Miss Carmel Sutton, Ballyrobin. He was the last of that family of Suttons, predeceased by his brothers, Peter, Narabane; Thomas, PC, Rahard; Patrick, Upper Kilmacow and Tramore, Co. Waterford; and a sister, the late Mrs Josephine Holden, Dun Laoghaire, Co. Dublin (mother of the Holden brothers who helped in no small way in the resurgence of hurling and football in the capital). He was a cousin of the Sutton families of Rossinan, and the Foskin families of Ballydaw and Rathcurby, Mooncoin. Politicians from all parties were represented at his funeral, headed by Minister for State, Mr Liam Aylward. Business, social and other sporting organisations also sent representatives to lay to rest one of the best-known hurlers in South Kilkenny.

JACK DUGGAN FARNOGUE (1902-1990)

Any search for a list of Mullinavat All-Ireland Senior Hurling medallists will always start with the name of Jack Duggan. Jack was born in Farnogue, Mullinavat, and was an outstanding player of the 1930s. He played in seven All-Ireland SHC Finals: in 1931 (3 games), 1932, 1935 1936 and 1937. He won three All-Ireland Senior medals (in 1932-1933-1935), along with six Leinster SHC medals (1931-1932-1933-1935-1936-1937), the last of those as Kilkenny captain.

Jack was a Gaelic footballer of distinction also and played with Mullinavat in the 1935 county Senior football final, when we lost to Barrow Rovers, a combination team from Glenmore and Slieverue, 0-5 to 0-3. In an era of players representing clubs other than their native parishes, Jack went on to win:

5 Kilkenny SHC medals with Mooncoin (1927, 1928, 1929, 1932, 1936)
1 Kilkenny SHC medal with Eire Og (1939)

2 Kilkenny SFC medals with Tullogher (1930,1931)

2 Kilkenny SFC medals with Glenmore (1938, 1939)

Jack also won a National Hurling League title in Kilkenny in 1933, and, as a result, toured the USA with Kilkenny in 1934. Jack's brother, Larry came on as a substitute in the 1935 final, a great day for the brothers, both winning a Senior All-Ireland together. Jack died in August 1990, aged 87, a man who himself was a superstar in the era of the likes of Mick Mackey.

(Jack was an uncle of Tommie Duggan, who has given much service to the Mullinavat club in more recent times as a player, referee and Gaelic football officer roles over the years).

JOHNNY WALSH, BUCKSTOWN

Johnny Walsh was one of the best-known GAA people in South Kilkenny. He played Junior hurling for the club, was the first secretary of the Mullinavat fete committee, and Johnny served for 25 years as caretaker of Mullinavat GAA grounds. He is still fondly remembered. At the 1976 annual meeting of Mullinavat hurling club the field caretaker, from Buckstown, announced that he was retiring at the end of that year. He has been widely praised on many occasions by club teams using the Mullinavat venue, for his excellent care and layout of the pitch for games, in what was the headquarters of Kilkenny GAA in the south of the county.

He had been associated with the GAA for many years and was for a period a delegate from the Southern Board to the Kilkenny Co Board. During that time he devoted much care and attention to the upkeep and lay-out of the pitch for games, including many important county championship ties, and his efforts at all times won the approval and high praise of officials and players for his efficient work.

Johnny was also postman in the Mullinavat area, and after 20 years efficient service in that role, in March 1979 he retired from this position. To mark his retirement, he was presented with a colour television set by the people of the districts. His gift was presented by Rev Canon Hughes, PP, Mullinavat, Dean of Ossory, who paid tribute to Johnny for his long and dedicated service to the local community and wished him every happiness in his retirement. He was also presented with a silver watch on behalf of Mullinavat hurling club for his great work as caretaker at the Gaelic field for 25 years until his retirement.

KEITH MADIGAN, BALLINTLEA (1981-2001)

The tragic death of Keith Madigan in a road accident on the Ballyluskey Road, near Ballynooney, in the early hours of Monday (19/2/2001) caused great grief in

Mullinavat parish, and further afield. The 19-year-old then Waterford Institute of Technology student was equally talented in hurling and Gaelic football; Keith had helped Good Counsel, New Ross to win the 1999 All-Ireland Colleges Senior Football Championship. Showing his love for both codes, he had engaged in two Gaelic football games in a 48-hour period prior to his untimely death. On Saturday 17th February Keith played with Kilkenny Under-21 football team versus Wicklow in the Leinster Championship. On the following afternoon, Sunday 18th February, he had helped Mullinavat beat Graigue Ballycallan in a county Senior football league game. Keith had crammed a lot of activity into his young life, since scoring a goal in the 1993 Mullinavat Primary Schools B Hurling final loss to Ballyragget. When Mullinavat won their first Kilkenny Under-21 Roinn A Football final (2000) held a few weeks before his death, on 28/01/2001, Keith was a vital part of a Mullinavat 1-8 to 2-4 victory over O'Loughlin Gaels. Keith's funeral was a poignant affair with his coffin flanked by guards of honour from teammates in Mullinavat, Good Counsel and Kilkenny jerseys. Keith was a quiet young man off the field and is still fondly remembered within Mullinavat GAA club to this day.

MICK HOLDEN (1954–2007)

The sudden death of Mick Holden, the former Dublin footballer and hurler, in 2007, cast a gloom over the GAA community in Dublin, but, also over his many relatives and acquaintances in Mullinavat. Here is a few memories of Mick, from an article by former Kilkenny librarian Jim Fogarty.

'Mick's father, Tom, from the Knockbrown area of Mullinavat, was one of the founders of the Cuala club in Dublin in 1961. Cuala is based in Dalkey within the administrative area of Dun-Laoghaire Rathdown, not an obvious catchment area for gaelic games. When Tom Holden moved from Mullinavat to take up a job with Boland's Bakery in Grand Canal Street, he joined the Erin's Own hurling club which trained in the Phoenix Park. Holden on being transferred to Dun Laoghaire, had a 16-mile journey by bicycle to play with his club.

'Marriage to Josie, also a native of Mullinavat, led to involvement with juvenile hurlers (including his three sons) in the Dun Laoghaire area. Through mergers with existing clubs, Cuala was born. Mick, together with his brothers PJ and Vinny, spent many happy holidays around Mullinavat. He was related, among others, to the former Kilkenny midfielder, John Sutton, the former Kilkenny centre-back, Brian Hogan, Shamrock's corner-back, Pádraig Holden and through marriage to All-Ireland winning double captain, Liam Fennelly. Mick's preference was for hurling rather than football. It was playing the latter game that he won an All-

Ireland Senior football medal in 1983, starring at corner-back. He also played on the Compromise Rules team which defeated Australia in 'Aussie Land' with Jack O'Shea as captain, and Kevin Heffernan as manager.

'Mick lost a finger in a Leinster football game when an opponent stood on his hand. He won 4 Leinster football medals (in 1979, 1983, 1984 and 1985). Hurling, however, was Mick's real passion. He played, at the age of 17, in the 1972 All-Ireland Under-21 final which Dublin lost to Galway. His brothers PJ and Vinny were also members of that team. He scored 2-3 from play against Kilkenny in the 1979 Leinster Senior Hurling Championship. The Cuala club won their first county Senior hurling title in 1989 defeating St Vincents by 2-8 to 1-5. JJ Barrett in his Evening Herald match report wrote: "In the left corner-back position was Mick Holden. I don't think there is a more popular man in Dublin than Mick Holden". Vinny Holden was full-back. The other brother, PJ was brought on as a substitute, and with time running out he struck the most important goal in Cuala's history.

'The Holden's father, Tom, was one of the three selectors of the 1989 team. In 1991, Cuala won their second county SHC in three years when defeating Craobh Chiaráin in a replay. Mick and Vinny were again on the first fifteen with PJ, who had lost 80 percent vision in one eye, as a sub. Cuala won their third title in 1994, defeating Crumlin in the final. It was a sweet success for Mick and Vinny Holden, both now over 40. Mick's popularity is evident from the many tributes paid to him, over the last week or two. All followers of gaelic games in Kilkenny will wish that the sod of his beloved Baile Atha Cliath will rest lightly on him in the graveyard by Shanganagh cliffs.

'Go ndéana Dia trócaire ar a anam dílis.'

FR J GALLAVAN

Father Gallavan was curate in Mullinavat from July 1952 to 1968. When he arrived in the parish, the hurling club was at a low ebb and needed reorganisation. After several years without a properly functioning club, Fr. Gallavan arranged a meeting at the Old School House on October 28th, 1952. This meeting resulted in the reformation of Mullinavat hurling club. Within three months, the club was back in hurling action, after several years absence, albeit only in a home and away challenge game with Kilmacow Hurling and Football Club. Mullinavat hurling club was back and were already getting ready for the 1953 Kilkenny Junior Championship. Leg one was played in Mullinavat on December 7th, 1952, with a Mullinavat win, by eight points, 6-4 to 4-2. Leg two, a week later was played in Ballykeoghan, Kilmacow, with the home side winning by 10 points. During his time in Mullinavat Fr Gallavan can be credited with being a driving force in the purchase of the original hurling field as a trustee and won many friends from his time in Mullinavat.

MONSIGNOR TOMMY MAHER (1922–2015)

Heroes do not always wear capes, and proof of this was the Gowran cleric who was PP in Mullinavat from 1983 to 1998. He coached Mullinavat out of the Junior grade in 1984, and the club's first team hasn't returned there since. Before this, he had led Kilkenny to seven Senior All-Irelands between 1957 and 1978. He is credited as being the man who changed Kilkenny hurling so much with renegade thinking.

At the Mullinavat AGM in 1987 Monsignor Maher announced his retirement from active participation in the GAA. Those present at the Mullinavat Hurling Club at the 24/11/1986 meeting, without possibly realising it, witnessing the end of an era in hurling in Kilkenny. Before he finished his address to the meeting, Monsignor Maher announced that the time had come for him to retire as trainer, and so after 50 years of active participation in hurling, both on and off the field, the man known to all lovers of the game, wherever they may be, as 'Father Tommy Maher', had finally decided to call it a day.

It was back in the Summer of 1936 that he played his first competitive game at hurling. Later on he became a member of the Kilkenny team for a number of years in the 1940s. But it was as a trainer that his name became a household word. For 21 years he trained Kilkenny teams, winning seven All-Ireland titles in the process. By this time he had become President of St Kieran's College, and during these years the boys of St Kieran's were a force to be reckoned with. When he was transferred to Mullinavat as PP he immediately took up the challenge to train the Mullinavat Junior hurling team. In his second year as trainer the team won the Junior County Championship and in 1986, the year that he decided to retire, he went out in a blaze of glory, having trained the Mullinavat Special Junior Team to win a county championship. For those in the Mullinavat club, who were privileged to know and work with him, their only wish was that Father Tommy Maher's company would continue to be present at the hurling field in Mullinavat for many years to come.

On 17/7/1998 Mullinavat parish honoured Rev Monsignor Tommy Maher, on the Golden Jubilee of his ordination, and on his retirement from the pastorate of the parish. Rev Laurence Forristal, Bishop of the Diocese of Ossory, presided over a Mass of thanksgiving, to mark the golden jubilee of the ordination to the priesthood of Rev Monsignor Thomas Maher P.P. Mullinavat in St Beacons Church, Mullinavat on that Friday evening. Here's an excellent piece of poetry, by Tony Fitzpatrick, commemorating Fr Maher's productivity, during his time in Mullinavat.

On this your Golden Jubilee, we congratulate you Fr. Maher,
To have a leader such as you is very rare by far.
You came here as Parish Priest in nineteen eighty-three,
and ever since the day you came, you've been busy as a bee.
Fr. Carrigan was the first Curate, and then came Fr. Dunne,
Now we've Fr. Purcell, who's well liked by everyone.
Your housekeeper's name was Nora, to her it was no bother,
She cared for you, as if she was your own beloved Mother.
The hurling club did not delay, and fast they did approach.
to ask the new parish priest if he would be their coach.
You took them on and very soon, the plugs began to spark,
and by the end of eighty-four, they were on for Nowlan Park.
Well then t'was down to business, as you put on your thinking cap.
on and bit by bit, Mullinavat, was coming on the map.
You extended the new graveyard, and the car park, both were small,
You swapped a field with Bernie, and the work was free for all.
The convent it was getting shook, the boy's school was no better.
So, you said you'd build a new one, with the boys and girls together.
Now the new school it is built, it's admired by one and all.
You can enter it from Buckstown Hill or down by Harneys Hall.
The Parishioners they were happy, as things were looking good.
But it wasn't all in Mullinavat, you also had Bigwood.
You called aside the unemployed, with those you picked your teams.
The work they done were second to none, they were known locally as the schemes.
The boys school now was vacant, it looked so damp and cold.
You replaced it with sixteen houses, which accommodates both young and old.
Although you are our Parish Priest, held in high esteem by all.
For had you been our Taoiseach the dole queues would be small.
So, God bless you Fr. Maher, for all that you have done.
Many years of health and happiness till your Final Day will come.

– Tony Fitzpatrick, July 1998

MICK HEFFERNAN, AYLWARDSTOWN, GLENMORE

Mick Heffernan was one of the few Mullinavat players to feature in two Kilkenny Senior hurling finals. Before the parish rule was introduced to Kilkenny hurling in 1954, there was nothing unusual about players choosing neighbouring teams. A good example of this was Mick Heffernan, the well-known hurler from Aylwardstown, Glenmore. Mick won Minor and Junior Kilkenny Championships with Mullinavat. The famous 5-0 to 3-1 victory over Freshford in the 1939 Junior final, included a solid performance from the Glenmore import, thus breaching a famine that went back to 1917. Mullinavat has only ever featured in two county Senior hurling finals, 1940 and 1943. On both occasions Mick was in the half-forward line.

Mick had previously won a Leinster Minor medal in 1937 while with Glenmore but was a great addition to the Mullinavat team in the period 1939-1943. He would later feature at Junior and Senior grade with Kilkenny. While working at Jimmy Hanrahan's premises in New Ross, Mick threw in his lot with Geraldine O'Hanrahans club, winning two Wexford Senior hurling and one county Junior hurling championship. By the time he finished his career Michael had the unique distinction of playing inter county hurling with Kilkenny, Waterford and Wexford.

He would later move to Clover Meats, stay there as a sales division staff member for 36 years, and return to his native parish club.

MICK CARROLL, ROSSINAN

It was a really sad night for Mullinavat Gaels when Mick Carroll passed away, having attended the Intermediate Hurling League tie with Dunnamaggin, at Mooncoin on 10/5/2014. Mick had been the club's delegate at county board meetings for decades. Mick played for the club many years previously, and was unfortunately struck down with polio back then, which cut his playing career short. This did not stop Mick dedicating his life to the GAA, particularly in Mullinavat, as a gate collector, club official, selector of both camogie and hurling teams, and other tasks, too many to mention. When the club won its only Roinn A Under 21 hurling title in 2013, Mick was there as a selector that day. He had previously served as chairman of the club for four years, 1982-1985. Mick is still fondly remembered by all involved in Mullinavat GAA.

THE HURLER'S PRAYER

This is a prayer often said at churches in Mullinavat and Bigwood before big games.

♣

Grant me O Lord, a hurler's skill,
With strength of arm and speed of limb
Unerring eye for the flying ball
And courage to match whate'er befall.
May my stroke be steady, and my aim be true?
My actions manly and my misses few
No matter what way the game may go
May I rest in friendship with every foe?
When the final whistle for me has blown
And I stand at last before God's judgement throne.
May the great referee when he calls my name?
Say, you hurled like a man; you played the game.

♣

Faces Down Through the Years

CLOCKWISE: FROM TOP LEFT

PAT AYLWARD (BALLYOGREEK)
Pat was captain of the 1939 County Junior hurling winning team, who won the club's third junior title.

BOB BARRY
Conducted a shoe-making business on the Main Street of Mullinavat– the premises doubled as a selection headquarters in the clubs early years from 1913.

NED DELAHUNTY
Chairman of the club in 1960.

PAT DELAHUNTY
Pat was treasurer of the club in 1960 and 1961, and later chairman in 1965 and 1966.

CLOCKWISE: FROM TOP LEFT

DENNY DUGGAN
Right Half Forward on the 1928 All-Ireland Junior hurling winning
Kilkenny team versus Tipperary, 4-6 to 4-4.

PETER FOSKIN
Following a long career as a player Peter also served as chairman for four years (1961-1964).

JAMES KEEGAN
James was a garda and gave great service to the club. He trained Mullinavat to their only
County Minor A championship in 1938, and also trained the team who contested our
second, and last, County Senior hurling Final, a loss to Carrickshock in 1943. From 1936 to
1945 James was active as secretary, chairman and treasurer of the club.

RICHIE KENNEALLY
Richie was a member of the 1915 and 1916 County Junior
championship winning hurling teams.

CLOCKWISE: FROM TOP LEFT

PAT POWER (GARRYGAUG)
Pat played on the 1915 and 1916
Kilkenny County Junior winning teams.

JIM PHELAN
Jim featured on the 1915 and 1916 Mullinavat
Junior Hurling Championship winning sides.

JOHN PURCELL
The man from Garrandaragh was chairman
of the club for seven years (1912-1919).

JOE SULLIVAN
Was a goalie on the 1915-16 Junior-winning panel
and also played for the Kilkenny Junior side.

FROM TOP LEFT:

JOHN SUTTON (ROSSINAN)
John acted as club chairman for two years, 1967 and 1968.

MICHAEL SUTTON
Michael was a versatile player who starred on various
Mullinavat Junior hurling teams of the late 1960s and early 1970s.

SEAMUS SUTTON
Another who has given great service to the club as both a player and administrator.
Secretary from 1961-1975 and was also a trustee of Mullinavat Gaelic field.

JAMES AYLWARD
On the formation of the Southern Board in 1919, James Aylward was the first chairman. He was secretary of the Kilkenny County Board from 1917 to 1918. He became Mayor of Waterford in 1935. He reportedly always referred to Mullinavat as the Capital of Europe.

BILLY HOBAN
Secretary of the hurling club in 1948 and later a Southern Board delegate.

JOHN HOLDEN
Club secretary from 1957 to 1959.

LARRY DUGGAN
Larry won a Senior All-Ireland hurling medal for Kilkenny versus Limerick in 1935. His brother Jack was also on the team. Along with playing for his native parish, Larry won two Kilkenny Senior Championship medals with neighbouring Mooncoin.

MARTIN CROTTY
Martin was a National School teacher, acted as trustee to Mullinavat hurling field for twelve years (1954-1966) and was club secretary in 1955 and 1956.

MAURICE MURPHY (BUCKSTOWN)
Maurice featured on the 1915 and 1916 Junior hurling winning side and was involved with Glenmore Senior football side who won Kilkenny titles in 1915, 1916, 1920 and 1922.

PADDY TYNAN
Paddy was a forward with the Junior team when Fr Gallavan reorganised the club in the early 1950s, and acted as club secretary in 1953 and 1954.

PAT FOSKIN
Treasurer of the club from 1953 to 1959.

PATRICK O'BRIEN
Patrick was part of the committee who reorganised the club in the 1950s.

TOM SUTTON
Chairman of the hurling club in 1958 and 1959 and also prominent as both a player and prominent referee.

WILLIAM KAVANAGH
Chairman of the club in 1956 and 1957.

Below: Murt McCarthy, Farnogue; John Power; Eily Walsh; Pat McEvoy. Kneeling – Patricia Walsh, Tom Delahunty.

Above: John Murphy and Tommy Flynn.

The official opening of our new clubhouse.

Jim Conway hard at work for Mullinavat, and receiving due recognition for his service to the GAA (including 43 years as treasurer of Mullinavat GAA Club) in Áras an Uachtaráin when he was honoured by President Mary McAleese (also photographed is Jim's sister, Margaret and Martin McAleese).

Normally he can be found on duty as an umpire at games in the local field. But last week one of the most discreet workers in sport in Kilkenny enjoyed tea with the President. Mullinavat GAA club official, Jim Conway, discarded the white coat of an umpire and instead donned his finery for a meeting with President Mary McAleese.

Mr Conway of Killandrew, Mullinavat, was one of the chosen few honoured during a Day for Sports Volunteers in Áras An Uachtaráin. Mr Conway was nominated for the honour by Kilkenny County Board in recognition of his dedication to his native club and parish. "His contribution has been immense, but you will never find him looking for praise," offered GAA Development Officer, Barry Hickey when he informed the monthly meeting of the 'Board of the honour accorded Mr Conway. He has served as treasurer of Mullinavat GAA club for 43 years. He organised the famous Gold Watch tournament in the town which attracted teams for all parts of the country for over 28 years.

And he has been caretaker of the club grounds virtually since he was able to push a pitch marker.

Mr Conway has been an umpire for over 30 years, and only recently he was on duty by a post during a Kilkenny camogie final at Nowlan Park. Anything that needed doing in Mullinavat, Jim Conway was prepared to put his shoulder to the wheel. "He has gracefully given his life to the GAA," Mr Hickey added. "He is a gentleman, a person any club would be proud to have involved." "If you ever want to find him he will be the umpire on the duty at the right hand post of the goal at the town end in Mullinavat on match days," advised County Board chairman, Ned Quinn. "The GAA is blessed to have people like Jim Conway in its ranks," he added.

From KILKENNY PEOPLE

Jim and his sister, Margaret, are pictured here with President Mary McAleese, and her husband Martin, in Áras an Uachtaráin.

Monsignor Maher

Neddy Aldridge

Pat Holden

Tommy Duggan

No. 171—WILLIE JOE CLEERE

Newspaper correspondent and publicman, but not a publichouse man, and no friend of Milady Nicotine. Headed the poll for South Kilkenny area in Kilkenny County Council elections of 1942, and held the further distinction of being the youngest member. Had the renewed confidence of his admirers by re-election in 1945. Now seeks higher honours as candidate for Dail Eireann in the postponed election in the Carlow-Kilkenny Constituency, and hopes to gain a "clear" majority again. There is no better known Gael in his native county, and hasn't the wind-up that his colleagues will let him down. Was Secretary of Kilmacow Football Club which won the Kilkenny County Championship in 1942. Consistently defends the underdog, though his bark is worse than his bite. Is no wire-puller, but is sought after as a fiddler in his social sphere.

Three Club Legends in the company of the Liam MacCarthy Cup: Ned Haberlin, Pete Foskin, Willie O'Dwyer.

Above (left): *Ned Haberlin, Tom Reade, David Brown, Liam Kenneally, Packie Wall.*
Above (right): *Packie Wall, Tom Anthony, Tom Reade, Joe Anthony, Ned Haberlin, Johnny Haberlin (kneeling) at Feile in Offaly.* **Below:** *Mullinavat in Kilkenny jerseys during the 2019 Leinster Intermediate club campaign.*

Kilkenny GAA Club of the Year award 2019 is accepted on behalf of the club by PRO John Power at David Buggy Motors.

KCLR

2019
KCLR &
David Buggy Motors
Kilkenny
Sport Star Award
Club of the Year
Mullinavat GAA

The story continues for Mullinavat, with the next generation on their way, travelling to 2019 Feile.

PART · TWO

HURLING
1887-2024

CHAPTER 1

1887-1919

'The re-born GAA became more efficient and business-like, but it also acquired a new ideological purpose. It aligned itself with the rising tide of cultural nationalism and, in 1902, reinstated a ban on GAA membership for anyone who played rugby, soccer, cricket or hockey – games that were characterised as Anglicised and alien to native culture. It was a move that effectively scuppered any prospect of a harmonious co-existence between the GAA and any sport it considered its rival. In Kilkenny, as elsewhere, sports like cricket got caught in the cultural crossfire.'

1887-1919

The first question concerning hurling clubs in Mullinavat, Kilkenny or further afield is, 'What happened to shift the power balance between cricket and hurling?'

By the mid 1890s, there were almost 50 cricket clubs in Kilkenny, and such was its pre-eminence within the local sporting life that it was easily the most popular sport in the county.

1884: GAA founded at Hayes' Hotel, Thurles, Co. Tipperary.

1885: The Rules of Hurling were printed in United Ireland Newspaper. The first ever game of Gaelic football was played in Callan this year.

1887: The first Kilkenny Senior Hurling Championship was held with just four entrants, Castlecomer, Confederation (Kilkenny City), Mooncoin and Tullaroan. Football ruled in Kilkenny with 19 teams in the football championship. Teams were 21-a-side.

1889: Hurling was gaining in popularity in the county with 12 teams competing in the Senior Hurling Championship.

1890: Mullinavat Independent Cricket Club were participating in both Waterford and Kilkenny leagues.

1890: No GAA games were played during Lent as per a request from the Bishop of Ossory.

1892: Teams were now 17-a-side.

1893: Mullinavat Independent Cricket Club beat Inistioge by one run. Team: T Holden, A Aylward, R Duggan, J Dobbyn, J Aylward, J Murphy, P Gilbert, P Aylward, T Thompson, J Tovey, W Cashin. Kilkenny played in their first hurling All Ireland in this year, losing to Cork (played the following year).

1895: A request was made through the pages of the Kilkenny People for cricketers to help out the GAA by turning out for football and hurling teams during their winter off-season.

1896: Mullinavat hurlers played a game v. Kilmacow.

1897: On 14th February it's reported that the first hurling game for many years was staged in the parish between Mullinavat and Kilmacow. The field was very rough and not conductive to a hurling contest, but still, hundreds showed up that afternoon. At the interval Mullinavat led 1-2 to 0-2. In a tough and bruising second half Mullinavat prevailed for a 2-4 to 0-4 victory. It's reported that the game had a referee from both parishes, J Kealy (M) and W Walsh (K).

1898: Mullinavat (Green Linnets) cricket team were very successful. Team: T Ryan (captain), R McDonald (treasurer), P Foley (secretary), J Murphy VC, J Ryan, J Mackey, J Reilly, P O'Shea, T O'Shea, T Mackey, J Walsh.

1900: There was still more cricket clubs than hurling clubs in Kilkenny. The Wexford People newspaper said there is far more interest in the GAA in County Kilkenny, albeit mainly still Gaelic football, than in neighbouring county Wexford, if you take the entries in the county championship as a guideline. The GAA began to repair itself in the early 1900s after a dismal decade of division and decline which followed revelations of Charles Stewart Parnell's extra-marital affair and the consequent split in the Irish Party and wider nationalist movement. Led by a new cohort of officials, among them Kilkenny's James Nowlan as President, the GAA received an administrative overhaul which saw, amongst other things, the introduction of Provincial Councils, each with a responsibility for running its own football and hurling championships. The reborn GAA became more efficient and businesslike, but it also acquired a new ideological purpose. It aligned itself with the rising tide of cultural nationalism and, in 1902, reinstated a ban on GAA membership for anyone who played rugby, soccer, cricket or hockey – games that were characterised as Anglicised and alien to native culture. It was a move that effectively scuppered any prospect of a harmonious co-existence between the GAA and any sport it considered its rival. In Kilkenny, as elsewhere, sports like cricket got caught in the cultural crossfire. The effect was evident in the decline in the number of cricket clubs, and in the hardening of attitudes to the sport among GAA members. In 1900 newspapers were the main source of news in this era and Kilkenny had three, namely the Kilkenny People, Kilkenny Journal and Kilkenny Moderator.

1901: Eight teams entered the Kilkenny Senior Hurling Championship.

1902: Eleven teams entered the Kilkenny Senior Hurling Championship.

1903: Eleven teams entered the Kilkenny Senior Hurling Championship. Mullinavat held a hurling tournament involving neighbouring teams where a win was recorded for Kilmacow, beating Tullogher 4-3 to 0-0.

1904: Sixteen teams entered the Kilkenny Senior Hurling Championship. Mullinavat were now involved, as were Piltown, Mooncoin and Ferrybank.

1905: Again sixteen teams entered the Kilkenny Senior championship, but Mullinavat were no longer involved, replaced by Graine.

1906: Seventeen teams entered the Senior Hurling Championship.

1907: Seventeen teams entered the Senior Hurling Championship.

1908: Twelve teams entered the Senior Hurling Championship.

1909: Twelve teams entered the Senior Hurling Championship.

1910: Cricket was still very popular in the Mullinavat area and here is a Munster Express summary from June 1910 on Plebestown v. Clonassy: 'An interesting cricket match was witnessed at Clonassy on a June Sunday in 1910, when the Pleberstown team travelled there to play the home team. They arrived at two o'clock and got a cordial welcome from all interested, and were immediately marched to the barn, given kindly by Mr John Aylward, Cloonassy, where they were treated generously. After taking refreshments, both parties proceeded to the field. Cloonassy won the toss and took the bat. A good evening's sport was witnessed. Both sides played well, Cloonassy winning by 14 runs. The stumps were drawn at 6 pm, and both clubs returned to the tent and a jolly time was spent in singing and dancing until 12 o'clock, when the Pleberstown men left for home with many a goodbye from the Mullinavat cailini.'

1911: Nine teams entered the Senior Hurling Championship.

1912: September 14th at Metropole Hotel, Kilkenny a decision was taken to finish the 1911 championship and start the 1913 campaign in the Autumn, with no 1912 championship. The Kilkenny GAA Convention of this year unanimously agreed that the championships of this year be dropped altogether. From here on, the hurling history of Mullinavat is very much linked with the origination of the Southern Junior Hurling Championship, which commenced the following year. Coincidentally this was also the year that the 15-a-side games we know today started. The initiation of the Southern Championships in both hurling and football meant that teams had far less to travel and probably explains the appearance, if brief, of new teams in the area not long afterwards.

1913

JUNIOR

South JHC R1: Mullinavat beat Piltown by 2 points (Waterford Sportsfield)

'The Junior hurling tie between Mullinavat and Piltown produced a win for Mullinavat, this in an area more noted for Gaelic football. Football was always the game that found acceptance in Mullinavat, and it is only recently that hurling has taken hold. Piltown were favourites for this contest but appeared to play below form on the day. Whilst possibly possessing greater skills than their Rod Iron neighbours, Piltown made errors, for which they were duly punished. Piltown were to the fore early on, but midway through the half Mullinavat settled into the game. Kennedy was prominent in the midfield area for Mullinavat.'

'The play was end to end before Piltown recorded the game's first score with a point. After the break it was still back and forth, a Kennedy effort was cleared by Ward for Piltown. The Rod Iron defence were under pressure for periods of the second half but defended manfully. It wasn't until the final few minutes that Mullinavat recorded a late goal which gave them a two-point lead. Piltown did apply a few bouts of pressure after this major score, but to the delight of their supporters it was to be Mullinavat's day.'

South JHC R2: Mullinavat 1-1; Kilmacow 1-1 (Harristown)

'The morning was beautifully fine, and this was something for which to be thankful, considering the downpour that fell all day long the previous day. Light-hearted and gay, the men on blue and green, in six jaunting carts left Kilmacow village at 12 noon. They were fancied for the event but did not succeed in pulling it off. The Kilmacow contingent, considerably augmented by those of their kindred who travelled in inside traps, on foot or on bicycles were the first to arrive at the venue. A change came over the day in the afternoon and the warmth of the sun which we so delightfully basked in all the faded away before a cold and continuous cutting gale that commenced to blow over the playing pitch at 2.30pm.'

'Mr Pierce Barden (Harristown) was referee. The popular Pierce, who knew his duty, and did it without fear or favour kept both teams well in hand. It was an easy task however as both teams played a straight, sporting game. Frees were kept to a minimum which spoke well for the play of both teams. Kilmacow were first on the field and their opponents joined the May 3pm, with the rival seventeens evenly matched from a physical standpoint. Mullinavat won the toss and elected to play against a slight incline but were favoured by the fast-blowing breeze. The cold was intense and the players with chattering teeth eagerly awaited the throw-in of the sliotair which took place at 3.05pm. The Mullinavat men, to the tune of "up the rod iron" took possession and challenged the Kilmacow back division.'

'Mullinavat scored the goal, and the Rod Iron contingent cheered their team's fine effort. The visitors livened up somewhat after this but when the sliotair was sent to the forward line the scoring machine was out of action. Mullinavat were playing a fine game and added a point before the half-time whistle blew leaving the Kilmacow boys scoreless against the opponents four points.'

'Kilmacow began to press almost all of the time, but their forwards were shooting wide on almost every occasion. No doubt, the defence was good. So the battle waged until ten minutes to go when things were looking bad for the men in blue and green.'

'"What are you doing", came calls from the sideline as with dismay written large on their faces, they saw defeat looming large in the distance. The Mullinavat boys were indeed jubilant. The play was waging fast and furious until at last Kilmacow scored a solitary point. Not a cheer – nothing to cheer about. Five minutes to go, could Kilmacow make the breakthrough for an equalising goal?'

'In attacking the Mullinavat goal a desperate mix up ensued. A surging crowd in multicoloured jerseys, a miniature forest of waving, clashing and smashing ash, sods flying, and men hitting off each other without fear or favour. Another scramble and in goes the equalising goal. The game is saved and defeat was snapped from the fire. The men from the 'mill of the sticks' replied and swept the decks once more but without avail. The Kilmacow team was playing much better now. With the scores level at four points all both sides made a play to win the match outright. The full-time whistle went with the match ending all square.'

'Judging the match on its merits one team seemed as good as the other. Mullinavat were a surprise packet and a force, which will now have to be reckoned with. Power, Kenneally, Freaney, Murphy, Foskin, Walsh and Whelan gave splendid exhibitions of hurling and the rest of the team were very useful indeed.'

South JHC R2: Mullinavat 1-6; Kilmacow 1-1 (Rathkiernan)

'All roads led to Rathkiernan on Sunday last. Crowds flocked in hundreds from Glenmore, Slieverue, Ballyhale, Waterford, Piltown, Temploerum, etc on bicycles, sidecars, horses and shank's mare and in wagonettes, common cars and traps of every colour and make, to see the replay of the semi final of the Kilkenny Junior hurling championship. The game was played on a splendid field kindly lent for the occasion by to the Gaels of Moondharrig by Mr Richard Brennan (Ashgrove). In the hands of the Mooncoin hurling club the arrangements were admirable. The Doyle brothers, Joe Kelly, Jim Quinn, Drug and the rest, not forgetting Dick Walsh (manager) worked like Trojans to have everything ready and make a success of the occasion.'

'Kilmacow were not disgraced. They looked winners right up to the final whistle. There was so much interest in the game that it was predicted that the vanquished would be in mourning for a week. Mullinavat deserved full credit for their win. The hurling was thrilling and exceptionally brilliant throughout the entire game. There was some changes from the previous drawn game with Kilmacow having John Doody (vice captain), Ned Keeffe and Willie Walsh. Mullinavat improved their team by adding Johnny and Pa Whelan (Clonassey) and Aylward and Raftice all of which strengthened the Rod Iron considerably.'

'The outstanding players for the winners was Johnny Whelan of the Thomas Francis Meagher team (Waterford County Champions) who gave an exhibition showing how he helped the Meaghers win the Waterford championship. Johnny scored from centre field and played havoc with the Kilmacow defence with every opening that came his way. He was a fast hard-hitting and scientific hurler. Every time he hit the ball; he made the most of it. His brother Jim played at left half back and also gave a fine exhibition. Richie Kenneally, a boy of modest disposition fair, fast and slim, was also to the forefront for the whole hour. His play was grand to watch.'

'Mick Foskin, the Mullinavat captain properly known as "the jar" at full back played with his usual ability and played a big part for his team in their worthy win. When congratulated on the victory, like a good sport replied, "There will be another day." Maurice Murphy at centre of the field played well and stemmed a number of Kilmacow attacks.

Letter (7/06/2013)
To the Editor – Munster Express
Mullinavat Hurling Club
June 3rd, 1913

Sir,

My attention has been drawn from time to time to the misleading statements in your popular paper regarding Mullinavat Hurling Club and I think I am justified in contradicting some of these statements on behalf of my club.

Mullinavat played a drawn game with Kilmacow at Harristown on Sunday, 2nd March, 1913 and with a little luck should have won. But could have been awarded the match had we objected as the Kilmacow team is illegally constituted, but the boys from the Rod Iron City were too honourable to disturb the friendly relationships between the two parishes that were formerly one. Secondly, we replayed the game at Mooncoin on Sunday 27th April 2013, and beat Kilmacow to the tune of 1 goal 6 points to 1 goal 1 point. We were all very much surprised to see Kilmacow, who were always manly on a gaelic field, taking their defeat so badly, viz Jack Maher, and W Walsh coming into the Rod Iron camp anxious for a pugilistic encounter with the Mullinavat chaps, and therefore breaking one of the strictest rules of the GAA that would enable Mullinavat to get Kilmacow suspended, if they desired to do so, but were too Irish for that. Lastly Kilmacow, when all fruits failed, objected to Mullinavat being awarded the match, on the grounds that one of the quartette Phelans, namely John, played Senior hurling with T F Meagher's in Waterford, but were unable to prove if at a meeting of the Kilkenny G.A.A held on Sunday, 24th May, 1913. He (John Phelan) being called before the meeting, could not give a satisfactory explanation, and therefore the majority of the delegates present voted for a replay, but were not in power to do so, when his objection was not proved.

Then I, on the instructions of my club, proposed that Kilmacow be awarded the match, but got no seconder. Therefore, the Kilmacow men will not get the third chance in the championship.

In order to renew the friendly relationships between the two parishes, Mullinavat H C suggests that the two teams play a friendly game, either in Mullinavat or Kilmacow, half the proceeds to go to the Connemara Fund, and the other half to help to pay the debt on the Parish Priest's house at Mullinavat, who is a Kilmacow man. But under no circumstances will my club play Kilmacow the third time for the 1912 Championship.

Yours sincerely,
JER Foskin (captain)

(Kilmacow had pointed out to Mullinavat prior to match two that they believed they had an illegal player, and post match lodged an objection to the secretary of Kilkenny County Board. The county board ordered a third game to be held at Waterford Sportsfield)

South JHC R2: Mullinavat 6-0; Kilmacow 0-2 (Waterford Sportsfield)

'On Sunday last before what a wit described as "fourteen pounds" worth of spectators, the above tie in the Kilkenny County Junior Championships was decided. The arrangements in the joint hands of the Glenmore and Slieverue Gaels were admirable and left nothing to be desired. Mr Mick Doyle, of Moondharrig and All-Ireland hurling fame, was the official referee, but he was away in "Glasgow town", after having upheld the name and fame of the Kilkenny Gaels in his brilliant style, on the day previous. In his absence, Mr Tom King, of the TF Meagher Waterford, made a right loyal referee. His coolness, tact, and keen judgment on many occasions was a soil on turbulent waters. The play of the Mullinavat fifteen demonstrated clearly that they were sixteen points a better team than the Gaels who did duty for Kilmacow. Tis hard to write it, but the truth is generally bitter. From start to finish of the game on Sunday, the Kilmacow team was like the man that fell out of the aeroplane, "not in it".'

'Mullinavat played again with John Phelan in their ranks, although it was on his account that the objection to him was upheld by the Kilkenny Co. Board. Still, his inclusion did not influence the result. Mullinavat won well on their merits, and in a large measure this was due to the splendid play of John, Pat, and Jim Phelan, P Power, Paddy Foskin, R. Kenneally, McDonald, Cashin, Aylward and last but not least "Captain Jer" J Maher.'

'The match was scheduled to start at 1.30 pm but It was 3 pm before it commenced. Mullinavat began in promising style, scoring four goals to nil in the first twelve minutes, a twelve-point lead at the rate of one point a minute. The play was decidedly, and, to my mind, unnecessarily rough during the opening moiety, culminating in a regrettable incident when the referee had to put a Kilmacow player and a Mullinavat player from the field of play. The referee simply did his duty, a rather unpleasant one. We are all Irishmen and sportsman, and we must control our tempers on all trying occasions. No one felt for the two men, and two good men on Sunday as I did.'

'The scores at half-time read: Mullinavat six goals; Kilmacow nil. Mullinavat scored an additional goal in the opening stages of the second half. Kilmacow immediately responded with their first score, a point per Michael Reid. In the concluding stages, P Walsh, Kilmacow, from an open stroke near the Mullinavat goal, scored a point, for which Mullinavat replied with a goal. That put "the tin hat" on the whole shooting match. We were fed up with it, and the cheers that rent the air at the conclusion of the game could be heard on "the plains of Sweet Rockhall".'

Mullinavat: Michael Foskin (captain), P Sullivan (goal), Patrick Foskin, Patrick Whelan, M Whelan, James Power, P Power, W Power, M Dunphy, P Kenneally, W McDonald, W Walsh, W Cashin, J Aylward and John Whelan.

South JHC Final: Mong 0-01; Mullinavat 0-00 (unfinished, Mong awarded title)

'Mullinavat winning the toss elected to play with the incline, wind and sun in their favour. When Dick Holohan threw in the ball at 3.15pm a goodly throng had gathered. Johnny Whelan immediately got going and shot the leather towards the Mong backs. The latter quickly transferred, only to have Kennelly and M Murphy renew the attack. The defence was good, and despite the continued and splendid attempts of John Phelan to score, Mullinavat send the ball over the goal line. Mullinavat were showing best so far. The goal delivery was "up in the sky" as Joe says, but Hanrahan and Mullins assisted the leather in its flight, and among came along, moving in grand style. The play was now really good. Fast footing and hard hitting was the order all the time.'

'Mong fought hard for a score, but Power was a terrible handful and cleared his lines frequently. Mong however sent the ball over, and this gave relief. Power's powerful drive put Paddy Foskin going, and he centred neatly to John Whelan only to have Murphy (Mong) regain possession and transfer play to the upper goal, where McKenna missed a score by inches. Mong kept the Southern backs busy but Kenneally (out of his place) with a beautiful drive send the leather flying to the other end, and his friends sent it over wide.'

'Mullinavat were defending 17 minutes from the start, Jim Whelan, the Mullinavat back, and one of the Mong defenders had a tussle for the ball in front of the Mullinavat goal. In endeavouring to clear himself from his opponent, Whelan shoved the Mong forward with his left hand and his right hand at the time held the hurley in the air in the readiness to strike the ball. Several thought the strike as a stroke deliberately given, and that the uplifted was to be used to strike the player. Evidently the referee was one of these. He whistled up the game, and immediately ordered Whelan from the field. To his credit be it said, Whelan walked towards the sideline, and the game started again. It then appeared as if Whelan's supporters amongst the spectators and players advised him to resume play and "Jim" stood in the arena once more. The referee, on seeing this, again blew his whistle and ordered Whelan to leave the field within one minute. The seconds ticked off 57-58-59-60 and as Whelan did not obey. Mong were awarded the match.'

'I do not wish to justify the referee's decision nor to back up Whelan's action. Personally, I thought the former's decision to be hasty and harsh, and that a caution would have met the case. I believe Jim Phelan is too much of a sportsman to deliberately and aggressively strike any player either with hand or hurley. However rightly or wrongly the decision of the referee which everyone ought to know, is final, had been given, and should have been obeyed. Jim Phelan is one of Mullinavat's best and he should have followed his own guidance and obeyed the referee a second time and question- if he thought fit – his decision in the proper place afterwards. Jim is not the first – no nor the ninety first – man that was ordered from the field. Anyway, the upshot of Sunday was that we did not get value for our time or our money and that Mong will contest the 1913 Kilkenny Junior Hurling Final.'

EN ROUTE FOR THE VENUE

'Six of us ensconced ourselves in a comfortable carriage at Kilmacow on Sunday, which was a gloriously fine day. We spoke of the match. If Mong's reputation made us fancy them, our sympathy and support were with our friends and neighbours from the '"Rod Iron" parish. A few songs fetched us into Mullinavat station, where a large crowd bound for Ballyhale were assembled. "Molly came after all," says someone, and we all had a laugh. More smoking and singing landed us at the next station, and we all got out. A short walk brought us to Knocktopher, and after some soda and cider and sherbet we sallied forth once more. Loud then were the lamentations at not having as much as a "deck" to while away our two hours of waiting. A good patriarchal Samaritan by cutting a small bit of a "kippeen" found us a way out of the difficulty, and we played the game until it, was time to go.'

'On arrival at the scene of action, my first exclamation was one of sheer surprise and delight at the magnificent field for the day's contest. Without a doubt, it was the finest field for a Gaelic game that I have ever seen in my life. I have been on the Dublin, Wexford, Enniscorthy. Cork, Limerick, Kilkenny, Thurles, Maryborough, Carrick and Dungarvan grounds, and the playing pitch at any of these venues could not approach the large, level and lovely field placed at the disposal of the Knocktopher Gaels by that generous sportsman and captain of the Knocktopher F.C., Ald. Dick Holohan. My next exclamation was that ninety nine out of every hundred on the field wore total abstinence badges. It was not long until our "big six" was augmented by an additional squad of Kilmacow Gaels and cyclists, and my readers may imagine our disappointment when the match had concluded as it did. Leaving the field, we took possession of an hotel and having refreshed the inner man we proceeded down the street in search of postcards and found, some lovely dainty flowers – cowslips – on our way. Having shaken the dust of ancient Knocktopher from our feet we marched on Ballyhale, a friendly fiddler playing "Brian Boru's March" before, us on the way. We enjoyed this treat immensely and reaching the station we were booked for the down train in second-class style, having made the most of our day.'

1914

JUNIOR

South JHC R1: Mullinavat 3-02; Kilmacow 0-01

'Sunday last (8/3/1914) was an ideal spring day and was a welcome change from the atmospheric conditions that have prevailed for the past ten or eleven Sundays. As I proceeded Kilkenny words via Dunkitt, I was delighted with another change steamrolling has not only commenced on the road from the cross up, but is already well under way, a splendid road now taking the place of the wretched boreen that has existed for years back from Dunkitt to Miltown. It will not take much time until the steamrolling of this road will be completed, and this will prove a great boon to everyone. However, I am out to talk hurling, not roadmaking. I soon met company, and on we jogged, a contented trio, to Ashgrove near Rathkieran; crowds who had journeyed miles to witness the day's contest, were now hurrying to swell the throng who were giving their mites to augment the coffers of the splendid Moondharrig club. We reached the venue in nice time, and then we parted temporarily. Mike Doyle, "Drug" Walsh, Dick Doyle, Dick Doherty, and last but not least, "Cousin" John Power, "the man in the know," were there, and I found them as usual in great form.'

'I was captured immediately by my friends in the Kilmacow hosting to get right down and place the men. Down I went, and I pitied the boys, no doubt. They had a team, and yet they hadn't. To cut it short, after much "coercion" and after a final warning: "Unless your team takes the field within three minutes, Mullinavat gets the match," the blue and green jersey clad men faced the cameras – 600 pairs of eyes, and walked across the green to meet their old-time friendly and worthy rivalries Mullinavat Gaels, attired in chocolate and green sweaters. It was exactly 100 minutes after the scheduled hour when the teams lined out, and my Kilmacow friends were largely to blame for this unusual and unnecessary delay.'

'The soil was delightful, and the playing pitch was nicely laid out; but the crowds kept very bad lines, and the field of play was encroached upon several times. To business – John Phelan put Mullinavat attacking with a lengthy drive, but Rockett checked. Murphy replied, and Phelan was again dangerous. Keeffe crossed nicely, and Kenneally getting possession sent in well. The game was fast and even. Murphy and Phelan, not to be denied, rallied their forces, and out of a mix-up in front of the Kilmacow goal.'

'Mullinavat scored first blood – a well directed shot beating Hunt cleverly. Mullinavat kept, up the pressure, and Quinn and Keeffe nullified their efforts. Rockett put in a good stroke, and Peter Phelan whipped across a fine shot, which Jim Phelan saved effectively. Power transferred play immediately. "Chopping" penalized Mullinavat, but Rocket's free was diverted by the breeze. Murphy and Kenneally returned for Mullinavat, but a grand burst by P Phelan, J Doody and Dalton put the chocolates in jeopardy, Maher making the Mullinavat custodian clear at the expense of a "70." Rockett centred nicely, but the Kilmacow forwards muffed the equalizer badly. Mick Phelan got his boys away with a grand drive, and Hunt cleared cleverly from Cashin. Rockett and P Phelan were holding up the Mullinavat men now, and Maher was in a fine scoring position when a "free" to Mullinavat spoiled his chances. John Phelan sent the ball with a magnificent stroke from the back division to the Kilmacow goal. Hunt ran out to clear, but Kenneally quickly returned. Merry, Quinn. Rockett, and Keeffe were now playing a grand defensive game. Another "free" at centre-field taken by Phelan, saw Hunt clearing in lovely style. Following the goal delivery, Peter Phelan and John Quinn sent in a few stingers, which Power, Jim and Mick Phelan saved. Doody now sent the leather out wide. Dalton swept up the field in the ensuing exchanges, and from a neat centre by Peter Phelan, Maher sent wide by inches. Phelan sent out finely, and Jim Aylward who was playing well, put in a well directed shot. A "free" to Mullinavat, close in, was sent over wide by a narrow margin. Still pressing the Mullinavat forwards kept Quinn, who was giving a fine account of himself, warm. P Phelan eased the pressure, and Michael Reid called on Jim Phelan to clear a hot shot, which he did nicely. Jer Foskin started now, and with a fine stroke placed the ball for Aylward to send it into the parallelogram, A mighty delivery from Keeffe soon saw play at the other end, when we had the first "check". Jim Phelan getting slightly injured accidentally. After first aid at the able and skilful hands of the referee, he resumed amid cheers.'

'Mullinavat soon got a "70" but John Phelan sent ball over wide. Hunt's delivery was great. Maher securing, flashed the leather to Matt Doody, who was but five yards from the goal and only the goalman to beat, when he sent the ball over wide. It was hard lines on his team certainly to lose a goal in this way. Mullinavat rushed the Kilmacow sticks soon afterwards but the defence of the six backs and goalman was perfect. From a "70" John Phelan's effort was magnificently cleared by Quinn, but almost in a moment John Phelan landed a lovely point for Mullinavat.

'Play was fast following the delivery and the next item unworthy of record was a second goal lost by Matt Doody, who was decidedly "off". The Kilmacow forwards were now having most of the play bur scoring was not in their line of business. They had not goaled or pointed in their stock-in-trade when the short whistle blew, the scores then reading Mullinavat 1-1; Kilmacow 0-0.'

'It was 4.20pm when the ball was again thrown in. Following a "free" which John Phelan neatly centred, Maurice Murphy put the ball nicely sailing over the lath, a point for Mullinavat from a left-hand ground stroke some thirty yards out. Mullinavat were still pressing, but again Hunt, Walsh, Merry, and Quinn was responsible for effective clearances. An accident to Ryan (Mullinavat) necessitated Raftice "subbing" him, and on went the game again. Keeffe was hurling a brilliant game throughout as was Peter Whelan, Moolum. Following a grand side-line movement, in which Kenneally was the central figure, Keeffe saved from Aylward when well placed, and Hunt running out to clear, nearly lost a goal, as Paddy Walsh saved sensationally and well merited the ringing cheers he received. A "70" to John Phelan followed, but an over resulted. A free to Rockett saw the play transferred by a grand stroke, but Jer Murphy and Cashin soon returned the leather. Hunt cleared his lines brilliantly on two occasions, but his posts fell to the tune of a goal in the next minute, and a green flag for Kilmacow.'

'Hunt's delivery was superb. Dalton got in a dandy stroke, which Jim Phelan and Power effectively, cleared. Some splendid play, in which Peter Phelan, who was playing a splendid forward game whenever the ball came his way, was very prominent, next resulted, and from a free close in Tom Dalton scored for Kilmacow. Keeping in to their fight, Peter Whelan, Reid, J. Doody, and Maher were now doing well, but they could not score. Following a "70" Mullinavat rushed a goal, which was hailed with great cheering. Sullivan saved his goal marvellously on a few occasions yet, despite several splendid chances, Kilmacow failed to score. Mullinavat, who were playing a winning, if not a brilliant game, now came along and put the issue beyond all doubt by scoring another goal.'

South JHC R2: Ballyhale beat Mullinavat
South JHC Final: Mooncoin 5-00; St Kieran's 2-01

1915

JUNIOR

South JHC R1: Mullinavat beat Kells.
South JHC Final: Mullinavat 3-00; Kilmacow 1-00

'On Sunday July 9th, 1916, Mullinavat and Kilmacow met in the 1915 Southern Junior Hurling Final at Waterford Sportsfield. Mullinavat were victorious by 3-0 to 1-0 to clinch a first South Junior Hurling title. There was a good attendance of spectators, who came in large numbers from the district, interested in each of the competing teams. The game opened very fast and continued so up to half time when the sides stood at one goal each. In the second half Mullinavat added two more goals lo their score. A very heavy shower of rain fell during this period and the ground afterwards appeared to be altogether in favour of the men from the "Rod Iron" village.'

'There is a rumour about that another match is to take place between the above teams. The Kilmacow boys think that but for the rain falling in the second half they would have won the game. However, if the match does come off if will, we are sure, be very interesting.'

County JHC Final: Mullinavat 2-04; Horse and Jockey 0-01

'There was not a very large attendance in St James Park on Sunday 06/08/1916, when the finals of the 1915 Junior hurling and football championships were decided. The day was threatening and was somewhat on the warm side and the sport provided did not reach anticipations. In the first half of the game especially, the vigorous defence which (the losing team) offered to the attacks of the Mullinavat forwards was beyond all praise, and on several occasions, they virtually took the ball out of the net. Their forwards however were somewhat on the weak side and some likely chances were allowed to go a begging.'

'Mullinavat were the first to appear and it was a good while after scheduled time when the hurlers were got going by Mr John Lalor the Board Secretary, who refereed. Mullinavat were the first to attack and registered a point and shortly after a similar score was registered following a "70". The "Jockey" lads scored a point a short time after, but Mullinavat replied with a goal after a great struggle and when the half-time whistle came Mullinavat had the advantage by four points. In the second half Horse and Jockey were obliged to play a defensive game and although they made several determined attacks they were unable to register.'

Mullinavat Panel: John Phelan (captain), Joe Sullivan (goal), J Power, Paddy Power, Walter Power, J Freyne, W Ryan, P Kennedy, Richard Kenneally, J Ryan, M Murphy, J Power, Jim Phelan, Jimmy O'Hanrahan, J Foskin, McDonald and Michael Holden.

1916
SENIOR

South SHC: Mullinavat w/o Horse and Jockey scr.
South SHC Semi Final: Mooncoin beat Mullinavat

(The 1916 County SHC Final wasn't played until 29/06/1919, and it was a draw – Mooncoin 4-1; Tullaoan 4-1 (5,000 attended at Knocktopher). The replay was staged at the same venue two months later, on August 24, 1919. Mooncoin won 5-2 to 2-3, the game again played at Knocktopher)

JUNIOR

South JHC Final: Mullinavat 5-03: Suirside Rovers (Mooncoin) 4-03

'The day was fine, and the fixture attracted a large gathering from the several neighbourhoods of the competing teams. The match was strenuously contested and played at a very fast pace all through. At the interval Mullinavat led by several scores, but on resuming the Mooncoin players rallied in great style and succeeded in reducing the margin between them. Play had to be suspended for about 20 minutes at this period in consequence of a dispute amongst some of the players. When the final whistle went Mullinavat emerged the victors by 1 goal.'

'Suirside Rovers (Mooncoin) objected to Mullinavat being awarded the match on the grounds of illegal players. There was a counter-objection of a similar nature by Mullinavat against Suirside Rovers. Mr Doyle contended that Mullinavat played Senior players, and it was a Junior championship match. After a lengthy discussion it was decided on the prostatic of Ald. Nowlan, that Mullinavat be requested to take off the team six players who played in the Junior final and that the match be replayed. The match was refixed for Waterford on Sunday 28th October,1917. Mr Doyle said Mooncoin were prepared to play Mullinavat for a set of gold medals, value £20, for the benefit of the County Board.'

South JHC Final: Suirside Rovers (Mooncoin) 6-01; Mullinavat 3-01

'On Sunday 25/11/1917 the replay in the final of the 1916 South Kilkenny Junior hurling championship between Mullinavat and Mooncoin was brought off at the Waterford Sportsfield. The weather though cold was fine and there was a good attendance of spectators from the districts concerned in the match. Although the game was timed to start at 3 o'clock it was almost 4 o'clock when the ball was thrown in, with the result that play had to cease within ten minutes of full time owing to darkness. Mooncoin won the toss and had the advantage of a very strong breeze in the first half during which they ran up 5 goals and 1 point to 2 goals for Mullinavat. In the second period the "Rod Iron" boys played up strongly, and after a short time scored a goal and a point. Mooncoin then added another goal after which there was some up and down play, the ball being at the time very difficult to see owing to the semi darkness. As already stated, the game had to be abandoned with ten minutes to go. At the time of cessation, the scores were: Mooncoin, 6 goals 1 point; Mullinavat, 3 goals 1 point.'

(Mullinavat were eventually awarded the title on an objection)

County JHC Final: Mullinavat 2-04; Dicksboro 1-02

'The contesting teams were Dicksboro, who won the North County Championship, and Mullinavat representing the South. In the opening stages of the play Mullinavat had somewhat the belter of the game but were assisted to a great extent by the strong wind blowing in their favour. At the half time the scores were Mullinavat 1 goal 2 points; Dicksboro 1 goal 1 point. In the second period the boys from the South played a much better game and defended the couple of onslaughts the Northerners made on their posts. In the closing stages of the game Mullinavat seemed to be all over their opponents, and the final whistle left them winners by five points.'

'So, for the second year in a row Mullinavat have won the Junior championship. At no time did the game reach the standard of excellence that one would expect from teams that have in turn beaten all that was best in hurling talent in the North and South of the county.'

'Mullinavat were the first to score and led at the interval by a small margin. On the change of ends it was believed that the city lads would make up the leeway but contrary to expectations they never seemed to get into their stride and many chances which would have enabled them to win were not availed of. However, they were not able to field their best team, they were two or three short of the fifteen that beat Conahy a few Sundays ago, and then again, the loss of Burke, the goalkeeper, who was knocked out after three minutes play, was a great setback, though a good substitute was found in Sparks. The superiority of the Mullinavat men in height and weight had also a good deal to say to the result, for the city lads were rather slow to tackle their opponents and when they did, invariably came out second best. Nevertheless, with all those disadvantages they got ample opportunities to win comfortably and if they showed anything like the form they displayed against Conahy a few weeks ago they would have won well with something to spare. Fennelly and Robert were about the best of the city lads, and Phelan, Hanrahan and Power did most for the winners. The latter gave a very finished hours play and he was never at fault.'

'The day was bitterly cold and the attendance was on the small side. The organisers were themselves to blame for this matter, as the match was very badly advertised. The southerners were the first to make an appearance. Mr D. Brennan, who refereed, lost no time in getting the teams together, Dicksboro defending the Freshford Road goal. Dicksboro were the first to get away, but they were driven back and Mullinavat attacked. Burke saved well but was again tested a moment after, and the ball skidding off his hand lodged in the net. One of the Mullinavat forwards challenged and he was obliged to retire, his place being taken by Sparks. Though the latter proved a good substitute, Burke's retirement had a bad effect on the city lads. On resuming a free was awarded to Mullinavat within scoring distance, and Power with a good effort scored a point.'

'An invasion by Dicksboro followed and they forced a "70" but nothing resulted. Power, the Mullinavat back, was doing well and he sent down the field again. Another free went their way but only an over followed. A nice passage by the Dicksboro forwards and Donnelly got in for Dicksboro's first score, a point. Nettled by this response, Mullinavat attacked and after a free forced a "70" which Power converted, giving Mullinavat a lead of four points. Following the delivery, they pressed again and Sparks was obliged to concede another "70". Power failed to convert on this occasion. It was followed with a similar free and the same result. A free to Dicksboro then followed but Mullinavat held up the attack and rushing to the other end got through for a point. Shortly afterwards a chance went Dicksboro's way and after some nice play by the forwards, McSweeney scored a goal. This raised excitement somewhat and it was intensified when two players lost their tempers and were "lined." The spectators rushed in and a considerable delay ensued in trying to clear the field. At the half time the scores were Mullinavat 1 goal 2 points; Dicksboro 1 goal 1 point.'

'At the change of ends it was thought that Dicksboro would most likely make up the deficit which was against them. Mullinavat made a redistribution of their defensive forces which had a very happy result. The ball being put in motion Mullinavat forced a "70" but nothing came of it. Mullinavat then settled down to defensive tactics and the game, except for brief packages, was uninteresting. Mullinavat scored twice (1-1) and Dicksboro once (0-1) and the Southern team won by a five-point margin. This is the second year for Mullinavat to win the Junior championship and they are to be heartily congratulated for the result.'

POLITICS AND THE GAA

'At the Kilkenny GAA Committee meeting held at the Assembly Rooms of Kilkenny town hall on Sunday 18/6/1916, a discussion took place on the GAA and Politics. Mr John Lalor informed the meeting that he took it upon himself to write to the County Inspectors of Kilkenny and Waterford regarding the holding of championship matches. He got no response from Waterford, but Mr Power, the inspector of Kilkenny, advised that provided the occasions were not used for political demonstrations or displays they had no objections to hurling or football games being played. However, he asked to be informed of the dates and places of these games'.

'This annoyed some delegates, such as Mr Aylward of Mullinavat:"I think that man seems be under a misapprehension altogether. Hurling and football matches are not held for political purposes or displays at all, and never have been held for such purpose in the history of the GAA. I think that idea should be removed out of his head; if he is not prejudiced it will be very easy to remove it." After a debate the meeting secretary John Lalor, and chairman Alderman James Nowlan decided to escalate the issue to Leinster Council.'

1917
JUNIOR
South JHC R1: Mullinavat drew with Callan
South JHC R1 Replay: Mullinavat beat Callan (at Thomastown)
South JHC R2: Mullinavat 5-02; Knockmoylan 2-00

'The match was very evenly contested throughout and though the "Rod Iron boys" were victorious, their win was by no means as easy as the scores would seem to indicate. A rather untoward incident occurred during the progress of the second half of the match which was calculated to rather mar what was otherwise a good game, but happily it was of short duration.'

Mullinavat: J Aylward, J Sullivan (goal), J Freaney, P Kennedy, M Hoban, M McDonald, J Power. Jim Ryan, M Foskin, P Neary, T Tobin, J Hanrahan, M Murphy, T Duggan and W Walsh.
(No South Junior or Kilkenny Senior Hurling Championships were completed in 1917)

1918

No South or Kilkenny Junior Hurling Championship completed.

In 1918, the British Authorities informed Luke O'Toole that no hurling or football games would be allowed unless a permit was obtained from Dublin Castle. The GAA, at their meeting of July 20, 1918, unanimously agreed that no such permit be applied for under any conditions and that any person applying for a permit, or any player playing in a match in which a permit had been obtained, would be automatically suspended from the association. In a further act of defiance, the Council organised a series of matches throughout the country for Sunday, August 4, 1918. Matches were openly played throughout the country with an estimated 54,000 members taking part. This became known as Gaelic Sunday.

GAELIC SUNDAY IN KILKENNY

At a meeting of the Kilkenny Co. Board, GAA, on Sunday 28/7/1918 last the following fixtures were made. The matches were played on Sunday, August 4th, at 3 o'clock in every parish in the county. In common with every other part of the country. Kilkenny staged 25 games, 9 in football and 16 in hurling.

FOOTBALL

Conagh v. Dunmore at Dunmore. C.Y.M.S. v. Grange at Grange. Kells v. Coolagh at Callan. Blanchfields Park v. Gowran at Paulstown. Hugginstown v. Kilmoganny at Hugginstown.

Cappagh v. Milebush at Milebush. Glenmore v. Tullogher at Ballyfacey. Mangan (the Rower) v. Coolcoe at Graignamanagh. Glenmore No 2 v. Bigwood at Bigwood.

HURLING

Foulkstown v. Dicksboro at St James' Park. Conahy v. Tulla United at Three Castles. Freshford v. Clomanto at Clomanto. Crosspatrick v. Horse and Jockey at Johnstown. Ballycloven v. Tullaroan at Kilmanagh. Callan v. Kilmanagh at Callan. Dunamaggin v. Ahenure at Dunnamaggin. Knockmoylan v. Mullinavat at Mullinavat. Lukeswell v. Killany at Killeen. Graignamanagh v. Mangan at Graignamanagh. Bennetsbridge v. Thomastown at Thomastown. Chapelhill v. Ballyhale at Knocktopher. Clogga v. Kilmacow at Kilmacow. Suirside Rovers (Mooncoin) v. Ramblers at Mooncoin. Piltown v. Temploerum at Piltown. Davidstown v. Slieverue at Slieverue

The following week the Munster Express reported:

'In common with every other part of Ireland, Sunday last was recognised as "Gaelic Sunday" in South Kilkenny, and each parish had its own game. At Clogga, Kilmacow played the home team, and an interesting match was witnessed. At Rathkiernan the Ramblers and Suirside Rovers met in friendly rivalry. A football match was played at Smithstown between Killahy and Lukeswell, which resulted in a draw. A hurling contest was subsequently brought off between Knockmoylan and Mullinavat and ended in a scoreless draw. At Ballyfacey, Glenmore beat Tullogher in a football match, and at Knocktopher, Ballyhale got the decision over Chapelhill. Hugginstown won from Kilmaganny in their trial at Hugginstown. A football match was played between Davidstown and Slieverue at the latter place. In the northern parish of the county similar events took place, each of which was carried out in a real Irish sporting spirit.'

GAELIC SUNDAY IN MULLINAVAT

Mullinavat had to overcome more obstacles than most clubs on this historic day. Mr Peter Foley owned a sawmill in Mullinavat Village. The local dance hall was also owned by Peter and was also the local hurling club's headquarters. Peter manufactured hurleys for several clubs in the area, selling them for approximately one shilling each. In fact, because of his allegiance to Mullinavat Club, many were provided for free to our players. The RIC Barracks was situated on Main Street, Mullinavat, and ahead of "Gaelic Sunday" the local police sergeant instructed the club chairman that none of the games were to go ahead. The club chairman countered by informing the sergeant that the games were going ahead regardless of directives. On receipt of the chairman's reply the local RIC decided to raid Peter Foley's sawmill, where they suspected at least 100 hurleys were stored. This would have made it impossible for the Gaelic Sunday fixture to go ahead. Luckily for the Mullinavat club, a local domestic cleaner at the RIC Barracks called Mary Mackey overheard this plan and informed Mr Foley. Mr Foley buried the hurls in eight feet of sawdust. The RIC did indeed raid the property the following morning and not a single hurl was found. The RIC knew they had been outwitted, and on Gaelic Sunday itself decided to surround the Mullinavat playing pitch to stop the fixture taking place. Again, Mullinavat were ahead of this, moved the fixture to an alternative venue a few miles away, and the game took place without a hitch. The game resulted in a scoreless draw. Several of the clubs listed above are either no longer in existence or are now part of a different club. It is noticeable that some clubs are listed to play two games. One can only assume that perhaps one was a hurling game and the other a football game.

1919

Southern Board commenced in 1919 with James Aylward, Mullinavat (chairman), Peter Walsh Temploerum (vice chairman) and John Ryan, Knockmoylan (secretary) as officers.

SENIOR
South SHC R1: Mooncoin beat Moondharrig (Mooncoin)
(The 1919 Senior championship was declared null and void when Tullaroan and Mooncoin could not agree on venue)

JUNIOR
South JHC R1: Moondharrig (Mooncoin) No.2 beat Mullinavat
South JHC Final: Knockmoylan 9-06; Temploerum 1-03

'The morning was beautifully fine, and this was something for which to be thankful, considering the downpour that fell all day long the previous day. Light-hearted and gay, the men in blue and green in six jaunting carts left Kilmacow village at 12 noon. They were fancied for the event but did not succeed in pulling it off. The Kilmacow contingent, considerably augmented by those of their kindred who travelled in inside traps, on foot or on bicycles, were the first to arrive at the venue.'

1913
South JHC
Mullinavat 1-1; Kilmacow 1-1

CHAPTER 2

1920s

'Many of the RIC barracks in South Kilkenny had been closed and/or burned down by the IRA. This included Mooncoin Barracks, Hugginstown, The Rower, Bennettsbridge, Inistioge, Glenmore, Slieverue and Rosbercon Barracks. These were all destroyed by 1921, with Mullinavat being the last to survive. This was garrisoned by about 20 men, composed of two RIC sergeants, eight or nine RIC constables and the remainder being "Black and Tans".'

1920s

1920

Townlands like Clonassy, Ballynooney, Garrygaug, Listrolin played against each other in this decade.

SOUTH

South SHC R1: Mullinavat drew with Moondharrig (Mooncoin)

(The Senior Championship was unfinished, in fact there was no completed Senior Championship again until three years later)

JUNIOR

South JHC R1: Thomastown beat Mullinavat
South JHC Final: Mooncoin 4-02; Knockmoylan 1-01

A SEPTEMBER 1920 NIGHT IN MULLINAVAT

(Munster Express)

'An extraordinary story of strange happenings in the village of Mullinavat comes to hand. We give us with all due reserve, though there seems to be no reason to doubt the authenticity of the source of information. It would appear that on Wednesday night, 16/09/1920 a number of "Black and Tans" who were stationed in Thomastown, proceeded with a couple of police to the village of Mullinavat, close on midnight, and entering the lodgings of Mr Nealon N.T. ordered him outside. Mr Nealon, who was clad only in shorts and trousers, and was in his bare feet, was escorted outside and compelled to march up the street to the school house, where he teaches. Here, it was stated, the "Black and Tans" proceeded to rip up the flooring boards, ostensibly in a search for arms. Finding nothing there it is alleged that Mr Nealon was brought outside, and placing him against the wall, fired three or four shots over his head from their revolvers, which they carried.'

'The firing over Mr Nealon, who was rather roughly handled, was then returned along the street and back to his lodgings. After this is a stated, the raiding party proceeded to the public house owned by Mr Murphy in the village. Mr Murphy, it is stated, has just come out of hospital having been ill for some time previously. He and his son, so the story goes, were taken out of bed, and accused of causing the police in the village to be boycotted. They then proceeded, it was alleged, to help themselves to whiskey and other drinks, and food, for which they paid in cash before leaving. They are also alleged to have questioned Mr Murphy as to why he refused to supply goods to the police, after which they proceeded to search him personally. In his pocket they found a medical certificate and asked him what it was about. Mr Murphy explained what it was. The raiders then turned to his son and asked him where we took the mails to. This evidently had reference to one of the recent raids on mail trains in the county. The young man replied he did not know anything of what they were talking of, and one of the "Black and Tans is then alleged to have said, "If you don't know that, then you know all about shooting a policeman? It is stated the men then took their departure. Next morning, the Mullinavat inhabitants found several doors in the village painted white, and numerous inscriptions painting on the walls, the majority of the mottoes being, "God save the King, down with the rebels".'

1921

There was no South or County Junior Hurling Championship completed in this year. This was the years of "the troubles", which were from 1920 to 1922 inclusive. In the main, normal life in Kilkenny continued relatively unabated throughout the conflicts of 1919-1923, although there was plenty of upheaval. GAA events were massively limited in 1921.

Twenty-three-year-old civilian James Hoban is shot accidently by Crown Forces on the Main Street in Mullinavat

Many of the RIC barracks in South Kilkenny had been closed and/or burned down by the IRA. This included Mooncoin Barracks, Hugginstown, The Rower, Bennettsbridge, Inistioge, Glenmore, Slieverue and Rosbercon Barracks. These were all destroyed by 1921, with Mullinavat being the last to survive. This was garrisoned by about 20 men, composed of two RIC sergeants, eight or nine RIC constables and the remainder being "Black and Tans".

On January 17th and April 11th there was two unsuccessful IRA attacks on Mullinavat Barracks. Less than a fortnight after the second attack, on April 19th, 1921, General Strickland, the highest-ranking British commander in the south of Ireland, visited Mullinavat Barracks. An armoured car was present as security for his visit, and the firing of bullets from this vehicle resulted in the sad death of James Hoban, from Glendonnell,

Mullinavat. He was in the village of Mullinavat with his uncle, James Walsh, on normal agricultural duties, selling pigs. Mr Hoban was just 23-years-old.

1922

JUNIOR

South JHC: Callan No. 1 beat Mullinavat (fixed for July 1923)
South JHC Final: Clonmore 10-02; Callan 1-00

CONVENTION

'The Kilkenny GAA Convention was held in the City Hall on Sunday 23/04/1922. Mr Thomas Walsh (Ballyfoyle) and subsequently Mr Sean F Gibbons president presiding. There was a large attendance of delegates. Mr Michael Moore secretary was present. Reference was made by a delegate to a set of medals which he stated was due to Mullinavat club In connection with the 1917 championship. The secretary said he knew nothing about these medals as he was not appointed secretary until 1919. So far as he could ascertain there was no record in the books relating to the medals. Mr Thomas Walsh said he did not think they would be in order discussing the matter at the convention. It was certainly a matter that the Mullinavat delegates should not lose sight if. The matter could be brought before the county board later on.'

EXECUTIONS BY FREE STATE AUTHORITIES

A bleak day in the history of the county occurred on December 29th, 1922, with the execution of two Kilkenny natives, namely John Murphy (aged 22, from Bennettsbridge) and John Phelan (aged 32, from Thomastown) by the Free State authorities in Kilkenny Military Barracks. They were the first such Free State executions to take place outside of Dublin or The Curragh.

The Kilkenny People reported, "Two men were executed in Kilkenny on Friday 29/12/1922. The following official report was issued from Army Headquarters: "John Phelan, Thomastown, Co. Kilkenny, and John Murphy, Bishopslough, Co. Kilkenny, arrested on the 13th December 1922 at Bishopslough, were charged with being in possession, without proper authority, of arms and ammunition, and further, with being concerned in a raid on Sheastown House, when property to the value of £180 was taken. The accused were found guilty of both charges and were sentenced to death. The executions were carried out at 8am."

"The two men were attended during their last moments by the Rev Fr. Kavanagh, Adm St John's, and the Rev M Drea, C.C. Chaplain to the military forces in Kilkenny. They walked steadily to the place of execution, and unflinchingly faced the firing squad. The volley was heard in all parts of the town. When the men fell, two priests rushed forward and annointed them. Death was practically instantaneous. Phelan was a married man and leaves a widow and two children. He was a labourer. Murphy was a farm worker, and a single man. An uncle of his named Kirwan, who lives near the barracks, was passing there on to his work when the deadly volley rang-out."

1923
JUNIOR

South JHC R1: A strong selected team made up from Glenmore, Kilmacow and Mullinavat players beat Slieverue
South JHC Final: Glenmore 5-02; Hugginstown 2-00

NATIONAL ARMY POST

On 26/3/1923 the post of the National army at Mullinavat was attacked by 25-30 men, but reportedly beaten off after 30 minutes, with no casualties on other side. By the middle of June the military posts stationed there had left, along with those at Fiddown and Mooncoin. By the end of the War of Independence in Kilkenny, seven IRA men were dead, seven members of the Crown Forces had been killed (including three who were Irish born), along with eight civilians fatalities (including those executed as informers), bringing to 22 the total number of fatalities.

1924
JUNIOR

Mullinavat did not compete.

Mullinavat played a challenge hurling game v. Slieverue at Bigwood on 8/6/1924 but when the fourteen team South JHC draw was made, whilst Mullinavat were one of 17 clubs affiliated along with six in football, they did not field in the championship in either code.
South JHC Final: Thomastown 8-00; Slieverue 2-00.

1925
JUNIOR

Mullinavat did not compete.
South JHC Final: Knockmoylan 4-06; Coolroe 4-03

CHANGING NAMES

Changing the names of clubs was a feature of the South Kilkenny GAA parishes in this period. On 26/4/1925 at the South Kilkenny AGM Mr Richard Houlihan (Knocktopher), the outgoing chairman, referring to the balance sheet, said that he noticed that there were several clubs in arrears with fixture fees. He wished it to be clearly understood that such clubs would in future be debarred from taking part in the championships unless the sums due were forwarded to the secretary during the coming week. It appeared that when some clubs were defeated in their championship matches, they forgot about paying their fees, and when affiliating for the following season they changed the name of the club and selected another representative in order to avoid responsibility for the money due to the Southern Board. That practice would have to cease and in future he would hold the representatives of the various clubs responsible for the debts of their predecessors.

1926
JUNIOR

Mullinavat did not compete.
South JHC Final: Knockmoylan 6-06; Collroe 3-01

1927
JUNIOR

Mullinavat were back in the South Junior for the first time in five years. The club played home games at land belonging to Mr Pat Raftice, Ballyluskey.
South JHC R1: Glory Rovers beat Mullinavat No.2
South JHC R1: Mullinavat No.1 beat Mount Juliet (at Dunnamaggin)
South JHC R2: Slieverue beat Mullinavat No.1 (at Kilmacow)

1928
JUNIOR

South JHC R1: Mullinavat beat Red Rocks (The Rower)
South JHC R2: Mullinavat beat Skeough
South JHC R1 Semi Final: Mullinavat beat Mooncoin
South JHC Final: Carrickshock 12-01; Mullinavat 1-01

Carrickshock qualified to meet the winners of the Northern area in the final of the county Junior hurling championship by defeating Mullinavat in the southern final at

Knocktopher Sportsfield on Sunday 6/1/1929 in rather easy fashion by 10-02 to 2-01. It was an uninteresting and one-sided game, and Carrickshock dominated the play all through, scoring as they pleased. Mullinavat never made any serious rally at any period of the game. They were completely outclassed, and their poor showing came as a great surprise to their many followers, who expected that their team would put up a better fight against their opponents, considering their fine displays in the preliminary rounds, when they defeated such prominent teams as The Rower, Skeough and Mooncoin.

Mullinavat Panel: Willie McEvoy (goal), John, Pat, Jimmy and Willie Aylward, Willie Sullivan, Willie, Pakie and Robert Walsh, Richard Kenneally, Jim Freyne, Maurice Murphy, Jimmy Walsh, Ned O'Neill, Tom Kelly, John Foskin, Ned and Jimmy Keeffe, Walter Walsh, Michael Hoban, Fr Pat Power and his brother, Walter.

1929

INTERMEDIATE

A new Intermediate grade for teams that survived Junior third round and beyond of the previous year was introduced. There was now four grades in the 1929 championships – Senior, Intermediate, Junior and Minor.

IHC R1: Mooncoin 4-01; Mullinavat 4-00

'Despite the inclement weather conditions that prevailed, a big crowd braved the elements to witness the match between Mooncoin and Mullinavat, played at Kilmacow on Sunday 28/4/1929, and which resulted in a rather lucky win for the former by the narrow margin of one point. The match took place in a field kindly given by Mr Michael Higgins, Skeard, and is in a convenient centre, close to the main road at Milltown. Lively midfield play followed the throw in, and then Tom Dunphy got possession to open the scoring with an easy goal for Mooncoin from far out, which was misjudged by the goalie. Mullinavat at the other end drove wide shortly afterwards. From a cut in near the Mullinavat goal Allen got possession in front of the posts, and though unmarked, sent badly wide, but the same player shortly after made no mistake in shooting through for a good goal from an opening. J McGuire and P Walsh were prominent at midfield for their respective sides. John Foskin sent well in for Mullinavat and was finished by Jimmie Foskin for a great goal.'

'Mullinavat were awarded a free, which was centred nicely, and amidst tense excitement the forwards broke through the Mooncoin defence to score the equalising goal, which was greeted with encouraging cheers from the "Rod iron" supporters.'

'Half Time Mullinavat 3-00; Mullinavat 2-01. Mullinavat again took up the running, and Aylward, with great dash, scored a goal. Mullinavat were now having the best of the exchanges, and their overhead play was good. They looked as being easy winners, but within ten minutes of the end Mooncoin got into their usual stride and fought on gamely till they gradually over hauled their opponent's lead. For the winners, the brothers Keane, William Dunphy, J McGuire and J Allen played well, while for the losers the Aylwards, the Walshes, O'Neill and Kenneally were outstanding.'

Mullinavat: R Kenneally (captain), W McEvoy (goal), John Foskin, P Walsh, M Keating, J Foskin, James, William, John and Patrick Aylward, R Walsh, E O'Neill, J Hanrick, J Freyne and W Walsh. Sub: P Foskin.

OBJECTIONS

Mullinavat Hurling Club subsequently objected to Mooncoin being awarded the match in the first round of the Intermediate Championship played at Kilmacow on April 28th, on the grounds that William Dunphy, one of the Mooncoin players, was ineligible to play, having played with the Senior team against Tullaroan on April 31st, in the Nowlan Park medal tournament; and (2) that one of the Mooncoin players was not properly togged, contrary to rule. The objection was not entertained on the grounds that the envelope containing it, did not contain the Irish watermark!

JUNIOR

JHC R1: Mullinavat w/o Skeogh No.1
JHC R2: Mullinavat 4-04; Floodhall 2-03

'The play on both sides was most exciting and interesting. The arrival the Floodhall players, dressed in "emerald green with white band" looked a picture of physical fitness and determination, as they filed out on the field. Then came the mighty caman wielders from Mullinavat in "blue and white" garb and from their appearance one could well imagine that they could make a great struggle for supremacy.'

MORE OBJECTIONS

'Floodhall HC objected to the Mullinavat team being awarded the match played at Skeough on 29th September on the grounds that Mullinavat played John Foskin, Patrick Walsh, William Walsh, J Aylward, etc., who were illegal players, having played against Mooncoin in the Intermediate Championship at Kilmacow on 28th April.'

Chairman – What have Floodhall to say?

Mr Carroll (Floodhall) – We have nothing further to say only that these men played in the Intermediate Championship.

Mr Conway (Mullinavat) – I thought the rule should be quoted in the objection.

Mr Carroll – We couldn't quote any rule because there is no definite rule on the point.

Chairman (to the Mullinavat delegates) – Did the men play in the Intermediate Championship? Now, give us your honest opinion?

Mr Conway – Well, we admit they did play on that particular occasion.

Mr R Houlihan TD Chairman – Well, then, I think we need not go further. I am very pleased at the way the Mullinavat delegates have met the case. They very manfully stated that the players concerned did take part in the Intermediate Championship and admitted the facts straight away, which showed a fine sport on their part. They did not try to baffle the Board in any way, as you will sometimes meet in other cases, and I admire them for their plucky action. Under the circumstances, I have no option but to award the match to Floodhall.

South JHC Final: Dunkitt 6-03; Thomastown 1-01

CHAPTER 3

1930s

***The Mullinavat team which defeated Freshford
in the 1939 Kilkenny JHC Championship:***
Back Row (from left): *Pat O'Brien, Danny McLoughlin, Willie Durney, John Walsh, Jimmy Bergin, Jimmy Foskin, Paddy Holden, Neddie O'Connor, Jim Keegan (secretary).*
Middle Row (from left): *Tom Durney, Jimmy Hendrick, Paddy O'Neill, Willie Walsh, Pat McDonald, Pat Aylward, captain, Peter Foskin, Andy Aylward, Tom Walsh, Dixie McSweeney, Nickie McSweeney.* **Front Row (from left):** *Philip Hoban, Mick Heffernan, Mick Doolan, Paulie Fitzgerald, Pete Sutton and Donie O'Brien.*

1930s

1930

In this decade many Mullinavat men played with Carrickshock, Kilmacow, Slieverue and Glenmore amongst others.

INTERMEDIATE
IHC R1: Mooncoin 3-02; Mullinavat 1-01

JUNIOR
South JHC R1: Mullinavat 6-03; Mooncoin No.2 1-02

'Mullinavat experienced some difficulty in getting their team together, and it was somewhat beyond the appointed time when the match commenced. Mullinavat won the toss and aided by a strong breeze, did most of the pressing in the opening half. Maddocks and Knox at centrefield kept the forwards well fed with the ball, and Mullinavat turned over with a comfortable lead of 10 points at half time. Mooncoin opened better on the resumption, but McEvoy and Keating were a brilliant pair in the Mullinavat defence and cleared several dangerous situations. Mooncoin continued to press but drove many overs. Mullinavat were away in surprising fashion and scored a goal and a point in as many minutes. Some fine passages of play by both sides were witnessed in the concluding stages, and though Mooncoin battled bravely to score, they were unable to overcome tho big lead of their opponents, who emerged easy winners by the wide margin of 16 points.'

Mullinavat: M Hoban (capt), T McEvoy, J Knox, M Knox, T Knox, P Holden, P Carew, D Maddocks, J Aylward, P Aylward, A Aylward, P McDonald, M O'Neill, M Keating and J Holden.

OBJECTION DISQUALIFIES BOTH TEAMS
'Mooncoin No.2 Hurling Club objected to Mullinavat being awarded the match played at

Dunkitt on June 29 on the following grounds:

(1) That the Mullinavat team was 25 minutes late in taking the field, contrary to Rule 8, page 75, Official Guide, 26 and 27

(2) that Mullinavat played a member (Michael Keating) not properly togged, contrary to rule passed at 1923 Congress. Mr T Dunphy, Mooncoin, stated his team took the field at the appointed time. At the expiration of half an hour Mullinavat lined up, and he made a protest to the referee. At least a half dozen Mullinavat players played in long pants, contrary to the rule quoted. Mr Maddock, Mullinavat, admitted his team was late owing to a breakdown in their means of conveyance and which was also responsible for some of their players not being properly togged, as they had not time to dress in knickers.'

'Mullinavat lodged a counter objection to Mooncoin on the grounds that the latter team included two unregistered players, Michael O'Brien and James Brophy, contrary to Rule 10, page 37 Official Guide. Mr Maddock said he applied to the acting Secretary of the County Board. Mr Cody, for a copy of the register of Mooncoin, and the names of the players named did not appear there on. Mr McDonald, Mooncoin, stated O'Brien was registered but admitted that owing to an oversight he omitted the name of Brophy. The Chairman said the representative of both clubs had admitted breaches of the rules and he must rule both out of the championship.'

South JHC Final: Crowraddie 8-07; Blue and Whites 3-04

1931
INTERMEDIATE

IHC R1: Slieverue 1-12; Mullinavat 3-04

'The play all through was characterised by dash and vigour and no quarter was given or taken. This was due to a large extent to the pitch being rather over grassy with resultant dangerous and close pulling, which had an irritating effect on the players. An unfortunate scene marred the concluding stages when a player from either side was sent off by the referee for breaches of the rules. Shortly after an altercation arose between two opposing players, and spectators rushed in from the sidelines; a general fracas arose between rival supporters, resulting in blows being struck and a most unpleasant melee followed which, however, was happily got under control after a short time and the game continued on uninterrupted.'

'Playing with a favourable breeze and a strong sun, Mullinavat piled up a lead of 12 points to nil in the opening moiety and were considered by many to be unlucky not to have retained the lead to the end. To say that they fought an uphill fight and succeeded in snatching the lead in the last ten minutes is a tribute to the excellent grit and determination of Slieverue, who, it goes without saying, did not hurl as well as in former games. Mullinavat fielded a vastly improved side from recent years, but they failed to last the strenuous pace as good as their opponents, who were a livelier, and more experienced side. Exciting play marked the concluding stages when two frees in succession to Slieverue from which scores resulted turned the tide in their favour, and though Mullinavat tried hard to get on terms, they were unable to break through a stern defence.'

'Midfield exchanges followed the start and Fabian Kinsella was away for Slieverue to send over. The Mullinavat defence was again assailed, and Power was obliged to concede a 70 from which Kinsella sent over, Aylward cleared from a free to Slieverue, and a free to Mullinavat brought no reward. Slieverue again pressed and Carroll centred neatly from the wing, but Phelan cleared from the danger zone. A free eased for Mullinavat, and Larry Duggan centred nicely from the puck out for the forwards to finish for the opening point. Mullinavat sent over from the delivery. Aylward and Durney and Kinsella and Penkert were conspicuous for their respective sides. Mullinavat were away again and Knox saved well in goal. From a free Larry Duggan added a goal for Mullinavat. W. Lynch centred for Slieverue but again Aylward distinguished himself on the back division by a brilliant clearance. Kinsella sent narrowly wide in a good try for a point, and Mullinavat broke away on the delivery, to send through a fast goal, followed by a minor shortly after. Mullinavat completely dominated the play at this period, and the Slieverue backs experienced a busy time. Just before the interval Mullinavat added a further goal and a point and led at halftime by 3-3 to 0-00.'

'Mullinavat broke away on the resumption and though playing against hill and wind, continued to press. Slieverue moved in from a free by Kinsella, but Duggan returned the leather from the danger zone. Exciting play followed at midfield, both sides contesting hard for supremacy. In a subsequent tussle two opposing players, T Penkort (Slieverue) and J Aylward (Mullinavat) were sent off by the referee for breaches of the rules.'

'Slieverue attacked and Frank Penkert sent over the bar from a neat ground shot for the first point for his side. Power conceded a 70 under sustained pressure, and from a well-placed puck the forwards rushed through for a goal. W Lynch added a second goal from a free close in shortly after. Hereabouts Slieverue made a splendid recovery and opened up in dashing style. The Mullinavat backs were now bearing the brunt of the battle and Slieverue continued on the offensive, Carroll (S) was injured but resumed. W Lynch centred neatly on a free to Slieverue, but Aylward cleared by a grand overhead stroke, but the forwards again returned, and in a fast bout of play Kinsella sent through for a goal. Slieverue again forced the pace from the delivery and Penkert added a further goal from a well judged free. Slieverue now led for the first time by a point and excitement and enthusiasm was intense,

Mullinavat again spoiled by fouling, and from the resultant free close in Penkert sent nicely over the bar. Determined hurling followed, both sides striving hard for victory. An exciting bout of play followed around the Mullinavat citadel, and Power saved a rasping shot in goal. The backs cleared to advantage, and play was transferred to midfield where an unfortunate incident, resulting in stoppage of play, developed (as already reported above). Spectators rushed in and it was some time before order could be restored, and after the pitch had been cleared the game was again resumed.'

'Only a few minutes remained to be played, Slieverue were away for a fast point on the restart. Mullinavat attacked but sent over. Larry Duggan sent well in from a free to Mullinavat and the forwards pressed hard to score the equalising goal but were well held by a stout back line. From a further free Duggan sent over. Kenneally sent over a good point for Mullinavat which reduced the lead to two points, and excitement was again renewed. Then Mullinavat attacked hotly to send narrowly wide. Mullinavat tried hard to overcome the lead, but in almost exciting and gruelling fashion Slieverue maintained their lead of two points to the final whistle. Play was at midfield at the end.'

Mullinavat: Jim Phelan (captain), J Power (goal), W Power, Tom Duggan, Larry Duggan, Pat Aylward, J Aylward, John Aylward, W Aylward, Tom Durney, R Kenneally, W O'Sullivan, M Hoban, Tom Walsh and W Walsh.

JUNIOR

South JHC R1: Mullinavat 6-02: Slate Quarries 0-01
South JHC R2: Mullinavat w/o Dungarvan
(Dungarvan objected to this and match was refixed)
South JHC R2 Refixture: Dungarvan easily beat Mullinavat
South JHC Final: Knockmoylan No.1 W/O Knocktopher No.2 scr.

1932

The club was struggling in 1932 and had to concede walkovers at both Intermediate and Junior grades. Meanwhile, off the pitch, in July Mr Pat Aylward, well known in Mullinavat and South Kilkenny GAA circles, opened a new carpentry establishment in the village, where he was assured of support and patronage from a wide circle of friends who wished his new enterprise every success.

INTERMEDIATE
IHC R1: Kilmacow w/o Mullinavat

JUNIOR
South JHC R1: Dungarvan w/o Mullinavat
South JHC Final: Knockmoylan 5-03; Knocktopher 4-00

1933
JUNIOR
South JHC R1: Dunkitt w/o Mullinavat
South JHC Final: Green and Whites (The Rower) 8-06; Mooncoin 2-04

1934
JUNIOR
Mullinavat did not compete.
South JHC Final: Ballyhale 8-6; Thomastown 1-1

1935
JUNIOR
Mullinavat did not compete.
South JHC Final: Slieverue 5-05; Black and Whites 0-00

1936
JUNIOR
Mullinavat did not compete.

While Mullinavat had pulled out of the South Junior Championship in 1932 and 1933, and were not fielding adult teams at all between 1934 and 1936, there was still major interest in hurling locally. This person wrote to the Munster Express proposing a look at the parish rule (something that wasn't properly implemented in Kilkenny until eight years later).

◄ MULLINAVAT GAA CLUB ►

Mullinavat, Jan. 21, 1936
To the Editor Munster Express

Dear Sir,

An interesting motion is down for consideration at Sunday's Kilkenny Co. Board Convention asking that the parish rule be enforced in the championships. The motion however, has various arguments for and against its adoption. The principal one for of course, is that it would give a chance to the weaker clubs to put up a better show in the championships, as at present when a good player is discovered on any team, his services are immediately sought after by a higher grade club, consequently to the detriment of his own. On the other hand, some players would never get a chance of inscribing their name on a medal were it not for the fact that they were taken up by an outside team, and if the motion were passed it would mean that those players would then have to turn out against their adopted club in the future, and it might so happen, too, that such players would not be allowed, through club prejudices or such like, to ever again turn out for the team they had previously reneged. All these matters are, of course only problematical, and whatever the decision may be, the motion ought certainly give rise to a very interesting debate. Apologising, Mr Editor, for taking up so much of your valuable space.

I am, dear sir, yours faithfully,
"MOUNTAIN DEW"

1937

JUNIOR

Mullinavat were back in the Junior Championship and qualified for a fifth South Junior final, which we lost by a point versus Mooncoin.

South JHC R1: Mullinavat No.1 w/o Glenmore, but then withdrew themselves.
South JHC R1: Mullinavat No.2 6-02; Kilmacow No.2 0-02

'Before a big attendance at Fiddown on Sunday 23/5/37 Mullinavat No.2 defeated Kilmacow No. 2 on the score of 6-2 to 2-2. The game was played in a good sporting manner and held lively interest throughout, despite the disparity in scores, but heavy rain in the last quarter held up play for some six minutes. Mullinavat was the heavier side, but their lighter opponents put up a gallant fight, the teams giving an interesting display which pleased the large attendance.'

Mullinavat No 2: P Aylward (captain), J Bergin (goal), J Aylward, William Aylward,

J Aylward, R Walsh, William Walsh, J Walsh, R Walsh, T Walsh, P Foskin, J Foskin, P Holden, P Fitzgerald and R Kehoe.

OBJECTION

'Kilmacow Hurling Club objected to Mullinavat No.2 being awarded the championship game played at Fiddown on Sunday 23/5/37. Mr Peter Barden, Chairman, presided, and the following delegates were in attendance: Messrs Martin Walsh. N.T. (Nore Rangers); Denis O'Doherty, N.T.; Edward Walsh; K Aylward; J Rohan (Moonrue); John Foskin, John Walsh, P Holden (Mullinavat); R Keating, E Norris, J Heneberry (Suir Rangers); D Kenneally. P Kelly, P Doyle, R Croke, P Cleere (Kilmacow); T Shefflin, Walsh (Blues and Whites); John O'Connor (Glenmore); Joe Lee (Thomastown); John Lonergan, M Brennan (Moonrue HC); Tim Maher, P Brennan (Blacks and Whites); R Wallace, P.C. (Graigue); Leo O'Connor, Martin White (Clover Brand), et cetera. Mr Seamus McKenna, Thomastown, Secretary, was also present. The following objection from Kilmacow Hurling Club was read: "On behalf of Kilmacow Junior HC, we object to Mullinavat No.2 being awarded the match played at Fiddown on 23rd May on the grounds that Mullinavat were ten minutes late taking the field, contrary to Rule 8, page 65, Official Guide."

John Foskin – Is the objection in order, Kilmacow have two hurling clubs, a No.1 and No.2, and it doesn't state which one.

Secretary – The objection is in order. It is the one club, but they have two teams, a No.1 and 2.

John Foskin – Who appointed the referee? Was he the official referee?

Secretary – No.

John Foskin – We weren't consulted about the referee at all, but we understood that the official referee was gone to Cork.

P Kelly – Is there any stipulation as to time, because Mullinavat were late taking the field? Didn't Mullinavat agree to the referee?

P Holden – Mullinavat were on the field at the appointed time, we asked Mr Walsh was he the official referee, and he said he was appointed by Kilmacow.

P Kelly – Mullinavat came on the field after time.

Chairman – What does the referee say in his report?

Secretary (reading report) – "The game was played in a sporting spirit by both teams. With 13 minutes to go rain began to fall heavily and play had to be abandoned for about six minutes. When play restarted Mullinavat scored a goal, but as the umpires had not taken up duty I did not allow any score. Mullinavat took the field at 2.32pm. I did not award the game to any team at the start" – John Walsh (Suir Rangers Hurling Club).

Chairman – Perhaps Mr Keating could tell us something about the matter.

Richard Keating – As a matter of fact, the Suir Rangers made a slight mistake that day, because we forgot all about the referee, and after asking two or three we finally got John Walsh to officiate at the last moment. It was 2.25pm then, and the match was started without Mullinavat being consulted.

P Kelly – Mullinavat were asked.

Secretary – The rule states that a referee cannot be appointed on the grounds unless with the consent of both captains.

P Cleere – By way of explanation, I may be permitted to say that Mr Keating approached me and said that the official referee was not available, so we endeavoured to obtain a suitable man to act. John Walsh said he would do it, and I took it for granted that he was a neutral man, and as Mullinavat had not raised any objection to him at the start of the game that they were quite satisfied to have him act as referee. I do not wish to enter into the discussion one way or the other, only to have this fact known by way of explaining what happened.

Chairman – I notice from the final scores that Kilmacow were rather decisively beaten and, taking everything into consideration, I would appeal to them to withdraw their objection.

P Kelly – I certainly say that any team late on the field should be dealt with according to rule. If a match is fixed for a certain time why not comply with that? So far as I see, the ruling is arranged in Mullinavat and not here. Any secret agreements outside this Board will not be tolerated so far as we are concerned.

(P Holden strongly resented the statement that the ruling was made in Mullinavat and called for further proof or a withdrawal)

R Wallace – If the official referee did not attend it is obvious that the match was null and void.

P Holden – It is a very flukey objection

P Kelly – The rules are there, and if a match is fixed for 2.30pm let it be 2.30pm. If Mullinavat objected to the referee, why did they not protest before the match or lodge a counter objection.

Chairman – I think there is no course open but to declare the match null and void, and although it will be holding up the championships, I rule that the match be replayed as the official referee was not present.

South JHC R1 Refixture: Mullinavat No.2 5-04; Kilmacow No.2 0-01

'Before a small attendance at Fiddown on Sunday 11/7/1937 Mullinavat No.2 defeated Kilmacow No.2 in the county Junior hurling championship replay on the score of 5-4 to 0-1. The half-time scores were 3-3 to nil. Rain fell heavily during the course of the game, but the winners were superior throughout and emerged easy victors.'

Mullinavat: P Holden (captain), J Bergin (goal), W Walsh, Richard Walsh, John Walsh, T Walsh, P Aylward, James Aylward, J Aylward, John Aylward, P Foskin, T Foskin, Edward O'Connor, Paul Fitzgerald and P Kehoe.

South JHC R2: Mullinavat No.2 3-02; Killarney 3-02

'Before a good attendance at Ballyhale on Sunday 19/9/37, Killarney and Mullinavat met in the second round of the County J.H. Championship, which resulted in a drawn game after an interesting contest, on the score of 3-2 each. Mullinavat led at half time by 3-1 to 1-2, and nearing the end held a three point lead, but a great goal by Paddy Cullen made the issue a drawn game. A feature of the match was the great goalkeeping of Tim Kelly for Killarney, who were also ably assisted by Fennelly, Murphy, Marnell, Fitzgerald and Cullen. Foskin, Aylward, Holden and Walsh were prominent for Mullinavat.'

Mullinavat: P. Aylward (captain), J Bergin (goal), T Foskin, J Foskin, P Foskin, W Walsh, J Walsh, T Walsh, J Aylward, P Fitzgerald, B Kehoe, P Holden, P Kehoe, J Purcell and J Aylward.

South JHC R2 Replay: Mullinavat No.2 v. Killarney

'The first-round tie of the South Kilkenny Junior hurling championship between Killarney and Mullinavat, played at Ballyhale on Sunday 17/10/1937, was marked by scenes of disorder. Fighting in which almost all the spectators participated broke out at intervals and became so general that the referee, Mr Bob Aylward, was obliged to abandon the game, his efforts to restore order being absolutely futile. Even the intervention of Rev Fr. Nolan, CC Ballyhale, failed to calm the tempers of the combatants.'

'The game opened in lively fashion, and keen hurling was the order until about midway through the 1st half hour a scuffle between two opposing players occurred and the crowd surged on to the pitch, hurleys were raised in a threatening attitude, and free fights amongst players and spectators presented the referee with an unenviable task. However, after considerable persuasion, he succeeded in having order restored and the crowd returned to the sidelines. The game was again resumed in spirited fashion but it was evident that the tempers of both players and spectators, had been by this time considerably ruffled. However, the first half-hour passed off without any further incident.'

'Shortly after the opening of the closing half of the game a melee in the Mullinavat goalmouth resulted in some people receiving nasty injuries. A considerable crowd surged around some of the players, but after a while order was restored. Play was again resumed but apparently some of the spectators must have thought their presence necessary on the pitch and it was with difficulty that the hurlers moved around. Shortly before the conclusion of the game the ball was driven down to the Mullinavat goalmouth and one of the Killarney forwards, in attempting to score was attacked by an opponent. The scene that followed which culminated in the abandonment of the game, was almost beyond description. From all parts of the field the crowd surged around two individuals who were forced to flee for safety. Hurleys waved in the air, blows were struck and a number could be seen to emerge with nasty head and facial injuries. For fully a quarter of an hour a crowd comprising practically all the spectators were huddled together. Mr Aylward abandoned the game and the scene ended. A number of the players appealed to the referee to continue the game, but he declined, saying, "I have given my decision on and I won't reverse it, when the game could not be played in the proper spirit." The abandonment came about ten minutes from the finish.'

'Mullinavat lead by 2-0 to 1-1 at half-time and when the game was abandoned in the second half only a point divided the teams with Mullinavat leading 2-2 to 2-1. Members of the Mullinavat team, Robert Walsh, and P. Roche, sustained nasty head injuries when struck with a hurley by a spectator, who subsequently received a rough handling before being escorted away. The players had later to be medically treated for their injuries.'

Mullinavat: J Bergin, J Foskin, P Roche, J Forristal, P Foskin, P Aylward, P Holden, W Walsh, J Aylward, J Hendrick, J Walsh, W Aylward, J Aylward, T Walsh, J Holden. Subs: P Fitzgerald and R Walsh.

South JHC R2 Second Replay: Mullinavat 7-02; Killarney 4-00

'Before a good attendance at Ballyhale on Sunday, Mullinavat defeated Killarney in their second replay of the Junior hurling championship on the score of 7-2 to 4-0. The game, which was played in a fine sporting manner, was well contested, but Mullinavat assumed superiority in the closing period to emerge worthy winners.'

Mullinavat: P Aylward (captain), J Bergin (goal), J Aylward, R Walsh, W Walsh, J Walsh, T Walsh, J Foskin, P Foskin, P Holohan, P Fitzgerald, J Forristal, J Hendrick, P Roche and J Walsh.

South JHC R3: Mullinavat 8-00; Blues and Whites (Ballyhale) 1-05

'At Ballyhale Sportsfield on Sunday 27/11/1937, before a good attendance, Mullinavat consolidated their position in the Southern Junior Hurling Championship by a decisive victory over Blues and Whites (Ballyhale) in the third round on the score of 8-0 to 1-5. The game was not as closely contested as anticipated, the winners running up a comfortable lead of seven points at the interval, when the score was 3-0 to 0-2. Mullinavat added five further goals in the closing moiety, to which their opponents replied with a goal and three points.'

'Whilst practically all the winners played their part in securing victory, it will not in the least be reflecting on the winners to say that the outstanding man of the side was Pat

Aylward, whose long-range drives at many periods throughout the hour were a source of continuous worry to the opposing defence. Bergin was cool and reliable in goal, bringing off some good saves under pressure, whilst the defence was sound throughout. The forwards also gave a satisfactory display, availing of every opening that came their way, whilst the clashes around centre field were a feature of the game, which was played in a fine, sporting manner all through. The winners were short the services of Robert Walsh, who was injured in the recent replay against Killarney, Willie Aylward coming on in his place.'

Mullinavat: P Aylward (captain), J Bergin (goal), J Aylward, W Aylward, T Walsh, W Walsh, J Walsh, P Foskin, J Foskin, P Holden, J Hendrick, J Purcell, P Fitzgerald, P Roche and John Forristal.

South JHC Semi Final: Mullinavat 5-02; Suir Rangers 3-02

'In a game which was productive of many exciting exchanges and pulsating passages, Mullinavat defeated Suir Rangers in the semi-final of the Southern J.H. Championship played at Kilmacow on Sunday 12/12/1937 on the score of 5-02 to 3-02. The winners got going early and ran up an interval lead of 7 points (3-0 to 2 points), but the Rangers made a wonderful recovery in the closing moiety, in the first ten minutes of which they sent through two fast goals to reduce the lead to the minimum margin. Excitement was intense as Suir Rangers assumed the lead with a swift goal only a point separated the teams once more when John Aylward had a point for Mullinavat from a free. Enthusiasm was again at fever pitch when Jimmy Hendrick, who played prominently throughout for the winners, levelled the scoring with the best point of the match. With time running out it was anybody's game, both sides battling every inch of the ground. Towards the end Mullinavat steadily gained the upper hand, securing two further goals to put the issue beyond doubt. Whilst not by any means over brilliant, the game, taken all round, readied a good standard, particularly in the early stages of the second half, and with the lead alternating, held the interest of the crowd to the final whistle.'

'The winners, on the general run of the play, deserved their victory, though they had a close call, which is not reflected by the six points margin, and many will agree that the Rangers experienced hard luck on a few occasions when the forwards lost some likely opportunities through over anxiety. Bergin, in the Mullinavat goal, was again, cool and reliable, saving his citadel at many critical moments when the fall of his net seemed imminent. The backs on both sides played well, whilst around centre field some hard and hectic hurling was witnessed throughout many periods of the hour. Midfield exchanges followed the throw in, John Aylward getting possession to put Mullinavat attacking, but the backs repulsed. Mullinavat returned to send over. The Rangers forced a "70" on the delivery, which brought no reward. Following a "70" to Mullinavat, taken by Pat Aylward, the backs cleared to the wing. From the resultant cut in John Walsh centred neatly to his brother, Tom Walsh, sending through for the opening goal.'

'Five minutes after the start, Paddy Holden was prominent around midfield and following fast exchanges, Mullinavat again moved in, Jimmy Hendrick slashing through for a second major to the joy of Mullinavat supporters. A free eased for Suir Rangers, which was cleared by Willie Walsh, and keen hard hurling followed, both ends being visited in turn. Roche cleared twice in succession for Mullinavat, whose last line of defence stood up well under pressure. Long and Heneberry sent well in for the Rangers, and the backs repulsed, but Mullinavat spoiled by fouling. Larry Gorman centred well from the free, but P Aylward cleared effectively. P Holden was injured by an accidental stroke from the ball, but resumed. The Rangers were away on the restart, Roche saving close in, but Long returned to send over the bar for a point. A further free, taken by Gorman, was beaten, off, and a free to Mullinavat (Aylward) was fouled, the Rangers sending over from the hop. Heneberry from a free at centrefield put Rangers attacking, but the forwards again finished weakly. Hendrick, Purcell and Walsh figured in a neat passing movement on the wing which ended in an over.' 'Mullinavat went on to the offensive again, a grand movement ending in a goal by Tom Walsh from a pass by Purcell. The Rangers sent over from the delivery. When the Rangers again pressed, Bergin conceded a "70" in saving, and Larry Gorman placed well, but Holden returned. J Aylward (Suir Rangers) retired, being replaced by J Bowe. From the hop Gorman sent well in, the Rangers finishing for a point after the ball had glanced off Bergin's hurley. Half time came with the scores reading Mullinavat 3-0; Suir Rangers 0-2.'

'On the resumption of play Suir Rangers forced a "70" which was taken by Gorman; but the backs repulsed. The Rangers again returned to the attack, Long finishing a grand effort for a goal. Following a free to the Rangers, an exciting bout of play ensued around the Mullinavat posts, ending in a further goal by O'Shea amidst intense enthusiasm. Only a point now divided the teams, and the Rangers were hurling with a speed and dash which swept the opposing defence momentarily off its guard. A further free to Suir Rangers was muffed, and when play veered round the Mullinavat forwards missed a likely opportunity close in. Hurling of a high order followed, and when Suir Rangers snatched the lead for the first time by a fast goal from Long, their followers went wild with delight. Heneberry and Keating cleared on a free to Mullinavat, and P Holden returned to send over. Mullinavat again moved in to send inches wide, and Rangers were wide of the objective at the other end after Bergin had saved in goal. W Walsh doubled on the delivery, but J. Walsh and P. Walsh nullified the attack, saving well under pressure. P Holden was injured but resumed. Mullinavat sent well in from a free, but Walsh and Foley cleared effectively. Paul Fitzgerald was injured in a collision with a colleague, but resumed after treatment. Rangers sent over from the hop, and Mullinavat were also wide of the objective in the next minute after Hendrick had eluded three opponents. J. Purcell was fouled in possession, and from the resultant free J Aylward had a point for Mullinavat, to again reduce the margin to the minimum.'

'Exciting play followed, the enthusiasm reaching a high pitch. Mullinavat forced a "70" following a hot onslaught around the Suir Rangers posts. From the "70" Holden placed well, but the forwards sent over. Walsh and Bowe cleared under pressure for the Rangers, but Hendrick picked up and levelled the scoring with a grand point, the same player giving his side the lead in the next minute with a great goal, which put Mullinavat supporters in jubilant mood. Mullinavat now seemed to have the upperhand, and a further goal by Tom Walsh, who received from Hendrick, clinched the issue. A free to Suir Rangers was muffed, and a further free in the closing minute was sent over.'

Mullinavat: P Aylward (captain), J Bergin (goal), John Aylward, William Aylward, William Walsh, J Walsh, T Walsh, P Foskin, J Foskin, P Roche, J Forristal, J Purcell, P Fitzgerald, P Holden and J Hendrick.

South JHC Semi Final Refixture: Mullinavat 9-01; Suir Rangers 3-00

'Mullinavat beat Suir Rangers convincingly in the South JHC Semi Final refixture held at Ballyhale. Suir Rangers Hurling Club had objected to Mullinavat being awarded the first match played on 12/12/37 at Kilmacow on the grounds of alleged illegal constitution. The matter came before the meeting of the Southern Board on 2nd January and this refixture was ordered.

South JHC Final: Mooncoin 0-03; Mullinavat 0-02

'The curtain has been rung down on the 1937 Southern Junior Hurling Championship, and the honours have gone to Moondharrig, who triumphed over Mullinavat in the final on Sunday 13/2/38 by the minimum margin, after a great game at Ballyhale. With the exception of a cold northerly breeze, the weather conditions were ideal for the match, the sod being in a good, dry condition.'

'The hurling was too close to be brilliant, but there were periods of exciting passages, which kept the big crowd at a high pitch of expectancy, and with the lead alternating it was anybody's game to the last minute. It is a tribute to the goalkeepers and backs on both sides that not one goal was recorded for the hour, though both teams had many overs. Mullinavat put up stiff resistance, but did not seem to last the hot pace set from the start and were apparently tiring towards the finish.'

'Twelve minutes of the opening half had elapsed before Mullinavat drew first blood! A point by John Walsh, and just before the call of half time Walter Crowley levelled up with a splendid shot. Mooncoin faced the sun in the second moiety and both sides had overs. Paddy Holden had an early point for Mullinavat and both ends were visited many times before Mick Fennelly picked up on the wing to send over the bar for the equaliser, amidst considerable excitement. Mullinavat defence spoiled by fouling, and Jimmy McGuire gave Mooncoin the lead with a point close in. Mullinavat pressed hard to secure the equaliser, but were held by a stout defence, and in a hectic finish, Moondharrig maintained their slender lead to the last whistle.

Mullinavat: P Aylward (captain), J Bergin (goal), R Walsh, William Walsh, J Walsh, T Walsh, P Foskin, J Foskin, J Hendrick, J Purcell, P Fitzgerald, J Aylward, P Roche, J Forristal and P Holden.

RUNNING COMMENTARY ON THE MATCH

A chairde Gaedheal, this is Ballyhale, the popular South Kilkenny gaelic centre. There is an enormous crowd present here for the Junior hurling game between Mullinavat and Mooncoin. In the throng I can see many old-time Gaels from all over the county, and I have spoken to some who have walked 10 miles to see the match. The pitch here looks in splendid trim, with a bare, dry sod, and freshly marked with white lines. There is a cold wind blowing across the ground, but otherwise the weather is ideal, and excitement is becoming apparent as the starting time is drawing near. Yes. Pierce Cleere, the referee, is now sounding the whistle, and the crowd is following the teams into the centre line to witness the usual preliminaries prior to the start. Jim Keegan is giving a few final words of advice to the Mullinavat boys, and Edmond Walsh, the tall, slim Moondharrig captain, is handing in his list of players, as is also Pat Aylward for Mullinavat. The coin is tossed and Moondharrig wins. The crowd now leaves to take up the best available positions around the pitch. Pat O'Brien races back to take his stand on goal at the village end, and Jimmy Bergin, his vis-a-vis is facing the sun at the railway goal. The backs are in position, the forwards are lined up at centre field, the referee is glancing at his watch, and the sun is shining brightly on the green and white and blue and white of the respective teams.

Hello! Hello! They're off! The great clash has begun and midfield exchanges follow the throw-in. Mullinavat are away, and John Walsh sends up to Johnny Aylward, but the Mooncoin backs have cleared to safety. When Pat Aylward is called on he responds gallantly and breaks up a spirited assault, Jimmy McGuire returning to scud over. Cleary has returned Bergin's delivery, and Paul Fitzgerald cuts to the wing. McGuire takes the cut in and the Moondharrig forwards are now racing in, but Fripps has driven wide of the objective. Cleary is again prominent around the halfway line and has sent well down to Fennelly, who crosses to Sean Maher, and Sean is narrowly wide.

Following a lengthy delivery there is now a fast bout of play, but a Mooncoin player is down injured, think it's Cleary. He is up again and play has been resumed. Willie Walsh secures possession from the hop and the Mullinavat forwards are now attacking. Johnny

OUR STORY (1887-2024)

Aylward is racing in and has forced away. Paddy Holden has sent narrowly from the puck in a good try for a point. Willie Walsh has returned the delivery and another "70" results. Paddy Holden's stroke falls short, but the forwards move in to force yet another "70". Pat Aylward is taking the puck this time and places well, but Cleary crashes his way through to make a splendid clearance. Mooncoin have spoiled by fouling, and from the free Paddy Holden centres well, but the backs have cleared effectively. John Walsh brings back the leather again and shoots over the bar for a grand point, the opening score, after 12 minutes play.

Foskin has cleared well in the backs for Mullinavat and hard, keen hurling is now the order. Cleary has been fouled in possession, and the whistle has gone for a free, which is being taken by Mike Crowley. The Mullinavat net looks in danger, the forwards are swarming in. No, Dave Quinn has sent over, and Mullinavat supporters are breathing a sigh of relief. There is a cut in to Mullinavat, but Johnny Aylward has finished for a wide. Mullinavat have returned for a further wide, shooting on both sides being somewhat faulty up to the present. Mooncoin have returned the delivery to send over, and Mullinavat have driven wide also after a sharp onset around the Moondharrig posts. Fennelly has sent well in for the Suirsiders but Foskin and Fitzgerald are sound in defence and Mullinavat have broken away to send wide once more. Paddy Holden and Tom Walsh have combined well in a neat movement, but O'Brien has raced out of his goal to pick up a hopping ball and clear well. The goalie has again cleared a strong shot from Holden, and Cleary is now playing a wonderful game for Mooncoin being all over the field, adapting himself to defence and attack as occasions demand. After the Mooncoin goalie clears again Mullinavat work back to send over. Holden eluded three opponents that time and sends well in, but Mooncoin is sound in defence, and when play veers round Walter Crowley picks up to send over the bar for a point, and scores are now level. Cleary has brought off a grand clearance once more and shows remarkable agility in screwing out of a tight corner. And there's the half time whistle sounding a truce, with the scores level at a point each.

Personally, I believe it's anybody's game yet, but from what I have seen of the first period both sides are a little erratic in their shooting and may have lost a few likely opportunities. The hurling, whilst not being over brilliant, has been keen and close, with not many loose advantages on either side. It would be a keen student who could as yet foretell the result, and Mooncoin will now be facing the sun in the last half. The teams are now coming to the centre line again, and in a few moments will be in action once more. The players are in their places, the stewards are busy keeping the crowd back, and the referee has thrown in the ball.

The teams are in motion again, and Paddy Holden has broken away for a point in the first minute, to give Mullinavat an early lead. Roche and Forristal cleared in the Mullinavat defence, but Fennelly returned with a grand centre which was finished for an over. Mooncoin pressed again from the delivery, but the forwards have sent wide of the mark. The Mullinavat defence cleared to the wing under sustained pressure, and McGuire was wide that time with a low, fast shot. There is a stoppage of play over near the sideline now, two opposing players being involved. The crowd has encroached, but the referee is whistling up for the restart of the game.

He has brought the two players concerned together and makes them shake hands, which is a happy termination to the incident. Mullinavat are away on the restart, but Tom Walsh, one of the forwards is down injured. He has resumed and from the hop Edmond Walsh puts his men in action, but Roche and Foskin cleared. Willie Walsh, Mullinavat, is down now having received an accidental injury. He is up again. From a free Paddy Whelan has sent wide. J Hendrick was prominent on the delivery and sent wide in a good try for a score. Hendrick and Walsh again moved in, but O'Brien is safe in goal and clears well. Jimmy McGuire is taking a free for Mooncoin, he sends up well, and Cleary and Fennelly are combining to advantage. The ball is out on the wing again, but Fennelly has picked up, and hello, hello! Yes, the leather is sailing between the posts for the equaliser. Two points each, and the cheering you hear now indicates the tense excitement at the moment. Mooncoin are pressing again, McGuire has centred well. The forwards are racing in. They're through It's a goal! No! Bergin saves on the line.

There is another hard bout of play in Mullinavat territory, but the backs have cleared successfully. There is another short stoppage to get the crowd back to the lines, so tense is the excitement it is hard to avoid encroachment. I see the Mayor of Waterford, who is an enthusiastic supporter of the Gaelic code, appealing to the crowd to avoid encroaching on the pitch and to give a fair chance to the players.

From the restart Mooncoin have moved in, but the Mullinavat backs have spoiled by fouling, and the whistle has gone for a free. Jimmy McGuire is taking the puck and steadying himself for the stroke. Mooncoin supporters are shouting to go for a point, and Jimmy, cool as the proverbial cucumber, lifts the leather and sends between the posts for a point. The white flag is waving in the breeze, and Moondharrig followers are jubilant, though it is still anybody's game.

Mullinavat were wide from the delivery, and when Mooncoin again returned to the attack Bergin cleared under pressure. Mooncoin forced a "70", and McGuire is taking the puck, but it falls short, and Willie Walsh clears. Fennelly of Mooncoin, is down injured, but is alright again. The game has again restarted and Cleary is showing up very prominently again. Roche was injured that time in a sharp onslaught on the Mullinavat posts, and is receiving treatment. He is up again and the game has been resumed. The hot pace from the start is now beginning to tell on the players, some of whom are showing signs of tiring. Mooncoin pressed from the restart, but Fripps sent over. Mullinavat are away again, but O'Brien has saved his citadel again.

The sun is now shining out brilliantly, and the end cannot be far off. Mullinavat are battling gamely to get the equalising point, but Mooncoin are striving might and main to retain their slender lead. The cheering is now terrific. Cleary is again in the picture and is doing great work for his side. The whistle is gone. Yes, it's a free to Mullinavat, and Pat Aylward is taking it. He sends well down, and Jimmy Hendrick is in position to send further on, but the backs are sound. Play veers round once more and the ball is now out on the wing.

Hello! Hello! The whistle has gone. Yes, the game has ended and Mooncoin are Southern champions for 1937 after a very close call from Mullinavat. I shall give you the final score again Mooncoin, 3 points; Mullinavat, 2 points.

Mr P Cleere. Kilmacow, was referee.

And that concludes the running commentary on the Southern Junior hurling final from Ballyhale Sportsfield. Good afternoon, folks, good afternoon.

1938

JUNIOR

South JHC R1: Mullinavat 9-03; Suir Rangers No.2 2-02

'Mullinavat had an easy victory over Suir Rangers No.2 in the opening round of the county Junior hurling championship at Kilmacow on Sunday 12/6/1938 last on the score of 9-3 to 2-2. The hurling was good for the first 15 minutes, and thereabouts, then the Rangers fell away, Mullinavat dominating the exchanges to win comfortably. Stoppages for injuries were frequent, no fewer than six subs being called on.'

Mullinavat: P Aylward (captain), J Bergin (goal), T Walsh, J Walsh, William Walsh, J Foskin, P Fitzgerald, P Holden, J Purcell, T Durney, J Aylward, M Heffeman, J Hendrick, P Roche and J Foskin. Sub: B Walsh and J Delahunty (for J Purcell and J Hendrick).

South JHC R2: Mullinavat 2-03; The Rower 2-01

'Mullinavat, had the services of Pat Aylward, the Kilkenny inter-county hurler who helped in the defeat of Laois the previous Sunday. With close scoring and the lead alternating, it was a keen struggle, though the hurling was not of a high order, with the exception of a bright spell in the closing moiety. The Rower held a lead of a point some ten minutes after the start of the second half, but Mullinavat, following a well-placed ball by Heffernan broke through for a goal to assume the lead, which they maintained to the end despite a gallant bid by The Rower, the issue being in doubt to the last whistle. Pat Aylward, M Heffernan, J Purcell and Tom Durney were conspicuous for the winners, whilst Martin Butler, J O'Brien, J Dunphy and Luke Grace were the pick of the losers.'

Mullinavat: P Aylward (captain), J Bergin (goal), T Walsh, John Walsh, William Walsh, P Foskin, James Foskin, T Durney, Paul Fitzgerald, P Roche, P Holden, J Hendrick, J Purcell, J Delahunty and M Heffernan.

South JHC R3: Mullinavat w/o Ahenure
South JHC Semi final: Mullinavat 4-03; Killarney 1-01

'The winners, with a favourable breeze, ran up an interval lead of 2-2 to nil, and though facing the gale in the second moiety had the better of the exchanges all through to the end, which found them easy winners. A high gale and intermittent cold showers imposed a severe handicap on the players, who, nevertheless, battled through a trying hour with commendable spirit. Mullinavat were well served in every department, particularly at centre field, where J. Purcell and Paddy Holden hit up a splendid partnership. Their long-range drives were the deciding turn in paving the way to victory, whilst the backs and forwards were always safe, even under pressure. Many anticipated a close finish when Killarney turned over with the strong breeze, but Mullinavat surprised even their most ardent supporters by doing most of the pressing and secured almost as many scores as they did in the opening moiety.'

'Mullinavat broke away from the throw in, and Purcell was narrowly wide with a grand shot from centre field. Fennelly drove wide at the other end after Bergin had saved in goal under pressure. Dannon cleared from a free to Mullinavat (Pat Aylward) but the forwards again moved in, Jimmy Hendrick opening the scoring with a neat point from a ground stroke, after five minutes play. A Mullinavat free close in on the corner (M. Heffernan) was muffed, but Tom Walsh gained possession to send narrowly over. Mullinavat dominated play at midfield and following a grand solo run on the wing by Purcell, Killarney spoiled by fouling. The resultant free, taken by Heffernan, was repelled, and a free to Killarney (M Fennelly) brought no reward. Mullinavat, aided by the gale, continued t o press, and Killarney backs and goalie were kept continually on the move. Mullinavat were over twice before Hendrick, trapping a high ball from Purcell, crashed home a great goal. Delaney was over for Killarney from the delivery. Mullinavat again broke away and Tom Walsh, with a neat corner shot, beat Kelly for a major. Rain now fell heavily, making matters unpleasant for players and spectators. Purcell was wide from a free, and from a further free Aylward centred splendidly but the backs cleared to the wing under pressure. Fennelly was wide on a free to Killarney, and just on the pip of half-time Hendrick sent over a point, leaving the half time score 2-2 to nil.'

'Though aided by the breeze, Killarney made no impression in this half, Mullinavat continuing the offensive. Fennelly had the opening score for Killarney, a point from a close-up free. Mullinavat continued to press, and Kelly in the Killarney goal conceded a 70 from which the backs cleared. From a free to Mullinavat close in Heffernan shot low for a try at goal, but the backs saved and Mullinavat returned again to force a further 70, which was taken by Pat Aylward, being finished for a point by Paddy Holden. Mullinavat now dominated the exchanges, and in a bout of whirlwind hurling, which left the Killarney defence powerless, Tom Walsh and Jimmy Hendrick had two swift goals which clinched the issue. A free eased for Killarney, but Mullinavat, hurling with great dash and elan, kept up the pressure despite the strong breeze, play for most of this period being in Killarney territory. Kelly saved from a grand centre by Hendrick, and when play veered round Killarney had a goal, when Bergin left his posts clear.'

Mullinavat: P Aylward (captain), J Bergin (goal) P Foskin, J Foskin, William Walsh, Tom Walsh, John Walsh, T Durney, P Holden, J Purcell, J Hendrick, M Heffernan, E O'Connor, P Fitzgerald and James Delahunty.

Gate receipts totalled over £12.

WHAT THE FINAL CAPTAINS SAY

Pat Aylward (Mullinavat) – 'Mullinavat are now at the peak of their form, and every player has reported fit and eager for the game. We consider we have a slight advantage in height and weight and were rather unlucky not to have won the Southern final last year. At the same time, we realise that in Bill Dalton's team we have worthy opponents who won their way to the final in convincing style. I anticipate a good, close game, but that Mullinavat should win. In conclusion I would say that which ever side wins should go on to annex county honours, and my final word is may the better side win'.

Bill Dalton (Blues and Whites) – 'Our team has improved with every game since the start of the championship and are anxiously looking forward to the final on Sunday. Although realising that Mullinavat have played consistently through the championship and will provide formidable opposition, I expect that on our display in the semi-final recently we should about win. I hope the game will be played in a good sporting spirit, and I can safely say that, whichever side wins, they will be worthy standard bearers of the South'.

South JHC Final: Mullinavat 5-03; Blues and Whites (Ballyhale) 3-03

'Before one of the largest attendances seen at this popular Southern venue for some time, Mullinavat defeated Blues and Whites in the Southern Junior hurling final at Ballyhale on Sunday by a margin of six points, on the score of 5-3 to 3-3. It was a keen hard-fought game in which the Blues and Whites had the better of the exchanges in the early stages, and it looked as if Mullinavat would be set a stiff task to hold this young, speedy and well-balanced team, whose first time pulling knocked their opponents off their usual balance. The sides were level at half time (1-1 each), but Blues and Whites took the lead by a point from a free shortly after the resumption. The locals continued to press again and had two swift goals, giving them a lead of seven points. Hereabouts the issued looked to be a foregone conclusion, but with that indomitable spirit which has always characterised the representatives of the Rod Iron parish, the Mullinavat lads staged a wonderful rally in the last quarter, and with a dash which swept all before it had two quick goals in as many minutes. With only a bare point in the difference and both sides going all out, the best hurling of the hour was witnessed, but was spoiled to some extent by frequent stoppages for minor injuries. Excitement was renewed when Heffernan levelled the scores with a grand point, and for a while it looked as if a draw would be the outcome, but Mullinavat were now definitely on top and with two further goals nearing the end put the issue beyond doubt in a hectic finish. It was a close call for Mullinavat, but it is a high tribute to their grit and tenacity that they never cracked up even when the tide went adversely against them. Their forwards, undoubtedly, missed a few chances, particularly in the opening moiety, but this is not to detract from the merits of the opposing backs, who carried off the honours of the day.'

'Bill Dalton in particular showing flashes of his old-time brilliance, his years of experience garnered from many a memorable clash proving a valuable asset. The other backs were also good but a reshuffling in the last half threw the whole line out of gear and upset the watertight combination which had been such a marked feature of the opening period. Honours were about even at midfield, where clashes were fiery between Paddy Holden and J. Purcell (Mullinavat). Kelly was a rare opportunist for the homesters, securing all of the three goals scored for his side, whilst his colleagues in the forward line combined well to advantage, being quick to draw on fast ground balls. Bergin kept a good goal for the winners, and at times saved his citadel when all seemed lost having to leave his posts on occasions to clear under pressure. The backs were solid and came through many anxious moments with flying colours, whilst the forwards, though finishing weakly at times, more than offset any earlier lapses by a gallant finish, which turned the tide at a critical moment.'

Mullinavat: Pat Aylward (captain), James Bergin (goal), William Walsh, Tom Walsh, John Walsh, Peter Foskin, James Foskin, Tom Durney, Paddy Roche, Paul Fitzgerald, M Heffernan, P Holden, J Purcell, J Hendrick and John Aylward. Sub: Robert Walsh.

The gate receipts amounted to £13 11.3.

RUNNING COMMENTARY ON THE MATCH

Mullinavat won the toss and elected to play from the village goal end. Fiery Barden (South Board Chairman) has the teams in motion and play is around the half-way line. Reade is away on the wing and sends across to Walsh, who slaps right into the Mullinavat goalmouth, but Bergin is alert and clears well, and when Blues and Whites return to the attack J. Walsh is fouled in possession. From the free, J Kelly had the opening goal after three minutes play.

OUR STORY (1887-2024)

Reade again attacked and J Foskin brought off a grand clearance for Mullinavat to break away, the forwards finishing for a wide. Pat Aylward broke up a spirited assault, and in a fast bout of play on the wing Paul Fitzgerald (Mullinavat) was injured and had to retire, being replaced by Robert Walsh.

Blues and Whites sent over following the hop and returned the puck out to send wide of the objective again. Bergin sent out a lengthy delivery which reached over 30 yards, but Eddie Neill returned the leather from the half back line, J. Walsh catching a flying ball to shoot hard and low, but Bergin and Durney saved in turn, the latter sending to the wing. J. Walsh sent over from the cut-in. Mullinavat were away on the delivery, and Purcell had a grand point from the wing. Blues and Whites replied with a similar score from the puck-out, Kelly crossing to J. Walsh, who sent neatly over the bar. After Mullinavat had sent over Durney cleared from a sharp onset initiated by Eddie Aylward and when play veered round Billy Dalton was prominent for the locals and stemmed repeated raids.

Carroll and Gorey put the homesters on the offensive again, Bergin being forced to leave his posts to clear under pressure. Heffernan and Walsh sent well in for Mullinavat, the forwards sending over after an exciting tussle. Blues and Whites again moved in, Reade sending in a high shot which Bergin slapped back. Pete Foskin cleared from a free to Blues and Whites, and in a fast bout of play around midfield Paddy Holden was injured, resuming with a bandaged head. Willie Walsh put Mullinavat attacking but Gorman cleared, and when Paddy Holden eluded two opponents on the wing he sent wide with a high shot from close to the half-way line. Billy Dalton was almost unbeatable at full back and saved time and time again when Mullinavat were almost through.

Back to midfield the leather came again, where clashes were very fiery. Players fell, hurleys flew and supporters cheered as both sides made every effort to gain superiority. Blues and Whites broke through the Mullinavat defence, and when Bergin lost his hurley he cleared with a handstroke. Mullinavat broke away on the wing to send over. E Aylward was injured but resumed after treatment. On the resumption of play Bergin again saved in the Mullinavat goal when Gorey, after receiving from Kelly, sent in a rasper. Pat Aylward cleared from a cut-in taken by Ed. Aylward and Mullinavat broke away for Jimmy Hendrick to level up with a great goal from the right wing when he neatly slipped the defence, the shot glancing off McBride's hurley. With the scores equal, excitement reached a high pitch and hectic exchanges followed.

After Johnny Aylward had sent over for Mullinavat, Paddy Holden got possession from, a cut-in and placed well, but the Blues and Whites' defence was sound. A free eased for the homesters, the backs saving from Gorman's shot, but the Blues and Whites again moved to send narrowly wide. John Walsh (Mullinavat) was injured but resumed. Pat Aylward, on a free to Mullinavat, sent the ball right into the goalmouth with a splendid high shot, but McBride caught the oncoming ball and made a splendid clearance, Blues and Whites breaking away to send over after a fast and exciting bout of play. The half time whistle sounded on the delivery leaving the scores level at 1-1 each.

Blues and Whites pressed on the restart, Bergin saving in the first minute. Mullinavat spoiled by fouling, and from the free close in Gorey gave his side the lead with a point. From a cut-in the homesters again gained ground, Kelly sending through for a swift goal. Willie Walsh and Heffernan put Mullinavat on the offensive, but the backs saved and Mullinavat returned to send wide. Purcell got the better of a stern dual at centre-field and sent a long shot all the way for a point, leaving the scores 2-2 to 1-2. Mullinavat again returned to the attack with renewed energy, Johnny Aylward crossing to Tom Walsh, who shot dead and true for the posts, but McBride was sound and affected a splendid clearance. Mullinavat returned to force a "70" which Pat Aylward sent over from a high stroke. Blues and Whites moved in per Corcoran, and Bergin brought off a fine save, coming out nearly 30 yards in clearing. Following a cut-in, Kelly finished for a great goal for Blues and Whites, and when Walsh added a point the homesters held a lead of seven points and looked as likely winners. Mullinavat, however, were undaunted and, true to tradition, came back with greater effort. Heffernan was narrowly wide with a high shot. A free eased for Mullinavat, which, however, brought no reward. Robert Walsh and Paddy Roche repulsed a spirited assault, and keen exchanges were witnessed around centrefield.

Mullinavat gained ground from a cut-in, and Billy Dalton in clearing slipped, the forwards coming back in a flash again to break through for a great goal. Fired with renewed enthusiasm Mullinavat came back again, Johnny Aylward sending narrowly over. An unusual incident happened on the puck out when McBrides hurley flew from his hands on the swing and he had to kick the ball from the ground. Mullinavat again returned to the attack, but the forwards spoiled by lifting, and when Blues and Whites broke away the forwards were whistled up for fouling. James Foskin took the free and sent well down, the backs clearing to the wing under pressure. Johnny Aylward slipped the defence again and crossed a ground ball in front of the Blues and Whites posts. Tom Walsh picked up and shot low and hard.

Hello! Hello! A goal! Yes, a goal! John Fitzgerald is waving the green flag and Mullinavat supporters are giving full vent to their enthusiasm. With only a point separating the teams' excitement was at fever pitch. O'Gorman was wide on a "70" to Blues and Whites, and Mullinavat, playing with rare dash now, had the balancing point in which Walsh and Heffernan shared the honours. Both sides had overs before Bergin brought off a good save from Reade. Robert Walsh retired injured find was replaced by Paul Fitzgerald, who had retired early in the first half.

Hendrick was wide from the hop, and after the delivery Mullinavat supporters were again jubilant when their team took the lead with a goal from far out which McBride apparently though, was rolling wide, but struck the pole and glanced through. The fast pace and hectic exchanges were how beginning to have a telling effect, and three players were down together for treatment, whilst play was also held up for a few moments to get the crowds back to the sideline, which was being encroached upon owing to the excitement. Following a cut-in McBride cleared from Heffernan, but Mullinavat again moved in, and Tom Walsh put the issue beyond doubt when he crashed home the last goal of the game, leaving Mullinavat winners of the Southern Junior hurling final of 1938 on the score of 5-3 to 3-3.

VIEWS ON THE GAME

Pat Aylward (Mullinavat captain) – 'It was a good, clean, sporting contest, and Blues and Whites seemed to have been well trained. Our boys finished well and never despaired, even when seven points behind. Our opponents deserve the highest praise for their fine display'.

Bill Dalton (Blues and Whites captain) – 'I thought we should have held the lead, but a draw would have been the most fitting result on the run of play. Well, we lost, but we are not downhearted, and we congratulate Mullinavat and wish them the best of good luck in the county final.'

FINAL PREVIEW: BRIEF SKETCH OF MULLINAVAT PLAYERS

Pat Aylward – Popular skipper of the side. Plays centre half back and a quiet and honest hurler who gives of his best in every game. Has assisted Kilkenny in the Leinster J.H. Championship this year and was previously with the Carrickshock Club. Pat is a carpenter as well as a farmer and can make a caman just as capable as he can handle one. He is also an accomplished footballer. Aged 27, weighs 11st. 2lbs. and stands 5ft. 9ins.

James Bergin (goal) – Jimmy hails from Coolnaleen and is one of the finest players on the team, standing 6ft. 4ins., being built in proportion. Gave a grand display in the Southern final recently and has a powerful delivery. Always cool and alert, and often comes out to make a splendid solo clearance along the wing. The Mullinavat net will be safe under Jimmy's guard on Sunday. Is attached to the G.S.R. and weighs 12st. 8lbs. He is aged 25 years.

Tom Durney – Fills the full back position and has a perfect understanding with the goalie. Hails from Bigwood district and formerly assisted Mooncoin Senior club. A stout defender who provides a difficult task for any full forward and has ample size and weight, as he turns the scale at 12 stone. Is a farmer by occupation, aged 27 years and 5ft. 9ins. in height. Tom is keen of eye and can size up an awkward situation in a flash, whilst the full forward is left dispossessed.

James Foskin – Left full back. Also hails from Bigwood district and comes from hardy hillside stock long identified with the Gaelic Athletic Association. Is a brilliant defender, with great strength and stamina, two vital assets to a hurler. James showed up well in the Southern final and effected some long range clearances when hotly tested. A farmer by occupation, aged 24 years, 6ft. in height and aged 24 years.

Paddy Roche – Right full back. A native of Glenmore, and has youth on his side, being only 20 years of age. A dour defender who always proves a thorn in the side of an opposing forward. As is to be expected, coming from such a renowned football parish, Paddy is also an adept player with the big sphere. He is now playing at the top of his form and should be heard of to advantage on Sunday. A farmer In occupation, weighs list. 7lbs. and 5ft. Qin. in height.

Paul Fitzgerald – Comes from Fahee and fills the left half back berth. Plays a cool, determined game and gave a grand display throughout the year. Sticks to his man like a leech and possessed of ample speed and stamina. Conies of hardy farming stock and knows no fear. Aged 21 years, weighs 11 stone 7 lbs. and 5ft 9in. in height.

Peter Foskin – Plays right full back and weighs nearly 14 stone. A brilliant and brainy defender who improves with every appearance. Combines in forming one of the best half-back lines in Junior ranks and will provide a strong Hindenburgh defence on Sunday which will allow little scope for openings. Pete is a farmer by occupation, aged 23 years and tips 5ft. 8 inches.

Paddy Holden – Comes of a well-known Gaelic family from Knockbrown and plays at midfield. Of splendid physique, weighing 14 stone and 6ft. 1/2 in. in height. His strength and reach prove a valuable advantage and his long-range drives are always a source of worry to an opposing defence. Knows no fear and revels in the thick of the fray. A farmer by occupation and aged 27 years.

James Purcell – Known to his hurling colleagues as "J" and partners Paddy Holden at centre field. Is also well known in Minor hurling ranks and led Mullinavat to victory in the southern final on Sunday. A youth of much promise and has assisted Kilkenny in the Leinster M.H. Championship. This is a splendid midfield pair and will be Mullinavat's strongest asset on Sunday. Of farming stock, weighs 12 stone, aged 17 years and 5ft. llin. in height.

Willie Walsh – Comes from Rossinan and descended from a prominent Gaelic family. His father, Tom Walsh, was one of Kilmacow's foremost players in the old football days of half a century ago. Willie is strong and active, as well as being an untiring worker who battles gamely to the last whistle. Weighs almost 12 stone, 28 years of age and 5ft. 9in. in height. A farmer by occupation. Plays centre forward.

Mick Heffernan – Hails from Glenmore and is a versatile player, having the distinction of playing Senior football, Junior and Minor hurling. Won the county Senior football title with Glenmore recently and has assisted Kilkenny inter-county Minor team. Played a prominent part in the victory of Mullinavat in the Southern Minor final on Sunday last. The winning of the Junior and Minor county championships would be the crowning of a brilliant record. Occupied as shop assistant at New Ross, aged 18 years, weighs 12st. 7lbs. and 5ft. 8in. in height. Plays right wing forward.

John Walsh – Operates on the left wing and is a splendid opportunist. Has youth on his side, being only 24 years of age. Hits fast and has a fine sense of direction, whilst speed is one of his strongest points. Always proves a handful for an opposing defender and co-operates well. A farmer by occupation; weighs 12st. 7lbs. and tips 5ft. 8ins.

Tom Walsh – Also a farmer and brother of John. Tom plays behind his brother as left full forward and there is a perfect understanding between the pair. Shared most of the honours in the defeat of Blues and Whites in the Southern final by securing two fast goals at a vital stage of the game, which turned the tide. Aged 26, weighs 11 stone and 5ft. 8in. in height.

James Hendrick – Jimmy plays right full forward and is a fast and elusive player who displays stylish wrist work. A keen and determined worker who, when he gets the bail, puts the opposing goal in danger, whilst his points from the most difficult angles are a spectacular feature. Has scored in almost every championship game this year and is a sporting and good-humoured player. Is employed as agricultural worker. Aged 28 years, weighs 11 st. and tips 5ft. 8ins.

John Aylward – Last but by no means least comes Johnny Aylward, who will act as spearhead of the attack. Shared in the scoring against Blues and Whites in the Southern final and has ample strength and endurance. A difficult handful for any full back and quick to seize on any openings. Has a happy knack of drawing out the defence and then doubling back to race in for a score. Johnny is a farmer by occupation, and a brother of the captain. Aged 28 years, weighs 11 stone and tips 5' 7".

TRANSPORT FACILITIES

'In connection with the county JHC final at Kilkenny on Sunday 19/11/38, a special bus will leave Bigwood at 11.30am on Sunday morning. Those intending to travel should hand in their names together with the fare. 2/6, as soon as possible to Paul Fitzgerald, Fahee, James Foskin, Rathnasmola, or P. Roche, Glenmore. A special bus will also leave Mullinavat immediately after second Mass, fare 2/6. As only a limited number of seats are available, intending followers desiring of travelling should send in names and cash as soon as possible to James Keegan, Mullinavat, or John Walsh, Mullinavat.'

COUNTY JHC FINAL: Ballyline 3-5; Mullinavat 2-4

'At Nowlan Park on Sunday 19/11/38 Ballyline defeated Mullinavat in the final of the county Junior hurling championship by 3-5 to 2-4. It was a strenuous, hard-fought game, featured by robust hurling and keen tackling, and while Ballyline deserved their four points win they had to fight every inch of the way to ensure victory. The hurling did not reach championship standard, and with the exception of a few passages of lively play the game could not he said to have aroused more than ordinary interest. In the first half the winners monopolised the play and turning every opportunity to account ran up a score of 3-3 without conceding a goal. In this half Mullinavat played with their backs to the wall, and while unlucky not to find the net on a few occasions they did well to notch three points. The interval score did not flatter the leaders, who at all stages, outplayed a harassed Mullinavat fifteen, but on the change of ends the fireworks started as the southern champions put all they had into the game, and when Ballyline had increased their score by 2 points the Mullinavat forwards got going in determined fashion and scored 2 goals and a point. It was only the splendid defence of the Ballyline backs that saved the day.'

'For the greater part of the second half Mullinavat hammered away at the opposing defence, and if the forwards had shown the same tenacity the result might have been different. Towards the end, the game was marred by an ugly incident, resulting in one of the Mullinavat players being ordered off the field by the referee. About ten minutes from the end a Ballyline player was injured and immediately a number of spectators rushed on to the field and blows were struck. The referee held the ball until order had been restored, when the game proceeded in the same friendly way as had existed up to this point. It was a regrettable incident though not of a serious nature, and officials would do well in future to prevent troublemakers from getting on to the sideline. Apart from this unfortunate interlude the game was played in a fine sporting spirit, which reflected credit on the players on both sides.'

'The game started in lively fashion and Ballyline were first to attack. Larkin, who was conspicuous, in the early stages narrowly missed for a goal. Ballyline kept up the pressure and a neat forward movement by P Giles resulted in a point which skimmed the crossbar, after five minutes play. Mullinavat next had a period of attack which proved fruitless. Nolan, Woodgate and Cahill figured in a determined effort by the Mullinavat forwards to get through. J Giles sent in a strong ground ball from the left wing and Shea stepping in finished to the net. Mullinavat fought back and when Aylward missed close in the ball came back to Heffeman, who sent over a point.'

'Exchanges were even for a time and Ballyline again attacked. A forward movement started by Paul Giles resulted in a point per Shea. Ballyline were now having the better of the play and in a return raid James Giles raised the white flag. The Mullinavat defence was having a busy time, and a long pass down the wing was intercepted by Larkin, who again found the net. Purcell from centrefield put Mullinavat attacking and in a desperate goalmouth duel failed to break through. There efforts were however rewarded when Purcell from far out sent over the bar. Ballyline now led by 2-3 to 0-2 and continued to do best. They had the advantage at centre-field where Nolan and J. Giles were seen to advantage. Nearing the interval Jimmy Hendrick scored a point for Mullinavat. J. Giles finished the scoring with a point to leave Ballyline leading at half-time by 3-3 to 0-3.'

'The second half-hour was featured by the splendid performance of the Ballyline defence, who kept the opposing forwards at bay for the greater part of the time. The Mullinavat forwards showed dogged tenacity in their endeavours to pull down the big lead. They put in some fine work and on the run of the play were deserving of more scores than eventually came their way. For the first five minutes they were held in their own half, during which time Ballyline had 2 points from Paul Giles and Shea. Mullinavat then got into their stride and kept up a veritable barrage on the opposing defence. Some lively duels were witnessed around the goal in which Mick Heffernan, John Aylward, Tom and John Walsh fought determinedly with Corcoran, Nolan and Woodgate assisted by Connolly and Cahill. When Jimmy Hendrick pointed for Mullinavat it seemed as if the pace was beginning to tell on the Ballyline defence.'

'Midway through the second half Walsh dashed through the centre and with a great shot got a goal. This lent courage to the whole Mullinavat fifteen and shortly afterwards followed up their success with a second goal scored by Aylward from close in. After the stoppage a free to Ballyline went goal-wards but the attack was beaten off and the ball returned to the Ballyline end, where a desperate encounter resulted in a "70." The ball was placed well but a wide resulted. Towards the end Mullinavat made a bold effort to pull the game out of the fire, but the sterling defence of the Ballyline backs frustrated their best efforts.'

Mullinavat: Pat Aylward (captain), Jim Bergin (goal), William Durney, Peter Foskin, P Roche, Jimmy Foskin, William Walsh, Tom Walsh, John Walsh, William Durney, Pat Holden, J Purcell, Jimmy Hendrick, Eddie O'Connor, Paul Fitzgerald and James Delahunty.

Ballyline: R Cahill (goal), Corcoran, J Nolan, R Woodgate, M O'Connell, P Cuddihy, P Cahill, J Nolan, James Giles, Paul Giles, T Larkin, Henry Giles, T O'Shea, J Donnelly and P Larkin.

1939

This was a great year for the hurling club. A fourth South Junior hurling title in our seventh appearance, followed later by a third County JHC title.

JUNIOR

South JHC R1: Thomastown beat Mullinavat No.2 by 6 points
South JHC R1: Mullinavat No.1 w/o Suir Rangers
South JHC R2: Mullinavat No.1 2-03; Killarney 0-02
South JUNIOR HC R2: Mullinavat No.1 2-03; Killarney 0-02

'The only score of the opening moiety was a Mullinavat point by Tom Walsh, following a cut in taken by Paddy Holden. Killarney levelled up shortly after the resumption when Boyle sent over the bar after hot pressure, the same player giving his side the lead by a further point in the next few minutes. Scores were even once more when Jimmy Hendrick, with a grand ground puck, shot over the crossbar from the right corner. Killarney who had given a surprising display up to that now faded out of the picture, and Mullinavat in a whirlwind finish had a brace of goals by the brothers Walsh, whilst Heffernan added a grand point when he doubled on a sky ball following a free taken by Pete Foskin and finished worthy winners.'

Mullinavat: Pat Aylward (captain), James Bergin (goal), Tom Walsh, John Walsh, William Walsh, James Foskin, Peter Foskin, Andy Aylward, Pat McDonald, William Durney, James Hendrick, Pat Holden, Mick Heffernan, Paddy Roche, and Edward O'Connor. Sub: Paddy O'Neill.

South JHC Semi Final: Mullinavat 5-04; Barrow Rangers (Goresbridge) 0-02

'The game was not as one sided as the scores would seem to indicate, although the winners were always in front and were never seriously challenged for supremacy. The Rovers, however, put up a good fight and contested every inch of the ground to the last whistle, some hard knocks being given and taken in true sporting spirit. The winners led at half-time by 3-2 to 0-1 and piled up a bigger lead in the closing moiety, to emerge deserving winners of a hard-fought game. Weather conditions were ideal and despite a counter attraction at Ballyhale, there was a good attendance the gate receipts totalling over £7.'

Mullinavat: Pat Aylward (captain), James Bergin (goal), Tom Walsh, John Walsh, James Foskin, Pete Foskin, Andy Aylward, Paddy Holden, Paul Fitzgerald, James Hendrick, Pat McDonald, Paul Fitzgerald, Paddy Roche, Edward O'Connor, and William Durney.

South JHC Final: Mullinavat 5-06; Hugginstown 3-01

'Before an attendance which was easily the largest seen at the popular Ballyhale centre for a considerable time Mullinavat retained their title as southern divisional champions for the second successive year by defeating Hugginstown m the Junior hurling final by a margin of eleven points, on the score of 5-6 to 3-01. It was a grand struggle throughout, with hurling of a high order at times which roused the crowd to enthusiasm, as man met man in deadly combat, but withal it was contested in a fine sporting spirit, despite keen rivalry, and reflected the utmost credit on the teams concerned. Taken all round, the game can be said to be one of the best seen in the south for some time and proved a fitting climax to the deciding tie in the southern Junior hurling championship.'

'Mullinavat showed two changes from the side which defeated Barrow Rovers in the semi-final, Mick Heffernan (who was then under suspension since the All-Ireland final against Galway), and Willie Walsh coming on in room of Paddy O'Neill and Paddy Roche. Mullinavat took the lead early and maintained it to the interval, when they turned over with a comfortable lead of 7 points, the scores being 3-1 to 1-0. Hugginstown made a great rally in the closing stages and at one period were only in arrears by 4 points, but Mullinavat piled on further scores to win well at the close of a hard-fought game.'

'Mullinavat won the toss. Pat Aylward and his boys electing to defend the village goal, whilst Martin Carty took up his position in the railway goal, facing a strong breeze. Mullinavat moved in from the start, John Walsh pointing in the first minute of the game. Jim Duggan cleared from a Mullinavat free, taken by Pat Aylward, and Hugginstown forced a 70 following a sideline puck by Peter Walsh. Martin Brennan placed well from the 70, but James Foskin made a splendid clearance in defence. Following a further free to Hugginstown (M Brennan), Bergin saved at the expense of a "70", which was cleared by Paddy Holden and when Mullinavat broke away Pat McDonald, the former London-Irish player, sent a grand shot all the way for a point from the wing. Mullinavat pressed from the delivery to send over, and when the "Rod Iron" representatives again returned to the attack, McDonald finished a grand centre by Holden for a great goal.'

'Exciting play followed, and as Bergin was slapping back a high ball from Connolly the whistle had gone for a free to Mullinavat out on the wing, Pat Aylward having been fouled. James Foskin sent well down from the free, Willie Walsh doubling on the ball, but Barron and Moore repulsed. Mullinavat again returning to send wide of the objective. A slight shower of rain fell but did not dampen the ardour or enthusiasm of the players or spectators. After John Walsh had been narrowly wide from a grand centre by Heffernan, O'Connor and Pat Aylward repelled a Hugginstown free, taken by Dick Connolly, and the forwards again broke through to send over. Hugginstown pressed from the delivery, and after Andy Aylward had cleared "Pa" Shea slipped through for a goal, the scores now reading Mullinavat 1-2; Hugginstown. 1-0.'

'Heffernan replied with a point from the puck-out. M. Brennan missed on a free, but sent in from a ground shot, which was cleared by Paddy Holden, and when play veered round Carty saved from Heffernan. The same player was wide on a free to Mullinavat in the next minute. Heffernan again slapped back the delivery and when Willie Walsh placed Tom Walsh, the latter pointed with a splendid grounder. Mullinavat were over twice before

Gorman missed on a free to Hugginstown, and when John Brennan sent in on Willie Durney was applauded for a spectacular clearance, and when Mullinavat again took up the running Tom Walsh finished a great drive to the net. Carty saved from Hendrick in the next minute, and immediately afterwards brought off a great clearance from McDonald, but the same player beat Carty shortly after for a major. Durney repulsed a fast onset, by Hugginstown following a free taken by Connolly, and when Daly returned the leather Paul Fitzgerald cleared to the wing, but Connolly again put his side on the offensive. A free for Mullinavat being taken by Andy Aylward, and the halftime whistle sounded on the drop of the ball, the scores reading: Mullinavat 3-4; Hugginstown 1-0.'

'Hugginstown pressed from a cut-in and when Peter Walsh placed Dick Shea, the latter crashed home a splendid goal. When Martin Brennan send back the delivery there was a hard bout of hurling around the Mullinavat posts which "Pa" Shea capped with a fast goal, amidst considerable excitement, Hugginstown followers going wild with delight. Only four points now divided the teams (3-4 to 3-0).'

'Some grand hurling was now witnessed, and so far it was still anybody's game. Duggan cleared from a free to Mullinavat (Pat Aylward) and on a free to Hugginstown close in Martin Brennan placed well. Bergin coming out to effect a fine clearance along the wing. When play swung round, Carty saved on the line from Tom Walsh at the expense of a "70" taken by Pat Aylward which was finished for a point by Heffernan, the Glenmore youth side stepping Duggan to send neatly over the bar. Willie Durney slapped back the delivery, and as the sun shone out strongly the sliotair was sent flying from end to end with lightning-like rapidity. Mullinavat battling strongly against the hill and sun to maintain the lead, whilst Hugginstown strove might and main to get on terms, being aided by a slight breeze, which had calmed down somewhat since the opening moiety.'

'From a free on the 21-yards line to Mullinavat, Tom Walsh shot low and hard for the posts, but the Hugginstown backs saved splendidly. Mullinavat returning to force a "70."' Pat Aylward took the puck, which fell short, but Heffernan picked up and following a grand solo run, passed to McDonald, who made no mistake for a point. Hugginstown pressed on the delivery, Bergin clearing well from Gaule to the wing. Hugginstown pointed from the cut-in and Tom Walsh was wide at the other end from the puck-out. Both defences proved sound under pressure, whilst the clashes around midfield between Paddy Holden and Willie Durney (Mullinavat) and W Daly and Dick Connolly (Hugginstown) were the highlight of the game. A free eased for Mullinavat (Pat Aylward) but was beaten off by a strong last line in which Power and Lonergan were prominent, but in the brothers Walsh had a big handful to contend with. Martin Brennan, the Hugginstown skipper, went down with a facial injury, but resumed after treatment. A free to Hugginstown taken by Martin Brennan led to a further free, the latter was charged before striking the ball. The second free, taken by T Barron, was finished for a wide. John Walsh, receiving from his brother Tom, was wide at the other end from the puck out. Paul Fitzgerald got possession on the delivery, but was fouled, and when Pat Aylward placed right in front of the posts from the free Jimmy Hendrick raced in to crash home a goal after an exciting bout of play. Heffernan again returned a long drive from far out in the next minute, which was finished for a further goal by Hendrick to leave Mullinavat leading by eleven points.'

Mullinavat: Pat Aylward (captain), J Bergin (goal), Tom Walsh, John Walsh, William Walsh, James Foskin, Pete Foskin, Andy Aylward, Paul Fitzgerald, William Durney, Paddy Holden, Pat McDonald, James Hendrick, Edward O'Connor, Michael Heffernan.

Hugginstown: Martin Brennan (captain), Martin Carty (goal), John Brennan, Edward Power. Frank Lonergan, Larry Gorman, W Daly, Richard Connolly, T Barron, J Moore, James Duggan, "Pa" Shea, Dick Shea, Peter Walsh and Luke Gaule.

Gate Receipts £13 11s 3d.

County JHC Final: Mullinavat 5-00; Freshford 3-00

'The Kilkenny County Junior Hurling Championships for 1939 were brought to a close at Nowlan Park on Sunday 10/12/1939 last when Mullinavat, standard bearers of the South, defeated Freshford. Mullinavat, thereby, compensated for their defeat at the hands of Ballyline in last year's decider, and recovered the county title after a lapse of 22 years, the victory being hailed with delight by their many supporters, who travelled in large numbers to cheer their favourites.'

'Three special buses from Mullinavat carried a large number of followers of the "blue and gold", whilst others made the journey to the Marble City by car and even bicycle. A number of the side which helped Mullinavat to win the 1917 championship were present to see the members of the younger generation win back honours after a long interim respite, and recalled the happy memories of the last victorious final with pride. Mullinavat, taking no chances from the start, settled down early and established a goal lead after ten minutes play, but three minutes later the sides were level when Freshford crashed their way to the net. Mullinavat had two further goals before the interval, to which the northern lads replied with a goal and a point, leaving the half-time score 4-0 to 2-1.'

'Some grand hurling was witnessed in the closing period, in which only two scores in total were recorded, a goal by each side, and it was only in the last ten minutes that the issue could definitely be counted upon as a foregone conclusion. Whilst all the winners played well throughout and acted as one individual unit in achieving success, credit for the victory gained will go in a large measure to the Mullinavat backs, who covered themselves with glory and stemmed many dangerous onslaughts time and again which threatened to sweep all before them. This was particularly true in the closing half, when Pat Aylward and his defenders rose to great heights, and held the opposing forwards at bay, whilst Jimmy Bergin in goal was practically unbeatable, saving shots from all angles, and was a real heart breaker to the Freshford forwards, who found their efforts foiled time and again by the brilliant work of the Coolnaleen giant between the sticks.'

'Paddy Holden and Willie Durney more than held their own at midfield against Paddy O'Brien and Nicholas Clifford, on whom great hopes were imposed by Freshford followers in view of the fine display of the pair in the Northern final, but they were firmly subdued by the two southern men, who succeeded in keeping the forwards well fed with the ball throughout and the latter made full use of any opportunities offered.'

'A strong breeze blew across the pitch, which was somewhat on the heavy side after the Minor game. Freshford moved in from the start, Dowling, who received a pass from Lawlor, sending over after Bergin had cleared a ground shot from O'Donnell. Mullinavat sent over at the other end, following a free taken by Pete Foskin. When Freshford moved in from the delivery, James Foskin effected a grand clearance in the Mullinavat last line. Holden, Heffernan and McDonald were prominent in a fast onset by the southern lads, which was nullified by Burke and Farrell, but Mullinavat again returned to force a "70" which Pat Aylward centred well, but Kelly and O'Donnell came out to effect a splendid clearance. Fitzgerald slapped back, Durney sending over the side-line, and following the cut-in taken by Paddy Obbins, Clifford sent wide of the objective for Freshford.'

'Exciting hurling ensued, and when Mullinavat got going from the puck-out John Walsh finished a great drive to the net after ten minutes of grand play. Andy Aylward repulsed a long shot from Obbins in the next minute and after a free to Mullinavat (W Durney), was beaten off, Freshford broke away on the left wing, a neat bout of passing being topped with a goal from a left corner shot by Molloy. Scores were now level, and intense excitement prevailed, both ends being visited in turn and things looked dangerous for Freshford when Tom Walsh, receiving unmarked, sent narrowly over. The same player however, made no mistake in the next minute, when, following a grand centre by Heffernan, he crashed to the net with a grounder, which sent southern supporters wild with delight.'

'After Bergin had saved twice in succession, Prendergast again returned to send over for Freshford. Mullinavat were further in the lead when, after a lengthy delivery by Bergin, Tom Walsh beat Farrell for a major. Mullinavat had a further goal when, following great work by Pat Aylward and Paddy Holden, Willie Durney beat the Freshford goalie with a ground shot, from far out. Bergin was applauded again for a great save, and Willie Walsh got the better of a hectic clash with Bill Farrell near the halfway line, but Clifford returned to send over for the northern representatives. Willie Durney (Mullinavat) went down with a hand injury sustained in a clash on the delivery, and retired his place being taken by Paddy O'Neill, who captained Kilkenny in the Minor All-Ireland final against Cork this year.

O'Neill went into the half-back line. Paul Fitzgerald coming out to mark Clifford at centre field instead of Durney.'

'Freshford attacked from the puck out, but shot over, Dooley sending over again in the next minute. P Prendergast (Freshford) retired injured, being replaced by Edward O'Gorman. Paddy Holden put Mullinavat on the offensive on the restart. Jimmy Hendrick eluding Kelly to put the southern lads attacking, but Burke came to the rescue to bring off a timely clearance. Holden sent over off a free to Mullinavat, and Heffernan was also wide of the objective in the next minute. Following a cut-in to Freshford in front of the stand, Molloy had a goal, after Bergin had cleared, and when Gorman added a point northern supporters were jubilant. Freshford were now playing better, Obbins sending well inwards from a free, but again Bergin proved the stumbling block, saving twice in succession, but O'Donnell returned the leather to force a "70" which proved fruitless. Freshford were attacking from a free when the whistle sounded for half-time, leaving the scores Mullinavat 4-0; Freshford, 2-1.'

'Burke, the Freshford full-back, cleared from Tom Walsh on the restart, and Farrell saved in goal from Hendrick. Both sides were over in turn before Freshford forced a "70", the puck, taken by Obbins, falling short. Andy Aylward was injured, but resumed. Paul Fitzgerald cleared from a "70" to Freshford and Gorman was over in the next minute, following a free (Clifford). Obbins cleared from a free to Mullinavat (Heffernan). and both defences were prominent in hectic hurling which followed, no quarter being given or taken, whilst supporters of the rival teams were keyed up to a high pitch of enthusiasm. Mullinavat were over twice before Pat Aylward put the forwards attacking from a free. John Walsh centring a grand shot which was cleared by Burke, but Heffernan returned the leather right into the goalmouth, where Farrell brought off a fine save. Following a cut-in to Mullinavat Paddy Holden sent to Heffernan and when the latter crossed to McDonald, the Bigwood player, unmarked, cut a grounder dead and true to the net after 23 minutes of the second half had elapsed. Clifford replied with a similar score for Freshford, after Bergin had saved.'

'Hard hurling ensued, in which the Mullinavat backs rose to great heights, stemming repeated onslaughts in brilliant fashion. Bergin saved from a close-up free taken by Obbins and O'Connor and Aylward cleared, the Mullinavat skipper being fouled in possession. From the free (P Aylward), Willie Walsh sent over. Freshford sent over from the delivery by Molloy and in the next minute the long whistle sounded.

Mullinavat: Pat Aylward, Ballyogreek (captain); Jimmy Bergin, Coolnaleen, (goal); Edward O'Connor; Andy Aylward, Ballyogreek; James Foskin, Rathnasmola; Paulie Fitzgerald, Fahee; Willie Durney, Bigwood; Paddy Holden, Knockbrown; Willie Walsh, Rossinan; Tom Walsh, Main Street, Mullinavat; John Walsh, Main Street, Mullinavat; Pat

McDonald, Ballyhomuck; Jimmy Hendrick, Deerpark; Pete Foskin, Deerpark and Mick Heffernan, Glenmore.

Freshford: Paddy Obbins (captain), J Farrell (goal), William Farrell, P O'Donnell, M O'Donnell, J Dowling, J Lawlor, James Molloy, P Prendergast, N Clifford, K Dooley, J Kelly, Dick Burke, D Lannan. Sub: E O'Gorman.

CAPTAIN'S TRIBUTES

'Speaking at a reception held at Butler's Hotel, Kilkenny after the game. Pat Aylward, skipper of the Mullinavat team, said he was proud to have captained the team which brought the honours to the parish after the long span of 22 years, and paid a high tribute to the players for their loyalty and co-operation throughout the year, and also their capable secretary, Jim Keegan for his efficient handling of the team, and to whom most of the credit was due for the success achieved. He also thanked the players from Glenmore parish who had given their services and who played a big part in the victory that day, and in conclusion paid a warm tribute to Freshford on their great display and especially on their splendid sportsmanship.'

CHAPTER 4

1940s

THE COUNTY FINAL

CARRICKSHOCK AGAIN CHAMPIONS

Game of Thrills

Carrickshock, 1—4.   Mullinavat, 1—2

By "AN LIATHROID"

"There was powerful slogging and no row" was how one enthusiastic townsman described Sunday's county senior hurling final as he left Nowlan Park after seeing Carrickshock defeat Mullinavat by two points. No one expected a low. It was only his way of saying that it was one of the manliest, cleanest and brightest finals ever played at the headquarters of the Marble County hurlers. "It was a great game altogether," he added, and in saying so expressed the opinion of the hundreds of spectators who witnessed it.

In congratulating Carrickshock on their merited victory, high tribute must be paid them and their worthy south-county neighbours and rivals who made so gallant a fight of it. The game was played in the finest sporting spirit and from every point of view reflected the greatest credit on the teams engaged.

It was preceded by the primary schools' hurling championship final for the Browne and Nolan Cup, in which St. Patrick's (De la Salle) defeated Thomastown by 2-0 to 1-1.

The exit of Eire Og from the semi-final of the championship cast a damper on the ardour of the Gaels which was reflected in the lack of customary enthusiasm for the final folders of the title, which they took from Carrickshock last year, the city team were strongly favoured for ultimate honours, but it was reckoned that Carrickshock would once them to narrow the margin. When the semi-final felt through a win for Carrickshock was regarded as a foregone conclusion. Nobody desired to cast reflection on the fighting spirit and skill of Mullinavat, but, it was argued, a team which had just emerged from junior ranks could not have acquired the experience and hurling necessary to carry them through against a side so well seasoned as Carrickshock and including up to 15 notorious players who had been actively in a number of All-Irelands. Mullinavat failed as expected by many outside the...

shout "Come on there, Mullinavat," and the next breath the same voice, "Ah, who are ye doing, Carrickshock." It was hard on those who were torn like that, but before the game ended many people who had cared seen Mullinavat, and never Carrickshock were in the same predicament.

The pitch was heavily green under cloudskies and the flags fluttering in the damp wind on the hour and beside the posts, had a washed appearance. Both teams were enthusiastically cheered when they emerged from the dressing-rooms. They were placed on the pitch by the James Stephens Pipe Band. Mr. R. Kelly (Conahy) was referee, and handled the game in a most capable manner.

No Frills.

There were no frills. There was no room for them, but it was all tasty hurling with plenty of hard hitting and a full hour...

G.A.A.

FOURTH SUCCESSIVE TITLE FOR CARRICKSHOCK

MULLINAVAT BEATEN IN COUNTY FINAL

POOR GAME AT NOWLAN PARK

Carrickshock, 3-6 (15);   Mullinavat, 1-3 (6)

Carrickshock secured the county senior hurling title for the fourth year in succession when they defeated Mullinavat in the final on Sunday at Nowlan Park by 3-6 (15) to 1-3 (6). It was an insipid game all through and did not by any means represent Kilkenny senior hurling at its best. Although Carrickshock deserved their victory it is only fair to Mullinavat to say that whatever little element of luck entered into the struggle was all in favour of the winners and it was generally conceded that the scores did not truly reflect the run of the play. Mullinavat made a hard fight for practically the whole hour but their forwards were unable to make any impression on a sound Carrickshock defence and it was in this sector that the champions were most impressive. Close tackling and spoiling tactics militated against brilliant hurling, while the greasy condition of the pitch did not help to improve matters. The low scoring helped to sustain the interest of the spectators for the greater part of the hour but nearing the end Carrickshock asserted their superiority and late scores clinched the issue for them.

Mullinavat's surprise victory over Eire Og in the semi-final helped to swell the hopes of their supporters, and they entered into the struggle fully confident. Heartened by their long list of successes in recent years the Carrickshock boys would not hear of defeat and made no secret of the fact that they were fully bent on adding another title to their list. It was the second time during the last three years that these two neighbouring teams have met in the final. Car-

---

Newspaper reports on Mullinavat's only two appearances in the Kilkenny Senior Hurling Championship final, in 1940 and 1943.

1940s

1940

For the 1940s Mullinavat were now up to the Senior grade for the first time since the 1920s. They had operated in the Intermediate Championship for four years (1929-1932) but this was a step up, and Mullinavat were to appear in their only two Senior hurling finals in the decade from 1940.

SENIOR

SHC R1: Mullinavat 4-02; Tullaroan 1-01

An incredible result for Mullinavat on their debut in the Kilkenny SHC.

'With all the grit, determination, and perseverance traditional of the "Rod-Iron" parish, Mullinavat created a first-class sensation in Kilkenny hurling circles by defeating a strongly fancied Tullaroan team in the opening round of the Senior championship at the Nowlan Park on Sunday by a margin of ten points, on the score of 4-2 to 1-1. Fielding five All-Ireland players, Tullaroan were strongly fancied to quality for the second round, but the southern representatives, hurling with dash and vigour which surprised even their most sanguine supporters, took the lead early, which they maintained to the end.'

'Mullinavat were in all respects deserving winners. Playing with the breeze in the opening half, Mullinavat did most of the pressing, Tom Walsh having a goal and Pat MacDonald a point early on, followed by a second goal after the Tullaroan goalkeeper had made a weak clearance. Jim Phelan replied with a minor for the northern lads, which was their only score in this moiety. Paddy Holden added a point for Mullinavat and the lead was further increased when Willie Walsh sent through for a great goal. Southern followers were again jubilant when Mullinavat broke through for a further major by John Walsh, leaving the interval score 4-2 to 0-1.'

'On resuming, Tullaroan, did most of the attacking, Paddy Phelan, the skipper, doing good work in an effort to rally his team, ably assisted by Peter Blanchfield, who had been moved from the defence to the forward line. After severe pressure Tullaroan had their first goal per Milo MacCabe, and it looked as if they were going to pull down the arrears. But the Mullinavat backs covered themselves with glory in the closing stages and repelled repeated onslaughts with great dash and brilliance in which each man in defence gave of his best. Hectic exchange characterised the closing stages. For Mullinavat, Jim Bergin was excellent in goal, Andy Aylward was the standout defensive player, aided by Pat O'Connor and Paul Fitzgerald. William Durney and Holden were dominating the midfield area and Pat McDonald, Michael Heffernan and Tom Walsh were the pick of the forwards.'

Mullinavat: Pat Aylward (captain), Jim Bergin (goal), Tom Walsh, William Walsh, James Foskin. P Holden, P MacDonald, Paul Fitzgerald, William Durney, Michael Heffernan, Edward O'Connor, John Walsh, Michael Doolan, Andy Aylward, Pete Foskin. Sub: Jimmy Hendrick (for Pat MacDonald). Not used: Richard Walsh, Tom Durney, P Holden, Tom Wall, J Purcell, D McLoughlin, P Hoban and P O'Neill.

SHC Semi Final: Mullinavat 5-01; Ballyline 3-07

'There was a lot of missing and faulty striking in a tame opening half, during which Mullinavat ran up a score of 3-1 to 0-2. Two of the goals were from ground balls far out, which easily beat the Ballyline custodian, and shortly after the restart, when Mullinavat went through for a further goal, the Ballyline culbaire came out to play at full-back, his place being taken in goal by Bobbie Woodgate. With the southern lads holding a lead of eleven points, it looked a foregone conclusion as to the outcome, and then fifteen minutes from the end, came the surprise of the hour, when Ballyline turned on steam and wiped out the big deficit in a wonderful finish, which found the sides level on the call of time. Both citadels had a narrow escape in the last few minutes of a hectic finish, and just on the call of time Ballyline forced a "70" which Coonan finished for a point to leave the scores level in a most exciting finish.'

'Mullinavat won the toss, and defended the City goal, being aided by a slight breeze. Jimmy Giles got possession on the break away, and sent well down, but Edward O'Connor repelled. Pat Aylward picking up to clear splendidly. Ballyline returned to send over. Following a great delivery by Jim Bergin, Mullinavat gained ground, but P. Cahill slapped back after a lively bout of play in Ballyline territory. Tom Larkin was injured but resumed, the same player having the first score of the game, a point, from a free out on the wing, close to the halfway line. A free to Mullinavat, taken by Pat Aylward, was beaten off by Coonan, who cleared to the sideline, where the ball rolled over. From the cut-in Tom Walsh was almost through for a goal, Cahill saving on the line, and in a hot onset round the Ballyline sticks John Nolan went down injured, but resumed. Cuddihy put Ballyline on the offensive from the restart, but Donnelly sent over from the corner. There was another stoppage for injuries when, following a sharp forward movement by Mullinavat, Tom Walsh was hurt, but was on his feet again shortly afterwards.'

'John Walsh, receiving from Willie Walsh, was wide at the other end, before Paddy Holden cleared well from a beautiful centre by Tom Larkin, and then play veered round Heffernan, with a ground shot from the corner gave Mullinavat the lead with a goal. Mullinavat were back again in a flash, Cahill saving a rasper from Tom Walsh at the expense of a "70" which Pat Aylward landed in front of the sticks, but Cahill again came to the rescue, Pat McDonald returning to send over. Paul Fitzgerald cleared from a "70" to Ballyline, taken by Henry Giles, and Woodgate missed on a free, Heffernan picking up to send over the bar for a point for Mullinavat. Paul Giles replied with a similar score from the delivery. Following good work by Pete Foskin and Pat McDonald, Mullinavat moved in, and in a neat wing manoeuvre John Walsh shot through for a goal with a grounder from the corner. Tom Walsh had a like score in the next minute when, following a long drive from around the halfway line by P Holden, he sidestepped his opponent and crashed to the net, to leave the interval score.'

Mullinavat 3-01; Ballyline 0-02

'When John Walsh, receiving from Heffernan, had a goal immediately on the resumption, Mullinavat had a lead of eleven points and looked all set for victory, but Ballyline replied with a like score. This was offset, however, by a further goal per John Walsh, following good work by Paddy Holden. Ballyline had two overs before Paul Giles had a rather lucky goal from a corner shot, the ball striking the upright and glancing into the net. Ballyline returned again from the delivery for Larkin to send wide of the objective. They were again back in the next minute, Jimmy Bergin the Mullinavat goalie, bringing off a good clearance at the expense of a "70". The puck was taken by Jimmy Giles, who placed well, but Andy Aylward the Mullinavat right full-back, brought off a lively clearance, T O'Neill returning to send over. Tom Larkin was injured but resumed. Pat Aylward and Paul Fitzgerald were prominent in the Mullinavat defence and repelled many dangerous raids by the opposing forwards, and when play veered round John Walsh sent over. Willie Durney slapped back the delivery, and in a fast onset Woodgate saved a grounder from Walsh, and moving up the wing the Ballyline forwards swept all before them in a headlong rush which Cuddihy finished by pointing. Jimmy Giles added a further point shortly afterwards after Bergin had brought off a great save, coming out the wing to clear. Ballyline, seemingly infused with new fire, swept back again, but Bergin was safe in goal, catching a flying ball to return.'

'There was thunderous cheering by Ballyline supporters when Tom Larkin finished a lightning raid to the net, and when the same player had a point immediately afterwards new life was instilled into the game, as only two points now separated the teams, with a few minutes to go. Some good bouts of hurling were witnessed now, and excitement grew as both sides put every ounce of energy into the game. Following a grand solo run by Jimmy Giles, who placed splendidly, Ned O'Connor brought off a brilliant clearance in the Mullinavat last line, but in a flash, Coonan was back to send a great shot over the bar from far out for a point. Only the minimum margin now divided the teams, and Ballyline who had staged a wonderful recovery, now seemed to hurl in winning vein. In a fast bout of play in Ballyline territory Tom Walsh (Mullinavat) was fouled in possession, and from the free Willie Hurney centred beautifully and in a fierce melee around the posts hurleys dashed in desperate combat. Mullinavat were all but through when the Ballyline backs, with a supreme effort, beat back the assault.'

'Hard hurling followed, in which both ends were visited in turn. Mullinavat sent over before Andy Aylward saved well under pressure in the last line of defence and when play swung round Bobbie Woodgate brought off a timely save in the Ballyline goal. Jim Bergin, his viz-a-viz, was also called upon to save in the next instant, clearing with his hand to the wing. Ballyline were back again in a flash, and in a sharp onset, forced a "70". Coonan came out to take the puck, and excitement was intense as Ballyline supporters shouted at him to go for a point, which would level the scores. Calm and steady, he settled himself for the puck, and with a grand effort sent the leather sailing between the uprights for the equaliser, leaving the issue undecided till another day.'

SHC Semi Final Replay: Mullinavat 2-08; Ballyline 1-03

'With a convincing win over Ballyline in this replayed semi final at Nowlan Park on 16/9/40, Mullinavat qualified to meet the winners of Eire Og v. Carrickshock in the final of the County Senior Hurling Championships. It was a much better game than when they drew on their first time of meeting. The hurling was well up to Senior standard and there was long bouts of spectacular play, especially in the first half. With the lead changing hands and every exchange closely contested there was plenty of excitement and spectators was given much to enthuse over. On the run of the play Mullinavat fully deserved their victory, though Ballyline put in a great show and fought gallantly in the end in spite of the fact that they were without the services of two of their best players, James Giles and John Nolan.'

'Ballyline were quickly away and with brilliant sun shining into their opponents eyes, found the net after a lively bit of play. From that on the game was fairly even with either side attacking in turn, but brilliant goalkeeping on both sides kept the scoring low. Nearing the interval their were stirring passages and top hurling was seen. Ballyline however made more of their opportunities and led at the interval by four points (1-2 to 0-1).'

'After the changeover, Mullinavat took up the running and drew level only to be overtaken again by a Ballyline team which appeared determined to fight every inch of the way. The presence of James Giles at centrefield might have made a big difference to Ballyline, but as it was Durney and Holden gained mastery in that sector and their good display exercised a big influence on the ultimate outcome of the struggle. Mullinavat gradually forged ahead and in the last quarter established a definite mastery and went on to win by a comfortable margin.'

Mullinavat: Pat Aylward (captain), J Bergin (goal), James Foskin, Pete Foskin, Tom Walsh, John Walsh, Willie Walsh, Edward O'Connor, Paul Fitzgerald, Andy Aylward, Mick Heffernan, Mick Doolan, Paddy Holden, Willie Durney and Pat McDonald.

SHC Final: Carrickshock 1-04; Mullinavat 1-02

'In a game which was punctuated by many pulsating passages and thrills and excitement in plenty, Carrickshock regained the Kilkenny Senior Hurling Championship by defeating Mullinavat in the current year's final at Nowlan Park on Sunday by the narrow margin of two points on above score. With even scoring throughout, and the sides level on three occasions, it looked as if a draw would be the outcome, but the greater experience and finesse of the Carrickshock men in the closing minutes proved the deciding factor. The brilliant display of the Mullinavat lads came as a surprise even to their most sanguine supporters, and though appearing in their first Senior final they hurled with a dash and elan which would have done credit to more experienced teams in the higher grade.'

'As it was, they went within an ace of creating a first class sensation, and turning over with a point lead at half time looked all set for adding a new chapter to Kilkenny's hurling history. The sides were level twice in the closing moiety, and in a great finish Jimmy Kelly and Tom Dalton sent over the winning points for Carrickshock. It was a grand game from start to finish, played in a most exemplary spirit, and though the teams hail from practically the same area, which added to the rivalry, there was not a harsh or discordant note throughout the entire game, which reflected the highest credit on the players concerned. From the spectators' viewpoint, it was equal to any of the finals seen at Headquarters in recent years, and those who came expecting a one sided match had a pleasant surprise to find that far from being a dull and lifeless affair, it kept the crowd in breathless expectancy to the last whistle, up to which it was anybody's game, with neither side capable of claiming superiority.'

'If Carrickshock were brilliant in victory, Mullinavat were glorious in defeat, and on their display they are certainly entitled to be ranked as equal to the best in the county at present, which shows that their form in the Senior grade on their first year of entrance was no mere flash in the pan. An excursion train, several special buses, cars and bicycles brought large numbers of followers from South Kilkenny, and the attendance included many well known Gaels, old All-Ireland hurlers of former years and prominent supporters from all over the county.'

'Mullinavat won the toss, and elected to play towards the city goal. Carrickshock broke away from the throw-in, Tom Dalton sending down but Jim Bergin, the Mullinavat custodian, came out to clear effectively, W Durney, working back for the forwards to send over. Paul Fitzgerald returned from cut-in by Bobbie Hincks, and some grand hurling was witnessed between the Mullinavat backs and Carrickshock forwards. Carrickshock had a cut-in which carried the leather into the Mullinavat danger zone, and Tom Dalton racing out swung on a fast ground ball, which crashed into the corner of the net to give his side the opening score after 12 minutes' play. Scores were level again, however, when following good work by Mick Doolan, Tom Walsh picked up to beat Malone with a rasper close in.'

'When Mullinavat again attacked Heffernan was fouled in possession, and from the free Tom Walsh put his side in the lead with a grand point, which brought a great burst of cheering from supporters. Jimmy Walsh and Tom Walsh were over in turn for their respective sides, before Hincks was narrowly wide off a free. A Carrickshock free (Jimmy O'Neill) was beaten off, and in the next minute Georgie Dermody forced a 70 taken by Jack Phelan, which was sent over by J Walsh. The halftime whistle sounded leaving the scores Mullinavat 1-1; Carrickshock 1-0.'

'Carrickshock pressed from the restart following a cut-in, but spoiled by fouling, Jimmy Bergin missed on the free, and following a hop, Bobbie Hincks got possession to shoot over the bar for the equaliser, and for the second time scores were level. Mullinavat pressed on the delivery, Malone bringing off a good save from Doolan and Walsh. Hectic hurling followed, in which both sides were visited in turn in a spate of grand individual work, with neither side having any advantage. Paul Fitzgerald was injured, but resumed after treatment. Pete Foskin and Andy Aylward saved splendidly in the Mullinavat defence, and when Carrickshock again moved in Bergin cleared, Paddy Holden picking up to send in a high shot right in front of the posts, but the backs cleared effectively to the wing when danger threatened. Heffernan raced out and picked up to send a beauty right across the parallelogram, where in a hard clash Paddy Donovan went down injured just as the whistle had gone for a free. When play restarted Pat Aylward gave Mullinavat the lead once more with a point off a free 21 yards out after eleven minutes of the second half had elapsed.'

'A free to Carrickshock (J Kelly) was finished for an over by the forwards. From a further free, Jack Phelan placed well and in a lively bout of hurling around the Mullinavat posts Luke Gaule forced a "70" from which Jack Phelan set the teams level once more with a grand shot which went all the way for a point. From a well-placed cut-in by Paul Fitzgerald, Mullinavat forced a "70" at the other end, which was repelled, J Walsh returning to send over. With time running out it looked as if a draw might be the ultimate outcome, but in a whirlwind recovery by Carrickshock, the forwards swept away for Jimmy Kelly to pick up a loose ball to send between the uprights from forty yards out to give his side the lead once more by the minimum margin. Two frees to Mullinavat in succession were repulsed, and after both sides had sent over in turn, Tom Dalton increased the Carrickshock lead with a further point.'

JUNIOR

South JHC: Barrow Rangers 2-03; Mullinavat 2-01

1941

SENIOR

SHC R 1: Carrickshock beat Mullinavat
County SHC Final: Carrickshock 4-05; Eire Og 3-07

JUNIOR

South JHC R 1: Carrickshock No.2 9-01; Mullinavat 4-04

'Before a big attendance at Earlsrath on Sunday 29/4/41, Carrickshock No.2 defeated Mullinavat in the opening round of the Junior hurling championship on the score of 9-1 to 4-4. The homesters led at half-time by 3-3 to 3-1. The winners included Jack Farrell and Pat Hartley, formerly of the London Irish team, whilst Mullinavat had the services of Jimmy Heffernan, Glenmore, and Henry Doolan, Shambogh, brother of Mick Doolan, the Mullinavat Senior player.'

Mullinavat: J Purcell (captain), T McDonald (goal), William Aylward, Richard Aylward, Paddy O'Neill, P Roche, J Heffernan, H Doolan, Philip Hoban, Joe Holden, Danny McLoughlin, Richard Walsh, Edward Kelly, Pete Sutton and Paddy O'Reilly.

1942

SENIOR

In 1942, there was to be a third meeting of Carrickshock v. Mullinavat. Whilst World War Two, aka "the emergency" was the topic of the day, this third meeting of neighbours in the SHC First Round was a welcome diversion, and here is a Munster Express preview of that game: 'The old neighbouring rivals, Carrickshock (holders of the title) and Mullinavat will meet at Waterford Gaelic Field on Sunday next in their tie in the initial round of the County S.H. Championship, which is exciting widespread interest. Mullinavat had a meteoric rise to fame since 1939, when they won the county Junior title, and on their promotion to Senior ranks in 1940, swept all before them to reach the final, in which they went within an ace of creating a sensation, as they only lost to Carrickshock by a bare point in a thrilling final.

Last year they went under in the opening round to Carrickshock in somewhat easy fashion, but the team has been considerably strengthened for the current year, and will include a number of players from Kilmacow and Ballyhale, some of whom are well-known in college hurling circles.'

'The team has undergone a three weeks' course of training, and there is a feeling of confidence in the "Rod Iron" camp that they will atone for the reverses of 1940-41 on Sunday.'

SHC R 1: Carrickshock 4-02; Mullinavat 2-02

'In the presence of a big attendance at Waterford Gaelic Field on Sunday 14/06/1942 last, Carrickshock (holders) defeated Mullinavat in the opening round of the Kilkenny county Senior hurling championship by a margin of six points. It was a keen, hard fought game, in which the champions were set a stiff task to pull through as Mullinavat opened up in lively style and had the better of the exchanges in the opening period to lead at the interval by a goal (2-1 to 1-1). It was still anybody's game up to the last quarter when the Carrickshock stamina, craft and experience gained the upperhand, and going into the lead they paved the way to victory by two quick goals, Mullinavat seeming to tire towards the close; they lost much of the pace and brilliant stick work which characterised their play in the opening stages. The champions were without Jack Farrell, Jimmy O'Neill and Tom Walsh of last year's team, whilst Mullinavat, fielding a number of newcomers, showed a vast improvement on the 1941 side, and appeared to be a well trained combination.'

'Carrickshock defended the city goal in the first half, and exciting midfield exchanges followed the throw-in. J. Kelly was over from far out, after Jim Foskin had cleared for Mullinavat. "Link" Walsh returned the delivery, but again the Mullinavat backs were sound, O'Neill and O'Connor clearing effectively, and when play veered round Michael Holden, racing through from the wing, had a great goal for Mullinavat to open the scoring.'

'The champions worked back to force a "70" (Jack Phelan), which was sent over. When "Link" Walsh slapped back the puck-out Jimmy Walsh was narrowly wide with a rasper. Exciting play followed at midfield, where duals between "Link" Walsh and Tom Wall (Carrickshock) and Paddy Holden and Willie Durney (Mullinavat) were the highlights of the game. Mullinavat spoiled by fouling, and from the free "Link" Walsh sent all the way to the net to level the scoring. Bergin was prominent in the next minute and caught a flying ball to send it sailing back to midfield, where Paddy Holden swung on it to put Mullinavat forwards again in action, but Bob Aylward and Pakey Butler cleared to the wing, the ball rolling over the line. The backs again repelled from the cut-in, but P. Holden was fouled in possession, and from the free Mick Byrne made no mistake for a point to put the "Rod-Iron" lads in the lead once more.'

'Mullinavat were away again from the puck-out and following grand work in the forward line Pat Aylward centred a beauty in front of the posts for Mick Heffernan to crash through for a great goal amidst the thunderous cheering from Mullinavat supporters. Mullinavat were now four points in the lead and were hurling in wonderful style. The rivals threw every ounce of energy into the struggle in reckless abandon. Broken hurleys flew in all directions as man met man in deadly combat, as it were, with each side striving hard for supremacy. Eddie O'Connor, who was playing a sound game at full back for Mullinavat, was injured, but resumed with a bandaged head. Holden and Foskin cleared from the restart, but "Lynch" Walsh picked up to send over. Carrickshock again broke away, Wall and Kelly putting the forwards in action for "Builder" Walsh to send over. Jim Heffernan, receiving from P Holden, was wide at the ether end in a good try for a point. Jimmy Kelly, receiving unmarked, pointed for the champions, and on the delivery Mullinavat broke away, following good work by Paddy O'Neill and Paul Fitzgerald, but Bob Aylward was sound in defence for Carrickshock, and cleared twice in succession; but the "Rod Iron" men were back in a flash again, J. Purcell sending narrowly over, following a grand solo run along the wing by Willie Durney. Mullinavat led at half time by 2-1 to 1-1.'

'P Holden and M Byrne opened up well for Mullinavat on the resumption. Eddie Quinlan came on for James Foskin, who retired, and a number of positional changes were also made, Pat Aylward going into the defence. Carrickshock had two overs after Andy Aylward and Eddie O'Connor had cleared. Malone saved well from Byrne when Mullinavat pressed. Andy Aylward was again applauded for brilliant defensive work under pressure, and when Carrickshock returned Luke Gaule sent over. Jim Heffernan, receiving a neat pass from his brother Mick, had the opening point in this half, after five minutes play, to stretch the Mullinavat lead to four points. Carrickshock, however, replied with a goal by Mick Walsh, and again only the minimum margin divided the teams.'

'Following a great cut in by Jimmy Kelly, Tom Dalton smashed his way through, for a major, which put Carrickshock in the lead for the first time, and when Jimmy Walsh added to point the champions appeared to be gradually gaining the upperhand, though the issue was still in the balance. Rain now commenced to fall, which spoiled play to some extent, and caused difficulty for players in keeping their feet. Paddy O'Neill was now prominent for Mullinavat, doing trojan work around mid-field. Bergin saved from Jimmy Walsh, after Jack Phelan and Fitzpatrick had repulsed a sharp onset by Mullinavat. Jimmy Kelly was away again for Carrickshock and sent in a beauty right in front of the Mullinavat posts for Luke Gaule to finish to the net.'

Mullinavat: Pat Aylward (captain), Jim Bergin (goal), James Foskin, Pete Foskin, Paddy Holden, M, Holden, Michael Heffernan, Jim Heffeman, Paul Fitzgerald, Edward O'Connor, Willie Durney. Michael Byrne, Andy Aylward, Paddy O'Neill and J Purcell. Sub: Eddie Quinlan.

County SHC Final: Carrickshock 3-02; Threecastles 2-03

1943

SENIOR

SHC R 1: Mullinavat 3-07; Threecastles 1-03

'Mullinavat were never really fully exerted by the display of an average Threecastles side. Both teams seemed to lack training and missing was frequent, whilst another notable factor which proved detrimental to anything in the nature of spectacular hurling was the bunching together of players, more especially in the forward lines, which left little scope for fine open work. Threecastles led at the changeover by 1-3 to 1-2, but this was hardly a true reflection of the play as the Southern men drove a lot of wides in the opening period. Mullinavat went ahead gradually from the restart and finished worthy winners in rather easy fashion. Played in a sweltering sun at a lively pace throughout, the game imposed a severe strain on players and both sides seemed to tire towards the close of the game.'

'Threecastles were away to a flying start up the wing, and when Kerwicke sent a grand shot in front of the posts, Matty Walsh smashed through for the opening goal in the first minute. Jim Heffernan was wide at the other end for Mullinavat. Pete Foskin slapped back the delivery but a free eased for Threecastles, from which Paddy Phelan send a long drive right into the half forward line, but Eddie O'Connor effected a splendid handed clearance, and when play veered round Tom Walsh and Paddy Holden were wide in turn. Ramie Dowling was applauded for spectacular hurling when he eluded two opponents to send well down, but the goalie saved from Tom Walsh.'

'From a free to Mullinavat, Dowling pointed, and in the next minute the same player had a similar score when Pete Foskin crossed from a cut-in. Both sides had overs in turn before Pat Aylward from a free, placed right in front of the posts but the backs repulsed, Dowling later picking up to send over. Mullinavat were again narrowly wide of the objective when Purcell doubled in a fast grounder. Following a cut in Jack Cleere got possession to score a grand point for Threecastles with an overhead stroke. Neary was wide off a free, and when the "Rod Iron" man got going once more there was a ringing cheer from Mullinavat supporters when Heffernan, receiving from Walsh, broke through for a well earned goal to give the Southern side the lead. In an exciting bout of hurling Matty Walsh set the teams level with a beauty over the bar from the wing. Just on the call of time Paddy Hennessy sent the Northern men in the lead again with a point off a free.'

'Paddy Phelan was prominent again on the resumption, but Joseph Holden and Andy Aylward cleared splendidly in turn for Mullinavat. Paddy Phelan was wide off a free on the restart. Following good work by Paddy O'Neill, Paddy Holden and Pete Foskin, the Southern men opened up in a fast spate of hurling which was finished by Tom Walsh for a point, to give Mullinavat the lead once more. The same player was fouled in possession in the next minute, and Dowling pointed from the free. Mick Heffernan added a further point in the next minute. Kevin Cleary saved twice in possession under pressure in the Mullinavat goal and in a flash Pat Aylward and Tom Walsh were away in a sharp onset which Jimmy Heffernan finished for a goal. Threecastles defence now wilted under sustained pressure, and when Pete Foskin had the last point of the match the result was practically a foregone conclusion.'

Mullinavat: Pat Aylward (captain), Kevin Cleary (goal), Tom Walsh, Joe Holden, Paddy Holden, M. Heffernan, J Heffernan, P Foskin, James Foskin, Andy Aylward, Paddy O'Neill, J Purcell, Edward O'Connor, Ramie Dowling and Tom Walsh. Sub: Willie Durney.

SHC R 2: Mullinavat 2-07; Mooncoin 2-06

'It was a neck-and-neck struggle throughout, and with the lead alternating, it was a thrilling contest despite the fact that the hurling as a whole did not attain to a high standard, but close play, keen tackling and hard hitting gave the crowd thrills and spills aplenty, particularly in the last few minutes, when the sides were level, the game being anybodys. The winners led at the changeover by two points (1-4 to 0-5).'

'Mooncoin broke away from the restart, and there was a terrific roar as they smashed their way through for a goal which set them in the lead by a point. Bill Dunphy cleared in the Mooncoin goal. John Mackey and Paul Crowley were wide in turn on frees and again both sides drove many bad overs. A Mullinavat free taken by Mick Holden was finished for an over. Mullinavat opened up again, and following good work by Pete Foskin, Pat Aylward and Willie Durney, Jimmy Heffernan finished a great drive to the net to put the rod iron representatives in the lead once more by two points, but excitement was intense as Mooncoin broke away for a goal after Cleary had saved, and again the Suirsiders were ahead by a bare point, 2-5 to 2-4.'

'Richard Cleary added a point from a free, and hereabouts some of the best hurling of the hour was seen, with deadly clashes, hard-hitting and close tackling. Excitement was at fever pitch as both sides went all out for success. John Hennebry sent wide for Mooncoin in a good try for a score, and when play veered round Willie Durney had a point, which left the scores 12 points to 11. Mullinavat forwards sent two bad wides in succession, but excitement was again intense when following a free to Mullinavat, taken by Pete Foskin, Mick Heffernan finished for a point to set the sides level once more. The issue looked like being a drawn when Paddy Holden sent over the bar for the winning point.

Mullinavat: Pat Aylward (captain), Kevin Cleary (goal), Joe Holden, Paddy Holden, M Holden, J Walsh, T Walsh, M Heffernan, J Heffernan, J Purcell, Willie Durney, P Foskin, Andy Aylward, M Byrne and Edward O'Connor.

SHC Semi Final: Mullinavat 5-05; Eire Og 3-09

'The men from the "Rod Iron" district started off well, and ran up an interval lead of 3-3 to 1-3, at which period supporters of the city team were feeling far from happy. At one period in the second half the winners led by ten points, but in a thrilling last quarter went all out to get on terms, reducing the lead to a bare point, and when the city backs moved in to help the forwards, the Mullinavat defence were sorely tried in the last few hectic minutes, but never wilted even under the utmost pressure. Mullinavat undoubtedly had the bigger following, and their victory was hailed with delight. They possess the nucleus of a vastly improving combination which, with attention to training, may make a bold bid to make history this year by adding its name to the scroll of fame as Kilkenny Senior hurling champions for the first time.'

Mullinavat: Paddy Holden (captain), Kevin Cleary (goal), Joe Holden, Michael Holden, John Walsh, Tom Walsh, M Heffernan, J Heffernan, Edward O'Connor, Paddy O'Neill, J Purcell, Andy Aylward, M Byrne, P Foskin and W Durney.

SHC Final: Carrickshock 3-06; Mullinavat 1-03

'Carrickshock secured the Kilkenny Senior hurling title for the fourth year in a row when they defeated Mullinavat in the final on Sunday 8/8/1943 at Nowlan Park by 3-6 to 1-3. It was an uninspiring game all through and did not by any teams represent Kilkenny hurling at its best. Although Carrickshock deserved their victory it is only fair to say to Mullinavat that whatever elements of luck entered into it was all in favour of the winners, and it was generally conceded that the scores did not truly reflect the run of the play. Mullinavat made a hard fight for practically the whole hour but their forwards were unable to make any impression on a sound Carrickshock defence, and it was in this sector that the champions were most impressive. Close tackling and spoiling tactics mutated against brilliant hurling while the greasy conditions of the pitch did not help to improve matters. The low scoring helped to sustain the interest of the spectators for the greatest part of the hour, but nearing the end Carrickshock asserted their supremacy, and late scores clinched the issue for them.'

'Though they did most of the attacking in the first half, Mullinavat lost numerous scoring chances through bad shooting, which was altogether in contrast with their display against Eire Og. Seldom has Carrickshock defence been seen to better advantage. Time after time determined raids were foiled. Even playing with the wind, Mullinavat were unable to break through. On the other hand the Carrickshock forwards did not come up to scratch and they too allowed many scoring chances to go amiss. Carrickshock led at the interval by 2-1 to 1-3. Mullinavat made a plucky effort in the first quarter of the second half which succeeded in reducing the lead to a point, but they then faded out completely and in a whirlwind finish the champions snatched a few quick scores which put the issue beyond doubt.'

JUNIOR

South JHC R 1: Hugginstown 3-01; Bigwood 3-01

'At Mullinavat on Sunday 11/4/1943, Bigwood and Hugginstown met in the opening round of the Junior Hurling Championship, the result being a draw, on the score of 3-1 each. Walsh from a free, had the opening point for Hugginstown but Dick Vereker, Paddy Wall and M Knox had goals for Bigwood, to which Dick Nolan replied with a major, leaving Bigwood in the lead at the interval by 3-0 to 1-1. Joe Gorman had two goals for Hugginstown on the resumption to put them in the lead, but Tom Sutton sent over the bar for the equaliser, following a free taken by P McDonald to leave the sides level in an exciting finish.'

Bigwood: Jim Vereker (captain), John Sutton (goal), Tom Sutton, P Sutton, P McDonald, Michael McDonald, Jack Knox, M Knox, Dick Vereker, John Wall, Joe Fitzpatrick, John Hokey, W Purcell, P Walsh and P Foskin.

South JHC Round 2 Replay: Hugginstown 5-01; Bigwood 3-03

1944

SENIOR

SHC R 1: Mullinavat 4-05; James Stephens 1-06

'The city lads were making a welcome reappearance in the Senior grade, after a very lean period since they last took the title in 1937. They were led by the old veteran of many a hard battle Paddy Larkin, who is still a force to be reckoned with, and was applauded for many fine clearances at centre-half back on Sunday. One of their best players, who gave a very promising display, was Tommy ("Dela") Murphy, a former Hugginstown and Carrickshock hurler, now in employment in the Marble City, and sent many long raking drives into the Mullinavat lines time and again, but the forwards finished weakly. Though the hurling was not over brilliant, there were some keen and exciting passages at times, especially in the opening period, when exchanges were fairly even, only two points separating the sides at half-time, Mullinavat 2-1; James Stephens 1-2.'

'The Rod Iron men opened up well in the closing period and emerged worthy winners of a hard-fought, but sportingly contested game. Three players of the Kilkenny All-Ireland team of the memorable 1931 final were in action, viz., Paddy and M ("Fleep") 'Larkin, with James Stephens, and Jack Duggan, who showed flashes of his old-time fire, with Mullinavat. Mick Holden was easily the best, of the winning side, and though pitted against such an old, seasoned campaigner as Paddy Larkin gave a very talented exhibition. The rest of the team also did well, but they will need to improve on Sunday's form if they hope to overcome the stiff challenge of Carrickshock (holders) in the next round.'

Mullinavat: Pat Aylward (captain), P Holden. Michael Holden, John Holden, Pete Foskin, James Foskin, Andy Aylward, Paul Fitzgerald, Jack Duggan, Jim Bergin (goal), Willie Durney, Tom Walsh, J Heffernan, Edward O'Connor and Edward Kelly. Sub: T McDonald.

SHC R 2: Carrickshock 4-04; Mullinavat 3-03

'It was a hectic game, with only a small margin dividing the teams throughout the hour. There was a good deal of erratic shooting on the part of the forwards of both teams, with the result that wides were numerous. The pitch was in excellent order and reflected much credit on the local Gaels. A heavy shower which fell during the opening half made the pitch rather slippery and militated to some extent against first class play. J. Kelly, opened the scoring for Carrickshock with a point, which was followed by a similar score for Mullinavat per M Holden. Hincks, from a free, put Carrickshock a point ahead. J. Walsh and Hincks registered a goal each in quick succession. J Heffernan scored the first goal for Mullinavat, and Duggan repeated the performance. Before the half-time whistle went, J Walsh put Carrickshock a further point ahead.'

'On resuming, P. Holden scored a point for Mullinavat, and a "70" taken by the same player resulted in a goal. Liam Long, who was prominent throughout, sent in a goal for Carrickshock, and Hincks added a point. M Holden registered a point with only a few minutes to go. The scores were now Carrickshock, 3-4; Mullinavat, 3-3. Following a hard struggle in front of the Mullinavat goal, Long secured an opening and sent to the net, leaving the issue no longer in doubt.'

Mullinavat: P Holden (captain), J Bergin (goal), E Connors, A Aylward, Paul Fitzgerald, Peter Foskin, William Durney, J Heffernan, M Holden, E Kelly. J Duggan, Thomas Walsh, P Aylward, J Foskin and R Aylward.

County SHC Final: Eire Og 7-09; Carrickshock 4-04

JUNIOR

South JHC R1: Bigwood 5-03; Nore Rangers (Inistioge) 3-02 (Nore Rangers objected)

'At Barrett's Park, New Ross, on Sunday 31/4/44, Bigwood defeated Nore Rangers (Inistioge) in the opening round of the Championship on the score of 5-3 to 3-2, after a great game, which was featured by bright passages of play throughout. Jim Vereker, Pete Foskin, Pete Sutton, John Wall, Jack Knox and Joe Fitzpatrick starred for the winners, who held an interval lead of five points. Murray, Tierney and Fitzgerald were the pick of the losers. Nore Rangers objected due to "illegal constitution" with the winners due to meet Callan in the second round.'

South JHC R1: The Rower No.2 w/o Mullinavat No.2 scr.

1945
SENIOR
SHC R 1: Mullinavat w/over Danesfort
SHC R 1: Carrickshock 6-04; Mullinavat 2-09

'Favoured with the wind, Mullinavat did most of the attacking in the first half, but great goal-keeping by McBride, coupled with the sound defensive work of the Carrickshock backs, kept the Mullinavat forwards at bay, with the result that Carrickshock led by two points at half-time, on the scores 5-1 to 2-8. A long spell of attack by Mullinavat in the second half brought no score, Carrickshock maintaining their two points advantage to finish strongly and increase their winning margin to seven points. For three quarters of an hour, the issue was in the balance, but Carrickshock's final rally gave them a deserved victory. They were unfortunate in the first minute in losing their promising young player, T. Murphy, who on this occasion was being tried at centrefield with Wall, Jimmy Kelly going in to the left half-forward position. The loss of Murphy brought on J Kelly, and Jimmy Kelly returned to centre field, Mullinavat put up a spirited fight. But the early failure of their forwards to get scores, coupled with some unsound defensive tactics, which resulted in goals, kept them fighting an uphill struggle.'

'Mullinavat defence was not as sound as that of their opponents, but A Aylward, J Heffernan and P Foskin were best. P Holden was prominent at centrefield, and in attack, M Holden gave a most outstanding display. His great efforts were worthy of more support. Durney and J Holden were also good workers.'

'At half-time the scores were 5-1 to 2-7 in favour of Carrickshock. After the interval, Jimmy Walsh pointed for Carrickshock, and P Holden replied with a minor for Mullinavat. A long spell of attack by Mullinavat failed to pierce a sound Carrickshock defence, and when play reverted to the other end, Jimmy Kelly, from a cut-in, centred, and Jim Walsh finished to the net to put Carrickshock leading by five points. From this until the final whistle sounded, Carrickshock dominated, and Jimmy Kelly had a point from a "70", to which he added with a like score when he received a nice pass from Jim Walsh, before the final whistle sounded.'

Mullinavat: J Bergin (captain), A Aylward, P Aylward, J Foskin, J Heffernan, P Foskin, P Fitzgerald, E Kelly, P Holden, J Holden, W Durney, M Holden, P Sutton, J Walsh and T Walsh.

Kilkenny SHC Final: Eire Og 2-07; Carrickshock 1-10
Kilkenny SHC Final Replay: Eire Og 4-08; Carrickshock 1-07

JUNIOR

South JHC R1: Mullinavat 6-02; Mooncoin 4-03
South JHC R2: Mullinavat 1-02 drew with Dunkitt Ramblers 1-02
South JHC R2 Replay: Mullinavat 4-02 drew with Dunkitt Ramblers 3-05
South JHC R2 Second Replay: Mullinavat 4-08; Dunkitt Ramblers 4-06 (AET)

'At Earlsrath on Sunday Mullinavat defeated Dunkitt Ramblers in their Junior championship second replay, after extra time, on the score of 4-8 to 4-6. The teams had met on two previous occasions, when drawn games resulted, and at the termination of play on Sunday, scores were level again at 4-3 each. During the extra half-hour, excitement reached fever pitch, and within a few minutes of the end the teams were even again with 1-3 each, but in the closing stages Dick Aylward and Michael O'Neill sent over two fast points for Mullinavat to give the homesters victory. The game was conducted in a fine sporting spirit, despite the fact, that some hard knocks were given and taken. Mullinavat were worthy winners of a match which made hurling history by reason of the fact that the teams played three drawn games, but the Ramblers were gallant losers by a narrow margin.'

Mullinavat: Tommy McDonald (captain), John Aylward (goal), Edward Holden, Jimmy Holden, M Hoban, Paddy Hoban, Pat Dungan, Buddy McDonald, S Foskin, J Grennan, Richard Aylward, Michael O'Neill, John Murphy, Paddy O'Reilly and James McDonald.

South JHC Group One Final: Glenmore 7-02; Mullinavat 6-01

'Before a big attendance at Earlsrath on Sunday 14/10/45, Glenmore defeated Mullinavat in the County J.H. Championship (group final) on the score of 7-2 to 6-1, after a keen hard-fought game. Mullinavat led at the change-over by 3-1 to 2-1, but Glenmore took the lead early in the second moiety to emerge deserving winners.'

Mullinavat: Tommy McDonald (captain), John Aylward (goal), Richard Aylward, Edward Holden, Jimmy Holden, James McDonald, P O'Reilly, Michael O'Neill, Richard Dunphy, Stephen Foskin, Pat Dungan, Jack, Grennan, Paddy Hoban, Michael Hoban and John Murphy.

County JHC R1: Mullinavat 6-02; Mooncoin 4-03 AET

'Before a fair attendance at Kilmacow on Sunday 29/07/45, Mullinavat defeated Mooncoin in the County Junior Hurling Championship on the score of 6-3 to 4-3 The winners led at the changeover by 3-1 to 3-0. Aylward, Foskin McDonald and Grennan were prominent for the winners, while Purcell, Cummins, Grant and Cleary did good work for the losers.'

Mullinavat: Thomas McDonald (captain), John Aylward (goal), Patrick Foskin, Stephen Foskin, Michael McDonald, James McDonald, Edward Holden, John Murphy, P O'Reilly, James Holden, Richard Aylward, James Farrell, Jack Grennan, Pat Dungan and Michael Hoban.

1946
SENIOR
SHC Round 1: Tullaroan 3-16; Mullinavat 2-03

'Tullaroan proved their superiority over Mullinavat at Thomastown on Sunday last in their tie in the first round of the Kilkenny Senior Hurling Championship, and within a few minutes of the final whistle were leading on the score of 3-16 to 2-3 when the game was interrupted by an incident in which players and spectators participated. As a result, the referee Mr D Treacy awarded the match to Tullaroan. Up to that the game had been played in a fine sporting spirit. Opening in strong fashion. Tullaroan did most of the attacking and it became apparent early on that they were the faster side and held a decided advantage in clever teamwork, which they used to good effect. It was only in the last quarter of the first half that Mullinavat registered their only score, a point before the turnover, when Tullaroan were out by 2-11.'

Mullinavat: J Aylward. A Aylward, E O'Connor, J Foskin, J Walsh, P Foskin, P Sutton, J Heffernan, P Holden, J Drennan, W Durney, J Sutton, M Hoban, John Walsh and T Walsh.

SHC Final: Thomastown 5-04; Carrickshock 4-05

JUNIOR
South JHC R1: Mullinavat 8-05; Mount Juliet 3-05
South JHC R2: Carrickshock beat Mullinavat

1947
JUNIOR

After seven years Senior it was back to South Junior in 1947. Kilkenny hurler Jimmy Heffernan moved teams from Mullinavat to Carrickshock in order to continue playing Senior club hurling.

South JHC R 1: Mullinavat beat Carrickshock No.1
South JHC R 2: John Lockes 3-07; Mullinavat 1-02
South JHC Final: John Lockes 3-10; Brandon Rovers 1-01

1948

JUNIOR

South JHC R 1: Mullinavat 6-05; St Leonard's, Dunnamaggin 1-01

'Mullinavat defeated St Leonard's (Dunnamaggin) in the initial round of the County Junior Hurling Championship after a rather one sided game, on the score of 6-5 to 1-1. The winners had the services of Paddy Crotty and Billy Hoban of St Kieran's College team, winners of the Leinster Colleges title.'

Mullinavat: Paddy Holden (captain), John Walsh (goal), Tom Walsh, Johnny Walsh, Billy Hoban, Michael Hoban, Andy Aylward, Richard Aylward, Pat Holden. Buddy McDonald, T McDonald, Nick O'Neill, Paddy O'Reilly, Paddy Crotty, J Holden.

South JHC R 2: The Rower beat Mullinavat
South JHC Final: Slieverue 4-06; Glenmore 3-03

1949

JUNIOR

South JHC R 1: Mooncoin beat Mullinavat
South JHC Final: Knocktopher 5-2; Glenmore 3-03 (Replayed following an objection by Knocktopher)

CHAPTER 5

1950s

The Kilkenny team which competed in the 1957 Leinster final.

1950s

1950
JUNIOR
South JHC R1: Thomastown 4-02; Mullinavat 3-01
South JHC R1: Bigwood 3-03; St Canice's 1-01
South JHC R2: Bigwood v. Thomastown
South JHC Final: Slieverue 5-06; John Lockes 2-00

1951
JUNIOR
Mullinavat did not compete.
South JHC R1: Mooncoin w/o Bigwood
South JHC Final Replay: John Lockes 5-07; Thomastown 5-04

1952

A three-parish rule was adopted at the Kilkenny GAA Convention, held at City Hall, Kilkenny on 14/12/1952. The motion for a three-parish rule was adopted by 97 votes to 68, was to be implemented in all grades, and now meant clubs could only draw players from their parish, along with two adjoining parishes. There was opposition from clubs such as Carrickshock and city clubs but smaller Junior clubs like Mullinavat got the motion through.

Mullinavat did not compete as seventeen teams entered the 1952 South Junior Championship.

Castle Rangers (Lukeswell) were formed in 1952. The club officers were John Fitzpatrick (Kilcready), Jimmy Walsh and Paddy Reade. They reached Round Three of the South Junior Championship but lost to Glenmore by 5-2 to 3-4. The club played at the

Saw Pit Field in Knockmoylan and the team v. Glenmore contained several players from Mullinavat parish: Matty Woods (goal), John Reade, Pat Keeffe, Dick Hogan, Pat Forristal, Denny Hogan, Jimmy Dermody, John Campion, Paddy Keeffe, Paddy Anderson, Tommy Campion, Nicholas O'Neill, Jim Forristal, Richard Forristal and Ned Campion. Subs - Owen Dermody, Fr Mick Dermody, Jim Keeffe.

South JHC Final: John Lockes 4-05; Glenmore 5-01

OCTOBER 28TH 1952: A DATE FROM HISTORY

This date is massively important in the history of the club. After several years without a hurling club, Fr. Gallavan, who had arrived in the parish in July 1952, and others, arranged a meeting at the Old School House on this date, which resulted in the reformation of Mullinavat hurling club. Paddy Tynan was made club secretary, Pat Foskin of Deerpark treasurer. The local creamery manager Nick McSweeney presented the revamped club with a set of jerseys. Within three months, the club was back in hurling action after several years absence, albeit, only in a home and away challenge game with Kilmacow Hurling and Football Club. So, Mullinavat hurling club was back, and were already getting ready for the 1953 Kilkenny Junior Championship.

Leg one was played in Mullinavat on December 7th 1952, with a Mullinavat win by eight points, 6-04 to 4-02. Leg two a week later was played in Ballykeoghan, Kilmacow with the home side winning by ten points.

Mullinavat: Tom Butler, Patrick Butler, Patrick Power, Larry O'Shea, Marty Grennan, Sean Gaulle, Pat Dungan, Séamus Foskin, Fintan Crotty, Thomas Holden, Paddy Tynan, Wattie Walsh, Patrick Delahunty, Martin Raftice and Tom McDonald.

1953

JUNIOR

Mullinavat were back, and fielded two teams in the Junior Championship.

Mullinavat No 1 Squad: John Sutton (captain), Dick Furney (goal), Pat Holden, Peter Foskin, Richie Aylward, Pat Holden, Tom Holden, Tod Holden, Paddy Sutton, Tom Sutton, John Walsh, Buddy McDonald, Larry O'Shea, Paddy Tynan, Wattie Walsh and Ned Kelly.

Mullinavat No 2 Squad: Tom Butler (goal), Patrick Butler, Paddy Daly, Patrick Power, Matty Grennan, Sean Gaule, Seamus Foskin, J Purcell, Fintan Crotty, Tommy Holden, Patrick Delahunty, Martin Raftice, Tom McDonald, Pat Dungan and Pat Raftice.

South JHC R1: Mullinavat 2-04; Knocktopher 1-04

South JHC R2: Mullinavat 3-07; Rower Inistioge 3-06
South JHC R3: Mullinavat 5-05; Thomastown Rangers 5-05
South JHC R3 Replay: Mullinavat 4-05; Thomastown Rangers 3-08
South JHC R3 Second Replay: Mullinavat 2-02; Thomastown Rangers 2-02
South JHC 3 Third Replay: Mullinavat 6-04; Thomastown Rangers 4-03

Mullinavat No.1 had beaten Knocktopher and Rower Inistioge before a four game epic with Thomastown that Mullinavat won on the playing pitch but lost in committee rooms. When the final whistle sounded at Ballyhale on Sunday 22/11/1953, Mullinavat had earned a well-deserved 6-4 to 4-3 victory over Thomastown. The first game ended in a draw, but on the occasion of their second clash the scores were level (3-5) at full time, and during extra time Thomastown put on three points and Mullinavat a goal, to make matters level again. This fourth clash therefore aroused more than ordinary interest, and a fairly large crowd turned up at Ballyhale, obviously in the hope that the issue would he decided. From the Thomastown supporters' point of view it was on the whole a disappointing game for at no stage did the local boys strike the form which they displayed in their earlier outings. Mullinavat on the other hand looked like winners from the start. An an early goal by Pete Sutton helped them to settle down quickly. T. Hanrahan had a point for Thomastown, but almost immediately P. Holden replied for Mullinavat. In the 10th minute, Sutton again struck to the net and W Walsh further increased Mullinavat's lead by a point. Having been well placed by P Holden, Sutton again found the net and just before the interval, he added a point, to leave the half-time score: Mullinavat 3-3; Thomastown 0-1.

In the opening minutes of the second half, T Hanrahan pointed for Thomastown but after a melee in the square, Mullinavat added a goal, followed shortly afterwards by another. At this stage, the winners appeared to combine better but after W Walsh had pointed from a free, a goal per T Hanrahan seemed to restore Thomastown's confidence. This, however, was short lived, as Sutton again raised the green flag. Joe Lennon had a point for Thomastown, and a good goal by Jimmy Kelly reduced the lead still further. Thomastown had two further goals, but by then it was a hopeless task and Mullinavat emerged deserving winners, having put up good performance, considering the absence from their ranks of John Sutton, who sustained an injury in the Cork-Kilkenny clash three weeks previously.

OBJECTION TO MULLINAVAT UPHELD

'A meeting of the Co. Kilkenny Southern District Board was held at Thomastown on Sunday 17/01/1954, Mr Sean Lonergan, Chairman, presided. There was a big attendance of delegates. The following objection, which was deferred back from the Co. Board, was considered. "A cara, on behalf of Cumann Baile Mic Anndain, (Thomastown Hurling Club), I object to Cumann Muilleann a bata (Mullinavat Hurling Club), being awarded the Junior Hurling Championship match played at Ballyhaie on Sunday, 22nd November for breach of Rule 17, page 51 Official Guide, 1950, which states: Each Club shall register annually in the Irish language with the County Registrar, its officials, players and distinctive club colours. The Club whose colours have been longest registered, shall have prior claim to markings. Failure to play in Club colours without official permission involves a fine of £1. A Club proved to have played an unregistered player shall forfeit the match on an objection."

"1. Contrary to above rule, Padraig O Roidgh, whose name appears as No.11 on players' list supplied by Mullinavat to the referee and given by the referee to Thomastown team, was not registered according to Rule 17, page 51, Official Guide, 1950."

"2. Kevin O'Connor and John Barron played with Mullinavat in above match and their names do not appear on players' list as required by above rule 17, page 51, Official Guide."

"3. Contrary to Rule 23, page 53, Official Guide, which states: A team which plays in a championship, a league or a tournament match, a player from another county, who has not fulfilled all the requirements of this rule, shall be automatically suspended for 12 months. The same suspension applies to the Officials, (chairman, secretary and captain) of the club playing such an illegal player. Kevin O'Connor, Killure, Waterford, a member of Erin's Own Club, Waterford, and John Barron, 94 Mornsson's Road, a member of Gael Og Hurling Club, Waterford, and also a member of De La Salle College Hurling Club, Waterford, who played with Mullinavat in above match were not eligible to play."

"4. Re three parish rule – Clubs must declare their headquarters to suit the three parishes so that two parishes shall touch their headquarters. Mullinavat declared Mullinavat as their headquarters and, as the above two players reside in Waterford, a breach of the three parish rule was committed."

"5. Padraig Sutton and Micheal Breathnach, whose names appear as No. 13 and 10 respectively, on list of players supplied by Mullinavat on 22/11/1953 to the referee, were ordered off the field during the match. Mullinavat v. Knocktopher played under the auspices of Knocktopher Fete Medal Tournament in Knocktopher on 14th July, 1953. According to Rule 115, page 101, Official Guide, 1950 a player ordered off shall stand suspended for at least one month. The said player, Patrick Sutton, played in a Football Championship match with St Senan's (Kilmacow) v. Glenmore, played at Mullinavat on 9th August, 1953 whilst under suspension according to Rule 63, page 75, Official Guide, 1950 which states: Suspension of member of Clubs under General Rules or County Bye Laws, means suspension from all functions privileges, and competitions under the Association; suspends shall be ineligible to take part in any capacity in the affairs of the Association; during such suspension and if included in a team, the team shall forfeit the match. Members who take part in competitions while under suspension shall be suspended for a period of at least six months, to take effect from the date on which they take part in such competitions.

Penalties imposed in one county shall be operative in all other counties. According to above rule, Padraig Sutton is not eligible to take part in the Association until term of suspension from 9th August 1953 has expired. Rule 37, page 10 Dhlighthe 1938, Kilkenny County Bye Laws states: that suspension by District Board and recommendations for reinstatement must in all cases, be ratified by Co. Committee. The reinstatement of Padraig Sutton and Micheal Breathnach was not recommended by the Southern District Board. According to Rule 30, page 9 Dhlighthe the Junior and Minor clubs in the southern divisions shall be under, the jurisdiction of the Southern Board. I herewith enclose copy of this objection." Peader Laffan.

'"The Chairman ruled that objection No.1 had been proved and upheld the objection. The match was accordingly awarded to Thomastown. Notice of appeal was lodged, but subsequently withdrawn.'

South JHC R1: Mullinavat No.2 lost to Brandon Rovers.
South JHC Final Replay: Glenmore 4-06; Thomastown Rangers 3-01

ONE PARISH RULE

The Kilkenny GAA convention on Sunday 20/12/1953 rescinded the three parishes rule and adopted a one parish rule for Senior, Junior and Minor hurling for 1954. The motion was proposed by Mr J Brophy (Valley Rangers) and seconded by Mr Liam Holohan (Eire Og). A hotly contested debate and subsequent vote of 83-67 was to change Kilkenny club hurling forever. The convention also decided to forward a motion to Congress asking for a ruling that Kilkenny City be regarded as four parishes.

PITCH PURCHASED

In June 1953, Mullinavat pitch was purchased for £590. This was the first official GAA pitch in the county outside of Nowlan Park. The Munster Express reported, 'Mullinavat Gaelic Field has now been purchased from the owner, Mr Bernie Kelly, by the local hurling club, and a big scheme of alterations and improvements is contemplated. It is proposed to erect an embankment and make the venue suitable for county Senior and Junior championship games. To help to defray the heavy outlay, it has been decided to hold a house to house collection in the district in the near future, when it is hoped that a generous response will be forthcoming in order to bring the proposals to a successful fruition. The members of the hurling club deserve to be warmly commended on their initiative and enterprise, which should be a great boon to the "Rod Iron" village'.

1954
JUNIOR

South JHC R1: Mullinavat No.1 lost to Knocktopher by 7 points
South JHC R1: Mullinavat No.2 scr. v. Brandon Rovers
South JHC Final Carrickshock 2-06; Knocktopher 0-03

1955
JUNIOR

South JHC R1: Mullinavat No.1 beat Thomastown Rangers
South JHC R2: Mullinavat No.1 3-08; Piltown 2-04
South JHC R3: Mullinavat No.1 drew with Dunnamaggin
South JHC R1 3 Replay: Mullinavat No.1 5-01; Dunnamaggin 2-05
South JHC Semi Final: Rower Inistioge 2-04; Mullinavat No.1 1-04

At a South Board meeting a fortnight later, on 11/12/55, Mullinavat objected to Rower Inistioge United being awarded the game played at Thomastown, on the grounds of alleged illegal constitution. Mr John Holden, representing Mullinavat club, stated that Richard McGrath of Rower Inistioge lived in New Ross, was on the electoral register there, and was therefore an illegal player. Mr T Lyng representing Rower Inistioge made a counter argument, and Mr Sean Lonergan (chairman) ruled in favour of the original match winners.

South JHC R1: Piltown beat Mullinavat No.2 by a wide margin
South JHC Final: Knocktopher 6-05; Rower Inistioge 5-04

1956
JUNIOR

South JHC R1: Mullinavat beat Thomastown Rangers

'At Ballyhale on Sunday 22/4/1955, Mullinavat beat Thomastown Rangers No.1 in the first round of the Junior hurling championship with Mr Jack Phelan (Ballyhale) as referee. Two weeks later Thomastown Rangers No.1 objected to Mullinavat being awarded the county Junior hurling championship tie played at Ballyhale on the grounds of alleged non-registration of a player. At a meeting of the Southern Board GAA on Sunday 13/5/56 the objection by Thomastown Rangers No.1 to Mullinavat being awarded the game on the grounds of non-registration of a player, was upheld, and the match awarded to Thomastown.

A counter-objection by Mullinavat was ruled out of order. Notice of appeal to the County Board was given. At a further meeting of Kilkenny County Board, held on Sunday 5/8/1956, Mullinavat appealed against the decision of the Southern Board awarding the match to Thomastown Rangers, on the grounds of non-registration of a player, Peter Foskin. After hearing representatives from both clubs, the acting chairman, Mr Martin Egan (Three Castles), ordered that the match be replayed.

South JHC R1 Replay: Thomastown Rangers 4-05; Mullinavat 4-03
'There was a large attendance at Ballyhale Sportsfield for the eagerly awaited replay of the Junior hurling championship match between Thomastown Rangers and Mullinavat. The meeting of the teams at the same venue a few weeks back resulted in a win for the Rangers. A subsequent objection by Mullinavat was overruled by the Southern Board, but on appeal to the county board a replay was ordered. Hence the more than ordinary interest in Sunday's clash, when the Thomastown boys again asserted their superiority, emerging worthy winners on the score, 4-5 to 4-3. The game was marked by somewhat rugged style exchanges from the throw in, but if hard, close tackling was the order throughout the hour, infringements were few and all in all both teams should be complimented for a creditable performance and on a display of restraint and sportsmanship which might well be emulated by some of their more excitable supporters.'

'There was little between the teams in the opening moiety, when repeated assaults on both goals were repulsed by sound defenders. Mullinavat turned over with a lead of just one point (0-3 to 0-2). On the resumption, Thomastown Rangers assumed control, and in the end of the third quarter when they clocked up a nine-point lead, seemed all set for a comfortable victory. Mullinavat however fought back valiantly, but although adding four goals to their first half tally, their all-out efforts for a vital score in the closing minutes were successfully foiled by their opponents back line.'

South JHC Final: St Senan's 6-02; Knocktopher 4-02

1957
JUNIOR

South JHC R1: Mullinavat beat Carrickshock No.2
South JHC R2: John Lockes, Callan 3-07; Mullinavat 1-02
South JHC Final: Tullogher beat Rower Inistioge by one point

KILKENNY SENIOR HURLING TEAM TRAIN REGULARLY AT MULLINAVAT

In May 1957, Kilkenny County GAA Board decided to make Mullinavat Gaelic field their main training centre in preparation for the upcoming Leinster SHC clash with Dublin on June 30. A preliminary meeting was held in Mullinavat on Monday night 27/5/57 to make the necessary arrangements with the officers of Mullinavat GAA Club. The meeting was attended by officials of the Co Board, including the Chairman Mr Bob Aylward M.C.C. and Secretary, Mr Paddy Grace, as well as representatives of the Mullinavat club. It was felt that as most of the players were from the Southern area Mullinavat would be a very central and convenient centre for training purposes, and would save a great deal of unnecessarily travelling in bringing the team to local headquarters.

1958
JUNIOR

South JHC R1: Bye
South JHC R2: Mullinavat beat Glenmore
South JHC R3: Knocktopher beat Mullinavat
South JHC Final: Knocktopher 3-05; Dunnamaggin 2-01

1959
JUNIOR

South JHC R1: Mooncoin No.1 beat Mullinavat
South JHC Final: Thomastown 10-03; Piltown 1-04

John Sutton of Rahard moved away from Mullinavat to Glenmore parish in 1959. John was a huge loss to the club, having played on the Kilkenny Senior Hurling team since 1951. John had an All-Ireland Senior medal from 1957, three Leinster Senior medals and numerous other awards.

CHAPTER 6

1960s

The Mullinavat Junior hurling team from 1960

Back Row (from left): Tom Sutton, Paddy Hendrick, Larry O'Shea, Ned Delahunty, Jimmy Reddy, Tommy Reddy, Matty Woods, Johnny Campion, Jim Conway. Front Row (from left): Philip Frisby, Ollie Aldridge, Paddy Hoban, Philly O'Neill, Seamus Sutton, Jack Frisby, Seamus Foskin, Johnny Walsh (official).

1960s

1960

JUNIOR

South JHC R1: Mullinavat beat Dunnamaggin

Games being abandoned through events like crowd incursions, and lost sliotars, were a feature of this era. Mullinavat's Junior campaign of this year began with a similar event. Legendary Kilkenny goalie Ollie Walsh was appointed to referee our first round game v. Dunnamaggin on Easter Sunday, 17th April, 1960 at Ballyhale. Ollie failed to turn up until 4pm, as the Thomastown man had been also playing a Gaelic football match for his club that afternoon. The game had started without a referee, but ended up being abandoned by the time Ollie arrived, much to the disappointment of a large crowd. Mullinavat eventually won the refixture quiet easily.

Mullinavat: Séamus (Ollie) Aldridge, Johnny Dwyer, Jack Frisby, Larry O'Shea, John Campion, Ned Delahunty, Paddy Hendrick, Jim Conway, Tommy Reddy, Paddy Hoban, Seamus Foskin, Jim Reddy, Seamus Sutton, Matty Woods and Phil Frisby. Subs: Richard Carroll, Michael Carroll, Richard Tobin, Tom Sutton, and Milo Foskin.

South JHC R2: Thomastown Rangers beat Mullinavat
South JHC Final: Knocktopher 4-08; Mooncoin 5-04

MULLINAVAT FETE

This year saw the staging of the first ever Mullinavat Fete from July 31st. The Aylward Cup was donated by James Aylward, a merchant in Arundel Square, Waterford, and 18 gaberdine overcoats was the winner's incentive. The very first game in the Fete's history was between Mount Sion and Castlecomer. Mount Sion won by five points in a game refereed by Paddy Buggy of Slieverue. The Mullinavat Fete is dealt with in a separate chapter.

1961

JUNIOR

South JHC R1: Thomastown Rangers beat Mullinavat
South JHC Final Replay: Mooncoin 3-03; Knocktopher 1-06

SENIOR

The county board introduced a break from the parish rule in 1961, which allowed Junior club players to participate in the Senior hurling championship as well as Junior. Four combination sides were allowed join the championship – the city, the North, the Near South and the Far South (Mullinavat were grouped in with the Far South selection, that included Carrickshock, Windgap, Piltown, Mooncoin and Carrigeen). Mullinavat had three players involved, Ned Delahunty, Seamus Foskin and Tommy Reddy.

SHC R1: Far South 7-08; Tullogher 3-12 (at Mullinavat)

Far South: E Fitzpatrick (goal), M Fitzpatrick, Edward Walsh J Murphy (Piltown), N Doyle, Wattie McDonald, Dick Holden, W Walsh (Mooncoin), Jimmy Murphy, J Nolan, PJ Molyneaux, P Barron (Carrickshock), J Walsh (Carrigeen), G Butler (Windgap), N Delahunty (Mullinavat).

SHC R2: Far South 0-10; Lisdowney 0-5 (at Nowlan Park)

This win gave a real boost to hurling in the South of the county. On this occasion the Far South team was made up of eight Mooncoin men, four from Carrickshock, two Piltown and one Windgap. Mullinavat and Carrigeen were not represented on the starting fifteen here.

Far South: R Dunphy (Mooncoin), E Connolly (Mooncoin), G Nolan (Carrickshock), T Nolan (Mooncoin), J. Delahunty (Mooncoin), J Murphy (Carrickshock), M Howley (Mooncoin), E Power (Piltown), W McDonald (Mooncoin), E Doyle (Mooncoin), Edward Murphy (Mooncoin), Liam Kelly (Carrickshock), G Butler (Windgap), J Murphy (Piltown), PJ Molyneaux. (Carrickshock).

SHC Semi Final: Freshford 3-10; Far South 2-13 (at Nowlan Park)

'This was a game which made up for in hardness, what it lacked as a spectacle… from the throw in to the very end Freshford were allowed to dictate their own special brand of terms. And to help them on their way the Southern team almost all the time insisted on too much lifting and fancy play. A lot of Kilkenny enthusiasts travelled to Nowlan Park on Sunday with a very high opinion of the Far South team, but not many came away with that opinion still intact. The halftime score was Far South 1-5; Freshford 0-6.'

'For the Far South, Liam Kelly was their principal scorer, although most of his tally came from frees. Apart from that he was always dangerous and combined well with others on the attack. Ned Murphy at centre forward got nothing soft, but asked for nothing, labelled that way. He played a sound, hard-pulling game all through, though a very little quickening in pace would make him really useful type for the 40.'

Far South: Dick Dunphy (Mooncoin), Seamus Ryan Carrickshock), Geoff Nolan (Carrickshock), Ned Delahunty (Mullinavat), Martin Howley (Mooncoin), Jimmy Murphy (Carrickshock), Eddie Connolly (Mooncoin), Wattie McDonald (Mooncoin), Ned Power (Piltown), Liam Kelly (Carrickshock), Ned Murphy (Mooncoin), Dick Holden (Mooncoin), Jeff Butler (Windgap), Jimmy Murphy (Piltown) and PJ Molyneaux (Carrickshock).

SHC Semi Final Replay: Freshford 2-9; Far South 3-5 (at Nowlan Park)
'A point by substitute Tommy Butler two minutes from full time gave Freshford a one-point victory in the replay. As a spectacle the game offered very little in the way of entertainment. The hurling was said to be scrappy and sub-standard, and for much of the hour did not have the usual competitiveness associated with a county final.

Far South: Dick Dunphy (Mooncoin), Seamus Ryan (Carrickshock), Tom Nolan (Mooncoin), Geoff Nolan (Carrickshock), Wattie McDonald (Mooncoin), Jimmy Murphy (Carrickshock), Eddie Connolly (Mooncoin), Ned Power (Piltown), Martin Howley (Mooncoin), Liam Kelly (Carrickshock), Ned Murphy (Mooncoin), Dick Holden (Mooncoin), Jeff Butler (Windgap), J Murphy Piltown), PJ Molyneaux (Carrickshock). Subs: Billy Walsh (Mooncoin), Ned Fitzpatrick (Piltown), S Foskin (Mullinavat), Ted Comerford (Windgap), John Delahunty (Mooncoin), Ned Fitzpatrick (Piltown), Tom Kenny (Windgap) and P Barron (Carrickshock).

1962
JUNIOR
South JHC R1: Thomastown beat Mullinavat by 4 points
South JHC Final: Thomastown 1-08; Thomastown Rangers 2-01

1963
JUNIOR
Pre the 1963 season 'Black and Amber' in the Waterford News & Star wrote: 'Good hurlers, good inter county men, learned their hurling in Mullinavat, but that unfortunately was not

yesterday. Today Mullinavat are a Junior team, and one that does not get that far in the championship. If there is a prominent reason why this should be it certainly escapes. The average onlooker can only see a hard-working, hard-pulling 15 doing the most to map themselves in Kilkenny hurling. It would appear to be lack of balance that keeps Mullinavat at the receiving end in most of the games. For without a doubt, the team has its fair share of talent. Perhaps the coming season will see Mullinavat in a better light, as fielding ex Minors could make all the difference in the Junior grade.'

South JHC R1: Rower Inistioge 4-11; Mullinavat 0-02
South JHC Final: Rower Inistioge 5-05; Thomastown Rangers 4-03

1964
JUNIOR

South JHC R1: Mooncoin beat Mullinavat No.1 by wide margin
South JHC R1: Mullinavat No.2 beat John Lockes (Callan) by 5 points

'Mullinavat had little difficulty in overcoming the challenge of John Lockes Callan in the opening round at Piltown on Sunday 19/4/64. Ahead by 7 points (1-11 to 2-1) at the interval, they looked like winners from early on. They were best served by Larry Whelan and Jim Conway in defence, and Liam Condon and Dennis Duggan in attack.'

Mullinavat: P Sutton, Liam Walsh, John Frisby, Peter Fitzgerald, Tom Duggan, Jim Conway, J Phelan, Liam Condon, Tommy Reddy, Paddy Hoban, Dick Carroll, Dennis Duggan, Seamus Freyne, Tom McGrath and Seamus Sutton. Sub: John Dwyer for Séamus Sutton.

South JHC R2 Mooncoin 6-05; Mullinavat No.2 3-05

Mooncoin were able to use some Senior players in this game, as per rules, due to the Senior game v. Bennetsbridge being later in the month. Helped by two early goals Mullinavat led 2-4 to 2-2 at the interval. Mooncoin were the better team in a robust second half, where both teams had a player sent off. A hat-trick by Tommy Ryan saw Mooncoin home.

Mullinavat: S Foskin, Peter Fitzgerald, John Frisby, Tom Duggan, N Delahunty, L Frisby, Tommy Reddy, R Carroll, Dennis Duggan, Jim Conway, L Condon, Liam Walsh, Tom McGrath and Paddy Hoban. Sub: J Irish.

South JHC Final Thomastown Rangers 3-05; Windgap 1-08

1965

JUNIOR

South JHC R1: St Senan's, Kilmacow beat Mullinavat No.2
South JHC R1: Windgap 2-13; Mullinavat No.1 3-05

'The 1964 Southern Junior Hurling finalists Windgap had many anxious moments before they overcame Mullinavat in a first round game at Piltown. The Piltown pitch, probably one of the best laid out grounds in the country, was in perfect trim, and the first half gave little indication of the thrills that were to come in the second period. Windgap dominated the first quarter to build up a lead of 2-2 to 0-0 after 16 minutes. Reddy then had two points for Mullinavat but Windgap were still well in command, and added a further five points as against one for Mullinavat, for a comfortable 10 point interval lead (2-7 to 0-3).'

'Mullinavat continued to look unimpressive as they dropped further behind after half-time, and their supporters could not have given them even the remotest chance of victory when they trailed by 2-11 to 0-3 with 20 minutes left to play. However, at this stage, it became apparent that Mullinavat would not go down without a fight, and putting great vigour and determination into the work, they set about what seemed like an impossible task. In an inspired quarter of an hour they scored 3-2 without a reply, to leave only a goal between the sides, when it seemed as if a badly rattled Windgap side would not hold out. Kieran Purcell, who had resumed following an injury, rallied his side, and they added two points in the closing stages. Mullinavat must be wondering why it took them so long to settle down. Goalkeeper Aldridge, P Fitzgerald, Frisby and Sutton were sound defenders. Conway was an outstanding figure at centre back and later in the forwards, and he got good assistance, particularly in the first half, from John Irish. Substitute Tom Duggan made a big impression and one could only wonder why he had not been on from the start. Liam Condon was their outstanding forward with Reddy and Sutton also showing up well.'

Mullinavat: J Aldridge, P Fitzgerald, J Frisby, J Sutton, N Delahunty, J Conway, J Irish, T Reddy, P Carroll, P Sutton, L Condon, D Duggan, S Sutton, P Hoban, and T O'Neill. Subs: S Freyne, T Duggan.

South JHC Final: Knocktopher 3-09; Mooncoin 3-06

1966

JUNIOR

South JHC R1: Mooncoin 4-07; Mullinavat No.1 2-05
South JHC R1: Carrickshock 4-09; Mullinavat No.2 1-07

1967

CHANGE TO BLACK AND WHITE

This was the year Mullinavat hurling club changed colours from green and gold to the current black and white. The Kilkenny People made the following appeal on behalf of the club in the paper's edition on 17/02/67: 'Mullinavat are sending out an appeal to friends and traders for a new set of jerseys'. By the end of March the news was: 'Mullinavat hurling club have acquired a new set of jerseys of all white, with black bands on the neck and sleeve. The former colours were green and gold'.

JUNIOR

South JHC R1: Glenmore No.2 8-03; Mullinavat 5-07
South JHC Final: Knocktopher 4-09; Ballyhale 2-03

1968

JUNIOR

South JHC R1: Thomastown Rangers beat Mullinavat
South JHC Final: Glenmore 3-11: Dunnamaggin 2-06

1969

JUNIOR

South JHC R1: Ballyhale 2-08; Mullinavat 1-08

'At Thomastown on Sunday 18/5/1969 Ballyhale accounted for Mullinavat on the score of 2-8 to 1-8 in the first round of the Junior hurling championship in a disappointing game. It was thought by many that this would prove to be the outstanding game of the Junior championship in the South as the teams had served up some brilliant fare in tournament games in recent years, and being from neighbouring parishes there is intense rivalry between the sides. Mullinavat never seem to produce their best form in the championship, and Ballyhale hadn't to reach any great heights on Sunday. After being led by five points, 1-7 to 0-5 at half time, they raised the tempo of the game on the resumption, and once they had levelled the game after ten minutes of the second half, and even though their winning margin was only one goal, they never again looked in danger of defeat. Mossy Murphy had a brilliant game for Mullinavat, but his great display failed to spark off any enthusiasm in his teammates. Aldridge in goal could not be faulted for the defeat as he brought off many fine saves. Jack Frisby, Tommy Reddy. T O'Neill, J Aylward and J Conway also tried hard for Mullinavat.'

Mullinavat: J Aldridge, S Freyne, J Frisby. M Sutton, D Aylward, J Irish, T Reddy, T Neill, L Kearns, P Hoban J Conway. Mossy Murphy (0-6), J Walsh, S Sutton, and JJ Aylward (1-1). Subs: O Conway for S Sutton, D Duggan (0-1) for J Aylward, S Sutton for J Walsh.

South JHC Final: Tullogher 9-05; Dunnamaggin 0-4

The Mullinavat Junior hurling team from 1961

Back Row (from left): Johnny Aldridge, unknown schoolboys, Willie Carroll (selector), Philly O'Neill, John Campion, Seamus Sutton, Tommy Reddy, Matty Woods, Eddie Freyne, John Sutton, Ned Delahunty, Paddy Tynan, Ollie Aldridge, Jack Frisby. **Middle Row** *(from left): Michael Carroll, Richie Carroll, Tommy Frisby, Denny Duggan, Jim Conway, John Foskin, Johnny Walsh (official).* **Front Row** *(from left): Seamus Foskin, Francis Shaughnessy.*

CHAPTER 7

1970s

'After trying hard in recent years with a number of narrow defeats, Mullinavat have now reached the county final after the long span of 35 years. It was as far back as 1939 since Mullinavat took Kilkenny county Junior championship honours when they defeated Freshford in the final. Sunday's game was not a brilliant one, mainly due to the prevailing high winds. Aided in the opening half, Mullinavat turned over with a lead of 1-5 to nil at the interval.'

1974
South JHC Final
Mullinavat 2-07; Tullogher 3-03

1970s

1970
JUNIOR

South JHC R1: Bye
South JHC R2: Mullinavat 5-14; Slieverue 3-09
South JHC R3: Mullinavat beat Carrigeen
South JHC Semi Final: Mullinavat 6-12; Glenmore 3-09

'In excellent weather conditions and in the presence of a big attendance of followers, the winners had the better of the exchanges in the first half, turning over with a lead of 15 points at the interval, when the scores were 4-8 to 5 points. The loss of their goalkeeper through injuries did not help Glenmore, though substitute Jim Ryan was sound, but Mullinavat were never fully extended in the second moiety and were the better side throughout.'

Mullinavat: Jimmy Murphy, John Sutton, Jack Frisby, Mick Sutton, Richard Aylward, Mossy Murphy (0-5), Andy Aylward, Dick Carroll (1-0), Tom O'Neill, Johnny Aylward (2-2), John Scully (0-2), Paddy Hoban (0-1), Jim Walsh, Seamus Sutton (1-0) and Jim Conway (2-2). Sub: Tommy Reddy (for J Scully).

South JHC Final: Windgap 2-13; Mullinavat 1-13

'In a thrilling and closely contested game, it was score for score throughout, and the sides were level on six occasions, but the winners can thank Kieran Purcell, the Kilkenny Senior inter county player, and Tommy Hearne, the former Ballygunner and Waterford Senior hurler, who were the chief architects in the downfall of Mullinavat. The Rod Iron men battled hard to endeavour to win in the southern division after the long span of 31 years but were frustrated in their gallant effort. However nobody will begrudge the success of Windgap, who already lost in two previous finals and on this occasion it was a case of "third time lucky." Mullinavat were in front by a single point at the interval, with the scores reading seven points to six, but the sides were level within five minutes of the restart. Jim Conway put Mullinavat in the lead once more with a point from a 21 yard free, but entering the last quarter the sides were once more on equal terms at 1-11 each.'

'Mullinavat forged ahead again with two successive points from frees, but the turning point in the game came shortly afterwards when Windgap sent to the net from a 21-yard free by Kieran Purcell, which proved a match winner. They were now in the lead by one point, and their opponents never rallied from the blow of that sensational goal, and Windgap added two more points before the end to make the issue safe. Scorers for Mullinavat were Mossy Murphy 1-6, Tom O'Neill and Jim Conway, a point each.'

Mullinavat: Jimmy Murphy; John Sutton, Jack Frisby, Mick Sutton; Dick Aylward, Mossy Murphy, Andy Aylward; Dick Carroll, Tom Neill; John Aylward, John Scully, Paddy Hoban; Jim Walsh, Seamus Sutton and Jim Conway.

1971

JUNIOR

South JHC R1: Mullinavat beat John Lockes Callan No.2
South JHC R2: Mullinavat beat Carrickshock
South JHC R3: Mullinavat 2-08; Tullogher 3-05
South JHC R3 Replay: Mullinavat 4-08; Tullogher 2-08
South JHC Semi Final: Mullinavat 3-15; Knocktopher 2-09

'At Piltown on Sunday 17/10/71 Mullinavat defeated Knocktopher in the southern Junior hurling semi-final by a margin of nine points, on the score of 3-15 to 2-9, and thus qualified for the divisional decider for the second successive year. The heavy overnight rain, which made the pitch heavy, as well as a strong wind, made matters difficult for the players. However, who stood head and shoulders over the rest was Kilkenny All-Ireland player Mossy Murphy, who was the star of the 30 players. His craft, allied to his ability to weave his way in and out between three or four opponents with the ball in his possession was a treat to watch, and without him the winners would be set a difficult task. His tally 1-9, including a goal and five points in the second half, set the seal on his side's success. The Army man, Wally Freyne, who was brought on as sub in the second game against Tullogher, retained his place at centre half back, where he gave a sound-display, especially in the first half, and others to shine for the winners were Jim Walsh, Dave Aylward, Jack Frisby, Dick Carroll, Paddy Hoban and Jim Conway, with Ollie Aldridge bringing off some fine saves in goal. Mullinavat led at half-time by 1-6 to 0-5.'

Mullinavat: J Aldridge, Liam Walsh, Jack Frisby, J Sutton, Richard Aylward, W Freyne, A Aylward, D Carroll. D Aylward, John Aylward (0-1), Mossy Murphy (1-9), Pat Hoban

(0-1), Jim Walsh (1-4), S Sutton Jim Conway (1-0). Subs: J Scully for S Sutton, T O'Leary for J Aylward, O Conway for A Aylward.

South JHC Final: Mullinavat 3-08; Graiguenamanagh 1-14

'In a game which the hurling reached a good standard at times and ended in a welter of excitement, Mullinavat and Graiguenamanagh, meeting for the first time in the south decider, played a draw in the Junior divisional final at Thomastown on Sunday. Mullinavat were away to a flying start and ran up a lead of 0-4 to 0-1 in the first 15 minutes. When they added a goal from a close in free, followed by a point, it looked as if the men from the extreme south were going to qualify for the county final for the first time after 32 years.'

'Both sides added a point before the changeover to leave the score 1-6 to 0-5, and Mullinavat had a bit of hard luck when the ball was crashed to the net, but the whistle had gone for a free just before the interval. Wally Freyne came on for Mullinavat at centre back for the second half. Mossy Murphy, the Kilkenny All-Ireland man, moved out to midfield, but disaster came for them shortly after the resumption when Freyne, injured in a previous match, was hurt again, and had to retire just as he was getting into his stride. This seemed to have an upsetting effect on the Mullinavat side, and as their defence was weakened by the alterations, as well as by the transfer of Murphy from the halfback line, Graiguenamanagh gradually got on top with a goal from a 21-yard free, and a point from far out, which left sides level after 10 minutes. When the Graigue men, now hurling with zest added two more points, their opponents were fighting with their backs to the wall. Characteristics of the Rod Iron parish tradition however, Mullinavat fought back, and regained the lead with a great goal from a 21-yard free, followed by a point, with only 10 minutes left the score was 2-7 to 1-12.'

'Graig came into the picture again and with only five minutes to go were ahead by two points. But a goal following a '70' (Dick Carroll) snatched the lead for Mullinavat once more by the minimum margin. Hurling was now intense, and the referee's whistle could scarcely be heard above the roar of the supporters as Graig levelled again with a point from Jack Connell, and the same player added further point to put them ahead. Mullinavat followers were disappointed as Mossy Murphy sent a free narrowly wide in a try for the equaliser, and shortly afterwards, Mullinavat made another determined raid in an effort to take the game out of the fire. Then the backs fouled, and in a thrilling finish, Mossy Murphy made no mistake in sending over the bar for the point which gives them another chance.'

Mullinavat: Jimmy Aldridge, Liam Walsh (1-0), Jack Frisby, J Sutton, D Aylward (captain), Mossy Murphy (1-4), Andy Aylward, D Carroll, Dave Aylward (0-3), Paddy Hoban (1-0), J Scully, J Aylward, J Conway, S Sutton, Jim Walsh (0-1). Subs: W Freyne for J Aylward, J Irish for W Freyne.

South JHC Final Replay: Graiguenamanagh 3-12; Mullinavat 2-0.

'Graiguenamanagh won their first Junior hurling cup when they beat Mullinavat by 3-12 to 2-08 in the southern final replay at Thomastown on Sunday. Despite the bitterly cold weather, a very big crowd attended, and they were treated to a hard and entertaining hour hurling. Graiguenamanagh's first breakthrough in the Junior championship was greeted with enthusiasm by the big contingent and their victory is certain to do a lot of good there. They were clearly the better side and well deserved to win. Their defence, in the first half, when they had to withstand a sustained barrage while playing to the very stiff wind, won high honours and it was certainly an indication of the shape of things to come when they turned over only two points down, 0-8 to 1-3.'

'Mullinavat faltered badly in the opening stages and despite having quite a lot of the play they failed to get the vital scores that would give them some leeway when they faced a wind in the second half. They were rather overanxious and over played the ball. Perhaps their great disadvantage was that the ball never went right for Mossy Murphy, the man on whom they depended to open the gaps in the Graig defence. But there were no gaps and try as they might the southerners were unable to pierce the sound Graiguenamanagh defence. Mullinavat were unable to get a goal in the first half despite many good efforts by Mossy Murphy and they were then forced to take their points. On the other hand Graigue made the best use of the opportunities in the first half and Jack Jones goal in the 17th minute was an inspiration.'

'The game started 20 minutes late which kept the big crowds an unnecessarily long periods in the cold, the pitch was in perfect conditions and the stewarding left no room for complaint. Jimmy Aldridge had a good game in the Mullinavat goal, and Jack Frisby, Liam Walsh and J Sutton stood up well to the strong Graiguenamanagh pressure in the second half.'

Mullinavat: Jimmy Aldridge, J Sutton, Jack Frisby, L Walsh, R Aylward (captain), W Freyne, Andy Aylward, R Carroll, T O'Neill, J Scully, Mossy Murphy, D Aylward, J Walsh, P Hoban and J Conway.

Graiguenamanagh: P Grace, P Cahill, J Bolger, S Grady, C McDonald, L Ryan, M Foley, P Cushen, M Walsh, P Kavanagh, M Kinsella, J O' Connor, J Dunne, T Foley (captain) and Mick Butler.

1972

JUNIOR

South JHC R1: Graiguenamanagh No.1 beat Mullinavat
South JHC Losers Group: Mullinavat beat Thomastown United
South JHC R2: Mullinavat 4-08; Carrigeen 1-14

South JHC Semifinal: Graiguenamanagh 4-10; Mullinavat 3-06.

'For the second year in succession Graiguenamanagh are in the Southern Junior hurling final. At Thomastown on Sunday 1/10/72, they outclassed and out-hurled Mullinavat before a good attendance. Mullinavat were flattered to lead in the first half on the score of 2-5 to 1-4 after they had thrown away many chances in a closely fought game. In this half we had skills not always seen even at Senior level, we saw hurlers who could adopt to ground and overhead striking, had passing and blocking with ease.'

'Hogan opened the scoring for Mullinavat with a nice point in the third minute, O'Connor replied for Graig after 5 minutes. Kavanagh added another for the winners after seven minutes and after a melee in the Graig goal, Grace, who had many fine saves, blocked a shot at the expense of a 70. It was taken by Mossy Murphy who lobbed the ball in the Graig square where it was blocked out to the incoming P. Hogan who finished it to the net to give Mullinavat back the lead. Murphy had two more points from frees. Conway had a point from play and Hogan's 21 yard free was finished to the net by O'Leary after a great save by Grace to give Mullinavat a commanding lead. Graig fought back and Butler and Kinsella had points and then came the refresher they needed when Kinsella had a great goal which left the half time score Mullinavat 2-5 to Graignamanagh 1-4. '

'Many thought that the leaders were home and dry at this stage, but they were not counting on the worthwhile efforts of the Graig mentors to rearrange their forward line and these moves paid off quickly, because the second half was only three minutes old when Butler and Kavanagh had two great goals for the winners, and after that Mullinavat were never in the running. Any fears that the Graig supporters had that they would not be able to hold the Mullinavat half forward line of the Murphy brothers and Tom O'Neill were dispelled early on because Liam Ryan more than held his own against the Kilkenny inter county player and he was ably assisted by Tucker, Foley and Colm McDonald.'

Mullinavat: J Aldridge, L Walsh, J Frisby, W Doyle, J Walsh, R Aylward, A Aylward, R Carroll, J Aylward, T O'Neill, M Murphy, J Murphy, T O'Leary, P Hogan and J Conway.

South JHC Final: Graiguenamanagh 3-08; John Lockes 2-08

1973

JUNIOR

It was decided to run the Southern Junior Hurling Championships on a league basis. Twenty teams took part, 4 groups of 5, with the winners of each group in the semi-finals. Losers group was abolished.

Group D: Mullinavat beat Dunnamaggin by 7 points

Group D: Mullinavat v. St Senan's
Group D: Mullinavat v. Glenmore No.2
Group D: Shamrocks No.1 4-07; Mullinavat 2-07
Did not qualify

South JHC Final: Shamrocks 0-12; Tullogher 1-07

The Intermediate grade was reintroduced to Kilkenny hurling in 1973. This was the first championship at this grade in almost 40 years, since 1930s.

1974

JUNIOR

Group B: Mullinavat beat Slieverue and Shamrocks and drew with Carrickshock.
South JHC Quarter Finals: Mullinavat 4-15; Slieverue 1-04

'At Piltown on Sunday, Mullinavat had a facile victory over Slieverue by 4-15 to 1-4 after a very one-sided game. The winners held an interval lead of 4-8 to one point. Mossie Murphy, Jim Conway, Dick Carroll, Andy Aylward, Tom and Joe Anthony were prominent for Mullinavat, while the Walsh brothers. Jim Dollard and D. Murphy played best for the losers, who were reduced to 14 players when Tim Murphy was ordered off mid-way in the second half.'

Mullinavat: P Fitzpatrick, R Aylward, J Conway, G Butler, T Anthony, M Murphy, N Fitzgerald, D Carroll, A Aylward, J Aylward, J Walsh, J Murphy, J Anthony, S Kelly and P Hoban.

South JHC Semi Final Mullinavat 2-13; Carrickshock 1-09

'At Piltown on Sunday Mullinavat beat Carrickshock by a margin of seven points, on the score or 2-13 to 1-9 after a well-contested game. The teams were level at the interval with the score reading 2-5 to 1-8, and 18 minutes of the second half had elapsed before the sides scored a point each. The sides continued level for a further period, but in the closing stages Mullinavat pulled out to send over seven points in quick succession, without reply, to give them a well deserved victory. Tom Anthony. Nick Fitzgerald. Andy Aylward. Jim Walsh and Paddy Fitzgerald on goal were outstanding for Mullinavat.'

Mullinavat: Paddy Fitzpatrick (goal), Tom Anthony, Joe Anthony, Mossie Murphy, Jimmy Murphy, Richard Aylward, Andy Aylward, Dick Carroll, Tom O'Neill, Nick Fitzgerald, Jim Conway, Paddy Hoban, Jim Walsh, George Butler and Seamus Kelly. Sub: John Aylward for Joe Anthony.

South JHC Final: Mullinavat 2-07; Tullogher 3-03

'After trying hard in recent years with a number of narrow defeats, Mullinavat have now reached the County final after the long span of 35 years. It was as far back as 1939 since Mullinavat took Kilkenny county Junior championship honours when they defeated Freshford in the final. Sunday's game was not a brilliant one, mainly due to the prevailing high winds, which spoiled play to a real extent, and made scoring accuracy difficult. Aided to some extent by the strong breeze in the opening half. Mullinavat turned over with a lead of 1-5 to nil at the interval. The margin was stretched to 9 points immediately after the restart when Tom O'Neill sent over the bar, but two fast goals for Tullogher in quick succession from frees put them back in the running again with 15 minutes left for play. Tullogher added a further point, but this was offset by a great goal by Ritchie Carroll. With time running out, the scores now stood at 2-6 to 2-3, and it was still anybody's game, but the forwards at both ends missed some likely chances, particularly Tullogher. Mullinavat worked back for a further point to make the lead pretty safe, but excitement was at fever pitch when Tullogher broke through for a fine goal from the wing which caught the reliable Paddy Fitzpatrick the Mullinavat custodian unawares. Tullogher strove might and main to get the equaliser, and in an exciting finish Mullinavat held on to their hair-breadth lead to qualify for the final.'

Mullinavat: Paddy Fitzpatrick, George Butler, Jim Conway (1-0), Dick Aylward, Tom Anthony, Mossy Murphy (1-3), Nick Fitzgerald, Dick Carroll, Andy Aylward (0-1), Jim Walsh, Paddy Hoban, Jimmy Murphy (0-1), Tom O'Neill (0-1), Seamus Kelly, Joe Anthony. Sub: Pat Phelan (0-1) for Joe Anthony.

VICTORY CELEBRATIONS AT MULLINAVAT

'The Mullinavat team, winners of the southern divisional Junior hurling final at Piltown on Sunday 27/10/74 were accorded an enthusiastic welcome on their return home to the Rod Iron village. Bonfires blazed and the Cup was filled a few times to recognise the fact that it was a long span of years since the parish reached the County final, the last occasion being away back in 1939 when Mullinavat beat Freshford in the decider for that year.'

County JHC Final: Muckalee-Ballyfoyle Rangers 4-17; Mullinavat 3-03

'Games are won and lost, but seldom will any county final be taken as easy as this one at Nowlan Park on Sunday. For the combined forces of Muckalee-Ballyfoyle Rangers proved much too strong for a gallant, but out of touch Mullinavat combination, that was never allowed to get to grips with the job in hand. Not to say that the losers were misfits, far from it, but they came up against an inspired team, that on the day had only one definition objective in mind, the 1974, county Junior hurling championship. The winners on this performance would prove a very big handful to most Intermediate teams, the rank they join next year.'

'From the start their all action, all purpose approach to the game, was far above anything the losers could muster. They are well balanced, heavily built outfit, who rarely look troubled by what the southerners threw at them. Their defence, stood strong and their forwards, snatched every half chance. But, is was the defensive qualities of this northern combination that subscribed enormously to the registering of the impressive 17 point winning margin. In the early stages of the second half, when the loser desperately tried to pull down the 12 point advantage the winners had totted up before the break, their class came through. In a half where Mullinavat had all to gain by going forward, something they did, throwing caution to the wind, the Muckalee-Ballyfoyle Rangers men stood firm. Indeed, so firm that the losers were 21 minutes without raising a flag. The lighter Mullinavat side were never in with a chance when the northern champions got first use of the strong breeze. Although the losers were well beaten by the call of time they never gave up the chase. Best for them was Jim Conway who started at full back and ended at full forward, Mossy Murphy was easily their number one man and he received good support from Tom Anthony, Richie Carroll, Jim Walsh, even when he moved from attack to defence, and Richie Alyward.'

Mullinavat: Paddy Fitzpatrick, G Butler, J Conway, R Aylward; T Anthony, M Murphy, N Fitzgerald, R Carroll (0-1), A Aylward, J Aylward, J Walsh (1-2), J Murphy, J Anthony (1-0), S Kelly (1-0), T O'Neill. Subs: L Walsh for J. Anthony, Pat Phelan for S. Kelly.

Muckalee-Ballyfoyle Rangers scorers: Brendan Morrissey (1-6, 0-3 frees), Tom Moran (2-1), Jack Nolan (0-5, 2 "70s" and 3 frees), Marty Coonan (0-3), Dick Nolan (1-1), Martin Nolan (0-1).

1975

JUNIOR

South JHC Group: Carrickshock beat Mullinavat by 5 points
South JHC Quarter Final: Mullinavat beat Dunnamaggin by 4 points
South JHC Semi Final: Mullinavat 3-04; Glenmore 1-10

'Mullinavat and Glenmore played a draw in the Southern Junior hurling semi-final in a game which never reached a high standard, in front of a large crowd at Slieverue. With conditions excellent, including bright sunny weather, hopes were high of a keenly contested match, but it was a disappointing display for spectators, with poor striking, a number of bad misses and some unaccountable wides by both sides. Glenmore faced a strong sun in the opening half, and missed a close in free in the first few minutes. Jim Walsh had a good goal for Mullinavat, but the sides were level when John Ennett from far out sent to the net after Paddy Fitzpatrick in goal had failed to hold the ball after catching it coming in. Paddy Murphy put Glenmore in the lead with two points, one from a sideline ball and the other from a free. Jim Walsh had a second goal for Mullinavat, followed by a point from a free taken by Paddy Murphy leaving the teams level again, 2-0 to 1-3. Although Glenmore had many bad wides in the last ten minutes of the first half, they went further ahead by two points from Denis Phelan and one from Paddy Murphy to leave the half-time score Glenmore 1-6 Mullinavat 2-0.'

'Hurling was poor and disjointed in the first quarter of the second half, during which the sides exchanged points, and with fifteen minutes left it was 1-8 to 2-2 in favour of Glenmore. The standard improved in the last ten minutes, but following an altercation between Johnny Phelan and Nick Fitzgerald, both were sent to the line by the referee. With only five minutes left, Glenmore looked likely winners, with the scores reading 1-10 to 2-3 in their favour, but Mullinavat put in a storming finish, and when Mossie Murphy goaled from 21 yards free, and had another point in the last moments, the teams finished level in an exciting climax.'

(The Tricolour was flown at half-mast, and prior to the throw-in of the ball a two minutes' silence was observed as a tribute of respect to the late Eamonn de Valera.)

Mullinavat: Paddy Fitzpatrick; Paudie Holden, Jim Conway, Noel Freyne; Richard Aylward, Tom Anthony, Nick Fitzgerald: John Aylward, Andy Aylward; Dick Carroll, Mossie Murphy (1-2), Jimmy Murphy; Jim Walsh (2-1), Paddy Hoban (0-1) and Tom O'Neill.

South JHC Semi Final Replay: Mullinavat 5-11; Glenmore 1-05

'Mullinavat had a rather easy win over Glenmore in the Southern Junior hurling championship replay by a margin of 18 points, on the score of 5-11 to 1-5. Losing their chance in the drawn game, when they were ahead by four points with only minutes left for play, Glenmore never really got going on this occasion and were no match for an improved Mullinavat side, which settled down early on and were in the comfortable lead of six points at the interval, with the scores reading 3-4 to 1-4. Mullinavat added 2 more goals and 7 points in the second half, in which Glenmore scored only one solitary point.'

Mullinavat: Paddy Fitzpatrick, Paudie Holden, Jim Conway, Noel Freyne, Richard Aylward, Mossy Murphy (1-2), Nick Fitzgerald, John Aylward, Andy Aylward (0-1), Tom Anthony, Paddy Hoban (2-0), Jimmy Murphy (2-5), Jim Walsh (0-1), Tom O'Neill (0-2), Joe Anthony. Sub: Dick Carroll for Tom Anthony.

South JHC Final: Carrickshock 1-14; Mullinavat 2-06

'Carrickshock, home of many famed Kilkenny hurlers in the past, and heroes of great championship victories in the Senior grade in the early 1940s, came to the forefront in the Junior section on Sunday, after a lapse of 21 years, when they took the southern title from Mullinavat (holders) at Piltown. While the winning margin was only two points, 1-14 to 3-06, Carrickshock deserved their success on the run of play, even though the forward line threw away numerous opportunities as indicated by the fact that they had no fewer than 19 wides over the hour. Billy Kearney, who was always a danger when he gained possession, and Kilkenny inter county Minor, Dick Power, were the stars in this section, while Dixie Burke was here, there and everywhere, helping attack and defence when needed in addition to his role at centrefield.'

'The defence was also sound, with Willie Power always reliable in goal. Mullinavat fought hard to retain the cup, but could only hold their opponents to level scores (1-3 to 0-6 for Carrickshock) with the aid of a strong wind in the first half. The teams were level again after 10 minutes of the second period with the scores reading 2-5 to 1-8, but Carrickshock added further points to hold a lead of 5 points nearing the end. However, Mullinavat fought back in determined fashion, and when Mossie Murphy broke through for a great goal, the outcome was still unclear with only a mere two points dividing the rivals, but the end came shortly afterwards, with Carrickshock retaining the narrow lead.'

'Mullinavat had a good goalie, fronted by a sound defence. Honours were about even at midfield, but the forwards, with the exception of Jimmy Murphy, Dick Carroll and Paddy Hoban, did not rise to their usual form. Though the hurling was tough, with exciting man-to-man clashes, the standard was never really brilliant, but the issue was fought out in a most exemplary manner between the neighbouring rivals, which reflected great credit on the participants, and also on the referee Ned Blackmore, who did an excellent job.'

Mullinavat: P Fitzpatrick, P Holden, J Conway, N Freyne, R Aylward, Mossy Murphy (1-3), N Fitzgerald, J Aylward, Andy Aylward (0-2), D Carroll, P Hoban, Jimmy Murphy (1-0), Jim Walsh (1-0), Tom O'Neill (0-1) and J Anthony.

Carrickshock: W Power; J Phelan, P J Roughan, P Power D Gaule, M Phelan, D Walsh, D Burke, Maurice Power (0-2), Dick Power (0-3), Jim Ireland (0-1), B Raggett, J Butler, Billy Kearney (0-8) and Martin Raggett (1-0). Sub: J Walsh for Butler.

1976

JUNIOR

South JHC Group B: Tullogher 2-13; Mullinavat 2-05
South JHC Group B: Mullinavat 3-05; Rower Inistioge 2-06
South JHC Group B: Glenmore 3-06; Mullinavat 3-05

Did not qualify for KO stages
South JHC Final: Carrickshock 0-17; Glenmore 2-09

1977
JUNIOR

South JHC Group B: Mullinavat 2-09; Carrickshock 0-11
South JHC Group B: Glenmore 3-13; Mullinavat 2-03
South JHC Group B: Dunnamaggin 2-08; Mullinavat 1-07
Did not qualify for KO stages
South JHC Final: Tullogher 4-12; Carrickshock 4-04

1978
JUNIOR

South JHC Group: Mullinavat 4-10; Slieverue 0-02
South JHC Group: Mullinavat 1-09; Piltown 1-07
South JHC Group: Glenmore 3-13; Mullinavat 3-09
South JHC Group: Mullinavat 4-05; Carrickshock 1-12
South JHC Semi Final: Mullinavat 1-11; Tullogher 1-11
South JHC Semi Final Replay: Mullinavat 3-13; Tullogher 2-05
South JHC Final: Mullinavat 2-06; Glenmore 0-11

'With a goal in the last seconds of the match, in a most exciting finish, Mullinavat took Southern honours in the Junior hurling championship at Piltown on Sunday 1/10/78 when they barely pipped Glenmore by a single point, on the score of 2-6 to 0-11. Despite perfect weather and an excellent pitch, the game never reached a high standard, with the forwards on both sides completely off target, as the number of wides indicate, 20 for Glenmore and 16 for Mullinavat, and the fact that most of the scores came from frees. The sides were level with a point each after ten minutes play, and it was deadlock again within five minutes of the interval, with the scores reading, Mullinavat 1-1 Glenmore 0-4, but Tom Murphy put his team ahead with a point to leave the interval scores 0-5 to 1-1 in favour of Glenmore, though Paddy Murphy missed a good chance of a point from a free close in just on the call of half-time.'

'Glenmore were in front by 4 points after 15 minutes of the second half, but Mullinavat gradually reduced the deficit and there was only six minutes left when the sides were level once more (1-6 to 0-9), but hereabouts Glenmore got on top again with two more points from Paddy Murphy and John Heffernan. There were some terrible wides on both sides, and when it looked as if Glenmore were well set on taking Southern honours for the first time in ten years, the lucky break came for Mullinavat. In the dying seconds of the match a high ball came in towards the Glenmore goalmouth, and a defender tried to grasp the sliothar but it glanced off his hand and the opposing forwards pounced on the rolling ball and finished it to the net.'

Mullinavat: Paddy Fitzpatrick, Nicky Fitzgerald, Paudy Holden, Tommy Duggan, Richard Aylward, Tom Anthony, John Joe Aylward, Andy Aylward, Pat Phelan, Tom Frisby (1-1), Mossie Murphy (0-4), John Aylward, Jimmy Murphy (0-1), Jim Walsh and John Fitzgerald (1-0).

Glenmore: Ollie Hartley; Mike Phelan, Christy Heffernan, Peter O'Connor, Mick Keogh, Paddy Murphy (0-6, captain), Tom Murphy (0-1), Bill Doherty (0-1), Mick Kirwan, Tom Phelan (0-1), John Phelan (0-1), Johnny Murphy (0-1), Paddy Culleton, Francis Ennett and Mick Heffernan. Sub: John Heffernan for M Heffernan.

County JHC Final: St Patrick's, Ballyraggett 4-06; Mullinavat 1-05

'After a topping first half, and a second that paled in comparison, St Patrick's (Ballyragget) emerged winners of the 65th Junior hurling championship at Nowlan Park on Sunday 12/11/1978. The winners collected their first title, and equalled a record by becoming the fifth consecutive Northern team to win this competition. Mullinavat, who in 1974 suffered the same fate in the Junior final, were held to a single point in the second half, though they played with the advantage of the strong breeze. St Patrick's, who now win promotion to the Intermediate grade, hurled with great aplomb, and when the need was greatest in the second half, displayed many team qualities. The losers were not as heavily beaten as the score line might suggest. A good goal in the 60th minute by centre-forward, Tommy Phelan loaded the scoreline against them, but there can be no doubt the better team won on the day.'

'St Patrick's, with Matt Ruth operating very effectively at centre-forward in the second moiety, absorbed tremendous pressure late in the match. Mullinavat won three 21 yard frees in front of goal and failed to get any reward from them. In the first half, the fare was comparable with the best in any grade in the county. Both sides showed plenty of ideas in attack despite the unfavourable conditions, playing attractive and action packed hurling. St Patrick's attacked the country end goal in the first half. They went into a commanding 2-3 to 0-2 lead after 15 minutes, but fine play by Joe Anthony, Richie Aylward, Mossy Murphy and John Walsh got the losers back within striking distance at the interval. The winners led by 2-3 to 1-4 at half time, an advantage they deserved on the run of play.'

'Matt Ruth goaled in the early minutes after Mossy Murphy (free) had opened the scoring with a point for Mullinavat. The winners score had a settling effect than just a single score.

Matt Ruth had a goal from play in the 13th minute that proved a big boost to the winners. For a while they owned the game, but then an Andy Aylward point pepped Mullinavat up once again, Jimmy Murphy banged home a great goal for them following a John Joe Aylward 65 in the 25th minute. Immediately, St Patrick's goalkeeper Patsy Trait brought off a wonderful save from Tommy Frisby to keep the rejuvenated Southerners at bay.'

'John Joe Aylward and Mossy Murphy added points before the break and bustling full-forward, Jim Walsh, had a goal disallowed for Mullinavat, who were enjoying their best spell. An important factor after the break was the siting of Matt Ruth at centre forward. His presence upset Tom Anthony, who had a sterling first half, but whose game seemed to suffer in the second because of an over awareness of who he was pitted against. Still he did not let the team down, but his contribution to the Mullinavat cause was not as great as it had been in the opening half. The game was not won and lost in this area. Mullinavat pressed hard, but they met with solid resistance, which if anything, grew stronger after full-back Sean Treacy was forced to retire injured in the third quarter.'

'Mullinavat's solitary second half score was landed by Mossy Murphy in the 36th minute (3-3 to 1-5). Afterwards, the winners had quick points through John Holland, Tommy Phelan and Matt Ruth. And just before the end the losers had a player sent off striking an opponent, but at that stage it made no difference one way or another.'

Mullinavat: P Fitzpatrick, N Fitzpatrick, P Holden, T Duggan, R Aylward, T Anthony, JJ Aylward, A Aylward (0-1), P Phelan, T Frisby, M Murphy (0-3, all frees), JJ Aylward (0-1, "65"), J Murphy (1-0), J Walsh and J Fitzgerald. Subs: M Reade for J Fitzgerald 48th minute, J Anthony for J Aylward 51st minute.

St Patrick's scorers: T Phelan (2-1); M Ruth (1-3, goal "65" and two frees); E Ruth (1-0); J Holland (0-2).

1979

JUNIOR

South JHC Group: Glenmore 3-6; Mullinavat 0-14

'A last minute point by Johnny Murphy secured victory for Glenmore when they played Mullinavat in the first round of the Southern Junior hurling championship at Piltown on Saturday 5/5/79. Mullinavat seemed to be in control throughout the game. They scored some good long-range points in the first half while their opponents had difficulty in finding the posts. The losers led by 0-8 to 0-3 at half-time. Glenmore played better hurling in the second half and got off to a good start with a Christy Heffernan goal. Throughout the remainder of the second half the game was very closely contested with the teams on level terms just on the call of time when Johnny Murphy pointed to give Glenmore a one-point victory.'

Mullinavat: P Fitzpatrick, R Aylward, P Holden, T Duggan, M Fitzgerald, T Anthony, JJ Aylward (0-2), A Aylward, P Phelan, T Frisby (0-2), J Walsh (0-4), J Murphy (0-1), J Anthony (0-1), M Murphy (0-4) and J Fitzgerald.

South JHC Group: Mullinavat 3-08; John Lockes, Callan 2-09
South JHC Group: Slieverue v. Mullinavat
South JHC Group: Carrickshock 4-12 Mullinavat 4-03
South JHC Group: Tullogher Rosbercon 3-10; Mullinavat 2-07
South JHC Final: Carrickshock 2-15; Piltown 2-08

CHAPTER 8

1980s

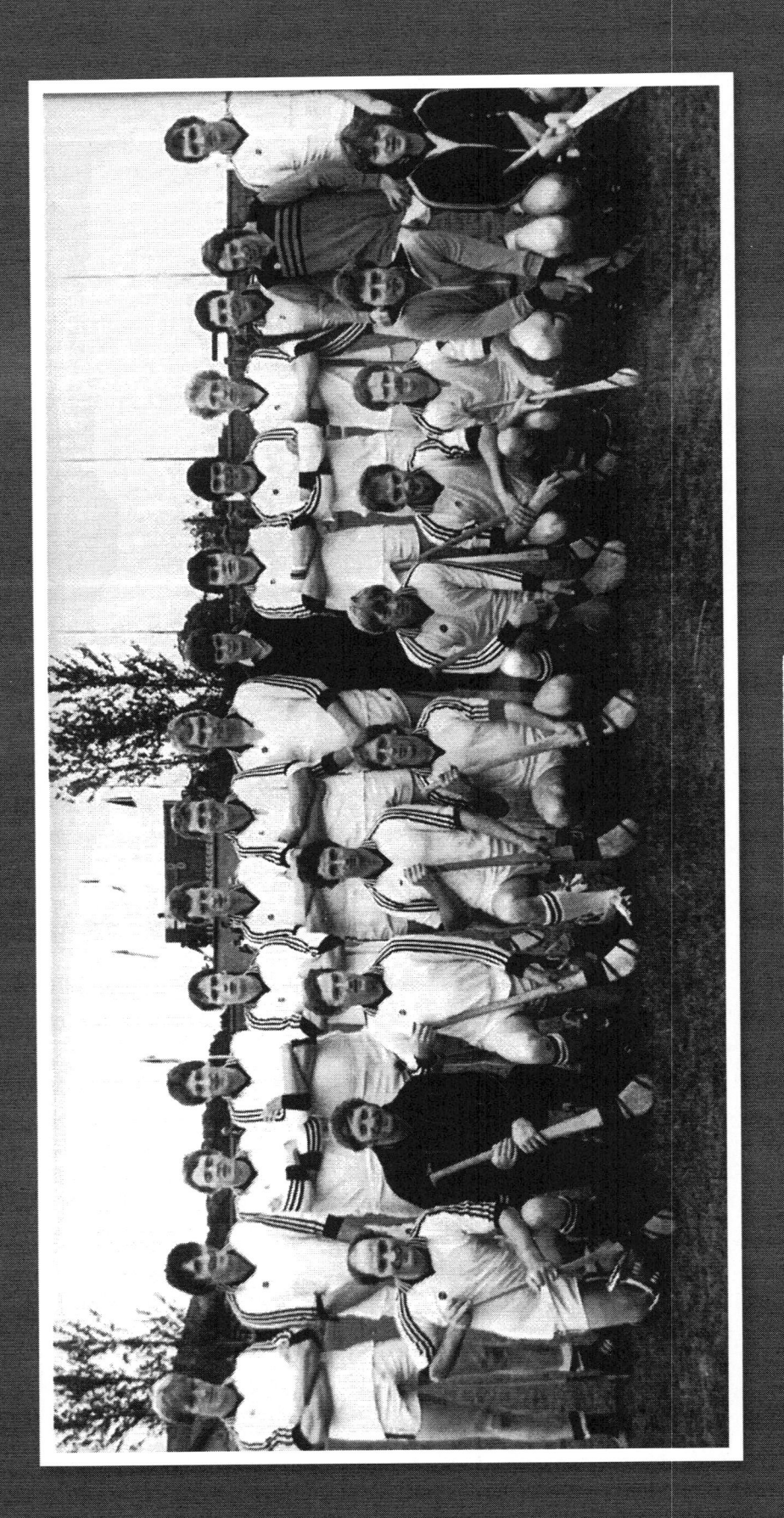

The Mullinavat team crowned Junior hurling county champions in 1984
Back Row (from left): Paudie Holder, Mossie Murphy, Joe Walsh, John Mc Donald, Paddy Frisby, Pete McDonald, Sean Walsh, Timmy Gough, Tomás Deegan, Dan Power, Stevie Foskin, Michael Law, John Haberlin, John Dumphy, Tom Anthony. Front Row (from left): Tommy Frisby (captain), Tommy Duggan, Andy Aylward, John Joe Aylward, Michael Fitzgerald, Paddy Fitzpatrick, Ned Frisby, Harry Waters, Michael Knox and Liam Law.

1980s

1980
JUNIOR

South JHC Group: John Lockes 3-10; Mullinavat 0-08
South JHC Group: Mullinavat 1-12; Carrigeen 2-05
South JHC Group: Mullinavat 1-10; St Senan's Kilmacow 1-10
South JHC Semi Final: Glenmore 5-12; Mullinavat 3-03

'A big crowd enjoyed excellent hurling in this entertaining South Junior hurling semi-final at Hugginstown on Sunday. The well drilled Glenmore outfit came out deserving winners The game was timed for 2pm but as the first ball was thrown in by referee Dick Dunphy at 2.15 the crowds were still pouring in. Inside six minutes big Glenmore centre forward Christy Heffernan had shook Mullinavat twice with fine goals. Ten more minutes and Glenmore led by 2-3 to 0-0. Further scores by Christy Heffernan made it 2-5 to 0-0. The good Mullinavat following was shattered. Then the losers made their first positional change with Tom Frisby going to midfield to try to stem the tide. Within minutes Mullinavat's most dangerous forward, Tom Foskin had the ball in the net. Mullinavat followers at last had something to shout about.'

'Mullinavat were playing into the Newmarket goal in the first half. It was now approaching half time. Johnnie Murphy added a point for Glenmore, followed by a point from Mossy Murphy for Mullinavat. Michael Heffernan added a Glenmore point and then on the verge of half time Andy Aylward, who had moved to the full line, passed to Jim Walsh for a goal. So the sides went in at half time 3-7 to 2-2.'

'The wind was now favouring Glenmore and they made use of it. Michael Heffernan opened the score for Glenmore with a point after 8 minutes. A lot of niggling went on and names could have been taken. The Mullinavat backs were hitting hard as the Glenmore forwards surged forward. Then Glenmore got loose. Bill Doherty, their Under-21 player sent over a point, followed by the fourth goal from Christy Heffernan. This was a gem of a goal that started at midfield when Francis Ennett, another player of outstanding merit, brought the ball to the 30 yards line. There he passed to Johnnie Murphy who drew the defence before passing to Christy Heffernan who gave the Mullinavat keeper no chance.'

'Mullinavat tried hard but they lacked fitness in all departments. Their midfield was at sea, even with all the positional changes they made. Some of their younger members did show up in particular John McDonald. The Glenmore team eased for a while in this half and left Mullinavat wondering whether they were trying at all. Mullinavat only snatched two scores in this half, a point from Mossy Murphy and a goal from the aftermath of a free that was taken by the same player, finished to the net by Jim Walsh. Mullinavat's goalkeeper could not be blamed for his side's defeat. Their backs were fighting a lost battle. They tried their best but their best was not good enough. Their midfield was also up against it as were their forwards.'

Mullinavat: P Fitzpatrick, N Fitzgerald, P Holden, T Duggan, R Aylward, T Anthony, JJ Aylward, A Aylward, P McDonald, S Foskin, M Murphy, J McDonald, T Frisby, J Walsh and J Anthony.

Glenmore: M Deady, J Phelan, P Murphy, E Aylward, S Boyle, D Ennett, T Murphy, M Kirwan, B Doherty, M Heffernan, F Ennett, M Connors, C Heffernan, J Murphy and J Heffernan. Sub: L Walsh for S Boyle (injured).

South JHC Final: Glenmore 2-18; Dunnamaggin 1-10

1981
JUNIOR

South JHC Group: Mullinavat 6-07; Tullogher Rosbercon 3-12
South JHC Group: Mullinavat 3-10; Carrigeen 3-06
South JHC Group: Mullinavat 4-08; Dunnamaggin 0-02
South JHC Group: Piltown 1-04; Mullinavat 0-07
South JHC Group: Mullinavat 0-10; St Senan's Kilmacow 0-09
South JHC Group Semi Final: Mullinavat 1-12; Dunnamaggin 2-04

'Mullinavat lined out without regulars Jim Walsh and Tommie Duggan, both out through hand injuries and Dunamaggin were without their great defender, Tom Phelan. Dunamaggin were first to score a point by Michael Moore, followed by a great point by County Minor John McDonald for Mullinavat. This man together with Mossie Murphy and his brother, Jimmie Murphy were the stars of this Mullinavat team. Jimmie Murphy was the man that put Mullinavat in front with a point and in this half he was the man that tried the most in the Mullinavat front line. From that Mullinavat went further ahead and the half time score was Mullinavat 0-8; Dunamaggin 0-1.'

'Dunamaggin began the second-half a little better and were again the first to score with a point from Stephen Martin. Mullinavat hit back with a point from Mossie Murphy, goals were scored in this half from Stephen Foskin for Mullinavat. This was as a result of a great effort from John McDonald. The first quarter of the second half is where Mullinavat really played but the switch at midfield after this time added to the scoring chances of Dunamaggin. Liam Law moved to the full-forward line and cut off a supply of the ball to the Mullinavat attack. The attack slumped and allowed Dunamaggin to come back into the game. John Ryan at No. 15 for Dunamaggin was the best of their forwards and in the half-line of attack, only Canice Mackey held his position for the hour, both Seamus Martin and Tom Hughes were replaced. In the half back line Dick Shea tried hard as did Paddy Fennelly and in the full line Jim Dunne was outstanding. He managed to go up the entire field and score a goal.'

'Dunamaggin used all three subs, Mullinavat used only one and that was 20 minutes into the second half so Mullinavat won well and they can thank John McDonald for passing the ball, Paudie Holden for containing anything that came, Liam Lawlor a good contribution at midfield and to Mossie Murphy and his brother Jimmy. There were good performances from half-back Andy Aylward, his brother John Joe and Tommy Frisby.'

Mullinavat: P Fitzpatrick, T Frisby, T Anthony, D Power, A Aylward, P Holden, JJ Aylward, M Fitzgerald, L Law, J McDonald (0-3), M Murphy (0-6), J Murphy (0-3), S Foskin (1-0), W Gahan, and T Gough. Sub: P McDonald.

South JHC Final: Piltown 1-17; Mullinavat 1-07

'At Hugginstown on Sunday 4/10/81, Piltown, the Model Village, lifted the Southern Junior Hurling Championship in splendid fashion for the first time in the history of the club. It was left to this great team, put together by the selectors and trained by former Tipperary All-Ireland hurler of five times, Joe English, to win this cup. Its captain, John Maher was a proud man when he showed the prize to his wild and enthusiastic supporters. Not since the club was formed in 1936 has the club won the Southern final. In fact, they have never won it in their history. This game against Mullinavat was won and lost in the first half. Mullinavat won the toss, but the team captain decided to play against the wind and try their luck in the second half. It never came, and from the time that man of the match Joe Sullivan, former Kilkenny Minor and Under-21 player, hit the score board after five minutes in the first half it was Piltown all the way. They were superb, in fact Theo English had them so fit that there was always an extra man around to help out in times of trouble. The whole of this Piltown team played above par. They chased all that came and Mullinavat must be wondering what went wrong.'

Mullinavat: P Fitzpatrick, T Frisby, T Anthony, D Power, A Aylward, P Holden, JJ Aylward, M Fitzgerald, P McDonald, J McDonald, S Foskin, J Murphy, T Gough, M Murphy and W Gahan. Subs: L Law, J Anthony.

Piltown: K Brennan, J Fitzgerald, P Brophy, J Maher, P Long, E Brennan, S Norris; N Culleton, T O'Shea; JJ Long, G Culleton, J Norris, L McCarthy, J Power, J O'Sullivan. Sub: P Dunne.

1982
JUNIOR

South JHC: Dunnamaggin 1-13; Mullinavat 1-08
South JHC: St Senan's Kilmacow 1-05; Mullinavat 0-05
South JHC: John Lockes 1-09; Mullinavat 0-07
South JHC: Mullinavat 3-11 Slieverue 3-01
South JHC: Mullinavat 2-08; Carrigeen 1-06
South JHC: Mullinavat 2-06 Mooncoin 1-06
South JHC: Mullinavat 2-17; Tullogher Rosbercon 2-08
South JHC Final: John Lockes 3-14; Dunnamaggin 4-10

1983
JUNIOR

South JHC: Mullinavat 6-09; Thomastown 0-06
South JHC: Mullinavat 1-15; St Senan's 3-08
South JHC: Shamrocks 1-07; Mullinavat 1-05
South JHC: Mullinavat 1-11; John Lockes 0-09
South JHC: Mullinavat 3-19; Carrigeen 1-10
South JHC: Mullinavat 2-13; Tullogher Rosbercon 2-06
South JHC: Mullinavat 1-14; Mooncoin 3-04
South JHC: Mullinavat 4-10; Slieverue 4-08
South JHC: Dunnamaggin 2-10; Mullinavat 1-07
South JHC: Semi Final Tullogher Rosbercon 2-09; Mullinavat 1-08

'The first of the Southern Junior Semi-Finals was played at Glenmore on Sunday evening 14/08/1983 The result was a very clear cut win over for Tullogher/Rosbercon over top of the table team, Mullinavat. The near neighbours and arch rivals Tullogher/Rosbercon deserved their victory in what was not the sort of game expected al this level and stage in the championship. At half-time with the winners playing with the breeze, they led by one point and most expected that the second-half would produce the kind of needle that is expected between these teams. Mullinavat opened the scoring with a good point from Liam Law, followed by a point from Mossie Murphy. By the close of the half, Mullinavat were reduced to 14 men.'

'The second half started with Tullogher on the attack and looking for a goal now that they had the extra man. They got the first of them with only 4 minutes gone in the second-half from a pass from Donie Lyng, centre-forward Seamus Murphy goaled. Their second came from Luke Bird after 16 minutes into the same half. Tullogher can feel proud of their achievement because they beat the firm favourites Mullinavat, and allowing for them to overcome only 14 men they can count themselves unlucky to go in only one point ahead at the interval. For Mullinavat, goalie John Dunphy had a good game as did Dan Power in the first half, Paudie Holden, Mossie Murphy and Timothy Gough.'

Mullinavat: John Dunphy, Andy Aylward, Paudie Holden, John Haberlin, Joe Walsh, Dan Power, JJ Aylward (0-1), Peter McDonald, Tom Deegan (0-1), Liam Law (0-1), John McDonald, Tom Frisby (0-1), Sean Walsh, Mossie Murphy (1-4) and T Gough.

South JHC Final: Shamrocks 3-11; Tullogher Rosbercon 0-18

1984

JUNIOR

Under the group system each club played 10 games, before the top four advanced to the South JHC semi-finals.

South JHC Group: Mullinavat 1-10; Thomastown 0-05
South JHC Group: Mullinavat 2-10; John Lockes 1-08
South JHC Group: Dunnamaggin 3-11; Mullinavat 2-05
South JHC Group: Mullinavat 3-12; Mooncoin 1-03
South JHC Group: Mullinavat 4-15; St Senan's 4-04
South JHC Group: Mullinavat 1-11; Rower Inistioge 1-09
South JHC Group: Mullinavat 1-10; Tullogher Rosbercon 2-05
South JHC Group: Mullinavat 2-16; Carrigeen 1-02
South JHC Group: Mullinavat 4-14; Slieverue 1-03
South JHC Group: Mullinavat 1-09; Shamrocks 1-07
South JHC Semi Final: Mullinavat 2-18; John Lockes Callan 0-08

'Never even stretched so far as to be forced to make a switch or substitution, Mullinavat cruised past a disappointing John Lockes (Callan) in this one sided second Southern Junior hurling semi-final at Hugginstown on Sunday. The winners got off to lightening start and

Mossy Murphy shot a brace of points inside a minute. That was a prelude of what was to come, particularly during the first half when Mullinavat scored some beautiful long range points. John Lockes did a reasonable job of containing the lively winners' attack in the early stages. But by halftime the evergreen Mossy Murphy had picked up five points, while the very impressive John McDonald hit three more to help Mullinavat into an 0-13 to 0-5 lead. Up front the losers found it hard to make progress, and apart from county Minor John Power, they were well held. As the match wore on they surrendered midfield, so their task was a hopeless one after that. The first three scores in the closing mostly fell to the winners, Joe Walsh (2) and Peter McDonald, which pushed them 0-16 to 0-5 clear. Jimmy Donovan had one for the Callan aide before Mullinavat hit back for another trio of scores.'

'The first one followed a classy piece of individual play by John McDonald. The county Under-21 star who had one of his most accomplished outings in ages, dashed on a 30 yard solo run before driving the ball left handed to the top corner of the town end goal (1-16 to 0-4). Scores were added quickly by Pat McEvoy and Sean Walsh to leave John Lockes 15 points behind.'

Mullinavat: J Dunphy, T Frisby, P Holden, A Aylward, P Frisby, D Power, JJ Aylward (0-2, one free, one"65"), J Walsh (0-2), P McDonald (0-1), P McEvoy (0-1), J McDonald (1-3), S Walsh (1-1), H. Waters, M Murphy (0-7, 0-4 frees) and M Law (0-1).

South JHC Final: Mullinavat 2-12; Dunnamaggin 2-06

'Benefitting from a few shrewd interval switches, Mullinavat slipped into a higher gear in the second half and eased past hard-trying Dunnamaggin in this entertaining Southern Centenary Junior hurling final at Piltown on Sunday.. Dunnamaggin were well beaten in the second half exchanges, which was in contrast to how they fared in the first. They opened well, and although they dominated territorially, they just couldn't reflect their efforts on the scoreboard. The surprising thing about the interval scoreline of 0-5 to 0-3 in favour of Dunnamaggin was how Mullinavat managed to get so close. The losers squandered a couple of good chances, and as well, they failed to make much use of a decided advantage gained at midfield and on their own 40. The winners were transformed after the change about. Contributory factors were the switching of Mossy Murphy to his more usual full-forward role and the siting of John McDonald at No. 11. Also, they stepped-up their efforts at midfield and by the 35th minute they were in front. Two goals in as many minutes after that by Harry Waters and Timmy Gough put them in a commanding 2-6 to 0-5 lead and really, they were never going to be beaten after that. It was the winners who opened the scoring in the third minute when Mossy Murphy pointed a free. After that they found it hard to make progress, and only at irregular intervals did they break up the field.'

'The Dunnamaggin half back line stood firm, and with Seamus Martin cleaning up at midfield, they got a good supply of the ball up to the front line. Here Jimmy Dunne posed the greatest threat, but he was well policed by a determined Tommy Frisby. Dunne still managed to grab three points (one free) while John Carroll and Seamus Moore hit one each before the break to give the losers a slim 0-5 to 0-3 lead after playing with the light breeze. The 2,500 spectators could hardly credit the sudden improvement in Mullinavat after the change of ends. Inside a minute Sean Walsh pointed. Then Mossy Murphy did likewise to leave them together at 0-5 each. Joe Walsh then shot a third point to put Mullinavat into the lead for the first time since the third minute. Dunnamaggin were backpedaling, and they got into a lot of trouble when Michael Law provided a pass for Harry Watters to palm a goal in the 37th minute. Two minutes later Timmy Gough pounced on a ball broken by Waters and slammed it into the net (2-6 to 0-5). A score from Mossy Murphy extended the lead to eight points with 20 minutes remaining, and all of a sudden Dunnamaggin were in serious trouble. They gave their supporters something to cheer about in the 42nd minute when Jimmy Dunne sent Johnny Murray through for a goal. However, they needed a second to bring them right back into contention, but when that eventually came six minutes from the end (2-10 to 2-6) it was too little too late to save the day. This was Mullinavat's seventh Southern championship success, and now they should make a bold bid for county honours. They had fine hurlers in Paudie Holden, JJ Aylward, Peter McDonald, John McDonald, Mossy Murphy, Sean Walsh and Dan Power.'

Mullinavat: J Dunphy, T Frisby, P Holden, A Aylward, P Frisby, D Power, JJ Aylward, J Walsh (0-1), P McDonald, J McDonald (0-3), M Murphy (0-7, 4 frees), S Walsh (0-1), H Watters (1-0), T Gough (1-0) and M Law. Subs: L Law, S Foskin.

Dunnamaggin: G Ryan, D O'Shea, M Hogan, L Costelloe, C Mackey, M Kelly, J Ryan, T Phelan, S Martin (captain), John Carroll (0-1), M Moore, J Reid, Seamus Moore (1-1), Johnny Murray (1-0) and Jim Dunne (0-4, 2 frees). Sub: J O'Dwyer, S Power.

County JHC Final: Mullinavat 3-09; Emeralds 1-05

'The well prepared hurlers from Mullinavat turned back the pages of history nearly 50 years when they scored this merited victory over game Emeralds (Urlingford) in the Junior hurling championship final at well attended Callan on Sunday. Way back in 1939 the Southerners recorded their last success. Now they have four overall, having also collected the glittering prize in 1915 and '16 and, of course, this Centenary year. This was a tough and gruelling encounter that was fought in tricky wind conditions and on a greasy surface. Three times in all these extremely fit teams were on level terms, but once Michael Law knocked home the winners second goal in the 36th minute, they took a positive grip and always looked like doing it afterwards.'

'In fairness to the Emeralds, they were desperately unlucky not to add to their goal tally, They tested the Mullinavat defence, including goalkeeper, John Dunphy, and even the woodwork, but they could not get the big score that might have rescued them. The 3,000 or so supporters were treated to a very close marking and low scoring first half. At the break the winners led by 1-3 to 1-2, but even at that they had impressed that little bit more than their opponents, particularly the way they moved the ball quickly and with an inventive use of the handpass. All the same, the Emeralds shot two quick points immediately after the change of ends to go in front (1-4 to 1-3) for the first time. They were instantly pegged back and then came Law's goal that put Mullinavat 2-4 to 1-4 in front and on the road to a memorable win. Now they gain promotion and will display their skill in the Intermediate championship of 1985.'

'In the opening three minutes the teams swapped points. That was the only time they were level in the half. After that came a 7th minute point from Mossy Murphy, but 21 minutes had passed before the next flag was sent flying. In between there was a lot of good hurling, but defences were mostly on top. Emeralds' goalkeeper, Dave Burke, although under no pressure, got it all wrong when dealing with a shot from 60 yards by Peter McDonald. Amazingly the ball ended in the net and the 'keeper and umpires alike examined the net to see had it gained entry through some unusual spot. It hadn't. But the Emeralds reply was fast and decisive. The experienced Frank Cleere had the ball in the net within 60 seconds (1-2 to 1-1). Before the break Mossy Murphy and Johnny Moriarty swopped points which left the minimum between them at the half-way mark. It was hard to know who gained advantage from the largely cross field wind. Anyway, it was the Emeralds who opened full of business in the new half and two points in as many minutes from John Tobin and Jimmy Queally put them ahead (1-4 to 1-3). This was the one and only time they made the running!'

'A 35th minute point from the lively Mossy Murphy squared the tie. Seconds later John McDonald was fouled 35 yards out to the left of the country end goal. Mossy Murphy's shot was poorly struck, but as it came across the square Michael Law got his hurley to it and knocked it into the Emeralds' net (2-4 to 1-4). For a while the exchanges became a bit nasty and three players were booked in quick succession, but when matters settled down the hurling all round was again full of commitment. Not long after that Law goal, Sean Walsh had the ball in the net again, and suddenly the title was moving away from the Northerners. The determined Johnny Moriarty pointed to keep the losers in touch, but that was replied to at the double by Mossy Murphy (3-6 to 1-5). Between Murphy's two scores David Burke brought off a smashing diving save from Joe Walsh that would surely have put the issue beyond all doubt. At the other end the Emeralds were out of luck. John Tobin missed a goal from point blank range and Michael Rafter had another fierce drive turned out for a '65'. Later Tom Frisby came to Mullinavat's rescue when he took the ball off the goal line, and after that Pat Ryan hit the woodwork. So the losers, really, were worth another few scores at least.'

'They didn't get them, but for that the Mullinavat defence can take a lot of credit They kept it tight, and star performers included John Dunphy, Tom Frisby, Dan Power and Paudie Holden, while further afield the versatile Mossy Murphy, Peter McDonald, John McDonald and Sean Walsh got through great work.'

Mullinavat: J Dunphy, T Frisby, P Holden, A Aylward, P Frisby, D Power, JJ Aylward, J Walsh, P McDonald (1-0), S Walsh (1-1), J McDonald, S Foskin (0-1), H Watters, M Murphy (0-7, 4 frees) and M Law (1-0). Sub: T Gough.

Emeralds: D Burke, J Tone, P Phelan. M Burke, J Hughes, L Cody, M Grace, P Ryan, J Tobin (0-1), E Holohan, F Cleere (1-0), J. Moriarty (0-3, one free), J Queally (0-1), M Rafter, P Tobin. Subs: H Grady and P Tobin.

1985

INTERMEDIATE

With only one win in five group games, Mullinavat had a baptism of fire in the Intermediate grade. A September win versus Barrow Rangers was one of the most important victories in the club's history. Since winning Junior in 1984, to this day, the clubs first team has never returned to the Junior grade, but this was a close shave.

IHC R1: Mullinavat 4-06; Galmoy 0-09
IHC R2: Dicksboro 1-12; Mullinavat 1-07
IHC R3: Conahy Shamrocks 2-08; Mullinavat 3-03
IHC R4: O'Loughlin's 2-11; Mullinavat 2-10
IHC R5: Graiguenamagh 3-16; Mullinavat 1-06
IHC Relegation Semi Final: Dicksboro 2-10; Mullinavat 1-09

'Dicksboro will be playing Intermediate hurling next year, but Mullinavat are just 60 minutes away from dropping back down to the Junior grade. After missing the chance in this match at Thomastown last Sunday to keep their Intermediate place, the Southerners will get another bite at the cherry when they face fellow strugglers Barrow Rangers in a second relegation play-off. Given the miserable weather on Sunday and the wet sod in Thomastown, it wouldn't come as a surprise to learn that this relegation play-off was a very poor affair hurling wise. But that won't worry Dicksboro. It has been a disappointing season for the city side who seemed set for a promising run this year. Mullinavat always faced an uphill struggle on Sunday after Dicksboro scored a goal in the second minute, and the city side went on to lead by seven points at half-time. The losers pressed very hard in the second half when aided by a strong wind, but some poor shooting, coupled with some magnificent defensive displays by a number of the Dicksboro backs, meant they never got nearer than four points. Dicksboro had beaten Mullinavat by four points when the sides met in the championship proper, and soon set about repeating the dose. They got off to a flier when Simon Walton got through for a goal after only two minutes and, backed by the wind, dominated the first 30 minutes.'

'Left-half forward Tom Bawle was in majestic form, hitting points from frees and play, and was well supported in the first half by Michael Hogan at centre-field and John Joe Cullen and Walton in the half forward line. With points from Hogan and Benny McGarry tacked on to Bawle's tally, Dicksboro led by 1-8 to 0-4 at the break. Mullinavat's hopes of pulling it back in the second half suffered a setback when Tommy Bawle hit a fine solo goal. Though John McDonald scored a goal at the other end and Dan Power and county Under-21 hurler Joe Walsh added points, Mullinavat failed to get on top of the winners' defence where John Marnell and Tom Maher were particularly effective.'

Mullinavat: J Dunphy; T Frisby, P Holden, A Aylward; P Frisby, JJ Aylward, P McDonald; J McDonald (1-0), P McEvoy (0-2), S Walsh, D Power (0-3), J Walsh (0-3); T Duggan, N Murphy (0-1) and H Waters. Subs: M Law, M Knox.

IHC Relegation Final: Mullinavat 1-12; Barrow Rangers 0-07

'Junior champions of last year, Mullinavat held on to their Intermediate status and dispatched Barrow Rangers (Paulstown) to the Junior grade when they won this hurling championship relegation play-off at St John's Park on Sunday. The winners started as if they had really missed the hurling action – it was over six weeks since their last championship game – and hit points per Mossy Murphy, JJ Aylward and Dan Power in the opening two minutes. They kept up a steady pace until the break, and even if they did hit only one score in the second period, they had done enough to carry the day. After scores from the trio mentioned above, Mullinavat conceded one to Michael Whitley. Then the experienced Mossy Murphy, who converted every free into a score, replied with two points before Pat Parcell hit another for the losers in the 7th minute (0-5, to 0-2).'

'The traffic was all one way, apart from a break for a 17th minute point from Michael Doyle, and by that stage the winners were 0-10 to 0-3 in front. Then in the 20th minute a free from 45 yards by Mossy Murphy went all the way to the net, and with one more score from the same player, the winners retired 1-11 to 0-3 in front at halftime. The losers had three scores during the third quarter, all from Michael Doyle, and then Pat Purcell had another in the 53rd minute. Mullinavat's lone score of the half was landed by Dan Power.'

Mullinavat: J Dunphy, T Frisby, P Holden, M Knox, P Frisby, P McDonald, JJ Aylward (0-1), P McEvoy (0-1), J Walsh (0-1), S Foskin, D Power (0-2), S Walsh (0-1), M Law, M Murphy (1-6, 1-4 frees) and H Waters. Sub: T Gough.

OUR STORY (1887-2024)

PARISH SURVEY

Total population of both Mullinavat and Bigwood: 1,449
Number of families: Mullinavat 289 Bigwood 69
Average number of persons per family: 4.0
Number of people living alone: 41
Number of adults under 65 years of age: Mullinavat 604, Bigwood 156
Number of children under 12 years of age: Mullinavat 321, Bigwood 81

1986

INTERMEDIATE

IHC R1: Mullinavat 1-08; Young Irelands 1-07
IHC R2: Mullinavat 3-08; Tullaroan 2-11
IHC R3: Conahy Shamrocks 1-09; Mullinavat 1-06
IHC R4: Mullinavat 3-13; Graigue Ballycallan 0-08
IHC R5: Mullinavat 2-10; Carrickshock 1-11
IHC Quarter Final: Tullaroan 5-8; Mullinavat 3-11

'A hard earned and at the same time somewhat lucky goal six minutes from time earned Tullaroan a thrilling victory over Mullinavat in this absorbing Intermediate hurling championship play-off at well attended Callan on Saturday. That vital score that won Tullaroan the ticket into the semi-final was knocked home by the skilful Jimmy Walton. In the lead-up it looked as if two defenders had done enough to prevent a score when first they bottled up an opponent, and then they hooked him. But somehow the ball broke to the unmarked Walton 15 yards in front of the town end goal. With one hand on the hurley Walton swiped at the ball and sent it on its way into the net. But the exciting and nail biting goalmouth action was far from finished at that. Within a minute the hardworking Stephen Foskin saw a sizzling shot for a goal went inches wide at the other end. A minute later the elusive John McDonald drew all the cover to the left of the posts and sent a beautiful hand-pass out to the unmarked Sean Walsh on the opposite side, but the laters rushed shot went high and over the bar. In the wind-up Bobby Sweeney scored a great point from an acute angle for Tullaroan, and that concluded what for me, was the most competitive club match seen this year.'

'The second half action was fast and furious, and with the scores so close, the chances were that in a helter-skelter finish any sort of score, lucky or otherwise, could make all the difference. It did, for Tullaroan. With the aid of one soft goal, and then three other good ones, Tullaroan opened up a 12 points lead (4-2 to 0-2) after just 25 minutes. From there to the break Mullinavat who had not been out hurled to the degree the scores might suggest, got their act together and at the break were somewhat better off when 0-7 to 4-2 behind.

'The new half was barely 20 seconds old when the losers goaled. John McDonald worked an opening for Pat McEvoy, but the latter was chopped down – the referee should have been more decisive in his action here – as he went for goal. From the penalty McEvoy netted. Jimmy Walton hit back with a point from a free for Tullaroan, but it wasn't enough to halt the charge of the Southerners. In Mullinavat's next attack Sean Walsh had a fine shot blocked out, and John McDonald picked up the rebound and netted. Then the same player hit an excellent left handed point from 40 yards before Mossy Murphy pointed to level the scores (4-3 to 2-9). By this stage both sets of supporters were urging their favourites to even greater deeds. For a while Tullaroan responded. They had points from Tom Gaffney (2), Pat Fennelly and Jimmy Walton without reply. Again Mullinavat took up the chase, and scores from Mossy Murphy and Sean Walsh (goal) – a great hand pass from John McDonald made it – levelled matters. Four minutes of fierce action followed, before a lucky break of the ball gave Jimmy Walton and Tullaroan the score that made all the difference. Mullinavat need feel no shame after this exciting effort. Had the lucky break gone their way, they could have made the semi-finals. They had stars too, but none did better than John McDonald, who shipped a considerable amount of punishment, the extremely competitive Dan Power and Joe Walsh, Andy Aylward, Paudie Holden and Sean Walsh.'

Mullinavat: J Dunphy, T Frisby, P Holden, A Aylward, P Frisby, J Walsh, JJ Aylward, D Power, P McDonald, P McEvoy (1-1, goal penalty), L Law, S Foskin (0-1), P Hoban, J McDonald (1-1) and M Murphy (0-7, 0-4 frees). Subs: S. Walsh (1-1) and M Law.

1987

INTERMEDIATE

IHC R1: Young Irelands 2-10; Mullinavat 0-04
IHC R2: Mullinavat 3-06; O'Loughlin Gaels 1-09
IHC R3: Mullinavat 3-07: Dicksboro 0-12
IHC R4: Mullinavat 2-08; St Lachtain's 1-07
IHC R5: Mullinavat 3-08; Carrickshock 0-09
IHC Semi Final: Graigue Ballycallan 1-15; Mullinavat 0-09

'Victory for either side would have meant an historic first appearance in the Intermediate hurling final, but the fare did not match the occasion, and Graigue-Ballycallan and Mullinavat played out a largely boring semi-final at Nowlan Park on Sunday. The exchanges were close and dour up to eight minutes from time when just one point divided the teams (0-10 to 0-9). The game needed something to shake it out of its mediocrity. An infusion of new blood by the winners in the shape of Pat Hayes provided just that. With his first touch of the ball, Hayes threw over a point for Graigue. With six minutes remaining the enigmatic Jimmy Ronan flashed over a good point after a piercing run by Tomas McCluskey carved out the opening. Within 30 seconds Pat Hayes slipped through to shoot home a fine goal, and Graigue were on the road to history and a flattering margin of victory.'

'Without doubt, Mullinavat missed the injured Mossy Murphy. His calming influence was missed from the front line, a point highlighted by the fact the Southerners went 26 scoreless minutes between the 23rd and 49th minutes. They had their good ones too, and Joe and Sean Walsh played particularly well. In the initial stages, Peter McDonald and Johnny Ronan exchanged points. During the next 10 minutes Mullinavat enjoyed the better of things, and opened up a 0-4 to 0-1 lead thanks to scores from Stephen Foskin, Michael Dunphy and Sean Walsh, who often found himself with plenty of space on the wing. Scores from Johnny Ronan and Kevin Hennessy brought the winners right back into the game but they were lucky to stay there. Because in the 14th minute 'keeper Adrian Ronan had to be at his best to block out a shot from Timmy Gough, and again in the 21st minute he saved the day when he deprived Pat McEvoy of what looked a certain goal.'

'At times during this half Joe Walsh cleaned-up at centre-back for the losers, and for a while they suggested they had the class to win through. Points from Stephen Foskin and Sean Walsh (2) had them 0-7 to 0-3 clear with barely five minutes left in the half. With an improvement in Kevin Hennessy's take from the midfield exchanges, came an improvement in Graigue's fortunes, and scores from Johnny Ronan (2) and Jim Maher, which this could have been a goal, left them just 0-6 to 0-7 down at the interval. In the opening seconds of the new half, Mullinavat guardian, Paddy Fitzpatrick did well to keep out a shot from John Teehan. But he couldn't prevent the equalising point in the 33rd minute from Johnny Ronan, who played like a man possessed during the early stages of the second moiety. The Southerners fell into arrears of three points nearing the end of the third quarter, but then scores from Pat Hoban, their first in 26 minutes, and Pat McEvoy, reduced the deficit to the minimum (0-9 to 0-10). Then up popped Pat Hayes, who shot a point for Graigue. Johnny Ronan hit another, and then came Hayes' goal that tilted the balance.'

Mullinavat: P Fitzpatrick, T Frisby, P Holden, A Aylward, P Frisby, J Walsh, JJ Aylward, M Dunphy (0-1, free), P McDonald (0-1), S Walsh (0-3), J Fitzgerald, S Foskin (0-2), P McEvoy (0-1, "65"), T Gough and P Hoban (0-1). Subs: D Power, and M Law.

1988

INTERMEDIATE

IHC R1: O'Loughlin Gaels 0-09; Mullinavat 1-05
IHC R2: John Lockes 3-12; Mullinavat 4-08
IHC R3: Bennettsbridge 0-15; Mullinavat 2-05 (54 minutes, unfinished due to disputed point).
IHC R4: Mullinavat 1-10; St Lachtain's 2-05
IHC R5: Mooncoin 4-11; Mullinavat 0-05

Did not qualify from Group

THE DISPUTED POINT

Mullinavat's season was affected by one incident in this year, which is remembered as the year of the disputed point! In a most unusual occurrence a Kilkenny hurling championship game was abandoned on 29/05/88. The Intermediate Round 3 tie between Bennetsbridge and Mullinavat at Thomastown was called off eight minutes from time when the referee was unable to continue the game. Apparently a Bridge effort for a point led to the confusion. The umpire at the nearest post felt the effort was a point, but his decision was hotly disputed by Mullinavat team members, officials and supporters. In the uproar that followed, the referee, Liam Dewberry (Dicksboro) called off the game. At the time the Bridge were leading by 0-15 to 2-5.

At the County Board hearing in June there was still no joy for Mullinavat. 'Mullinavat were warned as to their future conduct, and their player, Andy Aylward was suspended for two months following incidents at their abandoned game against Bennetsbridge. The referee, Liam Dewberry, called off that tie in the 54th minute when the Bridge were leading by 0-15 to 2-5. Mullinavat disputed a Bridge score, and their keeper, John Dunphy, who was also warned as to his future conduct, refused to puck-out the ball. The referee stated he was unable to start the game, and so abandoned it. Bennetsbridge were awarded the match by the Co. Board. Michael Carroll (Mullinavat) said losing the match was harsh on Mullinavat, and the suspension of Andy Aylward was unwarranted. He blamed the referee for all the trouble and said if the official had done his job properly nothing would have happened. "It is bad if the Co. Board accepts a club can be treated like this by any referee" he stated, and pointed out the loss of the match could cost Mullinavat relegation back to the Junior grade. He pointed out Mullinavat were nearly 40 years trying to win a Junior championship, and now something like this could push them back down. He appealed, but the appeal was rejected for Andy Aylward's suspension to be reduced to one month. He told the meeting that the umpire involved in the affair subsequently admitted his mistake, and the disputed Bennetsbridge effort was wide.

1989
INTERMEDIATE
IHC R1: Mullinavat 3-12; Barrow Rangers 3-10
IHC R2: Mullinavat 2-14; St Lachtain's 2-08
IHC R3: Piltown 2-12; Mullinavat 1-12
IHC R4: Mullinavat 1-11; Dicksboro 1-05
IHC R5: Mullinavat 2-17; John Lockes 1-10
County IHC Semi Final: Mullinavat 3-06; Mooncoin 2-08

'The vagaries in sport are unbounded! In a split second a villain can become a hero, and the reverse can be the same too. At Nowlan Park on Sunday 24/9/89, the former made the news of the day. With just two minute remaining on the clock in a tense finish to the Intermediate hurling semi-final between Mullinavat and Mooncoin the sides were level. There was no room for error. Then Mooncoin made a fatal mistake and conceded a free about 55 yards from their own goal. Mullinavat's Michael Dunphy stepped-up for the crucial free. It had not been his afternoon. His shooting had been way off, and he had missed the target much more often than he had hit it. From a good distance and into the wind, Dunphy duly converted probably the most difficult free he had faced in the hour, and he won the game for Mullinavat. Had his side lost, he could well have been a villain. That late strike made him a hero, a status he shared with team mate, Pat Hoban, who cracked home a dazzling 3-3 for the winners. Hoban was the real star. Dunphy was the late hero. Mullinavat celebrated a rare win over their more illustrious opponents.'

'This was a game that was dour and rarely opened up. The play was smothered because both sides had a healthy respect for each other, Too much so at times found the going hard.

Mullinavat had first use of the wind, but they found it hard to derive any great benefit from it. At half-time they were held to level terms (1-6 to 2-3), and but for the brilliant Pat Hoban, they would have been way behind. In that half hour Hoban slammed home 2-2, his first goal being a real dazzler. Mooncoin put the first two scores on the board, when Michael Walsh and Joe Wall pointed before six minutes had passed. Already Michael Dunphy had missed two possible scores from frees for the winners, and his confidence must surely have been undermined. Not so with Pat Hoban. In the 8th minute, he latched on to a drive from John McDonald and rounded his man at full speed before blasting a shot from 21 yards high into the net. 'Keeper David Bourke didn't even see the ball passing him (1-0 to 0 2). From here to the break the lead changed hands on several occasions.'

'Mooncoin had the ball in the net early in the second half, but play was called back for an earlier infringement, and Mullinavat escaped. They enjoyed a bit of luck again minutes later, when a scramble in front of their opponents net ended with Pat Hoban slipping the ball into the net. This score injected new life into the winners, and for a while they took a firm grip on the game. Mooncoin had a narrow escape in the 37th minute when Stephen Foskin blasted a low shot goalwards, out Joe Murphy's body saved the day. The winners produced their best hurling during this spell, and they had Mooncoin in considerable trouble, but they just couldn't get a safe margin ahead. They were looking good at the end of the third quarter when 3-5 to 1-8 clear, because their hurling was good. But they still couldn't finish their opponents off. Mooncoin had only their second score of the half in the 52nd minute when Michael Walsh converted a 21-yard free. Within seconds they launched another attack, and they goaled out of the blue. Joe Wall sent over a firmly struck drive from the right of the town end goal, and unlucky defender, Tom Frisby deflected the ball high into his own net. The teams were back level at 3-5 to 2-8.'

'Five minutes later came Dunphy's all important point from a free. In the dying stages Mooncoin mounted a frantic raid in a bid to save the day, but a well struck shot from 60 yards by Michael Walsh missed the target, and there wasn't even enough time for the puck out. Pat Hoban enjoyed the sort of day for Mullinavat when he could do no wrong. Everything he touched turned into a score, be it with his right hand or left. Other sterling performers were Dan Power, Tom Frisby, Pat McDonald and Stephen Foskin.'

Mullinavat: J Dunphy, T Frisby, P Holden, A Aylward, P Frisby, D Power, JJ Aylward, J Walsh, P McDonald, M Dunphy (0-2, frees), S Foskin, J McDonald, P Hoban (3-3), P McEvoy and S Walsh (0-1).

County IHC Final: Mullinavat 2-13; Young Irelands 0-14

'Conventional wisdom rarely gets things wrong, and the gem of conventional wisdom which says that a good big team will always beat a good small team isn't far out too often. The maxim wasn't far out at sunny Nowlan Park on Sunday 24/9/1989 either. Mullinavat were just that much stronger and bigger than Young Irelands (Gowran). And in the end that proved the decisive factor as the Southerners made the most of their size advantage to claim the county Intermediate hurling crown. Any of the 6,000 spectators who came hoping for a classic were disappointed, this final was never that. But the exchanges were close and tough and hard, and Mullinavat always had the edge in toughness and tenacity. Just as importantly, they had Mick Dunphy as freetaker with five frees, two 65s, a goal from a penalty, and two points from play for good measure, the winners' wing forward could not have given much more to the cause. Not surprisingly, he was named man of the match afterwards.'

'Yet for all that, Mullinavat needed the breaks. They were good enough to take them when they came, too, particularly in the second half. Break number one arrived seven minutes after the interval, John McDonald sending Steve Foskin in for a crucial goal against the run of play to leave the winners nine points to the good. Break number two came 10 minutes from time when John Dunphy saved point blank from the losers Mick O'Neill following a dazzling run by DJ Carey. Irelands had cut the gap to seven points by that stage, and who knows what might have happened if they'd coaled then.'

'Facing the lively breeze that swept into the country goal the losers stayed close to their opponents for most of the opening period. Mick Dunphy and Pat O'Neill exchanged early points from frees, Dunphy (65) and Charlie Carter did some more swopping and on 13 minutes the winners scorer-in-chief crashed them into the lead from the penalty spot after Pat Hoban was hauled down by a defender. Mullinavat, now 1-3 to 0-2 ahead, were never headed at any time in the match, and for the remaining 47 minutes always had at least three points in hand. Irelands, with Matt O'Neill having a fine game on the halfback line, steadied up for the next 10 minutes, and a 23rd minute John Brennan point left them only 1-5 to 0-5 behind. Then Mullinavat began to make their wind and territorial advantages pay off. Mick Dunphy landed a 65; Pat Hoban took a neat pass from Peter McDonald to add another; John McDonald set up Steve Foskin, a revelation at centre-forward, to hit a quick addition, and the inevitable Mick Dunphy rounded off the scoring with a free from 65 metres right on the blow of half-time. A seven point lead (1-9 to 0-5) was not unsatisfactory for the men from the south.'

'Seven minutes into the new half came the turning point of the final as John McDonald drew the cover in a rare Mullinavat attack. Steve Foskin was inside to grab the bandpass, and DJ Carey was left with no chance as the ball was palmed well wide of him (2-9 to 0-6). Dunphy nailed two quick frees, and the Southerners set sail for home with an 11-point lead. With Charlie Carter (Senior) coming on in goal, and Toss Farrell departing the scene, Carey was moved out the field in an attempt to save the game for Gowran. But not everyone can carry the weight of the world, as the song goes, especially when you're only 18 years old, and the hardened campaigners in the Mullinavat rearguard had too many years behind them to give the county man enough rope to hang them.'

'As it happened Irelands, helped largely by Pat O'Neill falling back from an attacking role, made a good fist of a comeback. Carter Junior was a danger whenever the ball could be fed into him, and a run of points began by himself from an acute angle on the left in the 43rd minute and continued by John Kennedy, Cathal Fitzgerald, Brian Farrell and Pat O'Neill (twice) brought the losers to within four points five minutes from the end. Only once did the Mullinavat citadel look like falling however, and that as already stated came when DJ Carey tore down the left flank and drove over a cross to the beautifully positioned Mick O'Neill. John Dunphy somehow stopped the shot and his colleagues managed to scramble the ball clear. When Mick Dunphy capped a Mullinavat breakaway by pointing a free minutes from the end, the siege was well sound in the last line and Matt O'Neill stood out at number five. But the midfield, though hardworking, fell down a little on the skill front and only Charlie Carter and Pat O'Neill posed a scoring threat in attack.'

Mullinavat: J Dunphy; T Frisby, P Holden, A Aylward; P Frisby, D Power, JJ Aylward, P McDonald, (0-1), J Walsh; M Dunphy (1-9, goal penalty, two 65's, five frees); S Foskin (1-1), J McDonald, P Hoban (0-1), P McEvoy and S Walsh (0-1).

Young Ireland's: DJ Carey, P Lennon, P Kennedy, J Midleton, Matt O'Neill, T Byrne, C Phelan (0-1), B Farrell (0-1), C Fitzgerald (0-1), T Farrell, J Kennedy (0-1), P O'Neill (0-5, three frees), J Brennan (0-1), M O'Neill (0-1), C Carter (Junior, 0-3). Sub: C Carter (Senior) for T Farrell.

CHAPTER 9

1990s

Paudie Holden became the first Mullinavat player to captain an All-Ireland winning side (Junior) in 1990 (Michael Dunphy, John Dunphy and Pat Hoban were also involved). Mick Carroll was one of Kilkenny's selectors.

1990s

1990
SENIOR

SHC R1: Shamrocks 1-18; Mullinavat 0-10
SHC R2: James Stephens 4-09; Mullinavat 1-08
SHC R3: Erin's Own 3-17; Mullinavat 3-05
SHC R4: Tullaroan 3-23; Mullinavat 3-05
SHC R5: Mullinavat 2-12; Conahy Shamrocks 1-09
SHC Relegation Semi Final: Mullinavat 1-10; Conahy Shamrocks 0-10

Mullinavat had lost four of their five Senior group games, only recording a win v. Conahy Shamrocks at Nowlan Park. They beat the same side in the relegation semi final at Callan to avoid the Senior relegation playoff game.

Mullinavat: J Dunphy, E Law, P Holden, T Frisby, P Frisby, P Hoban, JJ Aylward, B Walsh (0-1), P McDonald, M Dunphy (0-2), J McDonald (0-1), Joe Walsh (0-2), P McEvoy (1-5), M Law and S Walsh. Subs: W Carroll and L Aldridge.

1991
SENIOR

SHC R1: Mullinavat 3-07; Clara 0-10
SHC R2: Glenmore 3-14; Mullinavat 3-04
SHC R3: Tullaroan 0-12; Mullinavat 1-04
SHC R4: Mullinavat 2-08; Fenians 1-11
SHC R5: St Martin's 2-12; Mullinavat 2-04

1992
SENIOR

Mullinavat improved in 1992 under the coaching of ex-Ballyhale player Maurice Mason. We reached a first ever Kilkenny SHL final which we lost to Ballyhale Shamrocks.

SHC R1: Mullinavat 0-08; Tullaroan 0-07
SHC R2: Mullinavat 2-10; St Martin's 0-10
SHC R3: Graigue Ballycallan 1-12; Mullinavat 1-10
SHC R4: Mullinavat 0-11; Erin's Own 0-06
SHC R5: Mullinavat 3-08; Graiguenamagh 1-07
SHC Quarter Final: Glenmore 0-17: Mullinavat 1-06

SH League Semi Final: Mullinavat 3-12; Fenians 0-16
SH League Final: Shamrocks 2-11; Mullinavat 0-11

'Two goals without reply during the opening four minutes suggested there were going to be easy pickings for honour laden Shamrocks (Ballyhale), but events turned out much different afterwards as brave Mullinavat pushed their opponents all the way before giving best in a rather tame Senior hurling league final at damp Ballyhale on Sunday. Twice the challengers to last year's championship winners were on level terms, but although the Shamrocks were never at complete ease after taking up the running again with a point from Dermot Fennelly in the 32nd minute, they never looked in serious danger of being overtaken. After the early exchanges, only one outcome looked on the cards. In the Shamrocks first raid after 20 seconds, Dermot Fennelly planted the ball in the Mullinavat net. A few seconds more passed, and Jimmy Lawlor sent a sizzling drive across the face of the losers goal and wide. In the fourth minute Lawlor pulled a good ball back from near the endline onto the 14, and the in-rushing Tommy Shefflin swept the ball into the net. Mullinavat, with the fresh breeze in their backs, were two goals down before they knew what hit them. A Mullinavat collapse was a possibility, but they showed themselves to be made of sterner stuff and slowly inched their way back into the match. With their half-line defenders, Jimmy Roughan, Dan Power and Joe Walsh in top form, and midfielder Michael Dunphy out-classing all, the losers actually got on top and took the game to the opposition.'

'Dunphy, Michael Carroll and Dunphy again had points before 12 minutes passed. A close in foul on Pat Hoban gifted another point to Dunphy, and a like score in similar circumstances left the scores at 2-0 to 0-5 after 19 minutes. At this stage the Shamrocks mentors switched their midfielders, and pitted Ger Fennelly against the influential Dunphy. This move put a tight rein on the rampant Mullinavat man who was quieter afterwards. But it didn't stop his team getting back level at 2-1 to 0-7 nearing the rest. As ever, when the pressure was on, the

Shamrocks were able to produce something. This came in the shape of a snappy point from Dermot Fennelly, which left the winners 2-2 to 0-7 in front at half time.'

'The losers were much more with it at the start of the second half, and it was they who enjoyed a smart opening. Only seconds had passed when Michael Dunphy landed a great equaliser from a free from 75 yards range. Less than two minutes later Dermot Fennelly won back the lead for the Shamrocks, and John Shefflin stretched it in the 35th minute (2-4 to 0-8). Dunphy closed the gap to the minimum again The Shamrocks match winning burst followed. Unanswered points were picked off by Liam Fennelly, Tommy Shefflin and Ger Fennelly (free) to increase their advantage to 2-7 to 0-9. Thereafter they always had a bit of space, and a little comfort. Mullinavat hit back for a score, but two quick replies were landed by the more controlled county champions (2-9 to 0-10). From there to the finish the champions kept matters tight and edged out the opposition. All things considered, this was an improved effort by Mullinavat, who were contesting their first Senior final since the 40s. They played much better than in the semi-final win over Fenians (Johnstown), insofar as more thought went into their hurling. Keeper John Dunphy's second half puck outs were first rate, and the positive policing of potential destroyer Liam Fennelly by Eamon Law was most praiseworthy. The 40-line defenders faded somewhat after the change around, but the slack was then picked up by Paudie Holden and Tom Frisby had there been more penetration up front – only four scores came from play – they could easily have slipped one over the Shamrocks.'

Mullinavat: John Dunphy, Tommy Frisby, Paudie Holden, Eamon Law, Jim Roughan, Dan Power, Joe Walsh, Brian Aldridge, Michael Dunphy (0-8, seven frees), Pat McEvoy (0-1), Stephen Foskin, Harry Waters, Willie Carroll (0-1), Pat Hoban and Michael Law (0-1). Subs: S Walsh, B Walsh.

Shamrocks: K Fennelly, M Fennelly, F Holohan, S Ryan, D Walsh, P Phelan, S Fennelly, P Farrell, Ger Fennelly (0-4, frees), Tommy Shefflin (1-2), John Shefflin (0-2), T Phelan, Liam Fennelly (0-1), J Lawlor, and Dermot Fennelly (1-2).

1993
SENIOR

SHL R1: Dicksboro 0-11; Mullinavat 1-05
SHL R2: Young Irelands 2-15; Mullinavat 3-05
SHL R3: Tullaroan 1-14; Mullinavat 2-09
SHL R4: Erin's Own 0-21; Mullinavat 0-07
SHL R5: Mullinavat 1-13; Fenians 0-14

SHC R1: Mullinavat 0-13; Clara 1-05
SHC Quarter Final: Mullinavat 2-07; St Martin's 0-12

SHC SEMI FINAL PREVIEW

'This is prove it time for outsiders, Mullinavat and Dicksboro, who make up a most unexpected pairing in the Senior hurling semi-final at Nowlan Park on Sunday 10/10/93. Both are outsiders in the sense it has been so long since they featured at this stage of the competition. The Southerners are back for the first time in 50 years, while the 'Boro were last there when they won the championship in 1950. They went through the League without making a huge impact, but come the knockout competition, the teams blossomed and they earned the right to get within 120 minutes of a possible county title. Mullinavat opened the campaign on a terrible evening in Hugginstown, when they saw off Clara. In the quarter-final against St Martin's a mere two scores during the second half were enough to give them passage through to the semi-finals.'

'The 'Boro, who have one of the best under age set ups in the county, started tentatively against Young Irelands, when two late scores from Dan O'Neill were required to push them through. In the quarter finals they showed good form and an even better attitude, when seeing off old city rivals, James Stephens. This pair clashed in the opening round of the League on April 18. The 'Boro enjoyed the better of things and scored a narrow 0-11 to 1-5 win.'

'That is the only line of form of any consequence, but even that means very little because it was the first competitive game of the season. Such matches can often be misleading, insofar as teams are going through the final sorting out process before settling on the shape of things for the future. Mullinavat report Pat McEvoy has a bit of a hip problem. Otherwise, everyone is flying, and trainer Maurice Mason is delighted with the new found enthusiasm that has been generated by qualifying for the semi-finals. One of the main reasons for Mullinavat's vast improvement this season has been the shifting of 6'2" giant, Pal Hoban to centre-back Hoban was a reserve forward on the Kilkenny Senior panel in 1992. The way things are going, he could be back in the fold for the National League, this time as a defender. Such has been his huge influence on things for his club. His improvement has been equalled by others, including county man Joe Walsh, goalie John Dunphy, Jimmy Rohan, Raymond Carroll, Paudie Holden and Stephen Foskin, all of whom are going better than they have for a long time.'

'Mullinavat depend a lot on free taker, Michael Dunphy, whose shooting hasn't been up to the usual high standard of late. It must be a source of worry to team officials, that they landed only two scores, both goals, in the second half of the quarter-final against St Martin's. One was a penalty and the other an own goal. That tells its own story. The 'Boro, managed by former Kilkenny supremo, Pat Henderson, have been progressing in the right direction. That progress has been slow rather than dramatic, but the improvement has been noticeable. The main body of the team has grown together through the various grades and has won Under-21 and Intermediate championships in recent years. If the Boro can keep their feet on the ground, and produce the form of which they are capable, they should be looking forward to a county final appearance in two weeks' time.'

Mullinavat: John Dunphy, Tom Frisby, Paudie Holden, Eamon Law, Pat Rohan, Jimmy Rohan, Pat Hoban, Joe Walsh, Pat McEvoy, Michael Dunphy, Stephen Foskin, Sean Walsh, Jimmy O'Keeffe, Raymond Carroll, William Carroll, Jack O'Keeffe, Michael Law, John Joe Aylward, Derek Butler, John Fitzgerald, Dan Power, Richard Aylward, Brian Conway and Willie Delahunty. Selectors: Michael Carroll, Mossy Murphy. Trainer: Maurice Mason.

Dicksboro: Michael Walsh, Martin Hannck, John Marnell, David Beirne, Sam Morrissey, Tommy Bawlc, John Treacy, Ger Henderson, Donal Carroll, Tom Henderson, Mark Dowling, Liam Kerwick, Shane Prendergast, Michael Kennedy, Dan O'Neill, Scan Moore, Niall Lacey, Stephen Kennedy, Brendan Dalton, John Ayres, Ted Carroll, James Phelan, Jim Kerwick, Vinny Byrne, Eoin Begley, John Dwyer, Rory Derby, and Sean Fitzpatrick

Selectors: Seamus Fitzpatrick, John Cahill, Eugene Begley, Jimmy Mulroney, John Marnell. Trainer: Pat Henderson

SHC Semi Final: Dicksboro 4-11; Mullinavat 0-09

'Change goalies and we'll play you again!' That might well have been Mullinavat's cry after they failed the biggest test of their club careers at Nowlan Park at Sunday 10/10/93. The strange part about it is the Southerners didn't lose this Senior Hurling semi-final as badly as the scoreline suggests, and they could actually have been three goals ahead at half-time.'

'The key figure in this somewhat bizarre tale was the Kilkenny city outfit's net minder, Michael Walsh. Twice an All-Ireland medallist wilh the Black and Amber, and, generally acknowledged to be the best goalkeepers in the game today, the 1991 All Star produced an incredible first half display which made all the difference.'

'Following a sub-standard beginning to the season, Mullinavat had sprung into life as the knockout stages of the championship approached, and excellent performances against the battle hardened warriors of Clara and St Martin's saw them through to the penultimate stage. Now they were poised to turn a fine achievement into a famous one, and go all the way to the final. For quite a while it seemed as if they were generally agreed to be slight underdogs in a nevertheless open looking contest. The Vat began brightly and enjoyed a definite edge for the first 20 minutes. Pat McEvoy who wore the No 8 shirt, but lined out at full forward, opened the scoring in the 4th minute with a point from play after a good run by Stephen Foskin. Kilkenny Under-21 star, Dan O'Neill, levelled seconds later, and the teams stayed locked on 0-1 apiece for the next error-ridden ten minutes. Dicksboro, who had an early escape when alert corner back, Martin Hanrick nicked the sliotair away from the marauding Jimmy O'Keeffe, then got away lightly by virtue of a very good Michael Walsh save at his near post from Raymond Carroll, Michael Dunphy having sent in a dropping ball that cleared the last defender.'

'The third score of the match didn't arrive till the 19th minute, McEvoy converting a free which was quickly cancelled out at the other end by Shane Prendergast. The losers promptly went close again in the form of Stephen Foskin who worked his way through an unsteady Dicksboro rearguard and unleashed a fierce rising shot from close range; Walsh did exceptionally well to raise his slick and parry in a reflex action. That made two saves from right out of the top drawer. A third, even better, arrived with 25 minutes gone. Willie Carroll embarking on a, run, along the right and cutting in low released a tricky ground shot. Walsh, caught off balance, managed to reach out and divert the sliotar to safely. Even then the goalmouth action wasn't over, for shortly before the interval a long-range free by Michael Dunphy came off the upright and back into the square. Alas for Mullinavat, no forward was there to take advantage, and the most they could do was add points by Sean Walsh and Paul McEvoy (another free) in reply to earlier efforts by Tommy Bawie (free) and Sam Morrissey.'

'At the interval, therefore, the sides were locked at 0-4 each, and the southerners in the 8,000-attendance had to be feeling uneasy. Maurice Mason's charges might have been nine points to the good yet weren't. Had they perhaps punched themselves out, to employ pugilistic parlance? The answer was yes, and the evidence wasn't slow in revealing itself. Within 90 seconds of the restart the city crew had raised their first green flag – the Mullinavat defence got itself into a terrible tangle in trying to clear a cross and Tommy Bawle was on hand to lash the ball, home.. Still there was only that goal separating the teams. Any hopes the losers had of pulling back the deficit more or less disappeared, however, in the 37th minute when a clever flick by John Treacy set fellow corner-forward Sam Morrissey through to place the ball beautifully past a helpless John Dunphy. From there till the end, it was very much a case of one-way traffic. Dicksboro sprayed the sliotar around as they liked, picking out colleagues with ease and taking on goals per Shane Prendergast and Sam Morrissey, the only riposte came in the form of points by McEvoy and Willie Carroll. On a deeply disappointing afternoon when their big guns misfired and their championship dreams died a slow death, it was still impossible to forget what a satisfying and successful season this has been at Senior level for Mullinavat. They're not as bad, far from it, as this flop indicated. They have much to be proud of and gives the right attitude and a desire to go one belter, should be heard of once more in 1994.'

Mullinavat: J Dunphy, T Frisby, P Holden, E Law, P Rouighan, P Hoban, J Roughan, D Power, J Walsh, M Dunphy, S Foskin, S Walsh (0-1), W Carroll (0-1), P McEvoy (0-6, 5 frees) and R Carroll (0-1). Sub - J O'Keeffe.

Dicksboro: M Walsh, M Hanrick, J Marnell, D Beirne, G Henderson, D Carroll, T Henderson, M Kennedy, D O'Neill (0-3, 1 free), L Kerwick, S Moore, S Prendergast (1-2), J Treacy (0-1), T Bawle (1-3), and S Morrissey (2-1). Subs - N Dowling, for G Henderson; S Kennedy (0-1) for Moore.

1994

SENIOR

After five years in the Senior grade, Mullinavat were relegated back to the Intermediate championship in 1994. Having beaten John Lockes in the group stages the result was reversed in the play-off final.

SHL R1: James Stephens 3-17; Mullinavat 2-05
SHL R2: Fenians 1-15; Mullinavat 0-11
SHL R3: Dicksboro 1-12; Mullinavat 0-05
SHL R4: Erin's Own 4-11; Mullinavat 1-14
SHL R5: Mullinavat 3-11; John Lockes 0-09

SHC R1: Graigue Ballycallan 0-21; Mullinavat 1-13
SH Relegation Semi Final: Erin's Own 1-11; Mullinavat 0-08
SH Relegation Final: John Lockes 1-16; Mullinavat 2-08

'John Lockes (Callan), the doughty "labourers" of the Senior grade this term, at last got just reward for optimum effort when they out fought and out lasted dogged Mullinavat in a throbbing hurling championship relegation final at Hugginstown on Saturday 17/9/94. Lockes only win since they jumped up from the Intermediate grade last year earned them the right to stay among the elite clubs next season. Vanquished Mullinavat, Intermediate champions in 1989, make the drop down a division. The Callan crew, who, if reward were based on raw effort alone over the full season, would be crowned champions long ago, ended the fight to stay up with a battle to beat all battles. The first half hurling wasn't always pretty, and at the break Mullinavat were not too badly off when 0-2 to 0-7 down after playing against the fresh breeze blowing into the village end goal. They looked in a great position in the 38th minute when they were already back on terms (0-8 to 1-5). There was an exchange of minor scores after that. Then during the closing quarter the fear of losing the match and Senior status so consumed Lockes that they hit a new level of performance, and you would have to wonder would any team have lived with them. Mullinavat, full of effort and dearly wanting to stay up, tried really hard, but they were simply blown away. The winners had four scores from Declan Roche, two from Kevin Coffey and another from the all action John Power to make up their interval tally.'

'The losers, as ever, depended almost entirely on Michael Dunphy up front, and but for a 47th minute goal from Raymond Carroll, and a later point from Sean Walsh, he got all their scores. During the opening minute after the turn Michael Dunphy and Declan Roche traded pointed frees, and Lockes looked capable of continuing to take the lions share of possession. When the usually reliable Dunphy missed two reasonable chances from frees for Mullinavat, that feeling was reinforced. However, on his next visit to a free shot, Dunphy showed fair nerve. The effort was to the right on the 21 after a foul on Michael Law. The Vat sharpshooter went for broke, and he buried the ball in the net. A minute further on he punished a foul on Stephen Foskin, and after catching the puck-out following that score, he posted the equaliser (0-8 to 1-5) in the 38th minute. Suddenly it was John Lockes who were under pressure, and having difficult getting the ball past midfield where the Walshs, Joe and Sean had finally shackled the until then exuberant John Power and Philip Comerford. However, Power burst up the field moments later to make a score for Kevin Coffey. This was cancelled, inevitably, by Dunphy (0-9 to 1-6) in the 43rd minute.'

'This was the last time the teams were together. Power made another decisive break moments later, and after beating four men during a 35 yard solo run, he pointed John Lockes in the direction of the winning point. As if inspired by his partner, Philip Comerford then made a burst through the losers' defence, and this time David Lynch profited with a small score (0-11 to 1-6). Just into the last quarter Mullinavat looked dead when they made a bad error at the back and Stuart Donovan pounced to shoot to the net. However within 30 seconds the ball was in the net at the other end. This was only after a loose ball smacked home by Raymond Carroll. In the lead up Lockes keeper, Paul Morrissey pulled off a brilliant save from a Dunphy pile-driver. With the score at 1-11 to 2-6, and 13 minutes remaining, there was still everything to play for and the fireworks wasn't over by any means. The winners extended their lead via a good Stuart Donovan point from 30 yards on the left sideline. Dunphy tried to keep Mullinavat going with another point from a free. They were right back in the hunt when Sean Walsh sprinted up the right wing and casually picked off a point to leave the minimum between the teams with six minutes left (1-12 to 2-8). From there to the finish it was all John Lockes.'

'Mullinavat had their heroes, and none did better than Eamon Law, John Dunphy, Paudie Holden, Pat Hoban, Jimmy Roughan, Joe and Sean Walsh and of course Michael Dunphy, who did down the opposition on his own.

Mullinavat: J Dunphy, D Butler, P Holden, L Law, P McEvoy, P Hoban, J Roughan, J Walsh, S Walsh (0-1), R Carroll (1-0), M Dunphy (1-7, 1-3 frees, 0-1 "65"), S Foskin, W Carroll, M Law and Jimmy O'Keeffe. Subs: Jack O'Keeffe, R Aylward.

1995
INTERMEDIATE

IHL R1: Mullinavat 3-08; Carrickshock 0-09
IHL R2: Mullinavat 1-08; Graiguenamanagh 0-07
IHL R3: Bennetsbridge 0-14; Mullinavat 1-10
IHL R4: Mullinavat 0-10; Barrow Rangers 0-06
IHL R5: Tullogher Rosbercon 2-10; Mullinavat 1-07
IHL Semi Final: Dunnamaggin 2-09; Mullinavat 1-08

IHC Quarter Final: Carrickshock 1-14; Mullinavat 1-07

1996
INTERMEDIATE

IHL R1: O'Loughlin Gaels 2-14; Mullinavat 1-16
IHL R2: Mullinavat 1-11; Tullogher Rosbercon 0-04
IHL R3: Graiguenamagh 2-17; Mullinavat 1-07
IHL R4: Mullinavat 1-15; Clara 1-07
IHL R5: Mullinavat 1-11; Rower Inistioge 1-05

IHC R1: St Lachtain's 1-08; Mullinavat 1-05
IHC Relegation Semi Final: Mullinavat 2-10; Conahy Shamrocks 0-11

'Mullinavat ensured their survival in next year's Intermediate grade when they overcame Conahy Shamrocks In the relegation semi-final in Bennettsbridge on Sunday 21/9/96. The winners looked the more confident side from an early stage. Conahy failed to capitalise on the advantage of a stiff breeze In the opening half. A brace of goals by Mullinavat were to prove crucial and once they edged ahead the Southerners were never in any danger. The early exchanges were even, the game took a dramatic turn after 20 minutes when the Conahy defence was caught out for two soft goals. The first from Willie Carroll came when he took advantage of a hesitant Conahy reargaurd to shoot a fine goal. Another defensive error, when a forward was left unmarked, saw Ray Carroll rattle the net. These goals left Conahy dazed. They could never recover from such stunning blows. The winners were the more committed side, and deserved their win. Joe Walsh and Pat Hoban showed years of experience in a solid defence, and were rarely beaten. Michael Dunphy roamed far and wide to good effect with the Carroll's, Willie and Ray were more than a handful to Conahy.'

Mullinavat team and scorers: J Dunphy, J Walsh, E Law, S Holden, J Roughan, P Hoban, Murphy, J O'Keeffe, P Roughan, M. Murphy, M Dunphy (0-5), J O'Keeffe, W Carroll (1-1), R Carroll (1-3), O Alyward. Sub: S Foskin (0-1).

1997
INTERMEDIATE

IHL R1: Bennettsbridge 1-14; Mullinavat 2-05
IHL R2: Clara 1-9; Mullinavat 0-4
IHL R3: Mullinavat 2-11; Shamrocks 1-14
IHL R4: Mullinavat 0-12; Piltown 1-09
IHL R5: Mullinavat 1-20; Thomastown 0-17

IHC R1: Mullinavat 1-10; Thomastown 0-09
IHC Quarter Final: Mullinavat 3-16; Clara 2-13
IHC Semi Final: Shamrocks 2-12; Mullinavat 0-10

'Shamrocks played their way past Mullinavat's challenge and into a Intermediate hurling final showdown against Graignamanagh. The fare on offer in both semi finals at Nowlan Park, on Sunday 5/10/97, left something to be desired. Shamrocks were the better team but they didn't have to be great to beat a disappointing Mullinavat fifteen. The men with the distinctive black and white trooped jerseys didn't play up to expectations and indeed their opponents seemed to have a psychological edge. Both sides were short a number of first-choice players. Mullinavat's Eamon Law was out with a torn ligament, Jimmy Rohan was nursing a broken arm, and Kenny Butler was sidelined with a broken ankle. But it didn't seem to affect them at all as they raced into a lead in the early stages. Points from Mick Dunphy and Pat Hoban had the fans cheering and Shamrocks certainly looked vulnerable. The absence of the injured Padraig Farrell in defence and of Henry Shefflin up front, was of some concern to the Ballyhale following, but their misgivings took a back seat when John Shefflin drove home his side's first goal. The ball came out to John Shefflin and, he took, his chance well. Soft it may have been, but they all count and this one wiped out the Mullinavat lead at a stroke.'

'Pat Hoban responded with an immediate reply to make the score 0-4 to 1-0 near the end of the first quarter... But their lead was short-lived. Conor Harrington levelled matters from a free. Exchanges became a bit hectic at this stage. The clash of the ash was punctuated by one or two "personality clashes"" as the second quarter progressed. One of these resulted in a Shamrocks free which Conor Harrington duly converted to give his side a lead they never subsequently relinquished. Noel O'Keeffe and Oliver Aylward exchanged points. Stephen Foskin had a good chance of a goal for Mullinavat but his low shot, went wide of the post. At that stage, Shamrocks held a slender one point lead and a major score then might have revived flagging Mullinavat fortunes. Back at the other end, Shamrocks were soon putting fresh pressure on the Vat defence, Seamus Holden fouled Dermot Fennelly and Conor Harrington pointed from twenty-five yards out. Tommy Shefflin added another to make the half time score 1-5 to 0-5 in favour of the winners.'

'After the restart Dermott Fennelly took advantage of an astute pass from John Shefflin and gave John Dunphy no chance between the posts. From, that moment on, there was only going to be one outcome. The sides exchanged points and then, the Shamrocks went further ahead with a flurry from their midfielders, Sean Fennelly and Bobby Aylward. The latter embarked on a good forty yard solo effort before posting the ball between the uprights. Pat Hoban got one back a minuter later, to leave the score 2-S to 0-7 in favour of the Shamrocks. Mick Dunphy and Conor Harrington exchanged points from frees, and then Damien Mason added another to the Ballyhale total. In between Mullinavat had their chances, but failed to take full advantage of their opportunities. Sound goalkeeping by John Drennan kept them out twice in the closing stages.'

Mullinavat: John Dunphy, Joe Walsh, Pat Butler, Seamus Holden, Paul Aylward, Pat Phelan, Liam Murphy, Ray Carroll, (0-1), Oliver Aylward (0-1), Michael Dunphy (0-5 frees), Stephen Foskin, Michael Murphy (0-1), William Carroll, Pat Hoban (0-2) and Maurice Murphy. Subs - Martin Knox for William Carroll, P J Aylward, Liam Aylward, Andrew McGovern, Joe Kelly, Paul Conway, Tony Duggan. Trainer: Tommy Frisby.

1998
INTERMEDIATE

IHL R1: Mullinavat 0-10; Rower Inistioge 1-06
IHL R2: Mullinavat 2-12; Piltown 0-07
IHL R3: Mullinavat 2-09; John Lockes 0-07
IHL R4: Mullinavat 2-12; Mooncoin 2-06
IHL R5: Clara 2-6; Mullinavat 1-07
IHL Semi Final: Thomastown 1-13; Mullinavat 0-07

IHC Quarter Final: Clara 1-14; Mullinavat 0-14

1999
INTERMEDIATE

IHL R1: Mullinavat 2-10; Graiguenamanagh 1-11
IHL R2: John Lockes 0-10; Mullinavat 0-05
IHL R3: Mullinavat 0-12; Rower Inistioge 1-06
IHL R4: Mullinavat 2-17; Blacks and Whites 1-14
IHL R5: Mullinavat 1-16; Bennetsbridge 3-10

IHC R1: Mullinavat 1-09; Piltown 1-08
IHC Quarter final: Mullinavat 2-09; Dunnamaggin 0-13
IHC Semi Final: Mullinavat 3-11; St Lachtain's 1-08
County IHC Final: John Lockes 0-15; Mullinavat 1-09

'John Lockes came back from a four point deficit to overcome Mullinavat at a blustery Nowlan Park on Sunday. The conditions made for a gritty game of hurling, which was never going to be pretty as the harsh breeze and difficult drizzle made the chances of skilful play near impossible. At the end of an eventful Intermediate hurling final, John Lockes (Callan) were left singing in the rain and celebrating a return to the Senior grade next season.'

'Mullinavat struck first with the game's opening point. A foul on full forward Maurice Murphy gave Michael Dunphy the chance to open his account with a free from 22 yards out. Lockes took until the eighth minute to equalise when a poor puck-out from P. J. Aylward was punished with a well taken point by PJ Coady. They took the lead for the first time in the game when their influential centre forward John Power found a bit of space and put over his first point. The game was destined to swing to and fro as the teams fought for supremacy. Dunphy and then Michael Murphy restored Mullinavat's slender lead before the Callenmen put their tally up to four points with contributions from David Lynch and Andy Power after 13 minutes. The game was balanced on the sharpest of knife-edges before the Southerners seized on a Callan mix-up midway through the half. A defensive slip by Keith Doheny proved costly as Ray Carroll skipped through, sidestepped the advancing Paul Morrissey and had the simplest of tasks to put the ball in the back of an empty net. Mullinavat were now on top form. However, Lockes refused to lie down and hit back with a Robert Jackman free, but the Vat added to their lead with points from Dunphy and Maurice Murphy.'

'Mullinavat held a tight defensive ship, refusing to give the Callan half-forward line time to pass, or more importantly, shoot. After 19 minutes, Liam Egan made a great foray into the forward line and clawed back the deficit ever so slightly with a point after a neat one-two with Power. But Mullinavat put over three points in as many minutes to strengthen their position. It seemed as if Lockes would never recover. Power was given no room to move and any time he got the ball his chances at goal were snuffed out as Mullinavat double-marked him at all times. Lockes came close to scoring a goal with only four minutes left in the first half. A great pass from David Lynch put PJ Coady on a clear run at goal. His shot was driven low and hard, but Aylward was equal to the save, deflecting the ball over the bar. A point apiece for either side, through Donal Maher and Mullinavat full forward Maurice Murphy left Callan facing a little mountain of four points to ascend in the second half.'

'The second half started in poor fashion. The opening minutes were peppered with wides. It seemed as if both sides had left their shooting sticks in the dressing room. Lockes were guilty of some glaring misses, which could really have proved costly at the end of the game. Lynch notched up the first score of the half on 34 minutes. He scored his third point after 39 minutes, in between which the 'wide virus' spread to Mullinavat's normally reliable Michael Dunphy. Lockes edged their way back into the game with a 65-yard point by JP Corcoran after 40 minutes. Four minutes later, they were level. Pat Butler was penalised for travelling. Up stepped centre back Declan Roche who drove his effort from the half-way line straight and true between the posts to send the Callan support delirious. On 46 minutes Lockes completed a comeback Lazarus would have been proud of. Lynch crowned a great never-say-die display with his fourth point. The game had turned full circle and this time Mullinavat were powerless to reply. With ten minutes left, John Power added his second point of the game to extend the gap to two points. Mullinavat were in need of a goal to snatch back their lead and could have done so in dramatic fashion. The combined attack of Keith Madigan and Maurice Murphy was stopped bravely by Lockes' guardian of the net Paul Morrissey. The resulting-65 was dropped in dangerously around the area where it fell invitingly to the waiting Andy Power. He pulled on the sliothar first time, but looked on in despair as his goalbound effort was saved by a combination of Morrissey and his crossbar. On 55 minutes, Murphy tried his luck again, attempting to burst through the Lockes defence, but by this stage the Callan side were supremely confident and stopped him with ease. With just three minutes left, a Jackman pointed free put the cap on a marvellous second half performance for John Lockes.'

Mullinavat: PJ Aylward, J Walsh, K Butler, T Duggan, W Burke, P Butler, L Murphy, M Dunphy (0-6, 0-4 frees, 0-1'65'), P Aylward, Michael Murphy (0-1), P Hoban, K Madigan, W Carroll, Maurice Murphy (0-2) and Ray Carroll (1-0). Subs: S Holden for W Carroll (47 minutes).

John Lockes scorers: D Lynch (0-4), R Jackman, PJ Coady, J Power (0-2 each), L Egan, D Roche, JP Corcoran, D Maher and A Power (0-1 each).

Senior hurling county semi-finalists in 1993
Back Row (from left): Tommy Frisby, Paudie Holden, Sean Walsh, Pat Hoban, Joe Walsh, Pat McEvoy, Raymond Carroll, Jimmy Rohan.
Front Row (from left): Willie Carroll, Dan Power, Stephen Foskin, Mick Dunphy, John Dunphy, Pat Rohan and Eamon Law.

CHAPTER 10

2000s

The champions come home in style after defeating Clara in the 2001 county Intermediate hurling final.

2000s

2000
INTERMEDIATE

IHL R1: Mullinavat 1-13; Blacks and Whites 2-06
IHL R2: Mooncoin 4-10; Mullinavat 2-07
IHL R3: St Lachtain's 2-11; Mullinavat 1-11
IHL R14 Mullinavat 1-12; Thomastown 2-06
IHL R5: Mullinavat 2-19; Bennettsbridge 1-12
IHL Semi Final: Dunnamaggin 3-06; Mullinavat 1-11
Aylward Cup All County Hurling League Final: Mullinavat 0-16; St Martin's 1-12

IHC Quarter Final: Mullinavat 1-10; Bennettsbridge 1-07
IHC Semi Final: Dunnamaggin 1-12; Mullinavat 2-06

'Dunnamaggin overcame the elements and the stiff challenge of Mullinavat to go through to the Intermediate hurling final at a windy and rainswept Nowlan Park on Sunday. Mullinavat made the better start when they put the ball into the net after only after three minutes. Maurice Murphy rounded full-back Jim Hickey before blasting the shothar to the net. A Pat Hoban point a minute later gave the southerners a four-point lead in as many minutes. Battling against the teeming rain, Dunnamaggin started slowly, but got off the mark when County centre back Eamon Kennedy pointed a 65. They quickly set about restoring parity with a brace of frees from Colin Herity, before Kenneth Moore levelled the match in the 16th minute. Mullinavat swung back into the lead a minute later when Ray Carroll scored a point following a pass from Pat Hoban, but they were rocked by a swift Dunnamaggin comeback in the 23rd minute. Fallowing some good interplay between brothers Denis and Noel Lahart, Niall McCormack made a surging run into the Vat's danger zone. He made a quick pass to Michael O'Neill, who drilled a low shot across John Dunphy and into the net. Mullinavat tried to gain the upper hand again, and scored a point through a Michael Dunphy free. However, two more points from Colin Herity frees left Dunnamaggin three points clear at the break (1-6 to 1-3).'

'Backed by the breeze, Dunnamaggin jacked up the first scores of the new half. First Kenneth Moore picked off a great point from along the wing before Niall McCormack and Sean Ryan, with another long range effort, doubled their half-time lead to six points. Mulhnavat struck for goal in an effort to get back into the game. However, they found that Dunnamaggin were in no mood to concede soft scores After bursting through on goal, Maurice Murphy lofted the shothar over David Herity and towards a seemingly empty net. However, corner-back Noel Hickey was on hand to scoop the ball off the line and away to safety. Murphy tried to follow up with a rebound, but after being fouled by keeper Herity, the Vat settled for a point from Michael Dunphy The sides went through a scoreless stalemate for a lengthy period and began to rack up a number of wides. The miniature deadlock was finally broken when Maurice Murphy was again brought down after a foray around the Dunnamaggin area. Again Michael Dunphy stepped up to take the free but this time his shot was true and his searing drive found the roof of the net, despite the best efforts of four Dunnamaggin backs and the goalkeeper. Dunnamaggin remained undeterred and quickly retorted through a point from Ken O'Shea.'

'With the game entering the final ten minutes, Mullinavat began to attack in droves. Dunnamaggin countered the action by bringing back corner forward Michael O'Neill as an extra back, as they battled to keop then slender three point lead (1-10 to 2-4). Despite all the attention an their own goal-line, Dunnamaggin managed to break away and virtually seal the gamn on 53 minutes when Kenneth Moore collected a long clearance and shot the hall over the bar.'

Mullinavat: J Dunphy, J Walsh, K Butler, J Rohan, P Butler, W Burke, L Murphy, M Knox, P Aylward, Maurice Murphy(1-0), P Hoban (0-1), M Dunphy (1-4, 1-3 frees), R Carroll (0-1), P Butler, and Michael Murphy. Subs: K Madigan for M Knox, 23 minutes, J P. Dungan for J Rohan, half-time, W Carroll for D Butler, 39 minutes.

2001

INTERMEDIATE

IHL R1: Mullinavat 1-11; Mooncoin 0-13
IHL R2: Mullinavat 4-12; James Stephens 0-10
IHL R3: Mullinavat 2-17; Thomastown 1-15
IHL R4: Mullinavat 2-18; St Martin's 2-10
IHL R5: Mullinavat 4-14; Bennettsbridge 1-08
IHL Semi Final: Mullinavat 4-12; Clara 1-15.

OUR STORY (1887-2024)

IHL Final: St Lachtain's 1-14; Mullinavat 1-11

'Seven minutes from the end of an all-action Intermediate hurling league final St Lachtain's (Freshford) looked to have cut down the opposition when they shot an excellent goal, but brave Mullinavat rose again at Nowlan Park on Sunday went right down to the wire. Creeping into the 53rd minute St Lachtain's looked to have broken their opponents when they goaled to open out a good 1-13 to 0-11 advantage. Ollie O'Connor, who entered the final with 40 points to his credit, and left it seven better off, arrowed in a sideline cut from 40 yards on the right towards the county end goa.l The towering Damien Anderson rose above backs and forwards alike, and he diverted the ball into the Mullinavat net, to take his side five points clear. Lachtain's first league win looked in the bag. Mullinavat weren't prepared to give in just yet however. Five minutes from the end Andrew McGovern punched a hole in the St Lachtain's defence, and powered in a drive at 'keeper, Joe Dernody. The latter did well to block the shot, and divert the ball out for a '65'. The '65' by Michael Dunphy dropped on the edge of the square, and Mossy Murphy swept the ball home to throw the issue wide open again. The game finished in a welter of excitement as the Vat poured forward in search of a big score, which would have been a winner. They nearly got it when Andrew McGovern got a shot on target, but again Dermody was equal to the demands. Virtually on the hour Damien Anderson pointed to secure victory for Freshford and make them the eight club to put their name on the league title.'

'The losers opened like an express tram. They had four points on the board before the winners knew what hit them. After that it was Lachtain's turn to dominate, and scores on the bounce from Ollie O'Connor, Noel Hickey and Pat Hickey left them the minimum behind after 18 minutes. After losing another score to Willie O'Dwyer, St Lachtain's eventually caught up at 0-5 each in the 24th minute. The fast and open exchanges continued at a hectic pace up to the rest, at which stage a Michael Dunphy point from a free divided the teams (0-6 to 0-5). Less than two minutes into the new half had passed when Ollie O'Connor, Seamus Holden and O'Connor again landed scores to leave the teams tied at 0-7 each. However, the initiative was very much with St Lachtain's, and they constantly drove back the opposition'. 'The points were piled up, with O'Connor (2), one an absolute smasher from a 40 yards sideline cut, Damien Anderson, James Kavanagh and Jonathan Doheny joining in the scoring as the Vat were left 0-13 to 0-7 behind by the 13th minute. For no apparent reason, the wheel of fortune swung back in favour of Mullinavat. They slowly but surely themselves out of trouble, with Michael Dunphy (3) and Seamus Holden harvesting scores to slice the arrears to 0-11 to 0-13. Then up popped Anderson to stitch the ball in the back of the Southerners net, and shove Lachtain's 1-13 to 0-11 clear. Far from that effort signalling the end, it injected new life into proceeds, and added fizz to the fare right to the finish. Impressive for the losers were Michae Dunphy, Walter Burke, Joe

Walsh, J.P. Dungan and Seamus Holden.'

Mullinavat: P J Aylward, J Walsh, K Butler, J P Dungan, K Aylward, W Burke, L Murphy, M Dunphy (0-5), P Aylward, D Conway, J Roughan (0-1), S Holden (0-2), Michael Murphy (0-1), Mossy Murphy (1-0) and W Dwyer (0-2). Sub: Andrew McGovern.

IHC Quarter Final: Mullinavat 1-19; Bennettsbridge 1-11
IHC Semi Final: Mullinavat 1-11; Mooncoin 0-13
County IHC Final: Mullinavat 1-05; Clara 1-05

'In the end it was only fair Sunday's Intermediate hurling ended all square. On a day when the game and participants were well and truly battered by the elements, neither side deserved to lose. The first sign that the weather would play a big part in proceedings came in the second minute. After struggling to keep their footing during a brisk opening, Clara managed to separate the sliotair from the sticky sod and blast it into the forwards in front of the St John's Park end. The sliotair skidded past Mullinavat goalie John Dunphy (or was it the other way around?) allowing John Fitzgerald to slide in and scramble the loose ball to the net. A muddied Fitzgerald also ended up there. But any hope the spectators had of the scores coming as freely as that were soon halted. The next score didn't materialise until the ninth minute. This was a good goal as well.'

'After taking time to fix their sights on goal, Mullinavat finally found the mark. When Michael Murphy dropped the sliotair in towards the Clara goal, the young Willie O'Dwyer found space and flicked the sliotair past goalie JJ Ward, who was literally rooted to the spot. Mullinavat shot a point through Michael Dunphy (free) shortly afterwards before O'Dwyer added a point to his tally. With a quarter of an hour elapsed, the Southerners held a 1-2 to 1-0 lead. Understandably, it took Clara a little longer than usual to get back into the game. But they did so in determined fashion. Ger Prendergast converted two late frees to claw Clara back level, before Rory Moore shot them in front with a long range free in the 25th minute. Michael Dunphy then kept his sharp shooting skills honed with a free in the 27th minute to restore parity. It looked as if the sides would stay level until the break, but an injury-time free was gratefully accepted by Prendergast. That gave Clara a lean 1-4 to 1-3 at the interval'.

'Conditions steadily worsened after the restart. Conditions became so bad that there wasn't a score for more than 20 minutes. And that wasn't the fault of two hard trying teams! Clara went close to breaking the deadlock in the 48th minute, when John Fitzgerald was sent through on goal. The forward pulled, but the sliothar merely ploughed its way towards the goal. With the speed taken out of the ball, goalkeeper John Dunphy had time to turn and scoop the ball that had already beaten him away from the goal to safety. It was a frustrating experience for the Clara fans. Their nerves weren't helped when Richard

Nolan was adjudged to have over carried the sliothar when he tried to clear his lines in the 51st minute. The free gave Michael Dunphy an easy way to draw his side level. He made no mistake. Clara was stung into action by that free, and they won back the lead within a minute. From the puck out Rory Moore pucked the sliotair on to John Fitzgerald. His cross was pulled on by Conor Phelan, but somehow Kenny Butler foresaw the danger and got back on the line to block the shot. Clara kept up the pressure after the clearance, and Robert Shortall drilled the sliotair over the bar. Mullinavat also had a chance of a goal as the game entered the closing five minutes'.

'Another slip at the back, this time by Richard Nolan, allowed Seamus Holden to rob the full back of possession and head for goal. Holden shot low and hard. What a mess of maroon trout players dived in front of the ball preventing us from hitting the net. However, they were powerless to stop substitute Andrew McGovern from catching the clearance and sending this sliotair over to bar for the leveller. Mullinavat got a new lease of life during the closing minutes and attacked the Clara goal. Their opponents dug deep and defended as if their lives depended on it. It looked as if their efforts would be in vain when Mullinavat were awarded an injury time'65'. For once Michael Dunphy was off target.'

Mullinavat: J Dunphy; J Walsh, K Butler, JP Dungan, K Aylward, W Burke, L Murphy, J Rohan, P Aylward, M Dunphy (0-3, all frees), S Holden, D Conway, Michael Murphy, Maurice Murphy and Willie O'Dwyer (1-1). Sub: A McGovern (0-1) for Conway (halftime).

Clara scorers: J Fitzgerald (1-0), G Prendergast (0-3, all frees), R Moore and R Shortall (0-1 each).

County IHC Final Replay: Mullinavat 2-10; Clara 2-07

'A five star first half performance fron Michael Dunphy helped Mullinavat to the Intermediate hurling title at the second attempt at Nowlan Park on Sunday. Dunphy's bunch of five points, coupled with a brace of goals from Michael and Maurice Murphy helped the Vat make up for the heartbreak of 1999 and step back into big time hurling. All the promise of a cracking game of hurling was duly delivered, as both teams lived up to their tags of entertainers, thrilling the crowd on a sundrenched afternoon. Clara struck first with a Ger Prendergast point, but they were quickly put in the shade by Mullinavat. They exploded from the blocks, notching up 1-2 in three minutes. Two points from Michael Dunphy in quick succession cancelled out Prendergast's opener, before Michael Murphy pounced for the first goal of the game. The move was instigated by Dunphy, who lofted a teasing ball towards Willie O'Dwyer. He crossed the sliothar to Maurice Murphy, who knocked it down for brother Michael to scoop past J.J. Ward and into the country end goal. The score seemed to knock Clara for six. They struggled to move forward and found themselves pinned back in their own half. Mullinavat's dominance was impressive, and it yielded a second goal in the 12th minute, after Maurice Murphy chased a long ball towards goal.'

'Faced with a one-on-one with the goalkeeper, Murphy managed to finish to the net, but not before he was brought crashing to earth by JJ Ward. Referee Pat Dunphy allowed the goal to stand, and Ward escaped with just his name being taken. Clara had taken a real beating in that first quarter, but still they kept fighting. Points for John Fitzgerald and Ger Prendergast (free) gave them a glimmer of hope, but another Michael Dunphy free sandwiched in between kept Mullinavat well in front. They went even further ahead when Dunphy added two more points to his tally, through a free and a 65. They added another score for good measure before the breakthrough Seamus Holden, their first point from play, Clara had tried to stop the rot by making changes to their half-forward and half-back lines, but they didn't work in time. At the interval, they trailed Mullinavat by 2-6 to 0-3.'

'There was a change in Clara's game plan as they started the second half. They had but one option left, hit Mullinavat with everything they had. Clara were given a gilt edged opportunity to get their second half off to a flying start when Conor Phelan was fouled just on the 21 yard line. It looked like a certain score, but Ger Prendergast appeared to be caught in two minds – goal or point? – and sent his shot wide. Their next free, which was awarded in the 34th minute, saw sub Gerry Byrne take on the mantle of free-taker and he scored with his first shot at the target. However, they were unable to gain any momentum from that score, as Mullinavat stormed back. They thought they had scored a third goal after Andrew McGovern fed Seamus Holden in front of goal, but his blistering shot was excellently deflected away from the net by JJ Ward. Michael Dunphy pointed the resulting 65, but it could have been worse for Clara.'

'The men in maroon got back on the scoresheet with another Gerry Byrne free, before Andrew McGovern retorted for Mullinavat. After 36 minutes, Mullinavat still had a stranglehold on the game with a 2-8 to 0-5 lead. It looked as if Mullinavat were cruising to victory. Suddenly, they were rocked by a spirited Clara comeback. A surging run forward from Ger Prendergast was brought to a juddering halt by Kenny Butler in front of the Mullinavat goal. Gerry Byrne stepped up to take the free, and rattled the back of the Vat net.

Spurred on by that strike, Byrne added a point to his ever increasing tally with a 43rd minute free. Four minutes later, they had the sliothar back in the Vat net. Rory Moore's long free dropped dangerously in front of John Dunphy's goal. Conor Phelan tried to flick the sliothar goalwards, but it fell to Robert Shortall, who made no mistake from close range. To this point the final had been a dream for Mullinavat, but now they were in danger of waking up to a real nightmare. Willie O'Dwyer tried to restore his team's great lead with another surging run towards goal, but he was felled by another robust challenge from Ward. This time referee Pat Dunphy awarded the penalty, but Ward was lucky to escape with only a yellow card, as he could have easily walked for either of his two hard tackles that day. Michael Dunphy was given the task of taking the penalty, but he opted to take his point, rather than go for goal.'

'With less than ten minutes left in the game, the title was there for the taking. However Mullinavat were determined not to let it slip from their grasp, and a fine point from an acute angle by Walter Bourke gave them that extra bit of breathing space required. Clara continued to throw everything at Mullinavat, and they nearly got through for a third goal. Robert Shortall's pass back to sub Pat Fitzgerald brought him right to the edge of the Vat square, but his effort was blocked by goalkeeper John Dunphy, who rushed out to make a vital save.'

'Clara had a chance to draw closer from the 65, but Byrne's accuracy rate took a slight knock as the dead ball went wide. He went close again a minute later after catching a poor clearance from Dunphy, but again missed the target. Now it was Mullinavat's turn to get pegged back, as Clara searched for a route to goal. It all combined for a tense end to the game, and was not made any easier by a late Clara point from Byrne.'

Mullinavat: J Dunphy, J Walsh, K Butler, JP Dungan, W Bourke (0-1), P Butler, L Murphy, J Rohan, P Aylward, M Dunphy (0-7, 0-6 frees, 0-1 65), S Holden (0-1), A McGovern (0-1), Michael Murphy (1-0), Maurice Murphy (1-0) and W O'Dwyer.

Clara: J J Ward, P Brennan, R Nolan, M Fitzgerald, K Ryan, E Phelan, T J Fitzgerald, R Moore, B Phelan, G Prendergast (0-2, 0-1 frees), B Barcoe, J Casey, R Shortall (1-0), C Phelan and J Fitzgerald (0-1). Subs: J Phelan for E Phelan, 23 minutes, G Byrne (1-4, all frees) for J Casey, 27 minutes, P Fitzgerald for B Barcoe, 36 minutes, D Nolan for K Ryan, 43 minutes, M Shortall for J Fitzgerald 59 minutes.

2002
SENIOR

SHL R1: Mullinavat 1-10; Erin's Own 1-10
SHL R2: Glenmore 1-12; Mullinavat 1-05
SHL R3: Mullinavat 2-08; Shamrocks 1-08
SHL R4: Tullaroan 1-20; Mullinavat 1-09
SHL R5: Mullinavat 2-12; James Stephens 0-12

SHC R1: O'Loughlin Gaels 1-18; Mullinavat 0-10

2003
SENIOR

SHL R1: Mullinavat 1-08; Glenmore 1-08
SHL R2: Mullinavat 1-11; James Stephens 0-13
SHL R3: Fenians 7-09; Mullinavat 2-10
SHL R4: Shamrocks 1-17; Mullinavat 0-13
SHL R5: O'Loughlin Gaels 4-06; Mullinavat 0-15

SHC R1: Dicksboro 2-14; Mullinavat 2-14
SHC R1 Replay: Dicksboro 2-09; Mullinavat 0-09
SHC Relegation Final: Dunnamaggin 3-11; Mullinavat 1-09

'Dunnamaggin, the champions in 1997, avoided the drop in emphatic fashion when they scored a handsome win over Mullinavat in the SHC Relegation Final at windy Ballyhale on Saturday 4/10/2003. The winners faced into the closing half eight points behind after only scoring twice in the first half. Within ten minutes of the new half they had erased the deficit. Four minutes later a blocked Ken O'Shea ground shot was finished to the net by John Hickey, which left Mullinavat in trouble and they couldn't arrest the slide back to the Intermediate grade.'

'The winners opened brightly against the wind with Ken O'Shea pointing at the Knocktopher end within a minute. John Hickey had a goal shot saved by Mullinavat goalie John Dunphy shortly afterwards. Dunphy was vital for Mullinavat throughout the openings half, making further saves from John Hickey in the 12th and 25th minutes. After Dunnamaggin's promising start, Mullinavat settled and played good hurling in this fast and competitive game. However, shooting nine wides in the opening half, was to eventually cost them. Still, with Dunphy utterly dependable in goal, Tomas Frisby a driving force at wing back, Jimmy Roughan a disruptive centre forward, and Joe Walsh making fair use of the ball up front, they took the game to the opposition. After shooting five wides, they led 0-4 to 0-2 turning into the second quarter. Their next score, in the 20th minute, was a lovely goal from Joe Walsh, who planted the ball in the left corner of the net after shooting on the turn. For a while Mullinavat could do no wrong. Uplifting points from Walter Burke and Michael Murphy, before Joe Walsh found himself in front of goal again, but this time he lifted the sliotair over the bar (1-7 to 0-2). Moments later, substitute Conor Conway whipped the ball wide from in front of goal as Dunnamaggin hung on for dear life. Neither side added to their total before the break but the Vat looked well placed, even if it was mainly due to the heroics of keeper Dunphy.'

'Dunnamaggin led by the brilliant Seaghan O'Neill, who had moved into midfield, tore the opposition asunder from the second half throw in. O'Neill pointed within seconds, Dunphy saved a goal attempt well from the same player, and Ramie Cahill tacked on two further Dunnamaggin points, and the ball never reached the other end of the field. Seaghan O'Neill rowed in with two further points, Ken O'Shea was set up by Liam Heffernan for the equalising goal from an actuate angle on the right (1-7 each). Mullinavat's second attack of the half came in the 41st minute but Willie O'Dwyer blasted right of the the right post after bursting his way through. The winners hit the front a minute later when Sean Ryan pointed. Andrew McGovern of Mullinavat worked hard to equalise. When John Hickey put rampant Dunnamaggin a goal ahead (2-8 to 1-8) you feared for the opposition, and within 90 seconds they were gone. A defender missed a catch when he moved smartly to try and gather a clearance from the opposing defence. Ken O'Shea was in full stride towards the goal, and the ball fell into his hand. There was no doubting what was going to happen. He shot Dunnamaggin into a 3-8 to 1-8 lead. Game over.'

Mullinavat: J Dunphy, T Duggan, K Butler, L Murphy, T Frisby (0-1, free), S Farrell, K Aylward, W Burke (0-1), D Butler, J Roughan, A McGovern (0-2), W O'Dwyer, E Maher, Michael Murphy (0-4) and J Walsh (1-1). Subs - C Conway for E Maher, Maurice Murphy for S Farrell, R Raftice for L Murphy, S Holden for J Walsh.

2004

INTERMEDIATE

IHL R1: Mullinavat 1-12; Piltown 0-11
IHL R2: Mullinavat 1-12; Clara 1-11
IHL R3: Mullinavat 2-13; Graiguenamanagh 1-07
IHL R4: Mullinavat 2-14; St Lachtain's 1-09
IHL R5: Mullinavat 2-12; Rower Inistioge 0-09
IHL Semi Final: Mullinavat 2-14; Mooncoin 2-11
IHL Final: Mullinavat 1-13; Graiguenamanagh 1-10

'Mullinavat made sure their season had a silver lining at the finish when they lifted the Intermediate hurling league title at Nowlan Park on Sunday 7/11/2004. After winning every game in the group stages, Mullinavat kept up their unbeaten run in the competition, beating a Graiguenamanagh side who had their chances but could never get too far in front. The Vat made most of the early running, chalking up the opening scores through Paul Aylward and Michael Murphy (free). Graig had to wait until the seventh minute to get off the mark with a Ger Walsh free, and after conceding another to Murphy, they put a string of points together to steal ahead. Hughie Flood did the damage with a treble, but their lead lasted for all of a minute. Parity was restored when Michael Murphy dropped a long ball over the bar in the 21st minute. He added another, before Jimmy Rohan tacked on a point, but again Graig hit back. With half-time drawing close, Graig stepped up the pace as they went searching for some scores. A probing move pegged back the Vat defence, who were forced into fouling Eddie Walsh. Ger Dowling made them pay, drilling the 21-metre free to the net. That could have cost the Vat, but they didn't panic. They used the closing minutes to good effect, shooting two late points following a quick solo from Jamie Fennelly and Dinny Butler which saw them win the lead back at the break (0-8 to 1-4).'

'The tight play continued into the second half. Midfielder Brendan Foley brought Graig level with the first attack and score of the half, but a long free from Tomas Frisby and one closer to the posts from Michael Murphy had Mullinavat back in front two minutes later. The sides continued to share the points. Hughie Flood (free) and Paul Aylward shot another score each, but that still left two between the teams as the game moved into the final quarter. Mullinavat had a great chance to bag a big score when a Paul Aylward hand-pass put Jimmy Rohan through. Keeper Ronan Dowling dashed off his line to block the effort with his feet just as Rohan was about to pull the trigger That missed chance proved costly, especially when another Flood free left just a point between the sides. Mullinavat made better use of their next chance. After a Michael Murphy free came back into play off a post, the loose ball was seized upon by Jamie Fennelly. The corner-forward quickly passed it back to Murphy, who rounded his marker before smashing the sliotar to the net. Graig responded with another brace of Flood frees. Conceding that goal had cost them dearly. Tomas Frisby swapped frees with Flood, before sub Andrew McGovern ensured Mullinavat's victory with one more point in the last minute of normal time.'

Mullinavat: P Jones, G Anthony, K Aylward, T Duggan, S Farrell, W Burke, L Murphy, T Frisby (0-2), D Butler (0-1), J Rohan, Mossy Murphy (0-1), P Aylward (0-2), W O'Dwyer, Michael Murphy (1-5, 1-4 frees) and J Fennelly (0-1). Subs: JP Dungan for Anthony, A McGovern (0-1) for Rohan, C Conway for Aylward

Graiguenamanagh: R Dowling, H Roberts, M Blanchfield, L Blanchfield, J Cahill, J Bolger, C O'Neill, B Foley (0-1), P Hamilton, G Walsh (0-1), G Dowling (1-0, free), E Dowling, H Flood (0-8, 0-7 frees, 0-1 65), C Dunne and E Walsh. Subs: A Morrissey for Cahill, M Dunne for E Dowling, A Foley for O'Neill, D O'Neill for Flood.

IHC Quarter Final: Mullinavat 0-09; St Lachtain's 0-07
IHC Semi Final: Carrickshock 3-11; Mullinavat 0-12

'Carrickshock's quest to become a Senior club once again kept going as they sealed their place in the Intermediate hurling championship final at Nowlan Park on Saturday 16/10/2004. Opponents Mullinavat had been on track for a return to the top flight after one season out, but found their journey cut short by a determined 'Shocks. It didn't look like that at the start, as Michael Murphy (free) and Dinny Butler shot the Vat into a two point lead by the ninth minute. However they were given a sign of Carrickshock's determination when Jamie Power batted a Michael Rice sideline cut to the net after 12 minutes. Mullinavat did get their lead back with two points from Michael Murphy, but as the first quarter ended so too did their time at the helm, as two Richie Power frees had Carrickshock back in front minutes later. The Vat came back with a spirited point from Willie O'Dwyer which came from a free after his mazy 20th minute run was cut short by a foul. A John Dalton free from halfway edged Carrickshock ahead once more, but when Paul Aylward caught and pointed the resulting puck out it was a drawn game again. With the game in the balance both sides went hunting for the vital score to give them the advantage. It was Carrickshock who got it with six minutes left in the half. Richie Power floated in a teasing ball, which brother Jamie grabbed, and used to attack the Mullinavat backs. Curving the defence open he could have gone for a shot, but opted to pass out to Seanie Gibbons, who rifled the sliotar past PJ Aylward.'

'Mullinavat did come back with two points before the interval from Michael Murphy (free) and another solo effort from Willie O'Dwyer, but one in between from Shane Power ensured Carrickshock had the cushion of a two point lead at half-time (2-4 to 0-8). That cushion became even more comfortable as the second half started. Shane Power tacked on another point, this time finishing after a good break from midfield. Richie Frisby followed suit, battling his way down the Paddy Grace stand touchline before taking a point. The Shock kept pressing for more scores, and it paid off with then next attack. Jamie Power knocked a high ball down into Seanie Gibbons' path, but a shot into the ground looked easy for PJ Aylward to deal with, It didn't work out that way though, as the sliotar wriggled its way out of the keeper's grasp and rolled over the line. After seven second half minutes Carrickshock were seven points ahead (3-6 to 0-8). At that stage it looked like the distance was too much to make up. Willie O'Dwyer fought back with a brace of frees for the Vat but that still left them with a lot to do. They kept looking for points, but simply found themselves replying to scores from Carrickshock. Richie Power (free) traded scores with Tomas Frisby (65), before swapping another with Mullinavat captain Paul Aylward. That was as close as Mullinavat would got to a place in the county final.'

Mullinavat: PJ Aylward, T Frisby (0-2), G Anthony, JP Dungan, W Burke, K Aylward, L Murphy, J Rohan, S Farrell, P Aylward (0-2), D Butler (0-1), W O'Dwyer (0-4, 3 frees), Maurice Murphy, Michael Murphy (0-3, 1 free) and Jamie Fennelly. Subs: T Duggan for Dungan, R Raftice for Anthony, A McGovern for Butler, S Holden for Fennelly, C Conway for P Aylward.

2005
INTERMEDIATE

IHL R1: Mullinavat 5-21; Piltown 2-07
IHL R2: Mullinavat 2-17; Mooncoin 0-11
IHL R3: St Lachtain's 2-12; Mullinavat 1-10
IHL R4: Mullinavat 0-14; Rower Inistioge 0-11
IHL R5: Galmoy 1-16; Mullinavat 0-16

IHC R1: Mullinavat 2-09; Graiguenamanagh 1-12
IHC R1 Replay: Mullinavat 1-12; Graiguenamanagh 0-12
IHC Quarter Final: Mullinavat 0-13; St Lachtain's 0-12
IHC Semi Final: Mooncoin 3-11; Mullinavat 1-15.

'Two goals in three minutes paved the way for Mooncoin to return to the Intermediate hurling final. Beaten finalists in 2004, the goal for the men from the South has always been to avenge that defeat by Carrickshock and return to the top flight in the county. However, the dream looked like it would have to wait another year, at least if the opening minutes of Sunday's semi final against Mullinavat was anything to go by. Keen to make a return to Senior fare themselves (they were relegated in 2003), the Vat looked very strong from the word go.. A quick shuffle of the pack before the game seemed to have the desired effect. With Willie O'Dwyer and Michael Duggan holding the reins in midfield, the Vat looked a solid prospect for county honours early on. Yet, after opening up a two point lead and limiting Mooncoin to minimal time on the ball, the wheels came off the Mullinavat wagon in devastating style. After misfiring from the start, Mooncoin got a real break when Eoin Henebery was given room to advance from his right half forward role in the eight minute. A deep delivery was gathered by Michael Purcell, who made an angle for himself, and then turned the sliotair across the city end goal. The shot appeared to have little pace behind it, but the sliotair bounced just in front of keeper PJ Aylward and ended up in the far corner of his net. If that left the Vat reeling then the next blow left them shaky on their feet. Before they could recover, Diarmuid Mackey had rushed in to rattle the net for a second time in the tenth minute.'

'The two goal scorers were to have a dream day at Mooncoin. Of their teams 2-11 tally, Purcell and Mackey bagged all but one point (Niall Mackey was the other Mooncoin man on the scoreboard). That quick goal blast left Mullinavat game plan in tatters. They tried to rally the troops with points from Dinny Butler, Conor Conway and Michael Murphy, but a brace of Mackey scores left them trailing by four points after 20 minutes (2-3 to 0-5). Mooncoin began to look comfortable in their position at the helm, but a clinical strike from young Mullinavat forward Paddy Raftice gave them a rude awakening. Raftice, a member of this year's county Minor panel helped himself to a 24th minute goal that shook Mooncoin to their boots. After watching a long Michael Murphy free bounce off a Mooncoin hurley at the edge of the square, Raftice met the ball with a first time pull at waist height. The crack as stick met sliotair was as loud as the gasps from the crowd as the ball bulged the net. More impressively a team that had looked down and out just minutes before was now just a point behind (2-3 to 1-5). The Vat build on that and soon had the advantage, thanks to Duggan, Andrew McGovern and Murphy. However history quickly repeated itself as Mooncoin came storming back. Points from Niall Mackey and Purcell had Mooncoin back on level terms by the last minute of normal time. There was better to come from their side though as Purcell pushed them back into the lead when he batted a Diarmuid Mackey cross into the net two minutes into injury time. Dinny Butler responded with a long range point for the Vat, but from leading the game they were now two points down at half time (3-5 to 1-9).'

'The second half saw more of the same. Mullinavat opened brightly, shooting early scores through Michael Murphy (free) and Michael Duggan, but conceding four points to Diarmuid Mackey, appeared to have Mooncoin home and hosed by the 50th minute (3-9 to 1-11). With a place in the final at stake, it was no surprise to see both sides hurl at full pace for the last 10 minutes. Another Michael Murphy free ended a barren Vat spell in the 51st minute, but two scores in a minute from Diarmuid Mackey and Michael Purcell seemed enough to tip the game in Mullinavat's favour. The celebrations were put on ice for a while though. Two more Michael Murphy frees, each one either side of a Dinny Butler point, ensured Mooncoin had a nervous wait before the final whistle confirmed their place in the final.'

Mullinavat: PJ Aylward, S Farrell, W Burke, T Duggan, P Aylward, K Aylward, L Murphy, W O'Dwyer, M Duggan, A McGovern, D Butler, J Fennelly, C Conway, Michael Murphy, and P Raftice. Sub: Maurice Murphy for Conway (31 minutes).

2006

INTERMEDIATE

IHL R1: Clara 3-09; Mullinavat 0-15
IHL R2: Mullinavat 0-11; St Lachtain's 0-09
IHL R3: Mullinavat 2-13; Mooncoin 1-13
IHL R4: Mullinavat 2-13; Rower Inistioge 2-09
IHL R5: Mullinavat 3-13; John Lockes 2-12
IHL Final: Mullinavat 0-10; Emeralds 3-06

'When Mullinavat look back at this game on Saturday 23/9/2006, they can point to two reasons as to why they ended up being beaten by five points by Emeralds of Urlingford in this Intermediate hurling league final. In the first half with the wind in their backs they shot an incredible 14 wides in the opening period. From a meagre enough number of chances, the Emeralds shot 1-4 to the very poor return of Mullinavat, who had only 0-6 on the scoreboard at the half time break. It was still all to play for and when Willie O'Dwyer set up Paul Aylward for the levelling point in the fourth minute of the new half, we felt like we would be having a great game on our hands. Then an utter twin disaster for Mullinavat. Firstly a free from Aidan Fogarty was deflected into his own net by veteran goalkeeper John Dunphy, who was deputising for holiday tied PJ, Aylward. It got worse a minute later when Dunphy fumbled a high, lobbing ball dropping underneath his crossbow, and Austin Cleere was in like a flash to finish to the net. Game, set and match to the Emeralds, but in truth Mullinavat never looked like pulling the game out of the fire afterwards. True, they fought it out to the end but their only rewards were points by Dinny Butler and Willie O'Dwyer, and even at the death, a 20 meter free by Willie O'Dwyer was well saved by the rock solid Emeralds defence. The standard of hurling never rose above the ordinary, and yet there was some fine individual performances on the day. In the re-jigged Emeralds defence, Derek Lyng was absolutely magnificent. He was to use an old cliche, monarch of all he surveyed, with as fine an exhibition of centre back play as has been seen for some time. In the air or on the ground it mattered not a whit to the all Ireland star who made a major contribution to the Emeralds success, with his brilliant hurling. On the Mullinavat team, the crafty, speedy young, Paul Aylward caught the eye as he ran himself into the ground in an endeavour to swing the game his sides way. If only, they had a few more of his determination and drive the result could well have been different. But on the day Emeralds had the touch of class necessary to give them the league title, which on the run of play they just about deserved.'

Mullinavat: John Dunphy, Tomas Frisby, Ger Anthony, Seamus Farrell, Kevin Aylward, Walter Burke, Damien Aylward, Liam Murphy, Paul Aylward (0-4), Michael Duggan, Dinny Butler (0-2), Willie O'Dwyer (0-3), Conor Conway, Michael Murphy (0-1) and Jamie Fennelly. Subs: Paddy Raftice, Andy McGovern and Richie Raftice.

IHC Quarter Final: Mullinavat 1-15; Mooncoin 1-11
IHC Semi Final: Mullinavat 1-18; St Lachtain's 3-09
IHC Final: Mullinavat 1-21; Clara 2-11

'From the minute that referee Paddy Neary threw in the ball to start this Intermediate final on 4/11/2006, Mullinavat went about their business in a determined and well co-ordinated fashion. Faster to every ball, there was hardly a section of the field where they were not on top right throughout the game. Very often in finals, both county and inter county the big guns on the team fail to deliver on the day. Not so with Mullinavat, as their top stars were firing on all cylinders and this, coupled with great back up from their colleagues meant that hapless Clara was fighting a losing battle from early on. When Michael Murphy struck for his side's first goal in the fifth minute the warning signs were there, and it went from bad to worse for Clara as the game progressed. The gulf that existed between the relative merits of both teams meant that it was a one sided and somewhat disappointing end to what had been a good Intermediate championship. Not that it mattered one whit to Mullinavat who were as good a prepared hurling team as we have seen in Nowlan Park this year. Their running game, first touch, swinging the ball from wing to wing and excellent conversion of scoring opportunities meant that whoever came up against them would find it very hard to upset this match winning formula. They won on Saturday in impressive fashion carrying the tag of pre match favourites lightly and there was no danger of an upset at any stage of the game.'

'Leading by 1-11 to 0-6 at the break they had by then laid the foundation for their ultimate seven point victory. It could have been more as it was only in the last seconds of the game that Clara sub Michael Bergin goaled which only served to take the bad look off the scoreboard. The Rod Iron men were fast away from the throw in and Dinny Butler fired over a great point in the second minute. Robert Shortall equalised from a free. Then Michael Murphy came through on a defence splitting solo run and blasted the ball past a helpless Michael Barcoe in the Clara goal. The Mullinavat captain Liam Murphy then put his name on the scoreboard with a fine point. Robert Shortall pointed another free but then Mullinavat went into overdrive. Willie O'Dwyer (8 minutes), Nicky Anthony (9th), Willie O'Dwyer (11 and 12) with points put them on the high road to ultimate victory. Ger Prendergast interrupted the flow with a Clara point but it was only a brief respite. Dinny Butler struck for his second point of the game and Michael Murphy added another from a free. Austin Murphy raised the white flag for Clara but the on fire Dinny Butler replied in like manner. TJ Fitzgerald and Ger Prendergast tacked on two points in a brief spell of Clara resistance but Mullinavat finished the half as they began it with further minors from Dinny Butler and Michael Murphy to leave the half time score Mullinavat 1-11; Clara 0-6.'

'There was a hint of a Clara revival at the restart when Ger Prendergast pointed a 65, this coming after a good save from PJ Aylward in the Mullinavat goal. But the winners raised the momentum again and Jamie Fennelly kicked a good point to which Michael Duggan added another (which meant by then all six Mullinavat forwards had scored). Austin Murphy shot a simple goal for Clara with the keeper possibly unsighted and Robert Shortall pointed another free. Jamie Fennelly raced through for a fine point at the other end but Robert Shortall again neutralised. Michael Duggan pointed in the 46th minute only for Clara sub Lester Ryan to pick up a good point from the puck out and then Niall

Prendergast had one from a 65 after another good save from Aylward. Sending that a historic victory was now clearly within their grasp Mullinavat made a final surge that very few teams could contain. Points rained over from Nicky Anthony, Willie O'Dwyer and Michael Murphy again, before Michael Bergin got a goal back for Clara. Fittingly the Mullinavat men had the last say with another point from the mercurial Michael Murphy to leave the final score. It was a delighted captain Liam Murphy who accepted the trophy on behalf of his team from the Chairman of the County Board Mr Ned Quinn. Mullinavat who had hardly a weak link throughout the field were well served by PJ Aylward in goal, Tony Duggan, Ger Anthony and Ritchie Raftice were an excellent fullback line. Walter Burke gave an exhibition of centre half back play ably assisted by wing men, Kevin Aylward and Thomas Frisby. The ever improving Paul Aylward and team captain Liam Murphy won their midfield battle hands down. the three top hurling amigos Dinny Butler, Willie O'Dwyer and Michael Murphy stole the show with superb displays. Then Jamie Fennelly, Nicky Anthony and Michael Duggan too can feel chuffed with their efforts as each of them got on the scoreboard at different stages of the game. It was nice to see Richie and Pat Raftice collect their medals so soon after the sudden death of their father Paddy, for whom a minute's silence was observed prior to the start of the game.'

Mullinavat: PJ Aylward, Tony Duggan, Ger Anthony, Richie Raftice, Kevin Aylward, Walter Burke, Thomas Frisby, Paul Aylward, Liam Murphy (0-1), Jamie Fennelly (0-2), Dinny Butler (0-4), Willie O'Dwyer (0-4), Michael Duggan (0-2), Michael Murphy (1-6) and Nicky Anthony (0-2). Subs: Pat Raftice for J Aylward (48 minutes), Conor Conway for M Duggan (57 minutes).

Clara scorers: Austin Murphy (1-1), Robert Shortall (0-4), Michael Bergin (1-0), Ger Prendergast (0-3), Niall Prendergast (0-1), TJ Fitzgerald (0-1), Lester Ryan (0-1).

2007
SENIOR

SHL R1: James Stephens 2-16; Mullinavat 2-09
SHL R2: O'Loughlin's 1-17; Mullinavat 0-12
SHL R3: Tullaroan 0-13; Mullinavat 1-08
SHL R4: Young Irelands 2-12; Mullinavat 0-12
SHL R5: St Martin's 1-27 Mullinavat 1-20

SHC R1: Dunnamaggin 2-06; Mullinavat 0-12
SHC R1 Replay: Dunnamaggin 0-23; Mullinavat 0-14
SHC Relegation Final: Young Irelands 1-11; Mullinavat 0-13

OUR STORY (1887-2024)

'It may have been only the Senior hurling relegation play-off, but boy, what a game Young Irelands and Mullinavat served up at sun-baked Nowlan Park on Saturday. This was mighty stuff where only the bravest of the brave would survive. It had everything, classic scores and wonder saves, hairs-breadth misses, top class sportsmanship and fast fluent hurling. Both teams deserve the highest credit for the magnificent spectacle they providers, and pity was there had to be a loser in the end. Charlie Carter, got possession and weaved and ducked his way into position for a shot at the post and levelled the game at 1-10 to 0-13. Mullinavat keeper, Paddy Jones, who had replaced PJ Aylward at the interval, took a quick poke out as referee, Eamon Mansfield, looked at his watch, and send it into an open space where Young Irelands' Tom Drennan lay unmarked, and he fired the ball high between the post for the winning point. Fans who had come along to see DJ Carey (possibly for the last time) and Charlie Carter were not disappointed as the "terrible twins" turned in a virtuoso performance. While the speed of old may be gone, their hurling brains still remain intact. The uncanny understanding between them was a joy to watch, the movement which led to the side's only goal was poetry in motion. Carey blocked down an attempted clearance and careered away on a defence pressing solo run. Meanwhile, Carter drifted away from his marker and when that old trademark handpass arrived from Carey, Charlie got the ball and smashed it past PJ Aylward, who hadn't a snowball's chance of saving it. Old memories were revived in brilliant fashion.'

'But, fair play to Mullinavat, they dug deep and were only two points behind at the break despite Willie O'Dwyer missing a sitter, and Michael Murphy badly off target from two scoreable frees. Michael Murphy opened the scoring with a point from a free, and then the Young Irelands' goal had a miraculous escape. Murphy set up Willie O'Dwyer who somehow squeezed his left-handed shot just wide of the upright. Charlie Carter shot a beauty of a point from way on the right wing in the third minute, and this was followed by another from DJ Carey from the '65.' PJ Aylward paid the penalty a poor puck out when Tom Drennan availed of the gift chance and pointed. It was all Young Irelands now, and the lethal DJ bisected the posts from a free some 60 metres out. Michael Murphy replied for Mullinavat and Paddy Raftice cut the lead to the bare minimum with 13 minutes gone. A swerving solo run and a deadly finish by Carey lifted the crowd as the hurling was now fast and furious and they were entertained a minute later by as good a move and as deadly a finish as one could wish to see. Carey block down an attempted clearance, went on a solo run, the offload to Carter, and the finish was sublime. Far from lying down Mullinavat thundered back into the game and Michael Murphy punished indiscretions by the Young Irelands' backs with three pointed frees. The margin between the teams was down to one, with another point from the hard working Dinny Butler for Mullinavat. DJ had the last say when he put over a free to leave the score at break Young Irelands 1-06, Mullinavat 0-07.'

'Willie O'Dwyer (now at midfield) send over a massive point from under the new stand after a fine piece of combination play. Michael Murphy from yet another free tied the scores again. The hurling by now was top class with Carey and Nicky Anthony exchanging points. DJ popped over another free. Michael Murphy tied the scores once more, but not for long as Dick Carroll put Young Irelands one up again. Willie O'Dwyer, fought for, and won possession at midfield, and shot a point and the teams were on level times once again. So, who could find a winning score? It looks like Mullinavat had got it when Nicky Anthony put the ball between the Gowran posts for a brilliant point. But there was another twist to the tail, as Charlie Carter dodged and ducked and then shot a beauty to balance matters. It fell to a bad decision by the Mullinavat goalkeeper to eventually decided issue. His poorly placed puck out went to Tom Drennan, who flashed the ball over the bar for the final and most valuable point of the whole game. This preserved his teams Senior status for another year, and sent a gallant Mullinavat back down to the Intermediate grade.'

Mullinavat: PJ Aylward, T Duggan, G Anthony, S Farrell, K Aylward, W Burke, T Frisby, L Murphy, C Conway, W O'Dwyer, D Butler, N Anthony, P Raftice, M Murphy and J Fennelly. Subs: P Jones, A McGovern and R Raftice.

2008
INTERMEDIATE

IHL R1: Mullinavat 3-16; Graiguenamanagh 2-15
IHL R2: Mullinavat 2-12; Mooncoin 2-08
IHL R3: Mullinavat 0-11; Erin's Own 0-11
IHL R4: Emeralds 2-13; Mullinavat 0-12
IHL R5: Mullinavat 1-14; St Lachtain's 1-14

IHC First Round: Danesfort 2-14; Mullinavat 3-09

2009
INTERMEDIATE

IHL R1: Mullinavat 2-14; Tullogher Rosbercon 2-11
IHL R2: Mullinavat 1-16; Graiguenamanagh 1-08
IHL R3: Rower Inistioge 1-13; Mullinavat 0-12
IHL R4: Mullinavat 1-15; Conahy Shamrocks 1-12
IHL R5: St Lachtain's 1-10; Mullinavat 0-13

IHC First Round: Mooncoin 1-13; Mullinavat 1-10

CHAPTER 11

2010-2024

John Walsh celebrates as he stars for Kilkenny in the 2014 All-Ireland Minor Championship.

2010-2024

2010
INTERMEDIATE

IHL R1: Mullinavat 1-10; Mooncoin 0-05
IHL R2: Mullinavat 2-16; Emeralds 0-09
IHL R3: Mullinavat 1-18; Young Irelands 1-14
IHL R4: Mullinavat 1-15; Glenmore 0-12
IHL R5: Tullogher Rosbercon 0-12; Mullinavat 0-10
IHL Final: Mullinavat 2-10; Danesfort 0-11

'Already both sets of players would have erased the memories of this Intermediate hurling league final from their minds. It wasn't a particularly good contest at Ballyhale on Sunday 19/9/2010 and shortly after the final whistle thoughts turned to the upcoming championship. The obvious differences in the end between the two sides were the goals scored. Danesfort for large proportions of the game, particularly during the first half, shot numerous wides and squandered good scoring chances. Danesfort practically owned the ball during the opening 10 minutes, but they just couldn't muster up a score as the Rod Iron men were on target through Jamie Fennelly (2) and Conor Conway from a free. Paddy Hogan finally pointed a free to open Danesfort's account in the 16th minute, but they proceeded to shoot seven wides during the opening 20 minutes. The Southern men took full advantage of their opponents misery. Mullinavat's opening goal in the 22nd minute was one of the rare pieces of decent skill on show. A brilliant crossfield delivery from the left corner by Jamie Fennelly flighted the ball to Paddy Raftice, who rifled a low shot to the net giving keeper Frank Manogue no chance. Richie Hogan (free) and Robbie Walsh added points for the losers but the winners exerted control, and a Michael Murphy goal in the 29th minute after being set-up by Ian Duggan stretched the advantage further (2-4 to 0-3).'

'Ian Duggan and David Forristal exchanged points late in the half as Mullinavat were in control going in for the rest. Danesfort clawed their way back into contention during the third quarter. They outscored their opponents by 0-5 to 0-1 by the 43rd minute. Richie Hogan added three pointed frees while Robbie Walsh scored two, and a beauty from long range by Paddy Hogan saw the 'Fort charge gain momentum. However, the fare during the last quarter, like the majority of the game, was largely forgettable as the winners outscored the opposition by 0-4 to 0-2. The highlight during this period was a great score from wing-back Damian Aylward in the 54th minute.'

Mullinavat: James Culleton, Tony Duggan, Seamus Farrell, Joe Fennelly, Damian Aylward (0-1), Walter Burke, Michael Malone, Conor Conway (0-3, frees), Ian Duggan (0-1), Michael Murphy (1-1, 0-1 free), Dinny Butler, Padraig Gahan, Paddy Raftice (1-0), Willie O'Dwyer (0-2) and Jamie Fennelly (0-2) Subs - Nicky Anthony, Andrew McGovern.

Danesfort: Frank Manogue, Gavin O'Keeffe, Liam Forristal, Oisin 'Daly, Ben O'Connor, Paddy Hogan (0-3, 2 frees), John Doheny, Paul Murphy, Jim Phelan, David Forristal (0-1), Robbie Walsh (0-2), Cathal O'Neill, Richie Hogan (0-5, frees), Phily Walsh, and Richard Troy. Subs - Michael Cunningham, Marty McMahon, Padraig Forristal.

IHC Quarter Final: Mullinavat 0-17; Rower Inistioge 0-14
IHC Semi Final: Mullinavat 0-15; Danesfort 1-09
IHC Final: Dicksboro 2-12; Mullinavat 2-11

'They played with the verve and free spirit of the Harlem Globetrotters when turning in a class performance during the opening half, but subsequently Dicksboro were made to look like Ragged Rovers before holding out for a nail-biting win in the Intermediate hurling final at Nowlan Park on 17/10/2010. If ever a team left a county final with serious regrets it was Mullinavat. They played the opposition up a stick during the closing half, but a staggering 11 wides, to take their tally to 15 in all, left them agonisingly short at the last whistle. Young and talented Dicksboro most certainly are, but they gave their fans in the 5,028 crowd on Sunday a rollercoaster ride. The majesty of their hurling during the opening half drew gasps of appreciation from the entire crowd, and they weren't at all flattered by a healthy interval lead of 1-8 to 0-5. Indeed, they could easily have been two goals better off.'

'Mullinavat may have been made look second class, but after the rest they hailed down the opposition and proceeded to dominate. Their halfback line of Damien Aylward, he was magical, Walter Burke and Michael Malone dominated completely. On top of that, the 'Boro hardly got a look in at midfield where Conor Conway turned on the power and did fantastic work to try and drive his team to victory. Willie O'Dwyer was wonderful too. But sadly for them, Mullinavat couldn't find the target often enough. After nine minutes of the second half they had shot five wides. The 'Boro were hanging on, desperately it must be added, to a 1-9 to 1-6 lead. As the game edged into the last quarter the Mullinavat wides tally hit nine. The difference was still three points (1-10 to 1-7). Their luck, poor shooting or whatever way you want to put it, didn't improve. A minute into injury-time the losers missed a handy enough free from 50 metres, the ball going across the face of the goal and wide. Dicksboro conceded the final score to Dinny Butler, a point in the 62nd minute, which made the miss from the free moments earlier all the more costly. It was that sort of miserable, unlucky, disappointing day for Mullinavat.'

'The losers opened with all guns blazing and Nicky Anthony and Michael Murphy had points. The breeze assisted 'Boro then hit the go switch and before the third minute was reached, they had turned the tables and were 0-3 to 0-2 in front thanks to scores from Adrian Stapleton, Cillian Buckley and Eddie O'Donoghue (free). Things got even better for the winners in the seventh minute when they put together the move of the match. It ended with the scoring of a lovely goal. The ball was moved at pace from in front of their own goal by Darren Tyrrell, on to Dan Kenny and then on to wing-back Michael Fagan, who aimed a diagonal ball into the left corner at the county end. Adrian Stapleton snapped up the arriving sliotar, beat his man and planted the ball in the bottom left corner of the net. To add to that, O'Donoghue converted a free to leave Mullinavat 0-2 to 1-3 down. The 'Boro were flying. Turning into the second quarter the 'Boro were 1-5 to 0-2 clear. Minutes earlier Vat goalie James Culleton had done well when killing a goal chance on Cillian Starr and on 18 minutes O'Flynn prodded the ball wide from no more than three metres after Starr knocked down a delivery from O'Donoghue. Had the 'Boro turned those chances into goals it would have been game over. Still, there was an awful lot to admire about their hurling when they went in for the rest leading by 1-8 to 0-5, even after registering seven wides.'

'The losers didn't mess about in the new half. They took over from the start after Conor Conway pointed a free within 50 seconds. The 'Boro's Cillian Starr pointed after Ollie Walsh created the opening, but Mullinavat caught such a hold on the match the opposition rarely got within threatening distance of the opposing posts. In the 36th minute Conor Conway aimed in a free from midfield, and the ball appeared to come off a defender and sailed into the net (1-9 to 1-6). The Vat were on top, but their shooting was awful. Moments after, the losers posted their fifth wide, Derek O'Gorman but through a gap to shoot a 'Boro point after O'Donoghue had dug out possession. Conway posted a reply. By the time Damien Aylward registered the losers' next score in the 47th minute (1-10 to 1-8) they had shot wides eight and nine. A wonderful Nicky Anthony minor from 80 metres sliced the divide to two points and Dicksboro were under serious, serious pressure. They needed something special to lift them. O'Flynn provided it. He won a ball in the air on the '40', driven from his own defence. He galloped up the left wing before layoff an inch perfect pass as the cover closed in. Stapleton lashed to the net from nearly 20 metres (2-10 to 1-9). Mullinavat didn't have time for the disappointment or shock to sink in. They had the ball in the net within 30 seconds. Paddy Raftice took the honours. Within a minute they shot their

10th wide. In a very rare 'Boro attack, sub Tom Manning out-foxed the cover but his tame shot from the right was easily dealt with by goalie Culleton. Not long afterwards Derek O'Gorman was gifted possession from a Mullinavat puck-out and he arrowed the ball back in and over the bar (2-11 to 2-9). Michael Murphy and O'Donoghue, in that order, traded minors as the game galloped towards the finish with Mullinavat chasing furiously. After that O'Donoghue score the losers missed a decent chance from a free before landing one point. In the end the minimum divided them. Was it that Dicksboro were lucky or Mullinavat unlucky?'

Mullinavat: James Culleton, Tony Duggan, Seamus Farrell, Joe Fennelly, Damien Aylward (0-1), Walter Burke, Michael Malone, Ian Duggan, Conor Conway (1-5, 1-3 frees, point 65) Michael Farrell, Dinny Butler (0-1), Willie O'Dwyer (capt), Nicky Anthony (0-2), Michael Murphy (0-2) and Jamie Fennelly. Subs: Paddy Raftice (1-0) for I Duggan; Padraig Gahan for M. Farrell; Andrew McGovern for Jamie Fennelly.

Dicksboro: Sam Morrissey, Darren Tyrrell, Kieran Cuddihy, Philip Hogan, Michael Fagan, Danny Kenny, Enda Malone, Cillian Buckley (0-1), Derek O'Gorman (0-2), Martin Gaffney, Eddie O'Donoghue (captain – 0-6, five frees) Ollie Walsh, Cillian Starr (0-1), Paul O'Flynn (0-1), Adrian Stapleton (2-1). Subs: Tom Manning for Starr; Shane Maher for O'Gorman; Conor O'Loughlin for Stapleton.

2011

INTERMEDIATE

IHL R1: Mullinavat 1-18; Tullogher Rosbercon 1-08
IHL R2: Mullinavat 1-10; Danesfort 1-07
IHL R3: Mullinavat 3-11; Graiguenamanagh 1-10
IHL R4: Emeralds 1-08; Mullinavat 0-06
IHL R5: Mooncoin 1-15; Mullinavat 0-14

IHC First Round: Mullinavat 1-16; Young Irelands 1-10
IHC Quarter Final: Rower Inistioge 2-13; Mullinavat 1-12

2012

INTERMEDIATE

IHL R1: Mullinavat 1-14; Glenmore 0-07
IHL R2: Clara 1-19; Mullinavat 0-09
IHL R3: Mooncoin 0-12; Mullinavat 0-07

IHL R4: Mullinavat 0-22; John Lockes 0-09
IHL R5: Rower Inistioge 0-14; Mullinavat 0-09

IHC R1: Young Irelands 2-14; Mullinavat 2-12

2013

INTERMEDIATE
IHL R1: Mullinavat 1-14; Tullogher 2-09
IHL R2: Rower Inistioge 1-10; Mullinavat 0-07
IHL R3: Glenmore 0-12; Mullinavat 1-08
IHL R4: Mullinavat 5-10; Emeralds 4-12
IHL R5: St Lachtain's 3-15; Mullinavat 1-13

IHC R1: Mullinavat 1-15; Conahy Shamrocks 1-10
IHC Quarter Final: Dunnamaggin 1-17; Mullinavat 0-14

2014

INTERMEDIATE
IHL R1: Mullinavat 3-11; St Lachtain's 1-12
IHL R2: Mullinavat 1-11; Dunnamaggin 1-08
IHL R3: Mullinavat 5-17; Lisdowney 1-11
IHL R4: Mullinavat 2-20; Emeralds 1-14
IHL R5: Mullinavat 1-15; Graigue Ballycallan 0-10
IHL Final: Mullinavat 2-16; St Patrick's 0-18

'Mullinavat shot into the lead in the race for promotion when they clinched the Intermediate hurling league title in dramatic fashion on Saturday 13/9/2014. Their potent forward line was crucial as they grabbed the scores at the right times to swing the game in their favour against St Patrick's (Ballyraggett). Mark Mansfield was the driving force behind the Southerners, who have beaten all before them so far. The game didn't start in such fashion, however. After just 12 minutes Mullinavat trailed by 0-8 to 0-2, having failed to start the match on the front foot. It was Patrick's instead who dominated the early exchanges with Joe and Geoff Brennan making huge gains for them. Sean Mooney got the first score of the game, the full-forward shooting over from what seemed an impossible angle after just 20 seconds. Points from the Brennan brothers quickly followed, and Ballyraggett quickly took a hold on the game. Joe Brennan was the one stealing the spotlight in the opening exchanges, and the county hurler was certainly living up to his reputation. Kevin Kelly calmly shot over Ballyraggett's eighth point and all of a sudden, they found themselves six to the good over a hesitant Mullinavat team that never got going in this quarter. The signs were there that Mullinavat had begun to find their rhythm when Joe Gahan was denied a goal by Ballyraggett goalie James Gannon. A John Walsh free, and a fine effort from Marl Mansfield got Mullinavat into gear and they started to take control.'

'Mansfield was again instrumental as Mullinavat got the all-important goal that swung the game their way. The lightning quick midfielder spotted Willie O'Dwyer at full forward. O'Dwyer had lost his marker nicely. He received the pass from Mansfield and made no mistake as he planted the ball in the back of the Ballyraggett net. Sean Mooney went close to cancelling out O'Dwyer's goal when he harassed the Mullinavat goalie Jim Culleton, and nearly bagged a goal. Blocking down the number one, Mooney then attempted to kick the ball home but saw his shot trickle wide of the right-hand post. The game then seemed to slow down which was a surprise after such a frantic start. Neither team was able to get on top, and with just a point between them, the next few minutes were crucial as both tried to impose their will on things.'

'It was Mullinavat who got on top once more, and after a point from Joe Gahan levelled the match, they took the lead for the first time through a goal from wing forward Ger Malone. Malone appeared to shoot for a point, but an unfortunate slip meant that the ball dropped on keeper Michael Gannon, who saw the sliotair slip out of his grasp and into the net. Just like what happened after the first goal, Ballyragget then had a chance to hit back immediately. Kevin Kelly broke into the space behind the full back line, and time seemed to slow down as the ball bounced across the face of goal and wide. At the break Mullinavat led by 2-7 to 0-8.'

'They had totally outclassed their opponents in the fifteen minutes before half time. Ballyragget hadn't scored since the 12th minute. Their forward line was struggling to create chances. They changed their approach as soon as the second half started, however. Kevin Kelly was to the fore as they went in search of the goal which would bring them back into the game. He slotted over a number of frees and added another from play, but the Mullinavat forward line was growing in belief all the time. Ian Duggan slotted two points in quick succession. Mark Mansfield was making things happen, giving an excellent display in midfield. A point from Jamie Fennelly in the 38th minute meant that all of Mullinavat's forward line scored. Their movement and link up play caused Ballyragget all sorts of trouble. As the game entered the closing 10 minutes, there was still no sign of Mullinavat letting up.

Kevin Kelly was Patrick's best player. He received great help from Joe Brennan, who pointed his fourth score. The deficit was back to just two points, but Mullinavat still had a firm hold on the game as their midfield was dominant. Ballyragget made a late rally with chances from Joe Brennan and Sean Mooney, but keeper James Culleton was having a near perfect game and he blocked all attempts on his goal. Ballyragget showed signs of improvement in the second half, but their midfield had been outclassed by a rampant Mark Mansfield.'

Mullinavat: James Culleton, Joe Fennelly, Thomas Aylward, Seamus Farrell, Robbie Malone, Pauric Gahan, Simon Aylward, Dinny Butler (0-1), Mark Mansfield (0-5, 0-1 frees), Ger Malone (1-2), Ian Duggan (0-2), Joe Gahan (0-2), Jamie Fennelly (0-1), Willie O'Dwyer (1-1) and John Walsh (0-1 free). Subs - Darren Kenneally for Simon Aylward, Paddy Raftice (0-1) for Jamie Fennelly.

IHC Quarter Final: Mullinavat 2-18; Young Irelands 4-10
IHC Semi Final: Mullinavat 2-13; Tullogher Rosbercon 1-13
IHC County Final: Mullinavat 0-17; St Patrick's 0-14

'In a season when Mullinavat caught many a late bus to victory, they did the same when blasting to a terrific win in a high class Intermediate hurling final on Sunday. Points from young tigers Joe Gahan, John Walsh and Mark Mansfield during a sizzling closing six minute blast snatched the prize from gutsy St Patrick's (Ballyragget) just as they appeared set to drive on to victory. The previous four scores were all picked off by strong motoring St Patrick's as they got on top in what was an up and down battle. Those four scores brought them back level at 0-14 each, and momentum was firmly with them. However, Mullinavat, who have made a habit of surviving in tight battles this season, came up was another late party trick and three lovely scores to complete a magnificent league/championship double at Nowlan Park, plus earn promotion back to the Senior division. The nail-biting finish was in keeping with the general trend of a match that overflowed with classy deeds and moments of individual brilliance. Some of the points scoring from top scorers, John Walsh and Kevin Kelly was of the highest order. Mark Mansfield played like a man inspired as did Michael Brennan for the opposition. The winners opened backed by the fresh breeze, but as the game exploded into an open, skilful, and fast flowing affair, there was nothing between the teams during the half. They were level five times during the half, the last time at 0-7 each, in the 26th minute, when Kevin Kelly flashed over a free for St Patrick's. A great 29th minute point, and nothing short of that description, from midfield by Mark Mansfield edged Mullinavat 0-8 to 0-7 ahead at the break.'

'Within 50 seconds of the restart, it was all square again, thanks to a Joe Brennan dash and William Tell-like shot at the target. Mullinavat didn't even blink. They bounced back to claim the next three scores through John Walsh, a gift for Ger Malone after a puck-out was wrongly posted, and Mark Mansfield after a lovely catch from Willie O'Dwyer, who placed Joe Gahan to provide the scorer with possession (0-11 to 0-8). Kevin Kelly sneaked a score to keep St Patrick's chasing strongly at close quarters.'

'Ger Malone upped the divide in the 41st minute before John Walsh (free) stretched it further (0-13 to 2-9). Kelly and Ian Duggan traded scores before St Patrick's hit full pace between the 47th and 53rd minute when scores from Kelly (2), following fouls on Joe Brennan and Michael Brennan; Phil Staunton, a magnificent effort after a charge up the field, and Michael Brennan brought them back level as 0-14 each. Is there sink or swim time for Mullinavat. Just as they did against Young Irelands (Gowran) and neighbours Tullogher Rosbercon in the semi-final, the Rod Iron men showed nerves of steel. They plundered three lovely scores to win: capping off a wonderful season and opening a path into the Leinster club championship. Pauric Gahan, long serving skipper Willie O'Dwyer, Ger Malone and others have reason to look back with pride on this huge achievement.'

'However, immediately afterwards they were looking forward to the many and varied challenges that could lie ahead. "There is no point in finishing hurling next week," was the subtle message of intent from manager, Declan Wall, who plotted the league/championship double success for the club with fellow selectors Tommy Frisby, John Dunphy and Pakie Wall. "The Leinster club championship can help us develop even further, if we can get things together and do well in it," Mr Wall added. "That competition will open a whole new level of competition to us. I want these guys to succeed, to win as much as they can. Look what the provincial club competition has done for so many Kilkenny clubs down the years? It can help us develop like it did many others. The 35 guys on the panel were the guys who won the medals. There is no point in being satisfied now. We are carrying the Kilkenny flag now. We will enjoy this moment, but we can think it is the end of the season for us. This is our 25th game in all competitions, challengers and so on. We won 22 of those matches."'

Mullinavat: James Culleton, Joe Fennelly, Thomas Aylward, Seamus Farrell, Robert Malone, Pauric Gahan, Simon Aylward, Dinny Butler, Mark Mansfield (0-3), Joe Gahan (0-1), Ger Malone (0-3), Ian Duggan (0-1), Jamie Fennelly, Willie O'Dwyer, and John Walsh (0-9, 6 frees, 1 penalty). Subs - Liam Fennelly, Brian Phelan, Paddy Raftice.

St Patrick's scorers: Kevin Kelly (0-9, 6 frees), Michael Brennan (0-2), Bill Staunton, Joe Brennan and Seoirse Kenny (0-1 each).

2015

SENIOR

SHL R1: Danesfort 2-13; Mullinavat 2-09
SHL R2: Mullinavat 1-17; St Martin's 1-05
SHL R3: Rower Inistioge 1-15; Mullinavat 1-14
SHL R4: Mullinavat 2-15; Fenians 1-15

SHL R5: Shamrocks 4-12; Mullinavat 2-16

SHC First Round: Mullinavat 2-16; Carrickshock 1-13
SHC Quarter Final: Mullinavat 2-16; Rower Inistioge 0-12
SHC Semi Final: Clara 1-23; Mullinavat 0-14

'A fast-moving Clara showed Mullinavat no mercy in this Kilkenny Senior hurling semi final at Nowlan Park. The 2013 champions were too sharp in the opening half stringing together nine unanswered points in a run which took them a long way towards the finishing line. Although the Vat sparked into life early thanks to Mark Mansfield, Joe Gahan and Willie O'Dwyer, they were quickly stifled as Clara found their rhythm. Playing fast and fluent hurling they popped over a series of scores in quick succession to race well clear of their rivals. David Langton, Liam Ryan (2), John Murphy, Conor O'Shea (2) and Keith Hogan were all on target as Mullinavat found themselves 7 points behind after 19 minutes. The remainder of the half did not get much better for the Vat and Mullinavat led 0-15 to 0-5 at the break.'

'Clara didn't hit the same heights in the second half as they did in the first, but they did enough to keep Mullinavat at arms length. Chris Bolger brought a great save from goalie James Culleton before Hogan converted the resulting 65 to make it a ten-point game with 43 minutes on the clock (0-17 to 0-7). Mullinavat did narrow the gap thanks to two swift scores from Mansfield and Ian Duggan but a return of four points in as many minutes saw Clara all but rubberstamp their county final berth. There was still time for Clara to raise a green flag. Hogan did that rushing in to finish after James Culleton could only swat Chris Bolger's shot into his path. There was a late flurry from Mullinavat in response, Mansfield led the way with three of their five scores, but Clara was too far ahead by then.'

Mullinavat: J Culleton, J Fennelly, R Malone, S Aylward P Gahan L Fennelly, B Phelan, D Butler, M Mansfield (0-8, 3 frees, 1 sideline, 1"65"), I Duggan (0-1), J Gahan (0-2), M Malone, J Fennelly, W O'Dwyer (0–1) and G Malone (0-1). Subs: A Mansfield for Butler (45 minutes), M Jones (0-1) for O'Dwyer (45 minutes).

2016

SENIOR

SHL R1: Mullinavat 3-14; Danesfort 1-11
SHL R2: Shamrocks 3-22; Mullinavat 5-07
SHL R3: O'Loughlin Gaels 3-14; Mullinavat 0-10
SHL R4: Mullinavat 0-18; Clara 1-14
SHL R5: Mullinavat 0-13; Erin's Own 0-13

SHC First Round: Mullinavat 3-16; Bennetsbridge 4-13
SHC First Round Replay: Mullinavat 2-15; Bennetsbridge 0-15
SHC Quarter Final: Ballyhale Shamrocks 3-20; Mullinavat 1-11

'Mullinavat were rabbits caught in the headlights as Ballyhale Shamrocks secured Saturday's second semi final berth, and in devastating style, as they scored a 3-20 to 1-11 win over Mullinavat in Thomastown. Although the Shamrocks were without the likes of Michael Fennelly and James "Cha" Fitzpatrick they still had a galaxy of stars and had too much for Mullinavat to contend with. Ballyhale wasted no time stamping their authority on the game TJ Reid taking just two minutes to break through the Mullinavat defence and crash to the net. In fact everything they hit in the first quarter turned to gold. With Ronan Corcoran and Richie Reid also in impressive form the Shamrocks took control of the game and were 1-7 to 0-1 in front after just 12 minutes. Mullinavat with Ger Malone and Willie O'Dwyer leading the way did string four points together but Eoin Reid and Brian Cody finished to the net as the Shamrocks trooped in at half time 3-10 to 0-5 in front. Mullinavat were facing an uphill task, but didn't give in. John Walsh (1-2) and Mark Mansfield (0-2) tried to raise their sides spirit, but Ballyhale were never going to let the game slip.'

Mullinavat: James Culleton, Joe Fennelly, Thomas Aylward, Ian Duggan, Robbie Malone, Liam Fennelly, Pauric Gahan, Simon Aylward, Michael Malone (0-1), Willie O'Dwyer (0-2), Joe Gahan, Ger Malone (0-1), Jamie Fennelly, John Walsh (1-4, 0-1 free, 0-1 "65") and Adam Mansfield. Subs - Mark Mansfield (0-2); Brian Phelan, Mikie Jones (0-1), Ryan Bland.

2017
SENIOR

SHL R1: Erin's Own 2-18; Mullinavat 2-11
SHL R2: Mullinavat 1-17; O'Loughlin Gaels 1-17
SHL R3: Mullinavat 3-11; Rower Inistioge 2-14
SHL R4: Mullinavat 2-28; St Martin's 2-12
SHL R5: Carrickshock 1-17; Mullinavat 1-16

SHC First Round: Mullinavat 2-14; Bennetsbridge 0-10
SHC Quarter Final: Dicksboro 2-14; Mullinavat 1-17
SHC Quarter Final Replay: Dicksboro 2-18; Mullinavat 2-16

'Composure and cleverness saw Dicksboro overcome Mullinavat to become the third city team to earn a semi final berth. Boro had to fight hard to see off a stubborn Mullinavat in this replay at Callan. Having scored the equalising free in the drawn game, Shane Stapleton was to the fore again, shooting three late points as Dicksboro led 2-18 to 2-16. The city side roared out of the traps and stormed ahead as goals from Oisin Gough and Robbie Fitzpatrick helped them take a 3-5 to 0-5 lead in the first quarter. However, Mullinavat were no slouches either. John Walsh blasted a goal in a purple patch that yielded 1-4 but Dicksboro were back in front by half time (2-7 to 1-9). The game was tight in the second half, but Mullinavat crept ahead with Liam Fennelly bagged a 52nd minute goal (2-14 to 2-12). Mullinavat had stayed in touch throughout and were now two points clear with eight minutes remaining, but the city side refused to panic. The pressure was on Dicksboro, but they kept calm, Stapleton getting their late run of points, including the equaliser from a 60th minute free that turned things their way.'

Mullinavat: Jim Culleton, Joe Fennelly, Tom Aylward (0-2 frees), Paudie Gahan, Robbie Malone, Simon Aylward, Mark Mansfield (0-1), Michael Malone, Willie O'Dwyer, Ger Malone (0-2), Ian Duggan (0-8, 0-6 frees, 0-2"65s"), Liam Fennelly (1-0), Jamie Fennelly, John Walsh (1-3) and Joe Gahan. Subs - Darren Kenneally for J Gahan (31 minutes), Adam Mansfield for J Fennelly (54 minutes).

2018
SENIOR

SHL R1: Mullinavat 4-18; James Stephens 0-12
SHL R2: Mullinavat 1-18; Carrickshock 1-15
SHL R3: Mullinavat 2-17; Clara 0-16
SHL R4: Dicksboro 2-22; Mullinavat 1-12
SHL R5: Mullinavat 2-14; St Patrick's 1-17

SHC First Round: Mullinavat 2-14; Rower-Inistioge 0-16
SHC Quarter Final: Bennetsbridge 1-17; Mullinavat 2-08

'A teak tough defence and a smart forward line proved to be a winning combination as Bennetsbridge advanced to the Senior Championship semi finals with a six-point win over Mullinavat, 1-17 to 2-8. The former Junior and Intermediate All-Ireland champions had to do it the hard way, coming from four points down at half time (2-6 to 0-8), but were sent on their way when Austin Cleere recorded a quick 1-1 after the restart. Mullinavat fared well in the opening half, scoring goals through Jamie Fennelly and goalkeeper James Culleton (penalty). With John Walsh in point scoring form, they impressed but could only score two points in the second half as a wind assisted Bennetsbridge took over. Aidan Cleere (1-6) and Nicky Cleere (0-5) did most of the damage, while Robert Lennon led the way in what was a strong defensive performance from the winners.'

Mullinavat: James Culleton (1-0, penalty), Pauric Gahan, Joe Fennelly, Daren Kenneally, Robbie Malone, Michael Malone, Ian Duggan, Ger Malone, Mark Mansfield, Jamie Fennelly (1-0), Willie O'Dwyer, Adam Mansfield, John Walsh (0-8, 0-6 frees), Liam Fennelly and Oisin Knox. Subs - Simon Aylward for Gahan (39 minutes), Joe Gahan for Knox (52 minutes), Michael Murphy for J Fennelly (58 minutes).

2019
SENIOR

SHL R1: O'Loughlin Gaels 2-21; Mullinavat 2-12
SHL R2: Mullinavat 0-24; James Stephens 0-18
SHL R3: Mullinavat 4-12; Bennetsbridge 1-21
SHL R4: Mullinavat 2-12; Shamrocks 1-14
SHL R5: Clara 1-18; Mullinavat 1-16

SHC First Round: Graigue Ballycallan 1-10; Mullinavat 0-13
SHC First Round Replay: Mullinavat 1-18; Graigue Ballycallan 1-13
SHC Quarter Final: O'Loughlin Gaels 0-12; Mullinavat 0-12
SHC Quarter Final Replay: O'Loughlin Gaels 1-14; Mullinavat 0-13

'It was far from the perfect effort, but O'Loughlin Gaels have been searching for a performance of merit that might kick on their season, and that might just have unearthed it here. This seriously competitive SHC quarter final against well versed Mullinavat took a bit of winning. Three unanswered points deep in injury time from the gutsy Danny Loughnane, sub Cian Loy and ace marksman Mark Bergin after taking a short, smart delivery from cool goalie Stephen Murphy, before hitting the target from 85 metres, won the match for O'Loughlin's. At that stage Mullinavat had been reduced to 14 men after their great servant and massive performer, Willie O'Dwyer had been red carded. It wasn't necessarily the difference in numbers that turned things. By the time O'Loughlin's had attained such a high pitch of energy and efficiency that momentum and their good hurling saw them through. Apart from John Walsh and Willie O'Dwyer Mullinavat lacked natural scorers which hurt.'

Mullinavat: Mikey Jones, Joe Fennelly, Tom Aylward (0-1, free), Darren Kenneally, Robert Malone, Michael Malone (0-1), Pauric Dempsey (0-1), Mark Mansfield, Ian Duggan (0-2), Jamie Fennelly, Ger Malone (0-1), Adam Mansfield (0-1), Joe Gahan (0-1), John Walsh (0-3, 2 frees) and Willie O'Dwyer (0-2). Subs: Oisin Knox, Brian Phelan, Conor Duggan.

2020
SENIOR

SHL R1: Mullinavat 0-20; Erin's Own 1-17
SHL R2: Mullinavat 1-15; Rower Inistioge 0-18
SHL R3: Mullinavat 0-18; Graigue Ballycallan 0-13

SHC First Round: Mullinavat 5-27; Danesfort 1-25
SHC Quarter Final: James Stephens 1-21; Mullinavat 1-16

'In the most competitive of the 2020 County Senior hurling quarter finals, James Stephens qualified for the Kilkenny SHC semi finals with a five-point victory over Mullinavat on 6/09/2020 at Nowlan Park. Eoin Guilfoyle led the way with three late points, one from a free, as the Village held back a late Mullinavat comeback to win by five points, 1-21 to 1-16. In front from early on a Niall Brassil penalty and five Cian Kenny points left Cheddar Plunkett's men eight points up at halftime. The Vat reduced the margin considerably with a John Walsh goal leaving them breathing down James Stephens' backs, but Guilfoyle's late scoring burst helped the Village to advance.'

Mullinavat: Sean Fitzpatrick, Padraic Gahan, Tom Aylward, Darren Kenneally, Robbie Malone, Michael Malone (0-1), Simon Aylward, Ger Malone, Mark Mansfield, Padraig Dempsey (0-2), Willie O'Dwyer (0-2), Ian Duggan (0-2), Oisin Knox, Liam Fennelly, and John Walsh (1-9, 7 frees, 1 "65"). Subs: Brian Phelan, Adam Mansfield, Joe Gahan, Conor Walsh.

2021
SENIOR

SHL R1: Clara 1-26; Mullinavat 1-15
SHL R2: Mullinavat 1-19; O'Loughlin Gaels 2-13
SHL R3: Mullinavat 2-22; Erin's Own 2-16
Shield Final: James Stephens 2-21; Mullinavat 1-15

SHC Quarter Final: O'Loughlin Gaels 2-19; Mullinavat 0-19

'O'Loughlin's were the first team to book a place in the Senior championship semi finals when they beat Mullinavat by 2-10 to 0-19 on Saturday 9/10/2021. An explosive first quarter performance was key to much of the city side's success. They made a dream start, defender turned forward Paddy Deegan grabbing an early goal that helped push the side into a 1-2 to 0-2 lead inside five minutes. They kept the advantage thanks to a fine save from Stephen Murphy and points from Jack Nolan and Jordan Molloy. They strengthened their grip of the tie just before the water break. Mark Bergin grabbing a second goal after some fine work from Owen Wall as the Gaels opened up a five-point gap (2-4 to 0-5). With Bergin (2) and Deegan to the fore O'Loughlin's maintained their lead, but three John Walsh frees and two points from Ger Malone meant Mullinavat were still in the reckoning by halftime (2-9 to 0-10).'

'Mullinavat made a good start to the third quarter and had closed the gap to two points by the 45th minute (2-11 to 0-15), John Walsh (0-3) leading the way before a Mark Bergin free gave O'Loughlin's some breathing space (2-12 to 0-15). Bergin was a steadying influence, adding two more frees to cancel out more Walsh scores as the game moved into the last ten minutes. Mullinavat continued to look for a way back but couldn't find the space needed to trouble net minder Murphy. O'Loughlin's closed the match out, Bergin (free) and Paddy Butler on target in a polished display.'

Mullinavat: Sean Fitzpatrick, Michael Walsh, Robbie Malone, Joe Fennelly, Simon Aylward, Michael Malone, Pauric Gahan (0-2, 0-1 free), Ger Malone (0-3), Adam Mansfield (0-2), Joe Gahan, Brian Phelan, Bill Dempsey, Liam Fennelly, Willie O'Dwyer (0-1) and John Walsh (0-10, 0-6 frees, 0-1"65"). Sub: Padraic Dempsey (0-1) for Phelan (40 minutes).

2022
SENIOR

SHL R1: Lisdowney 2-15; Mullinavat 0-12
SHL R2: Shamrocks 1-26; Mullinavat 1-13
SHL R3: Mullinavat 2-18; Tullaroan 1-17
SHL R4: Mullinavat 1-20; Clara 0-19
SHL R5: Mullinavat 2-12; Erin's Own 1-18

SHC R1: Mullinavat 3-09; O'Loughlin Gaels 1-14
SHC Quarter Final: Dicksboro 3-19; Mullinavat 1-11

'A blistering start paved the way for Dicksboro as they claimed a 14-point victory over Mullinavat in the quarter finals of the Senior hurling championship at UPMC Nowlan Park on Sunday 25/9/2022. From the moment Timmy Clifford found the net within 20 seconds it was mainly plain sailing for the winners, and with Andy Gaffney scoring 1-13, they can move into the semi finals with plenty of confidence. Dicksboro didn't have to be brilliant to advance either. After beating O'Loughlin Gaels a week earlier, it was a very disappointing performance from a Mullinavat side that was always chasing their tail. Of

Mullinavat's 1-11 tally, only 1-4 of it came from play. In essence that lack of cutting edge up front was largely the difference between the sides. Mullinavat have largely struggled when playing in UPMC Nowlan Park in recent years and their mood wouldn't have improved when Clifford netted in the opening minute after Mark Nolan found the youngster in space and he finished to the top corner in style. Andy Gaffney then knocked over three successive points from play and almost in the blink of an eye, the city side went 1-3 to 0-0 ahead within six minutes of play.'

'John Walsh scored 1-7 in total for Mullinavat, and he got his side off the mark with an eighth minute free but despite playing against the breeze they looked in a bit of bother when Gaffney converted successive frees. The Boro led by seven at that stage and while Mullinavat replied with efforts from play by Ger Malone and Padraig Dempsey, it didn't affect the city side all too much as Gaffney, Clifford and Liam Moore added to a scoreboard which read 1-9 to 0-3 in favour of the winners. Walsh and Dempsey briefly kept in touch but when Liam Moore goaled on the other side of a brace of frees from Gaffney, the game looked done as Dicksboro went into the dressing rooms leading by 2-11 to 0-5.'

'Like Dicksboro in the opening half, Mullinavat got in for an early goal chance on the resumption. John Walsh had two attempts to score but after his first effort was blocked, Boro goalkeeper Darragh Holohan then saved well to deny him as he helped the sliotar past the post. While Walsh knocked over the subsequent 65, Gaffney then cancelled it out with a long distance free. Mullinavat did look a lot livelier than they were in the first 30 minutes and Walsh got his reward with a goal in the 33rd minute. The former Kilkenny Minor star then knocked over another free to reduce the gap to eight points before the turning point of the half arrived when Walsh again broke free after being released by Ger Malone, but Holohan stood tall to deny the Mullinavat corner-forward. A goal there would have reduced the gap to five points and with a bit of momentum behind them Mullinavat may have fancied their chances, but after Holohan's save they defeated side only scored four more points in the remainder of the game. In contrast, Dicksboro scored 1-7 in the final quarter as they eased clear of Mullinavat on the scoreboard.'

Mullinavat: Sean Fitzpatrick; George O'Connor, Tom Aylward, Simon Aylward; Rob Malone, Michael Malone, Padraic Gahan; Padraig Dempsey (0-2), Brian Phelan; Adam Mansfield, Willie O'Dwyer, Ian Duggan; Ger Malone (0-2), Liam Fennelly and John Walsh (1-7, 0-6 frees, 0-1 65). Subs: Conor Walsh for Phelan, 52 mins; Mikey Jones for Fennelly, 52 mins; Peter McDonald for R Malone, 56 mins; Robin Davis for Mansfield, 59 mins.

2023
SENIOR

SHL R1: Mullinavat 0-24; Danesfort 0-16
SHL R2: Tullaroan 6-21; Mullinavat 1-09
SHL R3: O'Loughlin Gaels 1-15; Mullinavat 1-10
SHL R4: Dicksboro 2-20; Mullinavat 1-19
SHL R5: Clara 4-19; Mullinavat 1-15

SHC R1: Mullinavat 4-11; Erin's Own 0-10
SHC Quarter Final: O'Loughlin Gaels 0-18; Mullinavat 2-10

'O'Loughlin Gaels' third quarter dominance, in which they scored eight consecutive points without reply, proved most decisive as they overturned a five point half-time deficit to lead by three points before running out eventual winners following late points by Jordan Molloy and Sean Bolger. However, Mullinavat were dominant throughout the first half and displaying great desire and determination, they deservedly built up a seven-point lead by the 25th minute with John Walsh on target with five points from placed balls – including a point from a 65 – to lead 1-7 to 0-3 as himself and Oisin Knox were proving a thorn in the O'Loughlin's defence. The goal came in the 9th minute as Oisin Knox kicked the sliotar to the net following great work by Ger Malone. Ger Malone was excellent throughout the opening-half as he did trojan work around midfield, and his point from play in the 24th minute was deserved for his magnificent efforts. Oisin Knox also added a point from play in the 16th minute, while Joe Gahan was on target in the 29th minute as the South Kilkenny men led 1-8 to 0-6 at half time. Mark Bergin scored 0-4 – three from placed balls – throughout the opening-half as they stayed in touch at the interval.'

'Brian Hogan's charges were an entirely different proposition during the second half as they came out with all guns blazing. Mark Bergin pointed another free, before wing back David Fogarty – who was one of O'Loughlin Gaels better players in the first half – surged upfield to score two glorious points from long distance in quick succession, as just two points separated them, 1-8 to 0-9. Further points came from another Mark Bergin free; Paddy Butler and Bergin as the O'Loughlin men now took the outright lead in the 40th minute (0-12 to 1-8).

Inter-county Senior All Star Mikey Butler led the way for O'Loughlin Gaels throughout the second half with a highly immaculate display, as he regularly thundered forward out of defence. His monster point from play from about 100 yards – his own 45 metre line – was hugely inspirational, and when goalkeeper Stephen Murphy pointed a long free from a similar distance, they appeared to be in total control heading into the closing quarter as they now led 0-14 to 1-8.'

'However, Mullinavat got an unexpected lifeline totally against the run of play in the 44th minute. A long ball was sent in towards the O'Loughlin Gaels' goal, and Oisin Knox managed to flick the sliotar beyond the advancing Stephen Murphy to bring them level, 0-14 to 2-8. Only six scores came throughout that final quarter as O'Loughlin Gaels outscored Mullinavat 0-4 to 0-2. Both Mark Bergin and John Walsh exchanged a brace of points each between the 45th and 52nd minutes, with both players on target from play and placed balls. With less than three minutes remaining, the teams were level (0-16 to 2-10) and extra-time appeared to be an increasing possibility. However, Jordan Molloy struck over a great point to give the O'Loughlin men the lead once again in the 58th minute following a surging run upfield by Mikey Butler, while a puckout from Mullinavat goalkeeper Sean Fitzpatrick went straight to Sean Bolger and he calmly slotted over the bar as they went on to grind out a hard fought victory and march towards the semi finals.'

Mullinavat: Sean Fitzpatrick; George O'Connor, Tom Aylward, Robin Davis; Ian Duggan, Michael Malone, Padraic Gahan; Padraig Dempsey, Joe Gahan (0-1); Ger Malone (0-1), Willie O'Dwyer, Adam Mansfield; John Walsh (0-7, 0-4 frees, 0-2"65s"), Liam Fennelly and Oisin Knox (2-1).

COVID 19 & the Kilkenny SHC

2020 was constantly referred to as 'a year like no other'.

On 12th March 2020 the GAA announced the lockdown of all activity including matches and training with immediate effect. What started out as a short-term measure for a number of weeks would last until the ban on training was lifted on 29th June. So, we had the unprecedented situation of having to lock our gates for over three months and not allow anyone to use the pitches. For a while it seemed as if we would see no GAA games at all, but thankfully the lockdown restrictions were eased, and action resumed. The lockdown forced the GAA to radically restructure the playing season and the clubs were given a condensed but very welcome playing season, which was to last from August until October, when the inter-county season restarted.

However, one of the conditions meant that spectator numbers would be monitored, and clubs were initially restricted to 100 spectators per game. This would be further restricted as the year progressed, until eventually matches were played behind closed doors. For supporters of clubs such as Mullinavat this was a cruel blow which was to some extent compensated by streaming of our games. The Kilkenny County Board organised live streaming of all Senior games played in Nowlan Park, and our club organised private streaming of some games when required.

The league stage of the championship was diluted to three games per club, and the Kilkenny knockout championship itself consisted of just 14 games. Few people saw very many of these games due to an outright ban on spectators in the early phases, mitigated to a maximum of 200 as the restrictions eased.

Although only a few short years ago, it is worth recalling the Mullinavat GAA year of 2020.

ST. CANICE'S CREDIT UNION
MLM MICHAEL LYNG MOTORS
J.J. Kavanagh & Sons
KILKENNY GAA ADMISSION TICKET
St. Canice's Credit Union Senior Hurling League
MULLINAVAT
versus
ROWER INISTIOGE
FRIDAY 7th AUGUST at 7.15pm
Venue:
THOMASTOWN
TICKET €5
Ticket No: 183
Cill Chainnigh

ST. CANICE'S CREDIT UNION
MLM MICHAEL LYNG MOTORS
J.J. Kavanagh & Sons
KILKENNY GAA ADMISSION TICKET
St. Canice's Credit Union Senior Hurling League
GRAIGUE BALLYCALLAN
versus
MULLINAVAT
(Match Being Streamed Live)
SATURDAY 15th AUGUST at 3.30pm
Venue:
UPMC NOWLAN PARK
TICKET €5
Ticket No: 159
Cill Chainnigh

'The closing five minutes of this game was as frantic and exciting as any supporter is ever likely to witness. This was a full-blooded encounter with both teams going all out for victory in front of a partisan crowd inside St. Lowman's Park, Mullingar on Sunday... Willie O'Dwyer stepped up to a free 70 yards from the goal on the sideline and with the Raharney supporters in full voice, he coolly slotted the ball over the black spot, to push his team a point ahead.'

2006
Leinster IHC R1
Raharney (Westmeath) 2-9;
Mullinavat 1-11

Leinster Hurling Campaigns

2006

INTERMEDIATE

Leinster IHC R1: Raharney (Westmeath) 2-09: Mullinavat 1-11

'The closing five minutes of this game was a frantic and exciting as any supporter is ever likely to witness. This was a full-blooded encounter with all teams going all out for victory in front of a partisan crowd inside St Lowman's Park, Mullingar on Sunday 12/11/2006. First Raharney corner forward Niall Flanigan took the paint off the Mullinavat left-hand upright with a screamer of a shot from the 21-yard line with the sides locked as 1-9 each. Then in the 58th minutes, Willie O'Dwyer stepped up to a free 70 yards from the goal on the sideline and with the Raharney supporters in full voice, he coolly slotted the ball over the black spot, to push his team a point ahead. From the puck out the ball was played into impressive substitute Paddy Raftice, who kept his composure to pass to Michael Murphy, who pointed. Two points in thirty seconds gave Mullinavat a winning look. But Raharney continued to battle, and when a Mullinavat player spilled the ball in midfield, they shifted the sliotair quickly into the Mullinavat goalmouth. Francis Boyle spoiled dashed out and caught the ball, turning quickly the Raharney number 11 forced the visitors defence to commit a foul, just outside the 21-yard line. The clock registered 60 minutes of play. Centre back Brian Connaughton was summoned to take the free and he hit an unstoppable shot past five defenders on the goal line. The place erupted with the Raharney supporters screams of joy. There was still another minute of action, but significantly it was the winners who kept possession and never allowed the visitors get beyond the halfway line in the 60 seconds that remained.'

'This was as hard and exciting a game as one could ask, without any rancour or malice. The tackling was ferocious, and the work rate of both teams was brilliant. Mullinavat will be very disappointed to go home empty handed after this clash, although they never reached the hurling heights of their county final display eight days earlier. Despite being at odds with their game, they look to have done enough to win the game until that sensational last score.'

'Raharney opened brightly with three unanswered point, a Brian Smith free, and points from play by Brendan McKeogh and John Shaw. Willie O'Dwyer opened Mullinavat's account in the tenth minute with a pointed free, but John Shaw availed of a poor free from the visitor's defence, to point from to put the home team ahead 0-4 to 0-1 after 14 minutes of play. Paul Aylward and Nicholas Anthony landed great scores from distance to bring the Vat men back into it, without ever really hurling well. John Shaw had a point from a place ball, before Dinny Butler and a Michael Murphy free levelled the game in the 23rd minute. Mullinavat were improving, and a long-range free was fielded by Michael Duggan, who was quickly grounded, and the referee Brian Gavin awarded a penalty. Willie O'Dwyer planted the ball in the back of the net. However the referee awarded two soft frees to the Westmeath champions, which saw Brian Connaughton convert one for 80 yards, and dropped the other one short from a similar distance, as Mullinavat went in 1-5 to 0-6 ahead at the break.'

'Michael Murphy planted a free for the Mullinavat men in the 32nd minute, and five minutes later John Shaw landed a reply for the winners, to leave the minimum between the sides. Jamie Fennelly was fouled as he bore down on goal and Murphy pointed. A quick reply from Brian Smith reduced the arrears again, and then the Mullinavat men last position in midfield, which saw the ball send goal wards, with Francis Boyle fielding on the 14-yard line, and kick to the net in the 38th minute, 1-8 to Mullinavat's 1-7. Centre-back Walter Burke was hurling up a storm all through for Mullinavat, and he literally kept his team in the game in times of crisis. Substitute Paddy Raftice hit a point from the left wing on the 21-yard line, and Michael Murphy pointed a free, to put the Mullinavat men back in front 19 to 1-8 after 51 minutes of play. Raharney switched full back Paul Greville to full forward, and he set up Francis Boyle to level the game, with six minutes remaining. Then came the dramatic closing five minutes, which saw the Westmeath men turn certain defeat into a sensational victory, was virtually the last puck of the game.'

Mullinavat: PJ Aylward; Tony Duggan, Ger Anthony, Seamus Farrell; Kevin Aylward, Walter Burke, Tomas Frisby; Paul Aylward, Liam Murphy; Michael Duggan, Dinny Butler (0-1), Nicky Anthony (0-1); Willie O'Dwyer (1-2, frees), Michael Murphy (0-5, 4 frees), Jamie Fennelly. Sub: Paddy Raftice (0-1).

2014
INTERMEDIATE
Leinster IHC Semi Final: Mullinavat 2-19; Coill Dubh (Kildare) 1-08

'Mullinavat scored an easier than expected victory over Kildare Senior champions Coill Dubh in a one-sided Leinster club Intermediate hurling championship clash at St Conleth's Park, Newbridge on Sunday 16/11/2014. The Kilkenny champions took control from the start and were rarely troubled. The forward line was brilliantly led by captain Willie O'Dwyer, whose work rate was exemplary. Mullinavat led after 50 seconds when a county minor, John Walsh pointed after a good pass from O'Dwyer. Willie then set up Ian Duggan for another point in the second minute. Mullinavat were totally dominant at this stage, and Jamie Fennelly finished to the net in the fifth minute after great work by Liam Fennelly and Ger Malone. The winners could afford the luxury of shooting five wides by the 10th minute before they got on the scoresheet again when Willie O'Dwyer found Ian Duggan with a pass for another point. John Walsh then set off on a searing run and Coill Dubh' keeper, Damien Byrne did well to party his shot, but Jamie Fennelly was alert and finished the ball to the net for his second goal. Robbie Malone got on the scoresheet with a fine point. Coill Dubh were finding it hard to get any traction, but Mark Delaney got them off the mark when he pointed a free in the 16th minute. The visitors replied with points from Ger Malone and John Walsh. Mark Delaney pointed another free and Jonathan Byrne finished off a good Coill Dubh movement with their third point in the 25th minute. Mullinavat were in control with Pauric Gahan and Thomas Aylward marshalling the defence. Pauraic found Jamie Fennelly with a well-placed delivery and Jamie pointed. Joe Fennelly found Willie O'Dwyer with a great clearance and Willie pointed. Damien Behan and Ger Malone exchanged points just before the break, at which stage they led by 2-9 to 0-4.'

'Coill Dubh began the second half in determined fashion. They opened with points from Jonathon and Thomas Byrne. Mullinavat keeper, James Culleton had to be alerted to keep out a whistling shot as Coill Dubh upped their game. Great work from Willie O'Dwyer set up Ger Malone for another point in the 35th minute. From the puck out Coill Dubh went on the attack and were rewarded with a 20-metre free. Mark Delaney's low shot squeezed past the Vat defence. The home side suddenly looked threatening. The winners sensed the danger and took control again. Ian Duggan and Dinny Butler took a grip on midfield and Mullinavat reeled off nine points, before Coill Dubh added to their tally. Paddy Raftice, who was a half time replacement for Jamie Fennelly, started the sequence. Willie O'Dwyer added a brace, Ian Duggan, Paddy Raftice, Simon Aylward ("65") shot fine efforts before Joe Fahan and John Walsh (free) saw the Vat home.'

Mullinavat: James Culleton; Joe Fennelly, Thomas Alyward, Seamus Farrell; Robbie Malone 0-1), Padraic Gahan, Simon Aylward (0-1, "65"); Dinny Butler, Ian Duggan (0-3); Joe Gahan (0-2), Ger Malone (0-3), Liam Fennelly; Jamie Fennelly (2-1), Willie O'Dwyer (0-3) and John Walsh (0-3, 1 free). Subs: Paddy Raftice (0-2), Brian Phelan, Darren Kenneally, Pat Mulhearne, Adam Mansfield.

Leinster IHC Final: Mullinavat 1-13(16); Kiltale (Meath) 0-13

'Jamie Fennelly's goal two minutes before half-time proved the difference as Mullinavat took the title at Pairc Tailteann. In an absorbing contest, the Kilkenny men were pushed all the way by the Meath standard-bearers, who belied their tag of rank outsiders. Kiltale started in determined mood and had raced into a three-point lead within six minutes. Jack Regan, named Meath hurler of the year recently, got the hosts off the mark from a free. He added another point from play shortly after captain Peter Durnin had hit the target. Liam Fennelly opened Mullinavat's account and minor star John Walsh and Thomas Alyward, from a long-range free, left the sides level on 13 minutes. Joe Gahan pointed the visitors ahead for the first time but that score prompted Kiltale to raise their game again and they hit back with three more points in succession, including two from county football panellist Mark O'Sullivan. With five-times All-Ireland medal winner Willie O'Dwyer switching from full-forward to the '40' Mullinavat were a much more potent force and dominated proceedings in the 10 minutes before half-time. They outscored their opponents 1-4 to a single point during that productive spell to enjoy a 1-8 to 0-7 interval advantage.'

'The crucial goal came when Jamie Fennelly latched onto a long delivery and rounded his marker before blasting to the net from close range. Fennelly had come close on two earlier occasions to finding the Kiltale net. Kiltale produced a rousing second-half display and closed the gap to two points on four separate occasions. However, Mullinavat had the ability to respond almost every time Kiltale got a score and with John Walsh and O'Dwyer getting vital points, they held out for a deserved win.'

Mullinavat: James Culleton; Joe Fennelly, T Alyward (0-2, 2 frees), Seamus Farrell; Robbie Malone, Padraic Gahan, Simon Alyward; Dinny Butler, Ian Duggan (0-1), Joe Gahan (0-1), Ger Malone, Liam Fennelly (0-2); Jamie Fennelly (1-0), Willie O'Dwyer (0-2) and John Walsh 0-5 (3fs, 1 '65'). Sub: B Phelan for Duggan (58).

All Ireland IHC Quarter Final: Kilburn Gaels 1-10; Mullinavat 1-08

'Mullinavat's quest for an All-Ireland club title came to an end in cold and uninviting Ruislip on Saturday. The game Kilkenny Intermediate hurling champions were defeated by Kilburn Gaels (London) after a tense well contested match. Kilburn led from the second minute, and they were never headed. Their lead stretched to seven points at the three-quarter stage, and they had enough resolve to see off a determined late charge from the Rod Iron men to run out deserving winners. Mullinavat will have huge regrets. Their first half performance hurt them, because they racked up nine wides. When all the figures were added up at the finish, the "misses tally" stood out for all the wrong reasons. A heavy overnight frost made the Ruislip pitch extremely testing. The Gaels adapted better to the conditions. Their more direct approach yielded a better dividend, and Mullinavat were guilty of over elaborating at times. The grassy and slippery underfoot conditions made it extremely difficult to play skilful hurling, and despite referee Eamonn Hassan's best efforts to keep the game moving, the action never flowed.'

'Kilburn registered on the scoreboard in the second minute when Stephen Lambert pointed. He added a second point a minute later. Mullinavat's first score came in the fifth minute when Ian Duggan sideline ball was grabbed by Jamie Fennelly who put the ball over the bar. The visitors began to find their feet, but their good approach work was not reflected on the scoreboard. They drove three bad wides during the following few minutes. Stephen Lambert punished any indiscretions in the Vat defence with excellent free taking. He nabbed his third point from a free in the 13th minute. Mullinavat grabbed a much-needed point from a John Walsh free after 21 minutes. Liam Fennelly, who was Mullinavat's best forward, showed great vision to pick out Willie O'Dwyer, who levelled the game in the 23rd minute. Stephen Lambert converted a free to restore Kilburn Gaels lead. Back came Mullinavat. Padraic Gahan send a perfect delivery to Willie O'Dwyer, who levelled the game in the 26th minute. Kilburn edged in front just before the break with a point from their danger man Stephen Lambert. Half time score: Kilburn Gaels 0-5; Mullinavat 0-4.'

'Neither side could get a foothold during the opening minutes of the second half. The strong low Winter sun was shining into the Mullinavat goal. In the 37th minute a long range shot from Stephen Lambert was dropped by a Vat player, and Kilburn grabbed a fortuitous goal. They snatched the initiative when adding three unanswered points, one from Keith Killilea and two frees from Stephen Lambert within minutes to race into a commanding seven-point lead as the match entered the final quarter. Mullinavat were in trouble, but they responded gamely, just as they have done throughout the championship. John Walsh, now operating at wing forward, led the comeback. He foraged deep inside his own half and set off in determined fashion towards the Kilburn goal; leaving two defenders in his wake he soloed 50 metres to shoot an inspirational point. Mullinavat won a free which was brought forward for dissent and again John Walsh pointed. Kilburn responded and when Mark O'Dwyer broke through the Mullinavat defence a goal looked certain, but 'keeper James Culleton saved brilliantly. Pauraic Gahan, who was outstanding, found John Walsh with an excellent delivery and John fired over to reduce the gap to four points. In the 53rd minute a long delivery from Brian Phelan was grabbed by Willie O'Dwyer and he finished to the net. There was now a single point separating the sides with seven minutes of normal time left. Kilburn Gaels went on the attack and were awarded a free which Stephen Lambert pointed. Back came Mullinavat. Pauraic Gahan found Liam Fennelly with a long delivery, but Kilburn keeper Kris Finnegan made an excellent save. Kilburn were not going to be denied. Martin Duggan pointed in the 58th minute to put three between the sides. Brian Phelan found Willie O'Dwyer with a long ball, but Willie's rising shot went just over the crossbar. Normal time was up, three minutes of injury time was announced. Mullinavat went in search of a big score. They forced a free 30 metres out. John Walsh went for broke; his shot was saved, and Kilburn had done enough. The Londoners held out for a deserved victory. Mullinavat's great run had come to an end.'

Mullinavat: J Culleton; Joe Fennelly, T Alyward, S Farrell; R Malone, P Gahan, S Alyward; D Butler, I Duggan; J Gahan, G Malone, L Fennelly; Jamie Fennelly (0-1), W O'Dwyer (1-3), J Walsh (0-4, 2 frees). Subs: Mark Mansfield, Brian Phelan.

Best Mullinavat Hurling XV

1970-2024

Choosing a 'Greatest XV' list of any era was never going to be a straightforward task.

Throughout this book we have covered the teams who represented the parish in hurling, Gaelic football, camogie and handball. Although this club history spans decades, I have decided to select a best Mullinavat XV from personal experience.

Unlike choosing all time county teams, lack of video and statistical evidence immediately makes this task a little difficult. Furthermore, the hurling game of today is almost unrecognisable from what it used to be in the 1970s, when players participated more in tournaments than county championships. It also has to be noted that in terms of preparation, fitness levels, training methods, what happens 'today' is a distance away from 'yesterday'. The 'pain in the leg' of 1970 is probably the same thing as the 'hamstring' of today.

Training nowadays is more intense, fitness levels are much higher, the rules have undergone several changes, scores are much more frequent in games also – as the sliothar nowadays is both lighter and therefore travels further and at greater speed.

Even positions have evolved massively over the 50 years period we are looking back at here. The days of 15 players taking to the field and matching up with their opposing 15 for the entire game 'mano a mano' are long gone. In the 70s and 80s games, if a member of a full-back line wandered up-field as they do nowadays, they would probably be substituted quite quickly. Contrast that to today's game.

THE DREAM TEAM

★ JOHN DUNPHY

★ ANDY AYLWARD ★ PAUDIE HOLDEN ★ THOMAS AYLWARD

★ JOE WALSH ★ WALTER BURKE ★ MICHAEL MALONE

★ MICHAEL DUNPHY ★ IAN DUGGAN

★ MICHAEL MURPHY ★ PAT HOBAN ★ JOHN McDONALD

★ WILLIE O'DWYER ★ MOSSY MURPHY ★ JOHN WALSH

THE AUTHOR'S CHOSEN FIFTEEN FROM 1970-2024

1

JOHN DUNPHY

IN PICKING A Mullinavat team from 1970 onwards, John is selected as our No. 1. John was a top-class goalie and was a main reason why the club advanced through the grades, from Junior through to Intermediate, and eventually onwards to Senior. As a 19-year-old, back in 1984, the man who hails from 'Dunphy's Mill', guarded the net as the club ended a Junior title famine going back to 1939. John won Leinster and All-Ireland Under 21 hurling medals in the GAA centenary year (1984), Leinster Junior and All-Ireland hurling medals with the county from 1986, 1988 and 1990, and three Kilkenny Intermediate hurling medals with Mullinavat in 1989, 2001 and 2006 (as a 42-year-old substitute).

2

ANDY AYLWARD

ANDY FIRST CAME to prominence as a 16-year-old half back substitute in a narrow 1966 South Minor final loss to Ballyhale. Andy was a midfielder in the losing county Junior finals in 1974 and 1978, before featuring as left full back in that never to be forgotten Junior victory in 1984. Five years later, when the club won their first Intermediate title in 1989, as a 39-year-old, Andy still retained the same position. Andy also won a Kilkenny Junior football medal with Bigwood back in 1979. After retiring, Andy still had not put his 'hurl' away, featuring on the Kilkenny Over-40s Masters selections in three All-Ireland finals; a loss in 1994 v. Tipperary, followed by All-Ireland final successes in 1997 v. Wexford and 1998 v. Tipperary. Andy Aylward is a huge part of the Mullinavat club, an active member all his life, and a highly respected former Southern Board chairman. The family are steeped in club history with his dad, Pat Aylward, captain of the 1939 Mullinavat county Junior winning team.

3
PAUDIE HOLDEN

PAUDIE WAS A really tight defender who featured on the Mullinavat Junior winning side (1984) and the club's first Intermediate winning side (1989). Paudie is another steeped in hurling heritage, with his uncles being the famous All-Ireland Senior winning Doyle brothers of Dournane, Mooncoin. The Mullinavat farmer, who hails from Knockbrown, was still playing as a 34-year-old in 1993 when the club contested its first county Senior hurling semi-final in 50 years. He was a 1976 Kilkenny Minor player, and later won All-Ireland Junior hurling medals in 1988 and 1990. In the latter one he became the first Mullinavat player to captain an All-Ireland winning Kilkenny side. Paudie also holds medals with the famed St Kieran's College.

4
THOMAS AYLWARD

THOMAS HAS FEATURED in almost all Mullinavat hurling and Gaelic football successes of the past 14 or so years, having joined the Intermediate panel as a 17-year-old in 2010. When the club won the 2011 Minor B title, Thomas was full-back and two years later when Mullinavat won its only county Under-21 A title in 2013 he was in the same position. For the following year's Intermediate success, and ever since, Thomas has been the club's No.3. He helped Mullinavat to a Leinster Club Intermediate title in 2014 and won Leinster and All-Ireland Intermediate medals on 2016. He featured on the 2018 Kilkenny Senior panel that won that year's National Hurling League.

5
JOE WALSH

JOE HAD A really successful career for both club and county. As a 19-year-old he featured at midfield with Peter McDonald on the 1984 County Junior winning team. He also starred in the club's first two Intermediate title wins in 1989, again at midfield, and 12 years later in 2001 as a 36-year-old, now as a left full back. Joe was also a noted Kilkenny County hurler, he played Under 14 in 1979, and was a county Minor panellist at half-back in 1982 and 1983. At Under-21 in 1985, he showed his versatility as a corner forward, losing to Tipperary in that year's final at Walsh Park. Joe harshly blames himself for wasting a late goal chance in that Under 21 final. In 1988, he featured in the Kilkenny Junior hurling All-Ireland success v. Tipperary at Portlaoise, starting at centre forward. His career went both 'backwards and forwards' at the same time after that, both geographically and on the playing pitch. Joe went to Canada for veterinary studies in the late 1980s, but so important was he to the club, that he was flown back from there, for the business end of the successful 1989 Intermediate season. Joe made his Kilkenny Senior debut in May 1992 at the Shamrocks GAA club pitch opening v. Cork, and for the next four years he was a regular on the Kilkenny Senior panel. In 1993 Joe was involved in all Kilkenny's Leinster campaign, making his championship debut v. Offaly. He was considered quite unlucky not to get 'game-time' in that year's final. In 1994 and 1995, he was a regular starter, having slotted in for the likes of Eddie O'Connor, as some of the league/championship double winners of 92/93 had departed the county scene. He has also been involved in coaching both with our club and others in neighbouring counties. Joe Walsh had a distinguished career, many handball and hurling medals for both club and county, and is still noted as one of the best players to ever wear the Mullinavat jersey.

6

WALTER BURKE

WALTER HAD ESTABLISHED himself as a starter at right-half-back on the Mullinavat Intermediate team in 1999, as an 18-year-old, when they lost that year's county final to John Lockes. Walter then moved to the centre back position two years later as the club won its second Intermediate title. He was also involved in that year's County Under-21 B Final victory over Erin's Own, Castlecomer. He would go on to feature in the full-back position for the Intermediate victory in 2006, and was still there for the county final loss in 2010. Walter played as a right corner-back for the Kilkenny Senior team. In the period 2002-2004 Walter was a fixture on the County Senior hurling panel. He made several National Hurling League starts and was on the listed panel for both the All-Ireland semi-finals and All-Ireland finals of 2002, 2003 and 2004. During that time he won two All-Ireland winners medals as a non-playing substitute. He had joined the team during the

2002 championship and was a regular member of the squad until his retirement from inter-county hurling three seasons later. He played one SHC and 4 NHL games in the 2003 season. Walter was probably unlucky to be around in the era of JJ Delaney, Noel Hickey, Peter Barry, Michael Kavanagh and Tommy Walsh. Still though, 2 Leinster SHC, and two All-Ireland SHC medals, is a fair reward for this teak tough excellent defender. After finishing with the Seniors, Walter did some hurling with the Cats in the Intermediate grade from 2007-2009, including a half back line role in the 2009 All-Ireland final loss to Cork.

7

MICHAEL MALONE

MICHAEL CAME TO prominence at full-back when the club won the Roinn B Minor Hurling championship in 2006 versus Emeralds. He joined the Mullinavat Senior panel as a substitute in 2007. When Mullinavat reached their first ever County Junior A final in 2008 – a narrow loss to Clara – he was already established at centre back. He missed the 2014 Intermediate hurling final but has featured in several positions for our Senior team in recent years. A renowned footballer also, Michael has featured on both Senior county panels and holds a Leinster Senior hurling medal from 2016. Michael also won a Fitzgibbon Cup medal as a panellist with University of Limerick in 2011.

8

MICHAEL DUNPHY

THE DEERPARK NATIVE was a deadly accurate free taker for Mullinavat in the period 1987-2001. He featured at midfield in the 1987 Intermediate semi-final loss versus Graigue Ballycallan. Two years later came Michael's finest hour, the club's first Intermediate title in 1989. Michael was the unanimous choice as 'Man of the match', contributing 1-9 to his side's tally of 2-13, versus a star-studded Young Irelands, Gowran team. Michael put in a wonderful hour's hurling. He goaled from a penalty, pointed from two 65's, and also pointed five from frees and two further points from play. He was still going strong years later, in 1999, when, then a 32-year-old, he contributed 0-6 (0-4 frees, 0-1 play, 0-1 65) as we were beaten in the county final versus John Lockes. However, two years further on again, in the successful 2001 County Intermediate hurling final draw and replay versus Clara, he got 0-3 from frees in the drawn game, and 0-7 in the final replay (0-6 frees, 0-1 65s). At inter county level Michael featured for the 1990 Kilkenny All-Ireland Junior hurling winning side, scoring 1-4 (one free) in the final v. Tipperary.

9
IAN DUGGAN

IAN SHOWED EARLY promise as a member of the Kilkenny Under 14 Tony Forristal side in 2005. He was a starter with the Kilkenny Minor side in 2009, and a panellist on the Kilkenny Under 21 All-Ireland team in 2012. He also featured on the Kilkenny Intermediate panel in 2011, and later saw county action with the Senior panel. Ian won a County Minor B medal with Mullinavat in 2006, and has been an ever present on the Mullinavat Intermediate and Senior panels since 2008 in various positions, and holds an Intermediate medal from 2014. The schoolteacher also has numerous medals from Gaelic football, going back to his days as a student at Good Counsel, New Ross. Versatility to cover positions would be one of the main reasons why Ian features on this selection.

10
MICHAEL MURPHY

MICHAEL HAS ALWAYS been one of the top forward talents at the club. He was our top scorer with six points when the club won its second Kilkenny County Minor hurling Roinn B Final in 1988. He also featured on the county Minor panel that year. He was full forward the following year when the club won its second County Under-21B championship. When scoring 1-6 in the 2006 Intermediate final victory versus Clara, he was the standout forward and was rewarded with a place on the Kilkenny Senior hurling squad for 2007. Kilkenny went on to win that year's All-Ireland final and Michael got an All-Ireland Senior hurling medal. As a 30-year-old he was still effective in the 2010 campaign when we narrowly lost the County Intermediate final to Dicksboro. Michael was a versatile forward, and over the years played in all six forward positions for the club.

11

PAT HOBAN

PAT WILL BE remembered as a forward of note, and featured prominently on the Mullinavat Intermediate hurling winning sides of 1989 through to being a substitute on the 2001 Intermediate side. The big man took up central positions for the club over the years, namely centre back, centre forward and full forward. He first came to prominence at Juvenile and underage levels when representing Kilkenny with distinction at Under-14 in 1982, Minor in 1985 and 1986, and Under-21 grade in 1988. He was a substitute on the 1985 and 1986 Kilkenny Minor hurling team. Two years later in 1988 he won a Leinster medal with the Under 21 team as right full forward and played in that year's All-Ireland Under 21 final loss to Cork in 1988. On joining the Kilkenny Senior squad, he made a number of NHL appearances and was an unused substitute on the 1992 All-Ireland winning team. Hoban was also a two-time All-Ireland winner with the Kilkenny Junior team. Later, he was part of the Intermediate winning teams in 1989 and 2001. While Pat has a Senior All Ireland medal, from 1992, and has represented Kilkenny with distinction at Under-14, Minor and Under-21 grades, he has also built up an impressive CV as a Kilkenny Intermediate and Minor manager. Pat had his best year as a Kilkenny Senior hurler in 1992, and was part of the match day listed substitutes for that successful Leinster campaign, eventually winning an All-Ireland medal that year, along with club colleague Joe Walsh. Pat had also featured in NHL games and both Mullinavat men were selected for a winter 1992 game v. Cork in London. After his hurling club and county career ended, Pat got involved in hurling management. This led to the bank official being appointed Kilkenny Intermediate manager from 2007 to 2011. In this role, he led the Cats to All-Ireland wins in both 2008 and 2010. He advanced to the Minor manager position in 2013 and stayed in charge until 2016. One of the highlights of his management career to date was leading the Cats to All-Ireland victory in 2014 v. Limerick. In springing Mullinavat youngster John Walsh from the bench in the semi-final, and also starting him in the final, both proved master strokes. John finished MOTM with 2-05 in that final and Pat Hoban had justified his clubman's selection. In recent times he has been successful as manager of neighbouring club Shamrocks, Ballyhale.

12
JOHN MCDONALD

THE FIRST KILKENNY man to win a Junior All-Ireland, Under-21 hurling All-Ireland, and a county Junior championship all in the same year (1984). One of the few Kilkenny men to also line out in the Munster championship for Waterford (1987-1988). At club level John played in the 1988 Waterford Senior hurling final draw and replay for Ballygunner versus Mount Sion, in what was (hard to believe nowadays) the Gunner's first final in 20 years. John, from Ballynooney, was one of the best ever players to wear the black and white jersey of Mullinavat, and even though he went to Ballygunner and Waterford, it was always predicted that he would end up back with Mullinavat and Waterford, and so he did! The following year of 1989 when Mullinavat won the Intermediate County final, the Kilkenny People reported: 'John McDonald was a delight to watch. He gave Stephen Foskin a great pass which the Deerpark man executed beautifully to the net in the first quarter of the second half. McDonald did more than that, he contributed greatly, and at times he showed the skill that marks him out for county selection'. Onwards to 1990, we had the first Mullinavat man to bring a National Hurling League medal to the club. So back to the start, in his early career with the club, John won Under-12, Under-14 and Under 16 county championships, Under-13 football, along with Munster Under-17 Colleges medals. As left half forward in 1981 he won an All-Ireland Minor medal, and in 1983 and 1984 he was an Under 21 starter for the county.

13
WILLIE O'DWYER

WHEN THE PREVIOUS club history was produced in 1984, there was a little boy of six months or so, cutting his teeth in the parish. Willie went on to become the club's most decorated ever player. The fact that he started with the club in the 2023 County Senior quarter final speaks volumes for a man who has given a lifetime to the black and white Mullinavat jersey. Willie was a Kilkenny Minor centre forward 2001 and 2002, and he was part of the Kilkenny Minor team in 2002 that won that year's All-Ireland. He then moved on to the Under-21 team and played in the Under-21 All-Ireland final against Galway in 2003, versus Tipperary in 2004 where he received the 'Man of the Match' award in that victory, and versus Galway in 2005, As part of the Kilkenny Senior hurling panel (2003-2009) he played 2 NHL senior games in 2003 on his way to a star-studded career. Overall, Willie won 5 All-Ireland Senior titles and 4 Leinster Senior hurling titles. He came on as a sub when Kilkenny won the 2006 All-Ireland. He played in the corner forward position in the Leinster Senior final against Wexford in 2007, where he scored 2-3. He later played in the All-Ireland final where Kilkenny overcame Limerick. He remained on the panel for the 2008 and 2009 All-Ireland wins. Willie also featured on the 2011 Kilkenny Intermediate team. Having been living and working in Tralee for a number of year he joined up with Kerry for the 2012 and 2014 seasons but stayed loyal to the club. Willie also played with Waterford IT and Dublin IT in the Fitzgibbon Cup. Winning three Kilkenny Intermediate Hurling Championships with the club in 2001, 2006 and 2014 is still the highlight of Willie's career. This 1970-2023 team needs a captain, and we have him here in the club legend that is Willie O'Dwyer.

14

MOSSY MURPHY

THIS BUCKSTOWN MAN still has legendary status within the Mullinavat club. Mossy first came to prominence scoring five points from frees in the 1966 South Minor final loss to Ballyhale. His adult career with the club commenced shortly afterwards, culminating with the 1984 County Junior title success. Having represented the Kilkenny Seniors in the early 1970s, winning one All-Ireland (1972) and two Leinster Senior medals (1971 and 1972), this day is still the highlight of Mossy's career. As a then 35-year-old he scored seven points on that famous day at Callan when we beat Emeralds, Urlingford (four frees and three from play). He was still playing top level club hurling three years later. With Kilkenny, Mossy had been a county Minor in 1967, Under-21 in 1969/70 and Intermediate in 1970/71 before his arrival on a star-studded Kilkenny Senior hurling panel. Mossy has an All-Ireland Senior medal as a substitute in 1972 v. Cork, having started the year previously in the three-point All-Ireland final loss v. Tipperary. He also has Leinster Senior medals from both those years. In the 1971, All-Ireland campaign, Mossy scored 4-4, including 1-1 in the final, which finished Tipperary 5-17, Kilkenny 5-14. In the 1972 campaign, he came on as a substitute in the final, scoring a point as Kilkenny finished with an unanswered 2-7 to beat Cork – Kilkenny 3-24 Cork 5-11. He scored 1-1 in the games prior to that final.

15

JOHN WALSH

JOHN FILLS THE final position on our team. He has been involved with Mullinavat adult squads since 2011 and continues to be our 'go to' forward and free taker. John was on the Kilkenny Minor squad from 2012 and won an All-Ireland Minor medal in 2014, Leinster MHC championships medals from 2013 and 2014, Leinster Under-21 in 2017, and Leinster and All-Ireland Intermediate medals in 2016. He has also featured with Kilkenny Seniors a few times, though injuries have not helped his cause at times. Special mention must be made of John's Minor campaign in 2014. The corner-forward's mother sadly passed away in March of that year and he struggled to break into manager Pat Hoban's starting side. However, he was sprung from the bench in their last three outings and made the No 15 shirt for the decider. John Walsh had kicked a goal in the semi-final versus Waterford and used the same right boot 40 minutes into the Minor final. He scored 2-5 that day in a 'Man of the match' performance, despite being marked by Sean Finn, a now Limerick hurling great. John helped win our only County Under-21A title in 2013, scoring 0-4 from play in that final versus O'Loughlin's. He had also been on the Kilkenny County Minor B winning team in 2011. As an 18-year-old John scored 0-9, (2 from play, 6 frees, 1 penalty) in the 2014 Intermediate side. He also helped the club win that year's Leinster Intermediate final, scoring 0-5 versus Kiltale, (3 frees, 1 65 and 1 from play). The club has been Senior ever since, and in our last game before publication of this book, the County Senior hurling quarter-final of 2023, versus O'Loughlin Gaels, he was our top scorer with 0-7 (0-4 frees and 0-2 65s). John Walsh is the fourth current player on our team, a group that will play in the Kilkenny Senior hurling championship for the tenth successive year in 2024. (As an aside, all four have numerous football medals also).

* Based on the above, picking a best Mullinavat team 1970-2024 was a challenging task, and several others could definitely have featured, but I have no doubt that the XV players selected would match any XV from any club in the county. Our club will hopefully continue to produce great players in the years ahead. In the words of Cork legend Christy Ring, 'Let no one say the best hurlers belong to the past. They're with us now. And better yet to come...'

'This 1970-2023 team needs a captain, and we have him here in the club legend that is Willie O'Dwyer.'

Hurling
IN PHOTOS

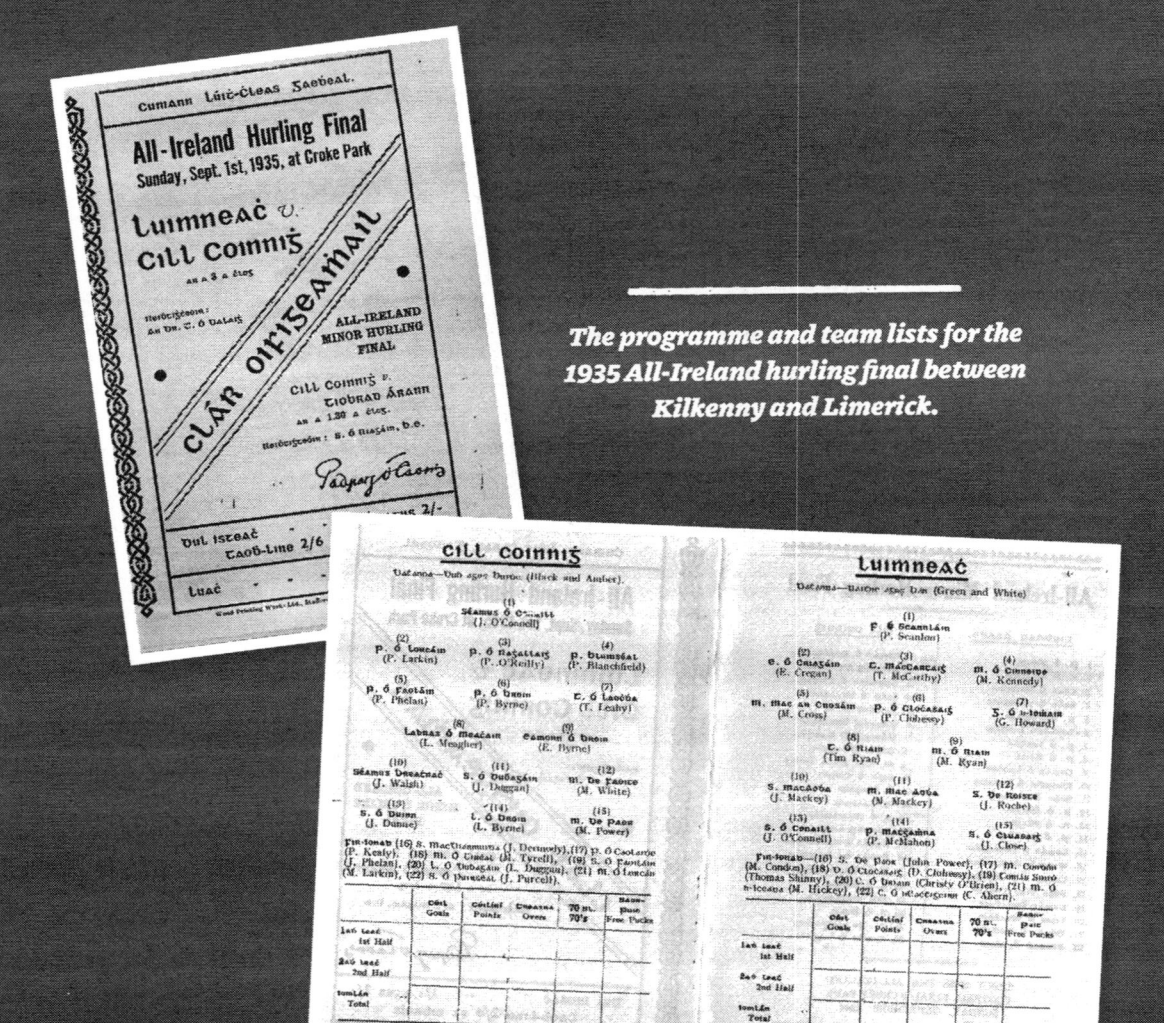

The programme and team lists for the 1935 All-Ireland hurling final between Kilkenny and Limerick.

Castle Rangers (Lukeswell) Junior hurling team from 1952

Back Row (from left): Pat Forristal, Mick Dermody, (partly hidden), Tommie Campion, Owen Dermody, Jim Forristal, Nick O'Neill, Jim Keeffe, (partly hidden), Richard Forristal, Matty Woods, Paddy O'Keeffe, John Campion, Jimmy Dermody. **Front Row (from left):** John Reade, Paddy Anderson, Neddy Campion, Denny Hogan, Pat Keeffe, Dick Hogan.

Intermediate hurling county champions 1989

Back Row (from left): Jim Walsh (trainer), Tom Anthony, Michael Law, Timmy Gough, Michael Dunphy, Pat Hoban, Pat McEvoy (captain), John McDonald, Paddy Frisby, Peter McDonald, Sean Walsh, Dan Power, Paudie Holden, Liam Aldridge. **Front Row (from left):** Bill Haberlin, Willie Carroll, Eamon Law, Mick Fitzgerald, Tomás Deegan, Andy Aylward, Joe Walsh, John Dunphy, John Joe Aylward, Tommy Frisby, Stevie Foskin, Harry Waters, Francis Conway.

The Kilkenny squads which won the Liam MacCarthy Cup in 1992 and retained the trophy in 1993. In the back row Mullinavat's Joe Walsh is third from the right, and Pat Hoban is five from the right. Joe is also third from the left in the front row (below).
Photo Credits: Tom Brett

Intermediate hurling team from 1997

Back Row (from left): Raymond Carroll, Joe Walsh, Liam Murphy, Pat Roghan, Pat Hoban, Stephen Foskin, Oliver Aylward, Pat Butler. **Front Row (from left):** William Carroll, Maurice Murphy, John Dunphy, Michael Dunphy, Michael Murphy, Seamus Holden and Paul Aylward.

JHC B final programme 2001

Fr Tommy Maher with the Mullinavat players after the 2001 Intermediate Hurling Championship victory.

IHC County champions 2001

Back Row (from left): Mossy Murphy (captain), Andrew McGovern, John Dunphy, Kenny Butler, Michael Murphy, Seamus Holden, Joe Walsh, Pat Butler. **Front Row (from left):** Walter Bourke, Jimmy Rohan, Paul Aylward, Liam Murphy, Willie O'Dwyer, JP Dungan and Michael Dunphy.

Photo Credit: Charlie Maher

The homecoming in 2001

Willie O'Dwyer (middle row, second from the left) with the Kilkenny squad which claimed the Liam MacCarthy Cup in 2003.

County JHC B champions 2006

Back Row (from left): Joseph Wall, John Farrell, Pat Hoban, Damien Reid, Alan Wall, Damien Aylward, Tommy Holden, Derek Aylward, Joe Kelly (selector) Pat Butler (selector). **Middle (from left):** Brendan Conway (trainer), Declan Duggan, Maurice Holden, Jim Holden, Pat Farrell, Damien Conway, NicholasAnthony, Pat Rohan, Richie Keneally (medic). **Front (from left):** Stephen Ryan, Liam Aylward, Brian Kenneally, Michael Farrell, JT Murphy, JP Dungan, Eoin Maher, Paddy Jones, Richie Raftice and Dermot Carroll. Kneeling in front Michael Jones.

Intermediate county champions 2006

Back Row (from left): Paddy Jones, Liam Aylward, Seamus Farrell, Derek Aylward, Alan Wall, Damien Aylward, JT Murphy, Eóin Maher, Andrew McGovern, Damien Conway. **Middle Row (from left):** Pat Farrell, Walter Burke, Tomas Frisby, Michael Murphy, Ger Anthony, Richie Raftice, Dinny Butler, Willie O'Dwyer, Paddy Raftice, Johnny Dunphy, Conor Conway, Brian Kenneally. **Front Row (from left):** Johnny Paul Dungan, Paul Aylward, Tony Duggan, Liam Murphy, PJ Aylward, Kevin Aylward, Nicky Anthony, Michael Duggan and Jamie Fennelly.

Intermediate hurling County finalists and League champions 2010

Back Row (from left): Brian Kenneally, Kevin Ayward, Paddy Jones, Ger Anthony, Damien Reid, Joe Gahan, Darren Kenneally, Michael Duggan, Ciaran Boyle, Brian Power, Liam Murphy. **Middle Row (from left):** Nicholas Anthony, Eoin Maher, Seamus Farrell, Michael Murphy, Tony Duggan, Dinny Butler, Michael Malone, Damien Aylward, Michel Farrell, Joe Fennelly, Pádraig Gahan, Andrew McGovern. Kenny Slattery. **Front Row (from left):** Simon Aylward, James Culleton, Conor Conway, Willie Dwyer, Jamie Fennelly, Ian Duggan, Walter Burke, Paddy Raftice, Mossy Jones, Ger Malone and Thomas Aylward.

Intermediate County Champions and League Winners 2014

Back Row: Ryan Bland, Conor Duggan, Nathan Malone, Ger Malone, James Culleton, Darren Kenneally, Conor Frisby, Adam Mansfield, Brian Phelan, Pat Mulhearn, Ian Duggan. **Middle Row:** Paul Ennis (coach), David Murphy, Joe Fennelly, Jamie Fennelly, Liam Fennelly, Paddy Jones, Robbie Malone, Dinny Butler, Seamus Farrell, Tony Duggan, Mark Mansfield, Liam Murphy, Declan Wall (manager), John Dunphy (selector). **Front Row:** Damien Aylward, Killian Dunphy, Ciarán Boyle, John Walsh, Mikey Jones, Willie O'Dwyer (captain), Thomas Aylward, Simon Aylward, Joe Gahan, Pauric Gahan, Paddy Raftice, Darren Waters. (**Inset:** Packie Wall and Tommy Frisby, selectors).

Willie O'Dwyer receives the 2014 Kilkenny Intermediate hurling trophy from Ned Quinn (County Board chairman) and Michael Lyng (sponsors). The club has remained in the Senior grade ever since.

Roll of Honour

HURLING

LEINSTER INTERMEDIATE HURLING CHAMPIONSHIP: (1) 2014
INTERMEDIATE HURLING CHAMPIONSHIP: (4) 1989, 2001, 2006, 2014
INTERMEDIATE HURLING LEAGUE: (3) 2004, 2010, 2014
ALL COUNTY INTERMEDIATE HURLING LEAGUE: (1) 2000
BYRNE CUP SENIOR HURLING LEAGUE: (1) 2017
JUNIOR HURLING CHAMPIONSHIP: (4) 1915, 1916, 1939, 1984
JUNIOR A HURLING CHAMPIONSHIP: (1) 2012
JUNIOR B HURLING CHAMPIONSHIP: (3) 1986, 1992, 2006
JUNIOR B HURLING LEAGUE: (1) 2010
UNDER 21 A HURLING CHAMPIONSHIP: (1) 2013
UNDER 21 B HURLING CHAMPIONSHIP: (2) 1981, 1999
MINOR HURLING A CHAMPIONSHIP: (1) 1938
MINOR HURLING B CHAMPIONSHIP: (4) 1981, 1998, 2006, 2011
MINOR HURLING LEAGUE DIVISION 2: (1) 1981
MINOR HURLING LEAGUE DIVISION 3: (2) 1992, 2003
UNDER 19 HURLING B SHIELD: (1) 2018
UNDER 15 HURLING B SHIELD: (1) 2018
UNDER 16 B HURLING CHAMPIONSHIP: (2) 1978, 1982
UNDER 16 C HURLING CHAMPIONSHIP: (4) 1977, 1991, 1993, 2015
UNDER 14 C HURLING CHAMPIONSHIP: (5) 1978, 1989, 2003, 2007, 2015
FEILE U-14 DIVISION C COUNTY WINNERS: (1) 2019

FOOTBALL

SENIOR FOOTBALL CHAMPIONSHIP: (7) 2007, 2017, 2018, 2019, 2020, 2022, 2023
SENIOR FOOTBALL LEAGUE: (3) 2005, 2010, 2022
INTERMEDIATE FOOTBALL CHAMPIONSHIP: (2) 2000, 2004
INTERMEDIATE FOOTBALL LEAGUE: (2) 1999, 2004
JUNIOR FOOTBALL CHAMPIONSHIP: (3) 1933, 1968, 1979 (WON AS BIGWOOD IN 1968 AND 1979)
UNDER 21 A FOOTBALL CHAMPIONSHIP: (2) 2000, 2011
UNDER 21 B FOOTBALL CHAMPIONSHIP: (2) 1998, 2005
MINOR A FOOTBALL CHAMPIONSHIP: (1) 1945 (BIGWOOD)
MINOR B FOOTBALL CHAMPIONSHIP: (2) 2007, 2010
UNDER 16 B FOOTBALL CHAMPIONSHIP: (2) 1996, 2004
UNDER 16 C FOOTBALL CHAMPIONSHIP: (1) 2006
UNDER 16 FOOTBALL LEAGUE DIVISION 2: (1) 2004
UNDER 14 A FOOTBALL CHAMPIONSHIP: (1) 2002
UNDER 14 C FOOTBALL CHAMPIONSHIP: (1) 2005
UNDER 14 FOOTBALL LEAGUE DIVISION 3: (1) 2005

COUNTY FINALS
(IN WHICH TEAMS FROM THE PARISH PARTICIPATED)

– SENIOR HURLING
1940 CARRICKSHOCK 1-4; MULLINAVAT 1-2
1943 CARRICKSHOCK 3-6; MULLINAVAT 1-3

– SENIOR FOOTBALL
1904 LAMOGUE MULLINAVAT
1905 LAMOGUE HARRISTOWN
1934 TULLOGHER 1-4; MULLINAVAT 0-1
1935 BARROW RANGERS (GLENMORE/SLIEVERUE) 0-5; MULLINAVAT 0-3
2007 MULLINAVAT 0-9; GLENMORE 1-6 (REPLAY MULLINAVAT 3-7; GLENMORE 0-11)
2012 MUCKALEE 1-10; MULLINAVAT 0-7
2017 MULLINAVAT 3-12; RAILYARD 2-5
2018 MULLINAVAT 5-11; MUCKALEE 2-09
2019 MULLINAVAT 1-07; RAILYARD 1-07 (REPLAY MULLINAVAT 1-13; RAILYARD 0-10)
2020 MULLINAVAT 5-07; MOONCOIN 1-04
2021 THOMASTOWN 2-06; MULLINAVAT 1-05
2022 MULLINAVAT 1-12; THOMASTOWN 0-08
2023 MULLINAVAT 3-7; THOMASTOWN 1-9

– INTERMEDIATE HURLING
198 MULLINAVAT 2-13; YOUNG IRELANDS 0-14
1999 JOHN LOCKES 0-15; MULLINAVAT 1-9
2001 MULLINAVAT 1-5; CLARA 1-5 (REPLAY MULLINAVAT 2-10; CLARA 2-7)
2006 MULLINAVAT 1-21; CLARA 2-11
2010 DICKSBORO 2-12; MULLINAVAT 2-11
2014 MULLINAVAT 0-17; ST PATRICK'S 0-14

– INTERMEDIATE FOOTBALL
2000 MULLINAVAT 1-4; O'LOUGHLIN GAELS 0-6
2004 MULLINAVAT 4-7; CONAHY SHAMROCKS 0-6

– JUNIOR HURLING
1915 MULLINAVAT 2-4; HORSE AND JOCKEY 0-1
1916 MULLINAVAT 2-4; DICKSBORO 1-2
1938 BALLYLINE 3-5; MULLINAVAT 2-4
1939 MULLINAVAT 5-0; FRESHFORD 3-1
1974 MUCKALEE-BALLYFOYLE RANGERS 4-17; MULLINAVAT 3-3
1978 ST PATRICK'S 4-6; MULLINAVAT 1-5
1984 MULLINAVAT 3-9; EMERALDS 1-5

– JUNIOR FOOTBALL
1914 BURNCHURCH 1-0; HARRISTOWN 0-2
1933 MULLINAVAT 6-3; MITCHELL'S (BALLYFOYLE) 0-3
1961 BARROWMOUNT 1-8; BIGWOOD 1-3
1968 BIGWOOD 0-6; BARROWMOUNT 0-6 (UNFINISHED) (REPLAY BIGWOOD 0-9; BARROWMOUNT 0-2)
1976 SARSFIELDS (CONAHY) 0-8; BIGWOOD 0-1
1979 BIGWOOD 3-2; DICKSBORO 1-5
1988 GRAIGUE BALLYCALLAN 2-6; MULLINAVAT 0-4
1989 BENNETSBRIDGE 2-9; MULLINAVAT 2-6
1990 DICKSBORO 0-9; MULLINAVAT 2-2
1998 YOUNG IRELANDS 0-9; MULLINAVAT 0-6

– UNDER 21 A HURLING CHAMPIONSHIP
2002 JAMES STEPHENS 0-11; MULLINAVAT 0-06
2012 ST LACHTAIN'S 2-11; MULLINAVAT 0-15
2013 MULLINAVAT 1-16; O'LOUGHLIN GAELS 0-14

– UNDER 21 B HURLING CHAMPIONSHIP
1981 MULLINAVAT 2-08; EMERALDS 1-09
1999 MULLINAVAT 3-07; ERIN'S OWN 1-05

– UNDER 21 C HURLING CHAMPIONSHIP
2022 MULLINAVAT 2-13; KILMACOW 1-15

– UNDER 21 A FOOTBALL CHAMPIONSHIP
2000 MULLINAVAT 1-8; O'LOUGHLIN GAELS 2-4
2001 ERIN'S OWN 1-5; MULLINAVAT 0-7

– UNDER 21 B FOOTBALL CHAMPIONSHIP
1998 MULLINAVAT 0-7; RAILYARD 0-5 (UNFINISHED – MULLINAVAT AWARDED TITLE)
2005 MULLINAVAT 3-8; MOONCOIN 2-4

– UNDER 19 HURLING
ROINN D
2021 MULLINAVAT 2-07; BARROW RANGERS 1-07

– MINOR HURLING
ROINN A
1937 EIRE OG 3-4; MULLINAVAT 2-0
1938 MULLINAVAT 4-5 DICKSBORO 2-3
ROINN B
1981 MULLINAVAT 1-8; LISDOWNEY 1-8
     REPLAY MULLINAVAT 5-5; LISDOWNEY 3-6
1998 MULLINAVAT 1-11; TULLAROAN 2-5
2004 ST LACHTAIN'S 2-16; MULLINAVAT 0-7
2006 MULLINAVAT 2-6; EMERALDS 1-3
2011 MULLINAVAT 2-9; ST PATRICK'S 0-4
2017 DUNNAMAGGIN 3-16; MULLINAVAT 2-11
ROINN C
1987 TULLAROAN 5-14; MULLINAVAT 3-1
1990 CONAHY SHAMROCKS 5-9; MULLINAVAT 2-3
1991 LISDOWNEY 2-6; MULLINAVAT 0-6

– MINOR FOOTBALL
ROINN A
1945 BIGWOOD 1-1; RAILYARD 0-3
1962 RAILYARD 2-6; BIGWOOD 0-4
1984 DICKSBORO 2-7; BIGWOOD 1-1
ROINN B
2005 RAILYARD 4-10; MULLINAVAT 2-4
2007 MULLINAVAT 3-6 GRAIGNAMANAGH 1-3
2010 MULLINAVAT 4-7; LISDOWNEY 3-4
ROINN C
2003 BLACKS AND WHITES 1-10; MULLINAVAT 1-9

– UNDER 16 HURLING
MULLINAVAT UNDER 16 B HURLING FINALS
1974 JOHNSTOWN 3-6; MULLINAVAT 2-3
1978 MULLINAVAT 4-5; ST LACHTAIN'S 2-0
1982 MULLINAVAT 1-12; GALMOY 3-3
2000 ST MARTINS 2-20; MULLINAVAT 0-7
2007 CLARA 1-8; MULLINAVAT 2-5
     REPLAY CLARA 0-15; MULLINAVAT 0-4
MULLINAVAT UNDER 16 C HURLING FINALS
1977 MULLINAVAT 5-5; GRAIGUE BALLYCALLAN 5-0
1989 DANESFORT 2-8; MULLINAVAT 3-5
     REPLAY DANESFORT 2-5; MULLINAVAT 0-4
1991 MULLINAVAT 3-6; EMERALDS 2-5
1993 MULLINAVAT 3-7; BENNETSBRIDGE 0-6
2015 MULLINAVAT 5-10; FENIANS 4-12

– UNDER 16 FOOTBALL
MULLINAVAT UNDER 16 B FOOTBALL FINALS
198 BIGWOOD 5-9; GOWRAN 0-2
1994 RAILYARD 3-5; MULLINAVAT 2-6
1996 MULLINAVAT 2-1; SHAMROCKS 1-2
1997 EMERALDS 3-10; MULLINAVAT 1-3
2004 MULLINAVAT 2-6; ST PATRICK'S BALLYRAGGET 1-4
2007 JOHN LOCKES 2-6; MULLINAVAT 2-4
MULLINAVAT UNDER 16 C FOOTBALL FINALS
2002 SLIEVERUE 5-3; MULLINAVAT 1-6
2006 MULLINAVAT 3-11; BARROW RANGERS 1-6

– UNDER 14 HURLING
1994 ROINN B TULLAROAN 1-13; MULLINAVAT 2-04
1977 ROINN C SLIEVERUE 3-02; MULLINAVAT 3-01
1978 ROINN C MULLINAVAT 6-05; GALMOY 1-01
1989 ROINN C MULLINAVAT 3-08; DANESFORT 2-06
2003 ROINN C MULLINAVAT 2-06; CONAHY SHAMROCKS 0-06
2007 ROINN C MULLINAVAT 3-12; WINDGAP 1-06
2015 ROINN C MULLINAVAT 5-07; MULLINAVAT 2-12
1984 ROINN D KILMACOW 2-5; MULLINAVAT 1-7

– UNDER 14 FOOTBALL
2002 ROINN A   MULLINAVAT 6-5; O'LOUGHLIN GAELS 4-7
2003 ROINN C   LISDOWNEY 2-3; MULLINAVAT 1-2
2005 ROINN C   MULLINAVAT 1-9; BARROW RANGERS 0-3
2013 ROINN D   ST LACHTAIN'S 5-5; MULLINAVAT 1-4

CLUB OFFICERS

– CHAIRPERSONS (1911-2024)
1911	MICHAEL HURLEY
1912-1919	JOHN PURCELL
1929-1932	ROSIE CARROLL
1932-1935	PAT MCDONALD
1936-1945	JIM KEEGAN
1953-1955	FR JOSEPH GALAVAN CC
1956-1957	WILLIAM KAVANAGH
1958-1959	TOM SUTTON
1960	NED DELAHUNTY
1961-1964	PETER FOSKIN
1965-1966	PAT DELAHUNTY
1967-1968	JOHN SUTTON (ROSSINAN)
1969	JOHNNY WALSH
1970-1973	MICHAEL CARROLL
1974-1981	ANDY AYLWARD
1982-1985	MICHAEL CARROLL
1986-2007	TOMMY FRISBY
2008-2010	PADDY FRISBY
2011-2018	BILLY WALSH
2019-2021	MICHAEL LAW
2022-	JOHN JOE AYLWARD

– SECRETARIES (1911-2024)
1911	PAT HOBAN
1913-19	JAMES AYLWARD
1927	JOHN FOSKIN
1932-1935	TOM CONWAY
1936-45	JIM KEEGAN
1946-47	PAT AYLWARD
1948	BILLY HOBAN
1953-54	PADDY TYNAN
1955-56	MARTIN CROTTY
1957-1959	JOHN HOBAN
1960	JOHNNY WALSH
1961-1975	SEAMUS SUTTON
1976-1988	NED CONWAY
1989-1992	ANDY AYLWARD
1993-1996	JOHN DUNPHY
1997-2004	ANDY AYLWARD
2005-2010	TOM REID
2011-2012	ANDY AYLWARD
2013	PAT ROHAN
2014-2018	BRIAN KENNEALLY
2019-	TOM DUGGAN (MILL ROAD)

– TREASURERS (1911-2024)
1911	MARTIN FORRISTAL
1927	JOHN FOSKIN
1936-1945	JIM KEEGAN
1953-1959	PAT FOSKIN
1960-1961	PAT DELAHUNTY
1962-2019	JIM CONWAY
2020-2022	ANDY AYLWARD
2023 -	BRIAN KENNEALLY

– PRO'S (1985-2024)
1985-1995	NED HABERLIN
1996-2004	TOM DUGGAN (MILL ROAD)
2005-2006	PAT ROHAN
2007-2009	TOM DUGGAN (MILL ROAD)
2010-2013	MICHAEL DUGGAN
2014-2017	JOHN DUNPHY
2018-	JOHN POWER

INTER-COUNTY REPRESENTATIVES

Below is a list of players from Mullinavat GAA club who represented the club on adult County hurling and Gaelic football teams (Championship, League, Oireachtas, Walsh Cup and other Inter County games). We are aware the list may have several omissions.

1914 - SENIOR HURLING · JOHNNY PHELAN

1914 - JUNIOR FOOTBALL · JOHNNY PHELAN

1916 JUNIOR HURLING · PAT POWER, R KENNEALLY, JOE SULLIVAN (GOAL), JOHNNY PHELAN, WATTIE POWER, JIMMY HANRAHAN

✦ 1922 SENIOR FOOTBALL · JIM PHELAN

1928 JUNIOR HURLING · DENNY DUGGAN

✦ 1931-37 SENIOR HURLING · JACK DUGGAN

1934 JUNIOR FOOTBALL · PADDY HOLDEN, JOHN FARRELL, JIMMY WALSH

1935 SENIOR HURLING · LARRY DUGGAN

1939 MINOR HURLING · PADDY O'NEILL, D MCLAUGHLIN, M HOLDEN, J PURCELL, PHILIP HOBAN, MICK WALSH

✦ 1940 JUNIOR HURLING · TOM WALSH, PAT AYLWARD, WILLIE DURNEY, PADDY HOLDEN, PAUDIE FITZGERALD

1941 SENIOR HURLING · TOM WALSH, WILLIE DURNEY

1942 SENIOR HURLING · ANDY AYLWARD

1943 SENIOR HURLING · M HEFFERNAN, MICHAEL HOLDEN

1948 MINOR HURLING · BILLY HOBAN

✦ 1951-50 SENIOR HURLING · JOHN SUTTON

1951 JUNIOR HURLING · JOHN SUTTON

1953 JUNIOR FOOTBALL · JOHN SUTTON

1953 MINOR HURLING · FINTAN CROTTY

1953 SENIOR HURLIN · BUDDY MCDONALD

1956 SENIOR HURLING · DICK DUNPHY

✦ 1960 MINOR HURLING · PHILIP FRISBY (SQUAD - ALL IRELAND WINNERS).

1962 MINOR FOOTBALL · TOMMY DUGGAN

1964 LIAM WALSH · MINOR HURLING

1964 INTERMEDIATE HURLING · PADDY HOBAN, TOMMY REDDY

1966 INTERMEDIATE HURLING · JACK FRISBY

1966 MINOR HURLING · JIM WALSH

1967-68 INTERMEDIATE HURLING · LIAM WALSH

1967-72 · MOSSY MURPHY (MINOR, UNDER 21, INTERMEDIATE & SENIOR HURLING)

✦ 1973 INTERMEDIATE HURLING · JIM WALSH & ANDY AYLWARD

1974 SENIOR HURLING · JIM WALSH

1976 MINOR HURLING · PAUDIE HOLDEN

1977 MINOR HURLING · TOMMY FRISBY (ALL IRELAND WINNERS)

1979 SENIOR FOOTBALL · JOHN FITZGERALD & MICHAEL FITZGERALD

✦ 1981 MINOR HURLING · JOHN MCDONALD (ALL IRELAND WINNER)

1982 MINOR HURLING · JOE WALSH & LIAM LAW

1983 JUNIOR HURLING · JOHN JOE AYLWARD, PAUDIE HOLDEN, MOSSY MURPHY

1983 - 84 UNDER 21 HURLING · JOHN MCDONALD

1984 JUNIOR HURLIN · JOHN MCDONALD

1984 UNDER 21 HURLING · JOHN DUNPHY (PANELLIST)

1984 UNDER 21 FOOTBALL · JOE WALSH & JOHN MCDONALD

1984 MINOR FOOTBALL · DARRAGH MCDERMOTT

1984 MINOR HURLING · PAT MCEVOY

1985 UNDER 21 HURLING · JOE WALSH, JOHN DUNPHY (PANELLIST)

1985 MINOR FOOTBALL · A WALSH (BIGWOOD)

1986 JUNIOR HURLING · JOHN DUNPHY (PANELLIST)

1985 - 1986 MINOR HURLING · PAT HOBAN

1985 SENIOR FOOTBALL • JOHN MCDONALD (BIGWOOD)
1986 SENIOR HURLING • JOHNNY MCDONALD
1986 UNDER 21 HURLING • JOE WALSH
1986 MINOR FOOTBALL • BILLY WALSH
1987 SENIOR FOOTBALL • EAMONN KELLY (BIGWOOD)
1987 UNDER 21 FOOTBALL • W HABERLIN
1987 MINOR FOOTBALL • BILLY WALSH
1988 UNDER 21 HURLING • PAT HOBAN
1988 JUNIOR HURLING • PAUDIE HOLDEN, JOE WALSH, JOHN DUNPHY, STEPHEN FOSKIN (ALL IRELAND WINNERS)
1989 JUNIOR FOOTBALL • L ALDRIDGE
1989-1990 SENIOR HURLING • JOHN MCDONALD (NHL WINNER 1990)

✦ 1990 SENIOR HURLING (WALSH CUP FINAL) • JOHN DUNPHY, PAUDIE HOLDEN, PAT HOBAN, STEPHEN FOSKIN
1990 JUNIOR HURLING • PAUDIE HOLDEN (CAPTAIN), PAT HOBAN, MICHAEL DUNPHY, JOHN DUNPHY (ALL IRELAND WINNERS)
1992 SENIOR HURLING • JOE WALSH, PAT HOBAN (ALL IRELAND SH WINNERS)
1993 SENIOR HURLING • JOE WALSH ALL IRELAND WINNER, HIS SECOND SH MEDAL)
1994 SENIOR HURLING • JOE WALSH, MICHAEL DUNPHY
1995 SENIOR HURLING (WALSH CUP) • MICHAEL DUNPHY
1995 SENIOR HURLING • JOE WALSH
1995 MINOR HURLING • DECLAN WALL
1996 JUNIOR HURLING • JOHN DUNPHY, PAT HOBAN
1997 INTERMEDIATE HURLING • JOHNNY DUNPHY
1997 UNDER 21 HURLING • JOHN DUNPHY
1997 MINOR HURLING • PAT BUTLER
1998 MINOR HURLING • PJ AYLWARD, MICHAEL MURPHY

✦ 2000 UNDER 21 & INTERMEDIATE HURLING • PAT BUTLER
2001 MINOR HURLING • WILLIE O'DWYER
2001 UNDER 21 FOOTBALL • KEITH MADIGAN
2002 SENIOR HURLING • WALTER BURKE (ALL-IRELAND SH WINNERS)
2002 UNDER 21 HURLING • WALTER BURKE
2002 MINOR HURLING • WILLIE O'DWYER & TOMAS FRISBY (ALL-IRELAND WINNERS)
2002 MINOR FOOTBALL • WILLIE O'DWYER & THOMAS FRISBY
2003 SENIOR HURLING • WILLIE O'DWYER & WALTER BURKE (ALL-IRELAND SH WINNERS)
2003 UNDER 21 HURLING • WILLIE O'DWYER (ALL-IRELAND WINNER)
2003 UNDER 21 FOOTBALL • WILLIE O'DWYER
2004 SENIOR HURLING • WALTER BURKE, WILLIE O'DWYER
2004 UNDER 21 HURLING • WILLIE O'DWYER (ALL-IRELAND WINNER)
2005 INTERMEDIATE HURLING • MICHAEL MURPHY, WALTER BURKE, WILLIE O'DWYER (ALL-IRELAND WINNERS)
2005 UNDER 21 HURLING • WILLIE O'DWYER & TOMAS FRISBY (ALL-IRELAND WINNERS)
2005 MINOR FOOTBALL • PATRICK RAFTICE & STEPHEN DUGGAN
2006 SENIOR HURLING • WILLIE O'DWYER (ALL-IRELAND SH WINNER 2ND MEDAL) 2006 INTERMEDIATE HURLING – MICHAEL MURPHY, WALTER BURKE
2006 MINOR HURLING • NICHOLAS ANTHONY, PADDY RAFTICE
2006 SENIOR FOOTBALL • DECLAN DUGGAN, MICHAEL DUGGAN
2007 SENIOR HURLING • WILLIE O'DWYER (ALL-IRELAND SH WINNER 3RD MEDAL) 2006 MICHAEL MURPHY (ALL-IRELAND SH WINNERS)
2007 INTERMEDIATE HURLING • DINNY BUTLER, MICHAEL MURPHY, PAUL AYLWARD, JAMIE FENNELLY
2008 SENIOR HURLING • WILLIE O'DWYER ALL IRELAND SH WINNER 4TH MEDAL)
2009 SENIOR HURLING • WILLIE O'DWYER ALL IRELAND SH WINNER 5TH MEDAL)
2008 JUNIOR FOOTBALL • DECLAN DUGGAN, KEN SLATTERY
2009 INTERMEDIATE HURLING • WALTER BURKE (ALL IRELAND WINNERS)

2009 MINOR HURLING · IAN DUGGAN, PADRAIG GAHAN
2009 JUNIOR FOOTBALL · MICHAEL MALONE, STEPHEN RYAN
2009 MINOR FOOTBALL · ANDY DELAHUNTY, JAMES CULLETON, IAN DUGGAN, BRIAN POWER, JOE FENNELLY

✦ 2010 INTERMEDIATE HURLING · IAN DUGGAN (ALL IRELAND WINNER)
2010 UNDER 21 HURLING · MICHAEL MALONE
2010 JUNIOR FOOTBALL · JAMES CULLETON, MICHAEL FARRELL, STEPHEN DUGGAN, MICHAEL MALONE, STEPHEN RYAN, PADDY RAFTICE, MICHAEL DUGGAN
2010 UNDER 21 FOOTBALL · MICHAEL MALONE, ANDREW DELAHUNTY, JAMES CULLETON
2010 MINOR FOOTBALL · SIMON AYLWARD, TOMAS AYLWARD, GER MALONE
2011 INTERMEDIATE HURLING · WILLIE O'DWYER, CONOR CONWAY
2011 UNDER 21 HURLING · IAN DUGGAN, PADRAIG GAHAN
2011 MINOR HURLING · MARK MANSFIELD
2011 JUNIOR FOOTBALL · JOE FENNELLY, PADDY RAFTICE, MICHAEL MALONE, JAMES CULLETON, MICHAEL DUGGAN
2011 UNDER 21 FOOTBALL · GER MALONE, JOE FENNELLY, JAMES CULLETON
2012 SENIOR HURLING (WALSH CUP) · PADRAIG GAHAN
2012 INTERMEDIATE HURLING · MICHAEL MALONE, IAN DUGGAN
2012 UNDER 21 HURLING · IAN DUGGAN
2012 MINOR HURLING · JOHN WALSH, MARK MANSFIELD
2013 2014 MINOR HURLING · JOHN WALSH
2012 JUNIOR FOOTBALL · JOE FENNELLY, JAMES CULLETON, MICHAEL MALONE, PADDY RAFTICE, STEPHEN DUGGAN
2012 UNDER 21 FOOTBALL · WILLIAM DELAHUNTY, JAMES CULLETON, THOMAS AYLWARD, JOE FENNELLY, IAN DUGGAN, PAT MULHEARNE
2013 INTERMEDIATE HURLING · MICHAEL MALONE, IAN DUGGAN
2013-2014 MINOR HURLING · JOHN WALSH

2013 JUNIOR FOOTBALL (BRITISH C'SHIP) · MICHAEL DUGGAN, STEPHEN DUGGAN
2014 INTERMEDIATE HURLING · WILLIE O'DWYER, IAN DUGGAN, THOMAS AYLWARD, PADRAIG GAHAN,
2014 UNDER 21 HURLING · MARK MANSFIELD, TOM AYLWARD, SIMON AYLWARD
2014 JUNIOR FOOTBALL (BRITISH C'SHIP) · MICHAEL DUGGAN, JAMES CULLETON, TOM AYLWARD, JOE FENNELLY, CONOR CONWAY, MICHAEL FARRELL
2014 MINOR FOOTBALL · KILLIAN DUNPHY, CONOR DUGGAN
2015 INTERMEDIATE HURLING · PADRAIC GAHAN, GER MALONE, MICHAEL MALONE
2015 UNDER 21 HURLING · MARK MANSFIELD
2015 JUNIOR FOOTBALL (BRITISH C'SHIP WINNERS) · JOE FENNELLY, MICHAEL DUGGAN, STEPHEN RYAN, STEPHEN DUGGAN, JAMES CULLETON, MICHAEL MALONE
2016 SENIOR HURLING · MICHAEL MALONE
2016 INTERMEDIATE HURLING · TOM AYLWARD, JOHN WALSH
2016 2017 UNDER 21 HURLING · JOHN WALSH
2016 JUNIOR FOOTBALL (BRITISH C'SHIP) · GER MALONE, JAMES CULLETON, JOHN WALSH
2017 SENIOR HURLING · MICHAEL MALONE
2017 JUNIOR FOOTBALL (BRITISH C'SHIP WINNERS) · JOE FENNELLY, GER MALONE, MICHAEL MALONE, TOM AYLWARD, JAMES CULLETON, IAN DUGGAN, MICHAEL JONES
2018 SENIOR HURLING (WALSH CUP V. KILDARE 7/01/2018) · GER MALONE, SIMON AYLWARD, MARK MANSFIELD, JOHN WALSH
2018 MINOR HURLING (NOW U17) · PADRAIG DEMPSEY
2018 JUNIOR FOOTBALL (BRITISH C'SHIP WINNERS) · JOE FENNELLY, MICHAEL MALONE, JAMES CULLETON, IAN DUGGAN, SHANE KELLY, JOHN WALSH, MICHAEL JONES, KILLIAN DUNPHY
2019 SENIOR HURLING · GER MALONE, THOMAS AYLWARD
2019 MINOR FOOTBALL · CONOR WALSH, DAVID MAHER
2019 JUNIOR FOOTBALL (BRITISH C'SHIP) · SHANE KELLY, MICHAEL JONES, JOE FENNELLY

✦ 2021 UNDER 20 HURLING · PADRAIG DEMPSEY
2022 UNDER 20 HURLING · CJ FITZPATRICK
2022 JUNIOR FOOTBALL (ALL IRELAND WINNERS) · KILLIAN DUNPHY, SHANE KELLY, GER MALONE, JAMES CULLETON, TOM AYLWARD, MICHAEL MALONE, ADAM MANSFIELD, JOHN WALSH, JOE FENNELLY, CONOR DUGGAN, MICHAEL JONES
2023 JUNIOR FOOTBALL (ALL IRELAND RUNNERS UP) · SHANE KELLY, GER MALONE, TOM AYLWARD, MICHAEL MALONE, JIM CULLETON, IAN DUGGAN, JOE FENNELLY, MICHAEL JONES, ADAM MANSFIELD

MULLINAVAT COUNTY FINAL REFEREES

Referees play a crucial role in maintaining fair play, and enforcing rules, during Gaelic football and Hurling matches, evolving their methods over the years to ensure the integrity of Gaelic games. Mullinavat have always been a prominent club in supplying referees within the county and beyond. From the 1930's onwards people like Pat Aylward and Tom Conway have taken charge of important fixtures in both GAA codes.

1940	PADDY WALSH (BIGWOOD) SENIOR & JUNIOR FOOTBALL FINALS
1943	PADDY WALSH (BIGWOOD) JUNIOR FOOTBALL FINAL
1954	JOHN SUTTON SENIOR HURLING FINAL
1978	RICHIE CARROLL MINOR HURLING B FINAL
1980	TOMMY DUGGAN SPECIAL JUNIOR FOOTBALL FINAL
1981	TOMMY DUGGAN JUNIOR FOOTBALL FINAL
1981	TOMMY DUGGAN SPECIAL JUNIOR FOOTBALL FINAL
1982	TOMMY DUGGAN SPECIAL JUNIOR FOOTBALL FINAL
1982	TOMMY DUGGAN UNDER 21 FOOTBALL FINAL
1982	TOMMY DUGGAN MINOR FOOTBALL FINAL
1983	TOMMY DUGGAN MINOR FOOTBALL FINAL
1985	TOMMY DUGGAN SENIOR FOOTBALL FINAL
1985	TOMMY DUGGAN MINOR HURLING A FINAL
1986	TOMMY DUGGAN SENIOR FOOTBALL FINALS DRAW & REPLAY
1986	RICHIE CARROLL JUNIOR HURLING FINAL
1987	TOMMY DUGGAN SENIOR FOOTBALL FINAL
1988	TOMMY DUGGAN SENIOR HURLING FINAL
1989	TOMMY DUGGAN JUNIOR HURLING B FINALS DRAW & REPLAY
1989	RICHIE CARROLL UNDER 21 HURLING B FINAL
1989	RICHIE CARROLL MINOR HURLING C FINAL
1990	TOMMY DUGGAN INTERMEDIATE FOOTBALL FINAL
1993	DINNY DUGGAN SENIOR FOOTBALL FINALS DRAW & REPLAY
1996	RICHIE CARROLL JUNIOR HURLING FINAL
2002	TOM DUGGAN JUNIOR HURLING B FINAL
2004	TOM DUGGAN MINOR HURLING C FINAL
2007	TOM DUGGAN MINOR HURLING B FINAL DRAW
2007	TOM DUGGAN MINOR HURLING C FINAL
2008	TOM DUGGAN INTERMEDIATE HURLING FINAL
2008	TOM DUGGAN INTERMEDIATE FOOTBALL FINAL
2013	TOM DUGGAN SENIOR FOOTBALL FINAL

Bibliography

Kilkenny GAA Yearbook 1972-2023

The Kilkenny People 1893-2024

The Kilkenny Voice 2004-2009

The Kilkenny Journal 1884-1965

The Kilkenny Standard 1978-1982

The Munster Express

Waterford News & Star

The Irish Independent 1939-2024

The Irish (Cork) Examiner 1931-2024

The Irish Press 1931-1995

Cooke, Senan, *A History of the GAA in Kilmacow 1884-2010* (2010)

Cumann na mBunscoileanna, Cill Chainnigh, Caoga Blian Og, *A History of Kilkenny Primary Schools Board 1939-1984*

Kavanagh, Dermot, *Kilkenny Senior Hurling County Finals 1886-2003*

Kelly, Michael & Kenneally, John, *The Shamrocks Story* (Perfecto Print, 2002)

McEvoy, Enda, *The Godfather of Modern Hurling, The Father Tommy Maher Story* Ballpoint Press (2012)

Mullinavat GAA History 1884-1984 (Munster Express 1984)

Murphy, James, R.I.P. *Tullogher 1988-1988, 100 Years of GAA history* (Kilkenny People, 1998)

O'Dwyer, Michael, *A History of Cricket in County Kilkenny, The Forgotten Game* (O'Dwyer Books 2006)

O'Neill, Gerry, *The Kilkenny GAA Bible* (Kilkenny Yearbook Committee, 2005, 2012, 2018)

O'Neill, Gerry & Dunphy, Dermot, *O Fhas go hAois, Cumann na mBunscoileanna, Cill Chainnigh 1989-2014*

Ryall, Tom, Kilkenny – *The GAA Story 1884-1984* (1984)

Phelan, Conor, *Fiche Cuig Blian ag Fas, Waterford Institute of Technology, GAA Club History 1981-2006* (WIT GAA Club, 2007)

Walsh, Jim, James Nowlan, *Athena Alderman and the GAA in his Time*

PHOTO CREDITS
Mullinavat GAA Club Archive
Kilkenny People Archive
Kilkenny Voice Archive
Munster Express Archive
John Power
Dylan Vaughan
Ray McManus/Sportsfile
Willie Dempsey
Tom Brett
Charlie Maher

Printed in Great Britain
by Amazon

68edb32f-da70-4b3f-a3d8-2d5f0c6ed488R01